P O P   C U L T U R E
GERMANY!

D0164570

Other titles in ABC-CLIO's series

Popular Culture in the Contemporary World

Pop Culture Latin America! Media, Arts, and Lifestyle, Lisa Shaw and Stephanie Dennison

Pop Culture Russia! Media, Arts, and Lifestyle, Birgit Beumers

Pop Culture Arab World! Media, Arts, and Lifestyle, Andrew Hammond

Pop Culture India! Media, Arts, and Lifestyle, Asha Kasbekar

UPCOMING TITLES

Pop Culture Caribbean! Media, Arts, and Lifestyle, Brenda F. Berrian

Pop Culture China! Media, Arts, and Lifestyle, Kevin Latham

Pop Culture France! Media, Arts, and Lifestyle, Wendy Michallat

Pop Culture Japan! Media, Arts, and Lifestyle, William H. Kelly

Pop Culture UK! Media, Arts, and Lifestyle, Bill Osgerby

Pop Culture West Africa! Media, Arts, and Lifestyle, Onookome Okome

P O P   C U L T U R E
GERMANY!

Media, Arts, and Lifestyle

Catherine C. Fraser
Dierk O. Hoffmann

A B C  C L I O

Santa Barbara, California   Denver, Colorado   Oxford, England

Images that do not contain source information within their captions are courtesy of Catherine C. Fraser and Dierk O. Hoffmann.

Library of Congress Cataloging-in-Publication Data
Fraser, Catherine C.
Pop culture Germany! : media, arts, and lifestyle / Catherine C. Fraser, Dierk O. Hoffmann, and Angelika Weiss.
p. cm. — (Popular culture in the contemporary world)
Also available on the World Wide Web as an eBook from ABC-CLIO.
Includes bibliographical references and index.
ISBN 1-85109-733-3 (hard cover : alk. paper) – ISBN 1-85109-738-4 (ebook)
1. Popular culture—Germany—History—20th century. 2. Germany—Civilization—20th century. I. Hoffmann, Dierk, 1963– II. Weiss, Angelika. III. Title.
DD239.F737 2006
306.0943—dc22
2006019413

09   08   07   06 | 10   9   8   7   6   5   4   3   2   1

ISBN-13: 978-1-85109-733-3   ebook 978-1-85109-738-8

This book is also available on the World Wide Web as an eBook.
Visit abc-clio.com for details.

Acquisition Editor: Simon Mason
Production Editor: Laura Esterman
Editorial Assistant: Gayle Woidneck
Media Editor: Giulia Rossi
Production Manager: Don Schmidt

ABC-CLIO, Inc.
130 Cremona Drive, P.O. Box 1911
Santa Barbara, California 93116-1911

Text design by Jane Raese

This book is printed on acid-free paper. ∞
Manufactured in the United States of America

Contents

Acknowledgments

In gathering material for this book, we were particularly fortunate to be able to consult frequently with Angelika Weiss and her daughter Pola. Their on-the-spot perspective, particularly regarding theater in Germany, as well as Angelika's collection of current articles and photos, kept us on track and up to date, and we are most grateful. For their personal insights into a range of topics, we would like to thank Seyhan Derin, Hans Lehmann, Klaus Meyer, Marlis Mueller, Ulrike Wittwer, and Harald Zils. For the photographs to supplement our collection, we are also indebted to Dieter Scholl and David Miller.

Finally, we thank our editors at ABC-CLIO for their encouraging and constructive feedback.

Chronology

1871	After the Franco-Prussian War, a number of German states was united under Prussian leadership.
1888	Kaiser Wilhelm II, grandson of Queen Victoria, came to power.
1914–1918	World War I. Germany was defeated and subjected to harsh terms under the Treaty of Versailles.
1918–1919	The kaiser was forced to abdicate (November 1918) and Germany became a republic (August 1919, known as the Weimar Republic).
1933	Adolf Hitler, leader of the National Socialist Party, became chancellor.
1939	Germany invaded Poland and World War II began.
1945	World War II ended with Germany's unconditional surrender. It was divided into four sectors under U.S., British, French, and Soviet command.
1946	The film *The Murderers Are Among Us* was shown for the first time in East Berlin.
	Carl Zuckmayer's play *The Devil's General*, which was to become the most frequently performed play of the postwar years, premiered in Zurich.
	Hermann Hesse received the Nobel Prize for Literature.
1947	The U.S., British, and French zones were joined into one economic unit and the European Recovery Program, or Marshall Plan, began.
	The news magazine *Der Spiegel* began publication.
	A group of writers met in the Alps and founded Gruppe '47.
1948	The Berlin airlift of supplies into West Berlin kept the city open in spite of a blockade by the USSR.

1949   The Federal Republic of Germany (FRG) was established in the west and the German Democratic Republic (GDR) in the east.

1950   Theodor W. Adorno and Max Horkheimer returned from exile in the United States and reestablished the Institute for Social Research at Frankfurt University—better known as the Frankfurt School.

A pilot television program was introduced in Hamburg and Berlin (*Nordwestdeutscher Fernsehdienst*, Northwest German TV service).

The era of the German *Schlager* (pop songs) began (Cornelia Froboess, Freddy Quinn, and others).

1953   Soviet forces sent tanks to quell riots by East German workers.

1954   West Germany was accepted into the North Atlantic Treaty Organization (NATO).

West Germany beat Hungary in the World Cup Soccer Championship.

1955   The high commissioners of the occupation powers declared the end of the occupation statute. The FRG's sovereignty was proclaimed.

The international art show *documenta* opened its doors for the first time.

1956   The first soldiers of West Germany's new conscription army began their service. In the GDR, a socialist army was created.

1957   The European Economic Community (EEC) and European Atomic Energy Community (Euratom) treaties were signed in Rome.

The last film of the *Sissi* trilogy about the Empress Elisabeth of Austria, starring Romy Schneider, was shown in movie theaters.

1958   The Central Agency of the State Judicial Administration for the Investigation of National Socialist Crimes was established (Zentrale Stelle der Landesjustizverwaltung zur Aufklärung nationalsozialistischer Verbrechen).

1961   The Berlin Wall was built by the GDR.

Adolf Eichmann was tried in Jerusalem by the Israeli government and subsequently executed.

1962   Beate Uhse opened her first sex store.

1963   The *ZDF* (Zweites Deutsches Fernsehen, Second German TV Channel) began broadcasting.

In December, the Auschwitz trials began in Frankfurt.

1965   Peter Weiss's play *Die Ermittlung* (The Investigation) was performed in theaters in East and West Germany as well as in London simultaneously.

Hans Magnus Enzensberger founded *Kursbuch*, which became the FRG's most influential magazine for intellectuals.

1966   Nelly Sachs received the Nobel Prize for Literature.

1967   Benno Ohnesorg, a student demonstrator, was killed by police in Berlin.

1968   German university students protested the authoritarian system and demanded reform.

The Red Army Faction (RAF), also known as the Baader-Meinhof gang, staged the first of its attacks.

1970   A new policy of reconciliation with the FRG's eastern neighbors was initiated by West German Chancellor Willy Brandt, who received the Nobel Peace Prize in December of that year.

1971   A school to train *Zivis*, those who chose to work in social services rather than serve in the army, was opened.

1972   The Grundlagenvertrag (Basic Treaty) was ratified, opening a new chapter in the relationship between East and West Germany.

Heinrich Böll was awarded the Nobel Prize for Literature.

1976   The singer and dissident Wolf Biermann was expatriated from the GDR.

1977   Student terrorists committed three murders against prominent members of the establishment.

Alice Schwarzer founded the feminist magazine *Emma*.

1979   Volker Schlöndorff won an Oscar for his film *The Tin Drum*, based on the novel by Günter Grass.

1980   The Taschen publishing company opened its first bookstore in Cologne.

Die Grünen (The Greens, or the "Green Party") was officially founded.

1981   Wolfgang Petersen had an international success with his film *Das Boot* (The Boat).

Elias Canetti (who was born in Bulgaria but wrote in German) was awarded the Nobel Prize for Literature.

1982   A successful vote of no confidence in parliament by the Christlich Demokratische Union/Christlich Soziale Union (CDU/CSU, Christian Democratic Union/Christian Social Union) brought about political change: Chancellor Helmut Schmidt (of the Sozialdemokratische Partei Deutschlands, or Social Democratic Party of Germany, SPD) was succeeded by Helmut Kohl (CDU).

1985   Richard von Weizsäcker, president of the Federal Republic, in a speech on the fortieth anniversary of the end of World War II, stated that Germany had been liberated from a terror regime.

1986–1987   The *Historiker Streit* (Historians' Debate, a series of essays in newspapers) questioned the uniqueness of Hitler's crimes.

1989   Following demonstrations and a mass exodus from East Germany, the Berlin Wall was opened.

1990   Germany was officially united on October 3 with Helmut Kohl as chancellor.

1995   The artists Christo and Jeanne-Claude wrapped the Reichstag building in Berlin with more than 100,000 square meters of fireproof polypropylene fabric, covered by an aluminum layer.

1998   Helmut Kohl and the CDU were defeated by Gerhard Schröder and the SPD.

Tom Tykwer's film *Lola Rennt* (Run, Lola, Run) starring Franka Potente was an international success.

1999   Günter Grass was awarded the Nobel Prize for Literature.

2003   The film *Goodbye Lenin* was an international hit.

Laws governing shop hours were modified to allow more evening and weekend shopping opportunities.

2004   Bernd Eichinger's film *Der Untergang* (Downfall), starring Bruno Ganz as Adolf Hitler, gained much attention but was not a major box-office success.

The Austrian writer Elfriede Jelinek was awarded the Nobel Prize for Literature.

2005   The Holocaust Memorial was dedicated in Berlin.

The CDU returned to power under Angela Merkel with a very narrow majority, which resulted in the first grand coalition (left-right) government in forty years. She is Germany's first female chancellor.

Introduction

Florian Illies and Constantin Gillies, two German authors with curiously similar sounding names and born in 1971 and 1970, respectively, have written books about their generation, a generation that in the United States would be classified as Generation X. Illies has entitled his books *Generation Golf: Eine Inspektion* (Generation Golf: An Investigation) and *Generation Golf zwei* (Generation Golf Two), whereas Gillies's title is *Wie wir waren: Die wilden Jahre der Web-Generation* (The Way We Were. The Wild Years of the Web Generation). The www alliteration is, of course, intentional.

Illies gives his readers a series of detailed snapshots of his childhood, teenage, and young adult years, beginning his first book with an image of a twelve-year-old on a typical Saturday evening. He takes his fellow Golfers (the reference is not to the game, but to the Volkswagen model that was introduced in 1974, shortly after his birth, and that gained popularity with these now thirty-plus-year-olds) on a nostalgia trip, reminding them of their favorite foods, fashions, trends, and tastes. Gillies, in contrast, focuses on his peers' dot-com careers, how they enthusiastically embraced the brave new world of computing and the Internet, how they founded companies, conducted business by their own rules, and, sadly, floundered as they discovered that their ideals lacked practical underpinnings.

Why it seemed necessary to chronicle a generation that still has to prove itself is initially unclear. As Illies was writing his first book (published in 2000), the German economy was still in good shape. The unification of the former German Democratic Republic with the Federal Republic of Germany had certainly made a dent in the smooth, comfortable way of life in the west, but most of the unemployment woes were in the east, where a certain level of adjustment had been expected. There were still adequate funds—and regulating policies—to ensure that the unemployed and those unable to work for reasons of health could be supported by a generous welfare system. But by the time *Generation Golf zwei* and *Wie wir waren* came out (both in 2003), this was no longer the case. As the new century was taking its first steps, it soon became apparent that the comfortable, secure life that generation had been born into was about to change. While Illies's first book has a lighthearted, affectionately mocking stance toward the goals and values of his peers, the later books have a darker tone and portray their fears and disappointments, and even their follies are discussed in a critical rather than sympathetic tone.

In this book, we will use this relatively sudden switch from carefree and comfortable to concerned and cautious as the prism for an examination of German popular culture since the end of World War II. It is not a grandiose attempt to trace the rise and fall of a nation as is done in studies such as *Deutschland. Der Abstieg eines Superstars* (Germany: The Decline of a Superstar), by Gabor Steingart. Rather, we will look at various aspects of culture and its manifestations, frivolous and otherwise. We will frequently move back in time (mainly to the early postwar years, but also to the prewar era) to examine the traditions on which German culture in the new millennium is founded, what it was that the parents passed on to their children, what each generation rebelled against, how the culture was shaped by the advent of the new technology and travel, and what people did, ate, played, wore, saw, and watched, and try to place all of this into some kind of context.

The parents of these young Germans belong to a group known as the '68ers, a name that refers to the year in which the students at German universities demonstrated against the way they were taught, the authoritarian way they had been brought up, and the political systems that were in place, which they considered to be too conservative. The '68ers also criticized their parents' generation—those born in the first three decades of the twentieth century—for their unwillingness both to confront the atrocities of the recent past and to distance themselves sufficiently from the fascist government of Adolf Hitler, a man they had elected to power either through active support or passive apathy. The issue of coming to terms with the past is one that surfaces again and again in many areas of everyday life and high culture in Germany, and the reader will find frequent cross-references both to this and to other topics to illustrate the interrelatedness of areas that are discussed separately. We also use such references to avoid repetition and to allow for nonlinear reading or dipping into the book for information on specific topics.

Reacting against their parents, the '68ers brought their children up with a strong antiauthoritarian bias, even offering them alternative versions of some children's books that they had read in their own youth. The chapter on literature offers more insights into what it was that children were given to read and how these books helped to form their character. Of course, Illies's and Gillies's schoolmates probably preferred television much of the time, and this, too, is discussed, along with film and theater. The latter might be considered high rather than popular culture to some, but in Germany, theater plays a major role in politics and city administration and as a barometer of attitudes and social change.

The three eras represented by the generations—the postwar years, the time of rebellion, and the present post-unification era—will be addressed throughout the book. We present both basic current information about the various topics, including the official structures, and a historical survey. The problems of the present day—that is, the years after the turn of the millennium—cannot be understood without considering the times that preceded them. In the main text of each chapter we offer an admittedly subjective, impressionistic survey emphasizing attitudes and examples; the sections entitled "From A to Z" near the ends of the chapters offer a more objective listing of facts and definitions to serve as a reference to the topics under discussion. Therefore, the main text uses quotations, summaries from popular magazines, descriptions from local papers, and comments by individuals, not necessarily experts, to explore various topics, whereas the "From A to Z" sections, which are sometimes quite extensive and detailed, focus on facts rather than perspectives. Here we also offer references to official brochures and Web sites. Additional Readings appear at the end of each chapter, and a Bibliography can be found at the back of the book. Our goal throughout is to present a balanced mixture of raw data and impressions and attitudes.

Additional Readings

Gillies, Constantin. *Wie wir waren. Die wilden Jahre der Web-Generation.* Weinheim: Wiley-VCH Verlag GmbH und Co.KGaA, 2003.

Illies, Florian. *Generation Golf. Eine Inspektion*, 5th ed. Frankfurt: Fischer, 2001. (1st ed., Berlin: Argon, 2000.)

———. *Generation Golf zwei.* München: Blessing, 2003.

Steingart, Gabor. *Deutschland. Der Abstieg eines Superstars.* München and Zürich: Piper, 2004.

POP CULTURE
GERMANY!

1

The Germans' Ambivalent Attitude toward Their Nation and Their Past

Overcoming Regionalism

"It is paradoxical," remarked Gordon A. Craig, the doyen of German cultural studies, "that the Germans, chronically torn and divided . . . throughout most of the modern period, seemed during the Middle Ages, and particularly between the tenth and twelfth centuries, to be politically more mature, and closer to establishing effective political institutions, than their neighbors. . . . Records dating from the tenth century speak of a *regnum teutonicorum* as an accomplished fact, which suggests that a recognizable national identity or self-consciousness also existed" (Craig, 1982, 16). However, this identity did not continue to develop because active commerce and the relatively early emergence of urban civilizations in the German states resulted in an increase of economic prosperity that also added "to the strength and pretensions of local princes, who were . . . restive under the domination of Imperial power" (ibid.). Today the legacy of these local princes can be seen in the number of small castles that dot the German landscape as well as in designations such as *Residenzstadt* (city of residence) for quite minor towns that once knew better days as seats of the local ruler. (See 1: From A to Z, "Historical overview, ancient to modern.")

The revival of the papacy from its earlier weakness and the political results of the Reformation led eventually to the dualism that has become so characteristic of German history, "the dualism between central authority and princely power, which, in the end, destroyed the former and fastened upon the realm the particularism that was to affect all aspects of German life in the modern period" (ibid., 16–17). Although one might argue that in the years since Craig wrote these words Germany has achieved some kind of central authority, a closer look reveals that each region has also retained its own characteristics and culture. In the

Germany's Layout through History

Augsburger Religionsfriede (Religious Peace Treaty of Augsburg) from the year 1555, the princes were even given the authority to determine the religion of their people. As a consequence, legal systems and many other aspects of daily experience were determined for Germans by the regions in which they lived (see 3: The Role of Religion). The region was the *Lebensraum* (living space) with which they identified, and to a large degree, it still is. (For detailed information on the various regions, with geographical data, see 1: From A to Z.)

Yet, this regionalism has never excluded an overarching cultural identity that is essentially German. Indeed, Germany may have even profited from the lack of political centralism, as the classical dramatist Friedrich Schiller (author of the Swiss "national" play *Wilhelm Tell*) remarked in his later years. "No capital and no court exerted its tyranny on German taste. There are as many lands and streams and customs, as there are own inclinations and types" (quoted in de Bruyn 1991, 22). These views were shared by many intellectuals in the eighteenth century. When the poet Johann Christoph Gottsched founded his "German Society" in Leipzig, when the dramatist Gotthold Ephraim Lessing tried to establish a theater in Hamburg, which was to belong to the whole German nation, when the intellectual Justus Möser from Osnabrück saw the regional pluralism of the Germans not as something disturbing but as something fertile, and when the philosopher Johann Gottfried Herder recognized that the language, the songs, the poetry, the customs, and the traditions are the essence of a nation, it became clear that this feeling of something uniquely German, the feeling of solidarity and the sense of a common bond, existed in spite of the political disunity (ibid., 21–22).

In the early nineteenth century, Napoleon's attempts to conquer more land for France contributed to the awakening of political nationalism all over Europe. In Germany, the new impetus was most distinctly and vividly expressed in the poem "Deutschland, Deutschland über alles" (Germany, Germany Above All [1841]) by Heinrich Hoffmann von Fallersleben, a poem later misunderstood by many (see 2: Symbols and Memorials). Hoffmann's verses did not imply a political world dominance—as many interpreted it after 1933—but only the desire to place the idea of a unified Germany over the many independent and rivaling principalities and cities, a dream that Otto von Bismarck was only partly able to realize at the end of the nineteenth century with the creation of the second German Reich (empire). But the nation that came into being under his rule was tainted, first by the emperor, Kaiser Wilhelm II, and then, of course, by Adolf Hitler. Hitler's Third Reich was designed to appeal to both the idea of nation and the idea of regionalism, that is, to regional history and customs as well as a united Germany that encompassed all. More than the Weimar Republic, which was founded as a confederacy of individual regions, it stressed the *Gau* (tribal districts). The boys and girls in the Hitler-Jugend (Hitler Youth) and Bund deutscher Mädel (Association of German Girls) learned all the traditional folksongs and dances, and traditions were exploited for nationalistic propaganda purposes. As a result, in the years following World War II, Germans had an even more difficult time coming to terms with their national identity. Not only did the more or less positive tension between centralism and regionalism continue, but now the term "nation" and national traditions were associated with and dominated by a cruel war and the Shoah (see 1: Coming to Terms with the Past; From A to Z, "Historical overview, postwar years"; "Holocaust").

The ambiguous attitude Germans have toward their own identity—Friedrich Dieckmann referred to *Negatividentität* (negative identity) in his study *Was ist deutsch?* (What Is German? 2003, 19)—can be observed frequently, particularly among the '68ers. But times are changing, and the younger generation, including the Golf group and their younger siblings, is more positive. (See 4: Lifestyle and Fashion, for the account of a designer who is doing her bit to change this attitude.)

On a larger political scale, however, this "negative identity" has been one of the driving forces behind the German effort to help create a new Europe (see 1: From Two to One). Many saw the introduction of the European passport as an emotional blessing that downplayed Germanness and stressed the membership in a larger geographical and political unit less tainted by recent history. A twist on the negative identity issue can be seen in the National Day of Mourning (Volkstrauertag, see 5: Holidays and Local Festivals). Whereas other nations commemorate their fallen soldiers, Germans remember "the victims of war and tyranny" as inscribed in Germany's central war memorial in Berlin. On a local scale, even monuments from the 1870/1871 Franco-Prussian War can be found hidden behind shrubbery or displayed prominently depending on the various prevalent attitudes in a given era.

This uneasiness with history has become so much of the German identity that even German textbooks for foreigners often in-

Typical monument for the 1870/71 War. The inscription at the base of the monument reads: *To the Brave Warriors 1870/1871—Our Souls to God—Our Bodies to the Enemies—Donated by the Citizens of Reinheim 1900.*

clude it in their culture sections. *Blaue Blume* (Blue Flower) (Eichheim et al. 2002) points out that before World War II, every German and Austrian village had a war memorial next to its cemetery where wreaths were laid on certain days. These memorials were demolished in both countries after 1945 because they could be interpreted as glorifying war and nationalism. In Switzerland, in contrast, a neutral country that has not been engaged in a war for 200 years, such memorials are still preserved. In this context, it should not be forgotten that most of the graves of soldiers killed in World War II are outside Germany and are tended by the War Graves Association. Today, when a former soldier is buried in Germany, a brass band plays the song "Ich hatt' einen Kameraden, einen besseren find'st du nicht" (I Had a Comrade, You Won't Find a Better One) rather than the national anthem (ibid., 177).

Yet another new twist to the age-old question of national identity was caused by the unification of the Federal Republic and the German Democratic Republic in 1990. It showed that Willy Brandt (whose goal as West German chancellor was to bring about a new relationship with the FRG's neighbors to the east; see 1: From Two to One) was correct when he spoke of two states and one nation, making the distinction between political entities and culture. In 1989, when the GDR had just celebrated its fortieth anniversary, the slogan of protest raised by the citizens of the GDR against their dictatorial and undemocratic government, "*Wir sind das Volk*" (We are the people), soon changed to "*Wir sind ein Volk*" (We are one people) when the possibility of unification emerged. And the emotional welcome of the GDR population by the West after the fall of the Berlin Wall confirmed the feeling of *one* nation. There were tears, hugs, and champagne, as at a family reunion. However, once the new Germany was legalized, the wall, this time as an imaginary divide in the minds of the people, was stronger than ever, leading over the years to an *Ostalgie* (nostalgia for the lost east, see 1: From Two to One), which is, in effect, a new version of regionalism.

Coming to Terms with the Past

Even after more than half a century, the shadow of Adolf Hitler has not disappeared (see Aust et al., 2004), although its impact is changing. (For a short general historical overview, see 1: From A to Z.) Richard Lord was only partly correct when he wrote: "For most Germans, history is a mega-nightmare that they can't simply awaken from" (Lord 2004, 40). Today, alongside the old feelings of guilt, a new sense of pride in the nation is noticeable among young Germans, as found in the German lyrics of bands such as the young Berlin group Mia (see 8: Music): "*Fragt man mich jetzt, woher ich komme, tu ich mir nicht mehr selber Leid*" (Now if someone asks me where I'm from, I don't feel sorry for myself anymore).

Yet, the wish to wipe out the twelve years of the Third Reich, to forget them, may have been one of the reasons that Konrad Adenauer, the first chancellor after the war, attained the stature that he did and remained pretty much unchallenged over the decades. He placed at the very top in popularity polls even as late as 2003, and, by a clear majority, he was still seen as the most important and greatest of Germans (see Knopp et al., 2003). Certainly, this selection was partly due to his willingness to continue business as usual during his term as political leader without forcing the nation to undergo a genuine reappraisal of its recent past. His was quite a different attitude from the one Theodor W. Adorno expressed in exile in New York City in 1944: "The thought that life could continue in a 'normal' way after this war or that even the culture could be 'reconstructed' again—as if reconstruction of culture were not in itself the negation of it—is idiotic. Millions of Jews have been killed, and that is supposed to be just an interlude and not the catastrophe itself. What is this culture actually still waiting for?" (quoted in Glaser 2002, 224). Pragmatism won the day. Continuity and stability characterized everyday life in the first thirty years after World War II. Most Germans simply wanted to forget and have others forget what had happened in the Nazi era. The media went along with this wish to fabricate an intact world in which the recent past had no place. The two broadcasting channels emphasized harmless entertainment, keeping to this pattern for years. Similarly, family life maintained its pattern, often reflecting the TV programs. Many households ate their supper at 8 P.M. to coincide with the nightly news, and every Saturday at about 10 P.M., water consumption would reach a peak: This was the hour at which the first segment of the evening's entertainment ended with the drawing of the lottery numbers, giving viewers a break to go to the bathroom (Eichheim et al. 2002, 207; see also 7: Radio and Television).

Political slogans of *"Keine Experimente!"* (No experiments), a carefully structured silence about fascist atrocities in school classrooms, and above all daily routines suppressed any unwelcome memories. And after the official Nuremberg Trials by the Allies and a few others in the 1950s and 1960s, indifference set in. In the early years (primarily in the late 1940s and 1950s), horrifying images and movies of past atrocities were shown to a few elementary and high-school children without any explanation of the context. There was little or no attempt made to explain the past atrocities or to educate the young people in their ethics, religion, and history classes about other cultures and religions in a detailed way. The opportunity to inform the new generation about Judaism and its customs and rites, holidays, and beliefs was missed, and the history curriculum always ended before reaching the years of the rise of fascism. A whole generation grew up without an official education about their recent past, which seemed as taboo a topic as sex. The '68ers searched for books on their own and tried to inform themselves without teachers.

Meanwhile, intellectuals suggested creating *Goethegemeinden* (Goethe societies) to help reinstill the most vivid examples of the German spirit, the most noble music and poetry, into the hearts of Germans (Glaser 2002, 224; see also 8: Theater and Dance). As the director of a cabaret explains to a *Kriegsheimkehrer* (returnee from the war) in Wolfgang Borchert's play *Draußen vor der Tür* (Outside the Door, 1947): "Be positive! Positive, my dear friend! Remember Goethe! Remember Mozart! Joan of Arc, Richard Wagner, Schmeling, Shirley Temple!" And instead of undergoing a soul-wrenching self-accusation and cleansing process of remorse, former Nazi officials were rapidly reintegrated into German life as fast as could be justified. The Allies followed the same pattern with Nazi scientists, integrating them into their research teams if they could advance their nuclear or missile programs, even though these very same scientists had used inmates of slave labor camps for their work (see "Concentration camps" in 1: From A to Z). If they were useful, their direct or indirect participation in the fascist system was overlooked. They were regarded as apolitical people who had only done their duty. Peter Weiss expressed this attitude explicitly in his play *Die Ermittlung* (The Investigation, 1965) when he had one of the accused say:

We all
I would like to emphasize again
only did our duty
even if it was often difficult for us
and when we almost despaired because of it.

Today

when our nation once again

has reached

a leading position

we should worry about other things

than about accusations

which come under the statute of limitations.

(Quoted in Glaser 2002, 247)

One could not expect everyone to become a hero like Paul Schneider, a priest who defended his Christian faith of brotherly love until his death in a concentration camp. Sixty years later, he is as forgotten as he was in the years after the war—at least in the general consciousness. Few resistance fighters and antifascists have experienced later fame or even recognition. An exception are the brother and sister Hans and Sophie Scholl, who were at the core of a student resistance movement, called "Die Weiße Rose" (The White Rose), in 1942/1943, and Claus Graf Schenk von Stauffenberg, who attempted to assassinate Hitler in 1944. They were voted among the top 100 greatest Germans in 2003.

In East Germany, the Nazi past was equated with capitalism, and the persecution of Communists by Nazis was emphasized. The new socialist GDR government abolished capitalism and stressed the fact that Communists were among the first inmates of concentration camps, thereby absolving itself of any responsibility for the Nazi era. West Germany had no such explanation, and its government had to accept the burden of the past. The FRG's relative silence about the fascist era during most of the first two decades after the war was an unpleasant stain on the fabric of the young democracy, though it was occasionally interrupted by official ceremonies and speeches that contained just enough an-

tifascistic rhetoric to satisfy any critic. In 1967, the psychologists Alexander and Margarete Mitscherlich analyzed the situation in hindsight in their book *Unfähigkeit zu trauern* (Inability to Mourn), stating that the German ability to avoid facing the past provided the foundation for the materialistic expansion that followed. The economic miracle (see 10: Consumer Culture versus Green Awareness) was possible only because of this pragmatic attitude. The loss of the historical conscience freed the nation from self-destruction, and the twelve years under Hitler could be interpreted as an aberration.

In his *Kleine Kulturgeschichte Deutschlands im 20. Jahrhundert* (Brief Cultural History of Germany in the 20th Century, 2002, 245), Hermann Glaser enumerated the most obvious shortcomings of the era, which were foreshadowed in the East German film *Die Mörder sind unter uns* (The Murderers Are Among Us, 1946; see 7: Film). There was Adenauer's close associate Hans Globke, who was a former legal commentator of the Nuremberg race laws of 1935. There was the banker Hermann Abs, who sat on many executive boards during the Nazi years as well as in the years after the war. In his influential positions, he had helped the Hitler regime in the *Arisierung* (literally Aryanization, the transferral of ownership from Jews to Germans) of banks and firms. In the postwar West German democracy, he became one of the financial advisers to the new government. There was Theodor Oberländer, who had been a member of the NSDAP (Nationalsozialistische Deutsche Arbeiterpartei, National Socialist German Workers' Party) since 1933 and had held important positions in the party. From 1953 to 1960, he was minister for refugees and exiles under

Adenauer until a public outcry over his past forced him to resign. There were only a few lawyers who survived with a clean slate, such as Fritz Bauer, who initiated the Auschwitz trials in 1965 (Wojak 2004, 814–830), and Martin Hirsch, member of parliament. But not one judge or prosecutor was sentenced under Adenauer because of judicial crimes committed during the Third Reich, although as many as 40,000 sentences of capital punishment may have been given to *Volksschädlinge* (enemies of the state) during the Hitler era. In 1951, a law was passed that guaranteed employment to almost all Nazi bureaucrats as well as compensation for their period of unemployment. Compensation for *Zwangsarbeiter* (slave workers), in contrast, was not regulated until the year 2000, when a bill established a foundation called Erinnerung, Verantwortung und Zukunft (Remembrance, Responsibility and Future). Finally, the various German firms involved were persuaded to contribute their share after long and cumbersome negotiations. Most of them had profited from the Hitler era and were bouncing back from their near-destruction in the postwar years, but they saw little connection between their present status and their past.

Not until 1958 did the ministers of justice of the individual German states establish a Zentrale Stelle der Landesjustizverwaltung zur Aufklärung nationalsozialistischer Verbrechen (Central Agency of the State Judicial Administration for the Investigation of National Socialist Crimes). But in spite of extensive investigations by its director, the resulting legal proceedings were minimal. In 1984, the newspaper *Süddeutsche Zeitung* took stock and remarked: "In spite of information stored in Ludwigsburg on more than 1.3 million index cards that were systematically evaluated, in spite of 4,802 pre-1958 and 13,000 preliminary proceedings since 1958—the final balance must be unbearable to all those victims who have survived Auschwitz or Majdanek, Theresienstadt or Treblinka. Out of 88,587 persons who had been accused of Nazi crimes by January 1, 1983, only 6,465 had been sentenced, 12 for capital punishment, 158 for a lifelong sentence, 80,355 were found not guilty and for 1,767 accused, the trial is still pending; but there is little expectation of further severe sentences" (quoted in Glaser 2002, 246; see also for general reference, Werle and Wandres 1995).

In 1987, Ralph Giordano spoke of a second guilt: the suppression and minimization of the Nazi crimes. Even now, the discussion on this topic has not been laid to rest, and many events, both small and large, have fueled the debate. In 1985, commemorating the fortieth anniversary of the end of the war, Richard von Weizsäcker, as president of the Federal Republic, made a point of stating that Germany had not lost a war but had been liberated from a terror regime. But there was also the *Historiker Streit* (Historians' Debate), a series of essays in prominent newspapers in 1986/1987 about the possibility of comparing Stalin's and Hitler's atrocities and thereby negating the uniqueness of the inhumanity of the Holocaust. Such academic arguments were seen by many as indications that a genuine understanding of the past was still lacking. "Vergangenheit, die nicht vergehen will" (The Past which Will not Pass Away), the title of the first article that began the Historians' Debate, seemed indicative of an attitude among many Germans that favored continuing the suppression of the topic, implying that there already had been too much emphasis placed on these years and that the emphasis ought to stop. It was argued that the past should not influence the current politics of the new Germany. This opinion also seemed to be at the core of a speech delivered by the writer Martin Walser when he received the Friedenspreis des deutschen Buchhandels (Peace Prize of the German Book Trade) in 1998. At least many understood him that way when he stated that the Holocaust should not be used as a political tool. Ignatz Bubis, president of the Zentralrat der Juden in Deutschland (Central Committee of Jews in Germany), left the room after Walser's remarks, which he regarded as a *"geistige Brandstiftung"* (intellectual arson). These controversies were full of complex nuances and only showed the difficulty Germans have had in coming to terms with their past; the anti-Israeli pamphlets distributed in 2002 by Jürgen Möllemann, a member of the Freie Demokratische Partei (FDP, the German liberals), were much more blatant and shocking in their attempt to cater to German right-wing voters.

In the early 1980s, Peter Sichrovsky, born in 1947 of Jewish parents who had emigrated to England during the war, sought to gauge the attitudes of Jews living in Germany and Austria forty years after the camps had been liberated. He published his findings in a set of narratives, or *Protokolle*, using a genre that had been developed in the German Democratic Republic as a cross between investigative journalism and literary writing. (In the GDR, Protokolle were often controversial, and authors often had difficulties finding publishers who dared to print them.) The somewhat cumbersome title of his book, published in 1985, would translate as *We Don't Know What Tomorrow Will Bring, We Know Well*

What Yesterday Was: Young Jews in Germany and Austria. Sichrovsky interviewed a number of people and wrote their responses (without including his questions) in the form of reflective autobiographical statements. Among those who were willing to talk about their status were Jews who had lived in Israel and chosen to return to Germany, married couples with different perspectives on the situation, and children of camp survivors who were angry about their parents' submissive attitude.

In a later book, *Born Guilty: Children from Nazi Families* (1987), Sichrovsky gathered statements from people whose parents had been supporters of the Nazi regime, asking them how this had affected their lives. One suffered from the burden of inherited guilt and wished to seek atonement for the sins of the fathers. Another Protokoll is given in the form of a dialogue in which a daughter defends her officer father against criticism from her dropout brother. In this case, the reader's sympathies tend to gravitate toward the daughter as she points out how well her father treated his family, in contrast to the son, who appears to take pleasure in shocking the bourgeois family but has no scruples about living off those whom he despises.

Nevertheless, in many communities the 1990s were also a time when ways of remembrance were discussed and ways found to take at least a first step. St. Georgen, once a farming village in Baden-Württemberg and today a suburb of the city of Freiburg, though it retains a village character, is a good example. Its local newspapers provide insights into everyday life, how customs are retained, revived, or modified, and how German culture is evolving in the twenty-first century. They also report about St. Georgen's dark side, a side some might wish to forget. During the Nazi era, the village was the location of a factory that made sacks and used forced labor from countries that had been invaded by Hitler's regime. Fortunately, this cloud has developed a rather special silver lining. In May 2004, one of these Zwangsarbeiter (forced laborers) returned to Freiburg for a reunion with others from the Ukraine, Slovenia, and France as guests of the mayor to unveil a memorial at the site of the camp where most of them had lived while working at the factory. Andrés Dirk Kylstra from Groningen, Netherlands, pointed out at the reunion that he was one of the luckier ones. Not only did he have the good fortune to live with a local family rather than in the camp, he was befriended by someone who made sure that he got to attend theater and concert performances. He also met his future wife in Freiburg. Later, Kylstra became a professor of older German literature in Groningen. He also suffered in his native Netherlands, however, in the early postwar years, when there was still animosity toward Germans. His mother was not happy about his marriage to a German woman, and for a long time being a professor of German literature aroused suspicion about loyalty to his home country. His fellow forced laborers from Eastern Europe also suffered when they returned home if they were suspected of having collaborated with the Nazis (*Der Sonntag*, May 9, 2004, 8).

One way in which the city of Freiburg—a city that had a Jewish population of around 1,400 in 1933 and was declared "free of Jews" ten years later—is dealing with its Nazi past is by literally tripping up its citizens as they walk the city streets. The Cologne artist Gunter Demnig came up with the idea of *Stolpersteine* (literally,

tripping stones), small cobblestones about 4 inches (10 cm) long that have a brass plate fitted into them that is engraved with the name and birth and death dates of individuals who suffered at the hands of the Nazis—Jews, Sinti and Roma gypsies, political enemies of the state, freemasons, and homosexuals. The stones are imbedded in sidewalks outside of houses the citizens are known to have lived in up to their deportation or flight. Demnig's idea gives the victims of the Nazi persecution a name and address and forces present-day citizens to confront the past and perhaps recall neighbors who suddenly moved away. In Freiburg, the decision to adopt Demnig's idea was made in December 2002, and the first stone was set in the *Goethestraße* (Goethe Street) outside the guest house of the university. It commemorates a professor of law (Robert Liefmann) who was deported with his two sisters, Else and Martha, and taken to Gurs, a camp in the French Pyrenees. He died there in 1941. In memory of that camp, there is a road sign in downtown Freiburg that looks like any

Example of a Stolperstein. Inscription reads: *Here lived/Kurt Adler/ Born 1918/Deported 1940/Dead on 26 January 1941 in/Gurs* (The usual abbreviation for "died" was not used.)

The Gurs Memorial is both the road sign to the location and the plaque in the foreground providing information. (The monument in the background is to a local dignitary, Carl von Rotteck.)

other but points to Gurs and bears a small plaque explaining its meaning.

As of May 2004, 170 additional Stolpersteine had been set in the sidewalks, all based on verified information, but there is a long waiting list of names and addresses deserving similar recognition. The city's coordinator for the program notices that many passersby avoid stepping on the stones, but she hopes to correct this. The brass plates need physical contact to make them shine and stand out to other passersby. If they are avoided or ignored, they will become dull and no longer stand out from their surroundings to catch the at-

tention of those who may not be aware of their hometown's involvement in the Nazi regime. The project is funded through private support with donations of 95 euros per stone, and has a Web site (www.freiburg-im-netz.de/stolpersteine) where one can check the location of the stones and the history behind those that have been laid thus far (*Amtsblatt*, April 30, 2004, 3).

On the one hand, guilt and shame are part of the German character; on the other, a new self-assuredness has reaffirmed itself in politicians such as former Chancellor Gerhard Schröder, Chancellor Angela Merkel, and President Horst Köhler, who were born at the end of the war or even after it. Symptomatic of the new attitude was the *Deutschland Kampagne* (Germany Campaign): Du bist Deutschland (You are Germany) that tried to instill pride and confidence into German citizens. In pop culture, representatives of this attitude may be seen in the group Virginia Jetzt! which proclaimed: "*Das ist mein Land, meine Menschen*" (This is my country, these are my people) (quoted in Aust 2005, 195). Germans remain ambivalent about the topic of remembering and forgetting, however, something Ernestine Schlant addressed well in her study *The Language of Silence: West German Literature and the Holocaust:*

> Germans—sometimes more than the citizens of other countries—have tried to address the Holocaust. They have done so not always convincingly, and they have been ambivalent and conflicted about their motives and their efforts. For half a century, literature has reflected these tortured, convoluted, even brazen and self-saving struggles and has fashioned many languages of silence to cope with the knowledge and the legacy of the atroci-

ties committed. While the private silences have become public debates, literature has begun to chart new areas. It has begun to express sorrow and mourning, and has started to acknowledge and include the Jewish presence in Germany. One should expect that as the seismograph of unconsciously held values German literature will persevere in its search for new articulations in its continuing efforts to come to terms with the Holocaust. (Schlant 1999, 243–244)

From Two to One

In 1945, before there were two Germanys, there was only one defeated and destroyed nation, physically and psychologically damaged, the *Stunde Null* (zero hour), as it was called by some historians. For most Germans at the time, it did not feel as if Germany had been liberated from an evil dictator by the Allies, but rather that they were regarded as a ferocious enemy and occupied in order to be subdued. According to the Berliner Erklärung (Berlin Declaration) by the victorious powers on June 5, 1945, Germany had to accept any and all demands that would be imposed then and in the future. All aspects of life, all governmental structures, down to the level of the community, were in the hands of the Allies. In Berlin, the Alliierter Kontrollrat (Allied Control Council) was in charge of all affairs in regard to Germany as a whole. The four supreme commanders were to make all decisions unanimously and then translate them into action at their discretion in the zones that they occupied. That was the theory, but their interests were too divergent and, in practice, each one of the four used the given discretion quite broadly in the respective zones.

Owing to the main difference between the occupying powers, which was in regard to the question of the reparations that Germany was to pay (the USSR was interested in large payments, whereas the West was more interested in getting the German economy working again), Germany was divided into two spheres of influence. Stalin emphasized again and again his support of a unified Germany (also driven by his desire to get his share of the future wealth of the Ruhrgebiet, the main industrial region in Germany), but at the same time he consolidated his hold on the eastern part of Germany, restructuring the whole region politically following the Soviet model.

When the United States feared in 1947 that Stalin's intent was expansionistic, its answer was to join the American and British zones into one economic unit and to begin the European Recovery Program, the Marshall Plan, which was accepted by the Western powers but rejected by the East. The currency reform in 1948 led systematically in 1949 to the creation of the Federal Republic of Germany (FRG) and the German Democratic Republic (GDR). In the West German Bundestag (lower house of parliament), Konrad Adenauer, leader of the Christlich Demokratische Union (Christian Democratic Union, CDU), was chosen as the first chancellor by only one vote over Kurt Schumacher, the leader of the Sozialdemokratische Partei Deutschlands (Social Democratic Party of Germany, SPD). The first election for the Volkskammer, the East German parliament, resulted in an overwhelming victory for the Sozialistische Einheitspartei Deutschlands (Socialist Unity Party of Germany, SED).

Both Germanys were organized into *Länder* (states) (see 3: The Political System). In 1952, the government of the Ger-

Regions of the GDR. *Source: Introducing the GDR*. Berlin: Panorama DDR, 1978:22

man Democratic Republic decided to restructure into fourteen districts (in 1961, Berlin became the fifteenth district) in order to adjust the state structure to the new economic necessities, to strengthen the central authority, and to widen the influence of socialist democracy. The Länder of the FRG were: Baden-Württemberg, Bayern, Berlin (special status), Bremen, Hamburg, Hessen, Niedersachsen, Nordrhein-Westfalen, Rheinland-Pfalz, Saarland, and Schleswig-Holstein. The districts of the GDR were: Berlin, Cottbus, Dresden, Erfurt, Frankfurt/Oder, Gera, Halle, Karl-Marx-Stadt (formerly and now Chemnitz), Leipzig, Magdeburg, Neubrandenburg, Potsdam, Rostock, Schwerin, and Suhl.

In the following years, the FRG did not officially recognize the existence of a sec-ond, Communist, Germany. West Germany's constitution regarded the division of Germany as temporary and saw the citizens of the GDR legally as citizens of the FRG. Therefore, they called the GDR the Sowjetisch Besetzte Zone (Soviet Occupation Zone, SBZ), or the "so-called GDR," in a policy formulated in 1955, the year of Germany's official return from an occupied territory to a sovereign state. Known as the Hallstein-Doktrin (Hallstein policy, named after the undersecretary of state, Walter Hallstein), it allowed all GDR refugees to the West to automatically receive a West German passport along with a small amount of financial startup support when they arrived. The Hallstein policy stressed that the Federal Republic alone had the right to represent Germany on the world stage and threatened to break off diplomatic relations with states that recognized the GDR (Müller 1986, 354).

The West German constitution was called the Grundgesetz (Basic Law), not the Verfassung (constitution), and Bonn was always regarded as a temporary capital (*provisorische Hauptstadt*). The preamble of the Basic Law, passed in 1949, stated that the population of the three western occupation zones also acted for those Germans who were not permitted to be involved. All German people were called upon "to complete the unity and freedom of Germany in free self-determination" (ibid., 332; for excerpts of the Grundgesetz, see Thiele 2004, 646–655). The constitution of the Deutsche Demokratische Republik (DDR, in English GDR) changed over the years. In 1968, the GDR still saw itself as a "socialist state of German nationhood" and its mandate as overcoming the division of Germany caused by imperialism; the constitution of 1974 avoided such references to

Left to right, Walter Hallstein (after whom the Hallstein-Doktrin was named), Chancellor Konrad Adenauer, Herbert von Blankenhorn (head of the political department in the office for foreign affairs) in 1954. (Bettmann/Corbis)

a German nation, and the republic defined itself only as "a socialist state of workers and farmers" (Armbruster 1981, 17).

The desire for unity was stressed on both sides, although only in political matters, and over the years the strength of the desire waxed and waned. It was not nurtured in the new generation, perhaps because both Germanys feared a nationalistic revival. As a result, even geographical knowledge of the other Germany was minimal in the youth growing up in their respective states. Maps in schoolbooks focused on the territories of the republic in which the book was published. The "other" Germany was *Ausland* (a foreign country), and maps produced in the GDR went so far as to have merely a blank space beyond the western borders.

Whereas East Germany was ravaged by the Soviets and had a difficult time building up its economy, West Germans enjoyed the results of the *Wirtschaftswunder* (economic miracle) based on U.S. help. West Berlin was kept artificially alive through its lifeline to the West. Even the Berlin blockade by the USSR in 1948 was not able to stop the support of this island within its territory. The importance of Berlin was demonstrated not only by the *Luftbrücke* (airlift) but also by the *Notopfer Berlin* (literally, sacrifice for Berlin in need), a special tax and a 2-pfennig stamp for every letter mailed inside Germany, starting in 1949 and lasting until 1956.

Berlin was not only an island of Western influence in the middle of communism but also a billboard advertising the wonderful world of capitalism, especially through its Kaufhaus des Westens (KaDeWe), the largest department store on the European continent. Like Harrod's in London, its major rival in terms of size, KaDeWe had a magnificent food hall with a dazzling array of meats, cheeses, breads, pastries, vegetables, and chocolate, much of it available for the shopper to sample. The contrast with the limited range of foods available in the eastern part of the city was striking, and intentionally so.

Just as West Germans looked longingly to the colorful, wealthy world they imagined in the United States, East Germans were fascinated by West Germany. And many came and stayed. Some 200,000 arrived in 1952, and 300,000 in 1953. The numbers did not diminish much after the Soviets demonstrated their ruthlessness in suppressing the riots by East German workers on June 17, 1953, sending tanks against people armed with a handful of pebbles. To stop the "brain drain" and not be faced suddenly with a state that had a government but no people, GDR bureaucrats decided to fortify their borders, to construct fences, and, in 1961, to close the last hole still existing on the border—to build, in Berlin, a 45-km-long wall with barbed wire and post armed guards along it. They called it the *antifaschistischer Schutzwall* (protective wall against fascist aggression). On the border between the eastern and western sectors, a so-called "death strip" was constructed from the Baltic to the border of what was then Czechoslovakia, a barren strip of land fenced with barbed wire on either side and planted only with landmines. Here too, border guards were posted in towers at intervals to watch for those trying to cross illegally. This was not so easy from the east,

Main entrance of Kaufhaus des Westens (commonly abbreviated KaDeWe).

since there was also limited access to the area just east of the border, and coastal areas of the Baltic were also put out of reach. One positive result of this is that Germans from both regions now enjoy some pristine beaches and countryside that remained undeveloped for many years.

All of these measures to strengthen the border seemed like the final step to an everlasting separation between the Germanys. And in 1968, the GDR gave itself a new constitution in which the socialist aspect of the state was emphasized, although it still saw itself as part of a German nation. In 1970, Willi Stoph, the prime minister of the GDR, continued the policy of socialist self-identification and of the separation of the two Germanys, claiming, "Today the socialist German Democratic Republic and the monopolistic capitalist Federal Republic exist as two separate independent states. Their citizens live and work under conditions completely opposed to one another. . . . In reality, the two sovereign states, GDR and FRG, cannot be united, because social orders contrary to one another cannot be united." But Willy Brandt, the architect of the new Ostpolitik in 1970, did not give up hope. He stated: "The concept of the nation forms the link that binds divided Germany together. Nation means more than just a common language and culture, more than a state and social order. The nation has its foundations in the ongoing sense of belonging together among the people. Nobody can deny that there is and there will be in this sense a German nation."

In 1972, the Hallstein policy was officially abolished and a treaty signed that affirmed the inviolability of the border between the two Germanys, as well as the fact that neither has the right to act in the other's name in its internal or external affairs. This treaty opened a new chapter in the relationship between the GDR and the FRG. The Berlin Wall lasted for a total of twenty-eight years. But then, in 1989, the year of the GDR's fortieth anniversary, the wall collapsed after another mass exodus of GDR citizens. This time they left their country not across the border from East to West Berlin but from East to West Berlin via Czechoslovakia and Hungary, the neighboring Communist states, which refused to serve as border guards for the GDR. The chief editor of the November 1989 issue of the *GDR Review*, published as the November/December issue a few weeks late owing to the upheaval in the GDR, wrote in his last editorial preface, "Speaking on Our Own Behalf":

Dear readers of GDR REVIEW and friends of the GDR in many countries!

. . . The last words to be put on paper for this issue are my own, the editorial. I find it difficult to formulate these words. . . . Along with most people in our country, we are struggling night and day for answers, explanations, admissions or rejections of guilt. What seemed valid yesterday is what we ourselves put in question today. I ask you, the reader, for your understanding in this respect.

. . . We, who have described to you the GDR in word and picture for years and in some cases decades, are now faced with the painful question: Have we deceived you, our readers, our friends, those who have placed their hopes for socialism specifically in **our** country, have we wilfully spread lies? For myself and my journalist colleagues I can and must reply with a clear conscience and a straight answer: No. But . . . [within] the scope given to us we painted a picture of the GDR which did not encompass all aspects of the reality.

New homes at low rents?—Yes, for millions of people, above all from the working class. But also the increasing dilapidation of buildings, particularly in the old town centres of which only a few have been restored. And therefore people continue to live under poor conditions.

No unemployment?—Yes, but at the same time weeks and months when working time has not been used to capacity in many enterprises, because the materials for production were not there, because fossilised economic structures prevented a feasible and necessary increase in work efficiency.

Participation from workers and employees in decision making?—What is the use of attested rights when bureaucratic, ossified and outdated leadership would recognise only what it wanted to hear?

We recognise **our** guilt in the acceptance of our condemnation to journalistic immaturity and speechlessness concerning the stated issues and many, many more.

The upheaval in the GDR was a completely unexpected turn of events. Just a few weeks before the events of November 9, 1989, Erich Honecker, the leader of the GDR, had given a speech in front of the wall that supposedly stood for his state's invincibility and proclaimed that it would stand for another century. He had underestimated the desire for reform that Mikhail Gorbachev had encouraged and also ignored the warning Gorbachev had given him during his state visit for the fortieth anniversary of the GDR: "Those who do not change with the times, will be punished by life."

The citizens who did not leave began to demonstrate. The most famous protests were the so-called Monday night demonstrations in Leipzig, when the chant "*Wir sind das Volk!*" (We are the people) resounded through the city and beyond. The question arose as to whether the GDR government should use force to subdue the protests, but there was no support for such an action by the Soviet Union. GDR officials realized that Honecker's time was over. The new reality was Gorbachev's *perestroika* (restructuring), and Egon Krenz replaced the outgoing Honecker. Krenz promised change. On the evening of November 9, 1989, the guards at the Berlin Wall apparently had been instructed to open the gates, and the rumor spread quickly. Within hours, thousands of people crossed the border. The Berlin Wall had fallen.

After decades apart, families were united. Tears of joy flowed as well as champagne. The slogan "*Wir sind das Volk*" had changed to "*Wir sind ein Volk.*" At the highest level of government, changes continued. Egon Krenz was replaced by Hans Modrow, the mayor of Dresden, who was seen by many as one of the leading reformers. Arrangements were made for the first free elections, which took place in March 1990. The eastern branch of the CDU scored a victory, replacing the SED as the largest single party. (The fact that bananas and oranges, something of a scarce luxury in the past, were suddenly being sold in eastern Germany, along with exotic looking products from the West, no doubt influenced many of the voters.) With amazing speed, driven by the fear that the window of opportunity might close again, the two Germanys moved toward unification. And on October 3, 1990, the forty-one-year-old division of Germany came to an end. It was not a true reunification but an expansion of the German Federal Republic of Germany: the addition of five new Länder. Many historians (and politicians), therefore, prefer the term 'unification' to 'reunification.'

Unfortunately, the politicians missed their chance to create the same sense of responsibility toward their fellow GDR citizens that they had once been able to muster for the Berlin citizens when they had established the Notopfer Berlin. Was the reason for this the timing, the fact that back then, in the early 1950s, people were still familiar with hunger pangs? Now in the 1990s, hunger was something suffered only far away in the Third World. Was it that the West Germans regarded the newcomers as a different kind of guest worker after the two states had officially recognized each other as the result of Willy Brandt's Ostpolitik? Or was it the fear that if they stressed the emotional aspect of the *one* people too much, a new nationalism would awaken? In any case, the spirit of the early postwar years had vanished. There was little talk of a new *Verfassungsversammlung* (constitutional committee) to work out a new joint *Verfassung* (constitution). The new Germany was not really to be a "new Germany" but only a larger West Germany. And the expansion happened fast: On November 9, 1989, the border opened; on July 1, 1990, the currency union became official (the GDR was given the deutsche mark); on October 3, 1990, the GDR was politically integrated into the FRG; and on June 20, 1991, the decision was made to select Berlin as the capital of the new Germany, now called the Berliner Republik.

Was it because of this purely political solution to an emotional question that the wall did not completely disappear, but instead was reerected in the minds of the people? There were the *Wessis* (westerners) on one side and the *Ossis* (easterners) on the other. One group (Wessis) felt superior, the other (Ossis) resentful because they had definitely been on the wrong side in this struggle. They were also the poorer cousins. Their run-down factories could not be compared with the world-class equipment of the other Germany. But they had worked hard under much worse conditions and they had built up a state that was a leading economic power in the environment they had lived in before unification came. They also could boast of some social and educational achievements. There were many ideas that might have proven beneficial to the West.

Since unification, many have left East Germany. The population has dropped by about 10 percent. According to Richard Lord, "In certain cities, the decline has been even more dramatic. For instance, the former heavy industrial bastion of Hoyerswerda saw its population plunge from roughly 75,000 to 45,000 in the 13 years following unification" (Lord 2004, 76). But

many of these relocated Germans have not adjusted to the West. They feel a loss of a certain human dimension. They miss camaraderie, the willingness to accept others on their own terms. After more than a decade, the division is still present in almost all aspects of life, as a detailed survey from 2004 in the magazine *Stern* proved. A chart reflecting the satisfaction people feel in regard to their home towns showed the dividing line as the old border between east and west. On the left of the map (the west), a green color indicating high to very high satisfaction was dominant; on the right (the east), yellow, orange, and even red were prevalent, where red meant deep dissatisfaction. On the next chart, which showed the degree of anxiety people had over losing their jobs, the division was very similar: low anxiety in the west, high anxiety (almost 60 percent) in the east. Not surprisingly, the same color distribution was also found in answers to the question about the social net: Should the individual or the state be in charge? The majority of the citizens of the new German states regard the state as the caretaker.

On other questions, some regions in the west concur with regions in the east and vice versa. But the difference in opinion between west and east is always more pronounced than the north-south comparison. No wonder that "Ostalgie" (an obvious word play on nostalgia) is so popular and has become an entertainment hit at the turn of the millennium. TV shows and films such as *Goodbye Lenin* have been box-office hits (see 7: Film). In March 2004, the *New York Times* offered readers of its Styles section a lighthearted perspective on recent German history in connection with a theater hit. The play in question was "I Am My Own Wife" by Doug Wright, about the transsexual Charlotte von Mahls-dorf, but the focus of the article was the toy model Trabant cars that Wright had bought in 1994 when in Berlin conducting research for the film. These little toy Trabis are described as one of the souvenirs available in the category of "East German relics," along with fragments of the Berlin Wall, Stasi uniforms and ID badges, and snow globes with zero visibility. The six-inch Trabis appealed to Wright as being the one "benign" memento among the "ominous" ones. He described the car as "the little comically inept Trabi that never ran." To one who recalls sitting with knees pressed against her chest in the back seat of one and smelling the fumes of many others puttering around, the image of them not running is distorted. They ran, but with attendant noise and polluting gases. The *New York Times* journalist David Colman talked of a more widespread urge to "paint over East Germany's blacker past with a drab coat of Trabi beige" and see the Trabi as "a dryly humorous stand-in for a reality many prefer to forget." He noted that production for the Trabi and its "two-stroke, smoke-belching engine" began in 1957 and that the basic model, the Trabi 601, went relatively unchanged until the car went off production in 1991. Nevertheless, there was a waiting list for the Trabis of up to ten years at times. Today the souvenir toy models are sold on e-Bay, reportedly fetching $15 apiece in March 2004. Colman remarked that "It's strange to see the Trabi aligned with reunification rather than Communism, but all's fair in memory and marketing" (*New York Times*, March 14, 2004).

In the years before the Berlin Wall fell, those in the West, with access to a wide range of consumer goods, would send care packages to their less favored friends and

relatives in the former German Democratic Republic, but it would seem that the situation has been reversed fifteen years later. A report in the online newsletter of the magazine *Brigitte* on November 22, 2004, with the heading "Ost-Päckchen" (East Packages), lists products that were well known in the GDR that are now available again for those who hanker after the good old days. Perhaps it is the popularity of recent films such as *Sonnenallee* and *Goodbye Lenin* that has made Germans from eastern and western states long for such products as Knusperflocken, a chocolate bar made of milk chocolate and crisp bread, or toothpaste with the cute name of Putzi. The signs that pedestrians followed when crossing the street—a little red man with a hat standing at attention, his feet together and arms outstretched, which commanded citizens to wait on the curb; and his complementary green man striding along, which encouraged those same citizens to cross the road (see 2: Symbols and Memo-

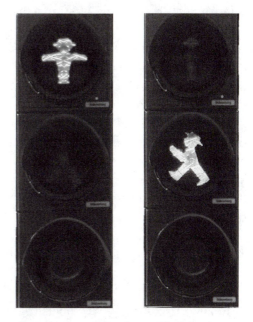

East German pedestrian traffic lights.

rials), have long been favorites on post-cards and T-shirts. They, too, are available online.

Of course, all the talk about Ostalgie has a negative side to it as well and may easily lead to a falsification and belittlement of a dictatorial regime that was responsible for murders and the incarceration of political opponents, whose suffering could easily be forgotten in such a rosy portrait of the former GDR (see Osang 2003, 212–222, and Haußmann 2003, 221).

From A to Z

Canals for shipping: The longest one in Germany is the Mittellandkanal in central Germany (321 km), followed by the Dort-mund-Ems Canal (269 km), the Main-Danube Canal (171 km), and the North Sea–Baltic Sea Canal (99 km).

Checkpoint Charlie: The Western Allies could not prevent the building of the Berlin Wall, but they could ensure at least access to East Berlin based on postwar treaties through the world-famous border control, Checkpoint Charlie (see www.mauer-museum.com). Haus am Checkpoint Charlie, a museum located in the last building before the wall, was established in 1963 and has been constantly expanded since then. Its exhibits are devoted to the theme of freedom and document the many escape attempts of GDR citizens. In 2005, the museum was in the headlines because of an argument between the city and the director of the museum over the maintenance of the display of the crosses for victims killed at the wall.

Climate: Germany has a moderate climate without extreme cold or hot periods. The northwest has a lot of rain, the southwest is known for its sunshine (Freiburg, Kaiser-stuhl). Eastern Germany has a typical con-tinental climate. Especially mild is the is-land of Mainau on Lake Constance, where palm trees, orchids, and citrus trees grow as well as other subtropical plants.

Concentration and extermination camps: Not all concentration and extermination camps were built outside German territory. Many were in everyone's view, even in the centers of German culture. Weimar was not only the cultural capital of Germany, as it has been proclaimed again today—the center of the German classic era and en-lightenment, the place where Johann Wolf-gang von Goethe and Friedrich Schiller lived and wrote—but also, during the 1930s, a conservative stronghold. In 1925, the progressive leaders of the Bauhaus school (see 9: Visual Arts; From A to Z) had to leave and move to Dessau. After his electoral victories, Hitler was welcomed with great enthusiasm. In 1937, Buchen-wald, one of the largest concentration camps, was established about 5 miles northwest of Weimar.

One of Buchenwald's subcamps was Dora-Mittelbau (also known as Dora-Nordhausen or Nordhausen) in the Harz Mountains, in legend famous for Walpur-ga's Eve (see "Tourist Attractions/places of myths and legends," below). It was the hor-ror place where Wernher von Braun (the later "father" of the U.S. moon landing, who was chosen in 2003 as one of the top 100 most important Germans) helped to develop the V2 rocket (*V* for *Vergeltung*, vengeance) built by forced laborers. One account reported: "Until the spring of 1944, prisoners were kept mostly underground, deprived of daylight and fresh air, and enclosed in unstable tunnels. The mortality rate was higher than at most other concentration camps. Prisoners too weak or ill to work were sent to Auschwitz-Birkenau or Mauthausen to be killed" (Holocaust Atlas, 162).

One of the very early camps was the Dachau camp 10 miles from Bavaria's capital, Munich. It was established in March 1933, one month after Hitler came to power, and remained operational during the entire period of the Third Reich, until April 1945. The Ravensbruck concentration camp, 56 miles north of Berlin and established in 1938, was the largest concentration camp for women. In addition to many other camps throughout Europe, Germany also had Sachsenhausen and Oranienburg even closer to Berlin, and Bergen-Belsen in the Lüneburger Heide (Lüneburg Heath), where Anne Frank died.

Dams: The largest dam in Germany is Bleiloch (Saale) (215 million cubic meters [m^3]), followed by Schwammenauel (Ruhr) (205 million m^3) and Edersee (Eder) (202 million m^3).

Deutschland Kampagne: (Germany Campaign) In the fall of 2004, an initiative with the title "Partner für Innovation" (Partners for Innovation) was begun by German companies. They collaborated in promoting Germany as the best country for foreign investment. They also discussed ways of overcoming the economic crisis of the turn of the millennium which had created a skeptical and negative attitude among the German population. Oliver Voss (b. 1966), of the advertising agency Jung von Matt, created the slogan: _Du bist Deutschland_

(you are Germany) which resulted in much controversy as it reminded many of the _Nazi_ years and the wrong kind of nationalism. The website of the campaign is: www.du-bist-deutschland.de.

Historical overview, ancient to modern: Many historians begin German history with Hermann or Arminius, a chieftain of the Germanic tribe of the Cherusker who defeated three Roman legions in 9 C.E. (see _Hermannsdenkmal_, monument of Hermann in the Teutoburger Wald [www.hermannsdenkmal.de]). The first internationally known historical figure is Charlemagne (Karl der Große), claimed by both French and Germans as a national hero. And the claim is not incorrect, because his empire embraced both what would become France and what would become Germany.

After his death, the empire was split, at first into three parts. But the middle section, Lorraine/Lothringen, did not survive for long, although even in the third millennium the claims for an independent nation have not died out completely in the Alsace Lorraine region. In 911 C.E., the eastern empire elected its own ruler, the first truly "German" emperor.

With the coronation of Otto I as Imperator Romanorum in 961, the Holy Roman Empire began, characterized by conflicts between the emperors and the church. Martin Luther's (1483–1546) Reformation, beginning in 1517, and the Thirty Years' War (1618–1648) stand out as particularly important examples of this ongoing conflict. In contrast to its neighbor, France, Germany was an empire in name only. The power rested primarily with the individual kingdoms and principalities (see also 1: Overcoming Regionalism).

After Napoleon had forced the last emperor of the Holy Roman Empire to abdicate in 1806, and after a failed attempt at establishing a democracy in 1848 (in the wake of a growing nationalism in all of Europe), Prussia forged a new German unification following victories over Austria in 1866 and France in 1871. The new Reich was proclaimed in Versailles outside of Paris; the Prussian king was annointed *Kaiser* (emperor), and Otto von Bismarck, who had orchestrated the whole event, became chancellor. The German parliament did not have much power, yet Bismarck was an intelligent statesman. He did not strive for German dominance in Europe but followed a policy of balance among the major powers. He also strove to avoid social unrest in the booming industrial era and introduced far-reaching social legislation (see 3: The Social Net).

By 1900, Germany was the second-largest industrial producer in the world, after the United States. It was a model for university education (see 3: The Educational System) and for science, research, and inventions (see 10: Innovation and Production). But in 1888, the emperor, Wilhelm I (1797–1888), died. His son, Friedrich (1831–1888), whose reign many liberals had looked forward to for a change of political climate, died in the same year after having been emperor for just ninety-nine days. His son, Wilhelm II (1859–1941), filled the void in this tragic *Drei-Kaiser Jahr* (Three Emperors Year). Under him, Germany began its actual rise as a military power and its fledgling attempts as a colonial power, stepping on British, French, and Russian toes. A clash of interests was predictable. World War I, the Great War in which the two old German powers (the Prussians and the Habsburgs) united against the rest of Europe, was the result.

After the war, in early November 1918, the first German republic was proclaimed—actually two different republics (which would be remembered and would be imitated after World War II). The social democrat Philipp Scheidemann proclaimed the Deutsche Republik (German Republic) from a window of the Reichstag, and the leader of the Spartakusbund (the forerunners of the Communist Party), Karl Liebknecht, proclaimed the Freie Sozialistische Republik (Free Socialist Republic) from the balcony at the Berlin City Palace. At that time, a division into two Germanys was avoided following both street fighting and parliamentarian discussions. But the turmoil forced the parliament to leave the capital in Berlin and convene in Weimar, which gave its name to the new republic: the Weimar Republic.

In Versailles, the place of the founding of the second German Reich, the peace was dictated by the Allies. The new German government, under the leadership of the moderate leftist Social Democratic Party, found itself with a difficult task to accomplish: It needed the support of the right-wing, antidemocratic military to help suppress the Communists. It even tolerated Freikorps (volunteer units) that had murdered two prominent and respected leaders of the radicals: Rosa Luxemburg and Karl Liebknecht. The new German government also needed to appease the Allies. The result was that the ruling politicians made themselves popular with the various factions of German society but barely survived a right-wing uprising, the *Kapp Putsch* (the putsch was mounted by a group of conservatives representing agrarian interests led by Wolfgang Kapp, director general of the East Prussian agricultural credit banks). The great inflation, the financial terms of the Versailles Treaty, and punitive reparations proved too much for politicians not well versed in democratic strategies and policies. The problem was made worse by the Weimar representative voting system, which allowed for many small parties. The result was an unstable government and bickering coalitions that could not agree on necessary decisions. The feeling that this type of democratic government could not deal with the problems of a modern society eventually led to the ascension of Adolf Hitler, a native Austrian who became a German citizen in 1932.

Historical overview, postwar years: May 8, 1945: Germany surrendered and the Allies took control of Germany (dividing it into four zones of occupation); May 23, 1949: The Federal Republic of Germany was founded in the three western zones (parliamentary democracy with a written constitution known as the Grundgesetz [Basic Law]); October 7, 1949: The German Democratic Republic was founded in the eastern zone (officially a parliamentary democracy, but dominated by the monopoly of power held by the governing SED).

1961: The Berlin Wall was constructed; 1966–1974: Willy Brandt's Ostpolitik prevailed (Brandt began as secretary of state and continued as chancellor; the new secretary of state was Walter Scheel); November 9, 1989: The fall of the Berlin Wall took place after a flood of refugees left the GDR and following the so-called "Monday demonstrations" for democratic reform; July 2, 1990: A monetary, economic, and social union was established between the two Germanys; October 3, 1990: Unification completed. Although the economic problems that followed unification did not

bring down Helmut Kohl's government in the elections of 1994, the second Grand Old Man (the first one was Konrad Adenauer) was defeated by Gerhard Schröder, the leader of the opposition party, in 1998. For the first time, the Grünen (Greens) entered the national government and became junior partners (see 10: Consumer Culture versus Green Awareness; 5: Holidays and Local Festivals; 5: From A to Z, "Days of Remembrance").

The new millennium brought more unemployment, and the reforms of the Red-Green coalition were seen by many as lacking a social conscience. Many left the SPD. Schröder called for a vote of confidence (see 3: The Political System), which he lost. The result was the announcement of early elections in September 2005, which brought no clear decision and much political maneuvering until the new *große Koalition* (grand coalition, meaning the coalition of the SPD and CDU) government with Angela Merkel as chancellor was established. In November 2005, Matthias Platzeck (b. 1953) was chosen as the new leader of the SPD. However, he had to resign shortly afterwards, due to health reasons. Since April 2006, the new leader is Kurt Beck (b. 1949), who has been Ministerpräsident (governor) of Rheinland-Pfalz (Rhineland-Palatinate) since 1994.

Historiker-Streit: Historians' Debate. While conservative historians (among them Ernst Nolte, Andreas Hillgruber, Michael Stürmer) demanded a relativization of the Nazi crimes, more liberal and leftist-oriented participants in the controversy (among them Jürgen Habermas, Martin Broszat, Jürgen Kocka, Wolfgang Mommsen, and Hans Mommsen) attacked these opinions, which they perceived as apologetic tendencies. The primary venue for the exchange of arguments was the press.

Holocaust: The term 'Holocaust' (from Greek 'holos', completely, and 'kaustos', burned sacrificial offering), rejected by some, became widely used in Germany after the American TV series *Holocaust* was shown on German TV in 1979. Before that time, Germans had used Nazi terms such as *Endlösung* (final solution) or *Judenvernichtung* (extermination of the Jews). The term "Shoah" (Hebrew for 'destruction' and 'catastrophe') is rarely used in Germany.

Inoffizielle Mitarbeiter: IM, unofficial collaborator. With unification and the opening of the records of the GDR secret police, many were shocked to learn how much information had been gathered about them by "unofficial collaborators." There may have been as many as 100,000 IMs, in addition to the 100,000 official members of the state security apparatus (Carr et al. 1995, 339).

Islands: The largest and best-known German island is Rügen (930 sq. km), followed by Usedom (445 sq. km; 373 sq. km belonging to Germany), Fehmarn (185 sq. km), Sylt (99 sq. km), and Föhr (83 sq. km).

Jugendweihe: Youth consecration. A secular act of consecration in the GDR, developed as a parallel ceremony to the Protestant *Konfirmation* (Confirmation) and the Catholic *Kommunion* (First Communion).

Lakes: The largest lake in Germany is the Bodensee (Lake Constance) (445 sq. km; 305 sq. km belonging to Germany), followed by the Müritz (110.3 sq. km), the Chiemsee (82 sq. km), the Schweriner See (60.6 sq. km), and the Starnberger See (57.2 sq. km).

Marshall Plan: An informal name for the European Recovery Program, named after U.S. Secretary of State George C. Marshall (1880–1959).

Memorials and museums: The psychological difficulty for Germans in dealing with the past became especially visible in the long, drawn-out debate about the Holocaust memorial in Berlin, prominently placed at the site next to the Brandenburg gate, designed by the American artist Peter Eisenman. It was dedicated on May 10, 2005, the sixtieth anniversary of the end of World War II (see also 2: Symbols and Memorials).

Mountains: The highest mountain in Germany is the Zugspitze in the German Alps (2,962 m), followed by the Watzmann (German Alps, 2,713 m), the Feldberg (Black Forest, 1,493 m), the Großer Arber (Bavarian Forest, 1,454 m), the Fichtelberg (Erzgebirge, Saxony, 1,215 m), and the Brocken (Harz, Thuringia, 1,142 m).

Nazi trials: In 1958, the Zentrale Stelle der Landesjustizverwaltung zur Aufklärung nationalsozialistischer Verbrechen (Central Agency of the State Judicial Administration for the Investigation of National Socialist Crimes) was instituted. It proceeded very slowly in its work because of bureaucratic obstacles, a questionable legal system that was still linked in many ways to the system of the Third Reich, and the difficulties its members encountered in locating reliable evidence and witnesses. Its most spectacular trial was the Auschwitz Trial in 1964. In

Israel, the Eichmann Trial in 1961 had ended with the execution of Adolf Eichmann, who had been in charge of deporting millions of Jews from German territory into the death camps. The reports on that trial by the philosopher and political theorist Hannah Arendt, compiled in *Eichmann in Jerusalem: A Report on the Banality of Evil*, were very controversial at the time of publication but have become a classic in the debate over fascism.

Population: With about 82 million inhabitants, Germany is the third most densely populated country in Europe.

Postal codes: As in the United States, postal codes in Germany consist of five digits (see also 10: Communication; 10: From A to Z, "Postal service"). Postal codes in Austria, Liechtenstein, and Switzerland have four digits. When mail is sent between countries in Europe, the international abbreviations that were first seen on car stickers are used for the country names. Examples:

D = Deutschland (Germany)
FL = Fürstentum Liechtenstein
A = Österreich (Austria)
CH = Confoederatio Helvetia, Schweiz (Switzerland)

Principalities: There has been a constant flux of borders within Germany over the centuries as principalities came into existence, merged, and disappeared. The most important ones were Prussia, Austria, Saxony, and Bavaria. The original Königreich Preußen (Kingdom of Prussia) was restricted to the former area of the duchy of Prussia that was not under the jurisdiction of the Holy Roman Empire. Yet, the kings of Prussia (who used the title of king rather than duke) were also the rulers of the *Kurfürstentum* (electorate) of Brandenburg. They expanded their domain in several wars, and the king of Prussia became emperor of the new German Reich in 1871 following the end of the Franco-Prussian War. This Reich collapsed after World War I. The Weimarer Republik (Weimar Republic) was its successor.

After Napoleon dissolved the Holy Roman Empire, the electorate of Saxony became the Königreich Sachsen (Kingdom of Saxony). Napoleon also elevated Bavaria (Bayern) to a kingdom, and both joined the new union with France. After the defeat of Napoleon, they were part of the new German union, and after 1871 they became part of the new Reich. Even today, Bavaria emphasizes its history and independence in using the term Freistaat Bayern (Republic of Bavaria), which is found on border crossings. Only in smaller letters does the information *Bundesrepublik Deutschland* (Federal Republic of Germany) follow. The Erzherzogtum Österreich (archduchy of Austria) became the Austrian-Hungarian Monarchy after the dissolution of the Holy Roman Empire in 1806, and after World War I the Austrian Republic.

Regions: Frankfurt is Germany's financial capital, the home of the nation's banking institutions and the European Central Bank. It is also known for its annual book fair (see 6: Publishers). Being situated on the river Main and featuring an almost U.S.-style skyline, it is also called Mainhattan. The Ruhrgebiet (Ruhr Valley) in the state of North Rhine–Westphalia is Germany's industrial heartland with its steel industry and coal mining. It is also known as the *Kohlenpott* (coal pot). The Schwarzwald

(Black Forest) in the state of Baden-Württemberg is one of Germany's best-known regions because of its cuckoo clocks and liquor-laced chocolate cake. The area around München (Munich) tops the polls for the best place to live in Germany. Berlin is seen as the most exciting city.

Resistance: Due to the German population's ambivalent attitude toward the Third Reich (in spite of the atrocities of war, the suppression by the Gestapo [secret police], and slowly emerging general awareness of the Holocaust, the myth of a well-run state looking after its citizens lingered on), the resistance against the Nazi regime was barely mentioned in the first years after the war. Only slowly did Claus Graf Schenk von Stauffenberg, leader of the plot to assassinate Hitler in 1944, and Hans and Sophie Scholl and their group, the Weiße Rose (White Rose), become part of the general consciousness. Since then, admiration and respect for them has grown. Johann Georg Elser's early assassination attempt in 1939 to prevent the war that he saw coming, in contrast, remained controversial. Resistance by well-liked generals such as Erwin Rommel, the *Wüstenfuchs* (desert fox), and Wilhelm Canaris, in charge of counterintelligence, became part of the legends about these German Nazi officers. Official groups such as the Kreisauser Kreis (Kreisau Circle), named after the estate of Graf (count) Moltke, and the Bekennende Kirche (Professing Church) were explained in history books, but many individuals, including priests and others, are forgotten or only mentioned on memorials.

Films about resistance and rescue of Nazi victims include Michael Verhoeven's *Die weiße Rose* (The White Rose, 1982),

Percy Adlon's *Fünf letzte Tage* (The Five Last Days, 1982) about Sophie Scholl, Hannes Karnick and Wolfgang Richter's *Rebell wider Willen. Das Jahrhundert des Martin Niemöller* (Revolutionary against His Own Will. The century of Martin Niemöller, 1985), Steven Spielberg's *Schindler's List* (1993) about Oscar Schindler, Eric Till's *Bonhoeffer—Die letzte Stufe* (Bonhoeffer—The Last Step, 1999) about the theologian Dietrich Bonhoeffer, Margarethe von Trotta's *Rosenstraße* (English title: Women of Rose Street, 2003) about German women who demonstrated in *Rosenstraße* in Berlin in 1943 for the release of their Jewish husbands, Volker Schlöndorff's *Der neunte Tag* (The Ninth Day, 2004), and Marc Rothemund's *Sophie Scholl—Die letzten Tage* (Sophie Scholl—The Last Days, 2005).

Rivers: The main rivers are the Rhein (Rhine, 1,320 km; 865 km in Germany), the Elbe (1,165 km; 700 km in Germany), the Donau (Danube, 2,858 km; 686 km in Germany), the Main (524 km), the Weser (440 km), the Spree (382 km), the Neckar (367 km), and the Mosel (545 km; 242 km in Germany).

SBZ: Sowjetisch Besetzte Zone (Soviet Occupied Territory). The term was used for the GDR by the West.

Stasi: Staatssicherheit (State Security Forces). The secret police of the GDR, founded in 1950, penetrated all aspects of life through an extensive network that also included unofficial informers (see "*Inoffizielle Mitarbeiter*," above). For decades, its director was Erich Mielke (1907–2000). Besides observing their own citizens, Stasi operatives were also responsible for external spying. Their most spectacular success was the placing of a spy, Günter Guillaume, in the office of Chancellor Willy Brandt, which led to his resignation in 1974 (the topic of Michael Frayn's play *Democracy*, 2003).

States: The following list contains the names of the states (with English names in parentheses where they differ from the German), followed by the capital (in city-states, it is the same name), its size in square kilometers, and its population, based on the official information from 2003 (Beck 2003). (1) Baden-Württemberg; Stuttgart; 35,751; 10,300,000. (2) Bayern (Bavaria); München (Munich); 70,552; 12,000,000. (3) Berlin; Berlin; 889; 3,460,000. (4) Brandenburg; Potsdam; 29,479; 2,600,000. (5) Bremen; Bremen; 404; 678,000. (6) Hamburg; Hamburg; 755; 1,700,000. (7) Hessen (Hesse); Wiesbaden; 21,114; 6,000,000. (8) Mecklenburg-Vor-pommern (Mecklenburg–Western Pomera-nia); Schwerin; 23,170; 1,800,000. (9) Niedersachsen (Lower Saxony); Hannover; 47,338; 7,800,000. (10) Nordrhein-Westfalen (North Rhine–Westphalia); Düsseldorf; 34,078; 18,000,000. (11) Rheinland-Pfalz (Rhineland-Palatinate); Mainz; 19,849; 4,000,000. (12) Saarland; Saarbrücken; 2,570; 1,100,000. (13) Sachsen (Saxony); Dresden; 18,337; 4,500,000. (14) Sachsen-Anhalt (Saxony-Anhalt); Magdeburg; 20,455; 2,750,000. (15) Schleswig-Holstein; Kiel; 15,729; 2,700,000. (16) Thüringen (Thuringia); Erfurt; 16,171; 2,500,000.

Stunde Null: Zero hour.

Tourist attractions/places of myths and legends: The Brocken, the highest mountain of the Harz mountain range (see "Mountains," above) in Saxony-Anhalt, is the place where, in German mythology, witches meet on the night of April 30 for Walpurga's Eve (see 5: Holidays and Local Festivals).

Burg Eltz, above the wine village Moselkern, belongs to the top ten tourist attractions in Germany even though it can only be reached on foot after a hike of more than an hour. It is well worth the ef-fort, however, because it is one of the best-kept medieval castles, with historical records dating back to 1157. The owners of

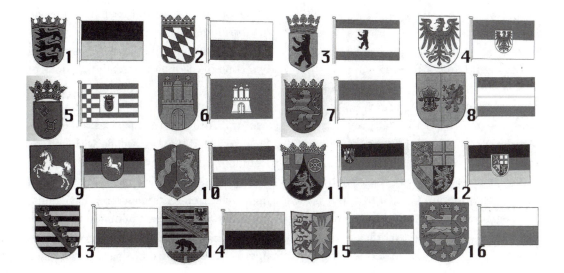

Burg Eltz on former 500 DM bank note.

Burg Eltz, fortunately, were sufficiently as-
tute over the centuries to avoid destruction
of the castle by diplomatically maintaining
connections to all sides in existing conflicts. Heidelberg, with its famous castle ruins (an important example of German Renaissance architecture), was the favorite
town of the Romantic poets. Many a tourist
has fallen in love with Heidelberg and "lost
his or her heart" there, as the song states:
"*Ich hab mein Herz in Heidelberg ver-
loren.*"

Neuschwanstein, the model for Walt Disney's castles and thereby the stereotype of
a storybook castle for many, was intended
by Ludwig II, king of Bavaria, as "a worthy
temple" for his "godlike friend" Richard
Wagner. The plans were drawn up by two
stage designers, Christian Jank and Angelo
Quaglio, inspired by the operas *Lohengrin*
and *Tannhäuser.* Built in 1869–1886, the
castle was financed to a large extent by the
new German Empire headed by the Prussian king, after Ludwig had agreed to with-
hold his name from consideration for emperor and accept instead money for his

architectural plans. His other famous castles are Linderhof, Herrenchiemsee (Neues
Schloss), and Hohenschwangau.

The Zwinger in Dresden, a place for festivals, is one of the remains of Dresden's
baroque buildings that caused it to be labeled "the Florence of the Elbe" and one of
Europe's most beautiful baroque cities before its destruction by the Royal Air Force
in 1945. The baroque Frauenkirche has
been restored and was rededicated by
Prince Philip, who brought as a gift from
Great Britain the magnificent cross crown-
ing the church.

Rothenburg ob der Tauber has always
been one of the major tourist attractions of
Germany because of its medieval appearance, which it has retained since the tenth
century. Although most cities and towns
have replaced their city walls with streets,
Rothenburg's wall is still accessible.

The Wartburg in Eisenach is not only an
important architectural site but of national
importance. Here, the famous song competitions—immortalized by Richard Wagner's
operas—are supposed to have taken place

in 1206/1207, gathering the best-known German poets of the time: Walther von der Vogelweide, Wolfram von Eschenbach, and Heinrich von Veldeke. It was also the hiding place for Martin Luther, who translated the Bible into German here in 1521–1522, laying the foundation for a unified German language and state, a historic fact that students picked up on in 1817 when they gathered in the Wartburg to celebrate the 300th anniversary of the Reformation and demand a unified and democratic Germany.

The Lorelei Rock near St. Goarshausen on Germany's most famous river, the Rhein (Rhine), has been the subject of legend, songs, and poetry: The beautiful maiden, a water nymph and German siren, who is combing her long golden hair, lured many a boatman with her beautiful songs.

Finally, Rügen is Germany's best-known Baltic island; its chalk cliffs have been immortalized by the Romantic painter Caspar David Friedrich (1774–1840).

Treuhandanstalt: Privatization agency. The Treuhand (as it was called in abbreviated form) served from 1990 to 1994 as an agency to privatize state-owned firms in accordance with free-market principles.

Vergangenheitsbewältigung: Literally, overcoming the past, a term used to describe the challenge of overcoming the legacy of Germany's Nazi past, which influences every facet of German life. Naturally, fewer and fewer personal questions are raised now than in earlier decades (such as the questions raised about the former chancellor, Kurt Georg Kiesinger, the former president, Karl Carstens, and the former prime minister of Baden-Württemberg, Hans Karl Filbinger). The number of embarrassing political events has also decreased over time (for example, the visit to the military cemetery in Bitburg, a town in Rhineland-Palatinate, by Chancellor Helmut Kohl and U.S. President Ronald Reagan in 1985, which caused a huge scandal because the cemetery also has graves of members of the Nazi Waffen SS [special Nazi forces in charge of the Holocaust]; the forced resignation of Philipp Jenninger as president of the German parliament in 1988 after he was accused of not distancing himself enough from the Nazis in his speech in remembrance of the *Reichskristallnacht* or *Reichspogromnacht* [Night of Broken Glass]). But, in many subtle ways, the fascist past is still part of the discussions on legislation from abortion to immigration laws. And, of course, it is revived through publications (such as Daniel Goldhagen's study *Hitler's Willing Executioners* [1996]) and exhibitions (such as one in 2002 that addressed war crimes committed by the Wehrmacht [regular German army]).

Zwangsarbeiter: Forced laborers. Although German industry was intricately connected to the Third Reich, and forced labor an important factor in its success, it took more than half a century for a satisfactory arrangement to be achieved between industry and the few survivors. For a long time, German industry defended itself by claiming a clear break between the management of the past and postwar personnel and policies.

Additional Readings

Armbruster, Frank. *Politik in Deutschland. Systemvergleich Bundesrepublik Deutschland—DDR.* Kollegmaterial Politik. Wiesbaden: Gabler, 1981.

Aust, Stefan, and Gerhard Spörl, eds. *Die*

Gegenwart der Vergangenheit. Der lange Schatten des Dritten Reichs. München: Deutsche Verlags-Anstalt und Spiegel-Buchverlag, 2004.

Büsch, Otto, and James J. Sheehan, eds. *Die Rolle der Nation in der deutschen Geschichte und Gegenwart*. Berlin: Colloquium, 1985.

Craig, Gordon A. *The Germans*. New York: G. P. Putman's Sons, 1982.

Dann, Otto. *Nation und Nationalismus in Deutschland. 1770–1990*. München: Beck, 1993.

Deutscher Bundestag, ed. *Fragen an die deutsche Geschichte. Wege zur parlamentarischen Demokratie*, 19., neu bearbeitete Auflage. Katalog der historischen Ausstellung im Deutschen Dom in Berlin. Bonn: Deutscher Bundestag, Referat Öffentlichkeitsarbeit, 1996.

Diem, Aubrey. *The New Germany: Land, People, Economy*. Ontario: Aljon Print-Craft, 1993.

Eley, Geoff, ed. *The "Goldhagen Effect": History, Memory, Nazism—Facing the German Past*. Ann Arbor: University of Michigan Press, 2000.

Fritsch-Bournazel, Renate. *Europe and German Unification*. Oxford: Berg, 1992.

Giordano, Ralph. *Die zweite Schuld Oder Von der Last Deutscher zu sein*. Neuausgabe. Köln: Kiepenheuer and Witsch, 2000.

Glaessner, Gert-Joachim. *The Unification Process in Germany: From Dictatorship to Democracy*. New York: St. Martin's Press, 1992.

Harold, James, and Marla Stone, eds. *When the Wall Came Down: Reactions to German Unification*. New York and London: Routledge, 1992.

Hoffmann, Christa. *Stunden Null? Vergangenheitsbewältigung in Deutschland, 1945–1989*. Bonn: Bouvier, 1992.

James, Harold. *A German Identity, 1770–1990*. New York: Sterling, 2001.

Jarausch, Konrad. *The Rush to German Unity*. Oxford: Oxford University Press, 1994.

Jarausch, Konrad H., and Volker Gransow, eds. *Uniting Germany: Documents and Debates, 1943–1993*. Oxford: Berghahn, 1994.

Jones, Alun. *The New Germany: A Human Geography*. Chichester and New York: John Wiley and Sons, 1994.

LaCapra. Dominick. *History and Memory after Auschwitz*. Ithaca, NY, and London: Cornell University Press, 1998.

Lewis, Derek, and John R. P. McKenzie, eds. *The New Germany: Social, Political and Cultural Challenges of Unification*. Exeter: University of Exeter Press, 1995.

Lohrbächler, Albrecht, Helmut Ruppel, Ingrid Schmidt, and Jörg Thierfelder, eds. *Schoa. Schweigen ist unmöglich. Erinnern, Lernen, Gedenken*. Stuttgart, Berlin, and Köln: Kohlhammer, 1999.

Marsh, David. *Germany and Europe: The Crisis of Unity*. London: Mandarin, 1995.

Merkl, Peter H. *The Federal Republic of Germany at Forty-Five: Union without Unity*. Washington Square: New York University Press, 1995.

Merkl, Peter H., and Gert-Joachim Glaessner. *German Unification in the European Context*. University Park: Pennsylvania State University Press, 1995.

Mitscherlich, Alexander, and Margarete Mitscherlich. *Die Unfähigkeit zu trauern. Grundlagen kollektiven Verhaltens*. München: Piper, 1967.

Mohler, Armin. *Vergangenheitsbewältigung. Oder, Wie man den Krieg nochmals verliert*. Krefeld: Sinus Verlag, 1980.

Osmond, Jonathan, ed. *German Reunification: A Reference Guide and Commentary*. Harlow: Longman, 1992.

Sereny, Gitta. *The German Trauma. Experiences and Reflections 1938-2001*. London: Penguin, 2001.

Wendt, Bernd Jürgen, ed. *Vom schwierigen Zusammenwachsen der Deutschen. Nationale Identität und Nationalismus im 19. und 20. Jahrhundert*. Frankfurt and New York: Peter Lang, 1992.

Werle, Gerhard, and Thomas Wandres. *Auschwitz vor Gericht. Völkermord und bundesdeutsche Strafjustiz. Mit einer Dokumentation des Auschwitz-Urteils*. München: C. H. Beck, 1995. (Beck'sche Reihe 1099.)

2

German Idiosyncrasies

Language, Script, and Gestures

The Language

Today, many Germans—and not only a few right-wing fanatics—are worried about the overwhelming influence of English on German. In 1989, one German journalist, after giving many examples of the use of English in German, wrote: "Where are we? In a colony of the US?" (Behal-Thomsen et al. 1993, 20). And she was not the only one to use such blunt language. In his book *Wie wir Amerikaner wurden* (How We Became Americans), Michael Rutschky begins his story with the statement: "How the FRG developed into a colony without realizing it" (Rutschky 2004, 9). Of course, in the new states in eastern Germany where a large portion of the population did not grow up learning or hearing English much at all, many wonder even more than in the west why they should, for instance, say "cash" when there is a perfectly good, German word for the same thing, *bar* (Lewis 2001, 240).

Besides the playful *Denglisch*, or mix of English and German, found in advertisements (for example, inside of McDonald's paper coffee cups), English expressions are found everywhere. Scholarly as well as newspaper articles are often blatantly filled with them. For instance, we find in the section "Uni&Job" in the *Süddeutschen Zeitung* (no. 95, April 24/25, 2004, 13) a reference to "Soft Skills," to "*Boomzeiten der New Economy*," to "*gejobbt haben*," and to the "*Recruiting-Chef*," a peculiar mixture of English and German. Another odd example of this insertion of a short English expression into a German phrase appeared in a report about a bakery that was short on space. The shop began serving coffee to accompany its pastries, but as it only had room for a few small tables and bar stools for customers to sit and enjoy their snack, the bakery introduced a "*Kaffee-to-go-Konzept*" (*Freiburger Wochenbericht*, June 16, 2004, 16).

In reference to the new media, it is a given to use an English expression. Very seldom does one encounter "*Netz-Nachricht*" (net message) for "*die E-Mail*." It is common to use "world wide web," "Internet,"

Advertising on the bottom of McDonald's coffee cups in Germany.

(Coffee is like beautiful women: suddenly gone.)   (That is nice that you've looked into it.)

"browser," "server" and "surfer," and "boom" and "zoom," as Hermann Bausinger noted (2000, 149). Older Germans living in rural areas sometimes feel helpless when they open the pages of their papers or watch television. Universities have "International Offices" instead of "*Akademische Auslandsämter,*" the trains are called "InterCityExpress" (ICE) or "CityNightLine" (CLN), information is now given at a "Servicepoint," and the annual card for rebates on first-class tickets by Germany's federal railway is called "BahnCard first." The telecommunications service of the German postal service is "Telekom-Service" instead of "*Fernmeldedienst.*" The list goes on and on and includes, besides strange combinations of German and English words, English terms that are not used by English speakers—for

example, "Handy" (pronounced "hendy") for the mobile or cellular phone, "Broiler" for a roast chicken, and "Dispatcher" for a project controller (Lewis 2001, 239), the last two examples being words from the former GDR vocabulary.

Often the words are used in a way that is either a distortion of English usage or sometimes downright incomprehensible to a speaker of English not familiar with the German language—for example, "Jeans-Dressing" (Behal-Thomsen et al. 1993, 19), which obviously is not a new form of salad dressing. An optician's clinic specializing in laser correction surgery uses the name "Realeyes" (*Freiburger Wochenbericht,* May 5, 2004, 23) and reports that more than 90 percent of its clients consider themselves to be in the "Happiness Zone" after treatment. An article about a "Funpark," a

Banner in Freiburg advertising bicycles.

large disco, reports on the opening of a "Chillout-Bereich," later referred to as a "Chillout-Zone," and regular Thursday "Wallstreetbörse" sessions (*Börse* is the German word for a stock exchange). On these evenings, the prices of drinks are determined by their popularity. Discos in neighboring communities collaborate for annual "Birthday Excess" evenings, when disco goers are allowed to attend all establishments (one is named "Inside") for a set price of 6 euros and travel between them in a free "Shuttle-Bus" (*Freiburger Wochenbericht*, April 21, 2004, 6). In another newspaper, under club announcements, the "Inside" disco lists "*Afterhour mit local DJ-Heros*" (*Der Sonntag Sport*, April 25, 2004, 20). One wonders whether it would make the listing too difficult if the lowly preposition *mit* (with) were also in English.

An ad for a resort area called Abenteuerland (Adventureland) in Bavaria describes its center as "Highway Hotel," from which one can visit "Jimmy's Fun Park" and "Western City," which has a "Saloon" and "Cowboys." One reader of *Brigitte* was so tired of the German/English mixture in the fashion pages of the magazine that she wrote a letter to the publisher to express her irritation. One way of expressing irritation in German is to say that the hairs (*Haare*) on the back of your neck (*Nacken*) are standing up. She wrote: "*Da sträuben sich meine Nacken-Hairs: Neben 'Must-Haves' nun auch 'Key-Pieces der Saison'. Bitte nicht!*" Further translation seems hardly necessary here! (*Brigitte* 19 [2005], 167). It is almost comforting to learn that the meals served in some restaurants are "*gutbürgerlich*" (traditional fare; see chapter 4: From Traditional Fare to International Cuisine) (*Der Sonntag im Breisgau*, May 2, 2004, 4). Sometimes, English words are misspelled—for example, *Sperrips* for "spareribs," or apostrophes misused in plural nouns.

Any American-sounding word or phrase signals to the German reader or listener "modern," "progressive"; the German word, in contrast, is associated with "old-fashioned," "boring," "provincial." On a small scale, the German auto industry tried to use the associative power of language in the 1990s by introducing the word "*Fahrvergnügen*" (pleasure of driving) in their English-language ads, relying on the fact that German products are still linked to such concepts as reliability and technical innovation. Unfortunately, most German expressions found in other languages are related to warfare. The remnants of Germany's leading role in the sciences and music is found only in such words as "angst," "gestalt psychology," "zeitgeist," and "leitmotiv." That "diesel" is also a German word going back to the inventor Rudolf Diesel (1858–1913) is probably not known by many.

In other eras, primarily in the eighteenth century, it was not English but French that infiltrated the German language, and many German nobles spoke better French than German. German not only survived this onslaught but became richer because of it. One should never forget that one of the reasons that English has become so influential is that it is a perfect amalgam of Germanic and French words, drawing on two large language reservoirs for expression. One may argue that the more international German becomes, the more robust it will also become. The many dialects will guar-

antee that the Germanic part will not be forgotten either.

Standard German is still relatively new. An important role in its development was played at the end of the nineteenth and the beginning of the twentieth century by Konrad Duden and his dictionaries. The name *Duden*, therefore, is synonymous with correct German, and the dictionary bearing his name is regarded as the authoritative source on questions of correctness. A new spelling reform, which caused an uproar in the general public, was passed in 1998 by the cultural ministries of Austria, Switzerland, and the individual German states. Although such state-sponsored attempts consolidate standard German, dialect use is alive and well, although less common than a century ago. From time to time—especially in the revolutionary 1960s—dialect use experiences an academic revival, and it has even been encouraged in schools, which are traditionally the foundation for spreading standard German.

The geographic mobility of modern times, television, the Internet, and the national mass media all seem designed to destroy dialects. Nevertheless, they persist (see also 1: Overcoming Regionalism). The further south one travels in Germany, the greater the acceptance of dialects, reflecting to a large degree the very ancient division of the three major dialect areas: Low, Central, and Upper German.

The phenomenon of resisting strong external trends is not that unusual. Hermann Bausinger remarked correctly in regard to globalization in general that there are various regional and national filters, in addition to each individual's very own culturally biased filter, that prevent an easy takeover by other cultures. Often, the

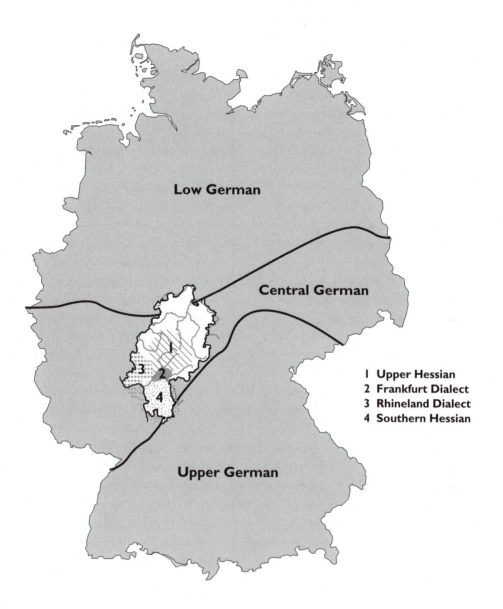

Low German

Central German

Upper German

1 Upper Hessian
2 Frankfurt Dialect
3 Rhineland Dialect
4 Southern Hessian

effect of globalization is just the opposite of what one might expect. The constant confrontation with the "other" may lead to a stabilization and confirmation of one's own culture (Bausinger 2000, 147). This is also true for language. The impact of foreign expressions is not a radical one and will only result in a slight modification of the original language. In an article in the *Fremdwörter-Duden* (a dictionary for foreign words in German), the authors stress: "It is an error to believe that the use of foreign words is able to influence the grammatical structures of German. As long as an English verb such as 'to download' is treated in a sentence as any other separable German verb (analogous to *herunterladen*) and follows the regular inflection pattern (*ich loade down, loadete down, habe downgeloadet*), the positive force of adaption works. As Goethe remarked: 'The power of a language is not that it rejects the foreign but devours it'" (Dudenredaktion 2001, 919).

In regard to dialects—as has been shown when refugees from one area have been forced into other geographical areas—this means that the dialect does not disappear, but only that a "milder" form of the original dialect develops, which then becomes more and more widespread, especially in urban areas. And this dialect can still be quite distinct from standard German, though not as pronounced as some geographically and socially very restricted varieties. New dialects reflect, on the one hand, the new economic reality, but on the other hand they are also proof of the continuing importance of regionalism in German society (see 1: Overcoming Regionalism).

A new—and quite different—language problem arose with unification (see 1: From Two to One). Not only did many East Germans find themselves suddenly deprived of free day care for children, day nurseries, state-subsidized housing, and a guaranteed workplace, but their language was stigmatized and they had to adapt to new forms of communication and bear the burden of linguistic reorientation. As Johannes Schwitalla remarked: "Along with a new political system, the complete political and economic lexicon of the FRG entered the eastern states" (Schwitalla 2001, 240). Many words changed their connotations radically from positive to negative and vice versa, especially those denoting bourgeois values and attitudes. Others, from all walks of life, suddenly sounded strange and ridiculous because the political and social basis for them had vanished. The language of the east was the language of the "loser," and many aspects of language use shifted. The former citizens of the GDR were used to a style of language characteristic of official speeches, formal declarations, and pronouncements, but they now encountered unaccustomed situations that required them to talk about themselves, such as job interviews. They had to learn to adjust their somewhat indirect language use, a use that involved not only a difference in choice of words but even of syntax. For instance, according to Schwitalla, they used to employ "the subjunctive more frequently in order to soften or qualify ideas," and their speech used to contain "more passive constructions" and to use "the impersonal *man* (one) more often instead of the self-referring *ich*-form" (ibid., 242).

In some cases, the reaction to this linguistic landslide by those from the former East Germany is overcompensation—using, for instance, even more English-sounding terms than those in the West—

but in other cases, the reaction is resentment. Words coined and used in the former GDR, such as *Plaste* for *Plastik* (plastic), *Kaufhalle* for *Kaufhaus* (department store), and *Broiler* instead of *Brathähnchen* (roast chicken), "have acquired the status of symbols of active German resistance to the west" (ibid., 244) (see Ostalgie).

The Script

German script, once a distinctive feature of the language, has pretty much disappeared in modern Germany. It evokes negative reactions and is dismissed not only as "obsolete" but also as "fascist," although it was regarded by the Nazis as "Jewish writing" and was abolished in 1941. This could have been a good reason to reintroduce it after the war, but the opposite was true. Perhaps the Allies feared—as the rumor goes—that Germans would have a secret code in this script. A good overview of German script is given by Marie Marcks (1984), who chose to draw on her training as a calligrapher as

Old German script, from a poem by the Prague poet Paul Leppin, 1878–1945.

well as a cartoonist in writing her autobiography, *Marie, es brennt!* (Marie, Something Is Burning!). The book is a facsimile copy of a handwritten text interspersed with illustrations, but it also includes copies of the diaries she kept as a child, her first attempts at writing, as well as the samples and illuminated poems her mother wrote for her. All of these offer examples of how German handwriting has changed and become more international over the years. The parts of the book that are new are relatively easy to read for one from another culture familiar with the language, but the diaries and the models from her school years in the 1920s and 1930s are difficult to decipher. The book also offers examples of font styles used in posters and proclamations from the Nazi era and includes examples of banners Marcks had to make as an artist in the youth workforce (Reichsarbeitsdienst). She explains that one illustration in the book of herself and her mother sitting at a drawing board does not depict them making painted tiles with popular German sayings to sell and make money as they often did, but rather shows them using their skills as calligraphers to counterfeit food-ration stamps.

Gestures

Germans are not known for lively gesticulations. Nevertheless, there are certain gestures and mannerisms that most Germans would immediately understand but that might well seem strange to others. For instance, one has to be aware that Germans smile much less frequently than Americans. As Hyde Flippo has pointed out: "This is not a sign that they are unfriendly or antagonistic, but it is merely a reflection of the European belief that 'unnecessary' smiling is superficial and insincere. Smiling at strangers for no reason is considered silly. A smile from an Austrian, German, or Swiss really means something. So you should not take offense at the lack of a smile" (Flippo 1999, 62).

The most frequently encountered gesture is that of tapping one's forehead with the index finger—a gesture usually seen on the road. It is the equivalent to shouting: "You idiot!" Instead of crossing their fingers for luck, Germans cover their thumb with the index and middle finger, which they call *den Daumen drücken* (press their thumb). Rubbing the thumb over the index and middle finger, palm up, indicates—as in many European countries—money. Counting begins with the thumb and not the index finger. The index finger is added for the number two, then follows the middle finger, the ring, and the little finger.

Primarily after lectures in a university setting but also in other meetings, applause is expressed by knocking with a fist on the table (as on a door) rather than clapping hands.

Stereotypes and Prejudices

When scientists found a mummified corpse in a glacier in the Alps in the Ötztal, apparently over 3,000 years old, they called him "Ötzi." But what nationality was he? The joke goes that he could not be Italian because he had tools with him. And he could not be Austrian because they had found brain tissue. Therefore, he had to be Swiss or German. Because he was found in a glacier, it was possible that he was Swiss. Yet, the ultimate proof that he had to be German was that he wore sandals. And no one but a German would wear sandals in the mountains.

While those outside the country have their own special stereotypes of Germans, the wealth of regional differences is one of the primary sources for stereotyping within Germany. There is the formal and stiff German from Lower Saxony, who does not like to utter a single unnecessary word, versus the German from Berlin, who sees himself as possessing not only a quick wit but also unrelentingly fast speech—the famous *Berliner Schnauze* (Berlin bigmouth) with *Berliner Tempo* (Berlin speed). People from Vienna in Austria and Cologne in Germany (the latter with its two famous legendary characters "Tünnes" and "Schäl") are both known for their reluctant attitude toward work. The Swabians are known for their easygoing nature, their *Schwäbische Gemütlichkeit*. This is typified in the two representatives of Swabia, "Pfleiderer" and "Häberle," whose names are typical of the local dialect, in which the diminutive suffix "le" is used for almost everything. Indeed, their speech is so slow that one could fall asleep while listening to them. Finally, the Bavarians are supposed to be, as Richard Lord put it, "the most open, fun-loving, rollicking and beer guzzling of all Germans. [Statistics amply support this last claim.]" (Lord 2004, 71). As with any stereotype, all these images are based on some verifiable facts, but distorted into caricatures.

Basic Characteristics

A Desire for Peace and Quiet. *Gemütlichkeit*, one of the key words used in talking about German culture, has no direct equivalent in English. Hermann Bausinger devoted a full chapter to it in his study *Typisch deutsch* (2000). It implies comfort and a pleasant ambiance but also contains a touch of nostalgia, of feeling cozy and protected, completely at home with one's surroundings and the other people present. It does not apply to larger spaces but rather to rooms bathed in soft light and radiating warmth. It excludes quarrels as well as intellectual discussions. Bausinger stressed that it is no surprise that the word *Eloquenz* in German is not a Germanic word, and that the equivalent *Beredsamkeit* and the adjective *beredt* are stilted and used infrequently. Only *geschwätzig* (talkative, gossipy), which has a negative connotation, is common.

From the beginning, parliament was branded as a *Schwatzbude* (a room for chattering). Too often in German history, decisions were not made through a democratic process, but by the aristocrats in power, the prime example being the fight for a republic with a constitution during the Napoleonic eras. The common people lost this battle, and it was another 100 years before a democracy, the Weimar Republic, could be established. The disappointed citizens withdrew into their private quarters and shunned public life. The family became the focal point of life. This period became known as *Biedermeier*—Meier (with its various spellings, Maier, Meyer, and Mayer) being a very common name (like Smith in English) and *bieder* implying "honest," "upright," and today, "conformist" and "unimaginative."

The word *Biedermeier* was coined by the German poet Victor von Scheffel in 1848. He created two philistine, petit bourgeois types, *Biedermann* and *Bummelmaier* (*bummeln* meaning to stroll, to take one's time), for a satirical leaflet in order to criticize this apolitical attitude. Today, Biedermeier furniture, with its delicate lines, as well as the Biedermeier paintings de-

picting scenes of idealized family life, originally conceived as an alternative to an elaborate style influenced by the French, are sought after collector items. When society changed, when it became necessary for the husband to go to his office to work as an accountant or to a factory, the wife was in charge of the children's education and the household and became responsible for creating a harmonious home for the leisure hours of the hardworking male. *Gemütlichkeit* is an expression of this withdrawal from public life and a focus on the private realm. The concept is expressed, for example, in embroidered wall hangings with sayings such as "*Trautes Heim, Glück allein*" (beloved home, pure happiness).

Yet, modern life is different. Families are not only smaller than in the past, and often childless, but the number of single households increases steadily (it was more than a third in 1998), and the functional division between work and household as a mirror of the male/female relationship has disappeared (see 4: Gender Equality). With these alterations, the word *gemütlich* has changed, too, but it has not disappeared. It lurks around every corner, although the new German event culture (see 5: Activities and Clubs) challenges its survival. The change in attitude has been commented on by foreigners who see Germans as lacking warmth and an understanding for others—comments found in various forms in many studies of German contemporary culture. The explanation given is that the foreigners saw Germans as too busy with their own lives to do anything else and trying to protect their own peace and quiet whenever possible (Behal-Thomsen et al. 1993, 53). Germany, like other nations, is experiencing a commercialization of society that leads to emotional detachment. One observer remarked pointedly that "in the East, there was one wall for everyone—in the West, a wall for each one" (quoted in Dieckmann 2003, 16–17) (see also 4: Multicultural Society).

The Home—Personal and Regional. Along with this sense of coziness goes the characteristic of being *seßhaft* (settled). Two-thirds of all Germans still live when they are old in the same town or region in which they grew up (Bausinger 2000, 54). Perhaps, as a study by Edward T. and Mildred R. Hall suggests, referred to in Bausinger's *Typisch deutsch*, the Germans cling to their homes because of the many devastating events they experienced over the hundreds of years of their history (ibid., 56). The importance of *Heimat* (homeland), always connected to the ownership of property, is reflected in legislation up to the nineteenth century. Those who owned land had a legal right to get married, to engage in trade, and to receive communal support. Those who did not own land were *heimatlos* (homeless), without any legal rights and without virtue. This was expressed well in Georg Büchner's (1813–1837) well-known play *Woyzeck* (written in 1835/1836), which addresses many social questions. The play received much attention in the postwar era, though it premiered in 1913 and was suppressed by the Nazis. (Alban Berg's [1885–1935] *Wozzeck*, which premiered in 1925, is based on this play and was designated *entartete Kunst* [degenerate art].) In Büchner's play, when the protagonist, Woyzeck, is accused by his superior of living a sinful life because he has had a child without being officially married, he states: "Yes, virtue, I don't quite get it yet. We common people, we have no virtue. We are just overcome by nature. I would like to be virtuous. Virtue has to be something beautiful. But I am a poor man" (scene 1: x–y).

It was not until the second half of the nineteenth century, when industrialization required more mobility, that the *Heimatrecht* (legislation based on property ownership) was replaced by the principle of the *Unterstützungswohnsitzes* (legislation based on place of residence). Under the new rule, everyone who had lived in one place for one or two years could count on communal support. This was also the time when Heimat had become very much a part of the people's emotional makeup. And the emotional aspect in life is more relevant to people's actions than other aspects. The dream of one's own home, and with it the feeling of security, is very much part of most Germans—even if they do not own a home but are renters. Germans are not, however, at the top of the list of homeownership, which only proves the importance of dreams. The statistical fact is that only about 40 percent of the population owns a home or an owner-occupied flat—which is a much lower percentage than in many other Western countries. And this is in spite of the emphasis on *Bausparverträge* (savings contracts with a building society; see 2: Thriftiness). There are many practical reasons for this. One is that large family units have to a large extent disappeared in Germany—in contrast to countries in the south of Europe—and the singles culture has increased in the six decades after World War II (see 4: Gender Equality). And although owning a home supports the need for security, the risk of making a long-range financial investment can be frightening.

A settled existence and the urge to travel are opposites, but in many ways they are also complementary, and Germans love to travel (see 5: Vacations and Travel). The tight living conditions (see 9: City Planning and Architecture) in Germany and the extremely regulated nature of daily life increase the longing for an *Ausbruchsversuch auf Zeit* (attempt at escape for a limited time), as Bausinger called it (2000, 59). People are not only looking for a beautiful landscape and the sun but also for freedom from the established conventions. The distances covered between the home and the vacation spot give tourists the feeling of being in another world. This desire is not contradicted by the fact that the tourists also carry a lot of cultural baggage with them: their eating habits, their general division of labor (the mother is in charge of washing the dishes), their desire to be with like-minded people, and to experience nature in relative comfort (in overcrowded campsites). And surprisingly, or not so surprisingly, many Germans return year after year to the same spot (or even own a vacation home)—fulfilling their need to lead a settled life even when traveling.

Domesticity.   The private sphere is sacrosanct for most Germans. This applies in its most visible expression to the home, marked off by gates, walls, fences, and hedges (space is rare in Germany; see 9: City Planning and Architecture). It also applies to personal possessions. Richard Lord observed that "borrowing and lending are not the casual matters in Germany that they are in many other places." He added, "Germans are loath to lend out anything of any value whatsoever to people they aren't close to, nor will they ask to borrow such items from these people. And it is essential that no matter from whom or what you do manage to borrow, you always return that

object in at least as good a condition as you received it" (Lord 2004, 43).

Apprehension toward strangers and protection of the familiar leads also to a strict separation of private and public life. Those who have had only casual contact with Germans would agree with Lord's observation that "work activities belong exclusively to the work sphere, while family life has its own unique sphere" (ibid., 45). He went on to say that friendships are carefully compartmentalized and that club activities are yet another sphere of social interaction (see also 5: Activities and Clubs). Those with more familiarity with Germans might see the matter as less clear-cut. Spouses are frequently included in official professional events in a way that is becoming less common in the United States. Business is rarely conducted on Sundays or official holidays, however, even with colleagues who are only in Germany for a limited stay.

The separation between private and public is also clearly maintained in language use. Older Germans, for instance, need time to accept use of the informal second-person address *du* (you), along with a first name, which used to be reserved for family and good friends, rather than the formal *Sie* (you), along with a title (*Herr* or *Frau*) and last name, when talking to new acquaintances, coworkers, or professional colleagues. It can happen that coworkers spend years of their lives together addressing each other in the formal style because there is a strict protocol about who can offer the informal *du* to the other person: It can be initiated only by the older to the younger or by the superior to the subordinate. To complicate matters even further, there are other possibilities and levels of formality. For example, *Sie* and the first name maintains a certain distance but acknowledges some informality and familiarity. If titles like *Professor* or *Doktor* are involved, the situation may get worse. The following dialogue is not as incongruous as it may appear:

Boss: Hello, Doktor Müller.
Assistant: Hello, Doktor Schulz.
Boss: We have worked together now for almost a decade on many successful projects, Doktor Müller, and I believe, I can say that we have a very cordial relationship.
Assistant: Thank you, Doktor Schulz. I would like to agree.
Boss: Perhaps the time has come to be less formal, Doktor Müller. May I suggest to you we drop the "Doktor," Herr Müller?
Assistant: With pleasure, Herr Schulz.

Yet another variation in this social minefield is that colleagues will use one form of address in the workplace—the formal—and be more familiar when they meet outside the office. Today, following trends toward less formal social interaction from the United States and other European countries, many young Germans do not follow these traditions and have already adopted the more informal first-name form of address, which is always accompanied by *du*.

Love of Nature.   The smell of freshly baked rolls in the early morning hours, the sound of steps on cobblestones, the ringing of church bells, the song of the nightingale perched on the gables of red-tiled roofs— none of these have changed over the past few decades. They were part of Germany right after the war, and they are part of many German villages and towns at the be-

ginning of a new millennium. And in small villages one can still find people who take a break from housework, lean over the windowsill, cushioned by a pillow, or stand at their garden gate and watch the neighbors walk by. There is still in many Germans a yearning for "naturalness," an unspoiled life of rural bliss and love of nature, especially the forest (see 10: Consumer Culture versus Green Awareness). It seems, as Bausinger states in his study *Typisch deutsch* (2000, 74–75), that everything that can be labeled "natural" can count on a strong resonance with Germans. This applies to domestic life as well as politics and to health issues as well as leisure-time activities (see 2: Health Issues and Sexuality; 5: Activities and Clubs).

Although doors, for Germans, were invented to be closed (partly because of the draft—a general fear of many Germans— but also for privacy), both windows and doors need to be opened at least once a day while one is cleaning the home to let fresh air come in, something that is done regardless of weather, temperature, or season and can strike non-Germans as bordering on the compulsive. A few people even continue to air their beds on windowsills in the morning to guarantee freshness. As odd as these customs may appear to the outsider, they have practical as well as historical reasons for existing, as Germans may point out. One rationale harks back to the hygiene (or lack thereof) of the eighteenth century, when evil "airs" played a more prominent role than in the modern days of bacteria and viruses; the other reflects the fact that most German houses are built of stone with airtight doors and windows. Natural circulation is, therefore, not a given.

The love of naturalness led also to a ready acceptance of the hippie lifestyle in

A typical romantic German village, Hirschhorn am Neckar.

Germany (see 4: Youth Culture and the World of Intellectuals), to vegetarian eating habits (see 4: Traditional Fare to International Cuisine), to homeopathy, and to the *Freikörperkultur* (FKK, nudist) movement (see 2: Health Issues and Sexuality).

Love of Toys and Gadgets.   To some it would appear that cars are Germans' favorite pets, though some would say cars are like children, and others would say cars are toys (see 10: Public and Private Transportation). Hermann Bausinger (2000) noted that when foreign correspondents write about Germany, they seldom miss taking a few ironic sideswipes at the almost fetishistic attitude Germans display toward their cars. Many Germans, he noted, do not get into a VW or an Audi in the morning, but drive their "Max" or their

"Happy" or "*Schnucki*" (sweetheart) out of the garage. The car is not just a commodity but a treasure. Weekends are often spent polishing the car until it gleams—including the bumper. Parking by using the bumpers as a means to navigate into tight spots is frowned upon in Germany and may even result in a ticket. In addition to being a great and practical gadget, which used to permit tinkering for hours (less likely in an age in which almost all features seem to be controlled by a computer), the car is, of course, also a status symbol. In Germany, a BMW or Mercedes is a sure sign of success, and a Porsche indicates both success and sportiness. The Golf Generation would argue that this generalization about cars does not apply to them but only to their parents. However, a cartoon in a 2005 magazine shows a man with his head bowed into the engine of a car, with tools and parts lying around behind him, telling a bored-looking woman sitting beside the car on a tire that when he thinks back to the weekends before he knew her, they seem so dull to him (*Brigitte* 18 [2005], 7). The couple does not look particularly old either.

The second topic mentioned by foreigners is the way Germans drive. The *Washington Post* used two German loan words in the headline of an article about traffic in Germany: "*Angst* on the *Autobahn*" (see 10: Public and Private Transportation). A journalist is quoted as pointing out sarcastically that in Germany the essence of democracy is not "free speech" but "free speed." As Americans continue to plead for their basic right to carry arms, Germans plead for "*Freie Fahrt für freie Bürger!*" (free driving speed for free citizens). A psychologist explained the need for unrestricted driving conditions on the Autobahn as a compensation mechanism for the many rules and regulations everyone is confronted with in daily life.

Humor. One of the standard and unfailing prejudices is that Germans have no sense of humor and that they are earnest and contemplative, always trying to puzzle out existential questions, such as: "What is typically German?" They are seen as taking themselves too seriously and needing to see everything in abstract and idealized terms (Dieckmann 2003, 17). It is also true that there are more serious philosophical tractates than comedies in Germany. The German textbook *Blaue Blume* cited a statistic from the *Süddeutsche Zeitung* of December 1997 that in 1956 Germans laughed an average of 16 minutes a day, whereas in 1997 the length of time had been reduced to 8 minutes (Eichheim et al. 2002, 199).

The decline may have many reasons and is not necessarily a sign of a humorless nation, but the fact that such a measurement was taken and reported supports the argument that Germans take even laughter a little too seriously.

German humor—and it does exist—follows some of the same basic genres that Anglo-Saxon humor follows in general, with, for example, series of jokes directed against various regional, national, or ethnic groups derived primarily from the depth of stupidity of such groups. This is evident in the jokes about residents of the east Frisian islands of the North Sea and, more recently, about the former German Democratic Republic, by those living on the western side of the border. The border police—the Vopos or Volkspolizisten—were the butt of jokes for those on both sides of the border. And, as in many countries, there are jokes about the stupidity of lower bureaucrats, who are often equated with *Schildbürger* (the mythical citizens of Schilda), going back to *Volksbücher* (folk tales) published in 1598. The *Focus* electronic newsletter of July 27, 2005, labeled a collection of odd and confusing traffic signs as *Schildbürgerstreiche*, tricks played by the citizens of that notorious town.

A typical German version of humor is *Schadenfreude*, which has no one-word equivalent in English. "Gloating" or "malicious joy" catch only part of the meaning. The more positive connotation has to do with one's general attitude toward the adversities of life and enduring them with humor. There is a proverbial German saying (by most people credited to Wilhelm Busch but in reference works to the writer Otto Julius Bierbaum) that "*Humor ist, wenn man trotzdem lacht*" (Humor is when one laughs in spite of everything).

One German form of humor that is difficult for Americans to understand—or rather to find amusing—is based on satires and parodies, juxtaposing a situation and the context or genre in which it is described. This type of humor has a long tradition in Germany, dating back in recent history to the magazine *Simplizissimus* of the outgoing nineteenth century with its satire about imperial Germany under Kaiser Wilhelm, and it continued through the Weimar Republic and was revitalized in West Germany by satirical magazines such as *Pardon* and in the 1990s by *Titanic* (see 6: The Press). In addition, there have been popular satire shows on radio and television (see 7: Radio and Television). From the beginning of German television in the 1950s, cabaret was popular: *Berliner Insulaner* (Berlin Islanders), *Berliner Stachelschweine* (Berlin Porcupines), *Kom(m)ödchen* (Little Chest of Drawers/Comedy), *Münchner Lach- und Schießgesellschaft* (The Munich Society for Laughing and Shooting). But the popularity of this form of humor was at the same time its inherent problem because it required a careful balancing act: The program had to be critical but not too critical; it had to be humorous, but it could not offend anyone too much. Sometimes, the balance was lost, ironically providing the highlights of such shows, the good moments justifying the genre. However, such moments were few and far between, and television—with its need to appeal to everyone—played a major role in the demise of cabaret in Germany. As Georg Seeßlen explained, the "broadcasts came close to the *Büttenreden* (carnival speeches) during Mardi Gras" (see 5: Holidays and Local Festivals); "the 'public jokers' had to deal with an audience which wanted to be amused whatever the cost but they did not want to be enlightened or pushed in the direction of change" (Seeßlen 1973, 141–142).

There were exceptions to this trend away from satire with such programs as the news magazine *Hallo Nachbarn* (Hello, Neighbors) broadcast by the Norddeutsche Rundfunk (North German Radio) in West Germany from 1963 to 1965. Individual skits, short films, and songs criticized the events of the day, and a satirical moderator linked the disparate elements together into a unit. One of the authors was Jürgen von Manger (1923–1994), who gained a certain notoriety and was criticized by the conservative newspaper *Die Welt* (The World; see 6: The Press). The result was a ban of *Televisionen eines Untertanen* (Television of an Underling), the subtitle of the show, and a title which recalls Heinrich Mann's (1871–1950) critical novel *Der Untertan* (The Strawman, 1914), itself a satire on the imperial era at the turn of the twentieth century. The TV show's short-lived rebirth lacked the brilliance of the early show. Television's self-censorship was clearly seen in a later series, *Abramakabra*, which avoided political topics and specialized in black humor and parodies of cultural fads.

Zeitvertreib (Passing the Time), broadcast by the West German ARD (see 7: Radio and Television), also escaped into the grotesque and nonsensical, with the exception of a few satires against a meritocracy, an achievement-oriented society, and the compulsion to buy, which were characteristic of the West Germans in the two decades after the war. The success of these shows was mixed. The show *Express*, however, which specialized in satirizing other TV shows, achieved respectable viewing figures during that period in spite of its late broadcasting time. One of the reasons for political apathy in the 1970s was the desire not to upset the ruling coalition of labor and liberals in West Germany (see 1: From Two to One). The comedians who themselves leaned toward the left were afraid that their criticism would be used by the conservatives to prevent further democratization of the society. Seeßlen wondered if these arguments were really true or if the escape into the use of gags and absurdity was actually a sign of resignation caused by the realization that satire was ineffective. A society that is content is inclined to find reasons for the absurdity of its existence in existential questions and not political reality. A satire about the vain smugness of a singer like Anneliese Rothenberger, a star of the 1970s (see 8: Music), was therefore more interesting than a satire about the dealings of Franz Joseph Strauss, minister of defense, who was involved in several political scandals (see 1: From Two to One) (Seeßlen 1973, 144).

One exception to the dying tradition of cabaret on television was provided by Dieter Hildebrandt, who, with *Notizen aus der Provinz* (News from the Countryside) in the 1970s and *Scheibenwischer* (Windscreen Wipers) beginning in the 1980s, created one-man shows that influenced critical popular opinion as much as magazines like *Spiegel* (see 6: The Press). Often, however, he was defamed as a *Nestbeschmutzer* (literally, a nest dirtier, a denigrator of his country).

Although there is a slight difference in style among the three German-speaking countries—German wit is often very earthy, Austrian humor has a touch of the macabre, and the Swiss favor self-irony—the political cabaret (*Kabarett*) can be found in all three, and in Germany it thrives best in small theaters. There is even an award, usually given to a politician who manages to incorporate wit and humor into his speeches, called the Orden wider den tierischen Ernst (Award against Dead Seriousness). In the late 1990s, Regine Hildebrandt (no relation to the satirist Dieter Hildebrandt) became one of the most popular politicians in Germany because of her lively sense of humor and a recipient of the award, though, sadly, not because of her political status (Eichheim et al. 2002, 199).

Published examples of satire, social as well as political (often verging on black humor), can also be found in the work of the well-known humorist "Loriot" and the writer Ingrid Noll. Germans chose Loriot (Victor von Bülow), whom Florian Illies refers to as the grandfather of the Golf Generation's humor, in 2003 as one of the most important Germans. He has written books of short prose as well as full-length feature films, all available on video and audio cassettes. Though they date from the 1970s, they are still frequently broadcast on German television. In one short story, *Advent*, that parodies the sentimental tales that might be read aloud during the pre-Christmas season as families work together on crafting Christmas gifts, the tone—with references to snow-covered trees, cute bunnies, and deer (described in the diminutive form)—contrasts sharply with the content. The forester's wife has murdered her husband because he got in her way around the house. She carves up the body, following prescribed rules for carving game into appropriate joints for cooking, wraps up the pieces, and gives them to Knecht Ruprecht (see 5: Holidays and Local Festivals) for distribution to the poor. To a German (and arguably also to those with a British sense of humor), the cruelty is rendered harmless by the totally unrealistic framework of the story (similar to the cruelty in fairy tales and works such as Wilhelm Busch's *Max und Moritz*). To Americans, the description of cold-blooded murder can be too horrific to be funny and tends to be taken at face value, as reality.

Similarly, in a novel by Ingrid Noll, *Der Hahn ist tot* (The Rooster Is Dead), the descriptions derive humor from the sheer unlikelihood of the character—a middle-aged woman besotted with a younger man—committing multiple murders, which she plots in order to remove anyone who gets in the way of her getting her man. Another Noll novel also renders a description of a murder humorous and, to a certain degree, harmless by the detailed description of sweat pouring down the victim's leg as the murderer lets it go, thereby causing the victim to fall from a high window. Perhaps it is the admission of a secret fantasy that creates the humor for the German reader, a fantasy that would be so impossible to realize that any semblance of reality is eliminated. The film versions of Noll's novels are less successful, perhaps because the visual reality of the medium confronts the viewer with the cruelty and the irony is lost.

Satire is also closely related to word plays, and this kind of humor is also very popular in Germany. In the Weimar years, it was Rainer Ringelnatz, and in the 1950s and 1960s, it was Heinz Erhardt who helped to shape German humor. Erhardt specialized in playing with familiar expressions in a literal sense. He would, for example, hunt around looking for the "lost thread" of a conversation, but most of his puns lose too much in translation to quote. He later experienced the sad fate of having a stroke, which destroyed the language domain in his brain. In the 1980s, Otto Waalkes,

though more blunt and with jokes verging on the cruel, was one of his successors.

As Sabine Schmidt noted in 1999, "Recent German comedy is frequently criticized for a perceived lack of sophistication but at the same time praised for an uninhibited nature not seen before, with performers like Helge Schneider and Wigald Boning walking the fine line between silliness and comic absurdity" (Sandford 1999, 495).

The Holiness of Order. One of the many annoyances for non-Germans is the constant requirement to register with different entities within the country—paperwork is required to do just about anything. Germans are accustomed to this and just accept the fact that they should register with the Einwohnermeldeamt (Communal Registration Office) when they take up residence in a town or village, and that there are many forms to be filled out when opening a bank account or getting a job. For them, it is understandable that the state strives for orderliness—just as they want to have order in and control of their own lives.

In the same way, Germans do not find it strange that most professions and occupations require practitioners to be certified by the state. It is a way to guarantee a society of highly qualified workers (see 3: The Educational System). Discussions about whether babysitters should have to pass a state exam might strike some as an extreme example of control. Others might well welcome this plan to safeguard children.

Order and control are also synonymous with security, from the German perspective. They guarantee it and eliminate chance and surprise in life. Another synonym for security (*Sicherheit*) is the term *Beamte* (civil servant). For some Germans, becoming a *Beamte* is seen as the ultimate goal in life. The *Beamtenstaat* (state run by civil servants) is an indication of an innate attitude in Germans: the fear of the unknown, the fear of risk-taking, a trait many see as "the major key to the German character" (Lord 2004, 40). As Bausinger remarked in *Typisch deutsch* (2000, 58), security is important for all areas of life. The quantity and the extent of personal insurance is especially high in Germany. Many people are insured for the same things two or three times over to be on the safe side. One of the major worries is the one about old age, and Germans tend to begin as early as possible to plan for retirement. Of course, one negative side of this need for security is the fear of entrepreneurship and risk-taking.

Frankness/Aggression versus Sentimentality.   Another commonly held prejudice about Germans is that they seemingly have an inability to participate in small talk—or at best a lack of appreciation of its function. Germans see themselves as having a purpose. In their greetings they tend to be brief and then get straight down to business. For foreigners, this can be a shock. They often find it impolite, although in fact it is not—at least, it is not intended that way.

In the same way, Germans may seem tactless. Their criticism is frank. As Richard Lord said, "They may even criticise you on things which happen to be personality flaws that are hard to remedy and thus pretty much taboo subjects in most other societies" (Lord 2004, 50). This is also true for discussions in university courses. While in the United States, students seldom criticize each other openly, in Germany it is considered perfectly acceptable to play the devil's advocate and attack another's opinions.

Lord sees this attitude as stemming from Germans' wish to be accepted as credible, whereas Americans wish more to be liked. It is also important for a German to base an opinion on rational arguments and to address a topic empirically, assembling all available facts. The downside of this is that the individual will then be convinced that the conclusion arrived at is the only valid one. Lord remarked, "It is not very profitable to argue with Germans about decisions they have arrived at after long consideration" (ibid., 52). The result is that they can appear aggressive and arrogant.

The flip side of the Germans' aggression is their apparent sentimentality and fundamentally pessimistic outlook. To quote Lord again: "Gloom is a staple of German life" (ibid., 53). This is not always so, however, as can be demonstrated by the popularity of festivals and organized jollity (see 5: Holidays and Local Festivals).

Secondary Virtues

There is a term that most Germans, especially those over forty, would accept as unremarkable. Moreover, they would generally agree on its definition. That term is *Sekundärtugenden*, which translates simply into "secondary virtues." These are not the grand and noble virtues of honesty, morality, integrity, and ethical high standards and do not deserve to be ranked up there with them, but, some might argue, they are the virtues that make everyday life livable: punctuality, respect for one's elders, saying please and thank you as appropriate, good table manners, cleanliness, and so on. But as the aging '68ers might add, these secondary virtues may be slipping into yet a lower ranking as the population becomes more diverse and the new millennium and the Golf Generation take over. Cleanliness, for instance, is not a primary characteristic of many German cities in the new millennium. Nevertheless, it is a major topic of discussion at all times. Questions concerning trash removal always find a large audience: The elaborate system of separating trash into different categories has become a science (see 10: From A to Z, "Recycling"). In many villages, the weekly sweeping of sidewalks has not changed for decades. Here a foreigner may find his stereotype of the clean and tidy Germans confirmed.

The virtues traditionally associated with Germany, such as *Disziplin, Zuverlässigkeit, Ordnungsliebe, Fleiß, Gründlichkeit, Sparsamkeit,* and *Pünktlichkeit* (discipline, reliability, love of order, diligence, thoroughness, thrift, and punctuality), have taken a roller-coaster ride over the past sixty years. They were certainly the basis for the economic miracle (see 10: Consumer Culture versus Green Awareness), with all its positive and negative aspects, but then, beginning in the late 1960s, these virtues began to lose favor. *Gesellschaftskritik* and *Selbstbestimmung,* in contrast to *Fremdbestimmung* (critique of society and self-determination instead of being ordered around by others), were the new guidelines. Surveys in the 1970s showed signs of a laissez-faire attitude toward one's job, avoidance of hard work and risk, a search for immediate gratification instead of striving for future goals, and the desire to spend money now instead of worrying about tomorrow.

With unemployment rising in the 1990s, the old values were revitalized (see Beyer et al. 2003). Diligence remains the number one typically German characteristic in the eyes of the French as well as the British: In a 2005 survey, French and British respondents, asked the question, "To what extent do the following statements apply to the Germans?" ranked diligence at the top, the French with 61 percent, the British with 56 percent (Aust 2005, 49, 51). Nevertheless, even today foreigners who are familiar with the "former" Germany observe that Germans have become less driven and more relaxed and easygoing. Perhaps the negative stereotype of *Sturheit* (stubbornness) is also vanishing. Pia Ampaw, a German model, related a characteristic example in an interview about typical German behavior. She was traveling by train with a colleague and the seat next to her was occupied. When Pia asked the passenger if he would switch seats with her so that she and her colleague could sit together, the German replied only that he had reserved that seat and therefore was not going to move (Weitz 2004, 24). This type of stubbornness is stereotypical of Germans, but the fact that Pia would question it is telling.

A trolley ride in any German city today can make a visitor very much aware of the shifting value of these secondary virtues in German society. On the surface, chaos seems more prevalent than order. The old saying "*Ordnung muß sein!*" (Order above all) seems not to be a driving force in the lives of the many youngsters who now noisily dominate the streetcars dressed in various torn outfits, showing much pierced flesh. The disorderly protagonists of Heinrich Hoffmann's *Struwwelpeter* (1845), one of the first children's books that showed drastic punishments for breaking rules, seem to serve more as models than deterrents. Yet, the well-organized public transportation system and German bureaucracy are still intact, suggesting that the situation is more complex than might appear on the surface. The Amt für öffentliche Ordnung (Office for Public Order) that takes care of the various types of registrations for both citizens and foreigners is as intimidating as ever and requires other German secondary virtues to survive it unscathed, namely *Kampfgeist*, *Ausdauer*, and *Härte* (fighting spirit, endurance, and toughness). These characteristics also are among those cited as typically German by both foreigners and Germans themselves, and one of the many Nazi slogans described young German boys as being as tough as leather, as fast as greyhounds, and as hard as steel from Krupp: "*Deutsche Jungen sind zäh wie Leder, flink wie Windhunde, hart wie Kruppstahl.*"

Thriftiness. The virtue of saving (*Sparen*) still has high priority among people in German-speaking countries. This special relationship to saving—collecting money on the one hand, and being mean about spending it on the other—has a considerable history. In the late nineteenth century, *Sparkassen* (savings banks) were founded in many villages and towns to provide ordinary folk and those employed in industry with an opportunity to set a little aside. People were encouraged not to tuck their earnings away in the so-called "savings stocking" under their pillow, but to take it to a public institution that would pay interest and channel the money into the economy for investments. Sadly, those who did this in Germany were out of luck. Because of the inflation that raged after the two world wars, money deposited in savings banks became almost worthless. After World War II, many people gave up saving in this way and instead put their money into *Bausparkassen* (building societies),

with the aim of exchanging it as soon as possible for a house or apartment. In addition, various laws were passed by the state to promote this form of saving. The visible consequence of these changes is that many towns and villages are now surrounded by new housing estates where all the houses look alike. The Swabian motto "*Schaffe, schaffe, Häusle baue, sterbe*" (Work, work, build a house, die—where *Häusle* is the diminutive form of *Haus* in the Swabian dialect) is still very appropriate in the new millennium.

Saving and thriftiness are even regarded as a sort of sport. So-called *Sparvereine* (savings clubs) often have their base in a pub, the members being regulars of the pub in question. There are also families who take comparison shopping very seriously. After comparing the offerings of the big supermarkets, they may well buy their Limburger cheese in a different place from their Emmentaler because it's cheaper. It is also customary to buy fresh food only in quantities people are sure of being able to eat to avoid wastage. Finally, if you go out for a cup of coffee with a German, be prepared for the fact that each will pay for his own, unless someone has said beforehand "*Ich lade dich ein*" (I am going to invite you).

Punctuality. The first and foremost of the secondary virtues for Germans is punctuality. Certainly, punctuality plays a greater role in Germany than anywhere else in the world, except perhaps its German-speaking neighbor, Switzerland. Bureaucrats and the military have done their share to enshrine the importance of punctuality in the hearts of all Germans—even the younger generation has internalized it, though not perhaps to the same extent as their parents. Still, there are two situations—when you have been invited to someone's house for a meal, and business appointments—when punctuality is a must. It is not unusual for guests at a large dinner party to all arrive together, challenging the hosts to take care of coats, find vases for the flowers that are still often brought as gifts, and greet everyone all at the same time. Punctuality for Germans is closely linked with courtesy: To arrive late for a meeting or meal can be interpreted as stealing the other person's precious time. Germans talk of being as punctual as *die Eisenbahn* (the railway, which still arrives and departs on the second most of the time). However, there is a negative aspect to this punctuality: Germans also talk of being "as punctual as *die Maurer* (bricklayer)." This means that they will not work a minute longer than is absolutely necessary (at least as employees). They have always also valued their free time (see 5: Activities and Clubs). Richard Lord observed: "Should you turn up at an office or store shortly before closing time (or the holy lunchtime break) so that it appears that your business might drag on past that magic hour, you will either receive chilly service or be turned away altogether" (Lord 2004, 47).

This attention to prescribed hours extends also to the sphere of education, from grade school to the university. At the latter, there is a recognized time period, known as *das akademische Viertel* (the academic quarter hour), designating how long students need wait for a tardy professor and giving them leeway for wandering into class a little late. So well established is this tradition that university schedules are listed *cum tempore* or *sine tempore*, with temporal leeway or without: 10:00 cum tempore means that you can be safe coming to the lecture hall at 10:15; 10:00 sine tempore means 10:00 sharp, and you would disrupt the lecture by coming in late.

This tacit acceptance of a quarter of an hour as the length of time one should wait for another person is valid beyond the halls of academe, too, and extends to personal meetings or dates as well as other educational settings. Teenagers have been known to exploit this silent agreement in classes outside the regular curriculum— for example, for Confirmation classes (*Konfirmandenunterricht*) where the teacher/preacher has to come from his home to the school. Lookout posts might be positioned along the teacher's route, and unwitting bystanders encouraged to talk to the teacher in order to delay him. And with the strike of the quarter hour everyone would vanish, even if the teacher was just approaching the schoolhouse.

Linked to the virtue—some might say the stereotype—of punctuality is that of early rising. When quite young, children learn the saying "*Morgenstund hat Gold im Mund*" (literally, The morning hour has gold in its mouth). In other words, to become rich, one needs to rise and shine at dawn. Once, it was the farmer who had to get up early in the summertime to till the fields. Today, it is also the factory workers, the bakers, and the butchers, since many small shops open at 7 AM to serve their customers fresh bread, rolls, cheese, and *Wurst* (sausages).

Symbols and Memorials

The German Flag
Citizens of countries such as Switzerland, Sweden, and the United States tend to fly

FRG flag. (Eye Wire, Inc.)

their national flag all year round. In Germany, the opposite was true until very recently. In part because of Germans' ambivalent attitude toward their nationality (see 1: Coming to Terms with the Past), the German flag was rarely seen except on official occasions. Even as late as 1994, only 60 percent of West Germans and 50 percent of East Germans reacted positively to the colors in a survey (Bundeszentrale für politische Bildung, BpB, Federal Central Agency for Political Education, www.bpb. de). The *Bundesadler*, or federal eagle, which is reserved for official use and therefore can be seen only on official documents and on a flag flown outside of official buildings, is somewhat more popular.

The colors of the present flag, black, red, and gold, have a somewhat mixed background. They were an obvious choice after World War II because they were the only colors from Germany's history that had more positive than negative connotations. They had been used in the democratic revolution of 1848, the result of which was the first German parliament, which gathered for a short time in the Paulskirche in Frankfurt on the Main. Black, red and gold had also been chosen for the national flag in the Weimar Republic, which, however, used the colors of the Prussian empire (black, white, and red) for its merchant flag and only inserted the colors of the national flag in the upper left corner. Black, red, and gold had been the symbol for a united and democratic Germany in 1832 at the Hambacher Schloß (Hambach castle) in the Palatinate, where 40,000 had gathered to demonstrate. As the colors of revolution, they were forbidden by the Deutsche Bund (German confederacy), whose reactionary policies tried to prevent just such a new

German flag with federal eagle. (Stefan Klein/istockphoto.com)

democratic Germany. Heinrich Hoffmann von Fallersleben, the poet of the national anthem, interpreted the colors as a red beam and golden light breaking through the blackness of night. The revolutionary refrain was sung: "*Pulver ist schwarz, / Blut ist rot, / golden flackert die Flamme!*" (Gun powder is black, / blood is red, / golden flickers the flame of revolution). In 1949, a parliamentarian summarized the reasons for their choice for the new democratic Germany, the Federal Republic of Germany: "The tradition of the colors black-red-gold is . . . *Einheit in der Freiheit* [unity in liberty]. The flag shall be for us a symbol that the idea of personal freedom is one of the foundations of our future state" (Bund Online).

Yet, the colors stood not only for democracy but also for the resurrection of the German empire, which had been destroyed by Napoleon in 1806. The colors had been used by the Freikorps (Volunteer Corps) under the command of Major Ludwig Adolf Wilhelm Freiherr von Lützow, who had enlisted men from all the regions of Germany to fight against Napoleon in the war of liberation. They wore black uniforms with red cuffs and lapels and golden buttons—colors that were interpreted by them as well as by the first German fraternity as the colors of the *Reichspanier*, the banner of the medieval German empire. It depicted a black eagle with a red tongue and red claws on a golden background. National aspirations were the main motivation for the activities undertaken by the Lützower Freikorps and the newly founded fraternity. Students and their professors had just celebrated the Wartburgfest in 1817 where the colors were prominently displayed (see colored woodcut in Pötzsch 1997, 135). It

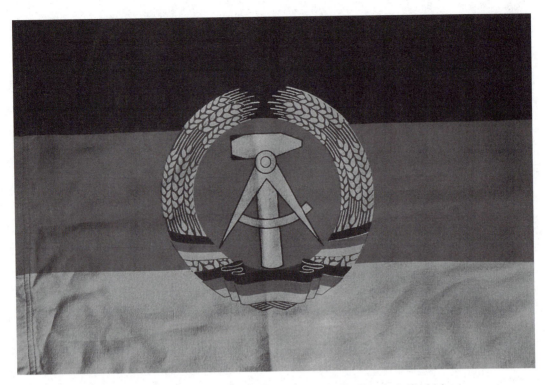

National flag of the historic German Democratic Republic. (Svenja-Foto/zefa/Corbis)

was on the Wartburg that Martin Luther had translated the Bible into German while hiding from the authorities. He was seen as the revolutionary and the champion of the German national cause. Therefore, the celebrations commemorated the 300th anniversary of the Protestant revolution of 1517 and at the same time the fourth anniversary of the defeat of Napoleon at the Leipziger Völkerschlacht (Battle of the Nations at Leipzig) in 1813.

German history is always complicated because of the many states involved, and the complexity continued after World War II. In 1949, two Germanys were created—although they did not officially recognize each other's statehood (see 1: From Two to One), and both states chose the same flag. In this way, the colors remained the only visible symbol of German unity until 1959, when the GDR added a coat of arms con-

sisting of a hammer (for the workers), a compass (for the engineers), and a sickle (for the farmers) to emphasize their political identity and sovereignty as the German *Arbeiter- und Bauernstaat* (state of workers and farmers).

The National Anthem

Only a little less confusing than the history of the German national flag—although in a different way—is the history of the German national anthem. The *Nationalhymne* (national anthem) is not accepted by everyone, although Joseph Haydn's music, the "Kaiserhymne" (Imperial Hymn), is appreciated as a wonderful piece of music. The problem is the accompanying text—or texts—as there are several based on two basic texts. The first basic one is the original text, "Gott erhalte Franz den Kaiser" (God Save the Emperor Franz). It was first performed in 1797 for the birthday of Kaiser Franz II, who was the last emperor of the Heilige Römische Reich Deutscher Nation (Holy Roman Empire of German Nations); Napoleon forced him to abdicate in 1806. Franz II then retained only his title as Franz I, Emperor of Austria-Hungary. The hymn served as a national anthem for the Austro-Hungarian monarchy until its fall in World War I. From 1797 to 1918, slight alterations were made in this text owing to the changing names of the emperors.

The second, completely different, text, "Deutschland, Deutschland über alles" (Germany, Germany Above All), chosen after World War I as the national anthem of the democratic Weimar Republic by its first chancellor, Friedrich Ebert, had a somewhat problematic history. The phrasing "Germany, Germany above all" sounded to many too nationalistic after the demise of the Weimar Republic and the Nazi era. However, its poet, Heinrich Hoffmann von Fallersleben, was—as Konrad Adenauer pointed out in 1949 in his defense of the anthem—"one of the best and first democrats" (Bausinger 2000, 101). Hoffmann von Fallersleben had only stressed the importance of a united Germany at a time of regionalism in 1841 when he wrote the poem. The Third Reich had, however, perverted its meaning by interpreting it from an extreme nationalistic point of view and demanding the integration of every piece of land that in the long history of the Holy Roman Empire of German Nations had been part of that empire at any time (see Overcoming Regionalism). In 1949, these words seemed totally inappropriate—even when read with a historical perspective.

Theodor Heuss, the first German postwar president, therefore asked for a new anthem, but the proposed "Hymne an Deutschland" (Hymn to Germany), by Rudolf Alexander Schröder and set to music by Hermann Reutter, found little support. The Federal Republic remained without a hymn for some years, whereas the German Democratic Republic in 1949 had adopted "Auferstanden aus Ruinen" (Risen out of Ruins), by Johannes R. Becher and set to music by Hanns Eisler. At sports events, the bands improvised by using drinking and carnival songs whenever a West German anthem was asked for. Finally, in 1952, a compromise was reached between the president and the chancellor of the Federal Republic: The third verse, which mentioned only *"Einigkeit und Recht und Freiheit für das deutsche Vaterland"* (unity and legality and liberty for the German fatherland), was adopted, and the first two verses fell into disuse. After the unification of both Germanys in 1990, the president, Richard von Weizsäcker, and the chancellor, Helmut Kohl, agreed to retain this innocuous third verse as an anthem for the new united Germany. Asked in 1997 to cite the first line of the German anthem, 58 percent of the West Germans and 21 percent of the East Germans repeated correctly the first line of the third verse. Only a minority recited the first line of the first verse or the former GDR anthem (BpB). And the missing percentages? Probably they did not know either verse.

The Eagle and the Deutscher Michel
In many cultures, the eagle, the king of the birds, has been an important figure in mythology and legends. Following the example of the Roman legions, Charlemagne adopted the eagle for his new empire when he was crowned in 800; official Germany has always proudly displayed a majestic eagle on its coat of arms ever since. After

German Chancellor Helmut Kohl addressing the first parliament meeting of the united Germany in the Berlin Reichstag in 1990 in front of the federal eagle. (Reuters/Corbis)

1433, the Holy Roman Empire of German Nations used the black, double-headed, imperial eagle on its coat of arms. This eagle's heads have red tongues, golden beaks, and crowns. Its wings are spread and it has golden or red claws, in which it holds the scepter and the orb. This image was used until the empire's demise in 1806. Austria kept this eagle during the Austro-Hungarian Empire. The new Deutsches Reich, the Prussian Empire, founded in 1870/1871, returned to the single-headed eagle. This tradition was so strong that even the Nazis' use of the eagle could not do the bird much harm; it was proudly displayed again as the official symbol of the new German democracy in the west during the postwar years and also decorated the front wall in parliament. It seemed to have lost its aggressive stance, however, and reminds many not of an eagle but of a plump duck.

Deutscher Michel from a 19th-century caricature.

That was the official symbol. The most popular symbol, however, is Deutscher Michel, the image of a man wearing a nightcap and gown who represents the German "everyman." Plumpness and naïveté, ponderousness and good-natured stupidity are the attributes of the Deutscher Michel, a real simpleton. Michel, a popular shortened version of Michael, is supposedly not related at all to the Old High German word *michel*, meaning "strong" and "large," as one might assume. The origin of the name is disputed, but the earliest reference is found in a collection of proverbs published in 1541 by Sebastian Frank.

Public Symbolism

The Third Reich's shadow has tainted official symbolism. For most Germans, it now smacks of nationalism and arouses cynicism. But fortunately for Germany, there were Jeanne-Claude and Christo, who were able to give public symbolism an aesthetic and popular facelift, to make it smile. The wrapping of the old Reichstag building in 1995 and its unveiling as the symbol for a new Germany became a folk festival. Even the motto "*Dem deutschen Volk*" (To the German People), glaring out from the portico where it had been installed in 1916, lost its stern associations, at least for a short time. A modern counterpart to this motto was created by the artist Hans Haacke. The artwork is a flat box (21 by 7 m) in which the parliamentarians, the representatives of the people and its different regions, are invited to deposit soil from their local districts. Across the center are large illuminated letters stating "*Der Bevölkerung*" (To the Population), stressing the inclusive democratic aspect of the new Germany. The German word *Volk* gained negative connotations during the Hitler era, and though the translation is simply "folk," the English does not convey the racist implications of a particular people—the Aryans. *Bevölkerung*, in contrast, implies the population as a whole, including its modern multicultural components. Rather than being placed in front of the stairs leading into the Reichstag, which would offer a balance to the older dedication, the Haacke installation stands in the courtyard, where, one can argue, it is at the heart of the building. It has its own website: www.bundestag.de/bau_kunst/kunst-werke/haacke/derbevoelkerung/index.html.

In a similar way, Sir Norman Foster's renovation of the Reichstag itself is filled with symbolism, integrating the old with the new as history merges old and new. Most pronounced is the cupola with its glass-sided spiral walkway, which leads to the very top of the building and is open to the public. It not only offers everyone—citizens and tourists alike—a great view of Berlin and the government buildings, but suggests symbolically that the people are in charge, that the parliament beneath them is subservient to them, that the political process is translucent, like the glass walls, which allow a view of the city as well as the parliament.

Holocaust Memorial in Berlin. (Photo by D. Scholl)

Memorials

Monuments used to be reminders of a proud past, of an attitude of defiance. For example, the *Cheruskerdenkmal* (monument of Armin, the Cheruscan) celebrates a Germanic victory over the Roman Empire in 9 C.E., the *Niederwalddenkmal* symbolizes defying France, and the *Walhalla* is a pantheon of famous Germans. But this changed in the postwar era. Monuments have become signs of warning, a reminder to avoid a repetition of atrocities. German has three words for monuments. Literal translations may sound clumsy, but they highlight both the similarities and the differences: *Denkmal* the word usually used for monuments, means, literally "a sign, a place to reflect"; *Mahnmal*, a word usually used for less grandiose structures, means "a sign, a place to admonish"; and *Gedenk-stätte*, used less for a structure than for a grave or plaque, means "a place of remembrance." This change in attitude toward monuments is well illustrated by the history of the Holocaust Memorial. The concept was first initiated in 1988 by the journalist Lea Rosh. Six years later, the request for proposals was made public and a heated discussion began, which continued even after Peter Eisenman's proposal was accepted in 1997. (A first round of proposals had ended in a veto by Chancellor Kohl in 1995.) The monument was dedicated on May 10, 2005, in commemoration of the sixtieth anniversary of the liberation of Germany, but the controversy surrounding the memorial continued. The Zentralrat der Sinti und Roma (Central Association of Sinti and Roma) stated their displeasure that the memorial was reserved for Jewish victims rather than being dedicated to all victims of the Nazi terror (see also 1: Coming to Terms with the Past; for information on other monuments, see 2: From A to Z).

Health Issues and Sexuality

Health and Fitness

"Be careful!" "That is much too cold! You will ruin your stomach with all that ice!" "It's not good for you to drink ice cold water!" "You can't run around like that with your midriff exposed. Pull your sweater down! Your kidneys will get cold." "Please close the door. You will catch a cold from the draft!"

Each culture has its own myths and prejudices about health and fitness, and Germany is no exception. The above warnings will sound very familiar, even normal, to Germans, though they may fit into the realm of superstition and myth for others. There seems to be an exaggerated fear of the ill effects of sitting in a draft among some members of the older generation in Germany. The phrase "*Es zieht*" (There's a draft), uttered with an annoyed tone and accompanied by a coat or jacket being buttoned up, can be very irritating to those seeking fresh air by opening a window on a train or bus. The prevalence of air-conditioning has reduced this problem to some degree, though it has created others—A/C vents are seen as sources of further drafts and colds. Another generally accepted risk to one's well-being, related perhaps to drafts, is that of allowing the kidneys to get too cold. Particularly young women in short jackets will be admonished to cover up and keep their kidneys warm— a real problem in a time when it is fashionable to display midriffs (see 4: Lifestyle and Fashion).

Until quite recently, pieces of fur from cats, about 12 inches square, were sold in German pharmacies or health food stores for placing on rheumatic joints for supposed relief. What was supposedly particularly beneficial about cats' fur—as opposed to rabbit fur or even dog skin—was not totally clear. As cats have gained in popularity as household pets, however, their value in a deceased state has diminished. Perhaps it is no longer as easy to find unclaimed cats, dead or alive. Are these concerns and cures valid for everyone in any country or are they specifically German health concerns?

Unfortunately, the topic of culturally based illnesses seems to be a topic not widely studied (but see Payer 1988 and Hackenbroch 2005). There is little empirical research on the subject and no real data. Nevertheless, words like *Kreislauf-*

störung are certainly used much more often in Germany than "poor circulation" or "problems with one's circulation" are in English-speaking countries. Such problems are seen as the basis of a range of ailments, with changes in the weather often blamed as the culprit. It is not surprising to learn that the diagnosis of low blood pressure as a condition requiring treatment was even known in the past, as Lynn Payer noted, as the "German disease." In other countries, the same condition is regarded as positive, a view gradually being shared by German doctors, too. But treatment of circulatory problems by the "Kneipp method" exists only in Germany (see 2: From A to Z, "Kneipp Kur"). Related to this concern is the undisputed fact that Germans are especially preoccupied with the heart. They don't complain about chest pains but *Herzschmerzen* (heart pain), and Payer's research showed that in the late 1980s Germany ranked highest worldwide in prescribing heart medication. The positive aspect of this preoccupation is that much heart research has been done in Germany.

In 2003, the women's magazine *Brigitte* had an article on the ten greatest fitness lies (*Brigitte* 14 [2003], 130–133). Some will be equally familiar to those in the English-speaking world, others less so. Each was refuted in turn by findings from modern research. But the myths that were stated provided insight into long-held beliefs, both those common to both cultures and some that may be particularly German. The discussion, purported dangers, and recommendations also highlight cultural differences.

One of the myths refuted was that women who work out would become overly muscular (untrue because of the small amounts of testosterone in the female body). Another was that during pregnancy one should not engage in sports. However, women were warned to avoid contact sports, skiing, and horseback riding. What was recommended was *"Walking,"* a term Germans have adopted for power-walking or walking at a faster than normal pace, no doubt with the walker clad in some kind of tracksuit (see 2: Language, Script, and Gestures), and gentle exercise of the muscles, particularly the back.

The myth about not eating for two hours after exercising if one wants to lose weight was described as a fairy story (*Märchen*), based on the fact that metabolism is speeded up after sport. Here one would think the direct opposite might be true—that one could take advantage of this faster rate by eating just after exercise rather than later. Similarly, the myth that fat is only burned off after 30 minutes of exercise was proven to be false. Here, the crux of the matter is the level of intensity of exercise. Those who run too fast will cause just carbohydrates to be burned—to get rid of fat, one needs a moderate pace.

Regarding exercising in general, the myth that just working out for an hour once a week is useless was refuted by a study conducted at the university of Bayreuth. Those who spent an hour "Walking," stretching, and following a short muscle-building program for a year had lower blood pressure and better blood sugar and cholesterol levels than those who did nothing.

The following three "fitness lies" are more familiar but the emphasis bears a distinctly German stamp. The old "no pain, no gain" adage was addressed in the article, and readers were warned not to lift weights that were too heavy as this could be a burden on the heart and circulation (see above). The belief that *joggen* (jogging) harms the joints was refuted as well, since the activity stimulates the production of joint fluids (*Gelenkflüssigkeit*) that nourish the cartilage and prevent arthritis. Those with knock-knees (referred to as X-legs in German) or bowlegs (O-legs) are advised to start an exercise regime with the much valued "Walking" to get their joints into condition. An Australian study from 2002 was used to refute the myth that stretching activities before sport are of no use in preventing aching muscles afterward—a condition that in German is called *Muskelkater*, literally a hangover of the muscles. Stretched muscles have better circulation (the golden key to German health, it would seem) and have more elasticity and recovery power.

The belief that recreational athletes need a special diet was exposed as another lie. They should have a balanced diet, the article said, with plenty of fruits and vegetables like anyone else. Special vitamin "*Drinks*" (yet another English term used in a specialized context) or vitamins are then unnecessary, but those who engage in sports are advised to keep up their fluid levels.

Natural cures and healing processes have a long tradition in Germany. Many foreigners are surprised when they go to a German doctor for the first time with a stomach disorder. Instead of receiving medication or a prescription, they may be advised to do a *Rollkur* (rolling cure), namely, to drink a cup of chamomile tea or a glass of *Kohlsaft* (cabbage juice) and lie down for five minutes on their back, then turn over to the side for five minutes, then lie on the front, and so on (see also 2: From A to Z, "Kneipp Kur"). Simon Richter even sees urine therapy as "indigenous to German culture," though most Germans would question this. But he

believes that it "nicely fits into the patterns and logic of the German culinary unconscious" (Richter 2002, 189). He cites as proof that titles such as *Urine: Your Body's Secret Elixir of Health; Urine the Ur-Nectar: The Inexhaustible Healing Power of Your Body's Own Pharmacy;* or *Urine: A Very Special Juice* can be found on the shelves of mainstream bookstores in Germany, noting that these are original German titles published by mainstream German presses in paperback format, indicating a broad readership. In addition, the Second World Conference on Urine Therapy was held in Gersfeld, Germany, a spa town in central Germany, in 1999. The first one was held in India in 1997, where urine therapy has a long tradition but gained more widespread publicity after India's prime minister in 1979, Morarji Desai, acknowledged that he was an adherent. As Richter emphasized, folk medicine has been cultivated in Germany for centuries. General reference articles for urine therapy alone date back to the mid-eighteenth century.

One area in which Germans, like most Europeans, seem less health-conscious than Americans is smoking, as many tourists and guidebooks have observed. As a result, there are few smoke-free restaurants or even smoke-free sections of restaurants in Germany. Hyde Flippo remarked that "more than 70 percent of Germans are opposed to legislation banning smoking in public places" (Flippo 1997, 70). While U.S. citizens worry about cholesterol and nicotine (both are becoming an issue in Germany now, too, because of U.S. influence), Germans worry about genetically manipulated foods. In this matter, it is the United States that lags behind Germany in the trend to seek out organically produced food and plants from heirloom seeds.

Sexuality

Magazines. Looking for a children's magazine in the children's section of a train station bookstore, a surprised traveler discovered many journals full of photographs and drawings of scantily dressed men and women. Had they been misplaced? Was the upper back row of the children's section, she wondered, actually a secret place for frustrated fathers pretending to search for reading material for their children?

The incident is symptomatic of the Germans' relaxed attitude toward sexuality and its public display since the 1960s. Not only are newsstands well supplied with soft-porn magazines with women's breasts clearly exposed, but Germans do not shy from displaying the nude body (both male and female), although strategically placed "natural" objects and shadows may be used in images designed for a general audience. At universities in the United States, German departments that subscribed to such news magazines as *Der Spiegel*, and particularly *Stern*, had to exercise censorship with many issues even in the 1970s and 1980s because the blatant display of nudity might have disturbed prospective parents considering entrusting their eighteen-year-olds to the care of the college.

Advertisements. Advertisements have long been erotically or sexually charged—not only for cosmetics, and not only in Germany. Yet, the Viennese photographer Andreas H. Bitesnich has reached new heights with a series of nude ballet dancer scenes advertising not only perfume but also mineral water. In one ad, for example, a nude female dancer dominates the page while the bottle of mineral water is placed unobtrusively in the right hand corner. The ad's slogan reads: "Water in its most beautiful form."

Bitesnich's credo, the display of cool elegance, inspired many German athletes to join their dancing colleagues in sharing their perfect bodies with a larger audience. The well-known and popular East German ice-skating star Katarina Witt, who decided to pose for photographs for the magazine *Playboy*, explained her decision as follows: "I'm sure that some of my skating audience, when they hear I've taken off my clothes for *Playboy*, will be shocked. They may be uncomfortable with it, or they might ask, 'Why?' I don't know what to say, except that I was ready to do this. But I also think that once people see the photos, they'll feel differently. The pictures are beautiful and pure and natural. They're nude, but they still have a feeling of innocence" (*Playboy* December 1998, 176).

Less stylized elegance but "naturalness" can also be found in ads breaking the pubic hair taboo, as an ad campaign for the fitness magazine for women, *Shape*, in which women take pictures of themselves with the help of a self-timing camera, illustrates. The headline reads: "Do Yourself a Favor: Like Yourself." The ad campaign, by the agency Jung von Matt, ran into legal problems—not because of the display of frontal nudity, but because the idea of having subjects take pictures of themselves with a self-timing camera was allegedly plagiarism: The same idea had already been used in a book by the Berlin photographer André Rival, *100 Frauen-Selbstansichten* (100 Women-Self-Portraits).

Although the display of the female body dominates, nudity includes both sexes and all ages. And it is not restricted to ads in magazines and newspapers or on TV. It also includes huge billboards as well as advertisements on the sides of trams that drive through both residential and business districts. This openness toward the naked body applies also to beaches, where it is considered perfectly acceptable to change into or out of a swimsuit without struggling to cover oneself with towels or bathrobes. The successful calendar made by the English Women's Institute, in which the group of middle-aged women posed tastefully in the nude, appealed to German sensibilities and has spawned several imitations in Germany, particularly one by the student athletes in Bremen (see 7: Advertising).

The Nudist Movement. The foundation for the sexually freer atmosphere was laid by Germany's long tradition of FKK (*Freikörperkultur*, literally, free body culture, nudist culture) going back to the reform movement of the turn of the twentieth century, which tried to address all aspects of life (eating habits, clothes, living, and health issues). Sunbathing was recognized as an especially healthy form of recreation, and the nude body was rediscovered as an expression of naturalness and true morality. In the Weimar Republic, the movement was accepted by the majority of the people and became part of mass culture. After a brief interlude at the beginning of the Nazi period in which FKK was forbidden, the movement reemerged in conjunction with the Nazi emphasis on physical fitness and the beauty of the body (as seen in Leni Riefenstahl's films), though it excluded all non-Aryans. After World War II, the Allies prohibited it again, yet the movement remained active, and one year later, in 1946, various FKK clubs were allowed.

In the repressive years of the Adenauer era, in which nudity was equated with pornography, however, the movement was unable to regain mass popularity in West Germany. It took the youth revolution of the late 1960s to change this attitude, but although sexuality was then in again, it was a different kind of acceptance of the nude, linked to the general breaking of social taboos and political restraints. The official FKK movement was marginalized. Instead, nudity (or semi-nudity) became part of the accepted form of sunbathing in areas even outside the official nudist colonies. Munich's English Garden (Munich's equivalent to New York's Central Park), which is close to major buildings of the Ludwig-Maximilian University, gained a certain notoriety in this regard. Students bathing in the nude have shocked many an unsuspecting tourist. Reason enough for Richard Lord to warn tourists in his travel guide: "Just because some sunbathers are fully stripped down, this does not mean that they are advertising their availability, or even looking for some companionship. Approaching someone engaged in solitary sunbathing is considered highly offensive, and can earn a sharp reproach from everyone around" (Lord 2004, 56).

In East Germany, in contrast, FKK continued and even expanded its mass appeal even though FKK clubs were not officially allowed. In the 1980s, a liberal bathing culture was reached—citizens could choose between FKK beaches and what was rather quaintly called a *Textilstrand* (textile beach) where swimsuits were worn. There was, however, an unspoken rule that one adhered to the customs of the beach—clothed individuals on the FKK beaches were just as unwelcome as nude bathers on a Textilstrand. With unification, the textiles began to dominate again at many beaches, and headlines announced another bathing culture war. In the new millennium, the non-club-oriented, laissez-faire attitude seems to have won over most people. From time to time, discussions about nudity flare up in the media, but in everyday life few people are offended to see someone strip completely, even in a public park.

The Sex Industry and Pornography. With the liberalization of public attitudes in the 1960s, the pornography, "sex education," and "sex-aid" industry also began to become more visible. The most prominent were the Beate Uhse chain stores (see 2: From A to Z, "Uhse [née Köstlin], Beate"). Over the years, Germany has become one of the leading producers of sex material and porn films as well as sex toys and medication. Sex fairs are held regularly in various German cities, and the "Venus 2000" in Berlin was one of the many big successes, demonstrating well the range of sexual preferences as outlined over 100 years ago by the first researchers on human sexuality (for example, *Psychopathia sexualis* [1879] by Richard von Krafft-Ebing, who introduced the terms "sadism" and "masochism" based on the novels by Donatien Alphonse François Marquis de Sade and Leopold von Sacher-Masoch, respectively). Liberalization neither increased nor decreased the preoccupation with the various forms of sexuality but only made the subject much more part of the general consciousness.

Child pornography and hard-core sexual violence—that is, forms of sexuality that victimize others—are outlawed. Germany, actually, "has some of Europe's most stringent youth morals protection laws in the audiovisual media" (Sandford 1999, 495–496). Soft-porn, however, can be watched during late-night shows on many TV stations.

Prostitution. Selling sexual services is not only legal in Germany but has been regarded as a "regular" business since 2002 (Holm 2002). John Sandford's reference work on German culture (1999) reported that German men in the 1990s spent an estimated 12.5 billion deutsche marks ($8.4 billion) per year "buying sex." Official and unofficial red-light districts with sex clubs, peep shows, and eros centers are found in all major German cities, often—as in Frankfurt am Main—near the main train station. Two major organizations fought for the rights of prostitutes, Hydra in Berlin and HWG (Huren wehren sich gemeinsam, Whores Resist Together) in Frankfurt am Main. The prostitutes did not understand why they should be required to pay taxes but also have their profession be regarded as immoral—as Stephanie Klee, one of the spokeswomen, stated (cited in Ehlers 2001)—and why they should not be granted official state benefits such as health insurance, unemployment benefits, or social security.

Of course, there always lurks the danger of slave trade and the maltreatment of women who are forced into such a life, as stressed by Alice Schwarzer (see 4: Gender Equality), who does not believe any woman should have to earn money in that undignified and inhuman way. Stephanie Klee and others—offering their services even in classified ads in family papers (*Knackige Großmutter sucht . . . :* ripe and juicy grandmother is looking for . . .)—disagree. They recognize the potential of misuse of women and the problem of forced prostitution, which has increased since the fall of the Iron Curtain, but they regard most prostitutes as voluntary "sex workers" who enjoy their profession and see it as a social act to help many frustrated men and women. Stephanie Klee explained to a reporter in an interview that in her twenty-six years as a prostitute, she has satisfied armies of men (more than 10,000); she has helped and saved them from their fixations and sent them back home to their wives or parents or empty apartments; and she has encouraged them, helped their self-esteem, and comforted them when they suddenly began to cry. She said, "I do not want to know what would happen in our society if there were suddenly no prostitution" (Ehlers 2001, 89).

From A to Z

Comedians and satirists: Wigald Boning (b. 1967) is known through the TV show *RTL Samstag Nacht* (RTL Saturday Night). Heinz Erhard (1909–1979) was one of Germany's best known comedians in the postwar era and is mentioned in the list of the 100 best Germans (Knopp et al. 2003). Dieter Hallervorden (b. 1935) achieved his breakthrough as a comedian in 1975 in a slapstick show *Nonstop Nonsens* as the character Didi. Dieter Hildebrandt (b. 1927) was the cofounder (with Sammy Dreschel) of the *Münchner Lach- und Schießgesellschaft* (Society for Laughing and Shooting) in Munich in 1956 and established himself as one of Germany's best-known and most influential political satirists. Helge Schnei-

der (b. 1955) had his breakthrough with such songs as "Guten Tach" (Hello) and "Katzeklo" (Litterbox). Films, mystery novels, and a musical (*Mendy—Das Wusical*) followed. Among his latest ventures are concert tours with a rock band called Helge Schneider and the Firefuckers. Otto Waalkes (b. 1948, known as "Otto") has long been one of Germany's most popular entertainers. He began his career as a stand-up comedian (after studying at the Hamburg Academy of Fine Arts). His wit ranges from political satire and ironic understatement to language humor. Live appearances, recordings, and his own TV show in 1973 followed. His work also includes the book *Otto: Das Buch* (Otto: The Book, 1980) and the films *Otto: Der Film* (Otto: The Movie, 1985), and *Otto: Der Neue Film* (Otto: The New Movie, 1987) which became "the two greatest successes in the history of German cinema" (Sandford, 633). (See also 7: Radio and Television.)

D: The international symbol for Germany is "D" for Deutschland. Whereas English speakers use "Germany" (referring to the generic term for all Germanic tribes), the French and Spanish selected the name of only one tribe, the Allemannen, their most direct neighbors living at the western borders of the German empire, as the designation for all Germans: "Allemagne" and "Alemania." The word *Deutschland* is a compound formed by the combination of an adjective and a noun: *deutsches Land*. The adjective *deutsch* derives from the Old High German, where *diutisc* came from the noun *diot*, meaning *Volk* (people). The adjective was used for the language that the common people of the German tribes spoke, in contrast to Latin and other Roman tongues.

Dialects: Dialects reflect Germany's regionalism and differ widely: Speakers of one dialect can barely understand the speakers of another (see 1: Overcoming Regionalism). Standard German began in the fifteenth century and had its source in the increasing importance of bureaucracy and the spread of Martin Luther's translation of the Bible. After World War II, the use of standard or High German was encouraged and became the language of the schools and formal public speaking. In general, Germany is divided into three dialect regions: the area north of a line running from Cologne in the west to Halle in the east (*Niederdeutsch*, Low German), the area between this line and a line running roughly from west to east through Frankfurt on the Main (*Mitteldeutsch*, Middle German), and the area south of this line (*Oberdeutsch*, Upper German). The differences include vowel as well as consonant changes, different word choices, and even grammatical variations.

Drugs: The use of soft drugs has been decriminalized since 1994. Hard drugs are handled differently in the individual states. Richard Lord warns, "Thus, in cities like Berlin, Frankfurt or Hamburg, you may be subjected to the spectacle of junkies shooting up more or less in the open as you walk through the major train stations and surrounding areas" (Lord 2004, 51).

Duden: For Germans, the term *Duden* is synonymous with correct orthography. The term is based on the name of Dr. Konrad Duden (1829–1911), a high-school teacher who authored a spelling dictionary in 1880. The impetus for his work came from initiatives of the newly established (1871) Prussian Empire to build a unified nation through standardization of the language. But it was not until 1901 that an official agreement between all the German states was reached at a conference for spelling reform in Berlin. Duden incorporated the results of this conference into his dictionary, which was soon regarded as the authoritative source for orthography, although it was not an official government publication. In contrast to most English dictionaries such as *Webster's*, *Duden* was short on definition. The emphasis was on spelling and grammatical information. Today, a series of *Duden* volumes cover all areas of language interest. Although Duden claimed that his dictionary was descriptive and not prescriptive, it certainly had the impact of prescriptiveness.

Over the years, the rules of German orthography in the *Duden* have become more and more complex. Beginning with the student revolt of 1968, which regarded a standardized orthography as repressive, the debate about a reform has gained momentum. In 1980, an international working group was established with members from West and East Germany, Austria, and Switzerland. In 1996, the various German-speaking countries agreed, after many conferences and discussions, to the introduction of a spelling reform (1998). But many citizens, publishers, and official organizations objected to the proposals, and the debate continued even after its official acceptance. The question was also raised as to whether government institutions have the legal right to undertake such a step. Even in 2006, the debate has not ended.

Einstand: Many businesses still expect a new employee to organize a small party at work or pay for drinks after his or her first working day is over. This is called an *Einstand* (Beck 2003, 213).

EU flag: In the 1950s, the Council of Europe adopted a circle of twelve gold stars on a blue background as a symbol of the unity of the European people. In 1985, it was finally accepted as an official emblem by all European Community (EC) members (see 10: Consumer Culture versus Green Awareness; From A to Z, "European Union"). The number twelve has nothing to do with the number of member states but was chosen because of its traditional symbolic meaning for "perfection" and "unity."

Fraktur: *Fraktur* is a German version of Gothic script developed in the 1500s that was used in German books for centuries. While the Roman type, the Antiqua, made inroads in most countries, the Gothic script experienced a revival in Germany in the first years of the Third Reich but was then condemned by Hitler as *undeutsch* (un-German) because it was supposedly derived from a Jewish source. In 1941, a version of Antiqua was introduced, but the change could not be implemented right away. Therefore, after the war, *Fraktur* was seen as a Nazi script, and the Roman script used in most other countries was introduced in Germany.

German language: German is the official language of Germany (Deutschland), Austria (Österreich), and Liechtenstein. It is one of four official languages of Switzerland (die Schweiz) and one of the three official languages of Luxembourg and Belgium. German is also spoken in regions of France, Denmark, Italy, the Czech Republic, Poland, Romania, Bosnia and Herzegovina, Hungary, Latvia, Lithuania, Estonia, Russia, and the Ukraine. Altogether, between 120 and 140 million Europeans speak German as their first language—more than the number of people in Europe who speak English as their first language. German is also spoken by many people as a first language in other countries, such as Brazil, Argentina, Canada, and the United States (Pennsylvania Dutch). Very few of those in the United States who claim German descent (over 50 million U.S. citizens, according to U.S. Department of Commerce figures) speak the language. In the African nation of Namibia, however, German is spoken by a sizable minority. It is estimated that outside of Europe, an additional 20 million people speak German as their first language. At present, approximately 20 million people worldwide are learning German in formal courses. Two-thirds of these people live in Eastern Europe (see MLA language map: http://www.mla.org/census_main).

Homeopathy: Homeopathic medicine is not only still popular in Germany but also gaining respect. It was the creation of Samuel Hahnemann (1755–1843), who "taught that drugs which produced symptoms in a person resembling those of a specific illness would cure the patient if used in smaller amounts" (Lyons et al. 1987, 524).

Institut für deutsche Sprache (Institute for the German Language): A research institute for contemporary German. It has no prescriptive power, however.

Kaiser-Wilhelm-Gedächtniskirche: The Emperor William Memorial Church in Berlin, located at the former center of West Berlin. It was not rebuilt after the war but its ruin left standing as a constant reminder of the horror of war. In 1961, a new octago-

Portrait of Samuel Hahnemann, German homeopathic physician. (Library of Congress)

nal church built of glass bricks, designed by Egon Eiermann, was built alongside the destroyed tower of the original church (known by the citizens of Berlin as *der hohle Zahn* [the hollow/decayed tooth]).

Kneipp Kur: The Kneipp cure. Sebastian Kneipp (1821–1897), a minister, apparently cured himself from tuberculosis when he was a student by combining hydrotherapy and medicinal herbs. Today, his name is primarily associated with the hydrotherapy, which alternates cold and hot baths to increase blood circulation.

Knigge: Anything in Germany relating to etiquette, such as table manners and appropriate dress and behavior, is associated with the name Knigge, after Adolph Freiherr von Knigge (1752–1796). Today, there are *Knigges* for everything, including drivers and vacationers. Though rules of etiquette are perhaps less and less important in a global, Americanized world, many Germans—at least of the older generation—

adhere to at least some of the rules they once learned as children. At the table, one had to sit upright and lay both hands on the table so that the wrist would more or less rest at the table edge. To put the elbow on the table was as impolite as putting one's hands in one's lap. When eating, one would hold the fork in the left hand, and the knife, which was used for cutting and to push food onto the fork, in one's right. Cloth napkins were often placed in personalized wooden or metal napkin rings so that they could be used for several meals. Once, saying grace was usual. Today it is rare, but the words *Guten Appetit* (bon appetit) are always said. Sometimes one may also hear *Mahlzeit*, although this expression (often accompanied by a knock on the table) is usually reserved for meals in a cafeteria in a firm or factory. Leaving food on one's plate was also considered bad form; today, it is no longer such a bad faux pas, partly because food is no longer as scarce. To signal that one is done eating, the knife and fork are placed side by side on the plate; a crossed knife and fork signal that one is just taking a break, or in a restaurant, that the waiter can serve some more. Originally, Freiherr von Knigge had not intended to write guidelines for correct etiquette. In his book *Über den Umgang mit Menschen* (About Interaction with People, 1788), he attempted to analyze human behavior and present observations that would serve as data for reflections. However, later editions simplified his intentions and transformed them into a guidebook for the (would-be) well-mannered.

Kolle, Oswalt: Kolle (b. 1928) is the German guru in regard to questions of sexuality. His films include *Das Wunder der Liebe, Sexualität in der Ehe* (The Miracle of Love: Sexuality in Marriage, 1968); *Deine Frau, das unbekannte Wesen* (Your Wife, the Unknown Being, 1969); and *Dein Mann, das unbekannte Wesen* (Your Husband, the Unknown Being, 1970). They influenced German culture at a time when a law that punished homosexuality with ten years in prison (the infamous paragraph 175 which caused the number '175' to stand as a synonym for 'gay') and another one regarding sex outside of marriage had yet to be abolished. The laws were finally changed in 1972.

Luftbrücken-Denkmal: This monument, in front of the Berlin-Tempelhof airport reminding everyone of the airlift of 1948–1949 (see 1: From Two to One), was dedicated on July 10, 1951. Due to its shape, it is colloquially known as the *Hungerharke* (the hunger rake).

Medical pioneers: German-speaking scientists and physicians have long been leaders in the medical field. Besides the well-known founders of psychoanalysis, the Austrian Sigmund Freud and the Swiss C. G. Jung, there are names lesser known outside Germany, such as Wilhelm Conrad Röntgen (1845–1923), Leopold von Auenbrugg (1722–1809), Robert Koch (1843–1910), Karl Landsteiner (1868–1943), Albert Schweitzer (1875–1965), and Felix Hoffmann (1868–1946), all of whom made important inventions or discoveries. Röntgen discovered X rays (in German, *Röntgen-Strahlen*). The Austrian Auenbrugg developed the diagnostic procedure of tapping a patient's chest or back to determine the amount of fluid in the chest. Koch won a Nobel Prize in 1905 for his work on tuberculosis and made many other important

contributions to medicine, among them research related to anthrax, diphtheria, and cholera. The Austrian Landsteiner discovered the four primary blood types in 1901. He came to the United States in 1922 and received the Nobel Prize for his work in immunology and viral diseases. Hoffmann, a chemist with the Bayer chemical firm, invented aspirin in 1893. Schweitzer, born in the German Alsace, is the embodiment of medical ethics. He spent most of his life in French Equatorial Africa caring for the native inhabitants and was awarded the Nobel Peace Prize in 1952.

Naturopathy: Especially popular in Germany, naturopathy is a method of healing by natural means such as using herbs, diet, water treatment, exercises, and warmth.

Orden wider den tierischen Ernst: Award against Dead Seriousness. This award has been given since 1950 by the Carnival's Association in Aachen to people who have shown humor in their official functions.

Registration: Anyone who spends more than a couple of months in Germany—even students spending a semester at a German university—is required to register with the Einwohnermeldeamt (Residents' Registration Office) within two weeks of moving into a community. The office must also be notified when one leaves, and the new residence has to be stated so that records can be verified with the office in the other community.

Schildbürger: Like the English village Gotham, which became proverbial for the foolishness of its inhabitants (the Gothamites), the German town of Schilda and its citizens, the Schildbürger, became synonymous with simpletons going back to folk tales published in 1598.

Schloss Bellevue: The official residence of Germany's president.

Sütterlin: The name usually associated with any older German script. The term goes back to Ludwig Sütterlin (1865–1917), who simplified the German script used in the nineteenth century. At that time, the newly introduced steel pen allowed the variation of thin upward and thick downward strokes, giving a certain aesthetic to the writing but requiring awkward hand positions. Sütterlin's script used a different pen that allowed only the same thickness for the various strokes but was easier for children to use. The script was adopted as the standard in Prussia in 1924 and a decade later in all states, but it was abolished in 1941 because it was seen as un-German. After the war, it was revived, but only in a few areas of Germany.

Titles and forms of address: Whereas in Austria, the "von" before a last name, indicating aristocratic ancestors, was abolished after World War I, it is still used in German (for example, Otto von Habsburg). Professional titles that may be unfamiliar to foreigners are: *Rektor* for a university president, who is addressed as *Magnifizenz* (from the Latin form *magnifice rector*). A *Dekan* (dean) is addressed as *Spektabilität* or *Spectabilis* (from Latin *spectabilitas*, meaning "honorable").

Uhse Beate: Uhse (née Köstlin, 1919–2001), was a champion for the sexual revolution and liberation, but also a somewhat controversial entrepreneur, and finally a millionaire. As the introduction to a biographical article on her states, she broke many taboos and had unusual insights into Germans' secret desires (Knopp et al. 2003, 290). At the age of eighteen, she became a professional pilot, and she later won prizes in international aerobatics competitions. She served in the German air force during the war and was the first woman to fly a German fighter plane. Legend has it that she steered the last plane leaving Berlin with her two-year-old son on board before the Red Army moved in.

Uhse settled in West Germany as a widow, her husband having been killed in an airplane accident in 1944. The Allies prevented her from flying again and she became a saleswoman for plastic articles. On her sales trips she encountered many women with unwanted pregnancies—a very real problem in the postwar years. As a result, she published *Schrift X* (Publication X) in 1946, with instructions on how to calculate safe days for birth-control purposes using the Knaus-Ogino-Method. The sale of sex products and, in 1951, the first catalog for mail orders followed. In 1962, after many legal fights and accusations about spreading immorality, Uhse opened her first sex store, beginning a remarkable postwar career. Before her death in 2001, she oversaw as CEO the world's largest chain of sex stores.

There are Beate Uhse stores in every major German city and in many other countries. After unification, she introduced mobile sex shops in the former GDR, where pornography had been banned. Annual sales reached into the millions, and the company began to offer shares on the stock exchange in 1999. In celebration of her fiftieth business anniversary in 1996,

Uhse opened a museum of erotica in downtown Berlin near the Bahnhof Zoo and the Kaiser-Wilhelm Gedächtniskirche.

Umlaut and ß: Besides the umlauts (ä, ö, ü), the diacritical marks indicating a change in the vowel sounds, German has another character that is not common in other languages, the "ß," called the *eszett* (sz) because it looks in Fraktur as if it originated from a combination of "s" and "z." In reality, it is "ss." German script had two forms of "s," a long one and a rounded one that was only used at the end of a syllable and word. The combination of the two led to the "ß."

Additional Readings

Ammon, Ulrich. *Die deutsche Sprache in Deutschland, Österreich und der Schweiz. Das Problem der nationalen Varietäten.* Berlin and New York: deGruyter, 1995.

Andritzky, Michael, and Thomas Rautenberg, eds. *"Wir sind nackt und nennen uns Du." Von Lichtfreunden und Sonnenkämpfern. Eine Geschichte der Freikörperkultur.* Gießen: Anabas, 1989.

Auer, Peter, and Heiko Hausendorf, eds. *Kommunikation in gesellschaftlichen Umbruchsituationen. Mikroanalytische Aspekte des sprachlichen und gesellschaftlichen Wandels in den neuen Bundesländern.* Tübingen: Niemeyer, 2000.

Bausinger, Hermann. *Typisch deutsch. Wie deutsch sind die Deutschen?* München: Beck, 2000.

Behal-Thomsen, Heinke, Angelika Lundquist-Mog, and Paul Mog. *Typisch deutsch? Arbeitsbuch zu Aspekten deutscher Mentalität.* München: Langenscheidt, 1993.

Clyne, Michael G. *The German Language in a Changing Europe.* Cambridge: Cambridge University Press, 1995.

Cullen, Michael S. *Das Holocaust-Mahnmal. Dokumentation einer Debatte.* München: Pendo, 1999.

Dieckmann, Friedrich. *Was ist deutsch? Eine Nationalerkundung.* Frankfurt: Edition Suhrkamp, 2003.

Dudenredaktion, ed. *Duden.* Vol. 5: *Das Fremdwörterbuch.* Mannheim, Leipzig, Wien, Zürich: Dudenverlag, 2001.

Elias, Norbert. *Studien über die Deutschen. Machtkämpfe und Habitusentwicklung im 19. und 20. Jahrhundert.* Frankfurt: Suhrkamp, 1989.

Flippo, Hyde. *The German Way: Aspects of Behavior, Attitudes, and Customs in the German-Speaking World.* Reprint with revisions. Lincolnwood, IL: Passport Books, 1997. (1st print: 1997)

Hendlmeier, Wolfgang. "Die deutsche Schreibschrift von Sütterlin bis zur Gegenwart." *Die deutsche Schrift* Nr. 69 (Herbst 1983): 20–29.

Heringer, Hans-Jürgen. *Tendenzen der deutschen Gegenwartssprache.* Tübingen: Niemeyer, 1994.

Hermersdorf, Martin. "Die Entwicklung der deutschen Schreibschrift." *Die deutsche Schrift* Nr. 19 (Oktober 1960): 1–20.

Heyll, Uwe. *"Wasser, Fasten, Luft und Licht." Die Geschichte der Naturheilkunde in Deutschland.* Frankfurt am Main: Campus, 2006.

Koch, Hans Jürgen, ed. *Wallfahrtsstätten der Nation. Zwischen Brandenburg und Bayern.* Frankfurt: S. Fischer, 1986.

Kuntz-Brunner, Ruth. *Sexualität BRD, DDR im Vergleich.* Braunschweig: Holtzmeyer, 1991.

Link, Jürgen, and Wulf Wülfing. *Nationale Mythen und Symbole in der zweiten Hälfte des 19. Jahrhunderts. Strukturen und Funktionen von Konzepten nationaler Identität.* Stuttgart: Klett-Cotta, 1995.

Lord, Richard. *Culture Shock: Germany.* Portland: Graphic Arts Center, 2004.

Lyons, Albert S., and R. Joseph Petrucelli II. *Medicine. An Illustrated History.* New York: Abrams, 1987.

Nuss, Bernard. *Das Faust-Syndrom. Ein Versuch über die Mentalität der Deutschen.* Bonn: Bouvier, 1992.

Payer, Lynn. *Medicine & Culture: Varieties of Treatment in the United States, England,*

West Germany, and France. New York: H. Holt, 1988.

Pross, Helge. *Was ist heute deutsch? Wertorientierung in der Bundesrepublik.* Reinbek: Rowohlt, 1982.

Richter, Simon. "Food and drink: Hegelian encounters with the culinary other." *Contemporary German Cultural Studies.* Ed. Alison Phipps. Oxford: Oxford University Press, 2002, 179–195.

Sillge, Ursula. *Un-Sichtbare Frauen. Lesben und ihre Emanzipation in der DDR.* Berlin: LinksDruck, 1991.

Steakley, James D. *The Homosexual Emancipation Movement in Germany.* New York: Arno Press, 1975.

Stern, Susan. *These Strange German Ways.* Bonn: Atlantic-Brücke, 1994.

Stevenson, Patrick, ed. *The German Language and the Real World. Sociolinguistic, Cultural and Pragmatic Perspectives on Contemporary German*, rev. ed. Oxford: Clarendon Press, 1997.

———. *Language and German Disunity: A Sociolinguistic History of East and West in Germany, 1945–2000.* Oxford: Oxford University Press, 2003.

Szarota, Tomasz. *Niemiecki Michel. Der deutsche Michel. Die Geschichte eines nationalen Symbols und Autostereotyps.* Aus dem Polnischen von Kordula Zentgraf-Zubrzycka. Vom Autor für die deutsche Ausgabe überarbeitete Fassung. Osnabrück: fibre, 1998.

Thomas, Carmen. *Ein ganz besonderer Saft— Urin.* Köln: Verlagsgesellschaft, 1993.

Wolfrum, Edgar. *Geschichtspolitik in der Bundesrepublik Deutschland. Der Weg zur bundesrepublikanischen Erinnerung, 1948–1990.* Darmstadt: Wissenschaftliche Buchgesellschaft, 1999.

3

Official Organizational Structures

The Social Net

Germany has been known since the end of the nineteenth century for its exceptional social security network. Otto von Bismarck realized early on that the best way for a politician (including a conservative one) to prevent unrest was to dispel any sense of dissatisfaction and despair among the citizens by providing the essential supports of life. He therefore introduced legislation in the 1880s establishing compulsory insurance for workers' health, employment-related accidents, and old age. This was extended in 1911 to include widows' and orphans' pensions. After World War II, the necessity to guarantee basic security became even more of a political priority. Reforms of the 1950s linked pension benefits to income growth. Fine-tuning followed in the 1970s and again after unification in the 1990s. The social security system developed in the Federal Republic was transferred almost unaltered to the new federal states (Länder) in 1990 (see 1: From Two to One).

GDR

In addition to the right to work, guaranteed in the constitution of the GDR, each citizen had the right to health and safety provisions at the workplace. Comprehensive health care for all was the basis of the social system. As an informational book for foreigners stated: "All citizens are guaranteed equal access to health care irrespective of social background, social situation and place of residence. All medical care is free of charge. Each citizen is free to consult a doctor of his or her own choosing" (Redaktion DDR im Überblick 1986, 225).

The social insurance scheme for workers and salaried employees was run by the Confederation of Free German Trade Unions (Freie Deutsche Gewerkschaftsbund, FDGB) and covered about 90 percent of the population. The remaining 10 percent, which included the agricultural and crafts cooperatives besides self-employed workers, was covered by a state-run organization. The contribution by those insured was about 10 percent of gross income. Voluntary supplementary insurance was also available.

The coverage encompassed everything from preventive treatment to surgery and from medication to hearing aids and other supports. Major benefits were as follows:

- Sickness benefits during illness and recovery
- Maternity allowance before and after delivery
- Financial assistance to single parents or parents with more than two children for leave from work to care for sick children
- Paid leave for women after the birth of a child for up to eighteen months
- Pensions for retirees and the disabled
- Payments for a transition period in case of a necessary job change to prevent an occupational disease
- Assistance to the blind
- A death grant

The overriding principle was, as the information book stated, "that the services provided should promote improvement in the health of the people, in the prevention of illness and in lowering the incidence of death in cases where it is avoidable" (ibid., 228).

Federal Republic of Germany

The *Sozialversicherung* (social insurance) system of the FRG that was transferred to all of Germany after unification is compulsory for all and has five subcategories: *Krankenversicherung* (health insurance), *Rentenversicherung* (pension insurance), *Pflegeversicherung* (nursing care insurance), *Arbeitslosenversicherung* (unemployment insurance), and *Unfallversicherung* (accident insurance). Monthly payments by employees and employers are the basis for this safety net. The amount paid depends on the level of income.

Health insurance provides financial protection in times of sickness and during maternity leave. The insurance also covers the spouse and children of the insured person, if these people have little or no personal income. Individuals can choose between various *Krankenkassen* (health insurers): *Allgemeine Ortskrankenkasse* (general compulsory medical insurance), *Ersatzkassen* (state health insurance), *Betriebskrankenkassen* (company health insurance), and *Innungskrankenkassen* (guild or union health insurance). The health insurers differ only slightly in the level of contributions collected and the services and coverage offered. The basic services covered are laid down by law. All employees below a certain income level are obliged under law to be publicly insured by their employers. In this way, at least 90 percent of the population is covered by compulsory nonprofit public health insurance. Individuals with higher incomes can choose between public and private health insurers (Beck 2003, 110).

Once upon a time, the German health insurance system, with its array of services, appeared to outsiders as a model. Doctors and dentists were relatively independent, and patients were able to choose freely among general practitioners and specialists. Yet, something went awry—expenses skyrocketed, and abuses of the system by both medical professionals and patients led to a review of the system.

The result was a succession of partial reforms that are still in progress. As in other industrial nations, cost containment has high priority. In 2002, the contribution rate (employer and employee contribute equally) was on average 14 percent of gross earnings (Lantermann 2003, 148). In general, patients are not aware of the exact charges for health services, but more and more frequently they are being required to make copayments, which may serve to curb some abuses. Though each health insurance scheme, or *Krankenkasse*, has different rules and regulations, one change common to all is that as of 2005 patients pay a flat fee per quarter of 10 euros to a primary physician, which authorizes that doctor to treat the patient and make referrals where necessary. Prescription costs are paid on a sliding scale based on income—some pay nothing, others the full amount. Only health specialists seem to understand the relationship between the insurance schemes, which act as a single purchaser of services, and the doctors and dentists, who are independent but at the same time must form regional associations for bargaining purposes. Some patients find the system both confusing and expensive, particularly with the recent changes. They feel that the new regulations are good for the insurance companies, but that the companies do not seem to have the patients' best interest foremost in their planning and reorganization.

For years, Germans recovering from various ailments would spend some time at a spa or sanatorium for a *Kur* (cure). They would drink the mineral waters, follow exercise regimes, take mud treatments, lie wrapped up in blankets in the sun at high altitudes (particularly if suffering from tuberculosis), and be entertained at the casinos and concert halls, which were often found in *Kurorte*—that is, towns designated as suitable for cures because of their elevation or healthy country air, even if they did not have mineral springs to earn them the distinction of being a spa (*Bad*). The setting for Thomas Mann's novel *Der Zauberberg* (The Magic Mountain, 1924) is a sanatorium in the Alps for tuberculosis patients, and the book offers readers insights into the rituals and culture of a stay in such a rarefied atmosphere. Nowadays, members of the Golf Generation, and their more hip parents, are likely to spend some of their vacation time at a "Wellness Hotel"—another example of an English-language term being used to update and modernize a concept that is traditionally German but had gained negative, or at least outmoded, connotations (see 2: Language, Script, and Gestures).

Compulsory health insurance covered such stays at spas until quite recently—and still does in special cases—but there has been a shift in cultural attitudes surrounding cures. In the nineteenth century, it was the wealthy, frequently women, who would spend the most time at the Kurorte, often several weeks at a time. The concept of *Kurschatten* (literally, cure shadow), healthy individuals who spend time at *Kurorte* to continue a love affair (usually illicit), is something generally acknowledged as part of the tradition. Wilhelm Busch immortalized this concept in 1872 in his illustrated tale of a young woman, Helene, who marries for money after realizing that the aunt and uncle who brought her up cannot keep her in the style to which she would like to become accustomed. Sadly, money and love do not go hand in hand, and Helene continues to hanker after her cousin Franz, who, though he has become a man of the cloth, still has a soft spot for pretty kitchen maids and women in general. Helene hopes for a child, but when she fails to become pregnant, she goes to a spa to improve her health. Franz also visits the spa, and soon after returning home, Helene apparently reaps the benefits of the cure. She gives birth to twins who bear a striking resemblance to their mother's cousin. As this is a cautionary tale, the ending is not a happy one. Helene's wealthy but dull husband chokes to death on a fishbone, and the widow seeks solace and pastoral care from her cousin. He, however, continues to have a soft spot for kitchen maids, is caught by the butler, who strikes him with a wine bottle, and dies. Helene finds comfort in alcohol and, in a drunken stupor, causes her house to burn and her own death.

What goes on at Wellness Hotels may or may not be as exciting. Whereas medicinal benefits were stressed at Kurorte, the benefits of a stay at Wellness Hotels are advertised in a more holistic manner. The Federation of Climatic Health Resorts of Germany (Verband der Heilklimatischen Kurorte Deutschlands) divides the types of resorts into various categories. "Health and Cure" is just one category, with subheadings that include various ailments and diseases. The "Wellness and Relaxation" category includes "Nutrition and Diet," "Fitness and Vitality," and "Beauty." The treatments are clearly as much for the outer self as the inner one. The food is designed to taste very good, unlike the water from the springs at spas. The locations of the hotels vary from remote country areas to coastal sites, and many of them are in renovated castles and grand houses. This is particularly true in the new federal provinces.

Some Wellness Hotels attempt to attract wealthy corporate clients as it is becoming difficult to defend payments from health insurance agencies.

The goal of pension insurance, the most important part of the social system, is to help ensure a secure old age for German citizens. Employers, apprentices, and certain groups of self-employed people are required to have public pension insurance. The pension insurers not only provide payment of pensions to the insured or their surviving dependents (spouse and children) but also incorporate medical and occupational rehabilitation measures. Certain conditions have to be fulfilled before pensions can be drawn: The insured individual must reach a minimum age, must have paid contributions for a certain amount of time, and must apply for the pension. Pensions are generally paid at the age of sixty-five, but it is also possible to receive an early pension or to work longer and receive the pension at a later age (Beck 2003, 112). The standard pension for a worker with forty-five years of contributions equals 70 percent of the net average income. Unemployment benefits range around the 55 percent mark of previous net income. In order to secure a comfortable standard of living in retirement, however, even according to the official handbook for foreigners, one must arrange for an additional private pension to supplement the state pension. In the state system, the current working population has to generate the income required to finance the pensions. The official manual for foreigners calls this mutual help "Solidaritätsprinzip" (principle of solidarity) (ibid., 13). Consumer advice agencies provide information on ways to fund private and company pension schemes.

Unemployment insurance provides financial help to the unemployed and assistance in acquiring new employment. Anyone who has paid unemployment contributions for a certain period of time and who then becomes unemployed is eligible for unemployment benefits. The Bundesanstalt für Arbeit (German Federal Employment Office) has a number of employment promotion schemes for employers and employees alike and endeavors to keep as many job-seekers as possible working (ibid., 114). However, the economic situation has worsened since the turn of the millennium, and discussion about the social net has increased.

In the early decades after World War II, the unemployment rate (over 10 percent in 1950) was eventually absorbed by the German economy, and even with 11 million refugees, the unemployment rate was less than 1 percent by 1962. But those days are long gone. Since unification, the unemployment rate has shot up, reaching even higher numbers than in the 1980s. Unemployment is around 10 percent in the west, with wide differences among regions. In the wealthiest federal states of Bavaria and Baden-Württemberg, it is only about 8 percent, but in the industrial area around the Ruhr, it is about 20 percent. In general, it is the densely populated areas, such as the Ruhr and Berlin, along with the eastern part of Germany, that have the highest number of people out of work. Simple statistics cannot give the real picture, however. A short-term unemployed citizen of the Golf Generation from the western part of Germany, Harald Zils, remarked in 2003 in a personal conversation:

At first you are optimistic and each new application seems like a lottery ticket, but then you realize what the chances of winning are. You hear that hundreds, sometimes even thousands, have applied for the same job. On top of that, you learn that the firms have not created new jobs but are just looking to replace people on leave—for a lower salary, of course. I know many people whose new jobs—when they actually found one—are way below the standard of their old ones and do not match their qualifications. Many were obliged to accept temporary jobs, especially when they were no longer even invited for an interview, either because of their age or the employer's fear of job protection. The fact that no job was secure any longer also led people to consume less and save more, neither of which is good for the economy. My generation is not having children at the same rate as earlier ones and that's because no one knows what tomorrow will bring.

In the eastern states of the former FRG, the causes of the persistent unemployment are—as is often stated—structural, and they are related to the economic transformation since unification. In 2004, 57 percent of the citizens of the former GDR worried about losing their jobs (Stern-Team et al. 2004, 50) and therefore had a generally bleak outlook on the region in which they lived.

Until the end of 2004, unemployed citizens first received *Arbeitslosengeld* (earnings-related benefits), at most 67 percent of the last net salary. After being unemployed for a longer period, they received *Arbeitslosenhilfe* (unemployment benefit), at most 57 percent. Beginning in 2005, the benefits were reduced drastically and depend on the financial situation of the individual, that is, if he or she has savings, owns a house, and the like. About a quarter of the unemployed will now receive no benefits at all. The rationale is that everyone affected will try harder to find work. Critics believe that those who tried to prepare for their old age by having a life insurance policy or a savings account will be the ones who get punished, while those who have spent all their earnings will be rewarded (Stern 29 [2003], 128–133).

Another West German citizen, Angelika Weiß, a baby boomer and single mother, has a long-term perspective on the issue. She wrote in August 2005 about her experiences as follows:

Many people have been required to make substantial contributions to unemployment insurance for years (for pensions and health insurance too) and now when they are out of work, after working without interruption for 20 or 30 years, they are only insured under the latest reforms and eligible for unemployment payments for one to one and a half years depending on age. After this time, everyone gets a so-called *Sozialhilfesatz* (social benefit) that is the same for everyone though the unemployment payments varied according to earlier earnings, which was fair. What is particularly bad and counterproductive is that once you move to the stage of the second type of unemployment pay (also known as Hartzy4) your financial situation must be made completely transparent. You are not allowed to have any savings, which is especially stupid because savings are usually for one's old age and politicians are constantly telling people they need them since pensions certainly won't be sufficient in the future. Recently there was a case in which a Hartzy4 payee had to go to court to be allowed to keep his car. With these new regulations there are people who at the age of 55, after working for 30 or 40 years, suddenly have nothing, too little money to live on, no

old age pension and no hope for any kind of work. Experience no longer seems valued— just youth.

Accident insurance reduces the negative financial consequences of accidents in the workplace or occupational diseases. It offers preventive advice on reducing potential dangers in the workplace as well as rehabilitation services (Beck 2003, 114). The nursing care insurance provisions grant citizens the right to financial aid for nursing care as inpatients or outpatients.

As outlined in the governmental manual for foreigners, German laws on social security state that the services provided are only available within the country. Nevertheless, it is possible to receive some social security benefits in other countries through international and bilateral social security agreements. Especially within the European Union, there is a legal foundation whereby social benefits can be paid to individuals residing in member countries (ibid., 115–116).

In spite of all the attempts to create a perfect social net, problems exist. Though Europe appears to be a wealthy continent, 14.3 percent of European households live below the poverty line. And although Germany is considered one of the wealthiest countries, there are still 1.3 million individuals without a permanent home. Some 360,000 people live either in parks, under bridges, or on the streets. Though unemployment, debt, and alcohol are often part of the problem, there are many complex causes for the situation. Charitable organizations and public initiatives attempt to deal with the issues, but the sight of people living on the streets and dependent on handouts seems to be becoming more familiar in Germany.

Another problem is the aging of the population, which is causing a considerable strain on the social system. While at the end of the eighteenth century, average life expectancy was between thirty-five and forty, 200 years later it has climbed to seventy-four for men and eighty-one for women. Yet, at the same time, seniors continue more than ever to carry their share of the burden. Each community needs volunteers to complement and support the organs of state. This work is being done more and more by retired people, who make up a sixth of the voluntary workforce.

The Legal System

Germany's constitution (*Verfassung*) is called the *Grundgesetz* (Basic Law), the term used for the provisional constitutional framework adopted in 1949 by the parliaments of the states of West Germany. Originally, it was intended to be changed whenever West and East Germany became united again and could freely determine a new constitution. But in 1990, no constitutional assembly was elected to formulate a joint constitution. The Basic Law underwent only minor revisions to accommodate the merger of the two Germanys, and even the name "Grundgesetz" was kept.

The Basic Law outlines the civil rights of Germany's citizens and the organizational framework of the state. Its rules are binding for all legislative and court decisions. Its basic principles—the establishment of a democratic and federal state based on a social commitment and the rule of law—cannot be changed. Modifications of other articles require a two-thirds majority in the Bundestag and Bundesrat (Lower and Upper House of the German Parliament).

Germany's supreme court is the Bundesverfassungsgericht, the guardian of the constitution, which also serves as the highest appeal court. Although highly respected, it is seen by its critics as a "surrogate legislator" and used by political parties as a means to block legislation by questioning the constitutionality of laws and treaties. In accordance with the German legal system, which distinguishes between *Zivilrecht* (civil law) and *Öffentliches Recht* (public law), the latter entailing *Staatsrecht* (constitutional law), *Strafrecht* (criminal law), *Strafprozessrecht* (criminal procedural law), and *Verwaltungsrecht* (administrative law), there are other federal courts that serve as the supreme courts for their specific areas, including the Bundesgerichtshof (federal law court) for all *ordentliche Gerichte* (criminal and civil courts) and four administrative supreme courts: the Bundesarbeitsgericht for the *Arbeitsgerichte* (courts for industrial law), the Bundesverwaltungsgericht for the *allgemeine Verwaltungsgerichte* (courts for administrative law), the Bundessozialgericht for the *Sozialgerichte* (courts for welfare law), and the Bundesfinanzgericht for the *Finanzgerichte* (courts for financial law). Subordinate to these supreme courts on the federal level are the courts on the state level—for example, *Oberlandgericht* (high court) and *Landgericht* (provincial court)—and on the regional level—the *Amtsgericht* (local or district court). It is not surprising that Germany has an unusually high number of judges and lawyers, who are kept busy by an increasing tendency of all parties to resort to litigation.

In addition to this very intricate legal network, there is the European layer, since German courts are integrated into the European Court of Justice and the European Court of Human Rights. A European law can override a national law. For example, one lawsuit involved a female German soldier who wanted to join a combat troop. Under German law, women were not allowed combat status. The woman sued before the European court, and because European law did not have this restriction, the woman won, and Germany had to change its laws accordingly and permit women to join the combat troops.

More important for most foreigners than these legal aspects is the German bureaucracy (known as *Behördendschungel*, administrative jungle), which has raised many a blood pressure and caused much frustration. Although visiting Germany as a tourist is unproblematic, establishing residence for even a limited time requires registration with a number of government agencies. As Richard Lord joked in his book for travelers and businessmen, "Like all who went before you, you will soon learn that in Germany there are three things that are inevitable—death, taxes and *Behörde*" (Lord 2004, 91). At the Auslandsbehörde (Immigration Office), which is part of the Ordnungsamt (Department of Order), one applies for an *Aufenthaltserlaubnis* (residence permit). This will be issued after a background check is completed and receipt from the Arbeitsamt (Employment Office) of a tentative *Arbeitserlaubnis* (work permit) based on a letter by a future employer. The Employment Office then grants the actual work permit. The next step is to register at the *Einwohnermeldeamt* (residents' registration office) of one's place of residence, a form of registration required of all residents, German or foreigner. In case of a move from one apartment to another, the process has to be repeated with notification of the old as well as the new address. One of the main problems in this process—and this applies to many aspects of German life—is the small window of time that officials make available for the process. Although shopping hours are being extended (see 10: From "Tante Emma Laden" to Shopping Mall), *Sprechstunden* (hours open to the public) of *Behörden* are extremely limited. Usually, offices are open to the public only three days a week and only in the morning hours between 7 or 8 AM and noon.

The Political System

Federal Republic of Germany

From the Platz der Republik (Square of the Republic) in Berlin in front of the Reichstag in 2005, a comparison of the old and new government buildings makes it apparent that Germany has come a long way since 1945. In the former provisional West German capital, Bonn, the architecture was much less grandiose. Everything about the Bonn parliament was an understatement intended to emphasize the provisional nature of the political situation. Now, in Berlin, "*Dem deutschen Volk*" (To the German People), a dedication from 1916, is again prominently displayed over the entrance to the Reichstag, so that a critical observer might initially ponder the attitudes of the democratic representatives working in that building. One might wonder whether they still believe in a nation based on a racial concept, as the word "Volk" implies. The Reichstag building is actually a good example of a successful blend of old and new and contradicts this first impression. Its cupola, designed by Norman Foster, the British architect in

Kanzleramt (seat of the chancellor). (Photo by D. Scholl)

charge of the renovation, is the most obvious example of this blend, with its union of aesthetics, functionality, and symbolism (see 2: Symbols and Memorials).

The planned Bundesforum (meeting place for citizens and politicians), situated between the Paul-Loebe-Haus (see 9: City Planning and Architecture) and the Kanzleramt (seat of the chancellor), has not yet been built owing to lack of funds. However, sufficient funds were available to construct the oversized Kanzleramt, which is an all-too-obvious symbol for the German form of democracy: a *Kanzlerdemokratie* (chancellor-based democracy) rather than a U.S.-style presidential democracy. The German president has primarily representative functions. For example, he or she represents Germany internationally, signs the laws that have been passed by parliament, and formally appoints the chancellor after his or her election by parliament. Though this position stands above party politics, the president can exert considerable moral authority in spite of the lack of direct political clout. The real power lies with the chancellor, however, who is the head of government. He or she is elected by a majority vote of members of the Bundestag, lays down the guidelines of government policy, and appoints the ministers without the assent of parliament. The ministers are in charge of their departments autonomously but are required to follow guidelines set by the chancellor and discussed by the cabinet.

Many aspects of the German political system illustrate a mistrust on the part of both the Allies and German politicians of the German citizens who had allowed Hitler to come to power. As a result, steps were taken to ensure that the new democracy would be stable and would have many safeguards to maintain a balance of power between the executive and legislative branches of government and between the federal and the state governments. To avoid a parliament made up of numerous parties that could not agree on action (as happened in the Weimar Republic), each party needs to win at least 5 percent of the votes to be represented in parliament. To avoid an ineffective government, a vote of no confidence was introduced to allow parliament

German parliament building in Berlin. (Photo by D. Scholl)

to force a chancellor out of office; yet, if this happens, parliament has to nominate a new candidate at the same time to prevent inaction. In addition, direct involvement of the people in the political process has been excluded. Unlike other European democracies, Germany has no provisions for a referendum on a federal level. Even after unification in 1990, this did not change, but the German answer to this situation is citizens' initiatives; vocal interest groups outside the established political parties focus on specific issues. Through publications and demonstrations they are able to achieve a political impact outside of parliament, good examples of which were the environmental and antinuclear movements that led to the formation of the Green Party (Die Grünen) (see 10: Consumer Culture versus Green Awareness).

The official political structures consist of the legislative branch—the Bundestag (lower house of parliament) and the Bundesrat (upper house of parliament, assembly of state representatives)—and the executive branch, the *Bundesregierung* (federal government). Since 1990, the Bundestag has had more than 600 members who are elected to four-year terms (see 3: From A to Z, *Wahlsystem* and *Wahlrecht*). The Bundesrat consists of 69 members. These are state government officials appointed by the state governments. Depending on the size of the state's population, the *Länder* (states) can send between three and six representatives. One of these will normally be the *Ministerpräsident* of the *Land* (minister president, head of the state government). The Bundestag enacts laws by simple majority after conducting thorough debates in committees, whereas the Bundesrat has only a limited legislative authority. Its primary role is in regard to legislation affecting the individual states. In this case, the Bundesrat even has absolute veto power.

German Democratic Republic

Although some in the former GDR miss what they considered the glory and hope of a socialist state, no one misses the *demokratischen Zentralismus* (democratic centralism), the absolute dominance of one party. The Volkskammer (People's Chamber) was the official parliament with—in theory—control of everything. But the members rarely met. Their main function was to inform their constituents of the government's plans, but the government was the Socialist Party (Sozialistische Einheitspartei Deutschlands, SED), and that is where the power lay. The SED Parteitage (party conventions), which met at five year intervals, elected the Zentralkommittee (ZK, central committee) to be in charge between the party conventions. The ZK chose the Politbüro (politburo being an abbreviation for political bureau/office, a small group of decision makers) as well as its chairman, the Generalsekretär (General Secretary), the most powerful man in the state. The ZK and the politburo worked closely together with the Ministerrat (Council of Ministers), the official executive branch, and its chairman, the Ministerratsvorsitzende. After the death of the GDR's first president in 1960, a small committee, the Staatsrat (State Council), officially headed the government. The chairman of this committee was the actual head of the state and was almost always the general secretary of the SED. On all levels, party and government overlapped.

The Educational System

In 2000, a Program for International Student Assessment (PISA) study sent shock waves throughout Germany. A similar wake-up call had been sounded in 1964 by the book *Die deutsche Bildungskatastrophe* (The Disaster in German Education) by Georg Picht. Germany was once an educational model for other countries. In the nineteenth century, German scholars were among the best in all fields. Even after World War II, German scientists, artists, and literati were sought after, and many emigrated to the United States, where they made noteworthy contributions. Now, however, German schools (with the exception of a few) appeared at the bottom of the list in an international comparison. What had gone wrong?

Although the Basic Law (Grundgesetz, Germany's constitution; see 3: The Legal System) charges the state with the supervision of its school system, the federal nature of Germany causes the task to be divided between the individual states (Länder) and the federal authorities. As is the case so often in German daily life, in education Hitler's shadow can still be felt. To prevent the possibility of one agency exploiting its power and changing education to indoctrination, and to ensure relative uniformity of standards across Germany, the Permanent Conference of the Ministers of Education and Culture (Kultusministerkonferenz, KMK) was created. Participants include the ministers of education and cultural affairs of the individual states who protect their state's interests. Furthermore, the KMK has only an advisory function. Consensus is based on the good will of all and not on hierarchical authority or majority decisions.

Primary and Secondary Education in West Germany

Normally, elementary education begins at the age of six (certain conditions allow par-

Boy with a Schultüte in 1949.

ents to apply for an earlier or later start). The first day in school is a very special day, and in Germany, the uniqueness is underlined by giving each child a *Schultüte* to sweeten the occasion. This is a large, decorated cardboard cone filled with chocolates and other candy. For all Germans, the picture taken on this day is an important one and proudly framed or at least preserved in the family album along with photographs of weddings and other such celebrations.

Four years later, when a child reaches the age of ten, a crucial time has arrived. In the first decades of the FRG, an exam decided the future of the child. The wishes of the parents also played a role in determin-

ing the course of the child's future, but in the case of a negative outcome on the exam, the determination could be made against their wishes. Three choices awaited schoolchildren: primary school (*Hauptschule*), secondary school (*Realschule*), and high school (*Gymnasium*). In the late 1960s, a fourth choice was added that served as a combination of these three types of schools—the comprehensive school (*Gesamtschule*)—to respond to the criticism of social inequality. (See Table 3.1 for an overview of how the different schools are organized and what qualifications can be earned from each type.) Basically, the school types reflected three social groups: (1) factory workers and craftsmen; (2) lower state officials, middle management, and engineers; and (3) higher state officials, future professionals (doctors, lawyers), and academicians. The argument against the existing system was that it encouraged a social status quo. Parents tended to send their children to the same type of school they had attended. In addition, the early decision for a school type did not take into account different developmental stages. Therefore, the Gesamtschule was intended to allow pupils to switch more easily from one type of school to another after the somewhat arbitrarily selected age of ten.

Schooling is mandatory in most states until the age of fifteen. Normally, the pupils in the Haupt- and Realschule graduate after ten years of schooling with a diploma (*Hauptschulabschluss* or *Mittlere Reife*). They then typically look for a job or an apprenticeship. If they become an apprentice (*Lehrling* or *Azubi*, from the German word *Auszubildender*, literally, one who needs to be trained), they enter a dual system of training for two more years, receiving

Basic (Simplified) Overview of Germany's Educational System listing the qualifications earned on completion of a step in the system (based on Lantermann 2003, 319)

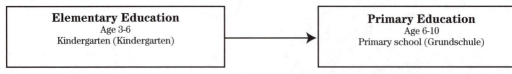

Elementary Education	Primary Education
Age 3-6	Age 6-10
Kindergarten (Kindergarten)	Primary school (Grundschule)

From age 10 to 12, students are assessed to determine which track will be most suitable for them. These two years are known as the "Orientierungsstufe", literally the "orientation step".

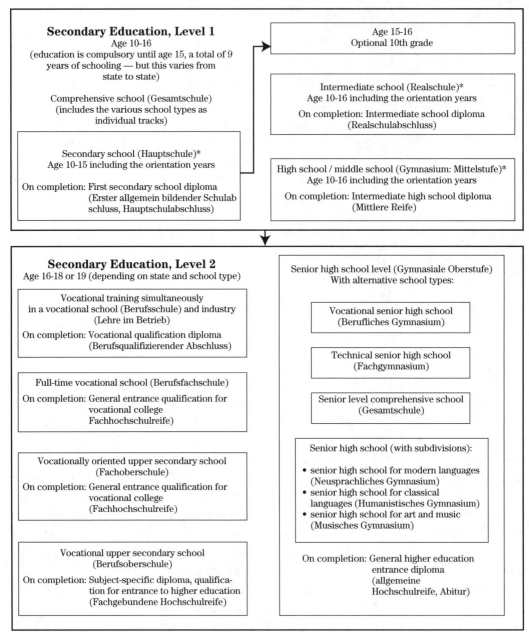

Secondary Education, Level 1
Age 10-16
(education is compulsory until age 15, a total of 9 years of schooling — but this varies from state to state)

Comprehensive school (Gesamtschule)
(includes the various school types as individual tracks)

Secondary school (Hauptschule)*
Age 10-15 including the orientation years

On completion: First secondary school diploma (Erster allgemein bildender Schulabschluss, Hauptschulabschluss)

Age 15-16
Optional 10th grade

Intermediate school (Realschule)*
Age 10-16 including the orientation years

On completion: Intermediate school diploma (Realschulabschluss)

High school / middle school (Gymnasium: Mittelstufe)*
Age 10-16 including the orientation years

On completion: Intermediate high school diploma (Mittlere Reife)

Secondary Education, Level 2
Age 16-18 or 19 (depending on state and school type)

Vocational training simultaneously in a vocational school (Berufsschule) and industry (Lehre im Betrieb)
On completion: Vocational qualification diploma (Berufsqualifizierender Abschluss)

Full-time vocational school (Berufsfachschule)
On completion: General entrance qualification for vocational college Fachhochschulreife)

Vocationally oriented upper secondary school (Fachoberschule)
On completion: General entrance qualification for vocational college (Fachhochschulreife)

Vocational upper secondary school (Berufsoberschule)
On completion: Subject-specific diploma, qualification for entrance to higher education (Fachgebundene Hochschulreife)

Senior high school level (Gymnasiale Oberstufe)
With alternative school types:

Vocational senior high school (Berufliches Gymnasium)

Technical senior high school (Fachgymnasium)

Senior level comprehensive school (Gesamtschule)

Senior high school (with subdivisions):

- senior high school for modern languages (Neusprachliches Gymnasium)
- senior high school for classical languages (Humanistisches Gymnasium)
- senior high school for art and music (Musisches Gymnasium)

On completion: General higher education entrance diploma (allgemeine Hochschulreife, Abitur)

*Possible as both an independent school or as part of a comprehensive school.

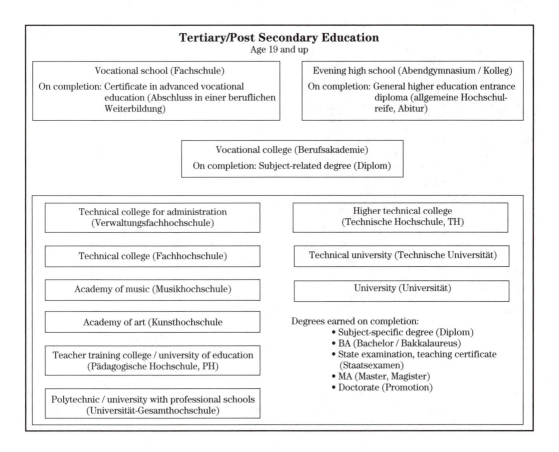

Tertiary/Post Secondary Education
Age 19 and up

Vocational school (Fachschule) On completion: Certificate in advanced vocational education (Abschluss in einer beruflichen Weiterbildung)	Evening high school (Abendgymnasium / Kolleg) On completion: General higher education entrance diploma (allgemeine Hochschulreife, Abitur)

Vocational college (Berufsakademie)
On completion: Subject-related degree (Diplom)

Technical college for administration (Verwaltungsfachhochschule)	Higher technical college (Technische Hochschule, TH)
Technical college (Fachhochschule)	Technical university (Technische Universität)
Academy of music (Musikhochschule)	University (Universität)
Academy of art (Kunsthochschule	Degrees earned on completion: • Subject-specific degree (Diplom) • BA (Bachelor / Bakkalaureus) • State examination, teaching certificate (Staatsexamen) • MA (Master, Magister) • Doctorate (Promotion)
Teacher training college / university of education (Pädagogische Hochschule, PH)	
Polytechnic / university with professional schools (Universität-Gesamthochschule)	

workplace training under a master craftsman (*Meister/Meisterin*), and go to a vocational school (*Berufsschule*) twice a week. After passing the *Gesellenprüfung* (apprenticeship exam), some continue the century-old tradition of *auf die Walz gehen* (traveling and working under master craftsmen in different locations—an activity retained in the English term "journeyman"; the phrase "auf die Walz gehen" means literally "to go on a journey," whereby the German word "Walz" is obsolete today and only retained in this particular phrase and context). Many still wear the old-fashioned black corduroy outfit that identifies them as journeymen during

this stage of their career. A young *Dachdecker* (roofer) and a *Zimmermann* (carpenter) questioned in 2004 about the tradition enthusiastically endorsed it, stressing the invaluable experience they gained by working for two years and one day (as the regulations state) in different regions of Germany with various masters. As a consequence, Germany is a society of highly qualified people. As Richard Lord remarked in his advice manual, "Here in Germany you can be reasonably sure that craftspeople will know their jobs pretty damn well" (Lord 2004, 41).

Coming from the Realschule, students can also enter a technical college (*Berufs-*

Journeymen in Germany in 2004.

fachschule) or an advanced technical college (*Fachoberschule*). Students entering the Gymnasium can choose from the outset between a regular Gymnasium or a *Humanistische* Gymnasium where the focus is on the classical languages, Latin and Greek (The German word for "humanist" is equated with "classical," that is the knowledge of classical Greek and Roman material). In the regular Gymnasium, students specialize during their last three years (*gymnasiale Oberstufe*) in one of several career areas: mathematics and science (*mathematisch naturwissenschaftlich*), humanities, art and music (*musisch*), or modern languages (*neusprachlich*). This means that they will take more courses in their specific areas of interest and discontinue other subjects. For instance, they may drop a foreign language and add more mathematics and physics courses, or do

the opposite. The Gymnasium ends with the *Abitur* (in Austria, *Matur* or *Matura*), which is a comprehensive standardized oral and written exam. For many years, it was regarded also as the entrance exam to a university.

Until 1967, the school year began at Easter. But after two transitional years, the Federal Republic finally adopted the international model and shifted to the fall for the beginning of the academic year. In the 1950s, schools were plagued by a lack of space. The schools improvised to deal with the problem, instituting two shifts of classes, with different schools often sharing the same buildings. One would occupy the building during the morning hours, and the other in the afternoon. Fortunately, the instructional system allowed for such sharing of buildings because most German schools are half-day operations: Lessons are given in the morning, and the afternoon is reserved for extracurricular activities. In the early postwar years, the extracurricular activities could be eliminated. The 1960s and 1970s saw a great deal of school construction and expansion, and the days of the two-shift classrooms were over.

Looking at the daily schedule could give one the impression that schooling in German-speaking countries is less strenuous than elsewhere. In most places, formal instruction is over by one o'clock. But the afternoons are not entirely free for hobbies or even part-time jobs for older schoolchildren. Homework is required, and it strongly influences one's grades. Students are given several tests a year in each subject, and depending on the average grade on the tests—both oral and written—and the grade from homework, they are either moved up to the next class or made to repeat a class, something that bears the quaint euphemistic description *sitzenbleiben* (literally "remain seated"). Though such an assessment is not welcome, the system does ensure that schoolchildren and their parents are informed as to their progress. Tests throughout the year also provide warning signals to all. A downside of the German system is that parents who work full-time have to make arrangements for younger children to be supervised in the afternoons and are not always around to help out with homework. (Some might, of course, see this as an upside.)

At the university level, this system is almost completely reversed. Students are regarded as adults who have to learn to budget their own time and be aware of their academic progress—or lack thereof. Therefore, the emphasis is then placed on independent research (and not classwork) as well as on final comprehensive exams and extensive research papers.

Postsecondary Education in West Germany

Similar to the secondary level, the tertiary level of education offers a variety of institutions: the university (humanities, sciences, medicine, law), the technical university (engineering), the pedagogical university or university of education (teacher training), music and art academies, and other variations, including the comprehensive university (*Gesamthochschule*), which combines several of the above-mentioned institutions. Students graduate with various degrees, ranging from *Diplom* to *Magister* (MA), and up to the doctorate. There is also a state certification program for teachers (*Staatsexamen*). Doctors (Ph.D. or MD) who want to teach at the university level

have to continue their education to complete a second thesis and pass a second exam in order to become *Dr. habil.* (abbreviated from *habilitatus*, that is, doctor with postdoctoral university teaching qualifications). A student who reaches this point then becomes a *Privatdozent* (lecturer) and can be appointed to a professorship.

In the new millennium, a university reform has begun and many universities have introduced a highly structured bachelor's degree program patterned after the U.S. system.

Alternate and Adult Education in West Germany

Because educational decisions have to be made so early in life (through the choice of school attended), the system needs to accommodate those who want to change a career path at a later stage. Thus, a second entry path to higher education (*zweiter Bildungsweg*) is possible—evening study courses leading to university entry qualifications. Though such classes can be demanding, and frequently the students have previously worked all day, people who opt to take this alternate route are often the most motivated students.

In addition to the career-oriented institutions that adults can attend is the rapidly expanding sector of continuing and adult education, with personal enrichment as the major goal, which is funded through federal, state, and private initiatives. The main providers are the *Volkshochschulen* (VHS, literally, people's universities), which offer a wide range of daytime and evening courses, from foreign languages to history and philosophy and art and vocational subjects. Because these are regarded as local centers of learning and culture, the courses are open to everyone. In addition, large companies such as Siemens or Telekom offer their employees a range of courses, many of which take the form of in-house training.

Education in East Germany

In the former German Democratic Republic, where individuals were seen as *zoa politica* (innate political beings) in the Greek sense, educational institutions played a very important role. They not only had to prepare students for a profession but also had to instill in them a sense of responsibility toward society. As a result, the central government, rather than individual local governments, was in charge. All private schools were abolished.

The Gesetz zur Demokratisierung der deutschen Schulen (Law for Democratization of German Schools) of 1946 introduced eight years of compulsory school attendance in the GDR. Curricula were identical across the Sowjetische Besatzungszone (Soviet Occupation Zone, SBZ). After graduation, when the students were fourteen years old, education was continued in a professional school (*Berufsschule*) to complete their training as skilled workers with a certificate of proficiency. Most then entered the working world, but about 20 percent went on to high school and studied for another four years to prepare themselves to attend a university after the *Abitur* (graduation). In 1965, the number of years of compulsory education was raised to ten. This was combined with an *Unterrichtstag in der Produktion*, a day in which students got an impression of what life was like in important jobs in industry and agriculture. In the following years, the linkage between professional life and schooling became even tighter. Students could study for and earn the Abitur and also become certified as skilled workers.

Education in a United Germany

Unification changed all of that. The West German system was adopted in the east with only minor modifications. The main difference in the new states was that the Abitur examinations could as before be taken after twelve instead of thirteen years, as in the West. Due to the introduction of the U.S.-type bachelor's degree at the university level, the schools in the former West Germany are also reducing their curriculum from thirteen to twelve years of schooling. In conjunction with this change, the Abitur is not now the only key to a university education. The tendency to require specialized entrance exams in individual subjects is increasing. The result of these exams is factored into the Abitur grade-point average to become the basis for acceptance or rejection.

There probably was no period in postwar Germany in which there was not some sort of discussion about the school systems, the slight differences in the different states, and some kind of reform. A slogan circulated: The shortest time unit is not a second but the time span between one school reform and the next. This has not changed in the new millennium. The main difference is that now Germany is no longer trying to find its own solutions but seems bent on imitating the United States without taking into consideration the social, cultural, and economic basis that makes the U.S. system successful—not the least of which is the attitude toward money and entrepreneurship in general, and sponsorship and patronage in particular. Highlights in these murky educational waters are a few private initiatives—for example, the Bucerius law school, the popular Waldorf schools, and Montessori-based kindergartens and high schools. Here, pedagogy still seems to be the driving force behind the curriculum.

Education financing is changing, too. Education was—more or less—free in the past for the individual student, as the taxpayer shouldered the bills. In primary and secondary education, even many of the textbooks used to be free. On the university level, too, the fees were minimal. The expenses the individual student had to pay for were primarily room and board, and those who could not afford these could get state support, consisting of loans and stipends, known as *BAföG* for short, which stands for Bundesausbildungsförderungsgesetz—the name of a law regarding grants for higher education.

The German Army

The author Kurt Tucholsky (1890–1935), a critic of the military, wrote in 1927 in his essay "Über wirkungsvollen Pazifismus" (on effective pacifism):

> More and more the real reasons for war become obvious: the economy and the dismal mental state of the unenlightened and manipulated masses. What is missing completely almost everywhere, however, is pacifist propaganda in everyday life, in the streets, in the four-room apartments, in public spaces— pacifism as a foregone conclusion. Four or five times a year we [pacifists] get together at conferences, often in meetings. And then everyone goes home and real life takes over

again; life—in this case that means the official state-sanctioned attitude that praises the war; the cinema that glorifies war; the newspapers that don't dare to show the real face of war; the church that urges believers to go to war (the Protestant church more so than the more perceptive Catholic church); the schools that distort the war into a bombastic spectacle; the university that celebrates war—everywhere war. (Tucholsky 1960, 908)

On the one hand, this text does not seem to be the most appropriate one to use for a discussion during a lesson on how to assemble a rifle in basic training in the Bundeswehr (literally, federal defense), the German armed forces. On the other hand, discussions about social instead of military questions were typical in the early years after the establishment of the new German army in 1956, though Tucholsky himself had committed suicide even before the war.

Initially, after 1945, no one wanted to think about a new German army. There was a general desire to keep Germany demilitarized forever (see the directive for the occupation of Germany, the memo JCS-1067, that was the basis for the Potsdam Conference) (Craig 1982, 237). When the Allied Control Council began its work in Germany in July 1945, the directives stated that Germans were prohibited from wearing uniforms, badges of rank, or military decorations. They were not allowed to own weapons, ammunition, or explosives. Military schools, military exhibitions, and military ceremonies were outlawed. Paramilitary sports clubs and similar organizations, as well as military research, were banned. Monuments, posters, street signs, and memorial plaques designed to inspire the German military tradition and glorify military events were to be destroyed. But as the Cold War began, followed by the Korean War, many politicians—Allies as well as Germans—reconsidered their beliefs. The Treaties of Paris in 1954 accepted Germany as a member of the North Atlantic Treaty Organization (NATO) and permitted the creation of an army of half a million men. In 1955, a decade after the end of World War II, the Bundeswehr, with the air force (Luftwaffe), navy (Marine), and army (Heer), was created as a conscription army in spite of much criticism on the part of many German citizens. In January 1956, the first soldiers of the new army began their work. About half a year later, 10,000 men from the Federal Border Guard (Bundesgrenzschutz) joined the army, and the first draftees arrived in April 1957. Germany was rearmed to support NATO against a potential attack by the Warsaw Pact— which might have resulted in the renewed destruction of Germany.

In January 1956, the GDR reacted to the developments in the west and passed a new law reorganizing its armed police force, which was already quartered in barracks, officially creating the Nationale Volksarmee (National People's Army, NVA). Just as the Bundeswehr was part of NATO, the NVA was integrated into the Warsaw Pact. Although the NVA stressed its complete disjunction with the Nazi past, Hitler's general Friedrich Paulus, whose capitulation in Stalingrad in 1943 was a turning point in World War II, became one of the main military advisors in building the NVA after his release from the Soviet prisoner of war camps in 1953. To avoid the danger of creating an organization that could easily become independent from the state, the GDR government tried to stress the break with the past. The NVA was, in the government's view, something new in military history because there had never before been a socialist German army. In contrast to the Bundeswehr, in the NVA the majority of officers came from the working class. The underlying connection between the military, capitalism, and landowners was thereby abolished.

At the head of the NVA was the Ministerium für Nationale Verteidigung (Ministry of National Defense). Real control was, however, in the hands of the SED through its committees and especially through the Nationale Verteidigungsrat (National Council of Defense), whose members all belonged to the Politbüro and the ZK. Its chairman was supreme commander. The position was usually given to the Generalsekretär of the SED. In addition, political representatives in individual military units guaranteed that the political opinions of soldiers were in agreement with the state. Political education was important. Officers were constantly observed by the Staatssicherheit (secret police). Border guards and special police units as well as other paramilitaristic groups also formed a power balance against the military.

The emphasis on socialism and a break with the past in the GDR helped to suppress outside criticism, but the situation in West Germany was different. Former Nazi generals served even in the headquarters of NATO—for example, General Adolf Heusinger and General Hans Speidel. To create a new kind of army for a democracy, new ideas needed to be found. Already in 1950, after the United States had realized that a demilitarized Germany was counterproductive, a new office was created under the leadership of Theodor Blank, known as Dienststelle Blank or Amt Blank (department Blank). Its task was to come up with a new model, new structures, and a new spiritual basis for a German army. The ideas of Colonel Wolf Graf von Baudissin, in particular, were influential in overcoming the gap between the military and civil society. The new army was not supposed to be a self-contained unit; nor was it to be a collection of robots and functionaries possessing weapons. It was supposed to be an organization of citizens in uniform bearing arms. While in the army, they would learn the newest technology, the necessary discipline, and team spirit without the degrading drills that had been characteristic of the German military in the past. In addition, courses in history and sociology would be part of the training. Freedom of opinion was a given, and a critical attitude and innovative ideas were to be encouraged. Individual rights and freedoms were to be respected, and complaints could be submitted to civil courts.

From the beginning, not only was the chain of command headed by a civilian, the secretary of defense (Verteidigungsminister), but the parliament was also involved. A committee was created to oversee the hiring of military personnel. Its members had belonged to the resistance and had fought fascism. The office of a *parlamentarische Wehrbeauftragte* (defense commissioner), who was seen as a kind of ombudsman, was created. Every soldier had direct access to him, and he had the authority to investigate any aspect of the military on his own initiative and report regularly to parliament.

It all sounded fine, but it was, nevertheless, a new army. The younger generation had no choice but to serve. They could volunteer for two years with a regular salary or be drafted for eighteen months, which would earn them only a *Wehrsold* (minimum pay for draftees). In spite of the financial incentive, many decided to remain idealists and not join the army on a voluntary basis. Although conscientious objection was a recognized alternative, this status was granted in the early years of the Bundeswehr only on religious grounds. Few in German society could pass the test to become a conscientious objector. Yet, many of the young soldiers who had been educated to be critical of authority resented the new army and the draft and made a point of exercising their right of passive resistance, gladly stressing the fact that they were not soldiers but "citizens in uniform." They wanted to make sure that this term, which had been used by the government to justify the new army, was taken seriously and that the lessons on social issues, and not only lessons in weaponry and strategy, were part of the training as promised.

And because of this fact, Tucholsky is actually a good author to cite in this context. Many of these "forced draftees" only played the role of soldiers: They sang louder than anyone else, they clicked their heels together with much more fervor, and they not only practiced looking to the left and the right but also up and down. They even became sergeants and officers and continued to read Tucholsky with their peers and subordinates. Luckily, no war broke out. Whatever the generals (many of whom were former Nazi officers) liked to think, the German Bundeswehr in the years between 1956 and the mid-1960s was not really ready for battle. Even the official statistics confirm that it was not until 1965 that the twelve divisions allowed under the Paris Treaty could be established.

Until the mid-1960s, each complaint received headlines, and most soldiers preferred not to wear their uniform in public. Officers had to be prepared to expect insults from the public, and a new attitude toward the past and German military tradition had to be formed. The *Traditionserlaß*, a study of tradition circulated by the secretary of defense, pointed out that German soldiers had always valued such virtues as love of the fatherland (in contrast to vulgar nationalism), conscientious fulfillment of one's duty without expecting reward or compensation for it, obedience and fidelity to the highest authority of the state, and preparedness to accept responsibility. It stressed also the political nature of the military. Finally, the report listed values that had shaped the German military throughout history: the ability to make decisions under stress and live with the consequences. Special qualities were generosity, chivalry, comradeship, compassion, bravery and the spirit of sacrifice, self-control, self-esteem in defeat as well as in victory, modesty, and discipline. Realizing the importance of symbols (see 2: Symbols and Memorials), the report mentioned the connection with the German past as expressed in the colors of the flag—black, red, and gold—the symbol of the responsibility of citizens and of Germans striving for unity, law, and freedom, the terms used in the national anthem. The eagle as the ancient symbol of sovereignty and legality, the iron cross as the symbol of bravery based on morality, parades, pledging allegiance, taps—these were all part of the tradition.

In a similar way, the new uniforms worn by the NVA soldiers in the GDR were attempts to establish a tradition. Willi Stoph, head of state at the time, pointed out that German soldiers and workers had expelled the emperor in 1918 in similar uniforms and had defeated the private armies of the Nazis. However, the GDR government also made use of the Prussian military tradition. In front of the Neue Wache, the former military headquarters in Berlin, which had become a monument honoring the victims of fascism and militarism, daily changing of the guards displayed the earlier splendor with the *Stechschritt* (goose step), legs raised high up in the air in unison and then lowered with a bang.

Times changed and attitudes changed. On one hand, the term "citizen in uniform" was mentioned less in West Germany, but on the other hand, the right to conscientious objection was firmly established. *Zivis* (*Zivildienstmachende*, civil service workers), working in social services instead of serving in the army, became an important element of German society. A federal commissioner for community service as an alternative to military service was established in 1969; a journal called *Zivildienst* (the first issues were called *Der Dienst*, The Service) was founded in 1971; and a school was opened to train the future Zivis.

From 1962 to 1989, the NVA in the GDR was also a conscription army (Bentzien et al. 2003, 111). There was no *Zivildienst* (civil service), only a *Wehrersatzdienst* (alternative national service), which allowed individuals to fulfill their military duty by serving in the Ministerium für Staatssicherheit (MfS, secret police) or the riot police. Christians who were serious in their belief, and claimed that their convictions did not allow them to use guns, were allowed to become construction workers in the military. A law to that effect was passed in 1964. Their epaulette displayed a spade (Bentzien et al. 2003, 126).

With unification, the former rival armies were merged, and the Bundeswehr was

GDR Military Honor Guard in the seventies.

reduced to half its size. Yet, at the same time, Germany regained its full sovereignty, and it was expected that it would live up to its new status and have the political will to deploy armed forces in other countries of the globe. The resulting crisis was short-lived. Former antimilitarists had "matured" and realized that pacifism only led to a support of dictators. Accordingly, the army had to be restructured. Heavy arms were no longer necessary, and there was no fear of an imminent attack by a Red Army, but the army's new role was as assistant policemen in a world increasingly fearful of terrorist attacks.

Just as Germany has not yet really found its new role in the community of nations, the Bundeswehr continues to question itself and to define its new image. It is not only financial problems that await answers, but also questions about the relationship between the Bundeswehr and German society—and with them the question of a conscription or a volunteer army. The drawback of a volunteer army is that there will be no more Zivis, and along with them an important part of the social system will disappear. Already in January 2004, it was announced that the length of service required from young people would be reduced from ten to nine months in the fall of that year to match the service of those serving in the armed forces, and there are plans for totally eliminating the service in 2008 (*Focus. de*, accessed January 12, 2004).

The Role of Religion

Although Christian churches in Germany, Austria, and Switzerland are rarely full—except on Christmas and Easter—Christianity (Catholic as well as Protestant) still plays a vital role in the social and cultural fabric of the German-speaking world, particularly through various church-sponsored activities such as *Kindergarten*, youth clubs, activities for senior citizens, and charitable organizations. Yet, times have changed since 1945 when the Christian churches offered moral support to millions in spite of their shortcomings during the Nazi era. Their coffers get emptier with each passing day. Churches are sold and turned into museums; church schools are closed; employees lose their jobs; ministers, priests, monks, and nuns cannot inspire enough young people to follow their example. And desperate appeals to the tastes and convenience of the congregations have failed. This was true in the 1970s when pop bands were introduced to accompany church songs instead of the traditional organ music, and it seems to be true again at the beginning of the twenty-first century. The current efforts to modernize in some cathedrals include placing TV screens on those Gothic columns that block the view of the altar. The idea behind this was to ensure that everyone would have the opportunity to watch the priest celebrate the Mass, but it is doubtful whether it will increase church attendance

Stephansdom in Vienna. The posters on the church steeple state: *Kein Haus ist für die Ewigkeit gebaut. Erste Sparkasse.* (No structure is built for eternity. First Savings Bank.) — *Keiner versteht Ihre Sorgen besser als wir. Städtische Versicherung.* (No one understands your troubles better than we do. Vienna City Insurance.)

and the collection. Some church fathers have even gone so far as to turn church steeples into the largest *Litfaßsäulen* (round billboards) by selling the covers that are necessary for renovations to advertising agencies, but here, too, it is doubtful whether it will bring in the necessary revenue for the upkeep of the building. It is too early to tell whether the fact that a German, Cardinal Joseph Ratzinger, was elected pope in 2005 will bring about a religious revival in Germany.

Christian churches in Germany always had a special status because they were directly linked to the state tax code going back to the Napoleonic era. Secularization had robbed them of their property and of the right to collect a tenth of the income from their parishioners. They had therefore been compensated by a new kind of taxation connected to the state. This new arrangement is still valid today. According to Germany's Basic Law, state laws regulate the content of the tax, and the religious institutions set the amount, which is linked to income. But an individual has the right to leave a church and by so doing be exempted from the church tax. In contrast to West Germany, in the GDR the separation between church and state was a reality. Church taxes had to be collected by the church from its members. Religion was not taught in schools, and there were no priests or ministers in the military. However, the state supported the church's welfare organizations and historical preservation efforts. After 1968, theology again became a regular offering at the more traditional universities.

Although church members in the GDR were not persecuted, and the GDR constitution guaranteed freedom of religion, the relationship between church and government was not without tension. The church regarded itself as responsible for helping to fill the spiritual needs of all people regardless of belief and political affiliation, and the clergy were always willing to listen to outsiders. They opened their church doors to artists who were politically out of favor, for example. As a consequence, Christians who openly confessed their beliefs were shunned by most groups in society and had little chance of gaining influential positions in government or industry. But as the authors of the reference work *Fragen an die DDR* (Questions Addressed to the GDR, Bentzien et al. 2003) reminded their read-

ers, each society favors those who are in agreement with its basic philosophy. And atheism was an important part of Marxism. Its underlying assumption that religion is the opium of the people understandably came into conflict with some of the church's teachings.

At the same time, the demand for social justice and peace united the church and the government. A peaceful coexistence was achieved, although, until the 1970s, churches in the GDR were in close contact with their brothers and sisters in the West, from whom they also received financial support, something which awakened suspicion at the political level in the GDR. The Protestant churches were members of the Evangelische Kirche in Deutschland (Evangelical Church in Germany, EKD) until a new GDR constitution forced them to annul their membership and found a separate organization, the Bund Evangelischer Kirchen (Federation of Evangelical Churches, BEK), which described itself as "*Kirche im Sozialismus*" (Church within socialism) (see 1: From Two to One; 3: From A to Z, "Protestantism"). Whereas the borders of the Protestant church organizations were pretty much the same as political state borders, the dioceses of the Roman Catholic Church in Germany crossed the political boundaries at least de jure.

The 1960s produced a critical generation, and not only in the West. In East Germany, reform groups got together and demanded a different, better form of socialism, a socialism with a human face (as was also true in Czechoslovakia during the Prague Spring under Alexander Dubček). Pacifism was proclaimed on their banners. In 1982, the peace movement, *Frieden schaffen ohne Waffen* (Create peace without use of arms), achieved real success, reaching out to many segments of the society. And in 1989, the Nikolaikirche (Nikolai Church) in Leipzig became a symbol for reform. The prayers for peace and the demonstrations were originally not intended to bring about unification with the FRG. Rather, it was a revolt for the people and against governmental inflexibility and disrespect for the individual.

After unification, the BEK was dissolved and the state churches of the former GDR rejoined the EKD. Protestants and Catholics expected a revival after their successful survival under communism, but instead, after unification, more people left the church than before, following the West German trend.

In the early postwar years, as many people left the church as joined it; since the 1960s the rate of those leaving the church has accelerated, although many still hesitate because of family tradition, the wish to be married in a church, to have their children christened, and, finally, to be buried by a priest. Official church membership (the Protestant and Catholic churches have approximately 28 million members each [Beck 2003, 36]) is therefore still higher than the number of practicing Christians. In the 1960s, about 75 percent of all West Germans on the church membership rolls went to church on a regular basis; forty years later, in the larger, united Germany, only about 10 percent of the Catholics and 4 percent of the Protestants do the same.

But the emptiness of Christian churches is no real indication of spirituality. Even in a relatively secular Germany, 52 percent regard themselves as religious, 44 percent believe in a life after death, and 61 percent believe in some kind of higher spiritual being. Of course, this is lower than the 90 percent of 1967, but it is still a high percentage. In 1998, Chancellor Schröder omitted the phrase "as true as God will help me" (*So wahr mir Gott helfe*) in his oath of office; nevertheless, the statement by the German philosopher Peter Sloterdijk that the post-Christian era is a global fact (*Focus* 16 [2004], 131) is not quite true. Religiosity has only shifted from state churches (Catholic and Protestant) to an individualized search for spiritual values. Major church rituals such as marriages and funerals are still accepted by a majority, and many Christian holidays are still part of the secular state calendar (see 5: Holidays and Local Festivals). The theologian and former priest Eugen Drewermann, who was excommunicated because of his deviant beliefs, remarked: "People no longer tolerate a dogmatic structure of infallible officials" (ibid., 132). Therefore, the old mother religions—for example, worship of the goddess Ishtar/Astarte, or, in the Germanic pantheon, Ostara (who gave her name for *Ostern* in German, "Easter" in English)—are experiencing a revival, and Buddhism has reached the general public. The Dalai Lama's visit to Berlin in 2003 was a huge success. His message was spread further through the largest German newspaper, *Bild* (see 6: The Press), which published advice by his holiness for the common people for several issues every day during his visit.

With the influx of guest workers and the new European order (see 4: Multicultural Society), the Christian churches have also been challenged by official faiths such as Islam, in addition to various Christian splinter groups (Church of Latter-day Saints [Mormons], Jehovah's Witnesses, New Apostolic Church). The Christian Orthodox churches have about 1.5 million members; Islam about 3.2 million (the vast majority of Muslims are Sunni; Shiites and Alevites form a much smaller group [Beck 2003, 36]); Judaism about 180,000; Hinduism not quite 100,000; Buddhism about 220,000 (*Focus* 16 [2004], 131). In all, according to Marieluise Beck, "There are more than 160 different religious communities in Germany" (Beck 2003, 36).

From A to Z

Abitur: From Latin, *abire*, to exit. The Abitur (a standardized state exam) used to be the required diploma for admission to a university. It still has that function, but in specific disciplines additional entrance examinations are also being administered, a change that began in the 2004/2005 academic year. The Abitur was introduced in Prussia in 1788 as a kind of entrance examination to the university, but its format has changed over the years. Basically, the final grade is determined by a series of written and oral exams and the achievements in the basic and the advanced courses (*Leistungskurse*). In 1965, only about 5 percent of the student population received the Abitur. The percentage has increased steadily over the years such that in 1970 about 8.5 percent received it; in 1975, about 12 percent; in 1984, almost 22 percent (Hermand 1988, 34); in 1999, almost 37 percent; and in 2003, more than 39 percent (*Statistisches Bundesamt*).

Abortion: Under certain conditions, abortion up to the twelfth week of pregnancy is permitted in Germany after consultation with representatives of a pregnancy conflict advice center: (1) for medical reasons; (2) in case of rape; and (3) for personal and social reasons. Further information can be obtained from various agencies, including Pro Familia (Pro Family), Arbeiterwohlfahrt (Workers' Welfare Association), Donum Vitae (The Gift of Life), and Diakonisches Werk (Evangelical Welfare Work) (Beck 2003, 194).

BAföG: Bundesausbildungsförderungsgesetz, or Federal Training Assistance Act. This 1971 act was designed to increase equity among students and open the universities to students from lower income groups. The financial assistance, a combination of a grant and an interest-free loan, is contingent on academic performance.

Betriebsverfassungsrecht: Rights of Employees at their Workplace. Passed in 1952 and revised in 1972, this law regulates the relationship between employee and employer. Employees are represented by the Betriebsrat (Workers Council), whose members they also elect (see Beck 2003, 106).

BGB: Bürgerliches Gesetzbuch, the German civil code, first established in 1900. The code originally covered civil law, the law of obligations (contracts), property law, family law, and the law of succession. It now has been extended to include commercial law, corporate law, and labor law.

Bundesländer: Federal states. Three of the sixteen states are considered city-states: Berlin, Bremen, and Hamburg. The state parliament is called the *Landtag*, the government the *Landesregierung*. The heads of state government are called *Ministerpräsident* (state prime ministers), and in the city-states the head of government is the *Erster* or *Regierender Bürgermeister* (first/governing mayor). The legislative periods vary between four and five years. In the former GDR, the earlier *Länder* (states) were restructured into *Verwaltungsbezirke* (administrative districts). (See 1: From Two to One.)

Bundesprüfstelle für jugendgefährdende Medien: (Federal Control Agency for Media Harmful to Young People) It is part of the Bundesministerium für Familie, Senioren, Frauen und Jugend (Federal Ministry for Family, Seniors, Women and Youth). Freedom of speech and freedom of the arts are not absolute but are limited by others' basic rights, for instance, the protection of children. Indexing such materials is not the same as censorship because it can only be done after the fact, that is after publication of such materials.

Bundesrat: The upper house of the German parliament. Germany is a federal republic made up of sixteen federal states. They have their representation in the Bundesrat. Each state has at least three votes, and larger states have up to six votes.

Bundesregierung: The federal government—that is, the executive branch of government headed by the chancellor.

Bundestag: The lower house of the German parliament, the main legislative branch of government. Its members, called *Mitglieder des Bundestages* (MdB), are elected every four years through an electoral system that is a blend of majority voting and proportional representation (see "*Wahlsystem*," below). It has its seat in the capital, Berlin, in the building known as the Reichstag.

Bundesverfassungsgericht: The German supreme court, the country's highest court. It decides on constitutional cases and examines the constitutionality of new laws. It is located in Karlsruhe.

Charitable organizations: In Germany these include the nondenominational Arbeiter-Wohlfahrt (Workers Charity), Paritätische Wohlfahrtsverband (Parity Charity), and Deutsches Rotes Kreuz (German Red Cross). The Diakonisches Werk (Evangelical Welfare Work), an agency of the Protestant church, and Caritas, its Catholic counterpart, help anyone in need regardless of their religious affiliation.

Confessions: In percentage, the statistics for religious affiliation in 2005 stated that Christians make up 66 percent of the population (Catholics 33 percent, Protestants 33 percent); Muslims 3 percent; and Jews 0.1 percent (www.deutschland.de/aufeinen blick). Germany is therefore almost equally divided between the two main confessions, the Roman Catholic Church and the Protestant churches. Both had about 27.5 million members in 1996 (Sandford 1999, 100). For historical reasons, the Roman Catholics dominate in the west of Germany (Rhineland) and the south (see 1: Overcoming Regionalism). Protestants have a majority in the north and east of Germany, as the former GDR was the center of the Reformation. It is the location of such towns as Wittenberg, where Martin Luther, according to legend, posted his Ninety-Five Theses, and Leipzig, where Johann Sebastian Bach was church organist in the

Thomaskirche (Church of St. Thomas). (See also "Protestantism," "Roman Catholic Church," below.)

Council of Christian Churches: Besides the EKD (see "Protestantism," below) and the Roman Catholic Church, the Arbeitsgemeinschaft Christlicher Kirchen in Deutschland (Council of Churches in Germany) includes the Greek Orthodox Metropolitanate of Germany (450,000 members); the Bund Evangelisch-Freikirchlicher Gemeinden in Deutschland (Federation of Evangelical Independent Communities in Germany, Baptists) (87,000); the Evangelisch-Methodistische Kirche (Methodists) (68,000); the Russian Orthodox Church (50,000); the Selbständige Evangelisch-Lutherische Kirche (Independent Evangelical Lutheran Church, SELK) (39,750); the Syrian Orthodox Church (37,000); the Armenian Apostolic Church (35,000); the Alt-Katholiken (Old Catholic Church) (25,000); the Moravians (7,200); the Evangelisch-altreformierte Kirche (Evangelical Old-Reformed Church) (7,000); the Mennonites (6,875); and the Salvation Army (2,000).

DAAD: Deutscher Akademischer Austauschdienst, or German Academic Exchange Service. This organization provides information on education in Germany and sources for funding and scholarships and also actively offers support in the different disciplines. Its program includes language courses, work placement and fellowships, visiting lecturer services, and research grants.

Death Penalty: Like most Western countries, Germany has abolished the death penalty (1949). Yet many regard the German legal system as too lenient. Richard Lord wrote, "Obviously chastened by the viciousness and arbitrary nature of the Nazi-era courts, German judges of more recent vintage have bent over backwards (and beyond, according to some critics) to protect the rights of the accused and understand the motives of the convicted, assuring that no sentence should be seen as unfair or too harsh" (Lord 2004, 60).

Driver's License: It is relatively expensive (minimum of 1,500 euros) to obtain a driver's license in Germany because one requirement is that the individual must take a course at a driving school. Other EU licenses are accepted temporarily, but not an international license if one registers residence in Germany. Non-EU licenses are valid for one year only and require an official translation.

Elections: See "*Wahlgesetz,*" below.

European Union (EU): In 2004, the EU had twenty-five members. Germany was one of its founding members in 1992. Its parliament is elected every five years. (See also 10: From A to Z, "European Union.")

Goethe-Institut: According to one author, "The fusion of the Goethe-Institut with InterNationes in 2001 created Germany's biggest mediator of foreign cultural policy" (Briel 2002, 59). Legally, the institute is a *Verein* (registered association), although most of its budget consists of a grant from the German Foreign Office. It is well known for its many language course offerings both in Germany and throughout the world. In addition, it provides support on matters pertaining to the teaching of German language and culture to individuals and organizations and offers development courses for German teachers. Its centers all over the world are the "windows" to German culture for many.

Grundgesetz: Basic Law. This document was the constitution of the Federal Republic of Germany and now of the unified Germany. It has been in effect since May 24, 1949, and spells out the basic constitutionally guaranteed rights of all Germans. Its articles supersede all other German laws. Changes to the Grundgesetz require a majority two-thirds vote of both houses, the Bundestag (lower house of parliament) and the Bundesrat (upper house of parliament).

Hartz-Konzept: These proposals for a reform of labor-market policy were named after the chairman of the committee that designed them, Peter Hartz. In 2002, it recommended policies that were accepted by the government and divided into four steps, labeled Hartz I–IV, which were adopted between January 1, 2003, and January 1, 2005. The proposals streamlined the existing Federal Employment Office (Bundesanstalt für Arbeit/Arbeitsamt) but also placed additional responsibilities on employees. The former *Sozialhilfe* (income support) and *Arbeitslosenhilfe* (unemployment assistance) were combined to constitute an *Arbeitslosengeld* (unemployment benefit), which for many resulted in a reduction of benefits.

InterNationes: See "Goethe-Institut," above.

Islam: The Central Committee of Muslims in Germany (Zentralrat der Muslime in Deutschland e.V.) represents more than 3.2 million members of that faith, many of whom belong to the third or fourth generation living in Germany. Some 500,000 have German citizenship. The Islamic Charter adopted by the committee on February 3, 2002, states the fundamental philosophy of its members in twenty-one succinct statements, with a foreword noting that the duty of this large minority is to integrate itself into German society and to enter an open dialogue regarding its beliefs and practices. The statements cover the main goals and beliefs of Muslims as well as the desire for peace and a desire to abide by the democratic rights and responsibilities listed under the German constitution, particularly regarding the rights of women and religious freedom and pluralism (www.islam.de).

Kanzler: Chancellor. The German chancellors since 1945 in the FRG and then the united Germany have been as follows, with dates of their term in office followed by the name and then biographical dates and party affiliation: 1949–1963: Konrad Adenauer (1876–1967), CDU; 1963–1966: Ludwig Erhard (1897–1977), CDU; 1966–1969: Kurt Georg Kiesinger (1904–1988), CDU; 1969–1974: Willy Brandt (1913–1992), SPD; 1974–1982: Helmut Schmidt (b. 1918), SPD; 1982–1998: Helmut Kohl (b. 1930), CDU; 1998–2005: Gerhard Schröder (b. 1944), SPD; since 2005: Angela Merkel (b. 1954), CDU. (For the GDR, see "*Ministerpräsident,*" below. For full names of parties, see "Political parties," below.)

Kindergarten: Run by local and charitable organizations and churches, the *Kindergarten* in Germany is a mixture of preschool and day care for children between the ages of three and six. According to Marieluise Beck, "Every child above the age of three has a legal right to a place in kindergarten" in Germany (Beck 2003, 196). Fees depend on the parents' income. Only about 30 percent of the kindergartens offer care for the whole day, most only for half a day.

KMK: Kultusministerkonferenz, or Permanent Conference of the Ministers of Education and Culture. Because education is the responsibility of individual states, the KMK was created in 1948 by the ministers for education in the three military sectors administered by the United States, Britain, and France to provide a forum for collaboration and to ensure that educational compatibility was accomplished. The KMK is also the international representative for German education.

Koalition: Coalition. Because of the number of parties in parliament (see "Political Parties," below), parties often have to form coalitions to be able to gain a majority and establish a government.

Konstruktives Misstrauensvotum: Constructive vote of no confidence—the procedure undertaken by parliament to force a chancellor out of office. The vote of no confidence has been used twice in the history of the FRG: (1) on April 27, 1972, when an attempt by Rainer Barzel and the CDU to call for a vote of no confidence against Willy Brandt failed by two votes; and (2) on October 1, 1982, when Helmut Kohl succeeded Helmut Schmidt as chancellor. (See also "*Vertrauensfrage*," below.)

Labor laws: All employees have certain minimum rights independent of any existing contract of employment (see Beck 2003, 105).

Law and order: Crime rates more than doubled between the early 1970s and the early 1990s and continued to climb. Burglaries have increased threefold in less than ten years.

Matura: The Austrian term for *Abitur.*

Ministerpräsident: Prime minister (of the GDR); also called *Ministerratsvorsitzender* (chairman of the council of ministers). Although the Ministerrat (Council of Ministers) was the official executive branch of the GDR, the Staatsrat (State Council) took on many of the governing functions from 1960 through 1971 and again after 1976 (following a five-year hiatus in the wake of Walter Ulbricht's forced resignation as first secretary of the SED in 1971). The prime ministers, listed with dates of their terms first, followed by names, biographical dates, and party affiliation, were: 1949–1964: Otto Grotewohl (1894–1964), SED (formerly a member of the SPD); 1964–1973: Willi Stoph (1914–1999), SED; 1973–1976: Horst Sindermann (1915–1990), SED; 1976–1989: Willi Stoph; 1989–1990: Hans Modrow (b. 1928), SED; 1990: Lothar de Maizière (b. 1940), East-CDU (chairman). (For full party names, see "Political parties," below.)

PISA: Program for International Student Assessment. PISA's 2004 study was somewhat more favorable for Germany than the earlier one mentioned in the text, but not glowing either.

Political parties: Parties represented in the German Bundestag in 2005 are (in alphabetical order): Bündnis 90/Die Grünen (Alliance 90/The Greens) (see 10: Consumer Culture versus Green Awareness):

www.gruene.de; the CDU (Christlich Demokratische Union, Christian Democratic Union): www.cdu.de; the CSU (Christlich Soziale Union, Christian Social Union), a so-called "sister party" to the CDU (that is, the CSU and the CDU do not rival each other in the individual states; the CDU has organizations in all states but Bavaria, and the CSU functions only in Bavaria): www.csu.de; the FDP (Freie Demokratische Partei, Free Democratic Party, the Liberals): www.fdp.de; Die Linkspartei (The Left Party): www.sozialisten.de; and the SPD (Sozialdemokratische Partei Deutschlands, Social Democratic Party of Germany): www.spd.de.

In the GDR, a pseudo-democratic system was established that allowed the existence of parties without giving them actual political influence. All parties were joined in 1945 in the Einheitsfront der antifaschistisch-demokratischen Parteien (Unity Front of the Antifascist-Democratic Parties), and in 1949 the Nationale Front. The KPD (Kommunistische Partei Deutschlands, Communist Party of Germany) and SPD (Sozialdemokratische Partei Deutschlands, Social Democratic Party of Germany) united and formed the SED (Sozialistische Einheitspartei Deutschlands, Socialist Unity Party of Germany) in 1945. Other parties were an eastern version of the CDU, the LDPD (Liberal-Demokratische Partei Deutschlands, Liberal-Democratic Party of Germany), and two parties that were controlled by the SED and only created to be better able to cater to farmers and former military: the DBD (Demokratische Bauernpartei Deutschlands, Democratic Party for Farmers of Germany) and the NDPD (National-demokratische Partei Deutschlands, National-Democratic Party of Germany). In addition, mass organizations controlled by the SED gained party status. In 1990, in conjunction with unification, the SED was restructured and renamed as the PDS (Partei des Deutschen Sozialismus, Party of German Socialism). In 2005, due to the many reforms of the Schröder government, seen by many as too conservative and antisocialist, a new left-wing party was founded, the WASG (Wahlalternative Arbeit und Soziale Gerechtigkeit, Election Alternative: Work and Social Justice), and the PDS renamed itself Die Linkspartei, abbreviated Die Linke, sometimes with the addition PDS.

Präsident: President. The president is the German head of state, but the position is primarily a ceremonial one with little direct (but much indirect, that is, "moral") political influence. She/he is elected for a five-year term by a special committee (Bundesversammlung) composed of members of the Bundestag, the Bundesrat, and figures from public life. The following lists give the years of service as president, then the name with biographical dates, followed by political affiliation.

In the FRG: 1949–1959: Theodor Heuss (1884–1963), FDP; 1959–1969: Heinrich Lübke (1894–1972), CDU; 1969–1974: Gustav Heinemann (1899–1976), SPD; 1974–1979: Walter Scheel (b. 1919), FDP; 1979–1984: Karl Carstens (1914–1992), CDU; 1984–1994: Richard von Weizsäcker (b. 1920), CDU; 1994–1999: Roman Herzog (b. 1934), CDU; 1999–2004: Johannes Rau (1931–2006), SPD; since 2004: Horst Köhler (b. 1943), CDU.

In the GDR: 1949–1960: Wilhelm Pieck (1876–1960), SED (formerly KPD). After Pieck's death, the presidency was replaced by a Staatsrat (State Council) whose chairman had in fact the function of president.

1960–1973: Walter Ulbricht (1893–1973), SED. Until 1971, he was also the Generalsekretär (general secretary, from 1953–1976 renamed Erster Sekretär, first secretary) of the SED. During this time, the Staatsrat took on many of the governing functions that belonged officially to the Ministerrat. 1973–1976: Willi Stoph (1914–1999), SED; 1976–1989: Erich Honecker (1912–1994), SED, who took over as Erster Sekretär of the SED in 1971 (since 1976 named again Generalsekretär) and reestablished in 1976 the governing role of the Staatsrat that it had under Ulbricht until 1971. 1989–1990: Egon Krenz (b. 1937), SED; 1990: Martin Gerlach (b. 1928), LDPD (during the revolution preceding unification, the position of Staatsratsvorsitzender [chairman of the state council] and general secretary of the SED were separated, and Gregor Gysi [b. 1948] became chair of the reorganized and renamed SED, the PDS); 1990: Sabine Bergmann-Pohl (b. 1946), CDU, Volkskammerpräsidentin (president of the People's Chamber, the GDR parliament), became head of state because the Staatsrat no longer existed. (For full party names, see "Political parties," above.)

Protest Movements: These were always part of the history of the Bundeswehr from its beginning to the new millennium. Especially important were the "ohne mich!" (count me out!) movement of the 1950s, the cruise and Pershing missile protests under chancellor Schmidt in the 1980s, and post-unification deployments of Bundeswehr personnel to Somalia and Bosnia.

Protestantism: The Evangelische Kirche in Deutschland (Evangelical Church in Germany, EKD), founded in 1945, consists of twenty-four independent Landeskirchen (state churches) of different confessions: ten Lutheran, two Reformed (Calvinist), and twelve United (Lutheran and Reformed), which all partake also in international church organizations based in Geneva, Switzerland—for example, the World Council of Churches (WCC), the Lutheran World Federation (LWF), the World Alliance of Reformed Churches (WARL), and the Conference of European Churches (CEC). In the postwar decades, the EKD has also become a political force owing to the fact that several influential politicians have been active members. In contrast to much political maneuvering and suppression of the past by the general public and politicians, the EKD tried to raise the consciousness of the German population for its history and its responsibility and helped Germany to become accepted in the international community again. It also helped Willy Brandt's Ostpolitik to become a reality (see 1: From Two to One).

Reifeprüfung: Literally, examination of maturity. Another term used for Abitur (see "Abitur," above).

Roman Catholic Church: The Catholic Church has been less politically active than Protestantism in Germany and has had more difficulty in coming to terms with the past. Hitler's Concordat with the Catholic church was a heavy burden. Rolf Hochhuth's play Der Stellvertreter (The Deputy; see 8: Theater and Dance) further tainted its image. In addition, the Catholic Church's conservative attitude toward family planning (as manifested, for example, in Pope Paul VI's Humanae Vitae, prohibiting artificial birth control) alienated church members. This all could change following the election of Joseph Cardinal Ratzinger as pope in 2005. As a German, Benedict XVI may even have an impact on the Protestant church in Germany.

Schultüte: A cone-shaped, decorated cardboard container filled with sweets given to children on the first day of their first year of school.

Separation of church and state: This principle is a part of the FRG's Grundgesetz (Basic Law), Articles 4 and 140. Yet, some churches, above all the Protestant and Roman Catholic churches, have a special status as *Körperschaften des Öffentlichen Rechts* (corporate bodies under public law). In contrast to the former GDR (see text), in the FRG and in the unified Germany church taxes are collected by the state, and religious education is guaranteed in public schools. The theological faculty at universities, approved by the church, is appointed and paid by the state. The main churches belong to the Rundfunkrat (Broadcasting Council; see 7: Radio and Television) and have their own news network (epd, or Evangelischer Pressedienst, an evangelical/Protestant news service; and KNA, the Katholische Nachrichten-Agentur, or Catholic News Agency). The church welfare organizations Caritas (Roman Catholic) and Diakonisches Werk (Protestant) play an important social role (see 3: The Social Net).

Sitzenbleiben: To repeat a class. Because students do not choose individual courses but belong to a group that takes a preselected set of subjects, they have to repeat the class if they fail in a given number of subjects. This way, they lose a whole year

in their academic career and also have to repeat the subjects that they did not fail.

Spas: Some physicians still prescribe a period of stay at a spa, known as *Heilbäder* (healing baths) und *Kurorte* (places for a cure), for patients who need to recuperate from an illness or stress. The health-care system is less likely to cover such treatments in the new millennium, and many spas are reinventing themselves as Wellness Hotels.

Staatsratsvorsitzender: Chairman of the State Council, the title of the heads of state in the GDR. See Präsidenten above.

Tarifvertragsrecht: Collective labor agreements. Trade unions and employers' federations or individual employers can engage in their own labor agreements (regulating employees' wages, working hours, length of paid vacation, and period of notice) as long as they abide by the minimum standards.

Taxes: Germany has a progressive tax system. The major tax in Germany is the income tax, which depends on the amount of the gross income. Other factors are marital status, children, and other sources of income (for example, rent and interest). Taxes are deducted automatically from the gross monthly income. At the end of the year, a tax declaration is mandatory. For further information, see www.finanzamt.de and www.ofd.niedersachsen.de. A brochure entitled "Steuern von A bis Z" is available from the Finance Ministry and www.bundesfinanzministerium.de (Beck 2003, 118). The reforms of the German tax system in 2000 reduced the tax burden on both companies and individuals. One German study reported that "a married employee with two children in this country generally does not pay more tax than in the United States. Also for the average, representative company the tax load in Germany is almost identical to that in the United States" (Lantermann et al. 2003, 248).

Members of Catholic and Protestant churches also have to pay a church tax in Germany. There is no tax for members of other religions (Beck 2003, 119).

Vertrauensfrage: The call for a vote of confidence, which can be initiated by parliament or by the government. In this second instance, there is a danger of political maneuvering. Whereas in the parliamentary vote of no confidence the opposing side has to nominate a new chancellor to succeed the former chancellor immediately, the situation is different if the chancellor himself calls for a vote of confidence. When he/she loses the vote, he/she is not automatically replaced by someone else but has a choice between stepping down or asking the president to dissolve parliament and call new elections. Consequently, a chancellor may try to get rid of critics in his or her own ranks by manipulating the vote and losing intentionally.

In the history of the FRG, the vote of confidence has been called five times by a chancellor. Twice the chancellor was confirmed and three times he lost the vote, parliament was dissolved, and new elections called: (1) on September 22, 1972, by Willy Brandt, who lost the vote and won the following elections; (2) on February 5, 1982, by Helmut Schmidt, who won the vote; (3) on December 17, 1982, by Helmut Kohl, who had, just two months earlier, dethroned Helmut Schmidt by a vote of no confidence on October 1, 1982 (Kohl's ma-

jority was too slim to govern, and he therefore posed the *Vertrauensfrage* but asked his own government to abstain from voting; in this way, he lost the Vertrauensfrage and new elections were called in which he won); (4) on November 16, 2001, by Gerhard Schröder, who won the vote; and (5) on July 1, 2005, by Gerhard Schröder, who asked not only his government officials but also many parliamentarians to abstain. He lost the vote and hoped to win the new elections. The question of manipulation of democratic procedures was raised regarding this move but the supreme court allowed the elections to be held. Schröder had, however, miscalculated. His party was not able to gain a majority. The election was won by the CDU. After much maneuvering, the chair of the CDU, Angela Merkel, was able to form a grand coalition and became the first woman chancellor. (See also "*Konstruktives Misstrauensvotum,*" above.)

Verwaltungsbezirke: Administrative districts. In 1952, the original *Länder* (states) of the GDR were restructured into fifteen administrative districts to allow for more centralized control.

Vocational advice: Vocational Information Centers (*Berufsinformationszentren*) help students to find the best training for their needs and can be especially helpful for foreigners who are new to the German educational system (www.bildungsserver.de).

Wahlsystem and ***Wahlrecht:*** Voting system and voting rights. Elections are general, direct, free, equal, and secret. Citizens are eligible to vote and to be elected after the age of eighteen. Marieluise Beck noted that "since 1994, citizens of the EU have been allowed to vote and stand for election in local elections if they have been registered in the community for at least three months. EU citizens are also eligible to vote in European Parliament elections, if they choose to vote in Germany rather than in their country of citizenship" (Beck 2003, 65). For the Bundestag, each German citizen eligible to vote has two votes. The first vote is based on a majority voting system. The candidate is elected who has received the majority of the votes in his or her district. The second vote is based on proportional representation. Each party establishes a list from which they can send a number of representatives based on the percentage of votes they received. A party can only send members to parliament if they received at least 5 percent of the second ballot or were able to win three *Direktmandate* (direct mandates, that is, candidates elected through the first ballot).

Elections in the GDR always resulted in an extremely high number of votes for the ruling party, more than 99 percent. This was because citizens were presented with a unity list established by the Nationale Front, a joint organization of all parties. Voters theoretically had the right to delete names of candidates or even discard the whole list. But almost all ballots were cast unaltered to avoid repercussions.

Walz: The period after a young person's initial apprenticeship when the journeyman travels through the land to gain experience and training from different master craftspeople in different regions.

Zivis: (*Zivildienstmachende*) Germany's Basic Law states that no one can be forced to serve in the military and bear arms. As an alternative to compulsory military service, conscientious objectors are obliged to serve as civil service workers. Through their assistance to the old and sick, they make a valuable contribution to society. Current discussion about the abolition of compulsory military service and the creation of a professional volunteer army might, therefore, have negative ramifications for social services and health insurers in Germany. The grand coalition (formed in 2005) plans to continue with the civil service at least until 2010.

Additional Readings

Anweiler, Oskar. *Schulpolitik und Schulsystem in der DDR.* Opladen: Leske and Budrich, 1988.

Armbruster, Frank. *Politik in Deutschland. Systemvergleich Bundesrepublik Deutschland—DDR.* Kollegmaterial Politik. Wiesbaden: Gabler, 1981.

Bald, Detlef, and Reinhard Brühl. *Die Nationale Volksarmee—Armee für den Frieden. Beiträge zu Selbstverständnis und Geschichte des deutschen Militärs, 1945–1990.* Baden-Baden: Nomos, 1995.

Baudissin, Wolf, Graf von. *Soldaten für den Frieden. Entwürfe für eine zeitgemäße Bundeswehr.* München: S. Piper, 1969.

Baumert, Jürgen, and Kai S. Cortina. *Das Bildungswesen in der Bundesrepublik Deutschland. Strukturen und Entwicklungen im Überblick.* Reinbek: Rowohlt, 2003.

Beck, Marieluise. *A Manual for Germany. Ein Handbuch für Deutschland.* Berlin: Beauftragte der Bundesregierung für Migration, Flüchtlinge und Integration, 2003. Additional information available through the Federal and State Centers for Political Education (*Bundes- und Landeszentralen für politische Bildung*).

Besier, Gerhard. *Der SED-Staat und die Kirche. Der Weg in die Anpassung.* München: Bertelsmann, 1993.

Brunotte, Heinz. *Die Evangelische Kirche in*

Deutschland. Geschichte, Organisation und Gestalt der EKD. Gütersloh: Gütersloher Verlagshaus G. Mohr, 1964.

Bundesministerium für Gesundheit und Soziale Sicherung, ed. Lebenslagen in Deutschland. Armuts- und Reichtumsberichterstattung der Bundesregierung. Bonn: n.d.

Bundeswehr, www.bundeswehr.de.

Burger, Annemarie. Religionszugehörigkeit und soziales Verhalten. Untersuchungen und Statistiken der neueren Zeit in Deutschland. Göttingen: Vandenhoeck and Ruprecht, 1964.

Cortina, Kai S., Jürgen Baumert, Achim Leschinsky, Karl Ulrich Mayer, Luitgard Trommer, eds. Das Bildungswesen in der Bundesrepublik Deutschland. Strukturen und Entwicklungen im Überblick. 2. Auflage. Reinbek bei Hamburg: Rowohlt, 2005.

Dahmen, Thomas. Wehrdienst, Zivildienst. Das Buch zur Fernsehserie ARD-Recht. Frankfurt am Main: Suhrkamp, 1997.

First-Hand Information Department. Education in the GDR. Objectives, Contents and Results. Berlin: Panorama, 1987.

Fischer, Johannes, ed. Verteidigung im Bündnis. Planung, Aufbau und Bewährung der Bundeswehr, 1950–1972. München: Bernard und Graefe, 1975.

Fisher, Howard D. German Legal System and Legal Language: A General Survey together with Notes and a German Vocabulary. London: Cavendish, 1996.

Forrester, Ian S., and Hans-Michael Ilgen. The German Legal System. South Hackensack, NJ: F. B. Rothman, 1972.

Forster, Thomas Manfred. The East German Army: The Second Power in the Warsaw Pact. London: Allen and Unwin, 1980.

Foster, Nigel G. German Law and Legal System. London: Blackstone, 1993.

Foster, Nigel G., and Satish Sule. German Legal System and Laws. London: Blackstone, 1996; Oxford and New York: Oxford University Press, 2002.

Freckmann, Anke, and Thomas Christian Wegerich. The German Legal System. London: Sweet and Maxwell, 1999.

Frick, Joachim. Lebenslagen im Wandel.

Determinanten kleinräumlicher Mobilität in Westdeutschland. Projektgruppe "Das Sozio-ökonomische Panel" im Deutschen Institut für Wirtschaftsforschung, Berlin. Frankfurt and New York: Campus, 1996.

Führ, Christoph. Schools and Institutions of Higher Education in the Federal Republic of Germany. Bonn: Inter Nationes, 1989.

———. On the Education System in the Five New Länder of the Federal Republic of Germany. Bonn: Inter Nationes, 1992.

Führ, Christoph, and Iván Tapia. The German Education System since 1945. Bonn: Inter Nationes, 1997.

Gabriel, Oscar W., and Everhard Holtmann. Handbuch politisches System der Bundesrepublik Deutschland. 3., völlig überarbeitete und erweiterte Auflage. München and Wien: Oldenbourg, 2005.

Gaffney, John, and Eva Kolinsky. Political Culture in France and Germany. London: Routledge, 1991.

German Law Archive, www.iuscomp.org/gla.

Hach, Jürgen. Gesellschaft und Religion in der Bundesrepublik Deutschland. Eine Einführung in die Religionssoziologie. Heidelberg: Quelle and Meyer, 1980.

Helwig, Gisela, and Detlef Urban, eds. Kirchen und Gesellschaften in beiden deutschen Staaten. Köln: Edition Deutschland Archiv im Verlag Wissenschaft und Politik, 1987.

Hollerbach, Alexander. Verträge zwischen Staat und Kirche in der Bundesrepublik Deutschland. Frankfurt am Main: Klostermann, 1965.

Ilsemann, Carl-Gero von. Die Bundeswehr in der Demokratie. Hamburg: Von Decker's Verlag Schenck, 1971.

Klingemann, Hans-Dieter, and Max. Kaase, eds. Wahlen und politisches System. Analysen aus Anlass der Bundestagswahl 1980. Opladen: Westdeutscher Verlag, 1983.

———, eds. Wahlen und politischer Prozess. Analysen aus Anlass der Bundestagswahl 1983. Opladen: Westdeutscher Verlag, 1986.

Krummacher, Jo, and Hendrik Hefermehl. Ratgeber für Kriegsdienstverweigerer. Praktische Hilfe zur Vorbereitung auf das Anerkennungsverfahren. Stuttgart: Radius, 1996.

Langguth, Gerd. *In Search of Security: A Socio-Psychological Portrait of Today's Germany.* Westport, CT: Praeger, 1995.

Larsson, Rune. *Religion zwischen Kirche und Schule. Die Lehrpläne für den evangelischen Religionsunterricht in der Bundesrepublik Deutschland seit 1945.* Lund: GWK Gleerup; Göttingen: Vandenhoek and Ruprecht, 1980.

Littell, Franklin Hamlin. *The German Phoenix: Men and Movements in the Church in Germany.* Garden City, NY: Doubleday, 1960.

Ministry of Health, German Democratic Republic. *Health Care in the German Democratic Republic.* Berlin: Panorama, 1984.

Peisert, Hansgert, and Gerhild Framhein. *Das Hochschulsystem in Deutschland.* Bonn: Bundesministerium für Bildung und Wissenschaft, 1994.

Phillips, David, ed. *Education in Germany: Tradition and Reform in Historical Context.* London and New York: Routledge, 1995.

Picht, Georg. *Die deutsche Bildungskatastrophe. Analyse und Dokumentation.* Olten: Walter, 1964.

Raven, Wolfram von, ed. *Armee gegen den Krieg. Wert und Wirkung der Bundeswehr.* Stuttgart-Degerloch: Seewald, 1966.

Rothe, Klaus. *Politik verstehen, Demokratie bejahen. Politik und politisches System in der Bundesrepublik Deutschland.* München: Olzig, 2000.

Rüdiger, Robert. *Bundesrepublik Deutschland. Politisches System und Globalisierung. Eine Einführung.* Münster and New York: Waxmann, 2001.

Ruh, Ulrich. *Religion und Kirche in der Bundesrepublik Deutschland.* München: Iudicium, 1990.

Schmidt, Manfred G. *Das politische System der Bundesrepublik Deutschland.* München: Beck, 2005.

Solberg, Richard W. *God and Caesar in East Germany: The Conflicts of Church and State in East Germany since 1945.* New York: Macmillan, 1961.

Thränhardt, Dietrich. *Die Bundesrepublik Deutschland. Verfassung und politisches System.* München: Goldmann, 1968.

Tucholsky, Kurt. "Über wirkungsvollen Pazifismus." *Gesammelte Werke.* Band 2: *1925–1928.* Ed. Mary Gerold-Tucholsky and Fritz J. Raddatz. Stuttgart and Hamburg: Deutscher Bücherbund, 1960, 907–912.

Weißhuhn, Gernot. *Bildung und Lebenslagen. Auswertung und Analysen für den zweiten Armuts- und Reichtumsbericht der Bundesregierung.* Berlin: Bundesminsterium für Bildung und Forschung, Referat Publ., Internetred., 2004, Stand Oktober 2004.

Wickel, Horst Peter. *Ratgeber Wehrdienst.* Reinbek bei Hamburg: Rowohlt, 2000.

Zapf, Wolfgang, ed. *Lebenslagen im Wandel. Sozialberichterstattung im Längsschnitt.* Projektgruppe "Das Sozioökonomische Panel" im Deutschen Institut für Wirtschaftsforschung, Berlin. Frankfurt and New York: Campus, 1995.

4

Social Aspects

Lifestyle and Fashion

"Driving or walking through town, you start looking for Germans—the Germans you've always seen in picture books," wrote Richard Lord in his guide for travelers. "You know, men in cute *Lederhose* shorts, ruffled shirts and those funny hats favoured by Robin Hood and his merry men or women decked out like grown-up Heidis in *dirndl* skirts, even more ruffled shirts and precariously pointed shoes. And of course, everyone with at least one fist wrapped around a huge beer stein" (Lord 2004, 10). He warned readers not to be too disappointed that in most German regions you won't find these picture-book Germans—only in certain regions at certain festivals. German fashion is, in fact, very much a European and Western fashion.

The 1950s

After the horror of war and the hard times of the 1940s, the 1950s seemed like paradise to most Germans. As Hermann Glaser noted in his cultural study of Germany, they were never so much at ease with their country as during that decade. They felt content and secure at home (Glaser 2002, 256). The real fears and anxieties of the war were replaced by intellectual angst.

As a former professor of political science at the university in Stuttgart, President Theodor Heuss embodied the new respectability. He was well educated and dignified, but at the same time affable and gracious. He was the grandfather everyone had always wished for. His speeches were eloquent and sincere. His smile was genuine and he had a twinkle in his eye. He was the exact opposite of a stereotypical military man. He was ideal, and he fit in perfectly with the more easygoing lifestyle of this era, which found its visual representation in round and undulating shapes. The angularity of the Nazi symbols had disappeared, and waving forms, particularly the *Nieren-Form* (kidney shape), were characteristic of the furniture, the cars, and even the architecture of the period.

Magazines such as *Schöner Wohnen* (Living More Beautifully), *Das Schönste* (The Most Beautiful), and *Monatsschrift für alle Freunde der schönen Künste* (Monthly Magazine for All Friends of the Arts) were expressions of the new attitude and desires (see 6: The Press). After chasing after the bare necessities of life during the 1940s, it was time to think again of the visually beautiful, of some luxuries. Clothing was no longer something purely practical but a measure of good taste, and it became a status symbol in the newly affluent time of the *Wirtschaftswunder* (economic miracle; see 10: Consumer Culture versus Green Awareness). The new German fashion capitals were Düsseldorf and Munich. Fortunately, the many synthetics (nylon, Formica, PVC, and others) that flooded the market made fabrics more affordable. The French designer Christian Dior designed the "New Look" for women, and in her *Geschichte der Mode des 20. Jahrhunderts* (History of Fashion in the 20th century) Gertrud Lehnert described the style with such adjectives as "feminine" and "voluptuous," emphasizing the natural form of the waist and bust, a direct contrast to the almost shapeless dresses of the war period. These elegant clothes required a lot of material, but the synthetics, some of which closely imitated silk and taffeta, made it possible to keep the prices down. Gloves were a part of the New Look, as were hats, either close-fitting or with a wide brim. Dressy shoes were cut to show much of the foot; especially chic was the "Flamenco shoe," which exposed polished toenails. Heels became higher and higher over the years as well as thinner and thinner, culminating in the stiletto heel of the 1960s.

Everyday clothes for women featured suits with fitted waists and rounded col-

Cover of the women's magazine *Brigitte* (November 18, 1958).

lars. Combinations of often pleated, mid-calf-length skirts and blouses or fine-gauge twin-sets were also considered stylish. Low-cut evening gowns were popular, but shoulders could be exposed only for evening dresses, not for daytime clothes. New were the sleeveless but high-cut blouses. During the turn of the decade (from the 1950s to the 1960s), full, often hooped petticoats became fashionable. Casual clothes still had to follow a few rules, although these were no longer as strict as before the war. *Fischerhosen* (fishermen's pants) were especially popular. They were cropped at mid-calf, were relatively tight, and had a sporty look to them. Bathing suits provided more coverage of the upper leg than today's suits and often included a short skirt. Although the bikini had celebrated its birthday in the 1940s, it did not begin its real success story until the 1960s, when Brigitte Bardot, the French actress, made not only bikinis, but also gingham—known in Germany as *Vichy Karos* (Vichy check)—popular.

Important for men's clothing were suitability and unfailing correctness, high quality, and durability. In the daytime, men wore single- or double-breasted suits. Synthetic shirts were more often chosen than cotton shirts because they were easier to wash and dry and needed little or no ironing and thus symbolized modern times. Ties were narrow and understated. Hats were a must, and shorts were only worn at home or on the beach during vacation.

During the 1950s, department store chains were established, and Kaufhof, Hertie, and C&A had large clothing departments. Another popular option for buying clothes was through mail-order companies, with Quelle, founded in 1927; Neckermann (reestablished in 1948); and Otto Versand (1949) leading the way. Fashion magazines gained in importance, the main ones being *Constanze* and *Brigitte*.

In houses and apartments, rubber plants added a touch of nature to the living room, and it seemed that almost everyone had at least one of them beside the kidney-shaped sidetable. Yet, being natural was not synonymous with being dirty. A home had to be *gemütlich* (cozy) but clean. At that time, cleanliness was still a German virtue (see 2: Stereotypes and Prejudices). One of the most successful household tools became the vacuum cleaner. (The German word *Staubsauger* literally means "dust sucker.") Soon these came in various versions and colors. Not only rugs needed to be vacuumed but sofas and curtains, too. Often, one was interrupted in these important

tasks by the ringing of the doorbell because a door-to-door salesman had arrived to offer a better, more efficient model. These vacuum salesmen came as frequently as insurance salesmen or those selling encyclopedias. In general, household machines were the "in" thing. Warm water heaters that were installed above kitchen sinks, coffee makers, mixers, refrigerators, Dictaphones, and sunray lamps all became as ubiquitous as microwave ovens are today.

The 1960s

In Germany as well as elsewhere, those born after the war had a different relationship to the elitist world of haute couture than their parents did (see also 4: Youth Culture and the World of Intellectuals). These young people preferred to create their own fashions that both suited their lifestyle and were affordable. Teenage fashion became a new and lucrative branch of the garment industry, and boutiques with their own individual styles became the stores of choice, particularly for young shoppers. The British fashion revival—with Twiggy as the top model and personifying the ideal young woman—had a strong influence on German fashion and the public at large.

For those who did still follow the Paris couture, Yves Saint Laurent was the most popular designer, but he, too, had been influenced by the changes in London and introduced pantsuits for women. Even the elaborate hairstyles of the early years of the decade, often upswept, sometimes supported by additional hairpieces and held firmly in place by hairspray, followed the trends from across the channel. Short straight hair that was easy to care for became popular as well as the Vidal Sassoon–inspired "five-point cut," both of which gave women a more boyish look.

The British influence was not only visible among women—men imitated the Beatles' haircut, which seemed scandalous at the time because it was considered both effeminate and slovenly by the older generation. Coats (often with a belt) and suits were fitted more closely. Trench coats were popular. For the very progressive, suit jackets had a zipper instead of buttons. Often, lapels disappeared and jackets had a stand-up collar in Nehru-style. Besides the traditional tweed, corduroy was used often for jackets and pants. Turtleneck sweaters replaced the shirt and tie. If ties were worn with shirts, they were much more colorful than in the 1950s. Sleeveless tank tops over shirts replaced thick sweaters. The waistline of the pants moved down to the hipbone. The width of the trouser legs underwent several variations—from very narrow to very wide in the 1970s. When narrow, the trousers were often stuffed into boots. Jeans, whose success story began in the 1950s, became the generic pants for leisure time in Germany as elsewhere.

The hippie generation developed its own look: bare feet or sandals without socks, long hair for both sexes with bands or ribbons, necklaces and bracelets, jeans, shirts in bright colors and flower designs. Women often wore long, loose, shapeless dresses that touched the ground and long, often hand-knitted scarves.

Similar trends were true in regard to furniture. In the 1950s and 1960s many young people discovered their preference for *Safaristühle* (directors' chairs) and expressed their anticonsumer attitude, independence, and individuality by searching through bulky refuse deposited on the sidewalks before the garbage trucks hauled it away. The young rescued their grandmothers' old chairs, tables, and sofas, while their parents regarded contemporary Scandinavian furniture as both elegant and fashionable. These mainstreamers liked the warmth of teakwood but also colorful, practical pieces in blue, green, yellow, and white. Shelf systems that could be easily rearranged—for example, shelves held together by cords or wire frames—became popular.

But, according to Dieter Bahr, the standard living room of the Schmidts, Schulzes, and Meyers was the same as it had been for years. He is quoted by Herlinde Koelbl and Manfred Sack in *Das deutsche Wohnzimmer* (The German Living Room) as follows: "Between the glass cabinet and the Bel-air curtains with their dotted pattern in pastel colors (which give the room a touch of the atmosphere of a turn of the century brothel through the petticoat like lace) hangs the battery-driven cuckoo-clock from which a bird of death croaks" (Koelbl and Sack 1980, 14). The cuckoo as a marker of time, a reminder of inevitable death, may not be a familiar metaphor for the non-German reader but it can shed new light on these almost kitschy symbols of Germanic folklore. Bahr continued: "Under a rustic-looking wall-lamp with the appearance of an old petroleum lamp with a lampshade made from fabric usually used for dirndls, and next to the collected works of Peter Alexander and beside the electric heating system with its fireplace-look stands the inherited sideboard in Viennese Baroque style. It contains the twelve apostles of tea sets, the best china and silver cutlery, which is only used on Sundays or for the visit by the boss" (ibid.). To regard the cups and saucers of a tea set as the twelve apostles is perhaps Bahr's way of showing the reverence with which this special china

1960s modern furniture in Germany. Chairs suspended from the ceiling, an idea by Danish designer Verner Panton (1926–1998) to aid housekeeping by avoiding furniture legs cluttering up the floor. (Keystone/Getty Images)

was treated. Primarily, the living room had a similar function to the clothes one wore: It represented one's image. The German adjective *repräsentativ* goes beyond the obvious cognate meaning to include distinguished, or even high-class.

The 1970s

In the 1970s, sweaters, dresses, scarves in all lengths, hats, and coats were often knitted or crocheted. Edwardian-style blouses and long skirts, like those women used to wear on farms, were also popular, continuing some of the hippie fashions from the 1960s. Everything had a folkloristic touch. Eclecticism continued into the 1980s, enriched by spiky hair and various other individualistic creations. Self-styling was the mantra, and it extended to the body as well as to clothing. Everyone was encouraged to create her- or himself. The role model was the athletic, slender, muscular, ambitious woman, successful both in her career and in her private life—*die Powerfrau* (the superwoman). She was also very aware of her charismatic sexuality. The focus on fitness led to an increasing predominance of fashions for aerobics and other sporting activities: leggings, skintight jerseys and leotards, hairbands, and tennis shoes, all in bright colors. These leisure outfits also influenced everyday clothes and could be worn in different combinations in settings beyond the fitness center.

The slow infiltration of women into the business world (see 4: Gender Equality) was accompanied by clothing patterned after men's tailoring, which downplayed femininity and emphasized masculine competence in business matters. Costumes with padded shoulders, skirts touching the knees, or pants were worn that were simple and elegant, and accompanied by comfortable shoes.

Fashion in West Germany was primarily international, influenced by France, Italy, Great Britain, and above all the United States. There were not many German fashion designers in the 1970s. One of the exceptions was Karl Lagerfeld, who remains active and influential. The eccentric Lagerfeld, who is always seen with a ponytail, reminiscent of the young Mozart, and a fan, wearing an elegant suit, has proved himself to be a multitalented genius. He was professor at the University of Applied Art in Vienna and is also a photographer and an excellent fashion illustrator. He collects fans and is an expert in European art history.

In the "Women's Fashion" magazine that accompanied the Sunday *New York Times* on February 20, 2005, an article was devoted to Karl Lagerfeld with the headline "The Rootin' Teuton." Readers were given a biography and learned that the designer is a little coy about his age—claiming in 2004 to be sixty-six though apparently a baptismal record has been found listing his year of birth as 1933, which would make him 5 years older—that he is "the last of a line of rich, cultivated Swedes and Germans," and that "his Germanness still ranks as his most profound and unexamined quality." He is briefly compared to Thomas Mann, whose books he began reading at the age of eight and with whom he shares links to Luebeck and Hamburg.

What comes across from the author's series of interviews with the designer is his complexity and intellectual depth. His continued popularity is explained in part by the fact that though he established his own lines and was the moving force behind Chanel, he did not have his own fashion house—something that was "out of fashion" in the 1970s but left Lagerfeld "free and unencumbered" and thus able to evolve and explore new directions. His latest venture is designing clothes for the low-priced Swedish chain Hennes and Mauritz.

The 1980s

In the 1980s, according to one author, "designer clothing came into its own for the middle class, in particular the younger generation." Besides Lagerfeld, "labels such as Escada, Hugo Boss, Jil Sander, Wolfgang Joop, [and] Helmut Lang (Austrian)" became household names and flourished (Briel 2002, 40).

In describing the teenage fashions of his generation, Florian Illies (2001) zeroed in on variations of jeans as the central article of apparel. Though he stated that he and his peers had difficulty determining which was the ultimate brand to wear, he said it was clear to all but the nerdiest that stonewashed jeans were "out." To be more precise, it was the cut known as *Karottenform* that would condemn its wearers to ridicule—those with pleats and fullness at the waistband, and narrowing down to the ankles in a shape vaguely resembling a carrot. He described the shopping choices of the early to mid-1980s almost as a wasteland, with no Hennes and Mauritz, no Gap, and little on television to educate the youth in dressing to be cool. Women's hair was still being teased and permed, and the new color of choice was henna red, but it was still only females who experimented with coloring their hair. Their male counterparts had to content themselves with growing one thin strand of hair long at the nape of the neck, often braided, to contrast with the rest of the shortly cropped head. Parents even subjected young children to this odd fashion, but, like other youthful follies, it too passed.

In those pre-Gap days, the most popular brand of clothing was Benetton, particularly for sweaters and sweatshirts. It was cool to wear them with the brand name in large letters across the chest. Even Fruit of the Loom gained notoriety in Germany in this fashion. Brand names retained their importance as the Golf teens matured into Yuppies and university students, but their taste in fashion also matured and they no longer felt compelled to advertise for the firms they patronized. Unlike their parents' generation, the male Golfers wanted their clothing to be ironed, particularly their shirts, and they were even willing to pay for the service. Of course, these shirts had to be from certain firms, too—Van-Laack or Uli-Knecht. Socks had to bear the name Hugo Boss. To go with this fastidious attention to clothing, the Golf Generation showed an interest in the *Sekundärtugenden* of etiquette (see 2: Stereotypes and Prejudices). Illies even conceded that his generation began to shop in the same stores as their parents just as long as they were cool and stylish. However, by now the brands of choice were somewhat pricier—Gucci, Dolce and Gabbana, Joop, and Kookai—and some of the young female law students liked to show off their Hermès scarves.

Individualism was also the keynote for interior decorating in the 1980s. To give specific examples of how the Golf Genera-

tion furnished their homes, Illies described two contrasting apartments and the individual rooms of each in great detail. One was inhabited by a male friend and was located in a new apartment complex on the outskirts of an unnamed city—not quite suburbs but not city center. The other was an apartment in an older building, probably from the turn of the twentieth century, in Berlin, and was inhabited by a woman friend. Illies even ventured the theory that, gender aside, there are two types of people, those who like to live in newer buildings and those who prefer older ones. The new apartment was recalled as being the first Illies knew of to have a video recorder. The dominant piece of furniture in the bedroom was a television, complemented by a large armoire/wardrobe and a large bed, from which the resident would watch car racing on TV and eat snacks. In fact, Illies claimed that this room looked very much like the hotel rooms one would encounter in midsized German cities such as Heilbronn or Wolfsburg: white and practical. The living room had a tile floor and black leather furniture—not quite chic, but a definite reaction against the decor of most of the houses in the village where the resident had grown up. Instead of his parents' rubber tree, he had a ficus, a small dining table and chairs, and a large lamp in the shape of an orange gummy bear. To match the leather sofa and armchairs, there was a black shelf for the TV, video recorder, and stereo as well as a few books (Illies 2001, 104–109).

Books displayed on shelves from IKEA were the common denominator in the contrasting apartments, but there the similarity ended. The older apartment was more eclectic in style, with an old secretary that the friend's parents had discarded that often displayed bouquets of dried flowers or small wreaths in addition to books. The kitchen epitomized *Gemütlichkeit* (see 2: Stereotypes and Prejudices). Pots and kitchen utensils hung on shelves; pasta, garlic, and other staples were on view in glass jars; and there was a row of herbs in pots on the windowsill. There was also a shelf for cookbooks, a poster, and a botanical picture. All that was said of the living room in this apartment was that it had an old armchair that was gemütlich. But lest one jump to the conclusion that the woman who lived here was a frumpy spinster type, Illies also explained that she made social phone calls to her friends while inline skating through the city in the evening. Gemütlichkeit can be hip too (ibid., 90, 109, 115, 118–119).

IKEA made inroads into the German furniture market primarily in the early 1970s—at least for the young generation, which needed to stay mobile. It is more than a chain of stores selling well-designed, reasonably priced furniture and home accessories to the Golf Generation. Illies sees it almost as a way of life. He described how, on Saturdays, young couples would flock to the store, forget where they'd parked in the huge lots surrounding the stores, argue about what they needed, and buy items such as 100 tea lights because they were a bargain, even though they rarely used them. While there, they would gain insight into what names were fashionable for children. Since most parents would leave their children at the store's play stations while shopping, it was not at all unusual to hear loudspeakers announce that young Tabea or Frederic (or whatever other name trendy young parents called their offspring) wanted to be picked up. This is still true in IKEA stores today. In addition, each piece of furniture sold at IKEA is given a Swedish name, with the result that to young Germans Billy is not a person, but a bookcase.

The 1990s

The fashion of the 1990s was the fashion of the children born to the '68ers generation. Like their parents, they wanted to express themselves and their beliefs, but these were quite different from the beliefs of their parents. They did not need to fight for the protection of the environment. Recycling, solar panels, and windmills belonged to their daily lives (see 10: Consumer Culture versus Green Awareness). The return to nature had been tainted. So-called "natural materials" are often chemically treated, and some of the new synthetics seemed to be more environmentally friendly. Even more than in the 1980s, fashion "quoted" former styles. Revivals chased each other. The time span between them became shorter and shorter. Dress regulations seemed to have disappeared, and only individual preferences counted—influenced, of course, by peers, film stars, and singers. Navel showing and piercing of ears, eyebrows, noses, lips, and many other body parts were seen on German streets as well as in the United Kingdom, other countries of the European Union, and the United States.

Independent of all these changing styles, which were primarily accepted by the younger people and varied from region to region, some timeless styles based on *Trachten* (folk costumes) are worn by many. In the north, men may sport a fishermen's or captain's peaked cap, as did the former chancellor Helmut Schmidt, and in the south, many men (Edmund Stoiber, the governor of Bavaria, for example) may

Former Chancellor Helmut Schmidt with his trademark fisherman's cap in 1976. (Owen Franken/Corbis)

wear jackets with a cut similar to a *Trachtenjacke* (traditionally styled jacket), and even *Lederhosen* (leather pants), as shorts as well as leather knee-breeches. Both men and women continue to wear *Lodenmäntel* (loden coats). In Bavaria, women can often be seen in various types of *Dirndl* or outfits patterned after them.

In most German regions, full folk costumes are only worn for festive occasions and cultural events or for the sake of tourists. It is debatable whether a marked difference exists between the regions in regard to standard clothing. Richard Lord remarked, "If these claims are true [that there are differences], then well-dressed folks in Düsseldorf and Munich wear more colorful and chic clothing, well-dressed

Hamburgers favor the classically conservative styles, while fashion trends in Frankfurt follow more staid and functional lines" (Lord 2004, 70).

The New Millennium

In the twenty-first century, German fashion seems to be changing again—and Lagerfeld may have to face successors and rivals. It has become both a global and a tribal world at the same time. Holger Briel, in his book on German culture, even sees jeans, which many regard as timeless, as going out of style. He remarked: "If in the 1960s, blue jeans were *the* trademark of all hip young people, nowadays it is almost only these youths of yonder who are still wearing them. Today, all over the globe, 'Goths' wear tight black, Skins Doc Martens, Technokids sport utility clothing, and other groups specific designer clothing. Germany is no exception" (Briel 2002, 40).

In November 2003, the *Frankfurter Allgemeine Zeitung* (November 14, 2003) published an article under the rubric *Mode* (fashion) with a sly, punning headline: "Die Nation zieht an" ("The Nation Is Moving Forward," but can also be understood as "The Nation Is Getting Dressed," although a reflexive "sich" is missing). The secondary header read, "Deutschland ist in Mode" ("Germany Is in Fashion" / "Germany Is into Fashion"). Alfons Kaiser pointed out in the article that whereas German celebrities did not usually show up at the Milan fashion shows in the past, three well-known actresses, Heike Makatsch, Christiana Paul, and Maria Lara, were in Milan to view collections by Gabrielle Strehle for Strenesse. He went on to note that the new editor-in-chief of German *Vogue*, Christiane Arp, had published a volume with the theme "Szene Deutschland: Unsere Stars aus Kunst, Film, Musik, Literatur" (Scene Germany: Our Stars from Art, Film, Music, Literature) with Claudia Schiffer on the cover wearing a Strenesse outfit.

All of a sudden, Germany was fashionable, but the trend appeared to have begun outside Germany. Arp reportedly got the idea when traveling and being asked what was happening in Berlin. In February 2004, the Swedish daily newspaper *Svenska Dagbladet* stated "it is now cool to be German." (*Nu är det coolt att vara tysk*). The article began with a list of long-held stereotypical views: that the German flag is associated with the sound of marching boots, that terms such as "patriotism," "nationalism," and "fatherland" were misused by the Nazis, that Israel is a land that cannot be criticized, and that Germany is populated by bores. But change is in the air, led in part by a young fashion designer named Eva Gronbach, who frequently uses the colors of the German flag—black, red, and gold—in her collections, along with the federal eagle (*Bundesadler;* see 2: Symbols and Memorials). While in the Swinging Sixties in London, the Union Jack could be seen on everything from T-shirts to coasters, and Ralph Lauren features the Stars and Stripes on expensive sweaters as well as household linens in the United States, but use of the black, red, and gold in German products has been rare. Adoption of national symbols was previously left to unsavory fringe groups such as the skinheads.

In her early thirties (in 2004), the Cologne native Eva Gronbach belongs squarely to Illies's Golf Generation, but she did not stay in the land of the Volkswagen to develop her talents. She spent six years studying in London, Brussels, and Paris, and while working for John Galliano and

Design from Eva Gronbach's 2003 collection, *mutter erde vater land.* (Levon Melikiany)

Yohji Yamamoto observed how they referred to their cultures in their collections. That led her to speculate on her own connections to her native country, and in an interview with Anne Petersen of *Brigitte* published in February 2004, she came up with such wide-ranging images as the Rhineland, Joseph Beuys (see 9: Visual Arts), the fall of the Berlin Wall (see 1: From Two to One), Heinrich Böll's *Die verlorene Ehre der Katharina Blum* (The Lost Honor of Katharina Blum; see 7: Film), and, "naturally," the black-red-gold flag (see 2: Symbols and Memorials).

Although many Germans find these colors ugly and associate them with football stadiums, *Schrebergärten* (see 5: Activities and Clubs), and *Kleinbürgerlichkeit* (the petty middle class), Gronbach is hoping to see a change in such attitudes. For her the colors are clear and beautiful, and she would like it to be taken for granted that club members would wear T-shirts with the colors of Germany. Indeed, her 2001 collection bore the title *Déclaration d'amour à L'Allemagne* (Declaration of Love for Germany)—but the title was still in French and was the product of her final exam at the Institut Français de la Mode (French Fashion Institute). She earned high honors for the collection and then decided to move back to her hometown and country. The 2003 collection has a German title: *mutter erde vater land* (mother earth father land), though the German convention of capitalizing the nouns is absent. And it is on Gronbach's Web site—www.evagronbach.com—that one can find a collection of articles about this new positive attitude toward Germany and some of its symbols, including, of course, the rationale behind her collections and her plans to redesign the uniforms of the German police force.

In the *Brigitte* interview Gronbach noted that her generation is much more relaxed about issues of nationalism and patriotism than their parents, but that they are concerned about being cool ("*Der Jugend geht es gar nicht um Patriotismus, sondern eben einfach nur um Coolness*") (Brigitte online, February 16, 2004). When pressed to talk about political overtones in her work, Gronbach insisted that her use of the German flag and other symbols has nothing to do with national pride, adding that many of her customers are non-Germans. However, she did point out that the German avant-garde is gaining ground, and that DJs in Paris now play electronic music from her hometown of Cologne (see 8: Music). She would also like the current connection between the symbols she uses and the skinheads to be blurred, or better, eliminated. Her goal is to give existing symbols a new

meaning, a form of modern punk, as she says, and fashion is a sufficiently light-hearted and transient field in which to do this.

Youth Culture and the World of Intellectuals

The sound of the chains of tanks grinding on cobblestones is the unforgettable music that was imprinted on the memories of the generation born toward the end of World War II and growing up during the time of the newly emerging Germanys. "Chewing gum"—pronounced in German fashion *tsheving goom*—was the first American word learned by many as they stood alongside the streets while U.S. military convoys passed by. Michael Rutschky, born in 1943, described the mythical image of the American soldier: "the black GI in immaculately ironed uniform, sitting beaming on his tank coming down the street and distributing chewing gum and Hershey bars to the youngsters who run along in astonishment" (Rutschky 2004, 37). The diary entry of April 25, 1945, by the cartoonist Marie Marcks describes the arrival of the U.S. troops. Despite their athletic appearance, she remembered how their pants stretched across their ample buttocks. The children begged for candy, shouting out the mispronounced American words. The U.S. soldiers, sitting on top of their vehicles, smiled, laughed, and showered the young bystanders with goodies such as they had never before experienced. Marie Marcks's attitude toward the Americans' generosity was somewhat ambivalent, and she described the women who picked up the chocolate thrown down from the tanks as "undignified" (*würdelos*) (Marcks 1984,

77). Only years later, when Carnival became popular again (see 5: Holidays and Local Festivals), would the candy thrown by the *Karnevalsjecken* (members of Carnival clubs) into the crowd remind the former children (now parents) of these early days of childhood.

In spite of all the shortages, their *Schultüten* were filled to the brim when the first day of school arrived. Little did the children know that this first day was not a typical day at all, but a huge deception. School was not much fun and instead a lot of drilling. Punishments lurked around every corner. It could be very unpleasant, for example, to stand in a corner with one's arms extended while balancing a ruler on one's hands. After a short time, the arms would get tired, the ruler would fall to the ground, and this would result in a slap on the fingers or a rubbing of ears. The teachers often became the enemy. The result was an ongoing warfare between children playing tricks and teachers administering corporal punishment of one kind or another.

In some schools in the American occupied zones in the 1950s, schoolchildren were forced to watch many shocking movies with images of thousands of dead bodies piled up into huge heaps and starving concentration camp inmates. Early on, the young children were *entnazifiziert* (de-Nazified), confronted with unbelievable inhumane atrocities that they did not understand, and no one explained them. The visual images were accompanied by silence on the part of the teachers, who, in one way or another, were once involved in these actions themselves—even if it had been only by their passivity and silence (see 1: Coming to Terms with the Past). The result was a buildup of guilt, a mistrust of authority, and a sense of confusion and helplessness. Questions awaited answers that never came. Young people were surrounded by a wall of silence only sparsely punctuated by brief accounts of difficult past times. The chance to begin a process of education in the spirit of a multicultural society, to teach the customs and beliefs of Judaism and with it the value of and respect for other cultures, was missed.

The main school break between tedious classes, announced by the school bell, brought both emotional relief and food. Long lines were formed, everyone took his or her small lunch pot and waited for the dollop of porridge, the Quaker *Schulspeise* (school meal). The pictures one could have taken of these often gaunt and hungry German children would have been quite different from the ones Marie Marcks and her sister drew of the children who had accompanied the U.S. troops. Marcks and her sister used their artistic talents to earn money, producing pictures of castles as well as portraits of the children. In the book's illustrations, the children appear obese, the boys with crewcuts, and the caption describes them as "jelly fish children" (*Quallenkinder*) to emphasize the softness and excess flesh (Marcks 1984, 82). Even today, the German image of Americans is that they are frequently overweight.

After-school hours were filled with homework and innocent street-gang activities such as playing soccer in the streets, or chasing each other as robbers and police through the town, fields, and forests. In many families, the grandparents (primarily the grandmothers) were in charge of family life, as the fathers had been killed in the war (and often the grandfathers had been victims of World War I), were sick, or had not yet returned from prisoner-of-war camps. Mothers tried to earn a living to support the family by working in factories and offices.

Over the years, youth clubs became important, and gymnastics, soccer, and handball headed the list. Churches began to organize youth evenings, and the various boy scout organizations (Deutsche Pfadfinder [secular], Christliche Pfadfinder [the Protestant version], St. Georgs Pfadfinder [the Catholic version]) became active. The young boys of this postwar generation did not understand why so many adults were upset when they wanted to combine their bike tours with camping out in tents, flying flags, and marching around with drums. Only much later, when they saw pictures of the Hitlerjugend (HJ), Deutsches Jungvolk, and Bund deutscher Mädel (Hitler Youth, German Youth, and Association of German Girls), did they recognize the fateful connections. They also realized how the *Wandervögel* (hiking clubs, literally "migrating birds") of the early twentieth century had been used as a basis for organizations that would win over and brainwash the youth.

This ambivalent attitude toward the past pervaded the immediate postwar generation more and more as time went on. According to Holger Briel, "After the Second World War, largely due to the American influence, youths publicly began to take on a strong separate identity from their parent generation. Psychologists and sociologists have attempted to explain this fact with German post-war youths growing up without (often literally) a strong father generation" (Briel 2002, 152). They were skeptical and independent. They knew that they had to take care of themselves. The more they became aware of their surroundings, the more they mistrusted all types of ideologies or systems that tried to explain the chaos of the world. They mistrusted also

the order, the cleanliness around them. Otto Preminger's *Bonjour Tristesse* (1958) (see 7: Film), based on Françoise Sagan's novel, became a hit among young girls who were rebelling against pedantic rules and against being well-bred. They wanted to be wild cats, not domesticated ones. The boys were fascinated by American culture and its promise of adventure.

Starting with the chewing gum, the American influence increased steadily, although there was only very limited contact even in U.S.-occupied German territories between the German civilian population and U.S. soldiers. One center was the Rhine-Main area around Frankfurt, where, at times, as many as 200,000 troops were stationed. The village of Ramstein became the largest U.S. air base, with thousands of U.S. troops passing through. The Americans outnumbered the Germans, but there was little contact between them. The U.S. soldiers lived in their U.S. ghetto with their PXs, paying in dollars, and the Germans lived their lives independently, paying in marks. The military police had jurisdiction over the Americans, the state police over the Germans. It was only in the occasional pub that Germans were to be found alongside Americans, who rarely spoke much German. Only seldom was a German family able to invite an American guest to their home, which—when it did happen—was a festive occasion.

But the emerging communication age swamped Germany with American music and an awareness of American fashion and films (see 4: Lifestyle and Fashion; 7: Film; 8: Music). Even if the American Forces Network (AFN) had not existed, German youths could not have escaped the new American cultural trends. But it did exist, and it was a major part of the youth culture. Michael Rutschky described how bored he was listening to German radio stations. When he found AFN, that was it.

From then on, AFN did not stop playing. It was the background sound for homework in elementary and high school, it provided the background music to studies as a university student and the first professional years. Not before the late seventies was it turned off, but then radio in general disappeared from my room. In postwar childhood and postwar youth, AFN embodied a transcendence. One did not understand what the friendly voice was saying, comprehension developed slowly—the same way the school beginner dives into the world of letters—while English, which one learned as a first foreign language in high school (*Gymnasium*), became available. In this familiar, miserable, depressing world of the postwar years, the existence of another world could be felt. That this world could only be listened to but not seen only contributed to its utopian force. (Other people, remarks the Anti-American, call this cultural imperialism.) (Rutschky 2004, 16)

For this generation (as for the ones before it), America was a utopia, the dream, a perfect world. The result was imitation— from jeans to rock 'n' roll. Everyone listened to and sang "Rock around the Clock" on their 78-revolution record players. The term "teenager" was adopted and was discovered as a great marketing strategy for a new consumer group. "In any case, at that time the main offensive against the pocket books of young people began—between 1957 and 1960, the young people of the FRG spent annually about 200 million marks on records; ten years later the amount was already 475 million" (Kemper et al. 1999, 16). Jack Kerouac's *On the*

Road was a hit, James Dean's hairstyle and mannerisms were imitated. A small riot occurred when Bill Haley was on a concert tour in Berlin in 1958. The older generation was appalled. They feared that their children's emotions, desires, and drives would get out of control as they cheered, yelled, and behaved in a manner now considered normal at a rock concert. They regarded their children's reactions to the music as a loss of self-discipline and accused them of destroying what they had laboriously built up again in the postwar years. The young were derisively called *Halbstarke* (young hooligans, literally "half strong"), and they, in turn, regarded their parents as inhibited and mocked them. Had not their parents' generation caused destruction, war, and the Holocaust, and now they tried to exercise their authority and emphasize their "morality" to suppress an expression of freedom and vitality?

The youth protest of the 1960s in West Germany was both a revolt against the parents' generation and part of a worldwide protest movement against rigid social and political structures, against the establishment and its exploitation of underdeveloped countries, and against the Vietnam War. On the domestic level, young people criticized the materialistic attitude of their parents, the family concerns that primarily centered around material well-being and financial security. The parents' attitude was poignantly expressed in the political slogan of the CDU, which tried to maintain the status quo: "No experiments!" Spearheaded by the Sozialistischer Deutscher Studentenbund (League of German Socialist Students, SDS), the younger generation also addressed concrete issues such as education, primarily higher education. The best-known slogan was "*Unter den Ta-*

laren, der Muff von tausend Jahren" (Beneath the academic gowns is the stuffiness of a thousand years). From the world beyond Germany, Che Guevara became the symbol for a new kind of liberation, followed by Ho Chi Minh and Mao Tse-tung. It was a time of optimism marked by faith in the possibility of changing society and the globe. The Beatles climbed the charts following their first performance in Hamburg in 1962. Bob Dylan, Joan Baez, and Pete Seeger convinced young people that songs and art can make a difference. "Make love not war," was the slogan. The contraceptive pill helped to revolutionize sexual behavior and to break taboos. As Hermann Glaser remarked, "'Flower power' (Allen Ginsberg) joined together with pacifism and bestowed it with an exulted spirituality" (Glaser 2004, 240).

Summarizing the tone of this generation, Glaser continued:

The mood of this generation was one of desperate cheerfulness, a dogged idleness, of happy nihilism; their attitude was marked by indifference, carelessness, but also sudden attacks of vitality and helpfulness; they explored the sensuality of physical relationships, tenderness outside of conventionality; the preference for the vegetative and androgynous was balanced on the other hand by psychedelic states of intoxication—and both were cleverly marketed by the entertainment industry (for instance in the film "Blow up"). Nudity, both in the concrete and the metaphorical sense (in the latter case in the form of psychic exposure), proved to be the favored vehicle for emancipation; norms, taboos and repression (including repressive tolerance, i.e., a tolerance which was only superficially tolerant) were despised; pornography and obscenity were 'in.' (ibid., 241)

In the GDR, the "Regulation on Programs of Entertainment and Dance Music" of January 1958 had attempted to protect socialist cultural life from "manifestations of decadence" (see also 8: Music). Therefore, at all public events at least 60 percent of the works were to be by socialist composers. *Beat* (a term that included everything coming from the West) was, naturally, suspicious. It was seen by the older generation (in the GDR as well as in the West) "as atavistic, immoral, and potentially criminal" (Goodboy et al. 1995, 175). When enthusiasm for the Beatles and the Rolling Stones swept across the countryside, new restrictions were instituted. Axel Goodboy wrote that "in a historic misjudgement, Ulbricht fulminated at the Eleventh Plenum: 'Are we really dependent on the monotonous Western pop songs and dances? . . . The unending monotony of their 'yeah, yeah, yeah' is both stupefying and ridiculous'" (ibid.). Instead, young bands were encouraged to revive the *Singebewegung* (song movement) of the 1950s, which had promoted antifascist songs and folklore. In so doing, the party actually helped to turn the GDR into the birthplace of *Deutschrock* in the late 1960s (see 8: Music).

The feeling of freedom and empowerment the youth felt in West Germany also had to do with the increasing outspokenness of the intellectuals who had been part of the inner emigration or had actually lived in exile during the fascist era. Now they voiced their concerns on many issues, ranging from rearmament in the 1950s to unification in 1990 (see 3: The German Army; 1: From Two to One). Intellectual theories and systems became part of public discourse.

One of the first cultural theorists who influenced East and West Germany was the

Hungarian Georg Lukács. His programmatic essays—such as "Fortschritt und Reaktion in der deutschen Literatur" (Progress and Reaction in German Literature, 1945)—were welcomed in East Germany right after the war as a theoretical basis for creating a new antifascist culture. His argumentation for a new realism going back to the "progressive" literature of the eighteenth and nineteenth centuries seemed convincing to many. Yet, he encountered opposition early on by writers such as Bertolt Brecht who argued for the techniques of modernism. Often, Lukács saw himself wedged between two views: One side accused him of neglecting socialist realism, the other accused him of being too narrow-minded and not open to innovative ideas. The debate was not limited to literary and philosophical circles but had a political dimension. When his involvement in the failed 1956 Hungarian uprising became known, his name was put on the index in East Germany. Therefore, his later works—for example, *Wider den mißverstandenen Realismus* (literally, Contrary to the Misunderstood Realism; the English translation was entitled *Realism in Our Time: Literature and the Class Struggle*)—were only discussed in the West.

Besides philosophical, literary, and cultural theorists, there were writers who established themselves early on as the "conscience of the nation," in particular those in the Gruppe 47 (see 6: Popular and Belletristic Literature). Yet, though their criticism of the crass materialism of the 1950s' economic miracle was applauded, their apparent silence on other issues, including the Holocaust, was criticized. Individual writers, such as Hans Magnus Enzensberger, Günter Grass, Martin Walser, and

Peter Handke, continued to exert political influence and stimulate discussion; the group itself, however, dispersed after 1968 when the social and political atmosphere had changed and consensus was less likely.

Somewhat more enduring was the influence of the Frankfurt School, also known as Critical Theory, representing the most thorough critique of modernism and analysis of living conditions in the era of late capitalism. Their central focus was—as a title of a book by Max Horkheimer, playing on Immanuel Kant's "Critique of Pure Reason," stated, *"Kritik der instrumentellen Vernunft"* (Critique of Instrumental Reason), that is, criticism of goal-oriented rationality as it is manifested in modern society. Interdisciplinary in nature, Critical Theory addressed issues in social sciences, philosophy, psychology, aesthetics, music, and natural sciences. In 1950, Horkheimer and Theodor Adorno had returned from their exile in the United States and reestablished the Institute for Social Research (Institut für Sozialforschung) at Frankfurt University. Along with the Freie Universität (Free University, FU) in Berlin, it became the hotbed of student revolt in the 1960s.

In Berlin, the iconoclastic spirit was especially alive and well. The most notorious manifestation was Kommune I, an apartment sharing community based on free love, with its happenings intended to ridicule and provoke the authorities and society. But then there were also academic events at FU, such as the "Vietnam Semester" (1965), filled with inspiring lectures, protests, and discussion groups. In Frankfurt, the protest movement was fired up by Herbert Marcuse, who had been invited by the SDS in 1966 to a Vietnam congress. And he did what the students expected: He declared the war in Vietnam to be a typical example of Western imperialism. Although associated with the Frankfurt School, Marcuse embraced student activism much more than Adorno and Horkheimer did. Students could have used the work of the latter as intellectual justifications for their actions only by negating the complexity of Critical Theory and ignoring its pessimistic outlook, which had been expressed as early as 1947 in the *Dialektik der Aufklärung* (Dialectic of Enlightenment).

In the same year as the Vietnam congress, 1966, the already tense political situation worsened when it became necessary to form a *Große Koalition* (literally, "grand coalition," that is, a coalition that included both major parties). The CDU/CSU and SPD were ruling jointly, and there was no effective opposition in parliament. The protest movement saw itself called upon to take on this role as extra-parliamentary opposition (*außerparlamentarische Opposition*, APO). Street demonstrations were one of the major means of agitation and with it came the danger of violence. Peaceful demonstrations attracted hooligans, and the government, through its police force, displayed its intolerant and authoritarian attitude, indiscriminately beating demonstrators and bystanders. In fascist fashion, police marched in riot gear through the streets, and many helpless victims fled into doorways with bleeding heads, arms, and shoulders. A hatred of authority and police was instilled in many members of this generation and did much long-term political and psychological damage. Police brutality was exposed, particularly in 1967 with the death of Benno Ohnesorg (whose name ironically means "without sorrow"), a young theology student who was shot dead by a policeman when demonstrating in Berlin against the terror regime of the Shah of Iran.

A series of events divided German society even more. In 1968, the charismatic young orator Rudi Dutschke was attacked by a young unskilled worker, though many students accused the right-wing newspapers of being behind the attack. Others raised accusations on both sides of the political divide, citing the violent actions of the Rote Armee Fraktion (Red Army Faction, RAF) that terrorized Germany for many years (primarily in the 1970s, see 4: From A to Z, "RAF") and the halt in recruitment of teachers who had been sympathizers with the Communists in their student days. All were symptomatic of a Germany that had not really overcome its past. It was a fossilized society that contained elements that tried to break open the hardened layer with the same kind of authoritarian attitude that had characterized the fossilization. Revolutionaries as well as the government lacked both the skill and the desire to solve conflicts. It was also a society that created a new division between the people and the intellectuals. While talking about the rights of the common people and speaking in the name of the common people, the revolutionaries were actually more interested in an intellectual display of abstract theories and the presentation of their egos than in solving the problems at hand.

Adorno's lectures and seminars continued to be well attended because his "negative dialectics" seemed to contain the analytical explanations students sought. But in the end, it was Georg Lukács attacking Adorno's radical thought as a bourgeois gesture that won the day. Shortly before his death, Adorno had to face the experience of his own students turning against him. Female students danced around him, baring and shaking their breasts in front of his face, while leaflets were handed out stating "Adorno as an institution is dead." Sabine Demm described the situation:

"I will give you five minutes. Decide if you want the lecture to take place or not." The interruption of his lecture "Introduction to Dialectic Thinking" on April 22, 1969, is nothing new for Professor Theodor W. Adorno—and he is not the only professor who experiences these. Just when Adorno has finished his sentence, three female students with long hair and dressed in leather jackets step up to him. They surround him, try to kiss him and unbutton their jackets: there is nothing beneath their jackets but their breasts. That's more than a declaration of war to the more than 65-year-old professor. The initiators want to humiliate their teacher. Nothing that outrageous has ever happened to Adorno. Shocked, the philosopher of sociology grabs his briefcase, holds it in a protective way in front of his face and leaves the lecture room running. Behind him, he hears the howling and laughter of some of the students. (Demm 2001)

Adorno's demise was symbolic of the end of the actual student revolt. On the one hand, radicals continued to meet in small action groups that led to homegrown terrorism (RAF); on the other, the more moderate students decided that street action was not effective. The so-called "march through the institutions," a systematic infiltration and revamping of the system from the inside, began for the revolutionaries of the 1960s. Joschka Fischer, former secretary of state, and Daniel Cohn-Bendit, now a representative in the European Parliament for the Green Party, were both active

in the student movement. The SDS, of which the former Chancellor Gerhard Schröder was a member, dissolved, and some members joined the Jusos (Young Socialists). The Frankfurt School was carried on by Jürgen Habermas, Adorno's former assistant.

The 1970s brought terror and punks and the birth of the Golf Generation. The punks made the streets more colorful with their spiky red and green hairdos sticking up high in the air. "Groovies," in black, were less visible. They were the symbols of lost hopes, of a new withdrawal from politics by the new generation, while their elders began forming citizens' initiatives that became the hallmark of the outgoing 1970s and 1980s. The most successful movement was the Green Party (see 10: Consumer Culture versus Green Awareness). Ecology was the new catchword, *Waldsterben* (the dying forest) was in the headlines, and activism reemerged in a different form. But it was not the younger generation that took the lead. Universities were calm. Here, disappointment, disillusionment with reform, and an anti-utopian mood were widespread. The declining material wealth awakened a fear for the future, and observers could note an interesting generational swing. The older people were more liberal than the younger ones, in whose circles conservatism had taken root. The new intellectual stimuli did not lend themselves to a new revolution. Niklas Luhmann's works *Soziale Systeme* (Social Systems, 1984) and *Ökologische Kommunikation* (Ecological Communication, 1986) did almost the opposite by viewing the various functional areas of society (law, politics, economics, science, and art) as self-referential or "autopoieic" systems. That is, they have their own internal dynamics that can-

Collage of punks and groovies in Germany.

not be causally influenced, as Henk de Berg stated (Sandford 1999, 390). Peter Sloterdijk, in another play on Kant, argued in his *Kritik der zynischen Vernunft* (Critique of Cynical Reason, 1983) that the philosóphos—the lover of wisdom—was not the one to steer society but only to analyze failures. And with his later interpretation of humanism as Western civilization's biggest disappointment, he returned to a pessimism already expressed in Adorno and Horkheimer's *Dialektik der Aufklärung*.

After the dismal 1980s came the 1990s, complete with love parades (see 8: Music). As one participant stated: "My generation . . . everything runs somehow supereasy; all this revolution shit, that was being taken care of by the people before us. Weekends are just there to have fun" (Kemper et al. 1999, 11). Times had shifted from a protest culture to a fun culture, or, in the words of Peter Kemper: *"von der Protest- zur Ausdrucksgeneration"* (from the protest generation to the generation of self-expression) (ibid.). It sounded like a typical postmodern cliché. Sometimes the past

was quoted; at other times, there were references to a fictional past. Irony and self-irony played an important part. Music, besides fashion, was the main focus of interest and venue for self-expression without creating its own subculture. Dieter Baacke continued his overview, quoted by Kemper, with an observation that summarizes well the opinion of many:

> I belong to the generation of '68. At that time, we demanded: "We want to discuss all issues!" and we wrote on our banners the slogans of social change, that was the way of the sixties, and that changed radically in the seventies when the Punk movement began. That was when no one believed any more that you can bring about social change through music and a youth movement. And the slogan "No one asks, politicians respond!" expressed that attitude very succinctly. Today, one no longer expects that discussions can solve problems any more. And that leads to a second way, via autonomy, independence, originality, that is, gestures of expression, to catch a glimpse of one's real self and to present it to the outside world. Perhaps one can survive the social life in that way and make new cultural patterns bearable, perhaps even attractive. (Kemper et al. 1999, 19)

And what does the youngest generation of Germans, those born in the 1980s and beginning to enter the job market or university life in 2005/2006, think as they reach the age of revolt? This generation is technically sophisticated, but it is naïve and insecure in many other ways. They all have cell phones and probably have had them for years. (Most children of twelve or thirteen have one in Germany.) From the age of sixteen on, they can go to most discos on their own, though some are only open to those aged eighteen and above. Their drug of choice is alcohol, and, contrary to the image held by some in the United States that binge drinking is unknown in Europe because of more liberal laws regarding the consumption of alcohol, young Germans, especially those living in the country, regularly get drunk. Ecstasy is available at certain discos, and marijuana/cannabis is the basis for the formation of cliques in the high schools (*Gymnasien*), though, in general, illegal drug use is not as widespread as some fear. Some 50–70 percent of young people in their early teens smoke, but among university students the percentage has dropped to 30–50 percent. The difference in expected levels of maturity and responsibility between high school and university is, however, not as great as it once was. More and more, universities seem to resemble a continuation of high school (see 3: The Educational System).

As to the aspirations and fears of these young people, interviews published in magazines indicate that they have only one goal: to be the best, to survive the fierce competition they believe is everywhere. Their highest values are freedom, free time, and self-realization (Hurrelmann 2005, 47). It seems that they would like to have the chance to take it easy and sort out their lives before it actually begins, but sadly, this option is not available. They find themselves confronted with expectations of early career decisions, but the fear of unemployment after they have finished their education is a real and present one. Many become discouraged, feel cheated, and lapse into total resignation and inertia. This negative attitude can also lead to a certain conservative tendency, particularly among young women, and particularly away from the big cities. Because the job market is so tight, some focus on establishing a family and dropping out of the career rat race entirely. Those who pursue an academic career are not much better off—their chances of a professorship are slim, and many are forced to seek employment outside of Germany.

Gender Equality

Without the women—the wives, widows, mothers, and daughters of the soldiers—reconstruction of Germany after World War II would have been an impossibility. Therefore, the term *Trümmerfrauen* (rubble women) is synonymous with sacrifice and the determination to rebuild German society. These women worked without pay, clearing the rubble and setting the tone for the decade to come. Without their selflessness, the economic miracle would have never happened in the same impressive way. A job needed to be done, and it was done without regard for personal gain (see 10: Consumer Culture versus Green Awareness).

However, in spite of the dependence on women in West Germany, protests and demonstrations were necessary for lawmakers to enforce the statements found in the Basic Law in Article 3, Paragraph 2: "Men and women have equal rights. The state promotes the actual implementation of equal rights of women and men and works toward the elimination of existing disadvantages." These sentences were recommendations that paved the way for concrete legal implementations. These finally came about in an Equal Rights Law in the civil code in 1957 (see 3: The Legal System). It stipulated that a husband could no longer prevent his wife from taking a job or end her employment contract for her. Yet, as late as 1972, a married woman could only accept a job legally if it did not interfere with her main task in life—taking care of the family. Moreover, a man who opts to share family responsibilities with his wife and takes a leave from work to take care of the household and children—which is a legal possibility (see 4: From A to Z, "*Erziehungsurlaub*")—is frequently regarded as a sissy and may have a hard time continuing his career at the same level at a later time.

Everyone seems to be in favor of gender equality until it comes to questions of implementation. Most women in Germany are paid less than men in many professions, and it is symptomatic that even in 2005, about 47.5 percent of German university students were female, but of their professors, only 8.6 percent were women (including assistant positions the percentage was slightly higher, 12.8). Fortunately, in politics the situation is more positive, although still far from equal. Women representatives in the Bundestag in 1949 were a real minority, with 6.8 percent. In 2002, they reached 32.8 percent. In the professional world, the statistics are mixed. Of course, overall the workforce is almost equally divided: 45 percent of all workers were women in 2004. But a closer look reveals that the better the position, the more likely it is to be occupied by a man. The percentage of prosecutors of higher regional courts that are women, for instance, was about 19 percent, whereas the offices of secretaries were almost exclusively filled by women (78 percent). In regard to medical doctors and dentists, the percentage of women was relatively high in 2004, 38 and 36 percent, respectively. Assistants, however, were almost exclusively female (99 percent).

Those who care for the elderly were also almost all women (almost 87 percent). And women have always dominated the cash registers of supermarkets, as anyone who goes shopping in Germany knows. Jobs that do not require much skill or personal initiative or offer much intellectual challenge are usually filled by women. And these positions are the first to go in a recession.

In 1980, as was widely reported, the politician Eva Rühmkorf remarked that if women wait for men to change their minds so that the situation is improved for women, it may take another hundred years. And she added that only laws and penalties can bring about change. But she overlooked the fact that there should also be laws to make it possible for men to stay at home. The slogan of the women of the 1980s, "*Kinder, Küche, Heim, und Herd sind kein ganzes Leben wert*" (Children, kitchen, home, and stove do not make up a full life), was correct but could easily be misinterpreted. It glamorized the professional lives that the men led instead of laying the emphasis on real gender equality in all aspects of life. As a result, women entered the workforce—in 2004, about 66 percent were employed (making up 45 percent of the workforce, as mentioned above)—but few men dared to leave it. The abstract idea of progress—that is, financial success—was the driving principle, not a world of personal partnerships. It was the business world, the professional side of life, that dictated daily routines and societal structures. Therefore, instead of a different type of society evolving that valued personal relationships, women adjusted to what had formerly been exclusively a man's world. The family, the smaller unit, was sacrificed to the bigger one in the same way that small family stores disappeared because of the efficiency-based larger commercial units.

Only in very specific instances, such as the abortion issue, have women united. "*Mein Bauch gehört mir!*" (My belly belongs to me) was the slogan of many demonstrations. Feminine awareness was raised, especially in regard to sexual relationships and family, and the late 1960s brought about a major change. There was little room for the old orthodox and patriarchal idea of a society. In 1971, 92 out of 100 women under the age of thirty stated that they would share an apartment with a man without being married. Even in 1967, it had been just 24 out of 100 (Craig 1982, 166–167).

But the personal aspect of equality did not necessarily correspond to a professional one. Even in leftist organizations, many women (with the exception of a few superstars) often found themselves regarded as much less than intellectual partners. They were allowed to print flyers and make coffee, being pushed into the same assistant, secretarial role as their conservative counterparts. In 1977, Alice Schwarzer founded the feminist magazine *Emma* (see 6: The Press). She was correct in stating that women only got what men left for them, the crumbs falling from the table. But the struggle of the 1970s, influenced by American feminism, had its own strange slant, creating a subculture that centered around emancipation in opposition to the male instead of developing concepts of a gender-inclusive change of society. There were *Frauenkneipen, Frauenbands, Frauenchöre, Frauencafés, Frauentheater,* and *Frauenhäuser* (bars, bands, choirs, cafés, theaters, and houses just for women). All

were organized without men, excluding them. Man became the pariah. Certainly, the movement was important, because it removed the taboos from female sexuality and inspired more women to become artists and writers. The market reacted with the establishment of special sections in bookstores for women. There was a movement in state organizations and parliaments and also in larger firms to appoint *Frauenbeauftragte* (female representatives). There were even quotas established for the number of women who should hold high-ranking positions in the public and private sectors. The Green Party became primarily a party for women (see 10: Consumer Culture versus Green Awareness). But the movement was also to some extent a replay of the 1960s when the intellectual academics planned a revolution and only succeeded in alienating the working class through their snobbish attitudes and intellectual elitism. The result was a backlash in both cases. A more conservative and patriarchal stance within society at large returned, though on university campuses gender studies became established as a discipline.

In East Germany, in contrast, the equal role of women (although imperfect) was part of the socialist ideology, part of daily life. The GDR constitution of 1968 established not only gender equality in all areas of society but promoted it actively. The success of women in qualified professions was seen as a major goal of society, although, at the same time, the state burdened women with sole responsibility for household and children. Already in 1974, women constituted a third of the members of parliament, about 20 percent of the mayors, about 25 percent of all leading positions in industry, a third of the chairs of collectives, about 20 percent of the directors of schools, and about a third of the judges. In 1989, 78 percent of all women of working age were employed—in contrast to only 55 percent in West Germany. Although women in the GDR made up half the workforce, the percentage in West Germany was at that time below the 40 percent mark.

It was also claimed in the GDR that salaries were equal in reality and not only on paper. The difference in approach was felt after unification when the different understandings of feminism became obvious. Indeed, before unification, those who subscribed to a Western understanding of the movement were given the negative label *Emanzen*, derived from the German cognate of emancipation. After unification, many East German women experienced firsthand the loss of the practical social advantages they had had under the GDR system. There was massive loss of employment, reduction of child-care facilities, and little recognition of their former achievements. Sterilization rates increased as women sought new and better employment opportunities.

In Switzerland, the very model of democracy, it was not until 1971 that men, who up to that point had alone been eligible to vote, decided to grant women an active right to vote in federal elections. In some cantons this was not actually put into practice until 1990. Still, in 1999 a woman was elected president of the federation.

It is not only secularization, individualism, and the financial burdens of family life that threaten the German family—the reasons that are usually cited for high divorce rates and other problems. The typical business structure of Western society, based on the aggressive rather than the altruistic aspects of individuals, is also at the root of the family crisis. Legislation cannot, therefore, change the situation. In spite of the fact that the federal Basic Law puts special emphasis on the family and has even instituted a cabinet position for "Family, Older People, Women and Youth," traditional family life has deteriorated. Statistics show that in 1998 every fourth citizen of a large city lived alone, and about 36 percent of the households in the western part of Germany consisted of only one person. In 1950, the percentage was about 19 percent. In roughly the same period, the number of marriages declined from 750,000 to 423,000, and the divorce rate doubled. The idea of job sharing has not yet taken hold in the society, and part-time employment usually kills a career. Governmental promises to guarantee child-care for every three-year-old by 1996, which were part of abortion legislation, were not kept.

It remains to be seen whether alternative lifestyles that emphasize family values and combine them with an ecological and anti-consumer attitude will have a real impact on society and offer workable solutions to a pressing problem without the intellectual snobbism of earlier attempts. Freiburg, at the edge of the Black Forest in Germany and a haven for the "real" Green Party, presents at least one model worth considering for imitation. The district Vauban is characterized by "green" ideas such as the renovation of old buildings, the elimination of traditional hierarchical structures between landlords and tenants as well as genders, the integration of different social groups along with a combination of living and working spaces, and the creation of environmentally friendly homes (see also 10: Consumer Culture versus Green Awareness).

Multicultural Society

Germans have to learn to accept that the EU means that Germany will become a multicultural society, not only a society with "guest workers" from various nations as was the case in the first decade of the Federal Republic (1949–1959) when the economic miracle required more workers than the population could supply (see 10: Consumer Culture versus Green Awareness). Furthermore, in 1955 the Bundeswehr (the draft army) was initiated, "in effect taking a whole year's supply of 18-year-old men out of the economic cycle" (Briel 2002, 53). At that time, treaties with Italy, Spain, Portugal, Yugoslavia, Turkey, and Greece were signed allowing the entry of cheap labor. In East Germany, a similar arrangement brought workers from Cuba, North Vietnam, and Angola. The plan was to have them stay for a few years only, but that is not how it worked out. The workers' families followed, and when the recession of the 1960s began, tension grew, because now it seemed as if these guest workers were taking work away from the Germans. In the following decades—and especially since unification—things worsened. Besides guest workers, there have been asylum seekers. Their number more than quadrupled between 1980 and 1992, when it hit a record high of 438,191 (Lord 2004, 70). In 2004, workers and asylum seekers from different countries made up about 10 percent of the population. The largest group consisted of Turks. Some cultural studies and travel guides point out that

Berlin-Kreuzberg is the fourth-largest Turkish city after Istanbul, Ankara, and Izmir. In addition, a stream of illegal workers, mainly from Eastern Europe, have come across the borders into Germany.

Richard Lord remarked in his book for travelers: "Before long you'll realise that in many big cities, there are almost as many foreigners as Germans on the streets and in the shops. In fact, if you enter through Frankfurt, you should be aware that at least 30 percent of Frankfurt's residents are foreigners" (ibid., 11). The result of this development was that violent xenophobia has erupted, foreigners have been attacked, and houses set ablaze. Primarily, it was in the early 1990s, soon after unification, that this increase of violence took place. Plays such as John von Düffel's *Oi* (1995), in which the German population turns into fascist pigs, depict this vision, which was inspired by neo-Nazi skinheads, but luckily, this attitude was changed relatively quickly. This time, there were enough demonstrations against xenophobia by other Germans to stop the matter from escalating.

To raise cultural awareness of "the other," in schoolbooks, German textbooks, and in many public places, a poster is being displayed stating that much of what is familiar to Germans in daily life is not in fact German. Pizza, for example, is Italian, coffee is from Brazil, numbers come from Arabic, and democracy is Greek. Some cities have also established a Department of Multicultural Affairs to promote and coordinate activities by non-German cultural groups such as Turkish men's social clubs.

Like all Western nations today, Germany is faced with the question of integration of the other. And Germans are not handling the task well. It is extremely difficult to become a German citizen. Until 2000, the major criterion was the blood line. With the new naturalization laws, time of residence has begun to be accepted among the criteria. Legal immigrants can apply for citizenship after eight years, and children born to foreign parents in Germany are now automatically granted citizenship at birth if at least one parent has lived legally in Germany for eight years. Although dual citizenship is not generally possible for adults, such children are exempted from this rule until age twenty-three, when they have to make a decision for one or the other (see 4: From A to Z, "Citizenship," "Immigrant groups").

To guarantee that the more liberal naturalization regulations do not lead to an undermining of traditional German culture, the conservatives have coined the phrase *Leitkultur* (guiding or dominant culture), by which they mean that the German culture is the dominant one, and the newcomers have to adapt themselves to it. Another model would be the attempt to live side by side with each other and create a tapestry of cultures. For Germans, integration seemed the natural thing—as happened at the beginning of the twentieth century, when many workers from Poland settled in the coal-mining area of Germany, bordering on Belgium and the Netherlands, an area known as the Ruhrgebiet.

With the shadow of the Nazi era still fresh, the West German Grundgesetz (Basic Law) of 1949 appeared to reach out to foreigners and specifically stated that political asylum seekers were welcome in Germany. But over the years, the number of economic refugees has increased because of fewer border controls in the EU. Although Germany has not been doing very well economically at the beginning of the

new millennium, the standard of living is still much higher than in many other countries, and it remains an attractive country in which to find work. In contrast to political asylum seekers, economic refugees have had their applications rejected. Nevertheless, all these asylum seekers have cost the taxpayers huge sums while they waited for the outcome of their applications, a period during which they were forbidden to work. To reduce these numbers, modifications were made to the Schengen Agreement, an agreement originally signed by five EU countries in 1985 that opened the borders inside the EU.

The United States supposedly became a "melting pot"—although the population of a few areas retained their original customs (the Amish are an extreme example), and there may even be a general shift in the United States from the traditional Anglo to a Hispanic dominance occurring at the present time—but the EU, and especially Germany, will have to find their own solutions based on cultural plurality. Throughout history, most similar mergers of cultures have failed. One of the main reasons has been the lack of knowledge in the receiving culture of the cultures represented by the migrants—either through lack of information or through lack of motivation to learn—a situation that also characterizes the present situation in Germany at the beginning of the second millennium. More and more Muslims are part of the German population, but few Germans are familiar with their beliefs and customs. Of prime importance will be the earliest socialization phase of the children of all the cultures involved. A knowledge of and respect for the other's customs and language are the foundation of peaceful coexistence— the enlargement of the EU to a total of twenty-five national states may help to further this process of mutual respect.

In March 2004, the women's magazine *Brigitte* focused on the upcoming acceptance of ten new countries into the European Union on May 1, 2004. The "dossier" began with a map of Europe marking in different colors the established members, those just accepted, and those remaining outside the union. Switzerland stood out as being in the middle geographically, but it was marked in a neutral gray among the unified countries. Beneath the map were words of welcome to the newcomers and the observation that there is much to discover and experience for both newcomers and Germans. The articles on the upcoming changes in Europe began with general reflections on the opening up of the former Eastern bloc by a Hungarian author whose parents had moved to Germany in 1956. It should be noted that the term *Osterweiterung* (expansion into the east) is a loaded one for Germans because of its echoes of Hitler's quest for more space (*Lebensraum*) for the German people.

Information on individual countries in the article came from a range of perspectives. Some of it appeared to be from promotional material, but there were also personal reflections from citizens now living in Germany, including a Lithuanian woman who had married a German and moved to Hamburg; a diplomat serving in the Estonian embassy in Berlin; a Hungarian journalist working in Berlin; a scientist from the Czech Republic now working in Berlin; a secretary from Slovenia working at her country's mission in Munich; a Polish businesswoman living in Ravensburg; a Slovakian student working on her doctoral degree in Göttingen; and an au pair from Latvia who had just arrived in Heidelberg.

Each writer presented her country and compared it with Germany, emphasizing characteristics that were atypical in Germany. Nomeda from Lithuania described her fellow countrymen as *brav*, a word that is a false friend to language learners whose mother tongue is English. It does not mean "brave" but rather well-behaved or obedient and is generally used for children. However, *brav* or not, she told of how Lithuanians erected crosses on a hill to protest the Soviet occupation, noting that when the Russians bulldozed them flat, they set up new ones. Kaili, the diplomat from Estonia, compared her countrymen with those of Finland, remarking that their languages sounded similar, that mobile phones were everywhere in both countries, and that they shared a charming stubbornness that has brought them success. Hungary was described as a hot country—where the food is spicy and one sweats in the famous baths or on the dance floor of the many nightclubs in Budapest. Emilia, who lived in Berlin, found that the immense pride of her compatriots could be unpleasant but welcomed the energy and sense of change in the east. Germany seemed to her "*gesättigt und langsam*," slow and its hunger stilled. Darina from the Czech Republic missed the cozy bars of her homeland and the special humor and found that Germans take rules too seriously. Visitors to Slovenia were warned by Barbara not to wear comfortable sneakers or shorts in Ljubljana or they would look like Cinderella among the fashionable young people. She recalled her first summer in Munich, when she was shocked at Germans bathing either topless or naked in the Isar, and considered her countrymen calmer and perhaps more reserved. Justina from Poland feared that entry into the EU would bring financial problems to her country and that many would get into debt attempting to imitate the Western style of living. Zuzana said that German students socialize less than they would in Slovakia. She admired the clean streets, the environmental awareness, and the sense of responsibility in Germany but missed a certain spontaneity. Jeva, from Latvia, found the Germans somewhat lazy, based on her observation that they bought foods that are processed and prepared rather than making everything from scratch like the people of her home country. Ironically, this is a criticism one often heard in Germany about the United States in earlier times. These observations from the new citizens of the Union, taken together, paint an interesting picture of Germans—it is not the hard-working image that was a stereotype of the past, though being obedient and following rules still seems to hold true for Germans.

For Malta and Cyprus, there were no personal perspectives given in the magazine, just short impressions, presumably from German journalists, but for each new member country there was a set of statistics: number of inhabitants, size of the country, currency, average income, the price of a pound of coffee, the number of unemployed, strengths and weaknesses of the economy, and a collection of data under the heading "Chances and Problems." The selection of coffee for the price comparison seems curious at first glance, but it recalls the postwar years when Germany was recovering economically and its citizens were beginning to travel. They shopped for coffee across the borders in Holland, France, and beyond because it was comparatively expensive in Germany. Finally, *Brigitte* readers were given the phone number and Web site address of the tourist office of each country.

Besides the EU expansion, besides a new global market that changes the character of all nations, Germany is in an especially precarious situation at the beginning of the new millennium. The population is shrinking and aging drastically. Only immigrants and the realization of a truly multicultural society will be able to stop that trend, to some extent (Klingholz 2004, 89).

Literature in the German language by non-Germans writing in a second language has gained a special niche in recent years to reflect the current situation of language and culture. Since 1984, a special prize has been set aside for the authors of such works, the Adalbert-von-Chamisso Prize, named for the French-born author whose family fled to Germany during the French Revolution and who became known as a German poet of the Romantic era. Elias Canetti (1905–1994) is a more recent example. He was born in Bulgaria to a family of Sephardic

Elias Canetti (1905–1994). (Horst Tappe/Hulton Archive/Getty Images)

Jews, and his mother tongue was Spaniolo, derived from Spanish. At the age of eight, he began to learn German, and he later began to write in that language. He was awarded the Nobel Prize for Literature in 1981.

From Traditional Fare to International Cuisine

Food

Mealtimes—even breakfast—have always been a social event in German families. If time allows, and many try hard to make it possible, family members sit down together at the table, exchange their plans for the day, and share their worries. *Brötchen* (rolls), *Konfitüre* (jam), and coffee or tea are now frequently replaced or supplemented by *Müsli* (cereal) and orange juice. At work, there is the second breakfast or coffee break with a different social group, the family of colleagues. Lunch, usually at work in the *Kantine* (canteen), cafeteria, restaurant, or *mensa* (student dining hall)—depending on one's profession and social status—begins with the greeting of *Guten Appetit* or *Mahlzeit*. On weekends and holidays, lunch is often still the major meal at home, as it was on all weekdays in the past, when working hours in offices and factories included an extended lunch break allowing workers time to go home to eat. To most, especially the stay-at-home wives, this arrangement was a mixed blessing and its passing not mourned. They had to scramble to cook and serve a meal to fit into the time allotted for their husbands' break. (This schedule also constituted a subtle form of discrimination, making it difficult for women to hold a full-time job.) Coffee and pastry at around 4 PM was once

a regular part of the day, but now it is a luxury for most. The word commonly used for supper indicates the weight of the meal: *Abendbrot* (bread in the evening) was often just that, usually with cold meats and various cheeses. It still is, though it is becoming more substantial, both in its content and its function. As the midday meal becomes lighter, supper is becoming a time for relaxing with food and wine. More and more, Germans are eating out in restaurants in the evening as well as during the workday.

The chronicler of the Golf Generation stated that tradition ruled the menus of his childhood. He claimed to have surveyed his peers and come up with seven different menus that their mothers cooked, regardless of whether they came from Osnabrück or Heilbronn (Illies 2001, 142). This standard repertoire included: *Königsberger Klopse* (a variation on meatballs) with a sauce, rice, and green salad; lentil soup with sausages; liver with rice and applesauce; apple pancakes with jam; noodle casserole; spaghetti with a meat sauce; and on Sundays some kind of roast meat with potatoes. In the earlier generation, there was less uniformity: What was served in Osnabrück would have had different ingredients and flavor combinations from the meal served in Heilbronn and points south. Although today the food served in Germany is much more varied and lighter than it was in the Golf children's youth, let alone fifty years ago, traditions and variations from one region to the next persist, in spite of the British adoption of the label "Krauts" for Germans based on the (false) assumption that everyone eats sauerkraut.

Usually, the *Nationalgerichte* or *Nationalspeisen* (national dishes) listed on menus are local specialties, as Hermann Bausinger remarked (2000, 38–45). But

whatever the local specialty, the *gutbürgerliche Küche* (literally, sound middle-class cuisine) designation is standard throughout Germany even today when ethnic restaurants abound. In the Münsterland there may be *Töttchen* on the menu, in Westphalia *Blindhuhn*, in Schleswig-Holstein *Dickmusik*—names unfamiliar in other areas. *Töttchen* is a rich ragout of veal (*Kalbskopffleisch*); *Blindhuhn* a stew of bacon, potatoes, onions, green beans, carrots, apples, and pears; *Dickmusik* a stew of beans, peas, carrots, leeks, potatoes, and bacon. Sometimes local variations on a dish will be regarded as a specialty throughout a region—for example, in the north, the various meals with herring, in the south, meals with bacon and sausages. Some dishes have their local variety: Dumplings in central Germany are predominantly made from potatoes (*Kartoffelklöße*), and in the

south from bread (*Knödel*). The fried ground meatballs are called *Buletten* in Berlin and *Frikadellen* (mixed with bread crumbs and egg) in many other parts of Germany.

The best-known local dishes outside of Germany are probably the Bavarian dishes because it is the center of tourism. Pork is the meat that features most frequently on menus, one of the best-known traditional dishes being *Schweinshaxen* (knuckle of pork). Pork is also usually the basis for the many varieties of sausage that are served, either cold and thinly sliced, or hot and whole, as a fast food in a roll, as part of a meal, or in a soup. Beef and veal tend to be more expensive but are quite popular, as are chicken and turkey—particularly as a substitute for veal—especially with the trend toward lighter fare. More and more one finds sausages also made from turkey and chicken. One of the best-known German dessert items is *Rote Grütze*, made from a mixture of crushed berries, particularly red currants, that are stewed with a thickening agent. Another dessert frequently found on menus and featured in tourist guides is *Kaiserschmarren*, literally "emperor's sweet dessert," which falls somewhere between a crepe and a sweet omelet.

The food in the northern and western regions of Germany often has a sweet component with the nourishing main course. For instance, the *gefüllte Schweinerippe* is cured pork chop filled with dried fruit such as prunes. In Pomerania and Mecklenburg (northeastern Germany), dumplings are offered with plums, white beans with apples, *Blutwurst* (blood sausage) with raisins, or roast goose with apples and prunes. The *Königsberger Klopse* that Illies and friends remember from their childhood have capers in the sauce, leading to a certain sourness. In the Saarland and in parts of Hesse, *Obstkuchen*, a yeast-based dough topped with apples or prunes, is eaten together with potato soup. This is not as strange as it might sound to those who consider cake to be something very sweet. German cakes, particularly those with a yeast-based dough, are not heavy on sugar.

In the Rhine region, sauerbraten is served with raisins and apples (*Apfelkraut*). Bausinger (2000) explained this *Geschmacksgrenze* (taste border)—which is reminiscent of the linguistic border of consonant and vowel shifts—by the greater openness to colonial influences in the northwestern regions of Germany (see 2: Language, Script, and Gestures). Until the late eighteenth century, sugar was exclusively a product made from the imported and expensive cane sugar; the first sugar beets were harvested and turned into sugar in those same regions. The same is true for tea. Today, tea is consumed ten times as much in Ostfriesland as in the rest of Germany.

Coffee, in contrast, came into Germany not only from the north but also from Austria. Vienna, with its various connections to the Ottoman Empire, is well known for its coffee culture. Legend has it that the first coffeehouse was opened by the Polish spy Georg Franz Kolschitzky (Franciszek Jerzy Kulczycki, 1640–1694) after the Turkish army had fled Vienna in 1683. He, supposedly, had received for his services during the Turkish siege 500 sacks of coffee beans the Turks had left behind. He is remembered today with a small sculpture at the corner of Favoritenstraße and Kolschitzky-Gasse in Vienna. Official records, on the other hand, give the honor for the first coffeehouse to the Armenian Johannes Diodato (Deodat, 1640–1725) who received a license to sell coffee in 1685. In 2004, a small park in the Schäffergasse was named for him (see also Heise 1987, 104, and Teply 1980). In any case, when in Vienna one has to be very precise when ordering to distinguish between a *Brauner* (coffee and milk), *Melange* (mixture of coffee and hot milk), *Kapuziner* (black coffee with foamed milk), *Konsul* (black coffee with cream), *Türkischer* (strong black coffee), *Pharisäer* (strong black coffee with whipped cream and a glass of brandy), *Schlagobers* (strong black coffee with liquid or whipped cream), *Einspänner* (coffee with whipped cream in a large glass), *Kaisermelange* (black coffee with egg yolk and brandy), or the more familiar *Espresso*—to name just a few. In Germany, the ubiquitous cappuccino and latte are taking over, however, with latte macchiato being the coolest choice.

The farther south one travels in Germany, the more likely it is that there will be a flour base to a dish. In Swabia, one of the *Nationalgerichte* is *Maultaschen*, which are similar to large Italian ravioli—pockets made from pasta and filled with a seasoned meat, or sometimes a spinach mixture. The dominant side dish is *Spätzle*, a pasta variety in which the dough is made of flour, eggs, and in some areas with milk or cream and butter. Traditionally the finished dough is scraped from a special board (*Spätzlebrett*) into boiling water for cooking. Since the art of scraping evenly sized pieces of dough is not easily acquired, there are other tools to make the job easier—a sort of grater and a press are currently on the market.

This prevalence of pasta (flour) in the south versus potatoes in the north is similar to the sweet versus sour taste line, as

Hermann Bausinger mentioned—though such differences are no longer strictly adhered to. Naturally, there are potato dishes in the south and pasta dishes in the north. Nevertheless, the prime regions for the acceptance of the potato were Saxony and Prussia as well as the Palatinate. Frederick II of Prussia is well known, in fact, for his support of the potato. In the south, the potato still had the connotation of poor people's food even in the nineteenth century. People like to find borders, and Richard Lord mentioned the "*Weiß-Wurst*-Equator" between the two southernmost states of Bavaria and Baden-Württemberg, "a jocular reference to the blanched sausage beloved of Bavarians" (Lord 2004, 69).

Most of the local food specialties are, of course, determined by the geographical conditions. White asparagus is therefore the favorite dish in June in the Rhine Valley between the Black Forest and the Vosges with its sandy soil. Boiled or cured ham is often eaten with the stalks along with *Kratzete* (a torn-up pancake) and as an accompanying sauce either melted butter or Hollandaise is served with the asparagus. Nowadays one can also find green asparagus in supermarkets and on menus, and since it is easier to cultivate—not requiring banking up with sand to avoid the greening effects of chlorophyll—and has more vitamins, it is likely to gain in popularity.

Although locally produced food and regional specialties are still available in Germany and play an important role in the country's eating habits, most restaurants in cities, as well as an increasing number in villages, offer an international cuisine. The towns are filled with Italian and Chinese restaurants, pizzerias, McDonald's and Burger King fast food, other foods from various nations, and above all, Turkish *Döner Kebab*, veal or lamb grilled on a rotating pole.

Food writing has also created a new journalistic—if not literary—genre, and newspapers and magazines offer informational articles along with their recipes. The expansion of the European Union has inspired writers from a broad range of fields, and foodies have jumped on the bandwagon, describing specialties of the new member countries and offering recipes that would appeal to modern-day German tastes for lighter, more subtly flavored food. In a newspaper article written at the time that new countries were becoming members of the EU, the hearty soups and dumplings of the Czech Republic were described along with the varieties of beer, but the dish Germans were encouraged to try for themselves is *Quarkknödel mit Zimt*, a dessert dumpling made with *Quark* (see under "Dairy Products," below) and cinnamon. These should be served with a cherry compote. Polish cuisine was also described as rustic and hearty—just as not so many years ago the Anglo-Saxon world would have characterized German cuisine. The article described sausages, stews, and beers and offered a recipe for *Pierogi*, pastry pockets filled, in this case, with a mushroom mixture. Hungary is traditionally known for paprika, salami, and gulasch, but one German foodwriter encouraged his readers to try a light cold soup made with Tokay wine, cream, and eggs. For Slovenia and Latvia, the focus was on wines and liqueurs. To introduce readers to Estonian cuisine, a fish soup or chowder was described, and for Lithuania a bacon sauce to accompany baked potatoes. The cuisine of the new Mediterranean members, Malta and Cypress, was introduced with a bean dip and cheese.

Most traditional German specialties are nourishing and simple rather than refined. Refinement was the domain of the French; in Germany, the preference for the simple meal was an expression of national self-confidence and frugality. The Nazis made use of this attitude and turned the simple meal into a cult. The *Eintopf* (stew made in one pot) became the symbol of the *Volksgemeinschaft* (brotherhood of the people) (Bausinger 2000, 43).

As new cooking equipment becomes available, the emphasis on simply prepared food is losing importance, but healthy food is still very important to Germans. Early on, with the naturalist movement and with the popularity of hiking and the various alternative lifestyles that developed around the turn of the twentieth century, health food stores (*Reformhäuser*) became a common feature in German towns. Today they are usually called *Bioläden* or *Öko-Läden*. The products sold in these shops are grown without the use of pesticides and other chemicals. Germans have been health conscious for a long time, and their present opposition to genetically altered agricultural products has a tradition in their aversion to food additives and colorings and their attraction to organic food. It is surprising that the *Reinheitsgebot* (purity law) of the beer brewers is not part of Germany's Basic Law. It goes back to 1516 and states that only malt, hops, yeast, and water are allowed in the beer brewing process.

Wine and Beer

In spite of globalization, local food and drink traditions continue in many small inns and pubs, including the *Straußen-* or *Besenwirtschaft* (literally, bouquet or broom inns). These private eating and drinking establishments are found in Ger-

many's wine-producing regions and are opened by wine growers as soon as the new wine (known as *Federweißer*) has fermented and is ready to drink. Tradition has it that they go back to regulations established in 794 by Charlemagne. Depending on the region, a wreath, a bouquet of flowers, or a broom, sometimes decorated with a bunch of flowers, is placed in front of the door to indicate that the establishment is open for business. This custom gave rise to the names used for the inns. In Austria they are called *Buschenschenken* (bush bars). In Germany, they are only allowed to serve a maximum of forty customers at a time during specific times of the year totaling four months. They can only serve their own produce, both wine and food, which is usually excellent, and the prices are very reasonable. They are therefore extremely popular in Germany's wine regions.

Broom Sign for Straußenwirtschaft.

The primary reason for the existence of *Straußenwirtschaften* is the wine (not the accompanying food), and this confirms the image of Germany as having less of an eating than a drinking culture. Bausinger (2000) referred to Norbert Elias's study about the Germans, noting that regionalism is important in regard to drinking: There is a distinction between wine and beer areas, and there are different drinking traditions in the different regions. In drinking, the Germans compensated for their political weakness. Bausinger then added economic reasons: The large breweries as well as the vineyards were owned by landlords who encouraged consumption. And they did so by paying their laborers their wages in a share of the harvest or production. This kind of payment was also the norm for other kinds of work—including

A Maßkrug (beer mug or stein), a tourist favorite. (Matthias Nordmeyer/ istockphoto.com)

academic work. Peter Untucht wrote about Erasmus von Rotterdam's emotions when he taught in 1526 at the university in Freiburg, Breisgau, where he did not really feel at home. "We do not know whether the reason for his discomfort was also based on the not unusual payment in kind—the work by the professors was compensated among other ways in 'wine currency'. Already at that time, the university owned its own vineyards" (Untucht 2003, 36). Therefore, there was never a shortage of beer and wine. Conviviality in Germany was also very much a male culture. Military rituals were even part of academic life, as the still existing schlagende Verbindungen (dueling fraternities) demonstrate, and all of them encouraged drinking.

Because many North Americans equate Germans with Bavarians (partly, perhaps, because this was a major part of the area occupied by the United States after World War II and thus the land described to families back home), the *Maßkrug* (beer mug or stein) has almost become an international symbol for Germany. Beer is brewed not only in Bavaria, however, but everywhere else in Germany. There are hundreds of large and small local breweries, and though Bavarian beer is the best known, the highest quantity is produced in Dortmund, the actual beer capital of Germany. St. Pauli beer from Hamburg is also well known, especially in the United States, where the company's posters can be found in many student dorms.

Cologne is known for its *Kölsch* beer, which is clear and traditionally drunk out of a *Stange*, a tall cylindrically shaped beer glass. The *Berliner Weisse* has a slightly sour taste resulting from the addition of lactic acid bacteria during the fermentation process. One usually mixes it with a shot of raspberry syrup (*Berliner Weisse mit Schuss*).

In spite of all the German beer hype, Germany also produces many excellent wines—primarily white wines. German wine differs from the wines of other countries. As the Deutsches Weininstitut states on its Web site:

> It is light, lively and fruity, thanks to Germany's unique climatic and geological conditions. With the exception of Saale-Unstrut and Sachsen in the east, the wine-growing regions are concentrated in the south and southwestern parts of Germany. They are among the most northerly wine regions in the world and straddle the border between the humid Gulf Stream climate of the west and the dry Continental climate of the east.
>
> The long growing season and moderate summer temperatures bring forth filigree wines that are relatively low in alcohol. The diversity of German wine stems from the many soil types and grape varieties—there is no "uniform" type or style of German wine—and this diversity is reflected in Germany's 13 wine-growing regions. (www.deutscheweine.de)

Both the eating and drinking cultures are influenced by socioeconomic differences. The answer to the question of whether wine or beer is the preferred drink may depend on social status. Wine is the more noble drink, beer is for the common man. This distinction is, of course, less pronounced in beer- and wine-producing regions.

In typical German fashion, wine labels are quite precise in order to give consumers as much information as possible. They usually inform the consumer about the *Jahrgang* (vintage or year of harvest),

Ort und Lage (region as well as the exact location of the vineyard), the type of wine—such as *Weißherbst* (rosé), *Rotling* (red), or *Perlwein* (sparkling)—the type of grape (for example, *Riesling*), the *Alkoholgehalt* (percentage of alcohol), and the *Qualitätsstufe* (rank in quality). The standard levels in quality are *Tafelwein* (table wine, simple wine, or vin ordinaire), *Landwein* (a slightly higher grade), and *Qualitätswein* (wine of certified origin and quality) with its traditional subcategories: *Kabinett* (high-quality white wine), *Spätlese* (late vintage), *Auslese* (high-quality wine made from selected grapes), *Beerenauslese* (wine made from specially selected grapes), *Trockenbeerenauslese* (wine made from choice grapes left on the vine to dry out at the end of the season), and *Eiswein* (a very sweet wine made from grapes that have been exposed to frost). A few other terms besides these traditional ones are in use nowadays that have not yet really been accepted by all consumers—for example, *Selection* and *Classic*.

Although most wine regions use the standard bottle, the wines from Franken (Franconia) are immediately recognizable from the round, flattened form of the bottle, the *Bocksbeutel*. The shape imitates that of a Celtic bottle found near Aschaffenburg and dating back to 1400 B.C.E. It became popular in the region because of a glassworks in the Spessart region, which has produced these bottles since 1349—at least, that date is the earliest documentation of such a bottle.

Wine and beer are regularly drunk in Germany with meals; tap water is not and is rarely served either in restaurants or private homes. The only exception is in the Vienna coffeehouses, where a glass of water is served with the coffee because caffeine

A bocksbeutel from the Franken region.

tween sour cream and cream cheese in consistency and taste, is used in a range of recipes, from cakes to casseroles and a simple dish of potatoes, boiled in their skins. Quark was often eaten after the war when food was in short supply and is still recommended today as a simple, healthy dish. Related to Quark and without direct Anglo-Saxon equivalents are *Schmand* (a sort of sour cream), *Yogurt*, and *Kefir*, which is similar to yogurt. Now less popular are buttermilk and *Dickmilch*—a yogurt-like product that could easily be made at home before pasteurization was common by leaving milk to stand and separate. And then there is sweet cream with varying levels of butterfat and often appearing whipped, lightly sweetened, and dolloped on cakes and pastries with afternoon coffee.

dehydrates the body. Those who do request water in a German restaurant are given the choice of sparkling or flat mineral water, even a choice of brands, all of which add to the bill, and ice is not included.

Dairy Products

Germany cannot boast as many varieties of cheese as France, but it does have a broad range of milk products beyond cream, butter, and a modest selection of regional cheeses. The best known of the traditional German cheeses are Harzer and Limburger, but nowadays Mozzarella can carry the "Made in Germany" label, too. *Quark*, a soft dairy product that falls somewhere be-

From A to Z

Abortion: The right to terminate a pregnancy has been called by many "the women's rights question of the century" (Sandford 1999, 208). The original paragraph 218 of the criminal code, introduced in 1871, allowed abortion for medical reasons only. The fascists raised the resulting consequences to capital punishment. Although this was abolished after the war, illegality remained on the books. The punishment was reduced to prison sentences for up to five years for the woman and for up to ten years for the person performing the abortion. In 1971, public debate of the issue reached a new climax because of an article in *Stern*. Legal reform in 1972 rendered abortion no longer a punishable offense, and in 1974 a new law was passed. During the first three months of pregnancy, an abortion was permitted with prior medical consultation. A constitutional challenge arguing that abortion conflicted with the right to life of the unborn led to a revision in 1976. New restrictions were imposed, and abortions were allowed if the life of the woman was in jeopardy, the pregnancy was the result of rape, or severe social and economic conditions existed that would adversely affect the unborn child and mother. In the GDR, abortion was legalized in 1972. In 1995, a compromise was passed. Although the act of abortion is considered illegal, it is in all cases exempted from punishment within the first twelve weeks (*Fristenlösung*, literally, term solution) in combination with a mandatory consultation.

Abuse: Every form of abuse within a family is illegal. This applies to corporal punishment of children as well as domestic violence, and restraining orders can be obtained. There are women's shelters in most German cities and various organizations to safeguard the rights of children—for example, Kinderschutzbund (Association for the Protection of Children) (Beck 2003, 101).

Advice centers: Many cities have offices to give advice regarding specific support for women. Often, companies and political parties have special regulations—even quotas—to ensure that women are equally represented in decision-making positions (Beck 2003, 99).

AFN: American Forces Network Europe. The radio station began broadcasting in 1943 using BBC studios and equipment. After the war in May 1945, AFN Frankfurt sent its first signals from a mobile van. AFN Munich came next in June. Berlin, Bremen, and Nuremberg, and later Kaiserslautern and other stations, followed. And as long as there are U.S. bases in Europe, there will be AFN.

Aktionsrat zur Befreiung der Frau: (Action Committee for the Liberation of Women) Founded in 1968, this committee tries to raise the political awareness level of women and has inspired the formation of many other women's organizations.

Apartments: The way one describes an apartment and counts rooms in German-speaking countries follows a distinct pattern that can confuse those used to American or British conventions. A *Zweizimmerwohnung* (literally, two-room apartment), for example, has a bedroom and a living room as its two rooms—though each could be used in other ways—as well as a kitchen and bathroom. The latter two rooms are a given and thus not included in the room count, although an *Appartement* is the term used for a studio or efficiency apartment. Rents tend to be high in German-speaking countries, and thus shared apartments known as *Wohngemeinschaft* (WG, living communities) are popular. In these, each individual has a room—hence the emphasis on number of rooms rather than their function—and the kitchen and bath facilities are shared. This mode of living is particularly popular with students.

APO: Außerparlamentarische Opposition (Extraparliamentary Opposition). In the 1960s, the APO was a loose alliance of disparate groups, with the SDS as its primary force.

Asylum: Asylum seekers are permitted to stay in Germany as long as the asylum process is ongoing. Information is available from the Federal Office for the Recognition of Foreign Refugees (Bundesamt für Anerkennung ausländischer Flüchtlinge).

Brand names of food: Brand names of food that have become household names in Germany and are familiar beyond its borders are: *Bahlsen:* In 1891, Hermann Bahlsen invented the characteristic shape for his company's biscuits with 52 zigzags around the edges (four large ones at the corners and 14 and 10, respectively, on the long and short sides of a rectangle). He also introduced the word *Keks* (from English "cakes") for his product; *Dr. Oetker:* The firm began its success story in 1891 with its baking powder *Backin* and branched out over the decades into other areas related to baking; *Haribo:* The acronym was derived from the name of the founder of the confectionary company, Hans Riegel, and the city where he lived: Bonn. The golden jelly bear made from sugar and gelatine (*Gummibärchen* or *Goldbärchen*), which became an unexpected export hit and is one of the most popular sweets in Germany and abroad, was created in 1922 inspired by dancing bears and teddybears. (See also 7: Advertising.); *Kühne:* It is Europe's market leader for vinegar and known for its ready-to-eat red cabbage and other delicacies. The vinegar distillery was founded in 1722; *Maggi:* the spice, was named after its inventor, Julius Maggi, in 1886; *Ritter Sport:* known worldwide for its square bars of chocolate that fit into a jacket pocket; *Vivil:* the peppermint roll, was created in 1903 by August Müller who as a soldier during the tiring drill sessions had always yearned for something refreshing. The name came from his wife's family who was French.

Citizenship: Children who have at least one parent with German citizenship are automatically German citizens from birth. For detailed information about obtaining automatic German citizenship and naturalization, see Beck 2003, 96–97, and www.germany-info.org.

Designers: (not mentioned in the text) Frank Leder and Mari Otberg are young contemporary Berlin fashion designers, as are the Italian Ivan Strano (born in Switzerland) and the German Klaus Unrath, who came to Berlin after several years in various countries to form the independent design team Unrath and Strano. Well known worldwide is also the name of Anett Röstel. Annette Görtz is based in Gütersloh and has showrooms in many cities, both within Germany and in other countries. Heinz Oestergaard (1916–2003), cofounder of the design studio Schröder-Eggeringhaus and Oestergaard in Berlin, is one of the doyens of German design. He was also a consultant for many firms and pleaded for a democratization of fashion. Markus Lupfer (b. 1968) from Baden-Württemberg moved to London; Dirk Schoenberger from Cologne established himself in Antwerp; and Bernhard Wilhelm (b. 1972) lives in Paris. Anja Gockel (b. 1968) founded a label under her name in London in 1996 and a limited liability company (Gesellschaft mit beschränkter Haftung, GmbH) in 2000 in Mainz. (See "Fashion houses," "Fashion industry," and "Labels," below.)

Deutsches Modeinstitut: German Fashion Institute. It was founded in 1952 to develop a socialist culture of clothing for the GDR by redesigning international fashion for mass production. It gained recognition through its designs for the successful GDR Olympic teams (see 5: Sports) and the famous Leipzig Gewandhaus Orchestra (see 8: Music).

Disabilities: There are many special advice centers for disabled persons. They offer information on rehabilitation as well as the opportunities to receive financial aid and privileges (Beck 2003, 103).

Divorce: Since 1977, no-fault divorces have been possible under marital and family laws. The spouse with the higher income is responsible for alimony.

Erziehungsurlaub: Family leave for raising children. Companies are required to offer a three-year, partly paid leave after the birth of a baby. The provision is available to either parent and is dependent upon various employment conditions.

Family name: A law passed in 1977 allows couples to choose either the husband's or the wife's last name as the family name. It was modified in 1994 to allow both spouses to keep their names.

Fashion houses: Modehäuser became an important factor in the economic miracle (see 10: From Consumer Culture to Green Awareness). Many important ones were in Berlin and belonged, originally, as Mila Ganeva mentioned, to Jewish companies (Sandford 1999, 199). After the war, their chief designers, for example, Hans Seger, Gerd Staebe, Hans Gehringer, and Hermann Schwichtenberg, were in charge. After 1995, other German cities became important in fashion design, especially Munich with Heinz Schulze-Varell, Hamburg with Irmgard Bibernell and Hilda Romatzki, and Wiesbaden with Elise Topell. Düsseldorf became famous for its annual fashion show of women's clothing, and in Cologne men's fashion was presented. Since unification, Berlin has tried to establish itself as the city for young fashion designers. (See "Designers," above, and "Fashion industry" and "Labels," below.)

Fashion industry: In 1949, a women's outerwear association (Interessengemeinschaft Damenoberbekleidung, IGEDO) was founded by twenty-four companies. It helped to reestablish German fashion by organizing fashion shows in Germany and abroad, establishing fashion houses to attract foreign designers, and awarding fashion prizes. In 1982, the world's largest trade fair for ready-to-wear clothing, *Collections Premieren Düsseldorf*, was introduced, with a new marketing strategy to address more specific target groups. But volume, more than style, was the main focus. Today, Germany is one of the largest exporters of apparel in the world. Leading companies are Escada (founded by Margaretha and Wolfgang Ley in 1975 as a knitwear house); Rena Lange (with cofounder Peter Gunerth and Irish designer James Waldron); Joop! (founded by Wolfgang Joop); Jil Sander (founded in Hamburg in the 1970s, sold to a larger concern and later bought back by the owner); Hugo Boss (founded in Metzingen by Hugo Ferdinand Boss [1885–1948] in 1923 as a cloth factory that produced Nazi uniforms after Hitler's ascent to power—Boss was a party member early on, and though he was not an ideologue, his firm did employ forced laborers; the firm was continued by his son-in-law, Eugen Holy, and expanded by his sons Uwe and Jochen in the 1970s); and Strenesse (founded as Firma Strehle KG in 1949 and developed into the label Strenesse since 1970 by Gerd and Gabriele Strehle). (See "Fashion houses," "Designers," above, and "Fashion magazines" and "Labels," below.)

Fashion magazines: In the FRG, *Constanze, Brigitte, Film und Frau, Burda, Elegante Welt*, and *Madame* led the list; in the GDR, *Sybille* and *Pramo* were the leaders. *Burda Moden*, founded in 1950 by Aenne Burda (née Lemminger in 1909), became an important part of German culture because of the sewing patterns that were included in each issue. The practice encouraged a do-it-yourself approach to fashion. (See "Fashion industry," above.)

Fast food: For decades, fast food for Germans meant *Bratwurst* (fried sausage) with French fries, ketchup, and mayonnaise. Then came the McDonald's hamburger invasion and the Italian pizza. The pizza has become almost a national dish because of the many pizza delivery services. Herring sandwiches from the food chain Nordsee have also made inroads. In the new millennium, *Döner Kebabs* from Turkey also fit into this category. The kebab meat rotates on a spit and is then sliced and served on Turkish bread, often with onions and peppers, and is probably the fast food of choice for most young Germans.

Feminat: In 1984, the faction of the Green Party in the Bundestag (lower house of parliament) elected a party executive board consisting only of women. This was called a *Feminat* (see 10: Consumer Culture versus Green Awareness).

Frauenruheraum: Relaxation room for women. This was a special room for women in GDR factories to take a break from work in a quiet and peaceful environment. It was used especially by pregnant women (Sommer 2003, 187).

Frauensonderstudium: Special studies program for women. In the GDR, a program was established to encourage women to get a postsecondary degree to prepare them for upper and middle management positions. Among other benefits was a paid work release time for a certain number of hours to be set aside for studies.

Fristenlösung: Literally, solution in a specific time frame. See "Abortion," above.

Garçonnière: Traditionally, the apartment of a bachelor, a term used in Austria for a studio or one-room apartment.

Gummibärchen: (jelly bears) see Haribo in above section Brand names.

Homosexuality: A special law on the equality of homosexual partnerships defines them as being "almost equal to those of heterosexual marriages" (Beck 2003, 102). As this formulation indicates, partners in a so-called Eingetragene Lebenspartnerschaft (registered partnership for life) have the same legal rights as partners in a traditional marriage with very few exceptions that are still being debated in parliament, state legislatures, and in the courts.

Immigrant groups: In the seventeenth century, the Huguenots settled primarily in Prussia; in the nineteenth century, many immigrants from Poland settled as coal miners in the Ruhr area. In the late 1950s, the Federal Republic made agreements with several countries—for example, Italy, Turkey, Yugoslavia, and Morocco—to invite workers to fill the many vacant positions. The GDR invited workers from Vietnam and African states. Since the end of the 1980s and unification, more than 2 million ethnic Germans, chiefly from former Soviet Republics, have returned to Germany. In 2003, more than 7 million foreigners lived in Germany, almost 9 percent of the population, but one-quarter of those had been born in Germany to parents from other countries. The breakdown by nationality for the main groups was as follows: Turkey 42 percent, Italy 13 percent, Yugoslavia (Serbia/Montenegro) 12.5 percent, Greece 8 percent, Poland 7 percent, Croatia 5 percent, Austria 4 percent, Bosnia-Herzgovina 3.5 percent, United States 2.5 percent, Macedonia 1.5 percent, Slovenia 1 percent (based on Lantermann et al. 2003, 17 and web updates). Immigration is somewhat higher than emigration: 800,000 vs. 700,000 each year. Although immigrants play an important role in the economic and cultural life of Germany, their representation in the political sphere—communal parliaments, state parliaments, and the Bundestag (the German parliament)—constitutes a disproportionately small percentage.

Intellectuals: Some of the best-known German intellectuals of the postwar era have been: Theodor (Ludwig) W(iesengrund) Adorno (1903–1969), Walter Benjamin (1892–1940), Jürgen Habermas (b. 1929), Max Horkheimer (1895–1971), Niklas Luhmann (1927–1998), György (Georg) Lukács (1885–1971), Herbert Marcuse (1898–1979), Marcel Reich-Ranicki (b. 1920, a literary critic, known as the 'Literaturpapst,' literary pope), and Peter Sloterdijk (b. 1947).

Kommune I: This was a natural outgrowth of the intellectual climate of the 1960s with its belief that the nuclear patriarchal family was the basis for fascism and that the traditional interdependence of men and women did not allow for self-realization. Therefore, eight young men and women began to live together in 1967 in a free anarchistic relationship, that is, everyone was allowed to follow his or her whims and desires. The commune dissolved after two years. It entered the public awareness and German culture through the unforgettable image (reprinted in many books on German history and culture) of male and female members of the commune (including children) standing naked against a wall, their backs turned toward the photographer. One of its founders and most popular members was Fritz Teufel (b. 1943), often called the *Spaß-Revoluzzer* (playful revolutionary) because none of his actions were intended to harm people, only to attract attention, to provoke the authorities. He also wanted to highlight the discrepancies between official reactions in the case of minor annoyances such as he produced and the official reactions in the case of actual global terror and the civilian deaths in wars, euphemistically called "collateral damage." He was arrested several times but always found not guilty of the accusations. Especially well known are two typical events. One was his arrest for an attempted assassination of the U.S. vice president Hubert H. Humphrey in 1967 which made headlines in Europe and abroad. In reality he had just thrown pudding, yoghurt, and a bag of flour at him. The other was a remark that he made when asked by a judge to stand up and show respect for the court. He stood up with the reply, *"Wenn's der Wahrheitsfindung dient"* (If it serves in discovering the truth).

Kosher: Products that meet the Kosher and Islamic dietary guidelines are generally only available in specialized shops (Beck 2003, 137).

Labels: One of the most prominent German fashion labels was started in 1932 by Willy Bogner (five times Bavarian and eleven times German champion in skiing [Nordic combination]), who founded Willy-Bogner-Skivertrieb (Willy Bogner ski sales) with a friend. In 1936, he was chosen to say the Olympic oath at the winter games in Garmisch-Partenkirchen, and for the first time the German team was dressed in Bogner outfits (a tradition maintained in the Winter Olympics in Turin, Italy, in 2006). His wife, Maria, was the designer, and he was the manager. In 1950, the company's first men's collection was presented, and in 1955 Maria had the idea of having the "B" part of all zippers. With Willy Jr. becoming part of the team, the firm expanded to its present status.

There are many other popular German labels as well. The label Bless was founded in 1997 by Desiree Heiss and Ines Kaag. Florinda Schnitzel was set up in 2001 by Heike Ebner. In 1999, Daniela Goergens had the idea of bringing together creative pioneers from a variety of disciplines, such as fashion, photography, graphic arts, music, and film. The result was the founding of L.R.R.H. together with the Belgian photographer Frédéric Leemans. René Lezard was founded in 1978 by Thomas Schaefer. Philemon and Baukis in Berlin, founded by Günter Underburger, is the best place for fans of hats. For real individualists, the label to follow is SAI SO, founded by Ursula Brem and continued after her death by her husband, Martin Brem. *Sai so* means "reassembled" in Japanese, and that is what Brem and his team, Katja Allrich and Bettina Kredler, do: design new clothes from old kimonos. Thatchers fashion in Berlin was founded by Ralf Hensellek and Thomas Mrozek in 1995 and belongs, with Coration and Eisdieler, to the new Berlin labels. Uli Dzialas in Berlin plays with nostalgia. (See "Fashion houses," "Designers," and "Fashion industry," above.)

Leitkultur: Guiding or dominant culture, a term coined by German conservatives.

Pay: In 1980 and again in 1994, laws were passed to guarantee equal pay for women and a neutral description of job ads. Reality lags behind the laws, however, and pay for women is generally lower than for men.

Personalausweis: Identity card. The card, which is legally required of all adults over the age of sixteen, is valid only inside Germany and is the major means of identification. It is not required if the person has a passport instead.

Protection of minors: The Jugendschutzgesetz (Law for the Protection of Minors) states what minors are permitted and forbidden to do without parental supervision. For instance, children under sixteen are not permitted to smoke cigarettes, and they may not be served alcoholic beverages (depending on the alcohol percentage, the age limit may be eighteen). After 10 PM, they are only allowed in public places under certain circumstances. The Jugendamt (Youth Welfare Office) provides detailed information (Beck 2003, 201).

Quality control: Labels stating *Naturland* or *Bioland* guarantee a product's origin and quality. With diseases such as mad cow disease appearing from time to time, consumers have often relied heavily on such stamps of approval.

RAF: Rote Armee Fraktion (Red Army Faction), also known as the Baader-Meinhof gang. In 1968, as part of the general student revolution—in protest against the Vietnam War, the capitalist consumer society, and their parents' generation—an arson attack on a department store in Frankfurt on the Main began a series of bomb attacks against U.S. military facilities in West Germany, the police, and law courts and offices, as well as bank robberies. The masterminds behind this violence were Gudrun Ensslin (1940–1977); her boyfriend, Andreas Baader (1943–1977), an education student; the journalist Ulrike Meinhof (1934–1996); and the lawyer Horst Mahler (b. 1936).

Gudrun Ensslin was the daughter of a Lutheran pastor and a postgraduate literature student whose frame of mind was clearly expressed in her remark: "You can't talk to people who created Auschwitz." Ulrike Meinhof worked at the left-wing magazine *Konkret* and authored the TV play *Bambule*. She provided the intellectual justification for the group's violent actions. All three committed suicide in their prison cells, though questions were raised as to whether they really were suicides. Identifying themselves with liberation movements in the Third World, they saw themselves as urban guerrillas. In the beginning, there was much sympathy on the part of intellectuals for their goals (see 7: Film). After the arrest of many of the founding members in 1972, a second generation of terrorists continued the violence, which peaked in 1977 with the unsuccessful hijacking of a plane and several murders of influential members of the establishment, such as the chief federal prosecutor Siegfried Buback (1920–1977), the chief executive of the Dresdner Bank, Jürgen Ponto (1923–1977), and the president of the Employers' Federation, Hanns-Martin Schleyer (1915–1977). The terror continued through the 1980s. The gang's last victim was the president of the *Treuhand* (see 1: From A to Z, "Treuhandanstalt"), D. K. Rohwedder (murdered in 1991). After unification, it became obvious that many had found a refuge in the GDR, where a third generation was still active in 1993. In 1998, the group announced their surrender and conceded their mistaken approach.

Schengen Agreement: Named after the town Schengen in Luxembourg, the agreement established a Europe without border controls. It also regulates questions in regard to visa matters and asylum seekers and brought about a closer collaboration between the national police forces. It was signed in 1985 by Belgium, France, Germany, Luxembourg, and the Netherlands. Other European countries joined in the following years.

SDS: Sozialistischer Deutscher Studentenbund (League of German Socialist Students). Founded in 1946, the SDS was officially independent of the SPD, but it naturally had many ties to the parent organization and helped shape its policies. Only on a few issues—remilitarization, for example—did the young socialists continue to disagree with their older peers. Yet, such disagreements led to a split of the movement in 1960. Though the more conservative wing was accepted by the SPD, party membership in the SDS was seen as incompatible with that of the SPD. This sparked the SDS to become even more active and to reach out to international student movements and initiate a discussion on university reforms. Its most charismatic leader was Rudolf (known as Rudi) Dutschke (1940–1979).

Sexual harassment: As in many other countries, there are special laws in Germany protecting women and men from sexual harassment—that is, any sexual behavior that is not wished by the person concerned (Beck 2003, 100).

Spätaussiedler: Literally, late emigrants. The term refers to those of German heritage returning to Germany, mostly from states in the former Eastern bloc. According to the Basic Law, these people are Germans. Information is available from the German Representative for Immigrants of German Origin and National Minorities in Germany (Beauftragte der Bundesregierung für Aussiedlerfragen und nationale Minderheiten in Deutschland): www.bmi.bund.de, www.bafl.de, or www.bundesverwaltungsamt.de.

Specialties: Some of the regional culinary specialties in Germany are: *Frankfurter Würstchen* (sausages), *Grünkohl* (curly kale), *mit Pinkel:* cabbage with a sausage containing groats, a dish from northern Germany; *Leipziger Allerlei* (literally, all sorts of things from Leipzig): a dish of mixed vegetables; *Sauerbraten* (braised marinated beef); *Maultaschen* (filled pasta pockets); *Pfälzer Saumagen:* stuffed pig's stomach from the Palatinate; *Weißwurst* (white sausage), *Schweinshaxen* (knuckle of pork), *Spätzle* (homemade noodles), *Buletten* (a type of hamburger), *Salz-Hering* (salted herring, a fish specialty from Holstein), and *Kieler Sprotten* (Kiel sprats [a type of herring]). For more information, see main text, "From Traditional Fare to International Cuisine."

Stammtisch: A table for regulars is still very common in many pubs and inns. Political parties and trade unions also use this term for special political events, as in *Politischer Stammtisch.*

Tipping: Service is usually included in the price at restaurants. Nevertheless, a tip is welcome. Usually, one rounds up to the next euro. Ten percent of the total bill is very adequate.

Trümmerfrauen: Literally, rubble women. The term refers to the women of Germany who helped to rebuild the country after World War II.

VHB Exquisit: Vereinigte Handelsbetriebe der Bekleidung. The VHB was the GDR's fashion manufacturing organization for the more wealthy consumer.

Additional Readings

Ardagh, John, and Katharina Ardagh. *Germany and the Germans.* London and New York: Penguin, 1995.

Baacke, Dieter. *Jugend und Subkultur.* München: Juventa, 1972.

———. *Jugend und Mode. Kleidung als Selbstinszenierung.* Opladen: Leske und Budrich, 1988.

————. *Jugend und Jugendkulturen. Darstellung und Deutung*, 4th ed. Weinheim and München: Juventa, 2004.

Bade, Klaus J., ed. *Population, Labour and Migration in the 19th and 20th Century.* Oxford: Berg, 1987.

————, ed. *Migration, Ethnizität, Konflikt.* Osnabrück: Universitätsverlag Rasch, 1996.

Beinssen-Hesse, Silke, and Catherine E. Rigby. *Out of the Shadows: Contemporary German Feminism.* Carlton, Victoria: Melbourne University Press, 1996.

Böltken, Ferdinand. "Einstellungen zu Ausländern. Ein Vergleich zwischen den neuen und den alten Bundesländern." *Geographische Rundschau* 49, 7–8: 432–437.

Bücken, Hajo, and Dieter Rex. *Die wilden Fünfziger.* Reichelsheim: Edition XXL, 2001.

Cohn-Bendit, Daniel, and Thomas Schmidt. *Heimat Babylon. Das Wagnis der multikulturellen Demokratie.* Hamburg: Hoffmann und Campe, 1992.

Counihan, Carole, and Penny Van Esterik, eds. *Food and Culture: A Reader.* New York, Routledge, 1997.

Czyzewski, Marek, ed. *Selbst- und Fremdbilder im Gespräch.* Opladen: Leske und Budrich, 1995.

Farin, Klaus. *Jugendkulturen zwischen Kommerz und Politik.* München: Tilsner, 1998.

————, ed. *Skinhead—A Way of Life. Eine Jugendbewegung stellt sich selbst dar.* Durchgesehene, korrigierte, akualisierte Ausgabe. Bad Tölz: Tilsner, 1999.

————. *generation-kick.de. Jugendsubkulturen heute.* München: Beck, 2001. (Beck'sche Reihe 1407.)

Ferchhoff, Wilfried. *Jugend an der Wende vom 20. zum 21. Jahrhundert. Lebensformen und Lebensstile*, 2., überarbeitete und aktualisierte Auflage. Opladen: Leske und Budrich, 1999.

————, ed. *Jugendkulturen 2000.* Berlin: Sozialpädagogisches Institut, 2001.

First-Hand Information Department. *Young People in the GDR.* Berlin: Panorama, 1987.

Frevert, Ute. *Women in German History.* Oxford: Berg, 1989.

Großegger, Beate, and Bernhard Heinzlmaier. *Jugendkultur-Guide.* 2. Auflage. Wien: Öbv und hpt, 2004. (1st ed. 1002).

Hafeneger, Benno, and Mechtild M. Jansen. *Rechte Cliquen. Alltag einer neuen Jugendkultur.* Weinheim: Juventa, 2001.

Haines, Brigid, and Margaret Littler. *Contemporary Women's Writing in German: Theoretical Perspectives.* Oxford: Oxford University Press, 2004.

Heine, Norbert. *Deutscher Weinführer.* Stuttgart: Ulmer, 1998.

Helwig, Gisela, and Hildegard Maria Nickel, eds. *Frauen in Deutschland 1945–92.* Bonn: Bundeszentrale für politische Bildung, 1993; Berlin: Akademie Verlag, 1993.

Horbelt, Rainer, and Sonja Spindler. *Die deutsche Küche im 20. Jahrhundert. Von der Mehlsuppe im Kaiserreich bis zum Designerjoghurt der Berliner Republik. Ereignisse, Geschichten, Rezepte.* Frankfurt: Eichborn, 2000.

Hurrelmann, Klaus. "Youth 2005." *Deutschland: Forum on Politics, Culture and Business* 3 (2005): 40–47.

Kemper, Peter; Thomas Langhoff, and Ulrich Sonnenschein. *"Alles so schön bunt hier." Die Geschichte der Popkultur von den Fünfzigern bis heute.* Stuttgart: Reclam, 1999.

Koelbl, Herlinde, and Manfred Sack. *Das deutsche Wohnzimmer.* Mit einem Beitrag von Alexander Mitscherlich. München: C. J. Bucher, 1980.

Kohl, Helmut. *A Culinary Voyage through Germany.* Commentary by Chancellor Helmut Kohl. München: Verlag Zabert Sandmann, 1996.

Kolinsky, Eva. *Women in Contemporary Germany.* Oxford: Berg, 1993.

————. *Women in 20th Century Germany: A Reader.* Manchester: Manchester University Press, 1995.

Kuhnhardt, Ludger. "Multi-German Germany." *Daedalus* 123, no. 1 (1994): 193–201.

Lehnert, Gertrud. *Geschichte der Mode des 20. Jahrunderts.* Köln: Könemann, 2000.

Loschek, Ingrid. *Modedesigner. Ein Lexikon von Armani bis Yamamoto.* München: Beck, 2002. (beck'sche reihe 1249)

————. *Mode im 20. Jahrhundert. Eine Kulturgeschichte unserer Zeit*, 5th ed. München: Bruckmann, 1995.

————. *Reclams Mode- und Kostümlexikon*, 5th ed. Ditzingen: Reclam, 2005.

Marcks, Marie. *Marie, es brennt! Autobiographische Aufzeichnungen.* München: Frauenbuch Verlag–Weismann Verlag, 1984.

Mintz, Sidney Wilfred. *Tasting Food, Tasting Freedom: Excursions into Eating, Culture, and the Past.* Boston: Beacon, 1996.

Musall, Bettina. "Trash and Sensual Appeal." *The Germans. Sixty Years after the War.* Ed. Stefan Aust. Spiegel Special International Edition 4 (2005): 202–206.

Olszewska Heberle, Marianne. *German Cooking.* New York: Berkeley Publishing Group, 1996.

Plonka, Kay Alexander. *Mode in D, A, CH.* Köln: Tisch 7 Verlagsgesellschaft, 2006.

Protzner, Wolfgang, ed. *Vom Hungerwinter zum kulinarischen Schlaraffenland. Aspekte einer Kulturgeschichte des Essens in der Bundesrepublik Deutschland.* Stuttgart: Steiner-Verlag, 1987.

Richter, Simon. "Food and drink: Hegelian encounters with the culinary other." *Contemporary German Cultural Studies.* Ed. Alison Phipps. Oxford: Oxford University Press, 2002, 179-195.

Roth, Roland, and Dieter Rucht. *Jugendkulturen, Politik und Protest. Vom Widerstand zum Kommerz?* Leverkusen: Leske und Budrich, 2000.

Rutschky, Michael. *Wie wir Amerikaner wurden. Eine deutsche Entwicklungsgeschichte.* Berlin and München: Ullstein, 2004.

Sommerhoff, Barbara. *Frauenbewegung.* Reinbek: Rowohlt, 1995.

Stephan, Alexander, ed. *Americanization and Anti-Americanism: The German Encounter with American Culture after 1945.* New York and Oxford: Berghahn, 2005.

Strate, Ursula, ed. *Déjà vu. Moden 1950–1990.* Heidelberg: Edition Braus, 1994.

Teuteberg, Hans Jürgen, ed. *Essen und kulturelle Identität. Europâische Perspektiven.* Berlin: Akademie Verlag, 1997.

Teuteberg, Hans Jürgen, and Günter Wiegelmann. *Unsere tägliche Kost. Geschichte und regionale Prägung.* Münster: F. Coppenrath, 1986.

Weber, Christiane, and Renate Möller. *Mode und Modeschmuck, 1920–1970, in Deutschland.* Stuttgart: Arnold, 1999.

Wierlacher, Alois, ed. *Kulturthema Essen. Ansichten und Problemfeld.* Berlin: Akademie Verlag, 1993.

Zerrahn, Signe. *Entmannt. Wider den Trivialfeminismus.* Hamburg: Rotbuch, 1995.

Zötsch, Claudia. *Powergirls und Drachenmädchen. Symbolwelten in Mythologie und Jugendkultur.* Münster: Unrast, 1999.

5

Leisure

Activities and Clubs

Many Germans like to garden in the extended sense. Gardening for them is not synonymous with riding a lawnmower or wielding a weed whacker, but means planting vegetables and flowers as well as pruning bushes, propagating plants, and designing small pools with running water. And in some areas it also means finding the best spot for garden gnomes (*Gartenzwerge*) with their shovels, their rakes, or a lantern.

And when all is done, it is time for sitting or lying down in the all too infrequently seen sunshine, having a smoke and/or a beer or glass of wine, or having a barbecue party (*Grillfest*) with friends and neighbors. During the early and mid–nineteenth century, the beginning of the Industrial Revolution, the large apartment complexes built in cities for the many working families (*Mietskasernen*) did not allow for gardens. A solution was offered by an orthopedist, Daniel Gottlob Moritz Schreber (1808–1861), who was very health conscious and encouraged gymnastics for young people. He realized the importance of gardens for the well-being of the individual and suggested that cities lease small garden plots on their borders to families. These gardens still exist today all over Germany, Austria, and Switzerland and are called *Schrebergärten*. Often they are just a few meters wide and long, enough for a garden shed and a flower and vegetable bed. Foreigners passing by often mistake these assemblages of little huts for slums—even though they usually are well tended and only rarely neglected.

As important as a garden was the local swimming pool—immediately after the war as well as today—which became a second home to many children during the summer. A pool and the surrounding lawn area, referred to as a *Liegewiese* (literally, "meadow for lying down"), is the place to meet friends, for schoolchildren to do homework, for mothers with young children to meet and share child care, and for those not working to use as a social club. Passes that are valid for the whole summer make it cheap entertainment.

Garden gnomes. (Photo by A. Weiss)

For men, and nowadays also women, stand-up bars (*Stehkneipen*) still play a social function after work. The prototypes of these bars are found especially in towns in northern Germany in regions such as the industrial area of the Ruhrgebiet. Coalminers and steelworkers hot or dusty after work (called *Maloche* there, a word of Yiddish origin) used to come here to quench their thirst with one or more glasses of *Pils* (pilsener beer). These bars are not designed for comfort and are usually narrow, with just a few tables for resting the glass as one talks to a neighbor or the bartender. Sometimes customers may stay long enough to play a round of *Skat*, a card game that is popular in all regions of Germany, in cities as well as in the country. More congenial is the old country pub (*das Wirtshaus*), the meeting place for farmers in the early evening. Those making a name in local politics (or trying to) can often be found at the regulars' table (*der Stammtisch*) along with anyone else who treats the pub as a sort of second home. At the other tables, it is quite usual for strangers to talk to one another over their glass of beer or wine. The town/country distinction is no longer as sharp as it once was, and nowadays both pubs and bars are found in residential areas of towns, some staying true to older traditions, others aiming for a more hip crowd.

But it is said that if three Germans with the same interest get together, they will organize a club (*Verein*). And, certainly, Germany probably holds the top spot in the Guinness records in regard to the number and variety of clubs. The term *Verein* also has legal ramifications. The establishment of a club has a special status in the Basic Law and the civil code to make sure that fascist-type gatherings will not take place. Clubs are regarded as nonprofit organizations and therefore exempt from paying taxes. This status is indicated by the abbreviation *e.V.* after the name of an organization and stands for "*eingetragener Verein*" (officially registered club).

There are the various sports clubs (gymnastics, soccer, handball, and bowling as well as *Kegeln*, that is, bowling with nine pins, which can be placed in different configurations for different types of games). Then there is the voluntary fire brigade (*Freiwillige Feuerwehr*), which serves many as a club in addition to its main function, and card playing clubs (bridge and—above all—Skat). Skat is also played at the table for regulars at an inn, which, though not officially a club, serves a similar social purpose. Very important are the hiking clubs, which are usually named after the region in which their members hike (for example, Odenwaldklub, Schwarzwaldverein, Alpenverein). In the early decades of the Federal Republic, they played a social role for the whole family. Besides hiking for several miles together in a fairly large group on a Sunday, following the well-marked trails, the clubs organized social events at which decorations were handed out for the distance covered in a month or year. They were fastened proudly onto walking sticks, and each member's ambition was to have his or her cane plastered with decorations, just as generals had their uniforms covered with badges and medals of honor.

Hiking has remained popular in the twenty-first century—and not only as something for older people in loden green leather hiking pants. It is being promoted with newly constructed hiking paths. For example, in Willingen, in the northwest corner of Hesse, an area known as the "Upland," a 64-kilometer trail has been constructed over a two-year period. The area is not far from the large industrial cities of Dortmund, Kassel, and Frankfurt, but the trail is in the unspoiled countryside of the Hochsauerland and offers hikers a range of scenery, from moors and meadows to forests and lakes. Willingen is also a center for other sports, namely biathlons and rollerski championships, and a venue for ski jump contests. In addition, it boasts the highest heathland tower (*Hochheideturm*) and the highest outdoor climbing wall in Europe (*Stadtkurier*, May 5, 2004, 7).

As important as clubs, and even undergoing a revival in the new millennium, are choirs—men's and women's as well as mixed choirs and a cappella groups, which were influenced by the popular movie *Comedian Harmonists* directed by Joseph Vilsmaier. Besides the *Burschenschaften* (fraternities), these *Gesangsvereine* (and the *Turnvereine*, gymnastic clubs) also contributed much to the political movements in the nineteenth century that strove for a democratic and united Germany, and local history clubs (*Geschichts-*, *Altertums-*, and *Heimatverein*) helped to raise communal awareness.

In recent years, *Vereine* in smaller towns and villages in southwestern Germany have been established to support and follow the progress of families of storks. Frames for nests are provided on church roofs or other tall buildings, usually community owned, and small video cameras are installed to offer citizens access to the daily goings-on inside the nests. They can see when eggs are laid, keep track of how the brooding and hatching are proceeding, learn information as to possible predators,

Stork nest on church roof in St. Georgen, Breisgau.

and so on. Citizens watch the antics of the stork families in a designated shop window, read reports of them in local newspapers, and can contribute funds for their upkeep through bank accounts established by the clubs. The storks are banded for identification and named, so that following these attempts to revive the once endangered stork population becomes something like a local reality TV show. There even appears to be a certain element of competition between communities for providing better stork facilities and food. Subscribers to the *St. Georgener Bote*, a magazine with local news and advertisements distributed free to all living in the Freiburg suburb of St. Georgen, could read in the April 2004 issue that Baldur and Cili were taking turns in incubating five eggs. They also learned that an aggressive raven had attempted to storm the nest several times and destroy the brood, but were beaten off by Baldur with strong blows of his beak. This was, however, not the only hazard the family had to contend with. Because of the relatively dry weather, food supplies for local storks were in short supply and foreign storks were invading their feeding place. In the next issue of the same magazine, townspeople read of stork happiness on the morning of May 2 as the first chick broke out of its egg. That evening, the second chick checked out St. Georgen and with his or her sibling was fed worms by the parent storks. By the time the third chick hatched, Baldur and Cili had to resort to serving the fish provided by the townspeople. The parents were kept busy turning the remaining two eggs, fending off the mean ravens, and even driving away fellow "storkess" Amelie from nearby Wolfenweiler, who occasionally flew over to St. Georgen for free food. Five days later, all the eggs had been hatched and the long sought after rain had arrived, making more food available naturally to the storks. Relieved readers were encouraged to follow the family's progress in the window of a printing company (Meier Druck), and many sent donations to SOS Weißstorch e.V.

Finally, there is an infinite number of clubs based on hobbies: aquarium clubs, shawm clubs (*Schalmeien Verein*), model train clubs, clubs for breeding small animals (*Kleintierzuchtverein*), clubs for dog lovers and cat lovers, and clubs for gardening enthusiasts (*Kleingärtnervereinigung*). All together, about 60 percent of all adults are members in at least one club (Bausinger 2000, 67). Many clubs have a clear social agenda, as their members belong predominantly to one social class or another. Clubs are part of the social status game. Whereas members of soccer clubs belong predominantly to the working class, golf clubs are like a second home for the upper crust.

Church choir booth at wine festival in St. Georgen, Breisgau.

Clubs can also be political entities, such as SUSI e.V. (Selbstorganisierte Unabhängige Siedlungsinitiative, Self-Organized Independent Housing Development Initiative; see 10: Consumer Culture versus Green Awareness). In many small villages, they are the foundation of local culture and organize and sponsor events, parades, festivities, and dances.

Many of the clubs can boast of a long tradition, sometimes going back to the Middle Ages when they were the proud expression of the independence and initiative of the middle class. The *Schützenfeste* (fairs featuring shooting matches) were the middle-class equivalents of aristocratic jousts. Although times have changed, they are still celebrated in rural areas, particularly in Austria and southern Germany. The winner of the competition becomes the *Schützenkönig* (shooting king). In festive ceremonies, chains are hung around their necks and badges and plaques are awarded that the winners keep until the following year. Only after winning for a specified number of years, usually three, can the kings keep the prizes for good.

One of the basic characteristics of the various club members used to be their dedication. Sometimes, a club virtually replaced the family. The common German word *Vereinsmeier*, denoting one who devotes his life to clubs instead of something else, and who may be regarded also as a busybody, points out this negative side of clubs. Yet, this emotional attachment is decreasing and usually only found among older members. The new generation looks more at the functional aspect of a club, especially in the area of sports and fitness training. Florian Illies remarked in his book about his generation: "The evolution from being members of the Jazzdance Group and the Soccer-C-Youth-Organization to visitors of fitness centers with an annual membership contract, the ennoblement of the arduous endurance run to the delightful jogging, the metamorphosis of roller-skating, the sport for little girls, to in-line skating, these are three achievements which are clearly the result of the Golf generation. . . . We, however, the fanatics for general individualism, later will have to bear the responsibility for the end of the German club culture" (Illies 2001, 90–91).

Holidays and Local Festivals

Introduction

Even a reference work notes that "Germans have been dubbed the 'world champions of holidays.' Statistically, Germans take more holidays than any other nation in the world" (Briel 2002, 68). Almost all are religious holidays, but the number of actual days off depends on the state (see 1: Overcoming Regionalism). Many local celebrations that cause stores and factories to close or limit their working schedule are not even listed in the following overview of the official holidays (most of them of a religious nature). The standard German calendar does not quite reflect the new multicultural society (see 4: Multicultural Society), however—the holy days of Muslim, Jewish,

Table 5.1

Overview of Official German Holidays

January 1:	*Neujahr* (New Year) in all states
January 6:	*Heilige Drei Könige* (Epiphany) in three states
Varying dates:	*Karfreitag* (Good Friday) in all states
Varying dates:	*Ostern* (Easter) in all states
Varying dates:	*Ostermontag* (Easter Monday) in all states
May 1:	*Tag der Arbeit* (Labor Day) in all states
Varying dates:	*Christi Himmelfahrt* (Ascension Day) in all states
Varying dates:	*Pfingsten* (Whitsun, Pentecost) in all states
Varying dates:	*Pfingstmontag* (Monday after Whitsun) in all states
Varying dates:	*Fronleichnam* (Feast of Corpus Christi) in six states and a few communities in other states
August 8:	*Friedensfest* (Festival of Peace) only in the city of Augsburg
August 15:	*Mariä Himmelfahrt* (Ascension of Mary) in one state and predominantly Catholic communities in a second state
October 3:	*Tag der Deutschen Einheit* (Day of National Unity) in all states
October 31:	*Reformationstag* (Day of Reformation) in five states
November 1:	*Allerheiligen* (All SaintsíD ay) in five states that are not Protestant
Varying dates:	*Buß- und Bettag* (Day of Repentance and Prayer) in one state
December 24:	*Heiligabend* (Christmas Eve) a semi-holiday that is not on the official list, although the evening of December 24 is the time when Germans celebrate Christmas
December 25:	*1. Weihnachtstag* (1st day of Christmas) in all states
December 26:	*2. Weihnachtstag* (2nd day of Christmas) in all states

and other minority religious groups, such as the Islamic Eid ul Fitr and Eid ul Adha or the Jewish Rosh Hashanah and Yom Kippur, are not included as official public holidays and are therefore not listed here (Beck 2003, 36).

For many years, June 17 was a national holiday in remembrance of the 1953 uprising in the GDR. After unification, it was replaced by October 3, the day in 1990 on which East and West Germany were officially united. According to Marieluise Beck, "This national holiday is similar to 'Independence Day' on the 4th of July in the US or 'Bastille Day' on the 14th of July in France. In Germany, however, celebrations are much more muted. There are no military parades; just festivals and gatherings with political speeches in parliament and many town halls" (ibid., 39). Switzerland celebrates its national holiday, the *Rütli Schwur* (Oath on the Rütli), on August 1 with fireworks and blazing fires on top of many hills and mountains, and Austria has its national holiday on October 26. There are also a few other days of remembrance in Germany that are not public holidays (see 5: From A to Z, "Days of Remembrance"). For forty years, the former GDR celebrated various events with great enthusiasm, and although there were few days when the shops were closed and one could stay at home, the other usual benefits derived from public holidays. (See 5: From A to Z, "GDR Holidays" and individual holidays.)

Folk Festivals

"There is always a reason for celebration!" (Es gibt immer einen Grund zum Feiern) is a typical phrase in German. Germans love to party, and traveling through Germany, one can easily get the impression that Germans are *festsüchtig* (festival-addicted). There seem to be local *Volksfeste* (fairs) somewhere all the time, in addition to the nationwide festivals, many with a long tradition. In rural areas, they are usually related to church activities, local historical events, or seasonal dates and the annual cycle of farm work, and in the urban centers to workmen's guilds. Once these festivities were an expression of the pride of individual social groups. In the nineteenth century, they were encouraged and sponsored by communities as symbols for the emancipation of the middle class and national pride. Today the reason is primarily commercial. Most have become folkloristic, nostalgic tourist attractions that are an amalgam of several traditions and have little to do with the original motivation. Exceptions do, however, exist. Today's wine festivals (primarily in the southwest of Germany)—relatively unspoiled local events organized by the whole community with all its various clubs—are the most recent incarnations of the traditional local fair.

Wine festivals vary from one region to another, and though all include ample opportunities to taste the products of the local vineyards, usually accompanied by music, different groups are represented at these festivities. In Staufen, a town in Baden-Württemberg in the Markgräfler region, a four-day festival in 2004 celebrating the fiftieth anniversary of the event included music from several groups, with names that are neither really English nor really German, such as "Redhouse Hot Six Dixiland," and "Tanzmusik mit Fresh" (Dance Music with Fresh; see 2: Language, Script, and Gestures), along with more traditional-sounding groups such as the Trachtenkapelle (a band wearing tradi-

tional local costume) and the vintners'
band from a neighboring village. Parades
included the riding club, local people in
traditional costumes, and the wine "roy-
alty"—the wine princess for the year as
well as former princesses and dignitaries.
On the last day of the festival, the coopers
were to parade with the masters of the
wine cellars, the former wearing their
coopers' blouses (*Küferblusen*). While all
of this sounds very traditional, it should
not be forgotten that this particular festival
was initiated in 1954, nine years after the
end of the war when people were beginning to feel more comfortable about their
German traditions without immediately being branded as Nazis.

Sometimes it is the old traditions that
lead the way in innovations. One way that
the locals celebrated the festival in Staufen
was by keeping shops open on Sunday afternoon from 1 PM until 6 PM, something unheard of in Germany just a few years ago.
Shopkeepers benefited from the additional
visitors to the town, though shoppers had
to compete for parking spaces. During the
parade itself, shop doorways and windows
were blocked by spectators; however, a reception for former wine princesses and
other wine royals was also scheduled for
early afternoon, and one would hope that
the refreshments encouraged shopping
(*Stadtkurier* 30 [July 21, 2004], 10).

The *Kirchweih* (sometimes called
Kirmes, *Kerb*, or *Kerwe*) is another celebration that has remained relatively close
to the original spirit. It takes place every
year in villages, districts, or small towns
across Germany in commemoration of the
consecration of the local church. It may
last a weekend or for several days. Carou-
sels, roller coasters, shooting stands, numerous fast-food stands, and other attrac-

tions are set up on town squares, inviting
children and adults alike to take part in the
festivities.

Attractions that have become internationally famous are the various forms of
Fastnacht (*Fasnet*, *Karneval*) and the *Oktoberfest* as well as historical shows such
as the *Oberammergauer Passionsspiele*
and the *Landshuter Hochzeit*, which are
performed in fixed cycles (for a description of these holidays see below and 5:
From A to Z).

Christmas

Christmas is accompanied by various
Christkindl- or *Weihnachtsmärkte* (Christmas fairs) that draw large crowds each
year. These are held on the squares in front
of the main cathedrals or town halls of
cities and villages. At the same time,
Christmas is probably the most private,
family-oriented holiday in the year, with
Christmas Eve as its center. Even today,
when stores begin displaying Christmas
trees and playing Christmas carols in early
December, many German families keep the
old tradition of surprising children on the
evening of the 24th with the ringing of
small bells, signaling that the Christmas
tree has been finally decorated with candles and has been lit for the first time, usually in the living room. Even today, many
families still use real candles—a good reason for not setting up the Christmas trees
indoors before Christmas Eve.

To Germans, Christmas is not just a couple of days in December. The season begins with Advent (the Latin word means
"arrival"), and even those who have not
been inside a church in years will mark
each of the four Sundays of Advent by
lighting an additional candle on a wreath
displayed in the home and opening doors,

envelopes, or pockets on an Advent calendar to find small gifts or see new images. It is also not unusual for families to sit together and make gifts or decorations (*basteln*) and read stories and poems for the season as they work. The fact that the weeks before Christmas occur when daylight is in short supply and the weather cold and often unpleasant makes such cozy gatherings even more attractive. The word *basteln* is translated as "tinker" or "rig up" (Langenscheidt dictionary), "work at as a hobby" or "occupy oneself with a constructive hobby" (Cassells dictionary), but the very fact that German has a single word that captures different types of creative hobbies, including sewing and woodworking and therefore not at all gender specific, indicates a culturally distinct attitude toward such activities. Typical items to work on in the Christmas season would range from stars made from strips of paper—not unlike origami but traditionally German—wreaths of all kinds, decorations for the tree, which can be of fabric, wood, metal, paper, and the like, and the beloved *Hampelmänner*, often translated as jumping jacks. These are two-dimensional figures with jointed arms and legs that are connected by a string or cord. When one pulls on the cord that hangs down, the arms and legs move up and down. The figures can be animals as well as humans, but one of the most popular figures at this time of year is Nikolaus. These toys capture the imagination of adults and children alike.

According to a book published in 2003 by the popular women's magazine *Brigitte*, students and other young people feeling the pinch of Germany's economic downslide can earn "upwards of 50 Euro" for taking on the role of Nikolaus during the Christmas season (Herzog 2003). Nikolaus

A Hampelmann, allegedly made by a Russian prisoner of war and found in Bonn. The figure looks like a cross between a jolly Red Army soldier and Santa Claus.

might be considered the German version of Santa Claus or Father Christmas, but his duties differ somewhat from his Anglo-Saxon counterparts. He is one of a trio of gift bearers, along with the *Weihnachtsmann* (literally, the Christmas man) and the *Christkind*—a child who is part of the Christmas entourage but not the Christ child as the name might imply (and as is stated in some encyclopedias). Most of the time, the child is depicted as an angel. (A corruption of the diminutive form, *Christkindl*, is the basis of the U.S. term Kris Kringle.) Nikolaus and the Weihnachtsmann are almost identical in appearance, with red and white suits and long white beards, but whereas the Weihnachtsmann comes at Christmas (December 24–25) with major gifts, Nikolaus arrives on the night between December 5 and 6. He brings mainly chocolate, gingerbread, and nuts on a decorative plate.

The figure of Nikolaus is based on the fourth-century bishop of Myra known for his miracles and generosity, who became the patron saint of children. December 6, regarded as the date of the bishop's death, was declared in 1222 at the Council of Oxford as one of the main holidays. Two legends about him are especially well known and can explain how he could evolve into the benevolent St. Nikolaus/Santa Claus. One tells of a greedy innkeeper who killed two students because he believed they had money. He cut them up and hid the body parts in a barrel. But the bishop of Myra discovered this deed, reassembled the body parts, and resurrected the two. Another legend tells of a poor father who had three daughters but not enough money to give each one a dowry. So he sent them out onto the street to earn money as prostitutes. The bishop had pity on them, and on three consecutive nights he threw three pieces of gold into the poor father's small room, helping all three girls to get a good husband. In one version of the legend, he threw the pieces of gold through the chimney. They fell into the socks of the girls, who had hung them there to dry. This version is the basis for the tradition of placing shoes in front of the door or hanging stockings by the fireplace to be filled. In some regions, children also place a carrot for St. Nikolaus's horse into the shoes. In other areas of Germany, the father, a relative, or an older brother dresses up as St. Nikolaus, visits the children, and has them recite a religious poem or sing a song—a practice that also teaches the children about their religion. If they have been good and know their lessons, they receive apples and nuts. In southern areas, the faithful have traditionally been encouraged to keep records of their prayers and attendance at Mass. They were rewarded (and in many regions the traditions are kept alive) by St. Nikolaus with cookies called *Spekulatius* (akin to the word *speculator*, meaning "investigator, examiner"). In the late 1940s and 1950s, after World War II, when many families were without fathers, mothers and grandmothers took on this role; only years later, when these children had become adults, did they learn about the efforts of the women in the family to give them a "normal" childhood and family life.

St. Nikolaus also has a sidekick, Knecht Ruprecht (Knave Rupert), who has a sack and bundle of sticks and punishes naughty children. In Austrian tradition, he is practically synonymous with the devil and is called "Krampus." Some families still follow the tradition of having the children make their own *Zwetschgen-Krampus* out of dried prunes (*Zwetschgen*) stuck on wires for the body, legs, and arms with a nut for his head. In the 1973 poem entitled "Advent" by the German comedian Loriot, it is Ruprecht who travels around the countryside on a sleigh picking up gifts to be distributed. The black humor of the poem is juxtaposed against the cozy, sentimental tone of the season (see 2: Stereotypes and Prejudices).

Of course, the students—who, with good planning, can earn up to 400 euros on their Nikolaus rounds—have to do more than simply dress up. They must be willing to answer children's questions about their background, how it is they can visit so many children in one night, how they know whether the children have been good or bad, and so on. Since there is no reference to opportunities for working as Ruprecht, it would seem that it is hard to find families in Germany with children naughty enough to warrant visitations by him. Companies also hire people to impersonate the *Weihnachtsmann* or *-frau* (male or female versions of Santa Claus) or angels for office parties and families for Christmas Eve appearances. Payment is a matter of agreement but about 30 Euros is usual for a fifteen to twenty minute visit to a family. Student agencies, particularly the *Heinzelmännchen* agency in Berlin, have about 4,000 bookings per year. Their prerequisites are that individuals have their own costume (about a 50 Euro investment) and visit a school on how to handle sticky issues such as when children try to rip off a beard or ask about the reindeer sled.

Carnival

In some areas, there are festivals outside of the pre-Christmas and Advent season extending into January and February (see 5: From A to Z: "Reformation Day," "All Saints' Day," "Penance Day," "Martin's Day," "Epiphany," "Candlemas," "Valentine's Day"). In areas of Germany that have a Catholic tradition, the main celebration in February is *Fasching* or *Karneval* (Carnival or Mardi Gras). The highlight of the festivities is what is known as *Rosenmontag* (Crazy Monday—*rosen* derived from *rasen*, meaning running crazy). It is the Monday before the beginning of Lent, the traditional period of fasting before Easter. On this day, traditional processions are held in Cologne and Mainz and other western and southern cities. Many of the highly decorated floats display political themes satirizing local as well as global events and politicians. The *Jecken* (crazy people,

members of a carnival's club) throw candy, usually caramels, and fruits into the crowds lining the streets. In between the floats are individual *Schwellköppe* (swollen heads, that is, larger-than-life heads made from papier-mâché) and marching bands in costumes.

In some areas, the season officially begins as early as November, the eleventh month of the year, to tie in with an elaborate network of myths and symbolism surrounding the number eleven. These include:

- Symbolism of the equality of all members (a 1 next to a 1).
- Reference to the legend of the 11,000 virgins of Cologne, in which Ursula, the daughter of a British king, made a pilgrimage to Cologne with 11,000 virgins, all of whom were killed by the Huns upon arrival in the city. However, thunder and lightning sent by God scared the Huns away and saved Cologne. The grateful citizens made Ursula the patron of the city, built a church in her honor, and had eleven tears included in the city coat of arms below three crowns, the symbols of the Magi, whose relics are kept in Cologne cathedral.
- Acronym for *Egalité, Liberté, Fraternité*: ELF (eleven).
- Reference to the Babylonian god Marduk, who supposedly was accorded the number eleven. The fact that Babylon was known as the city of sin should not be forgotten.
- Creation of a *compagnie des fols* (association of fools) by the aristocrat Adolf Graf von Kleve, who signed the document as the eleventh person (although he could have signed it as the first one), and whose coat of arms contains the

A carnival float showing a papier-maché figure of former German Chancellor Gerhard Schröder dressed as Spiderman during the traditional Rose Monday (Rosenmontag) carnival parade in Cologne on February 7, 2005. (Alex Grimm/Reuters/Corbis)

words "*Ey Lustig Fröhlich*": ELF (Be in good spirits).

Whatever the reason, the number eleven is the reason that in some regions Carnival begins on November 11 (Martinstag) at 11 minutes past 11 o'clock.

However, the main celebrations begin on the Thursday before Lent, which is called *Weiberfastnacht* (Carnival for women). Women assume control of the city governments and, as a highly visible—not to mention suggestive—symbol of their temporary takeover, they have the right to cut off the ties of men who dare to wear one on this day. The festivities continue until the following Wednesday, *Aschermittwoch* (Ash Wednesday), the beginning of Lent, a period that traditionally involves forty days of fasting. It is not only the participants in the parades who dress up in costumes with fancy masks and gowns, but many of the bystanders too, especially in the lower Rhineland. The tradition stems from old customs celebrating the end of winter and the beginning of spring. (For the history of Carnival and more details see 5: From A to Z, "*Fastnacht/Fasnet/Fasching.*")

Easter

Ostern (Easter)—with *Palmsonntag* (Palm Sunday), *Gründonnerstag* (Maundy Thurs-

A "Tanzmariechen" (dancing Mary) is lifted up during the street carnival in Cologne on Carnival Thursday, February 19, 2004. The "Weiberfastnacht" (women's carnival) heralds the climax of the carnival festivities in the region along the River Rhine. (Rolf Vennenbernd/dpa/Corbis)

day; see 5: From A to Z, "Corpus Christi"), *Karfreitag* (Good Friday—the syllable *Kar-* comes from Old High German *kara*, which means mourning), Easter Sunday, and Easter Monday—is the most important festival in the Christian calendar in Germany. (For other holidays, see 5: From A to Z, "Ascension Day," "Pentecost," "Corpus Christi," and "Feast of Assumption," with celebrations that depend in part on the region.) Easter is celebrated on the first Sunday after the spring full moon. As in other countries, it has become very much commercialized, but in many families the children still hunt for colorfully decorated Easter eggs that have been hidden by their parents in the apartment or garden, though it was supposedly the Easter Bunny who

brought them. There are many theories about the symbolic connection between the eggs and the bunny. Certainly, heathen fertility rites play a prominent role. The egg as the origin of life; and the eggshell as the symbol of Christ's tomb, which he broke open as chicks do when they hatch, are common elements of these theories, but there are also very practical reasons for the use of the eggs. Easter is the end of Lent, the period of fasting. During that time, the consumption of eggs was traditionally forbidden. Therefore, they accumulated and needed to be used up. The painting of eggs goes back to the time when special eggs were blessed by the priest and needed to be marked, that is, painted for purposes of identification. Similar to the egg, the hare is a symbol of fertility. Three hares were also used in Gothic churches to indicate the Trinity.

In some regions, the Easter fire is also a part of the Easter festival. The fire is lit on the evening of Karsamstag (the night before Easter). Sometimes straw puppets are burned to symbolize the end of winter. In other regions, the *Osterwasser* (Easter wa-

The illustration is based on the Three Hares image at the Cathedral in Paderborn.

ter) is believed to heal illnesses. On Easter morning, the herds were driven into the creeks to ensure that they would stay healthy during the coming year. The *Osterspaziergang* (Easter walk), described by Germany's most famous writer, Johann Wolfgang Goethe (1749–1832), in his play *Faust*, inspired many Germans to do just that—to take a stroll in the fields—on Easter morning, when weather permits. Perhaps inspired by these Easter strolls, and to give them a significance in accordance with the Christian message of peace, pacifists organize protest marches against war and military proliferation during the festival of Easter. The first of these political Easter marches in Germany took place in 1960.

May Day

Because of the large military parades in Moscow during the May Day celebrations, in some parts of the world May 1 is sometimes better known as the International Socialist Labour Day. It is an official holiday in Germany today—but the political aspect (which was introduced in 1890) is actually secondary. Originally, it followed old traditions to celebrate spring and the month of May, the beginning of farm work (see also 5: From A to Z, "Candlemas"). A custom that has largely died out in the English-speaking world, but is still thriving in Germany, is that of raising a maypole, symbolizing the fertility of spring.

In the April 2004 edition of the *St. Georgener Bote*, the magazine for local news of

A maypole erected in the village of St. Georgen, Breisgau, in 2004.

the Freiburg suburb of St. Georgen, there is an invitation to attend a maypole event, which would be followed by festivities including refreshments and entertainment by the *Schalmeien Verein* (shawm club; see 5: Activities and Clubs), whose members still play the shawm, an ancient woodwind instrument, at village gatherings (they also march in carnival festivities). The following month readers found reports on the festivities, could see photographs of the 20-meter pole being set into place, and could read that the old May custom had been reintroduced in the village as recently as 1986. They also learned that wine and baked *Fleischkäse* (a sort of finely ground meatloaf) were served at the festivities and that it is becoming increasingly difficult to find trees of the appropriate height in the region for making a good maypole—thus the future of the custom may be in doubt. The description of the tree being stripped of its bark and decorated with branches and garlands, as well as with the coats of arms of the local crafts, matches almost identically the description of the maypole given in *Feste und Bräuche im Jahreslauf* (Festivals and Customs throughout the Year; Woll 1995, 52–56). Woll noted that the trees selected are usually pines or birches and that the custom goes back to the beginning of the sixteenth century, though it is documented only since the eighteenth. Villages competed for the tallest and most beautiful maypoles. Whereas in the past trees were felled, stripped, and set up in secret, today the erection of the maypole is a public event organized by the clubs of the villages, Woll said.

Woll's reports of May celebrations begin with *Walpurgisnacht* (see also 5: From A to Z, "Walpurgis Night") on the eve of the first of May, when tools and farm equipment were locked away to keep them safe from marauding youths. The destructive antics of the youths are based on much older traditions of witches riding through the night on their brooms and causing havoc. The evening before the first of May is the time for the traditional *Tanz in den Mai* (Dance into May) parties. It was also on the eve of May 1 that suitors set up birch or pine branches outside the houses of the young women they admired to indicate future weddings and engagements. The counterpart to these *Maien* (literally Mays) were *Schandmaien* (shame Mays) of brooms, bunches of twigs, thorny branches, or even straw figures that were set up at the windows or doors of less admired women. These were removed as early as possible the next day to avoid shame. May was also the time for seeking brides, and in the days before personal ads and online dating services, *Mailehen* (Mayfief) made it possible for young men to find partners for local dances. As the word "fief" implies, the girls had little say in the matter. Sometimes they were auctioned off by the community, although in a playful manner in later years. A few villages also selected a May king and queen who had special privileges. The custom apparently can be traced back to the thirteenth century, when *Ehezwangsrecht* (literally, the right to enforce marriage) allowed the aristocracy to marry the daughters of their subjects when they wished (Woll 1995, 55). Fortunately, St. Georgen does not appear to uphold these more embarrassing and inhumane traditions.

Oktoberfest

The *Oktoberfest* in Munich is probably Germany's largest and best-known festival. Yet, like so many, it is a local event. It lasts for sixteen days, ending on the first Sunday in October. Its origin is a horse race that took place in 1810 in honor of the marriage of Bavaria's crown prince, who later became Ludwig I.

Today the festival attracts more than 6 million people annually, who are entertained by roller coasters, fast food stands, and various other attractions. The main feature is, of course, the beer, and more than 5 million liters are consumed, along with upward of 200,000 pairs of sausages, all served in huge tents, large enough to seat the thousands who attend. The people listen to traditional Bavarian music as they drink their beer and eat their sausages. The bands join together for a concert and accompany the procession of brewers and landlords of the inns and pubs (Beck 2003, 54).

Company Outings

"*Das Wandern ist des Müllers Lust, das Wa-an-dern!*" (Hiking is the miller's pleasure, hiking). The song echoed from the walls of the gorge through which a small group of people dressed in hiking outfits walked—or, one might say, marched. It was not a weekend, and they were not members of a hiking club (see 5: Activities and Clubs) but employees of a publishing company. It was in the 1970s, and at that time, *Betriebsausflüge* (company outings) were popular and part of the social fabric. They could take many forms—from hikes to museum excursions or parties and dances (*Betriebsfeste*). These events helped to create a sense of belonging, just as the local festivities do.

The untranslatable term *Gemütlichkeit* was then, more than now, part of German society. It implied not only the very private sense of being comfortable with others with whom one felt a special bond of closeness (see 2: Stereotypes and Prejudices) but also the sense of belonging to a social sphere that included more casual acquaintances and even strangers. Although Germans used to be (and to a large extent still are) very particular in regard to the form of address, using a formal "Sie" in most cases and reserving the intimate "Du" for close friends and family (see 2: Stereotypes and Prejudices), they are, at the same time, outgoing and see themselves as part of a group. Therefore, in restaurants and even more so in pubs, one does not mind sitting with strangers. Gemütlichkeit occurs when everyone feels like a happy family. And the "happy family" can be a circle of friends; a social group bound together by the same interests, religion, or profession; employees of a firm; or even a group of strangers who get along just fine for whatever time span.

Vacations and Travel

Germans have not only more official holidays than other nations (about fourteen) but also the longest paid vacation time (about thirty to thirty-five days per year, compared to about twelve in the United States). They also work fewer hours per week than most other workers (about thirty-five). Although the hours of work per week have become again at the beginning of the new millennium a hotly debated issue (some firms reestablished the forty-hour work week in 2004), whatever the outcome, it probably will not change the fact that the many holidays and long vacations have turned Germans into the prime tourists of Western Europe. At any time, more than half the population, according to Hermann Bausinger (2000, 58), is on the

Working Time and Leisure Time 1840–2000

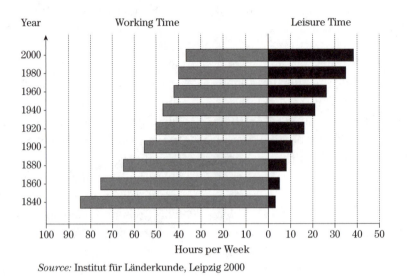

Source: Institut für Länderkunde, Leipzig 2000

Paid Vacation Days in One Year, 1950–1997 (Average)

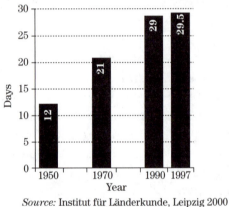

Source: Institut für Länderkunde, Leipzig 2000

Percentage of Travel Inland and Abroad during the Main Vacation Time, 1954–1998

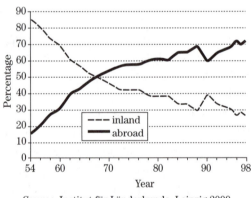

Source: Institut für Länderkunde, Leipzig 2000

road—about 35 million with their own cars, 12 million by bus or train, and another 12 million by plane. In 1995, German households spent an average of almost 1500 euros on their holidays (see Eichheim et al. 2002, 63).

The vacation budget is so important that even in financially difficult times, Germans cut their spending in other areas before they begin to cut down on vacations. They travel more often than other nationals, they travel further, they stay longer, and they seek a wider range of amenities or choices when they travel. A main topic of conversation among friends and acquaintances is where one has just been and where one plans to go. The main differences over the decades since 1945 are that the distances Germans travel have increased and that the photo albums with black and white pictures have been replaced first by colored slides and then by

Percentage of the Population using Vacation Time for Travel, 1954–1998

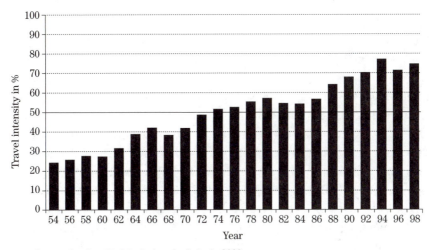

Source: Institut für Länderkunde, Leipzig 2000

videos and now by digitized still and moving images. Everyone is now a documentarist with the civic duty of educating friends and neighbors about the world.

Because there is not only one vacation time but several, one vacation is reserved for apparently well-deserved relaxation from work. This is usually the summer vacation and is often spent at a beach resort. The term *Teutonengrills* (Teutonic grills) has been coined for those beaches of the Mediterranean, Adriatic, and Mallorca—and, more recently, Florida—where many Germans migrate to lie in the sun. The North Sea and Baltic beaches cannot guarantee warmth and sunshine and tend to be favored by those who spend other vacations, usually winter ones, in sunnier climes. The goal of the other vacations is self-improvement and expansion of one's knowledge of the world. These are referred to as *Bildungsreisen* (educational journeys). Safaris, adventure tours, and even trips to experience the poverty of the less industrialized countries are high on the list for such trips. The tourist industry, domi-

nated by TUI (Germany's largest tourist agency at the beginning of the new millennium) and Neckermann (the former number one tourist agency), certainly helps the economy. At one time, domestic European flights were very expensive, and Germans tended to take the car or train to reach their vacation destinations. Cut-price airlines have changed the situation, particularly for the young and Internet-savvy, and jetting between European cities is no longer reserved for business travelers or the very wealthy.

Another thing Germans do with their long vacations is combine their respect for the environment (see 10: Consumer Culture versus Green Awareness) with a desire to stay fit (see 2: Health Issues and Sexuality) by going on bicycle trips, or "tours." This does not simply mean riding around the neighborhood, but traveling (by train or car) to a destination and then cycling for at least a week, staying at inns or hostels along the way and enjoying the local cuisine. In February 2005, when many were planning their trips to distant tropical climates, others were beginning to collect maps and information through the magazine *Brigitte* for their bicycle tours. In a subtle nod to the fairy tale about seven-league boots that help the wearer cover huge distances with a few steps (see 6: Popular and Belletristic Literature, Dime Novels and Comics), the magazine spread its series of routes and information over seven issues, supplying seven different routes and seven sets of tips on where to stay, what to eat, what to wear, how to fix a flat tire, and so on. Bike fans were also offered an online resource for checking such information while on the road. To make the concept even more appealing, special equipment was offered in the "Brigitte Shop," including a bicycle computer, no doubt to quickly check how to handle that flat tire (*Brigitte Newsletter*, February 9, 2005).

Sports

"Tooooooooooor!!" (Goal!) The decisive third goal against Hungary (final score 3–2) at the soccer world championship in 1954 was important not only for German soccer fans but also for the nation as a whole. The victory helped to give the still young German Federal Republic self-respect. The headlines announced: "*Wir sind wieder wer*" (We are someone again). Sepp Herberger, the coach, became a national hero, as did Fritz Walter, Max Morlock, and Helmut Rahn, the star players.

In sports, as in other aspects of daily life, the shadow of the Third Reich—with its successful Olympic Games in Berlin in 1936 and its emphasis on healthy living, which drove it to organize Germans into unions that made everyone "exercise for the *Vaterland* (fatherland)" (Briel 2002,

127)—loomed large for many years. Still, sport (besides hard work) was an area where one could forget one's troubles in spite of the fact that many of the prewar facilities were still in use. Hitler had not invented sports—just appropriated them for his own purposes. Stadiums and swimming pools had been built all over the country, so that even in rural areas, access was relatively easy. The new Germany renovated the old and built more public facilities, particularly public indoor and outdoor swimming pools, often combined with medicinal saunas, which had been popular in Germany since Roman times. These pools and saunas have since been developed into vast complexes, designed not just for a quick swim or soak but for a whole day of relaxing and refreshing activity. There one can relax one's muscles in whirlpool baths, get a massage on different parts of the body by moving from one jet stream to another at the sound of a gong, and finally, have hot water splash from a gushing waterfall onto the neck and shoulders. The more energetic can swim in warm water from an inside pool to an outside one and do laps in either, and nonswimmers can jump in artificially created waves.

For years, Germans both young and old have run, played ball, swum, bicycled, hiked, skied, climbed cliffs, practiced shooting at ranges, ridden on horseback, and glided through the air. However, in German fashion, they usually did all this in local, state, or federal sports associations (see 5: Activities and Clubs). Schoolchildren also had about two hours of supervised sports each week, gymnastics in winter and athletics and swimming in summer in the tradition of *Turnvater* (father of gymnastics) Friedrich Ludwig Jahn (1778–1852), whose name is synonymous with physical exercise. In many schools, each child—to the chagrin of some—had to pass a *Freischwimmer-Prüfung* (a test that proved that one could keep afloat—that is, swim or tread water—for at least fifteen minutes and jump into the water from the one-meter board) before graduation. Without this badge, which the children had to display on their swimsuits, they were not allowed to use the deep end of a public swimming pool unless supervised in some towns. Today, many restrictions have disappeared but young and old are still encouraged by swimming associations to pass swimming tests of varying degrees of difficulty. Badges are given for the display of one's skills.

Along with the expansion of the pool complexes, other facilities were updated. Shooting ranges were rebuilt. The hiking trails that crisscross all of Germany were groomed, and the signs freshly painted. Skiing experienced a boom beginning in the 1970s once Germans began to travel more. As a result, German ski resorts were developed and now offer trails for snowboarding as well as all the variations on skiing. Especially in the 1970s, the various clubs encouraged the local communities to add *Trimm-dich-Pfade* (get-fit-circuits), which were often sponsored by insurance companies. Balancing beams and pull-up bars in the woods and fields awaited the crowds of exercise-crazy Germans. Table-tennis tables were added to playgrounds.

The influence of many of the club sports has waned, and they have lost members while private sports, driven by advertisements and professional and commercial fitness centers, have expanded. The latter are still expanding. A private trainer is no longer uncommon. A few sports have been briefly in the spotlight at times when indi-

vidual German stars become popular, such as Boris Becker in tennis, or Katarina Witt in ice skating. Enthusiasm for biking and equestrianism, although also influenced by the ratings of champions, has remained relatively steady. Newer sports are also gaining popularity: inline skating, mountain biking, hang gliding, squash. Windsurfing has long been popular in Germany, perhaps because it allows people from a country with more lakes than ocean beaches a chance to experience the sensation of riding waves.

Motor racing has changed its character over the past half century. In the first decades after the war when the Mercedes team, the Silver Arrows (*Silberpfeile*), established international fame, motor racing also became a communal event with local heroes. Especially popular were the motorbike races with daredevil sidecar-drivers leaning out of their cars and almost touch-

Soap box racing in Darmstadt, Hesse, in the fifties.

Motorbike sidecar racing in Germany. (Matthias Stark, www.lukemarvin.com)

ing the pavement. And not to be forgotten in this context are the children's *Seifenkistenrennen* (soapbox derbies), preparing the future pilots of formula-1-races.

The one sport that is constant in Germany and remains above the whims of fad and fashion is *Fußball* (football, called "soccer" in the United States). Football training resumed in many German villages just days after the end of the war. As the researcher Tara Magdalinski discovered, "Organized clubs emerged only six weeks after Germany's capitulation" (Sandford 1999, 574). Twice in West Germany's history the *Autobahnen* were almost empty: One time was in 1973 during the oil crisis, and the other was in 1974 during the world championship match, Germany against the Netherlands (Germany won again after twenty years, this time 2–1).

The Deutscher Fußballbund (German Football Association, DFB), founded in 1900, is one of the largest sports' organizations in the world, with more than 6 million members and some 27,000 clubs. In the beginning, all clubs consisted solely of amateurs who played the sport in their leisure time. Since 1963, Germany has had a professional league, and since 1973 a second league, to guarantee that German players can compete internationally, and in the summer of 2006, Germany was the host to the soccer world cup.

In the German Democratic Republic, centrally organized sports were even more important than in the Federal Republic. Children were tested early for special abilities and then trained accordingly in special programs. Although a small nation, the GDR became one of the powerhouses in many sport disciplines. The high point of its achievements was in Seoul, South Korea, in 1988, when the East German athletes finished second overall in medals won at the Summer Olympics, behind the Soviet Union but ahead of the United States. With unification, it was hoped that the new Germany would be even more successful, but instead the widespread use of performance-enhancing drugs in the GDR was uncovered, leading to further shame for the citizens of the new provinces.

From A to Z

All Saints' Day: On November 1 and 2 as well as on the last Sunday before Advent, the dead are remembered in Germany. All Saints' Day on November 1 (which is a public holiday in Baden-Württemberg, Bavaria, North-Rhine Westphalia, and Saarland) was originally instituted by the Catholic Church to honor all saints, known and unknown, and to supply any deficiencies in the celebration of saints' feasts throughout the year. On this day, Catholic families pay a visit to the cemetery and place flowers and candles on graves. (Those who live far away from their family's graves order a floral arrangement or wreath from a florist or nursery.) Candles continue to burn on the graves until the next day, which is All Souls' Day. At that time, the celebration of the Mass, prayer, and fasting can help free the souls of the dead from Purgatory. Protestants initially rejected both cults. Since the nineteenth century, however, they, too, have remembered the dead on the last Sunday of the church year (*Totensonntag*, Sunday of the dead), the Sunday before the first Sunday of Advent. Finally, the state instituted a *Volkstrauertag* (national day of mourning) in 1952 celebrated two Sundays before the first Sunday of Advent.

April Fool's Day: April 1. April Fool's Day is not an official German holiday; nor does it have any traditions associated with it in Germany that are different from those known in the other Western countries. But it certainly is popular in Germany, and many people play tricks on others on this day. There are numerous explanations for this custom. Some see it related to Christ being sent to Pontius Pilate; others regard it as the birthday of Judas, who betrayed Jesus, giving the devil power over the world. To overcome him, one must trick him. The Romans also celebrated a fool's festival at this time, however, as did the people of India.

The most likely explanation for the tradition is one given in detail by Anthony Aveni. In 153 B.C., the Romans chose as the beginning of the New Year "the first sighting of the crescent moon in the west after sunset following the winter solstice." But the Christian church, "once firmly established, stubbornly clung to the spring equinox as the starting point of the solar cycle. Staid England and her colonies continued to designate New Year's Day as March 25 and refused to adopt January 1 until 1752. April Fool's Day is the remnant of the bogus new year created when Charles IX of France made the switch from the spring equinox to January in 1564. But because news traveled slowly, most rural folks continued to make New Year's calls and exchange gifts on the first of the month after the equinox. The situation gradually evolved into mockery, and it became the custom to hook a *poisson d'Avril* (April fish), named after the young fish more easily caught in streams at the beginning of the season, by offering up a silly gift" (Aveni 2003, 18–19).

Ascension Day: *Christi Himmelfahrt*, the fortieth day after Easter, represents the ascension of Jesus to his Father in Heaven. Ascension Day always falls on the Thursday nine days before *Pfingsten* (Whitsun). In many areas of Germany, Ascension Day is also celebrated as *Vatertag* (Father's Day). Primarily the young fathers come together and ride in coaches into the fields with sufficient supplies of beer to commiserate with each other about their lack of freedom as husbands and fathers. The custom probably developed from the processions in the fields that used to end with a meal for all participants.

Athletes: The names of numerous postwar athletes have become part of German culture. Max Schmeling (1905–2005) defeated Joe Louis in 1936 in boxing. This event was used by leaders of the Third Reich to support their superior race ideology. But Schmeling kept his distance from the Nazis, who disowned him after he lost the rematch in 1938. After the war, he became a symbol of fairness and great athletic achievement. Soccer legends include Fritz Walter (1920–2002), the center forward; Max Morlock (1925–1994), the most successful German player in the famous Berne-tournament in 1954; Helmut Rahn (1929–2003), the *Bomber*, who shot the winning goal at the soccer world championship game in 1954; and his coach, Sepp Herberger (1897–1977); Uwe Seeler (b. 1936), one of Germany's most consistent soccer players; Franz Beckenbauer (b. 1945), known as "der Kaiser" (the em-

peror), an admired strategist and a successful manager and coach; Sepp Maier (b. 1944), one of the greatest goal keepers of all time; Lothar Matthäus (b. 1961), captain of the successful world cup team in 1990; Oliver Khan (b. 1969), another of the colorful goal keepers; Jürgen Klinsmann (b. 1964), nicknamed the "Golden Bomber" (because of his long blond hair), who retired from the national team after the 1998 World Cup but returned in 2004 as the coach of the national team hoping to win the World Cup in 2006 when Germany hosts the tournament. Armin Hary (b. 1937) became the first man to run a 100-meter sprint in ten seconds in 1960 and was the first non-American since 1928 to win the Olympic gold metal in the 100 m dash in the same year. Bernhard Langer (b. 1957) was the most successful German golfer. Katarina Witt (b. 1965) is the greatest GDR (as well as the greatest German) ice skater and one of the most successful in the world, winning four world championships and two Olympic gold medals in figure skating. Boris Becker (b. 1967), the *Wunderkind* (child prodigy) of tennis, was the first unseeded and the youngest player ever to win the Wimbledon's men's singles title. He was voted several times West German sportsman of the year and revitalized tennis in Germany together with Steffi Graf (b. 1969). Michael Schumacher (b. 1969) is synonymous in Germany with Formula One racing. Heinz-Harald Frentzen (b. 1967) is one of his great rivals. Both are on the list of the 100 Best Germans, as are Jan Ulrich (b. 1973), winner of the Tour de France in 1997; Sven Hannawald (b. 1974), one of Germany's top ski-jumpers, world champion in 2000 and 2002; and Dirk Nowitzki (b. 1978), the best German basketball player ever and a very successful player in the United States, in the NBA (Knopp et al. 2003).

Bildungsreise: Educational journey. This is the term for vacations with an educational or self-improvement theme.

Bundesliga: The premier league in football (soccer), formed in 1963. It comprises eighteen football clubs. The highlight of the season is the championship. The title was won sixteen times in its forty years of history by Bayern Munich.

Candlemas: *Lichtmess*, a Catholic holiday celebrated on February 2. Its name indicates its function: the consecration of all candles needed for the upcoming year. It is a festival that takes place exactly forty days after Christmas (*Weihnachten*) and goes back to old Roman and Germanic spring festivals. It occurs at a time when the days are getting longer, the sunlight is getting stronger, and the workmen can stop using artificial light. Years ago it was celebrated by taking half a day off from work. For centuries, Candlemas was also the day when farmers took on their helpers, farm laborers, and maids, because the winter period was over and they could begin preparing for the cultivation of their fields. Therefore, this is the festival of those employed in agriculture. It predates May Day and Labor Day celebrations.

Carnival: See *"Fastnacht/Fasnet/Fasching,"* below.

Clubs: Membership in clubs and associations is quite high in Germany. The following list gives the percentage of the total German population that belongs to each type of club; many people belong to more than one club: (1) sport club (25 percent), (2) bowling club (12 percent), (3) labor union (8 percent), (4) church-related club (7 percent), (5) automobile club (7 percent), (6) Red Cross or other charitable relief organization (7 percent), (7) shooting club (6 percent), (8) glee club (6 percent), (9) club based on one's hobby (5 percent), (10) volunteer fire department (4 percent), (11) hiking club (4 percent), (12) club for the preservation of regional traditions (3 percent), (13) club to protect nature and animals (3 percent), (14) club for young people in rural areas (3 percent), (15) garden club (3 percent), (16) political party (3 percent), (17) professional organization (2 percent), (18) association of refugees and expellees (2 percent), (19) citizens' initiative (2 percent), (20) fan club (1 percent) (Behal-Thomsen et al. 1993, 87).

Corpus Christi: Literally, the body of Christ; in German, *Fronleichnam* (*fron* meaning Lord, *leichnam* meaning body). Corpus Christi, instituted in 1264, is a Catholic festival celebrated on the second Thursday after Whitsun. It is significant in the Catholic Church calendar around the world; in Germany it is celebrated with processions in Baden-Württemberg, Bavaria, Hesse, North-Rhine Westphalia, Rhineland-Palatinate, Saarland, Saxony, and Thuringia. The holiday is a reminder of the Lord's Supper on *Gründonnerstag* (Maundy Thursday) in the light of Christ's resurrection and ascension. Whereas the English term "Maundy" comes from the symbolic washing of the disciples' feet by Jesus, the German word *grün*, which seems to mean "green," actually comes from the German word *greinen* (to weep) and refers to the fact that the sinners and penitents who had been excluded from the community of believers, and therefore were weeping, are now forgiven. Chronologically, Fronleichnam should be celebrated on *Gründonnerstag*, but because it is a joyous feast, it seemed inappropriate to celebrate it in the *Karwoche* (week of mourning).

Days of remembrance: Some important dates in German history (some positive and some negative), often an occasion for official speeches are, January 27, the liberation of the Auschwitz concentration camp by the Soviet Red Army; May 8, the anniversary of the surrender of the German army in 1945, or, as FRG President Richard von Weizsäcker described it in his speech forty years later, the liberation day of the German people by the Allies; May 23, the date the Basic Law, Germany's constitution, took effect in 1949; June 17, see text; July 20, the failed assassination attempt of Hitler in 1944 by high-ranking German military officers, who were immediately executed; August 13, the first day of the construction of the Berlin Wall in 1961; September 1, the beginning of World War II in 1939 when Germany invaded Poland; October 3, see text; November 9, the anniversary of a collection of events, not all of which are cause for celebration (see below); December 10, passage by the United Nations of the International Declaration on Human Rights in 1948.

On November 9, 1918, the last German emperor, Wilhelm II, was forced to abdicate, and the first parliamentary democracy, the Weimar Republic, was established. On November 9, 1923, Adolf Hitler organized the *Marsch zur Feldherrnhalle* (known in English as the Beer Hall Putsch; the literal translation is "march to the hall of commanders" [a monument in honor of Bavarian military leaders, built in 1841–

1844]) in Munich, which failed. In 1938 on this same date, the *Reichskristallnacht* (Night of Broken Glass, today usually referred to as *Pogromnacht*), Nazis attacked synagogues and Jewish shops, smashing windows and setting them on fire. Finally on November 9, 1989, the border crossings from East to West Berlin were opened, which started the process of unification.

Deutscher Sportbund: German Sport Association, DSB. Founded in 1950, the DSB is the national organization for the various regional and local sports clubs that have financial and administrative autonomy. Its official goal is the Olympic slogan, "The most important aspect is not to win but to participate." In the GDR, the equivalent organization was the Deutscher Turn- und Sportbund (German Association of Gymnastics and Sport, DTSB).

Epiphany: Known in German as *Heilige Drei Könige*, (literally, holy three kings), the Epiphany on January 6 (at the end of the twelve days of Christmas) is especially celebrated in Bavaria, Baden-Württemberg, and Saxony-Anhalt. Epiphany is a feast day in the Catholic Church celebrating the coming of the Magi. On this day, children dressed as the Three Kings, or the Three Wise Men, write the letters C + M + B above the doors of houses. The letters stand for the names of the Three Kings, Caspar, Melchior, and Balthazar, as well as the expression *Christus Mansionem Benedictat* (Christ Bless this Home). Primarily in the Alps, one may encounter three frightening figures (sometimes just one) with horns and furs instead of the Magi. These figures are related to old Germanic nature goddesses representing the fury of winter. The positive aspect, the pleasant snow, is found in the image of *Frau Holle* (Mother Hulda), a mythical figure who shakes her featherbeds to cause snow to fall (see 6: Popular and Belletristic Literature, Dime Novels and Comics).

Fastnacht/Fasnet/Fasching: The nights before a period of fasting begins, a time of revelry in which, according to Germanic customs, fertility rites took place. The church tried in vain to stop the festival from taking place but only succeeded in limiting the period of indulgence by having it end on Ash Wednesday (the fortieth day before Easter, since the seventh century the beginning of an annual period of repentance, officially confirmed in 1091 at the council of Benevent). There are not only different names (Fas[t]nacht, Fasnet, Fasching, and Karneval [Carnival]) but also varying traditions.

The first part of the compound, *Fas-*, is related to words meaning "to dress oneself" and "to have fun" as well as to the word *faseln*, which could mean "to play tricks" or "to be fertile." The word *Fasching*, used in Bavaria and Austria, is documented for the first time in 1204. The term *Karneval* came to Germany via Italy in approximately 1700. It may be derived from "carne vale" (farewell to meat) or "carrus navalis" (carts in the form of ships), referring to the floats looking like ships.

The Fasching festivities in Vienna and Munich were influenced by aristocratic balls, and still are to some extent, especially in Vienna, whereas the Karneval tradition in Cologne is based on the medieval guilds. After 1385, Cologne was an imperial free city. The shooting guilds (whose activities were the craftsmen's equivalent to the joustings of the knights) played an especially important role. The officer calling the shots was usually very quick-witted, similar to the fool at royal courts. This led to the political satire found at the Carnival and executed in the *Bütt* (washtub), the lectern for Carnival speeches, in which everything is being "cleaned" that has become "dirty" during the year. The main Carnival events have been broadcast since the beginning of TV (see 7: Radio and Television), and the media have certainly influenced their character. But each century had already added its modifications. This is especially true of the last years of the French occupation at the beginning of the nineteenth century. At this time, the *Prinz*, *Bauer*, and *Jungfrau* (Prince, Peasant, and Virgin) were introduced as the official heads of the celebration. Also new at that time was the participation of various military guards, dressed in the flashy uniforms of the seventeenth century. Girls' dance groups began to perform in those years as well, though these were later influenced by the popular ballets of the 1920s. Finally, a board of eleven members was introduced to organize and run the event. (See 5: Holidays and Local Festivities, section on "Carnival," for the various interpretations of the popularity of the number eleven.)

In the old Allemanic regions in the southwest corner of Germany, the parades are smaller than in the big cities of the Rhineland (Cologne, Düsseldorf, Mainz), and the marchers are fully masked figures whose features and roles stem from a centuries-old lineage. There is the *G'schellnarr* (bell fool) with bells sewn onto his costume; the *Schaantle* (Disgraced one) with a frightening facial mask that has its origin in a caricature of the hated Jewish businessman; the *Fransenkleidle* (fringed dress); and the *Federehannes* (feather Jack) with a devil's mask, a costume covered with feathers and its wearer carrying a long stick with a fox tail. The parade itself is a strictly organized chaos that features a reversal of values (for example, bad becomes good) and the breaking of taboos. Though once these themes may have been a driving force in the culture, nowadays they are only theater.

In Basel, Switzerland, Fasnacht begins a week later than in most other towns—that is, after Ash Wednesday. The important day is Monday (one week after Rosenmontag), when, at 4 AM, a parade begins. Apparently, religious and military traditions came together in establishing this timing. The Monday after the traditional Fasnacht had been selected in the sixteenth century as the day when recruits had to report for duty, and this was a cause for celebration and parades. Because of the Reformation, however, Ash Wednesday had lost its religious importance, preparing the ground for this merger of two celebrations, religious and secular. But in Basel, as in Cologne, many of the characteristic features of the festival that remain are inventions of the nineteenth century.

For the *Morgenstraich* (morning parade), all the lights in the city center and in the streets of the inner town are extinguished, and the participants light lanterns that are placed on their heads. They also carry large lanterns that display pictures and satirical comments and verses. Every member of a *Clique* (club) wears a costume with a *Larve* (face mask). Many are set characters with a long lineage, as in the other Allemanic traditions. There is the *Harlekin* from the Italian *commedia dell'-arte;* the *Alte Dante* (old aunt); the *Waggis,* a dialect word describing an Alsatian farmer in a blue shirt, white pants, and wooden shoes wearing a face mask with a large nose and wild red hair; and many

more. They all play the piccolo or a drum, reminders of the military tradition, and start precisely at 4 AM, with the last strike of the clock. In contrast to other parades, the Basel one is organized as a crisscrossing of the groups through the town, a constant coming and going of small and large groups playing their instruments or carrying large lanterns, as well as individuals, some distributing *Zeedel* (leaflets with verses and commentary). Often, behind them follow family members and friends in an orderly line in their normal clothes. In the same way, the spectators do not wear costumes but are only encouraged to buy a *Plakette,* a decorated metal sign with a new design each year, as a symbol of their support for the Fasnacht. The restaurants are filled, and the special foods are the *Zwiebelwähe* (onion cakes) and Mehlsuppe (a brown soup thickened with flour). From time to time, so-called *Schnitzelbänk,* groups of satirists, will come to designated restaurants to deliver songs and verses. In the afternoon, a more traditional parade with floats and bands playing *Guggenmusik,* music just a touch off-key, winds through the main streets.

The word *Morgenstraich* for the parade echoes the military *Zapfenstreich* (literally, the tap on the plug to close the wine barrel for the night), the signal in the evening for all soldiers to return to the barracks.

Feast of Assumption: In German, *Mariä Himmelfahrt* (Mary's ascension to heaven), August 15. This feast of the Catholic Church celebrates the Mother of Jesus, Mary, being taken into Heaven by God, in body and soul. The Feast of the Assumption is particularly celebrated in Bavaria and the Saarland.

Gartenzwerge: Garden gnomes. These terra cotta gnomes (plastic ones are not the "real thing") are the symbol of kitsch and as German as the word *Kitsch*. Actually, some intellectuals regard them as kitschy to such a degree that they are no longer kitsch and have become a symbol for the "cool" intellectual. There are male *Gartenzwerge* and female *Gartenzwerginnen.* They have been used as art works, they have been objects of ridicule and legal arguments, and they caused an economic stir when cheaper, Polish-produced versions invaded the German market, resulting in the founding of the Association for the Protection of Garden Gnomes and a Eurognome-94 symposium (Sandford 1999, 244). The true origins of these figures are not quite clear, but researchers agree that it was Philipp Grieben who really began the craze with the founding of his own factory in 1874.

GDR holidays: Official holidays in the GDR included International Labor Day on May 1; the Day of the Republic on October 7; New Year's Day; Christmas; Good Friday; and Easter. In 1967, when the five-day work week was introduced, Easter Monday, Ascension Day, the Day of Repentance and Prayer, and the Day of Liberation from Hitler's Fascism on May 8 were taken off the list of days that people were off from work. Nevertheless, they were still seen as days to be honored. Other holidays included the Day of Post and Telecommunication Workers on the second Sunday in February; the Day of Civil Defense on February 11; the Day of Trade Workers on the third Sunday in February; the Day of the National People's Army on March 1; the International Day for Women on March 8; the Day of Metal Workers on the second Sun-

day in April; the Day of the Youth Brigades in May or June; the International Day of the Child on June 1; the Day of the Railway and Public Transportation Workers on the first or second day in June; the Day of Teachers on June 12; the Day of Cooperative Farmers and Workers in Socialistic Agriculture and Forestry on the second or third Sunday in June; the Day of Construction Workers on the third or fourth Sunday in June; the Day of the People's Police on July 1; the Day of Miners and Workers in the Field of Energy Production on the first Sunday in July; Peace Day of the World on September 1; the Day of Service Workers on the third Sunday in September; the Day of Maritime Traffic and Trade on October 13; the Day of Workers in the Food Production Industry on the third Sunday in October; the Day of the Great Socialist October Revolution on November 7; Youth Day of the World on November 10; the Day of Chemistry Workers on the second Sunday in November; International Student Day on November 17; the Day of Metalworkers on the third Sunday in November; the Day of the Border Guards of the GDR on December 1; the Day of Health Service Workers on December 11; and the Birthday of Pioneers on December 13. In addition, there were many celebrations for achieving the various economic plans and other milestones (Eulenspiegel-Verlags-Team 2002, 9–10). The fact that most of these holidays fell on a Sunday can be interpreted in at least two ways: They did not interfere with the work week and thus slow down production, and they offered secular celebrations that would allow people to gather together as they might otherwise have done in churches.

International Women's Day: A purely political celebration is the International

Women's Day on March 8, which took place for the first time on March 19, 1911. Millions of women in Germany, Austria, Denmark, Switzerland, and the United States took part. It was initiated by Clara Zetkin (1857–1933), the German woman suffragette. March 18 was a day of commemoration for the victims of the suppression of democracy in 1848. March 8 was chosen in 1921 in commemoration of the strike by female textile workers in Saint Petersburg in 1917.

Karneval: See "*Fastnacht/Fasnet/Fasching,*" above.

Landshuter Hochzeit: The wedding in Landshut, a historic reenactment of a wedding in 1475, which is performed every three years on four weekends in July and August.

Martin's Day: *Martinstag*, celebrated on November 10 or 11, depending on the region. Usually, children form a procession carrying lanterns and move from house to house, singing or reciting poetry and hoping for gifts. (The similarity to the American custom of children going door to door at Halloween, just ten days earlier, and hoping for candy may be more than just a striking coincidence.) The legend of the saint Martin of Tours tells that as a young soldier he shared his overcoat with a freezing beggar. Therefore, he is usually depicted as a knight on a horse with a sword in his hand cutting his coat in two halves. In some areas, "Martin's Fires" were lit, which symbolically burn away the summer to make way for the coming year. It was also the symbol for Martin's good deed that lit up the darkness of evil.

Mother's Day: Called *Muttertag* in German, Mother's Day is celebrated on the second Sunday in May. As in other countries, mothers are given flowers and presents by their children.

New Year's Day: Termed *Sylvester* or *Silvester*, in honor of the day of death and name day of Pope Silvester I (314–335), the new year is marked in all regions with the ringing of church bells and with fireworks. In a few towns, trumpets are still heard from church steeples. Even rarer nowadays are customs connected with singing and well wishing by going from house to house. Though New Year's Eve is certainly still a time for parties and good food and drink, games that attempt to foretell the future are less popular nowadays—for example, competing for who will end up with the larger part of a Brezel (pretzel) or interpreting the shapes that result from throwing a spoonful of melted lead into a bowl of cold water. The pig, the horseshoe, and the four-leaf clover are still often used as good luck omens. (Many customs are described in Schönfeldt 1980.)

Oberammergauer Passionsspiele: Passion Play in Oberammergau, performed every ten years since 1634 because of an oath by the citizens of Oberammergau to thank God for saving them from the plague.

Olympics: For Germany, the games in 1972 were especially important because they were hosted in Munich. The events that year were overshadowed, however, by the murder of eleven Israeli athletes and officials by terrorists. See Stephen Spielberg's film *Munich*, 2005.

Peace Festival: *Friedensfest*, held on August 8 in Augsburg, where the *Augsburger Bekenntnis* (*Confessio Augustana*, Augsburg manifesto) outlining a guarantee of religious freedom for Protestants was presented in 1530 to the emperor Karl V. This manifesto was the basis for the peace treaty between Catholics and Protestants in 1555, which stated that the rulers of the different regions could determine the religion of their subjects. This strengthened regionalism in Germany (see 1: Overcoming Regionalism). Yet, even this document could not prevent the Thirty Years' War (1618–1648). On August 8, 1629, a new wave of anti-Protestant sentiment began in Augsburg. All Protestant churches were destroyed. But after the *Westfälischer Friede* (Peace Treaty of Westphalia) in 1648, which ended the war, religious freedom returned. In commemoration of these times and as a plea for religious tolerance, the Friedensfest has been celebrated since 1650. Since 1950 it has been a public holiday in Augsburg and a time when both churches, Catholic and Protestant, join in ecumenical worship.

Penance Day: *Buß- und Bettag*, celebrated in the Protestant churches on the Wednesday before the last Sunday of the church year (*Totensonntag*). It is only a holiday in Saxony.

Pentecost: Also known as Whitsun (*Pfingsten*), celebrated on Whit Sunday and Whit Monday, the fiftieth and fifty-first days after Easter. It commemorates the appearance of the Holy Ghost to the apostles.

Reformation Day: October 31, celebrated by Protestants. It is a public holiday in Brandenburg, Mecklenburg-Western Pomerania, Saxony, Saxony-Anhalt, and Thuringia. The holiday commemorates the Reformation of the church by Martin Luther in the sixteenth century, which created the formation of a new religious group, the Protestant Lutheran Church.

Schrebergärten: The small gardens at the edges of the cities, leased and maintained by families. They are named after their founder, Daniel Gottlob Moritz Schreber. Although Schrebergärten (also called *Kleingärten*, small gardens) are a family-based activity, they are often organized by *Kleingartenvereine* (small garden associations). They were also extremely popular in the GDR.

Seifenkistenrennen: Soapbox derbies. Sponsored by friends and small companies and built in do-it-yourself style, these wooden racing cars without motors had to roll down a hill and were very popular among young people in the 1950s.

Silberpfeile: Literally, silver arrows, the famous Mercedes Formula-I racing cars that reestablished German car engineering on an international level.

Sports associations: Sports in Germany are organized primarily through associations. There are also private fitness and sports studios that offer a wide range of activities for a monthly fee.

Tourism: For global tourism, the major German travel agencies are TUI and Neckermann-Reisen. For national tourism, the main private organizations are Deutscher Fremdenverkehrsverband (German Organization for Foreign Visitors) and the Deutsche Zentrale für Tourismus e.V. (German National Tourist Office).

Travel in the GDR: Some see the travel restrictions on the citizens of the GDR as one cause for its collapse. The various efforts by the government to make travel possible, even to subsidize it, seem to have been insufficient. The Freier Deutscher Gewerkschaftsbund (Free German Trades Union) had its own—but not necessarily very exciting—vacation facilities. Limited travel inside the GDR and neighboring Eastern bloc countries could not make up for the global attractions that were out of reach.

Turnen: Gymnastics. In Germany, sports and the military have long been closely linked. This connection began with the defeat at the hands of Napoleon's armies and the decision of Prussian leaders to strengthen their youth through gymnastics organized by the *Turnvater* (father of gymnastics), Friedrich Ludwig Jahn, in whose honor many village streets have been named.

Valentine's Day: Some believe that Valentine's Day is an invention of the florist and chocolate industries. In reality, the celebration dates back to the fourteenth century in France and Great Britain. Perhaps its origin lies in a Roman fertility rite celebrated on February 14/15, the Lupercalia. The legend has it that St. Valentine, bishop of Terni living in the second or third century (dates in reference works vary), married lovers secretly against the wishes of the parents, who were more interested in a good financial deal than a love marriage. St. Valentine was also the chief saint to protect against epilepsy. Therefore, the town of Rouffach

in Alsace-Lorraine, where a skull relic is kept, was a center for pilgrims who wanted to be healed. Today, this tradition has died out, but St. Valentine's popularity increases each year because of U.S. influence. It may well be that there is subtle lobbying by purveyors of chocolate and roses.

Verbindung: Fraternity. Once German *Verbindungen*, called *Burschenschaften* (*Bursche* meaning a young male), played an important role in German politics as the standard-bearers of national liberalism against the Napoleonic occupation (see 1: Overcoming Regionalism). As their name implies, they excluded women. Today, they have lost their revolutionary glamour. The remaining groups are usually very conservative. Their main function is to aid the various members in their careers through their old-boy network.

Walpurgis Night: In German, *Walpurgisnacht*, the night when, according to legend, witches, cats, and goats ride on brooms to the Blocksberg, a mountain in the Harz region, in order to dance with the devil. Therefore, it is a night of magic in which things and people can be transformed. The legend is based on the oral tales that the Saxons, after having been baptized by force by Charlemagne, returned in disguise to this mountain to continue to honor their heathen gods. The Catholic Church tried to overcome this legend by dedicating the day to Walpurga, the patron saint of farm wives and maids. But the witch stories survived because—as some say—the young boys liked to make up horror stories to make the women and girls stay at home while they cut down the maypole and made preparations for the May Day celebrations (Schönfeldt 1980, 140).

Wanderlust: "A strong desire or impulse to rove or travel about" (*Random House Webster's Dictionary*, McGraw Hill edition, 1991) seems to be so much part of the German character that it has become a loanword in other languages.

Additional Readings

Bächtold-Stäubli, Hanns, and Eduard Hoffmann-Krayer. *Handwörterbuch des deutschen Aberglaubens.* 10 vols. Berlin and New York: Walter de Gruyter, 2000. (Original edition, 1927–1942)

Behal-Thomsen, Heinke, Angelika Lundquist-Mog, and Paul Mog. *Typisch deutsch? Arbeitsbuch zu Aspekten deutscher Mentalität.* München: Langenscheidt, 1993.

Deutsche Gesellschaft für Freizeit (DGF). *Freizeit, Sport, Bewegung. Stand und Tendenzen in der Bundesrepublik Deutschland.* Hannover: Medienpool, Gesellschaft für Wirtschaftswerbung, 1987.

Deutscher Bundestag, ed. *Materialien der Enquete Kommission. Aufarbeitung von Geschichte und Folgen der SED-Diktatur in Deutschland.* Vols. 3/1 and 3/2. Frankfurt: Suhrkamp, 1995.

Deutscher Sportbund, www.dsb.de.

Dieckert, Jürgen. *Freizeitsport. Aufgabe und Chance für jedermann.* Düsseldorf: Bertelsmann-Universitätsverlag, 1974.

Dreyer, Axel, ed. *Kulturtourismus.* München and Wien: R. Oldenbourg, 1996.

Frogner, Eli. *Sport im Lebenslauf. Eine Verhaltensanalyse zum Breiten- und Freizeitsport.* Stuttgart: Enke, 1991.

Fuchs, Peter, M. L. Schwering, and Klaus Zöller. *Kölner Karneval. Seine Geschichte, seine Eigenart, seine Akteure.* Zweite, auf den neuesten Stand gebrachte Auflage. Köln: Greven, 1984. (Erste Auflage 1972).

Gieseler, Karlheinz, and Jürgen Palm. *Sport–Gesundheit–Wirtschaft. Breiten- und Freizeitsport in der Bundesrepublik Deutschland.* Köln: Deutscher Instituts-Verlag, 1985.

Hartmann, Rudi. *Freizeit-Reisen und Tourismus in Deutschland und in den Vereinigten Staaten von Amerika. Eine interkulturelle Untersuchung.* Trier: Geographische Gesellschaft Trier, 1984.

Joel, Holger, ed. *Chronik des deutschen Fußballs. Die Spiele der Nationalmannschaften von 1908 bis heute.* Gütersloh and München: Chronik Verlag im Wissen Media Verlag, 2005.

Holz, Erlend. *Zeitverwendung in Deutschland. Berufe, Familie, Freizeit.* Stuttgart: Metzler Poeschel, 2000.

Huck, Gerhard. *Sozialgeschichte der Freizeit. Untersuchungen zum Wandel der Alltagskultur in Deutschland.* Wuppertal: Hammer, 1980.

Kluge, Volker. *Das große Lexikon der DDR-Sportler.* 2nd ed. Berlin: Schwarzkopf und Schwarzkopf, 2004.

Küster, Jürgen. *Wörterbuch der Feste und Bräuche im Jahreslauf. Eine Einführung in den Festkalender.* Freiburg: Herder, 1985. (Herderbücherei 1177.)

———. *Bräuche im Kirchenjahr. Historische Anregungen für die Gestaltung christlicher Festtage.* Freiburg: Herder, 1986. (Herderbücherei 1293.)

Nake-Mann, Brigitte. *Neue Trends in Freizeit und Fremdenverkehr und ihre Auswirkungen auf ausgewählte Feriengebiete in der Bundesrepublik Deutschland.* Bonn: Bundesministerium für Raumordnung, Bauwesen und Städtebau, 1984.

Naudascher, Brigitte. *Freizeit in öffentlicher Hand. Behördliche Jugendpflege in Deutschland von 1900–1980.* Düsseldorf: Bröschler, 1990.

Opaschowski, Horst W. *Freizeit und Lebensqualität. Perspektiven für Deutschland.* Hamburg: BAT Freizeit-Forschungsinstitut, 1993.

———. *Neue Trends im Freizeitsport. Analysen und Prognosen.* Hamburg: BAT Freizeit-Forschungsinstitut, 1994.

———. *Tourismus. Systematische Einführung. Analysen und Prognosen.* Opladen: Leske und Budrich, 1996.

Opaschowski, Horst W., and Paul Steinebach.

Literaturverzeichnis Freizeitsport. Essen: Kommunalverband Ruhrgebiet, 1980.

Palm, Jürgen. *Sport for All: Approaches from Utopia to Reality.* Schorndorf: Verlag Karl Hofmann, 1991.

Schildt, Axel. *Moderne Zeiten. Freizeit, Massenmedien und "Zeitgeist" in der Bundesrepublik der 50er Jahre.* Hamburg: Christians, 1995.

Schönfeldt, Sybil Gräfin. *Das große Ravensburger Buch der Feste und Bräuche. Durch das Jahr und den Lebenslauf.* Ravensburg: Otto Maier Verlag, 1980.

Tödtmann, Friedhelm. *Freizeitsport und Verein. Zur Situation nicht-wettkampforientierter Gruppen im Sportverein.* Frankfurt am Main: Haag und Herchen, 1982.

Ueberhorst, Horst, ed. *Geschichte der Leibesübungen.* Teilband 2: *Leibesübungen und Sport in Deutschland vom ersten Weltkrieg bis zur Gegenwart.* Berlin: Bartels und Wernitz, 1989.

Weber-Kellermann, Ingeborg. *Volksfeste in Deutschland.* HB-Bildatlas Spezial. Hamburg: HB Verlags- und Vertriebs-Gesellschaft mbH, 1981.

Woll, Johanna. *Feste und Bräuche im Jahreslauf.* Ulmer, 2. Aufl. 1995.

6

Print Media

Publishers

"Why do you want to give him a book for his birthday, he's already got one!" is a standard joke in the German-speaking countries showing contempt for people who read little or not at all and are presumably uneducated. In some people's living rooms, the well-stocked bookcase is the planned focal point, while the TV is hidden away in the corner or an annex. Books therefore still play quite an important role, both culturally and economically, in the country where the first books were printed by Johannes Gutenberg in Mainz in about 1450.

After Germany's liberation, the occupation forces right away began to control the book trade. Three days after the end of the war, on May 12, 1945, the printing, production, publication, dissemination, and selling of newspapers, magazines, books, brochures, posters, musical scores, and other printed or otherwise mechanically reproduced publications were prohibited. The next step in the reintroduction of publishing houses involved special permits (Wittmann 1991, 392). The approval stamps read, "Published under Military Government Information Control/License No. . . ." (Rutschky 2004, 10).

In East Germany, the revamping of the book market was executed by the Soviet censors as well as the German exiles—for example, Johannes R. Becher, who would later become minister of culture. The maxim expressed explicitly in 1951 by Otto Grotewohl, the prime minister, was: "Literature and art are subordinate to politics. . . . What proves itself to be correct in politics, has to be accepted by art" (Wittmann 1991, 395). After 1963, the highest authority was the Hauptverwaltung Verlage und Buchhandel des Ministeriums für Kultur (Head Administration Publishers and Book Trade of the Ministry of Culture). This office regulated matters regarding all publishers in the GDR, set the upcoming themes, did the annual planning for literature, and took charge of the allotment for all materials (for example, paper) related to printing and publishing. In addition, there were *Analysegruppen* (analysis groups) to observe and discuss current developments in the book market and make recommendations (ibid., 396–397).

In July 1945, three publishing houses were reestablished: (1) Dietz, the publisher for the Communist Party, publishing political and ideological tractates; (2) Aufbau-Verlag, at first the publisher for the new Kulturbund (Association for Culture), later for the SED (Socialist Unity Party of Germany), which tried to create a cultural bridge to the classical German literary tradition; and (3) Volk und Wissen, the centralized publisher of textbooks for the schools. Other publishers followed, however. All were owned by parties and mass organizations, of whom the most successful was the SED. After 1946, a few privately owned "bourgeois" publishers received a license to prevent the exodus to the West, but in the ensuing years the rights of the larger ones were continuously curtailed. They finally were declared *volkseigener Betrieb* (firms owned by the people) or placed under the control of the party. Of the 160 privately owned publishers that existed in 1949, only 17 retained private ownership until the end of the GDR (ibid., 394–395). Dissemination of books was handled by the SED's Volksbuchhandel (People's Book Trade) instead of private retailers (ibid., 399).

The organization behind the book trade was the Leipziger Börsenverein (Association for the Book Trade). The famous Leipziger Frühjahrsmesse (Leipzig Spring Fair) offered the best survey of new publications by GDR publishers and also included a few West German ones. According to official statistics, book production per year increased from about 2,000 titles in 1949 to more than 6,000 in 1989. Actually, the triple increase had already been

reached in the 1970s, when stagnation set in. Production volume increased from 33.4 million to 136.8 million. It stagnated again after 1980. The main areas of publication were political and sociological studies and fiction and poetry. Each had about 25 percent of the market share.

The United States, Britain, and France were interested in propagating their nation's publication mode as the model for a democratic understanding in West Germany and carefully selected (German) publishers that met their criteria. Licenses to publish were issued to Kurt Desch in the American sector, Peter Suhrkamp in the British sector, and Hermann Leins in the French sector. Ernst Rowohlt was the first to receive a license for all four sectors. With his cheap *Rowohlts Rotations Romane* (Rowohlt's Rotation Novels), abbreviated to *Ro-Ro-Ro*, he wanted to end the existing intellectual vacuum and offer food for thought to the new generation that had accepted the task of putting back on track what their parents had derailed. He used the newspaper presses (that is, rotating presses), which were more easily available than book presses. After 1949, when readers became somewhat tired of these surrogate books, Rowohlt began his *rororo-Taschenbücher* (paperbacks) with a new binding that glued the pages together, invented by Erich Lumbeck (ibid., 409–411). In 1949, a reader survey about the most popular publishers resulted in the following list: Insel, Suhrkamp, Desch, Rainer Wunderlich, Deutsche Verlagsanstalt (directed by Hermann Leins), Piper, Münchner Verlag, Bertelsmann, and Rowohlt (ibid., 411).

After the United States handed over the center of the German book trade, located in Leipzig, to the Soviets in 1945, a subsidiary was established in Wiesbaden, Hesse, the headquarters of the Allies. It published the *Börsenblatt*, the professional magazine for the book trade. In 1946, the office was moved to Frankfurt, and in 1948 the local and regional book trade groups united to form the Börsenverein Deutscher Verleger- und Buchhändlerverbände (German Publishers and Booksellers Association) with its main office in Frankfurt. It was renamed and reorganized in 1955 to become the Börsenverein des Deutschen Buchhandels (Association of the German Book Trade). In 1998, it counted more than 7,000 firms among its members, including publishers, retailers, book stores, and printers (ibid., 413). The association is also one of the organizers of the Frankfurter Buchmesse (Frankfurt Book Fair), founded in 1949, the largest book fair in the world. More than 360,000 books from over 100 countries are exhibited there annually in October. Each year there is a special focus on the book production of one particular country. This country is then given the opportunity to present its literature in a number of special events.

The time it took to reestablish a valid German book trade lasted from the currency reform in 1949 to the 1960s and included a steady increase of expansion. In 1951, about 14,000 titles were published; by 1970, the number of titles had increased to over 45,000. Publishing houses appeared and disappeared, and survival was not easy. In the years between about 1950 and 1955, one-third of the 850 originally licensed publishers had to close their doors. Many of the old established publishers returned, and important firms from East Germany, such as Brockhaus, Diederichs, Insel, Kiepenheuer, List, Meyer, Reclam, and several aca-

An employee of German publishing house Taschen prepares a display of oversized books for the 2004 Frankfurt book fair. (Kai Pfaffenbach/Reuters/Corbis)

demic publishers, resettled in the West. Many publishing houses were very small and fostered close personal relationships with their authors—for example, Max Niedermayer's Limes Verlag, the friends Eugen Claassen in Hamburg and Henry Goverts in Stuttgart, Joseph Caspar Witsch, who opened a branch of the Weimarer Kiepenheuer-Verlag in Hagen in 1948 (and later in Cologne), and Ingeborg Stahlberg in Karlsruhe. Geared for success were enterprises such as Erwin Barth von Wehrenalp's *Econ* publishing house founded in 1950, which emphasized nonfiction. In 1955, Werner Keller's *Und die Bibel hat doch recht* (The Bible Is Correct after All) was its first best seller. Its most popular author was Erich von Däniken in the late 1960s and early 1970s, with his speculations about extraterrestials (ibid., 416–417).

The fact that books are not only read by the so-called educated classes is a result of the early activities of the trade unions and the Worker Education Associations back in the nineteenth century. They ensured that people on low incomes would have ready access to world literature by means of cheap editions produced by the book clubs. Today, there is an association called Stiftung Lesen (Foundation for Reading) that promotes reading both in schools and in the home. The dissemination of books changed during the first two postwar decades (from about 1950 to 1970) with the popularity of book clubs and the increase in the production of paperbacks. Strict market analysis determined the choice of publications. Publishers formed consortia as a response to book clubs and produced cheap editions of popular titles that they marketed aggressively as publishers' suggestions. Bertelsmann AG, the largest media conglomerate in Europe, whose activities no longer focus solely on books, owes its success in large part to its Bertelsmann Lesering (Bertelsmann's Book Club), founded in 1950.

The most important role in the process of democratization of the literary culture after 1950 was played by the paperback. Rowohlt's success with its rororo books resulted in imitations. Starting in 1952, Fischer Bücherei (Fischer's Library) began production. Series by Ullstein, Herder, Heyne, Goldmann, List, Knaur, and Suhrkamp followed. In 1961, twelve publishers gambled on a new joint venture, founding the Deutscher Taschenbuchverlag (literally, German pocketbook publisher, dtv).

Only about half of the books published by this group are fiction and poetry. Since the 1960s, collected works (usually of traditional authors) have been offered in boxed sets. Encyclopedias followed, and today these sets even include scholarly editions. In 1996, 10,000 paperback titles were published in Germany and about 100 million copies were sold.

In the late 1960s, it was not only the political climate that changed (see 1: From Two to One; 4: Youth Culture and the World of Intellectuals). The era also marked the beginning of new organizational structures and a technological revolution affecting book production. Marshall McLuhan announced the end of the *Gutenberg-Galaxis* (Gutenberg galaxy), and new electronic methods of typesetting and printing set new standards. The new structures included *Verlag der Autoren* (literally, authors' publishing company), a type of corporation in which profits were shared by all—authors and publishers—and the company run by chosen delegates. Bertelsmann followed suit with its *Autoren-Edition* (authors' edition), in which each author had shares in the company. Klaus Wagenbach's experiments for his company ended in the splitting off of a small group from the rest of the company, resulting in the creation of Rotbuch-Verlag.

The death of literature was proclaimed along with the death of the traditional bookstore, the death of the publishers of fiction, the death of the capitalistic book trade, and the death of the book itself. Things did change, but not as predicted. In 1999, the book was still alive and well, and the publishers were busy, though the trend was clearly toward a concentration of a small group of publishers. Eight percent of the 2,000 publishers were responsible for three-quarters of the total turnover in Germany. The global player Bertelsmann, regarded as the largest and most profitable publisher in the world, was way ahead of everyone else. In Germany, companies owned by Bertelsmann include Blanvalet, Blessing, Goldmann, Knaus, Mosaik, Siedler, Berlin Publishing, and the academic publisher Springer. The group Holtzbrinck followed (seen by its top executives as the largest provider of printed literature on the German market). This group includes Droemer-Knaur, Fest, S. Fischer, Kindler, Krüger, Rowohlt, Metzler-Poeschel, Scherz, Schroedel, Wunderlich, Urban and Schwarzenberg, Gustav Fischer, and parts of Kiepenheuer and Witsch; the firm also has a partnership with Weltbild.

Next came the Langenscheidt Group, the Weltbild Group (owned by the Catholic dioceses in Germany), Heyne, Ganske (Hoffmann and Campe, Gräfe and Unzer), the Munich publisher Goethestraße (now owned by the press mogul Springer, who also owns Econ, List, Claassen, and Südwest), the Langen-Müller Group, Falken, Bastei-Lübbe, the Suhrkamp Group (with Insel), and Diogenes. The number of publishers without larger affiliations—for example, Hanser (with Zsolnay and Sanssouci), Luchterhand (with Limes, Volk und Welt), and Aufbau—has decreased. Academic and specialized publishers were headed by the Weka Group, followed by Bertelsmann Fachinformation, the scientific Springer-Verlag (not related to the Springer publisher in Hamburg), Süddeutsche Verlag, and C. H. Beck. The textbook market was dominated by the Cornelsen Group. It was followed by the Klett Group, Westermann, and Schroedel. Books for young people are dominated by the Egmont Group (ibid., 424).

Suhrkamp became one of the leading literary publishers. Its clever marketing strategies of its classic books, which appeared in collected, single, selected, and special editions—eventually evolving into the *Deutsche Klassiker Verlag* (German publishing company for classical/great authors)—was a solid basis for expanding the program's profile into an elitist and progressive disseminator of literature. The *edition suhrkamp*, founded in 1963, became especially important and included contemporary authors as well as theoretical tractates.

The smaller publishers developed special niches and patterns of success or failure. Wolfgang Schaffler's Residenz-Verlag was the home of modern Austrian literature until Schaffler's death. Diogenes had its first major best seller with Patrick Süskind's *Das Parfum* (The Perfume). Haffmann Verlag focused on the work of Arno Schmidt. Franz Greno appeared to realize a dream with his exceptional productions—for example, *Die andere Bibliothek* (a different kind of library) edited by Hans Magnus Enzensberger, which included a special free magazine with each volume—but the company failed eventually because of poor marketing.

A special success story is Taschen, a publishing company founded in Cologne in 1980, today a top publisher of art books. Benedikt Taschen was just eighteen years old when he began to sell his large collection of comic books in a tiny store. In 1984, he scored his first hit with an art book. He bought 40,000 copies of an English Magritte edition at a discount and sold them for a fraction of the original selling price. He realized that art books could be best sellers, but that they are usually too expensive for a wider audience. His conclusion was that it could be profitable to produce cheap art books. Beginning in the late 1980s, Taschen became a global player and added architecture, design, photography, and lifestyle books to his repertoire.

In 2000, the publisher came up with a new surprise: the most expensive book of the twentieth century. The first copy of Helmut Newton's *SUMO*, signed by more than eighty of the famous people depicted in the book, was sold at auction for $300,000. The book, with a list price of $5,000, is exceptional in almost every aspect. As an advertisement found in magazines and on the internet in various versions stated:

Weighing over 65 pounds, measuring more than two feet long, and breaking any previous size record in book publishing, *SUMO* contains 480 pages of every aspect of Newton's outstanding career in photography. Each copy of the book is bound by hand and numbered and signed by the artist. In order to showcase this colossus, the book is packaged with its own stand designed by Philippe Starck. This outsized volume contains the body of Newton's controversial yet iconographic work, documenting fashion, fetishism, and above all an overriding obsession with voyeurism that can make the viewer feel complicit or uneasy by turns. Newton himself describes *SUMO* as "terrifying and outrageous. I don't even look at it as a book. . . . I look at it as an object."

Today Taschen publishes books in more than twenty languages and is expanding its publishing houses and bookstores. A novelty appears almost every week. Looking at Taschen, one wonders why the German book trade cannot overcome the multitude of problems it faces. Publishers of scientific books, in particular, are seeking international collaboration as a necessity for survival. Books written in German are read less and less frequently, and publishers are forced to publish even original manuscripts in English translation. Textbook makers face many regulations imposed by the cultural ministries of the individual states. Free provisions of schoolbooks and equipment in most schools (the schools buy a certain number of copies, which are loaned to the students, who then return the books to be distributed to the next year's students), extensive copying by teachers and students alike, constant school reforms, and chaos in regard to guidelines, as well as the increasing expansion of multimedia learning, are just a few of the additional challenges to be met (Wittmann 1991, 425).

The Press

Newspapers

As Kurt Koszyk remarked in his detailed survey of the history of the German press since 1945, the Allies wanted a caesura, a clear break between Germany's past and its new beginning (Koszyk 1999, 31). As a result, all German newspapers were initially prohibited as part of an ambitious strategy to reeducate the German populace. The Allies planned to create model newspapers for the occupied zones with each ally in charge of its sphere of influence. But before these model newspapers (beginning with the *Tägliche Rundschau* [Daily Survey] published in Berlin by the Soviets in May 1945) could become established, regional newspapers began to appear that were controlled not only by Allied journalists but also by Austrian and

German emigrants who had returned to Europe and other German writers. The first of these newspapers was the *Aachener Nachrichten* (Aachen News), which made its debut in the territory that had been conquered by the Americans in January 1945. The British feared that such a paper with substantial German input might give the wrong signals to the German population at large and insisted that—beginning with the fifth issue—a subheading be added stating: "*Herausgegeben mit Genehmigung der alliierten Militärbehörde*" (Published with the authorization of the Allied military command). To make it clear to everyone who was in charge, a few so-called *Heeresgruppenzeitungen* (newspapers published by individual sections of the U.S. army) followed.

When the British entered the regions originally conquered by U.S. troops but now placed under British control, they continued most of these established papers, changed some, and added a few new ones. In all cases, German journalists were hired in addition to Allied journalists to give Germans the opportunity to prepare for the next stage in the process: the licensing of new papers run solely by Germans. The proposed new German papers were both approved and published swiftly in 1945, sometimes even before the official "model" paper for the specific zone appeared. For instance, already six days after the first appearance of the Soviet *Tägliche Rundschau* (Daily Survey, which continued publication until 1955), a licensed paper, the *Berliner Zeitung* (Berlin Newspaper), was added. And in August 1945, the French licensed the *Badener Tagblatt* (Baden Daily Paper) before its own French-language publication, the *Nouvelles de France* (published in Konstanz) ap-

peared (it followed a month later, in September). The German version of the French "model" did not appear until January 1947. Both were subsequently canceled in 1949 before the establishment of the Federal Republic.

Die Neue Zeitung (The New Newspaper), the official newspaper introduced by the Americans for their zone, appeared in October 1945, two and a half months after the first U.S.-licensed German paper, the *Frankfurter Rundschau* (Frankfurt Survey), was published. It was followed that same month by the *Süddeutsche Zeitung* (South German Newspaper), the second U.S.-licensed paper, although it bore the imprint "license no. 1." *Die Neue Zeitung*—together with the magazine *Der Monat* (The Month)—became especially important for the reemerging German culture (Glaser 2002, 254). It ceased publication in 1953 everywhere but in Berlin, where publication continued for another two years.

The exception in regard to early control by Germans were papers under British governance. The British did not begin licensing German newspapers until 1946. They continued the *Aachener Nachrichten* (founded by the United States in 1945) and the *Braunschweiger Zeitung* (Brunswick Newspaper), licensed in January 1946, but waited until April 1946 for the publication of their zone paper, *Die Welt* (The World). In 1948, a Sunday edition was added with the title *Welt am Sonntag* (the World on Sunday), and both became part of the Axel Springer publishing company in 1953.

In the U.S. zone, licensing was especially swift. The only conditions imposed on German journalists were that former publishers could not apply for licenses and that former newspaper names could not be used. Licenses were given to groups that had an unstained political background and consisted of members with differing political views. In this way, the Allies attempted to avoid political arguments between papers, as such debates had the potential for expanding into intellectual attacks on the occupying force. The provision that made a clear separation between news on the front page and opinion on the second page—a separation still practiced in many German newspapers today—was based on the same rationale: namely, to avoid blatant, front-page attacks on the Allies by German journalists. But these attempts at neutrality and objectivity were harder to realize than expected. It was difficult to find politically balanced groups of journalists, as the example of the *Frankfurter Rundschau* demonstrated. It clearly had a leftist leaning that became even more pronounced over the years, making it a favorite among students. As a result, the *Frankfurter Neue Presse* (Frankfurt New Press), more closely in line with the views of the conservative CDU (see 3: The Political System), was licensed. Both papers appeared in alternate turns twice a week, in one week two editions of the *Rundschau*, the next week two editions of the *Presse*.

The British, who were in closer contact with the emerging political parties in Germany, soon realized that the supposedly objective group principle for newspaper editors would not work. Instead they reached an agreement with the politicians to license newspapers affiliated with individual political parties, though even this decision was too radical. In a survey, three-quarters of the German public voiced their disagreement with these types of newspapers, and yet another solution had to be found. In addition to those with a party al-

legiance, the British encouraged the foundation in 1948 of independent regional newspapers. These included the *Norddeutsche Zeitung* (North German Newspaper [Hannover]), the *Westdeutsche Allgemeine Zeitung* (West German General Newspaper [Bochum and Essen]), the *Westdeutsche Zeitung* (West German Newspaper [Düsseldorf]), and Axel Springer's *Hamburger Abendblatt* (Hamburg Evening Paper). The French tried to follow this group newspaper concept by shifting the pluralism of opinion away from the publishers to the editorial staff. They also allowed a few party-affiliated papers.

The Soviets granted each political party its own newspaper and also encouraged several regional papers. While the large parties, the Communist and the Socialist parties (KPD, Kommunistische Partei Deutschlands [Communist Party of Germany], and SPD, Sozialdemokratische Partei Deutschlands [Social Democratic Party of Germany]), merged to become the SED (Sozialistische Einheitspartei Deutschlands [Socialist Unity Party of Germany]), the other parties split into smaller fractions (see 3: Political System; 1: From Two to One). The result was that there were many small newspapers of marginal importance, on the one hand, and one large, influential paper, on the other. This dominant paper was the *Neues Deutschland* (New Germany), a merger of the KPD's *Deutsche Volkszeitung* (German People's Newspaper, founded in 1945) and the SPD's *Das Volk* (The People). From 1950 to 1989, *Neues Deutschland* was the official paper of the ZK (Zentralkomitee [Central Committee]) of the SED; since 1989, it has been the daily socialist newspaper for the PDS (Partei des Demokratischen Sozialismus [Party of Democratic Socialism]).

Although there was no direct censorship in the early postwar years, there was an understood limitation on what could be reported. There was an unspoken agreement that some topics were taboo—for example, the expulsion of Germans from former German territories and the disagreements between or a critique of the occupation forces. However, after 1947 the United States allowed criticism of the Soviets, an indication perhaps that the Cold War had begun. This was also one of the reasons that denazification was considered to have been accomplished relatively early on and perhaps explains why—as Hermann Glaser (2004) noted—a surprisingly large number of the influential German journalists who shaped the new opinions and were active in prominent positions had formerly been nationalists or even national socialists. For a long time, the language of the journalists was marked by a distinct style—a kind of revised "Hitler German." A study of German journalism edited by Lutz Hachtmeister and Friedemann Siering showed that an "elite without consciousness" dominated the profession and tended to avoid investigating the contemporary situation. Because of this, a willingness to deal with the past (*Vergangenheitsbewältigung;* see 1: Coming to Terms with the Past) was delayed until the generation born at the end of the war was old enough to question their parents about what had really happened.

After the creation of the Federal Republic in September 1949, the licensing of the press by the Allies ended, and Paragraph 5 of Germany's new Basic Law took effect with freedom of speech and freedom of the press. The result was that many new newspapers began to compete with the licensed ones that had been established as regional papers and had built up a system of local support. The new papers tried several strategies to gain a foothold in the market. One was to form joint editorships. A larger paper would collaborate with smaller ones and furnish them with necessary information. Another strategy was the establishment of a consortium of editors to complement one another. The attempt to gain a national readership was limited to just a few newspapers. The most successful was the *Frankfurter Allgemeine Zeitung* (*FAZ,* Frankfurt General Newspaper), a daily newspaper published in Frankfurt, which continued the tradition of the liberal *Frankfurter Zeitung* shut down under Hitler and evolved from the German edition of the *Allgemeine Zeitung* (General Newspaper), Mainz, in 1949. From the very start, it established itself as a leader and as a "national" and "international" newspaper (*überregionale Zeitung,* supra-regional newspaper). It was characterized by detailed and trustworthy coverage of all issues, a moderately conservative outlook, and an avoidance of fads and controversy.

Even its appearance—which has changed little over the decades—signals respectability: Gothic print was selected for the title, no oversized headlines, no photos appear on the front page, and there are only a few inside, for many decades with no colors. The *FAZ,* as it is usually called, is known not only for its articles on politics and the economy but also for its *Feuilleton* (feature section) containing an overview of German culture. Sports and crime are barely covered. To guarantee journalistic independence, the paper is headed by a group of five editors. Only the *Süddeutsche Zeitung* and the weekly *Die Zeit* (The Times) can claim equally high intellectual standards. The *FAZ*'s advertisements are also unemotional and to the point, though often with subtle wordplays. A series of ads, which has become a classic, shows a reader behind a newspaper with the slogan: Dahinter steckt ein kluger Kopf (Behind it, there's always an intelligent head). The newspaper readers, although almost completely covered by the paper, are often well-known celebrities, identified only in a small by-line.

Other papers that appeared between 1945 and 1949, but had only a regional impact, were: *Nürnberger Nachrichten* (Nuremberg News), the *Münchner Merkur* (Munich Mercury), the *Stuttgarter Zeitung* (Stuttgart Newspaper), the *Stuttgarter Nachrichten* (Stuttgart News), the *Weser Kurier* (Weser Courier, Bremen), the *Rheinische Post* (Rhineland Post, Düsseldorf), the *Westfälische Rundschau* (Westphalian Survey, Dortmund), the *Hannoversche Presse* (Hanoveranian Press), the *Hamburger Echo* (Hamburg Echo), the *Kölnische Rundschau* (Cologne Survey) and the *Freie Presse* (Free Press, Bielefeld) as well as several papers in Berlin: *Der Tagesspiegel* (The Daily Mirror), *Telegraph*, *Der Kurier* (The Courier), *Der Morgen* (The Morning), *Nachtexpress* (Night Express), and *Berlin am Mittag* (Berlin at Noon).

In 1954, there were 624 newspaper publishers in West Germany. Among their publications was *Bild* (Picture, or Image), modeled after the English tabloid *Daily Mirror*. *Bild* began as a printed response to the emerging medium of television with its visual presentation of news (see 7: Radio and Television). John Sandford regards it as "the exception that proves the rules of German newspaper publishing: not only its countrywide reach . . . but its brash and sensational style . . . are quite atypical of the rest of the German press" (Sandford

1999, 446). It was first published in 1952 by Axel Springer with a circulation of 250,000 copies. Back then, the paper had just four pages and could be picked up without charge on the first day. After that, the price was set at 10 pennies. It was full of pictures (hence its name) and featured often sensational human interest stories, horoscopes, and jokes. From the outset, *Bild* used eye-catching layout techniques and bold headlines, often punning but on a less intellectual level than those in the more serious *FAZ*. From 1953 on, the circulation exploded, and after 1960 its anti-Communist political stance was one of its chief trademarks, besides stories about crime, sex, scandals, gossip, health, weather, and sports.

The erection of the Berlin Wall in 1961 provided stories and images of attempted flight that served both the human interest and the political agenda. Above all, *Bild* stressed the everyday concerns of the common citizen and depicted itself as the avenger of the oppressed. In the late 1960s, it spoke out against the student rebellion. Many regarded the increasing violence during these years as being caused by *Bild*'s inflammatory reporting style. The books by Günter Wallraff—for example, *Der Aufmacher* (Front-Page Story, 1977)—and the novel *Die verlorene Ehre der Katharina Blum* (The Lost Honor of Katharina Blum, 1974) by Heinrich Böll, which was turned into a film directed by Volker Schlöndorff (see 7: Film), show the controversy *Bild* caused at the time. In the new millennium, *Bild* is still the German newspaper with the highest circulation—almost 4 million copies daily, and it is read by even more people, with estimates ranging between one-fifth and one-third of Germany's population. Each day, twenty-three modified

A montage of German newspapers. Photographed in Berlin on Wednesday, Nov. 3, 2004.

city versions are printed, plus special editions for foreign countries.

Over the years, a *Bild* family has emerged: *Bild am Sonntag (BamS)*, a paper intended for the whole family, which began publication in 1954; *Bild der Frau*, which from its introduction in 1983 had the largest circulation for a women's newspaper in all of Europe; *Auto Bild*, the newspaper for the car enthusiast, which also became a European market leader with its first issue in 1986; *Sportbild*, which in 1988 repeated the success story of the other *Bild* papers; *Computer-Bild*, an illustrated paper for the computer addict, which appeared in 1996; *Computer-Bild-Spiele*, a paper for computer games that was introduced in 1999, becoming yet another Euro-

pean market leader; and *Audio-Video-Foto-Bild*, a paper for photography and popular music enthusiasts, first published in 2003. Stylistically, *Bild* has the goal of being as brief as possible, and almost 50 percent of the sentences in *Bild* have just four words or less, something almost incomprehensible to any student of German who has struggled with the long convoluted sentences of some of Germany's better known authors. However, because of its sensational character, many stories are overdrawn and sometimes incorrect.

By 1989, the year of Germany's unification, the number of newspaper publishers had diminished drastically from the high of the late 1950s. The reasons for this were mergers and closings and perhaps a stronger reliance on television as a source of news information. In the German Federal Republic there were only 338 newspaper publishers left, selling 1,344 papers with a total circulation of 20.3 million copies (Schütz 1999, 126). As a result of unification, two West German papers closed their doors right away: *uz. unsere zeit* (Our Times), published by the DKP (Deutsche Kommunistische Partei [German Communistic Party]), and *Die Wahrheit / Neue Zeitung* (The Truth / New Newspaper), published by the SEW (Sozialistische Einheitspartei Westberlins [Socialist Unity Party of West Berlin]). The other West German publishers saw the opportunity to extend their market share, and newcomers embarked on new and exciting publishing ventures. These newcomers did not have much of a chance, however, because the large West German publishers were able to seize hold of the old SED papers as well as their established reader base. Only eight new publishers survived from a total of 103; six of those were only able to survive by collaborating with former SED papers, now owned by dominant West German media giants.

The result of these dealings was that the total number of newspaper publishers in the new, larger Germany was just about 370 at the turn of the millennium—down by almost 50 percent of the figure fifty years before. And while in the western part of Germany, many small, medium, and large newspaper publishers coexist, the eastern part is dominated by a few large regional papers. These "former SED district papers, bought up by western concerns after privatization, have a virtual monopoly of the regional market" (Sandford 1999, 446). In addition, the number of publishers conceals the fact that only about a third of the papers published in Germany are independent editorial units. In many cases, various kinds of editorial collaboration reduce the real heterogeneity of opinion (Schütz 1999, 130).

Weekly Papers, News Magazines, and Periodicals

The licensing regulations for daily newspapers also applied to magazines and weekly publications. The first periodical to appear after the war was *Aufbau* (Construction), published for the first time in September 1945 in the Soviet zone. In the western zones this was followed by *Die Wandlung* (The Change) (Heidelberg, U.S. zone, September 1945), *Die Sammlung* (The Collection) (Göttingen, British zone, November), *Göttinger Studentenzeitung* (Götting Student Newspaper) (December), and *Die Gegenwart* (The Present Time) (Freiburg im Breisgau, French zone, December). As with newspapers, not all of the western publications continued after the end of the Allies' licensing phase. Among the more successful were *Dokumente* (Documents) (Cologne, first published in August 1945), *Die neue Rundschau* (The New Survey) (Frankfurt am Main, 1945), the *Frankfurter Hefte* (Frankfurt Notebooks) (April 1946), the *Deutsche Rundschau* (German Survey) (Baden-Baden, 1946), *Geist und Tat* (Spirit and Deed) (Frankfurt, 1946), *Merian* and *Merkur* (Mercury) (Stuttgart, 1947), and *Der Monat* (The Month) (Berlin, October 1948). Not one of these was able to compete with illustrated magazines, weekly papers, and news magazines such as *Der Spiegel* (The Mirror).

Der Spiegel began publication in January 1947 and "built up the reputation of having the best archive in the German media world and the best sources of information in the corridors of power" (Briel 1998, 326). It certainly worked hard at establishing its image as one of the most controversial and stimulating publications in the country. According to Holger Briel, "It became required reading for the intelligentsia through wide-ranging, snappy reporting, easy-to-read personalized writing, penetrating interviews (*Spiegel-Gespräch*), investigative work, liberal attitudes and insistence on democratic rights (giving space to views of leftist radicals around 1968 and 1977)" (Briel 2002, 126). Its publisher, Rudolf Augstein (1923–2002), made himself a name as an eloquent critic of many conservatives. In 1962, *Spiegel*'s investigative reporting led to the *Spiegel*-scandal, when Defense Minister Franz Joseph Strauß had the publisher's offices illegally searched. "Strauss was forced to resign while the journal was able to consolidate its reputation for accurate reporting and refine its own brand of aggressive and ironic journalism," Briel wrote (Briel 1998, 326). Even in the twenty-first century, with a formidable rival in the news magazine *Focus* since 1993, *Spiegel* still attracts many readers from the intelligentsia and continues to influence (as well as to report on) German politics. Statistics show that over the past six decades it has retained its percentage of readers. In 1954, about 10 percent of the adult population read *Spiegel* in the Federal Republic. In 1998, the number for the united Germany was just above 9 percent; the number in the west was more than 10 percent, whereas in the new states in the east it was only about 5 percent.

Back in 1932, Germany had had a rich magazine tradition, with about 7,000 titles; the magazine industry recovered only to a limited degree after the war. By 1953/1954,

the Federal Republic again had almost 5,000 titles and the GDR over 300. Among the first magazines were *Blick in die Welt* (Looking into the World, published in Bünde), *Heute* (Today, Munich), *Zeit im Bild* (Time in Pictures, Dresden), *Neue Berliner Illustrierte* (New Berlin Illustrated Magazine, founded in 1948 as *Das Ufer* [The River Bank]), *Kristall* (Crystal, founded in 1946 as *Nordwestdeutsche Hefte* [Northwest German Notebooks]), *Die neue Illustrierte* (The New Illustrated Magazine, Cologne, first published in 1946), and *Quick* (Hamburg, since 1948). Holger Briel, explicating the name of the latter, called it "[h]overing . . . between the English 'quick' and the German '*erquicken*' (to revive, to refresh)" (Sandford 1999, 516). It thrived on sensational news stories and scantily clad women on its cover.

Weekly papers included *Das grüne Blatt* (The Green Page, Dortmund, first published in 1948), *Heim und Welt* (Home and World, Hannover, October 1948), the *Neue Post* (The New Post, Düsseldorf, March 1948), *Diese Woche* (This Week, Düsseldorf, November 1948), *Wochenend* (Weekend, Nürnberg, September 1948), the Catholic *Rheinischer Merkur* (Rhineland Mercury), and the Protestant *Sonntagsblatt* (Sunday Paper), *Christ und Welt* (Christ and the World), *Echo der Zeit* (Echo of the Times), *Neuer Vorwärts* (New Getting Ahead), and *Stimmen der Zeit* (Voices of the Times). The paper *Ost und West* (licensed by the Soviets in 1947) was one of the few that attempted to bridge the widening gulf between the eastern and western parts of Germany. But the Berlin blockade in 1948 rendered its efforts futile. In a similar way, the *Ulenspiegel* (owl's mirror, a title using a name of a legendary prankster) (Berlin), first published in December 1945, failed in 1949. At the top of the circulation statistics was *Hör zu* (Listen), an illustrated magazine that contained the schedule for all the radio programs. It later added a television guide, interspersed with feature articles and human interest stories.

Hör zu also introduced a mascot by the name of Mecki, a cheerful-looking hedgehog—dressed at first in Lederhosen and featured on the cover in seasonally appropriate settings. Even today Mecki is still a part of the magazine, commenting on the season through a range of costumes, usually casual, but now with a hedgehog son who is given sound advice on becoming an upright citizen. One still can buy these figures in stores—Mecki almost rivaled Mickey Mouse in Germany as a friendly, anthropomorphized animal. The similarity in names may not be a total coincidence.

In 1954, *Hör zu* could boast 23 percent of the adult readers in West Germany, and even in 1998, a time of rough competition, it held its own, with about 12 percent. It has been published since December 1946 by Axel Springer. Rumor has it that the magazine was first offered to the well-known journalist Gerd Bucerius (1906–1995), who had declined it with the remark, "I don't publish schedules" (Koszyk 1999, 55). His ambitions were of a different nature, and his weekly paper *Die Zeit*, founded in Hamburg in the same year (1946), became one of the most influential and respected political and cultural papers in Germany and remains so up to the present day.

Although Bucerius was a CDU member of the Bundestag in the Adenauer years (1949–1963), his paper evolved as the voice of liberalism. It preferred in-depth reporting (in later years, with a special thematic *Dossier*—small magazine—in each issue) and investigative work, with an eye to issues rather than personalities. After Bucerius resigned as publisher, ex-chancellor Helmut Schmidt (SPD) became one of his successors, along with Marion Gräfin Dönhoff (1909–2002), a countess who held the status of grand old lady of German journalism. In 1993, in an attempt to woo a readership looking for something more colorful and catchy and less daunting than the earnest pages of *Die Zeit*, the paper *Die Woche* (The Week) was launched by the journalist Manfred Bissinger. The experiment was not successful, however, and publication ceased in 2002.

The women's magazine with the largest circulation, *Brigitte*, published every two weeks, began its success story in 1954. At least, 1954 was the year when the name *Brigitte* was introduced for this women's magazine, which was founded in 1886 and had reappeared in 1949 with the name *Das Blatt für die Hausfrau* (the Paper for the Housewife). Since 1952, the name *Brigitte* had been used unobtrusively in front of the main title. But from 1954 on, the name *Brigitte* dominated the page. In 1957, the *Constanze* publisher, at the time the market leader, acquired *Brigitte*, and in 1969 *Constanze* was merged with *Brigitte*, which is today's market leader, ahead of *Für Sie* (For You) and *freundin* (Girlfriend). As Hannelore Schlaffer remarked in her essay in honor of the magazine's fiftieth anniversary: "'Brigitte', this name with its two pointed vowels and the many exploding consonants, had the effect of an encouraging crack of a whip that woke housewives up from their post-war sleep." With the first copy of *Brigitte*, the circulation reached 200,000. The August 17, 2005, issue proudly proclaimed that each issue had a readership of 3.95 million, of which 3.62 million are women and 330,000 are men.

Brigitte is much more than a fashion magazine. It is an educational magazine geared primarily toward women. One example of this educational mission in the new millennium was a series of workshops in German cities (with an emphasis on the smaller ones) to introduce women to the Internet and its offerings. In 2005, the magazine introduced a new educational initiative, this time to reacquaint its readers with both modern and older literary classics. A series of audio books read by celebrities was offered first, and then a specially bound collection of books selected by the author Elke Heidenreich, published for readers of the magazine and promoted within its pages.

Another semi-educational aspect of the magazine is the page for children, which has been a regular feature of the magazine for years. The page contains some kind of puzzle. Young readers solve them by, for example, tracing lines to find who owns what in a drawing, labeling pictures to find rhyming words, or deciphering a text in which part of the word is a drawing. An egg (*Ei* in German) is often featured in these puzzles because of the frequent occurrence of the diphthong in German. Whatever the main puzzle is, there is always a tiny drawing of a mouse hidden away on the page. Solutions to the puzzles (but alas, not to the location of the mouse) are located on a different page in the magazine so that children (or their parents) are not tempted to cheat.

Like most modern publications, *Brigitte* maintains a Web site and offers free subscriptions to a weekly e-mail newsletter. In many ways, be it via its features on social

issues, fashion, food, travel, books, film, or music, the magazine is one of the best mirrors of German culture. Although *Brigitte* is also a magazine for the emancipated woman, the primary manifestation of women's emancipation in Germany is the magazine *Emma*, published twice a month and founded in 1977 by Alice Schwarzer (b. 1942), who is regarded as the leading spokeswoman for the women's movement in Germany. The magazine, according to the researcher Barbara Rassi, "defines itself as a magazine by women made for people. Questioning women's traditional roles and positions in society, it reports about and comments on a variety of women's issues. Subsequently the magazine has often provoked heated debates, be they on violence against women, pornography, unequal payment for women and men, or women and religious fundamentalism" (Briel 2002, 36).

The tradition of satirical magazines, which began at the end of the nineteenth century with the publication of the *Simplizissimus* (literally, the most simple person, the name going back to a novel of the Baroque era) criticizing the Wilhelminian *Kaiserreich*, continued after 1945 with *Pardon* from 1962 to 1982, which attempted a comeback in 2004; *Titanic*, the ultimate satirical magazine; and *Eulenspiegel* (literally, the owl's mirror, the name going back to a legendary prankster), a GDR satirical magazine founded before *Pardon* (an even earlier magazine was called *Ulenspiegel*, see above).

Over the past six decades, the range of magazines has increased along with an increasing focus on specialized audiences. The traditional general-interest titles, such as *Der Stern* (The Star) (founded in Hamburg in 1948 by Henri Nannen, since 1965 published by Gruner and Jahr), *Bunte* (Colorfully Illustrated), or *Neue Revue*, have lost market shares (in 1954, *Stern* had 22 percent of the adult population in West Germany among its readership, but in 1998, only slightly more than 11 percent of the adult population of the united Germany), as did the leader of youth magazines, *Bravo*. The special-interest titles—and even more so the highly specialized titles—have gained readers, although many, such as *Tempo* and *Wiener* (Viennese), glossy and irreverent urban magazines for the "yuppie" culture linking cutting-edge text and graphic design, have experienced only a short-lived boom. They gained a large market share in the 1980s among the twenty- to thirty-five-year-olds, as Briel remarked (Briel 1998, 327), but folded in the 1990s.

"Diversity" is the prime catchword at the beginning of the twenty-first century. There are today, in addition to general sports magazines such as *Kicker*, *Sport-Bild*, *Sports*, or *Bravo sport*, specialized journals such as *Fly and glide* for fans of hang gliding or *Runner's world*, the largest magazine for joggers (often the titles are in English to signal their trendy character; see 2: Language, Script, and Gestures). Next to technical journals such as *BW Bauwirtschaft* (Building and Construction Industry) are the very focused journals such as *awt* (*Abwassertechnik*—Sewage Technology). Besides *Geo* and *Geo special*, which present historical, scientific, and sociological topics for a general audience, there is also now *Geolino*, a magazine of adventure for young boys and girls between the ages of eight and fourteen. Often only known to insiders, about 240 so-called *Fanzine*, *Underground-* and *Szene-Magazine* (Magazine for the Alternative Culture)

are published in Germany with a circulation of about 2.5 million copies.

Not at all influential, but nevertheless part of German culture, are publications by and for those in need. One example is the monthly *BISS*, sold in Munich. The homeless earn a little by selling the publication—they keep 50 percent of the proceeds—and thereby help both themselves and others in a similar situation to get back on their feet.

Popular and Belletristic Literature

After 1945 and after the misuse of language for so many years by the Nazi regime, the question arose for many as to whether one could still trust language at all. The Gruppe 47 of writers who first met as a group in the Alps in 1947 attempted to find an answer. Hans Werner Richter, who was one of the founders of the group, wrote in a retrospective in 1981, "Each word which is read is being weighed to test whether it is still usable or perhaps obsolete, used up in the years of the dictatorship, the time of the immense wear of the language. Each sentence is being scrutinized. Each unnecessary ornament is being criticized. Rejected are the big words that are meaningless and have lost their content in the opinion of the critics: heart, pain, joy, sorrow. What is being accepted are the short statements" (quoted in Glaser 2002, 228–229).

For the very young who had just learned to read and write in the 1940s and 1950s and had not experienced the language misuse, literature as a subject was usually synonymous with boring lectures by authoritarian teachers. The literary canon with which these children were bombarded in school spoiled reading for many. *Groschen-*

hefte (dime novels), regarded as literary trash and the nightmare of all teachers, filled the need for entertaining light reading. The first ones that appeared right after the war were printed on cheap paper, with drawings on the title pages that looked amateurish, but the young readers did not mind the technical imperfections. In 1949, the series about *Coyote, Billy Jenkins,* and *Buffalo Bill* were again available at newspaper stands beside many other short novels of the sort. *Billy Jenkins* had 264 titles from 1934 to 1939 and 370 titles from 1949 to 1963, partly written by prewar writers.

One of the star writers was G. F. Unger, who made himself a name as a writer of stories of the Wild West. Beginning with title 100, photos of Bill Jenkins, as cowboy, marksman, handler of eagles, and so on, were shown on the inside of the cover page, creating the illusion that these novels were almost documentaries providing real information about the Wild West. In the fourteen years of publication, the price increased from 40 to 70 pennies and the pages from 32 to 64 per issue. *Coyote, the Rider with the Black Mask* was the first imported dime novel, but it was expensive: 1 deutsche mark (DM) per issue, a considerable amount for children at that time. Coyote, the Spanish nobleman, helped the poor in Robin Hood fashion and was similar to Zorro, made famous by Hollywood, and who also reappeared in films and novels after the war. *Buffalo Bill* represented the typical Wild West novel in a tradition going back to the nineteenth century. Many other series followed—for example, *Tom Mix* and *Sitting Bull.*

The anti-trash movement had a big task ahead of it and sometimes succeeded. Publication of *Buffalo Bill* was stopped in 1951 after issue no. 65 (Galle 1998, 184). Comics

such as *Mickey Mouse, Donald Duck, Tarzan,* and the ones featuring various superheroes were less controversial, as were the ever popular works by Karl May (see 6: From A to Z, "Karl May"). For many young teenagers of the postwar era in West Germany (though not in May's native East Germany, where his work was forbidden under the GDR regime), the price of one volume of his collected works became a standard currency unit for purposes of comparison: A loaf of bread cost half a volume, an engine for an electronic train set two volumes. For many years, the price of one of these volumes was DM 7.50. It seemed as stable as the exchange rate of the U.S. dollar to the deutsche mark, which was $1 to DM 4.20.

James Fenimore Cooper's *Der letzte Mohikaner* (The Last of the Mohicans) and *Lederstrumpf* (Leatherstocking) were also popular. But the prime source of young people's knowledge about the Wild West (as well as about the desert in Saudi Arabia) were Karl May's books of adventure. The superhero in his books, known as Old Shatterhand when he traveled in the Western Hemisphere and as Kara Ben Nemsi when he visited the Near East, was not only clever, strong, brave, and quick-witted but also humane. His best friend in the Wild West was Winnetou, the noble Indian. Together they defeated all evil. Almost half a century later, little has changed. Millions of copies of the collected works, now amounting to seventy-four volumes, are being sold (Lowsky 1987, xi).

The appearance of May's books is not as uniform as it once was, however, because the copyright has expired. In addition, Karl May's ouevre has become an object of academic research. The mystery that surrounded him has given way to discussions of his literary stature and has brought more attention to his early trashy novels (*Kolportageromane*) as well as to his late pseudo-mysticism. Yet, for most young readers, the stories about Indians and Arabs remain their favorite; they follow May into a dream world that he described in detail without ever actually having been there. Karl May, the fantasy writer and visionary, assumed the role of an ethnographic travel reporter. Only much later was he able to travel to soime of the places he had described so vividly. Perhaps one of the most sincere forms of flattery in mainstream recognition is the way his work is quoted in a recent popular movie: *Der Schuh des Manitu* (Manitou's Shoe; see 7: Film), which has familiar motifs from the books but also parodies such American television series as *Bonanza*. Attacked and praised from the beginning—his books despised as *Kitsch*—then regarded as the best German storyteller, both read and forbidden by Marxists and Nazis, May achieved a fame as colorful and confusing as his life. Only one thing is certain: Though his name is part of German popular culture, he is almost unknown outside of Germany.

The works of Wilhelm Busch and the Brothers Grimm, in contrast, are not only part of Germany's popular cultural heritage but also known in many countries in translation. When he wrote his cautionary tale about Max and Moritz, two mischievous schoolboys who played pranks on everyone, from their schoolmaster to the baker, Wilhelm Busch (1832–1908) could not have known that his refrain of "*Wehe, Wehe, Wehe, wenn ich auf das Ende sehe!*" (Woe, woe, woe, when I look ahead to the end of all this) would fit neatly into a book about the World Wide Web and the way it af-

fected a generation over 100 years later. The fact that the phrase with the three Ws jumped into Constantin Gillies's mind as he wrote about the way his generation responded to the new technology, how they set up their offices with childish equipment and games, such as scooters and table-top football, is, however, not so surprising.

There is a large collection of traditional children's stories that would be familiar to those born in Germany throughout the twentieth century. It goes way beyond the fairy tales of the Brothers Grimm, though these, too, are cited visually and verbally in everything from headlines to ads. A recent advertisement for the Deutsche Bahn (German Railways) shows a young woman wearing a red hood with a basket filled with food on her lap. She is sitting on a train next to a young man with a knowing smile on his face and a cartoon image of a wolf on his T-shirt. The caption under the advertisement is "Getting safely to grandmother's house." Some of the other old tales are still being used by dot-commers as they teach their children to read.

The fairy stories of the Brothers Grimm are known in the English-speaking world in a somewhat diluted form; only a relatively small number of them have become sufficiently well known to be used in current media in the way they are in Germany. Jakob Grimm (1785–1863) is also known for his work in the field of linguistics, especially as the author of Grimm's Law. This "law" shows that a process—the regular shifting of consonants in groups—took place once in the development of English and the other Low German languages and twice in German and the other High German languages. The first sound shift, affecting both English and German, was from the early phonetic positions documented in the ancient, or classical, Indo-European languages (Sanskrit, Greek, and Latin) to those still evident in the Low German languages, including English; the second shift affected only the High German languages—such as standard German. Grimm's Law shows that the classical voiceless stops (*k*, *t*, *p*) became voiceless aspirates (*x*, *þ*, *f*) in English and mediae (*h*, *d*, *v*) in German. This accounts for the initial sounds of the Latin ***p**ater*, the English *father*, and the German *V**ater* and the middle of the Latin word *frater*, as well as the English *bro**th**er* and the German *Bruder*. It also shows that the classical unaspirated voiced stops (*g*, *d*, *b*) became voiceless stops (*k*, *t*, *p*) in English and voiceless aspirates (*kh*, *ts*, *f*) in German—for example, the initial sounds of the Latin ***d**ecem*, the English ***t**en*, and the German ***z**ehn*—and that the classical aspirated voiced stops (*gh*, *dh*, *bh*) became unaspirated voiced stops (*g*, *d*, *b*) in English and voiceless stops (*k*, *t*, *p*) in German—for example, the initial sounds of the Sanskrit ***dh**ar*, the English ***d**raw*, and the German ***t**ragen*. But it is for the Grimm brothers' desire to preserve the traditional stories that had been passed on primarily orally that they are best known. They claimed to have traveled to the villages of their native province of Hesse, and later beyond, to write down tales they heard told by the local people, noting in particular a peasant woman in a village near Kassel who told them most of the tales published in the second volume. The tales appeared in a series of volumes beginning in 1812, with a seventh edition appearing in 1857.

Through an 1843 letter written by the younger brother, Wilhelm (1786–1859), to Bettina von Arnim, we know that a first edition was sent to Achim von Arnim (1781–1831) twenty-five years before. Apparently Arnim was concerned that the magnitude of the task would become too much for the brothers and might be abandoned, but, luckily for children and Walt Disney, his fears were unfounded. In a preface to the 1819 edition, the brothers told how they had eliminated expressions that were unsuitable for young, impressionable children from an earlier edition. However, they defended their decision to include tales that might frighten some in order to provide as complete a collection as possible. They also noted that local dialects had been preserved where possible to maintain the true flavor of the originals. They regretted the loss of some Hessian dialects and expressed admiration for those with which they were less familiar, from the *plattdeutsch* of the coastal areas of northern Germany to the Swiss tales included in the third edition. Though later researchers have questioned the claim that the stories were gathered through travels around the German-speaking provinces, making the counterclaim that most were told by a family servant, the image of the brothers traveling from village to village listening to the peasants is certainly an appealing one.

The didactic nature of the tales that was so important to the brothers has become part of the ongoing tradition of German children's stories. Though puns might be made on the word "grim," the brothers' name is not sufficiently common in the English-speaking world for neologisms to be formed with them implying a fairy-tale quality. Gillies wrote of *Grimmkalkulation* and *Grimmfaktor* to refer to what might be translated as the "creative bookkeeping" and unrealistic or "pie in the sky" business plans of the dot-commers (Gillies 2003, 99, 101).

In the popular English translations, the cruelty or brutality that is part of the Grimm stories has often been edited out, as in the case of Aschenputtel (Cinderella), whose ugly sisters cut off their heels and then toes to try to fit into the slipper the prince has found. It is not made of glass, however, as in the English language version. (One explanation of this odd material is that the English version was translated from a French one, and the word for mink [*vair*] was misread as "*verre*," meaning glass.) The German tale refers to a golden leather slipper that fits Cinderella as if it were poured on (Grimm et al. 1980, 144) and is contrasted with the heavy wooden shoe she takes off to try for size.

In the tale of Little Red Riding Hood (Rotkäppchen in German), there are two versions of how the big bad wolf meets his end. In the first, he gets to eat both the grandmother and then Little Red Riding Hood and falls asleep after he had "nursed his lust" (*sein Gelüsten gestillt*). It is the thoughtful hunter who decides not to shoot him but cut him open with scissors, releasing grandmother and granddaughter. Little Red Riding Hood fetches stones for filling the belly again. When the wolf awakes, the weight of the stones is too much and he falls down dead. In the second version, there is another wolf that comes to the house on the same pretense of bearing baked goods, but this time it is the crafty grandmother who gets the better of the beast via that staple of German cuisine, the sausage. After refusing to open the door to the wolf, she tells her granddaughter to carry out the broth in which the sausages have cooked and pour it into the water trough outside, knowing that the wolf is lurking around. Sure enough, from his perch on the roof, he stretches his nose to smell the sausage broth, slips, falls into the trough, and drowns. Wolves are thereby shown to be not only sexual predators, as the researcher Bruno Bettelheim (1976) has written, but also greedy good for nothings. Both hunters and grandmothers can be intelligent schemers. A current trend to reintroduce wolves into Germany as they migrate from Poland and points further east is meeting some resistance, no doubt because of these tales.

A tale that is sufficiently well known in Germany to be used in public service appeals for tolerance toward refugees and foreigners in the City of Bremen, though unfamiliar to most in the English-speaking world, is the one about the city musicians of Bremen ("Die Bremer Stadtmusikanten"). The Bremen office for integration of immigrants and for the welfare of foreigners has as its slogan: "What has given Bremen its fairy-tale fame is its immigrants."

In the tale, a donkey, a dog, a cat, and a rooster find themselves homeless and hungry and pool their resources to find something better than death. What they find is a robbers' house, and by braying, barking, meowing, and crowing they scare away the stupid robbers. (It should be noted that robbers are generally of limited intelligence in the Grimms' tales.) When the robbers attempt to reclaim their residence, the animals use their teeth, claws, hooves, and frightening cries to drive them away once and for all. One suspects that the city fathers of Bremen would rather gloss over the fact that the immigrants drove the original residents away—or perhaps they capitalize on the fact that it was only bad (and stupid) citizens who felt threatened by the newcomers.

A 1979/1980 film directed by Helma Sanders about a young mother coping with

Statue of the Bremen town musicians, which come from a brothers Grimm fairy tale. (istockphoto.com)

depression and the deprivations of World War II (*Deutschland bleiche Mutter*, Germany Pale Mother) uses the gruesome Grimm tale of the Robber Bridegroom (*Der Räuberbräutigam*) to reinforce an atmosphere of hardship and hopelessness and perhaps to warn of the dangers of marriage. To entertain her young daughter as she carries her through the bombed-out city, the mother tells this tale of a young miller's daughter whose father finds her a husband she mistrusts. At his urging, she visits him at his home in the forest (a setting that can be both magical and mysterious). Like her fellow fairy-tale figures Hansel and Gretel, the miller's daughter marks the path to the house by scattering lentils beside the path of ashes that the robber has described. When she reaches the house, she finds it empty except for a bird in a cage and an old woman, both of whom warn her to turn back. The miller's daughter continues, asks the old woman where her bridegroom is, and learns that he is one of a band of cannibal robbers.

Before the two can escape, the robbers return with a young virgin. Our heroine barely has time to hide behind the large cauldron that is used for cooking, and then she watches as the other young woman is plied with wine (red, white, and yellow) so much that her heart bursts. Her clothes are ripped off, and then she is cut up and sprinkled with salt. During the slaughter, one of the robbers notices that there is a golden ring on her hand and he hacks off the finger. It jumps in the air only to land in the lap of the miller's daughter. The old woman persuades the robbers not to hunt for the finger, gives them a sleeping potion, and thus saves a second young woman from a grisly death. Both women climb over the drugged robbers and flee the house. The ashes laid on the path by the robbers have blown away, but the lentils have sprouted and are visible even by moonlight, so that the miller's daughter and her rescuer can get out of the woods and back to the mill. The father is told what has happened but goes ahead with the wedding plans anyway. As all are sitting at the dinner table and making their speeches, the robber bridegroom asks his bride to speak. She tells of her walk to the house in the wood, repeating the tale the Grimm brothers have narrated, but stops with the account of the ring finger, produces it, and shows it to the assembled guests. The bridegroom pales and attempts to flee, but he and his fellow robbers are caught and handed over to the law. The retelling of the story is repeated over and over in the film, and the young daughter thereby learns of the cruelty of men and the dangers of marriage.

Another tale from the collection, that of a fisherman and his wife, has been cited and transformed in recent times by the Nobel Prize winner Günter Grass in his novel *Der Butt* (The Flounder). The original tale is of a greedy fisherman's wife who is never satisfied with her condition and constantly wants more. Luckily for her, her patient husband has established magical connections. One of the few fish he has managed to catch is actually a prince who has been put under a spell and begs to be let go. The fisherman is impressed by the talking fish and releases his catch, though he fears he will be scolded by his wife for coming home empty-handed. As expected, the wife berates him and asks why he didn't ask for something in exchange for his generosity. She suggests he demand a hut to live in rather than the chamber pot in which they now reside. The dutiful husband returns to the sea, finds the fish, and makes his request. It is granted, but the sea is no longer as calm. Soon the hut must be replaced by a stone castle, then the discontented wife wants to be a king (not a queen, as they had no power in those days) in a palace, then emperor.

Here the fisherman becomes worried. Though he is familiar with the concept of multiple castles and even kings, he knows that there is just one emperor. But the wife insists. The sea is now stormy, but the fish assures the fisherman that the wife's request has been met. Alas, her ambitions are not satisfied, and she wants to be pope. They argue and the wife prevails. The fisherman returns to the shore, where the sky and sea are dark and ominous, but the fish grants the wish. This is where the tale should end, but greed takes over one more

time. Next, the wife wants to be God. This, however, is too much, and the magical fish/prince transforms her back to where she was at the beginning, living in a chamber pot. In addition to teaching children the dangers of greed, the tale also illustrates the old hierarchy of a Germany still divided into small principalities with larger kingdoms subordinate to an emperor who, in turn, paid allegiance to the pope and ultimately to God.

The name Frau Holle is evoked in the province of Hesse whenever it snows—it is said that Frau Holle is shaking her featherbed—but in the Grimm fairy tale, the old woman with the witch-like appearance who bears that name actually seeks healthy, industrious young women to do the bed-shaking for her. She lives in some obscure region that is entered through a well shaft but has meadows, bakeries, and apple orchards just as one would find in Hesse. In the tale, a beautiful, industrious young woman accidentally enters Frau Holle's realm because her mean, widowed stepmother (who also has a lazy, ugly daughter) has given her so much spinning to do that her fingers become bloodied. When she seeks to wash them in the well, she loses her bobbin. The poor young maiden tells her stepmother of the loss but is scolded and ordered to fish it out of the well. In doing so, she falls in, becomes unconscious, and wakes up to find herself in a beautiful meadow on a sunny day.

The maiden sets off through the flowers and comes to a baking oven where the loaves of bread call out to be saved from burning. Being the good stepdaughter, she naturally pulls them out and walks on. She then finds apples calling from a tree to be shaken down, as they are ripe. Again she obliges and piles them neatly together. Finally, she comes to a little house where an old lady with enormous teeth is standing in the doorway. Perhaps she has heard the tale of *Red Riding Hood* and knows that wolves can often dress in drag, but the old woman urges her not to be afraid and promises to treat her well if she is willing to help in the house and shake her featherbed properly so that it snows down on earth. She introduces herself as Frau Holle. Once again, the maiden proves to be the better daughter and overlooks appearances, works diligently, and is treated very well, with good food and kind words. After a while, she becomes sad and realizes that in spite of the kindness she is receiving, she is homesick. She tells Frau Holle, who is understanding about her desire to go home and leads her to a great gate. When she stands beneath it, gold rains down on her and sticks to her clothing. Frau Holle tells her this is her reward for being so industrious and now returns the lost bobbin. The gate is closed and the maiden finds herself not far from her stepmother's house.

Because she comes bearing wealth, she is welcomed by both stepmother and stepsister. Upon hearing her story, the mother immediately seeks the same good fortune for the other daughter and orders her to sit and spin at the well. To save her from too much work and blisters, however, she advises her to prick her finger on a thorn. The lazy daughter then simply throws the bobbin into the well and jumps in after it. Like her stepsister, she lands in the meadow and encounters the bread and the apple tree, but she refuses to help out. Because she knows what the deal is with the old lady, she agrees to work and shake the bed, but already on the second day her lazy nature gets the better of her. Her work be-

comes sloppier, and on the third day she doesn't want to get out of bed. Frau Holle is disappointed, fires her, and accompanies her to the gate, where the lazy daughter expects to be showered with gold. Alas, instead she is covered in pitch (*Pech*) and goes home to her mother. She is unable to rid herself of the pitch for the rest of her life. *Pech* is also the colloquial term for bad luck.

At the same time as later versions and additional tales were being published by the Grimm brothers, others were writing their own stories to be read to children and to teach them rules for life. Heinrich Hoffmann (1809–1894), or, to use his nom de plume, Heinrich Kinderlieb (the last name means, literally, "fond of children"), published a series of cautionary tales in 1845 under the title of one of the characters, *Der Struwwelpeter* (Peter of the unruly hair). Dr. Hoffmann, whose primary occupation was as a psychiatrist, originally wrote the stories in 1844 as a Christmas gift for his three-year-old son, Carl Philipp.

One is about Kaspar, a young boy who refused to eat his soup and died of starvation, another about a child who always walked around looking up at the sky and falls into a river. He is more fortunate than Kaspar and is pulled out by two passersby. Another is about Philip, who couldn't sit quietly but fidgeted all the time and finally wasted the evening meal of soup and bread by pulling off the tablecloth as he rocked back and forth in his chair. The nickname *Zappelphilipp* (literally, fidgety Phillip) is still commonly used for a restless child. One of the cruelest is the tale of Konrad, who continued to suck his thumb in spite of his mother's scolding. As punishment, his thumb was cut off by a tailor with a large pair of scissors. One can't help con-

jecturing as to whether there is some sub-
liminal anti-Semitism in this tale, since
many tailors at that time were Jewish. A
parody from the 1930s shows the tailor
transformed into Hitler.

"The Tale of the Black Boy" ("Die
Geschicht von dem schwarzen Buben") is
an interesting plea for tolerance and an example of how St. Nikolaus (on whom Santa
Claus was based) played a role as an authority figure who could bring both rewards for good behavior and punishments
for bad outside of the Christmas season.
When the young boys repeatedly laugh at a
black child (portrayed in a way that some
would find offensive today), St. Nikolaus
dips them into a large inkpot and makes
them even blacker than the *Mohr* (Moor)
they had ridiculed. St. Nikolaus does wear
a long red robe, but he is not the fat, jolly
figure into which he has evolved in the English-speaking world. The boys are initially
portrayed playing with hoops, and one has
a flag, perhaps a sign of the desire for nationalism on which the failed 1848 revolution was based. Though eight of the ten
stories are about boys, one is about a girl
named Paulinchen (little Pauline), who
plays with fire and meets a fiery death. The
tenth tale, of less relevance to Hoffmann's
son, is about a hunter who is outwitted by
a crafty hare. Perhaps Hoffmann had an
aversion to sportsmen mistreating animals.
Wherever they appear in his stories—being
mistreated by one boy (Friederich) or
warning Paulinchen of the dangers of
fire—animals are shown in a sympathetic
light.

Contemporary authors are continuing
the tradition of rhyming tales established
by Hoffmann and Busch. One of these is
Elke Heidenreich, known as a journalist,
radio personality, and author of short stories. A children's book she wrote in 1998
entitled *Am Südpol, denkt man, ist es
heiss . . .* (At the South Pole One Would
Think It Would Be Hot . . .) tells the story
of penguins, always dressed appropriately
for the opera, who are visited regularly by
an opera ship from Vienna. The visit described in this book brings the three
tenors, Luciano Pavarotti, José Carreras,
and Placido Domingo, to perform *Tosca* because, as the narrator adds in one of the
many asides to the reader, everyone else
has had enough of the three singers. The
young penguins are not as excited as their
parents about the opera. Young Lotte, who
would rather hear the Spice Girls, is described in words that sound much like
those used by her predecessor, Suppenkas-
par, who stated *"Nein, meine Suppe ess'
ich nicht"* (No, my soup I won't eat):
"Nein, in die Oper geht sie nicht" (No, to
the opera she won't go), but eventually she
is persuaded to swim out to the boat with
the other penguins. Lotte is shown sitting
next to the penguin prodigy, Leo, who can
read and has developed the art of scalping
tickets. (The adult reader might suspect he
will use his promise to the impressionable
Lotte to bring the Spice Girls in on the next
ship to take advantage of her.) The book's
illustrations, by Quint Buchholz, contain
sly references to both high culture and contemporary issues. On one hand, the cliffs
before which Pavarotti's portrait is painted
are strongly reminiscent of Caspar David
Friedrich's paintings of the island of Rügen, in particular *Kreidefelsen auf Rügen*
(chalk cliffs on Rügen, 1820). On the other
(lowbrow) hand, the illustration of the
opera foyer inside the ship has icons to direct the penguins to various amenities. A
fish and a glass with a straw in it imply that
refreshments are available in one direc-

tion. In another, one sees back views of two penguins, one simply standing; the other appears to be sitting on a toilet.

Germans seem to have raised the issue of toilet etiquette to a public topic of discussion. Recently cartoons on posters and postcards have promoted a minor feminist campaign urging men to sit when urinating. The terms *"Sitzpinkler"* and *"Stehpinkler"* (sitting piddler and standing piddler) were used to describe the two positions. There have also been cartoons illustrating the apparent inability of German men to understand the goals of the campaign—to "get it." In one cartoon, a sign requests that men raise the *Brille*, a word that is used both for eyeglasses and a toilet seat, which has a similar, lens-like shape. The man raises his glasses to his forehead. The sign on another cartoon simply requests that one sit while urinating. The man sits on the floor. It is difficult to imagine these cartoons being as acceptable in North America as simply amusing as they are in Germany.

Judging by the high level of activity in bookstores, one would assume that the world of books is booming. However, studies on leisure research come to the conclusion that reading books occupies only the tenth place of the most frequent leisure activities, after watching television (80 percent), reading newspapers or magazines (62 percent), listening to the radio (59 percent), talking on the telephone (44 percent), having a cup of coffee or a glass of beer (42 percent), socialising with friends (37 percent), gardening (36 percent), sleeping late (36 percent) and listening to records or audio cassettes (33 percent). Not yet included in these studies was the ubiquitous use of the ipod.

From A to Z

Alternative press: According to Holger Briel, the alternative press "emerged in the 1970s in the wake of the German student movement which had voiced sharp criticism of the established press and inspired a counter culture of political action and communication" (Briel 1998, 326) (see 4: Youth Culture and the World of Intellectuals). *Pflasterstrand* (Cobble Beach), for example, founded by Daniel Cohn-Bendit (b. 1945), became a symbol of the student protest movement. Cohn-Bendit became known as the "Rote Daniel" or "Dany le Rouge" because of his political stance as well as his red hair. He made a name for himself in the May demonstrations in Paris 1968 and has represented the German as well as the French Greens in the European Parliament. *Tageszeitung* (known as *taz*) emerged as the preferred daily newspaper of the German counterculture. Briel remarked that "the media of the counter culture played an important part in highlighting environmental issues and contributed to the 'greening' of Germany" (see 10: Consumer Culture versus Green Awareness). He observed: "It could even be argued that the publishing ventures of the counterculture in Germany are forerunners of publications on the Internet in their attempt at revealing a hidden reality and breaking the monopoly of established communications" (ibid., 326–327).

Book clubs: Besides general book clubs (for example, Bertelsmann Lesering; Deutsche Buchgemeinschaft), an important academic book club that has its own line of publications is the Wissenschaftliche Buchgesellschaft (Academic Book Club) in Darmstadt.

Buchhandel: Book trade. Besides wholesalers (for example, Koch, Neff and Oetinger [KNO]; Lingenbrink [Libri]; and Bertelsmann), book chains (Hugendubel and Montanus Aktuell), and department stores (for example, Karstadt and Kaufhof), there are small, sometimes family-run bookstores that are only able to survive through outstanding customer service and their attempt to find a specialty niche.

Cartoonists and satirists: Among the many cartoonists and satirists being published in many papers (not only the satirical magazines) are Peter Gaymann, Robert Gernhardt, Bernd Eilert, F. K. Waechter, Chlodwig Poth, Hilke Raddatz, and Max Goldt.

Children's stories: Besides fairy tales, the children's canon still includes Heinrich Hoffmann's *Struwwelpeter* and Wilhelm Busch's *Max und Moritz*. Also popular today are Janosch's *Tigerente* and *Kastenfrosch*. The German counterpart to Joanne K. Rowling, the author of *Harry Potter*, is Cornelia Funke (b. 1958). She has written about forty novels, among them the bestsellers *Herr der Diebe* (The Thief Lord, 2000) and *Tintenherz* (Inkheart, 2003). In 2005, *Time Magazine* included her in their list of the 100 most influential people in the world.

Fairy tales: The most popular fairy tales probably are "Hansel and Gretel," "The Bremen Town Musicians," "Little Red Riding Hood," "The Star Talers" or "Star Dollars," "Rapunzel," "King Thrushbeard," "Snow White and the Seven Dwarfs," and "Sleeping Beauty."

Karl May (1842–1912): May's name has been alphabetized on purpose under "K" because his name is not just a name of a writer but a brand name that has continued its influence long after his death. The total sales of his books exceed 80 million, yet are limited to Germany. The adventures in his novels, in which good always wins, take place in the Wild West (with his heroes Old Shatterhand and the noble indian Winnetou) and in the Near East (with Kara Ben Nemsi and his servant Hadschi Halef Omar).

Magazines: The leading political weekly magazines are *Der Spiegel*, the more conservative *Focus* (published since 1993 by Burda), and *Stern*, which suffered a crisis of public credibility in 1984 when it promoted the "Hitler Diaries," later exposed as forgeries. The epitome of the magazine for the intellectual is the *Kursbuch* (Timetable) founded in 1965 by Hans Magnus Enzensberger. The leading leisure magazines are *Quick, Neue Revue, Das Goldene Blatt, Neue Post*, and *Bunte* (published by Burda, presenting the stories of the rich and famous). Leading the charts in youth magazines is *Bravo* (originally founded in 1956 as a magazine for film enthusiasts). The most prominent women's magazines are *Brigitte, Tina, Bella*, and German editions of international magazines such as *Vogue* and *Elle*, along with shelter magazines (for example, *Schöner Wohnen*, but often with English-sounding titles, such as *Living at Home*). According to Marieluise Beck, "There are a total of 20,000 press publications in Germany including numerous professional journal and trade magazines" (Beck 2003, 203–204).

Newspaper publishers: Bertelsmann/ Gruner and Jahr is one of the German media giants. Among its seventy-two maga zines and ten newspaper titles are *Stern, Capital, Brigitte, Frau im Spiegel, Berliner Kurier, Berliner Zeitung,* and *Hamburger Morgenpost.* Bertelsmann is now, since its acquisition of Random House in 1998, also the biggest publishing group in the English-speaking world. Burda is also one of the largest publishers in Germany, with over thirty magazines—for example, *Bunte, Freundin, Bild und Funk, Elle, Super-Illu* (founded in 1991 and aimed at East German readers, with advice columns and gossip about TV stars), and *Focus.* The publishing company was established in 1927 in Offenburg and has today diversified into several new media areas. Springer is the largest German newspaper publisher, with *Bild, Die Welt,* and *Berliner Morgenpost,* among others. It had a market share of 24 percent in 1991 (Peter Humphreys, quoted in Briel 1998, 333). Alex Cäsar Springer (1912–1985), its founder and owner until his death, became especially controversial during the 1960s because of his opposition to Brandt's Ostpolitik. Many blamed his publications, particularly *Bild,* for provoking the violence that led to the death of Rudi Dutschke, the popular student leader. The headquarters of the publishing house in Berlin was often targeted by demonstrators who saw it as "less a beacon of freedom and democracy than a symbol of entrenched power and of the continuities with Germany's fascist past" (Sandford 1999, 578).

Newspapers: For most Germans, the daily paper is the one published locally—usually a morning paper. The distribution of these papers ranges from a few thousand, the norm, to over 100,000, the exception. In 2004, the manual for foreigners listed the following newspapers as the most impor-

tant ones with nationwide distribution (*überregionale Tageszeitungen* [supraregional dailies]): the *Süddeutsche Zeitung* (published in Munich), founded in 1945, the largest national daily; the *Frankfurter Allgemeine Zeitung* (*FAZ*); the *Frankfurter Rundschau; Die Welt;* and *die tageszeitung* (*taz*) (published in Berlin). The financial daily *Handelsblatt* and the tabloid *Bild* are equally important. Although German papers have no explicit political affiliation, *Die Welt* and *FAZ* are regarded as more conservative, *Die Süddeutsche* and the *Frankfurter Rundschau* as left-of-center politically, and *taz* as an "alternative" paper. The most important weekly newspaper is *Die Zeit.* Of the few GDR papers, the *Wochenpost* survived unification by keeping its East German focus. (See text for translations of titles.)

Nobel Prize winners: After 1945, the Nobel Prize for Literature was awarded six times to German-speaking authors: In 1946 to Hermann Hesse (1877–1962, born in Germany, he became a Swiss citizen in 1924); in 1966 to Nelly Sachs (1891–1970) together with Shmuel Yosef Agnon (1888–1970), she observed that Agnon represented Israel whereas she represented the tragedy of the Jewish people; in 1972 to Heinrich Böll (1917–1985); in 1981 to Elias Canetti (1905–1994), born in Bulgaria, he wrote in German (his main language) and lived much of his life in Austria and Switzerland but adopted British citizenship in 1952; in 1999 to Günter Grass (b. 1927); and in 2004 to the Austrian Elfriede Jelinek (b. 1946). (In addition, Volker Schlöndorff's screen adaptation of Grass's novel *Die Blechtrommel* [The Tin Drum] won an Oscar in 1979. No Nobel Prize was awarded but global bestseller status was achieved during the outgoing 1990s by Bernhard Schlink [b. 1944], a professor of law and a practicing judge. His novel *Der Vorleser* [The Reader, 1995] was selected by Oprah Winfrey for her Book Club in 1999. This made Schlink the first German author to reach the number one position on the *New York Times* bestseller list. The novel deals with Germany's fascist past, the guilt of the perpetrators, and the bewilderment of the post-war generation.)

Publishers: Besides the large publishers (9 percent of publishers account for 80 percent of sales in Germany), there are many medium-sized and small publishers. Often they restrict their publications to specific areas. Examples not mentioned above include: Campus (primarily books in the fields of history, politics, economics, finance, and the humanities); Kohlhammer (emphasis on law and administration as well as various other academic fields); Max Niemeyer (humanities); Beltz and Gelberg; Ravensburger; Thienemann (children and young adults); Hirmer; Prestel (art); Du-Mont (art, literature, travel); Echter (religion); Kösel (psychology, family, and other areas); Baedecker; Polyglott (travel); Elfenbein (modern and foreign literature); Orange Press (culture and intellectual history); Erich Schmidt (law, economics, environment, philology, and technology); and Stroemfeld/Roter Stern (politics, sociology, and literature).

Regenbogenpresse: Literally, rainbow press. The term refers to the lower end of the German weekly magazine market, as Briel mentioned (in Sandford 1999, 524), and its "colorful" reporting practices and prolific use of photography. A good example is the magazine *Quick*.

TV guides: Well-known TV guides are *Hör zu* (Listen), *TV Hören und Sehen* (TV Listen and Watch), *TV Movie*, and *TV Spielfilm* (TV feature film).

Zwischenbuchhandel: Intermediate book trade. The German distribution system of books, with its intermediate book trade, allows customers to receive most books the next day after ordering if the individual bookstore did not have it on its shelves.

Additional Readings

Briel, Holger. "The media of mass communication: the press, radio and television." *The Cambridge Companion to Modern German Culture*. Ed. Eva Kolinsky and Wilfried van der Will. Cambridge: Cambridge University Press, 1998, 322–337.

Faulstich, Werner. *Grundwissen Medien*. 5th ed. München: Fink, 2004.

Galle, Heinz J. *Volksbücher und Heftromane. Ein Streifzug durch 100 Jahre Unterhaltungsliteratur*. Passau: Erster Deutscher Fantasy Club e.V., 1998.

Hachmeister, Lutz, and Friedemann Siering, eds. *Die Herren Journalisten. Die Elite der deutschen Presse nach 1945*. München: Beck, 2002.

Holzweissig, Gunter. *Massenmedien in der DDR*. Berlin: Holzapfel, 1989.

Humphreys, Peter. *Media and Media Policy in Germany*, 2d ed. Oxford: Berg, 1994.

Koszyk, Kurt. "Presse unter alliierter Besatzung." *Mediengeschichte der Bundesrepublik Deutschland*. Ed. Jürgen Wilke. Köln, Weimar, and Wien: Böhlau, 1999, 31–58.

Lott-Almstadt, Sylvia. *Brigitte, 1886–1986. Die ersten hundert Jahre. Geschichte einer Frauenzeitschrift*. Hamburg: Gruner und Jahr, 1986.

Meyn, Hermann. *Massenmedien in Deutschland*. Konstanz: UVK Verlagsgesellschaft, 2004.

Nusser, Peter. *Romane für die Unterschicht*.

Groschenhefte und ihre Leser, 5., mit einer erweiterten Bibliographie und einem Nachwort versehene Auflage. Stuttgart: J. B. Metzlersche Verlagsbuchhandlung, 1981.

Schütz, Walter J. "Entwicklung der Tagespresse." *Mediengeschichte der Bundesrepublik Deutschland*. Ed. Jürgen Wilke. Köln, Weimar, and Wien: Böhlau, 1999, 109–134.

Seegers, Lu. "Die Erfolgsgeschichte von *Hör zu!*" Pp. 151–232 in *Hör zu! Eduard Rhein und die Rundfunkprogrammzeitschriften (1931–1965)*. Potsdam: 2001. Available at http://www.mediaculture-online.de (accessed December 7, 2004).

Seeßlen, Georg. *Romantik & Gewalt. Ein Lexikon der Unterhaltungsindustrie*. Bd. 2. München: Manz Verlag, 1973.

Wilke, Jürgen, ed. *Mediengeschichte der Bundesrepublik Deutschland*. Köln, Weimar, and Wien: Böhlau, 1999.

Wittmann, Reinhard. *Geschichte des deutschen Buchhandels*. München: Beck, 1991.

Ziermann, Klaus. *Der deutsche Buch- und Taschenbuchmerkt, 1945–1995*. Berlin: Wissenschaftsverlag Volker Spiess, 2000.

7

Other Media

Radio and Television

During and just after World War II, German radio became identified with the *Volksempfänger* (people's wireless) and Nazi propaganda, the voice of Joseph Goebbels, and the sound of the trumpets and drums playing the Ride of the Valkyries to announce another victory. The Allied forces were well aware of the power of the medium and were set on using it for a better purpose, to build a democratic and antifascist society. They created broadcasting organizations patterned after their own national systems in the western part of Germany, resulting in *Anstalten des öffentlichen Rechts* (public corporations) that were owned neither by the state nor by private organizations and whose prime source of income was listeners' fees. Television and radio were put under the jurisdiction of the individual states, which worked together in the Arbeitsgemeinschaft der öffentlich-rechtlichen Rundfunkanstalten Deutschlands (Association of Public Broadcasting Institutions of Germany, ARD). The beginning phase in the history of West German broadcasting, the monopoly of ARD, lasted from 1952 to 1963. The governing body was the Rundfunkrat (Broadcasting Council), which consisted of members of the public and representatives of various political and religious groups. In East Germany, in contrast, a centralized broadcasting system was created, which was abolished after unification in 1990.

In the first two decades after World War II, the stations of the occupying forces were as important as the German stations for young people, especially the American Forces Network (AFN), which had a huge impact on German youth growing up at that time. When Elvis Presley was stationed with the U.S. Army in Hesse, teenagers listened even more avidly to AFN to hear his music firsthand. American English was learned in spite of vain attempts by teachers of English to impose British pronunciation on their students, and tastes were shaped (see 4: Youth Culture and the World of Intellectuals).

Throughout the latter twentieth century, as television became Germany's number one leisure activity, the importance of radio declined. In the new millennium, Germany, Austria, and Switzerland all have a broad range of stations, both public and private, many of which are local and independent. Examples are orange 94.0 in Vienna, Austria, and Radio Dreieckland (Three Corner Land), which serves Germany, Switzerland, and France and is based in Freiburg, Germany (Briel 2002, 113).

In 1948, the British military gave the approval for a German television network, and in 1950 a pilot program began in Hamburg and Berlin under the name of Nordwestdeutscher Fernsehdienst (Northwest German Television Service, NWDF). It aired a program three days a week for two hours: Mondays, Wednesdays, and Fridays from 8 PM to 10 PM. The decision to include Berlin in this test phase was politically motivated. Berlin was the *Schaufenster des Westens* (display window of the West). The official beginning date for German TV was 1952, although not all areas of Germany were able to receive the program that year. Wherever the opportunity existed, people flocked to the few restaurants and inns that owned a TV set—of course, in black and white. In this way, the 1953 coronation of Queen Elizabeth II became imprinted into the mind of a whole generation even outside Great Britain, and Germany's victory in the Soccer World Cup championship of 1954 became one of the most important sports events for Germans ever (see 5: Sports; 7: Film). By 1954, enough directional radio towers to cover all of Germany had been built. Now, television was the new window to the world. To display a TV in the living room and watch two to three hours of programming nightly seemed to be a national ambition.

The programs were produced in the various regional studios and then broadcast throughout Germany. The Hamburg studio dominated programming, and only on a few occasions did regional studios not broadcast this common program—for example, when the Cologne studio produced and broadcast the *Kölner Karneval* (Cologne Carnival; see 5: Holidays and Local Festivals), which was of prime interest to the Rhine region. Although the first TV initiatives came from the northern part of Germany, regional programs—in addition to the joint program—were an initiative of the studios in the south. The show *Von Rhein, Main und Neckar* (From the Rhine, Main and Neckar), produced and broadcast twice a week by Hessischer Rundfunk (Hessian Radio, HR), the Süddeutscher Rundfunk (South German Radio, SDR), and the Süd-West Funk (South West Radio, SWF), was one example. As with local newspapers, the regional programs tried to be in closer touch with their direct constituents. From 1959 on, all ARD stations had their own regional programming. Starting in 1956, Bayerischer Rundfunk (Bavarian Radio) also experimented with TV commercials, which became a standard feature for all broadcasters after 1957. A commercial segment was introduced between the afternoon shows for children and the evening program that began at 8 PM. From the very beginning, various national studios also began their collaboration to jointly broadcast special events of common European interest under the label *Eurovision*. In addition to the above-mentioned coronation of Elizabeth II and the 1954 soccer world championship, there was the annual Eurovision song contest, "Grand Prix d'Eurovision," the butt of many parodies, as contestants were rarely of the highest caliber and often wore modified national costumes as they performed.

Television broadcasting in the GDR by the Deutsche Fernsehfunk (German TV Broadcast, DFF) began in 1952 with about two hours of programming each day. Exceptions to this were Mondays, the day reserved for work in party and other organizations. In 1956, the directional radio network was more or less completed so that almost everyone was able to receive the new TV programs. Production of TV sets increased with the goal of having a set in every household. Besides the GDR's own programs, almost all viewers in the GDR could watch West German television, too, and it was very popular and considered more entertaining than the home stations. Historians have debated the role of West German broadcasting, with its focus on consumer goods, in creating discontent and a desire for a Western lifestyle among citizens of the GDR, a situation that contributed to the unrest leading to unification (Briel 2002, 133). There was one area that could not receive West German programming, and it was jokingly referred to as the *Tal der Ahnunglosen* (valley of the unsuspecting). However, in the 1950s and 1960s only about 5 percent of West Germany could receive East German programs. Some nevertheless feared an eastern TV offensive, which the GDR was only able to realize to a very limited degree. For instance, in 1957, when ARD broadcast children's programs or nature films, the GDR TV station aired the news magazine *Telestudio West*, which was especially geared to Western TV audiences.

One of the first TV stars in the West was Peter Frankenfeld, who with Conny Froboess moderated the first light entertainment program, *Eine nette Bescherung* (A Nice Mess), in 1952. He was regarded as the all-around genius of TV entertainment,

and his name had a 100 percent recognition rate by Germans (rivaled only by Adenauer). He was the first entertainer to be featured on the cover of *Spiegel* (1955) and was honored with an entry in the *Große Brockhaus* (Great Brockhaus, the standard German encyclopedia). Even a variety of roses was named after him. He established his own version of the American game show and invented a TV lottery to aid charitable causes. Wherever he appeared on stage, the show was sold out, and his trademark plaid jacket gave him instant recognition.

The second superstar was Hans-Joachim Kulenkampff, known as "Kuli," who began his career as an actor in classical roles on stage. To supplement his income, he also performed in radio plays, and his quick wit brought him to the attention of his superiors at the Hessian radio station. The result was that he became a quizmaster and host beginning in 1949. He was instrumental in transferring several shows from radio to the new medium of television. His biggest success was *Einer wird gewinnen* (Someone Will Win, soon known by the acronym EWG, the same acronym as used in German for the European Economic Community, Europäische Wirtschaftsgemeinschaft; see chapter 10: 'From A to Z' [EU]), which reached viewing figures of 90 percent. The first sequence of twenty-six shows ran from 1964 to 1966; a second series, with twelve shows, from 1968 to 1969; and a third one, with forty-four shows, from 1979 to 1987.

Robert Lembke was one of the longest-serving representatives of German TV, best known as quizmaster of *Was bin ich?* (What's My Line?), the longest running entertainment show. But he was also chief editor, sports coordinator, and finally director. One of the main characteristics of his work was consistency—for many years, the format of his show did not change. The panel, made up of a chief prosecutor, actors, and journalists from Austria, Switzerland, and Germany, sat behind their simple desks, dressed very conservatively and joking politely. Lembke had a small piggy bank in front of him into which he would insert the five-mark pieces whenever the candidate won one of the questions. No big money, no flashy stage, but down-to-earth, wholesome fun.

In contrast to West German TV, the East German TV stars displayed an explicit and affirmative political attitude and were much less narcissistic. The typical representative was Heinz Quermann, who could look back on a theater, radio, and TV career. His breakthrough as a TV entertainer came with the live broadcast of *Da lacht der Bär* (Then, the Bear Is Laughing) from Berlin, the most important show in the GDR in the 1950s and 1960s. It was a politically and culturally liberal show with good music, first-class artistic performances, and great cabaret.

Another typical representative was Heinz Florian Oertel, who made himself a name as a sports reporter as well as a talk-show host and music moderator. He was nominated seventeen times as the top favorite TV star between 1962 and 1989. His career began in 1952 with reports on the Olympic Games in Helsinki.

In 1963, a second channel, Das Zweite Deutsche Fernsehen (The Second German TV Program, ZDF), was created in West Germany (with its headquarters in Mainz), and ARD became known also as Das Erste (The First [Channel]). The expansion of the existing regional channels of ARD led to a third program. With this event, phase two in the history of broadcasting in West Germany was initiated. This phase, characterized by competition between ARD and ZDF, lasted for twenty years, from 1963 to 1983. Although ZDF was organized similarly to ARD, it was conceived by the then ruling "CDU government to provide a more conservative counterweight to the ARD" (Briel 2002, 133). Certainly, the broadcasting stations' complete independence from the state was reduced because politicians sat on the board of the new organization. Another difference was the method of financing. ZDF's contract with the state allowed it to raise money through advertising, whereas ARD, as a public institution financed by public fees, had not been allowed to sell air time in the past and had been forced to create *Werbefernseh GmbHs* (special private limited liability advertisement companies) that had to overcome many legal hurdles.

The commercials, aired at a set time between afternoon and evening programs, were part of the legal arrangement and changed the financing of both public broadcasting systems to a mixture of fees and revenues from advertisements. For the public, unaware of all the negotiations behind closed doors, the most obvious innovation was ZDF's introduction of *Mainzelmännchen*, six cartoon characters (Anton, Berti, Conni, Det, Edi, and Fritzchen) who played practical jokes on one another in short skits between the commercials. Before the first ZDF broadcast, the staff at the Mainz headquarters had worked as diligently as the little goblins in German folktales, known as *Heinzelmännchen*. The stories of these goblins, who efficiently did household chores during the night, were very popular. German children learned about them along with other fairy-tale characters and would wait for the little helpers to come and do their homework while they slept. It was a clever marketing strategy to build on that tradition and call the new characters created for the TV station located in the town of Mainz *Mainzelmännchen* (a name sounding very similar to *Heinzelmännchen*). Wolf Gerlach, the cartoonist who had created the figures, at the same time made fun of the Germans' predilection for garden gnomes (see 5: Activities and Clubs), but he made his figures younger and cuter looking and added an engaging giggle. This way, the *Mainzelmännchen* became an unforgettable symbol for the new station and a part of German culture. In 2003, forty years later, they underwent a makeover to keep up with the new millennium. Not surprisingly, this was the source of some controversy among those who resisted change.

By 1961, ARD had already experimented with a second channel to offer programs geared to different groups of audiences. The station, II. ARD, also served as a test channel for new shows before they became part of regular ARD programming. The political magazine *Panorama* was tested that way, as was the U.S. series *77 Sunset Strip*. The managers of both ARD and ZDF had not yet totally forgotten television's cultural and social responsibilities. Both channels continued, according to Holger Briel, "to co-operate in many areas, such as jointly securing the rights for major sporting events, making sure that their programming structures [were] compatible and not overly competitive, etc." (Briel 2002, 153). Yet, both stations became increasingly entertainment-oriented, especially ZDF, which relied more than ARD on advertising revenues. TV became the competitor of the cinema (see 7: Film). One could stay at home, be comfortable on the couch with a glass of beer, and watch a movie. More and more, television became the focus of an ever-expanding entertainment center. Once the portable TV set was introduced, it was possible to watch television in the kitchen and on the balcony. Between 1964 and 1970, leisure time for Germans increased by 10 percent, time spent at home by 24 percent, and the time for watching TV by 58 percent. Watching television became the prime form of relaxation and entertainment.

Vico Torriani, with his show *Der goldene Schuss* (The Golden Shot, 1967–1970); Caterina Valente with *Bonsoir, Kathrin* (Good Evening, Kathrin, 1957), the first personality show of German TV; Lou van Burg with *Sing mit mir, spiel mit mir* (Sing with Me, Play Games with Me, 1961–1962); and Peter Alexander with his *Peter Alexander präsentiert Spezialitäten* (Peter Alexander presents specialties, 1970) were all characteristic of this era. These foreign-born stars—Torriani from the Rhaeto-romanic part of Switzerland, Valente from Italy but raised in France, van Burg from the Netherlands, and Peter Alexander from Austria—added a cosmopolitan touch and demonstrated Germany's openness to the world. Color television was introduced in 1967. Global broadcasts were no longer the very special events they had been in 1962, when the first U.S. satellite, Telstar I, was the primary device facilitating such broadcasts, but they became a regular feature from 1968 on. Most of the shows were apolitical and superficial and seemed to offer a counterpoint to the political upheaval of the 1960s, a protest against the protest, an affirmation of the status quo. Helga Hahnemann added an "exotic" touch to GDR TV in the 1960s and 1970s—

in a way comparable to the foreign-born stars on West German TV during the same period—because of her nonconformist mockery and daring irony. Karl-Eduard von Schnitzler, in contrast, sought to address the problem of GDR citizens watching and being influenced by Western television with his program *Der schwarze Kanal* (The Black Channel). He portrayed West German TV as being engaged in antisocialist political manipulation. In the wake of unrest in the GDR, he was forced to resign after twenty-nine years. His last show aired on October 30, 1989, less than a month before the fall of the Berlin Wall (see 1: From Two to One).

Deregulation set in during the 1980s. After heated debates, the strict broadcasting laws that existed in the Federal Republic were changed. Finally, it became possible to establish private stations. The years 1984 to 1991 championed the model still in use today: a dual broadcasting system—that is, the coexistence of public and private broadcasting stations. And at the beginning, both channels, ARD and ZDF, had a hard time competing with the new private stations such as SAT1, PRO7, and RTL; of course, both lost their monopoly, though they were able to retain their leading ranking for prime-time news shows: *Tagesschau* (ARD) and *heute* (ZDF). Meanwhile, program offerings had expanded to twenty-four-hour coverage. The TV evening had become a TV day. There were children's programs in the morning and news, soap operas, talk shows, and quiz shows throughout the day—something for everyone.

The average total viewing time had increased as well as the percentage of viewers making use of the varied programming. Whereas 36 percent of the population

watched television for more than three hours per day in 1974, 49 percent watched the same amount by 1990. The number of stations that offered entertainment increased, with cable and satellite TV helping to enlarge the choice of programs. Channel surfing became the new trend. Instead of seeing themselves as having a primarily cultural obligation, the broadcasters' priorities shifted to commercial concerns. Viewing numbers dictated the types of shows and financial success, and advertising revenues set the parameters. The most popular programs were murder mysteries and soccer matches, followed by entertainment shows. New stars who appealed to all members of the family were added to the lineup, and gradually the boundaries between the types of shows became blurred. Hosts incorporated various new elements into their game and quiz shows. This was true of Wim Thoelke's *Der Große Preis* (Win Large, 1974–1992) with its cartoon figures by Loriot—Wum, a dog, and Wendelin, an elephant—as well as of Hans Rosenthal's *Dalli Dalli* (Quick, Quick, 1971–1986), which included many casual interviews with guests; Frank Elstner's *Wetten, dass . . . ?* (Let's Bet that . . . ? 1981–1987), in which contestants wagered that they could accomplish various outlandish tasks within a certain time, and which also included acting interludes, and later the continuation of that show by host Thomas Gottschalk (1987–1992, 1994–present); and Rudi Carrell's *Am laufenden Band* (Nonstop), always good for a surprise. Television shows became the new social glue, allowing families and other groups to experience a joint media consumption.

The opening chapter of *Generation Golf* by Florian Illies begins with a typical Saturday evening of the author's childhood in the early 1980s. After his bath he would watch *Wetten, dass . . .?* on television, knowing this was exactly the right show to be watching to keep up with his friends. Illies reported this with a touch of nostalgia, regretting that in later years he was unable to recapture this sense of security; part of this was due to the way television offerings changed in the 1980s and 1990s (Illies 2001, 9).

Though there were clearly recognized stars with family appeal, the concept of stars for target groups eventually developed. In the 1990s, television followed the same trend toward extreme diversity as popular music, fashion, lifestyles, film, literature, art, and architecture and design (see 4: Lifestyle and Fashion; 6: Popular and Belletristic Literature, 7: Film; 8: Music; 9: City Planning and Architecture). Everything was allowed. The result was an immense juxtaposition of styles and directions. One of the early stars for a specific audience was Heinz Schenk with his *Zum Blauen Bock* (By the Blue Goat, 1966–1987), seen as a show for the working class. The name of the show referred to a pub patterned after an *Äppelwoi-Wirtschaft* (inn that serves apple cider) in Frankfurt-Sachsenhausen. It exhibited a simple kind of humor. Dieter Thomas Heck created a show for all those Germans who did not like Anglo-Saxon rock music. He rediscovered the German popular song (*Schlager*) in his *ZDF-Hit-parade* (1969–1984). Anneliese Rothenberger was the representative for "high culture" on television for the educated middle class (see 8: Music). She presented opera and operetta stars. Dieter Hildebrandt was the resident TV cabaret artist (see 2: Stereotypes and Prejudices). Alfred Biolek was— and still is—the sensitive talk-show host for the intellectual with a touch of exclusivity,

an elaborate style, and the image of the cultivated citizen. In the west, Carolin Reiber represented the successful middle-class conservative yuppie with a flair for folk music; Petra Kusch-Lück was her GDR counterpart. Jürgen von der Lippe, a proletarian with an aristocratic-sounding name who makes fun of the upper classes, was the spokesman for the lower classes. Finally, Margarethe Schreinemakers introduced gossip, sex, and sensationalism and made voyeurism acceptable on television.

After unification, the West German system was expanded to include the new states, a process that could be regarded as the third phase of German broadcasting history, lasting approximately from 1991 to 1997. Most of the programs and performers of the former GDR were absorbed by West German radio and television. Typical examples were *DT 64*, a radio program from the 1960s, which was canceled in 1992, and the youth program *Elf 99* (Eleven 99), which had started just before the revolution in 1989. At that time, it was controversial for its open political criticism and its Western look and appeal. But in 1990 it was reduced to a harmless entertainment show. Only two television stations in eastern Germany still broadcast GDR movies and series just before the millennium.

One of the regional channels from the former East Germany, Mitteldeutscher Rundfunk (Central Germany Broadcasting, MDR), produced a nostalgic show in 2000 reminding viewers of how creative they had been when they lacked the choice of products and services that came with unification. The show's title was *Der Mangel macht erfinderisch* (Shortages Make One Inventive). Two commentators, speaking the dialect of Saxony, reported on a range of examples of making do with what was available. The old Trabi car was rebuilt into a bicycle, a camper, and a stretch limo; a sauna was built out of an old wardrobe, and one particularly creative handyman built a revolving sunhouse to catch the optimum rays.

After 1997, the dual broadcasting model was modified when the government specified the maximum market share allowed for each group of private broadcasting stations (limited to 30 percent), while guaranteeing the continuation of the two public stations, ARD and ZDF. But meanwhile, television now had close to 100 TV broadcasters, which were now competing with other new media, including videos, toys such as Nintendo and Game Boy, and the World Wide Web. One could use the television like a computer to call up information. It had become interactive. Moreover, the look of TVs had changed, with the huge monster sets giving way to slim picture frames in the new millennium.

The new type of showmaster was represented by Harald Schmidt, who made it in 2003 onto the 100 greatest Germans list. Television was not only the medium for, but the subject of, his analyses. He made fun of himself, of television rituals, and the audience in such a subtle way that all felt included rather than excluded. From his high-school days he had been a quick-witted, mischievous, multitalented trouble maker. He led the church choir, was organist, studied acting, became a member of the satirical group Düsseldorfer Kom(m)ödchen (combining the words for "chest of drawers" and "comedy" with the diminutive suffix "-chen"), and landed his first engagement as showmaster in 1988. But at first he was too confrontational, and the quotas sank. He overcame the low approval ratings and established himself as one of Germany's best TV entertainers. Florian Illies devoted considerable space to Schmidt in his chronicle, describing him as the great teacher and educator of the Golf Generation (Illies 2001, 121, 175). Schmidt's criticism of the generation's political apathy—that they found the weather too cold for engaging in political demonstrations (ibid., 163)—is cited, along with the way he seemed to be a barometer of the generation. In the early days, he wore his hair long and joked with the chief editor of *Mad* magazine, but later he came to distance himself from the children of the 1970s and joked *about Mad* (not *with*). He cut his hair, wore Hugo Boss suits, and generally made fun of people who took themselves and their efforts to improve society too seriously (ibid., 179–180).

Besides Thomas Gottschalk and Harald Schmidt, the third unrivaled name in TV entertainment at the beginning of the new millennium is Günther Jauch. His top shows are *Wer wird Millionär?* (Who Will Become the Next Millionaire?) and *Stern TV*. In contrast to Gottschalk and Schmidt, who are known for good humor and cynicism, respectively, Jauch represents respectability. Many can identify with him and love his laid-back understatements. When, in 1998, a goal collapsed in a championship soccer game between Real Madrid and Borussia Dortmund and the game was delayed for over an hour, his remark was, "*Für alle Zuschauer, die erst jetzt eingeschaltet haben, das erste Tor ist schon gefallen*" (For the viewers who have just turned on their TV sets: the first goal has already fallen). The line contained a pun, since *ist gefallen* can mean to score as well as to fall or to collapse. Not surprisingly, he was voted in a survey in January 2005 as the best-loved German.

Although not a German invention, reality TV has been a success story on German TV. Two participants who became national heroes were Zlatko Trpkovski (b. 1976) and Daniel Kueblboeck (b. 1985). Zlatko, an unemployed automechanic, made himself a name through his stupidity and his inability to hit the right note in singing. This was the basis for his singing career after leaving the Big Brother container. His name even entered the German vocabulary. *Zlatko-isierung* (zlatkotization) means a fad that occupies one's time with completely unimportant topics and people. Daniel Kueblboeck, voted the most annoying German in 2003, also began an acting and singing career following a reality TV performance.

Film

Although Germany had an outstanding film tradition in the early days of the medium, the country has enjoyed only a limited success in this area in the postwar years. The fate of the Babelsberg film studio (named after the location, between Berlin and Potsdam) is pretty much a mirror of the ups and downs of German cinema. In the first decade of the twentieth century, it was the production center of German classics such as Paul Wegener's *Der Student von Prag* (The Student of Prague, 1913) and his *Golem*, 1915. Then, after a short period of decline caused by World War I, it became the home of the films of the "Golden Age of German Cinema" and Europe's largest film studio. Universum Film AG (UFA), founded in 1917, was the only serious competitor to Hollywood's hegemony. After World War II, Babelsberg became the production center for Deutsche Film AG (DEFA), the GDR state film company. Following unification, Treuhand (the trust company in charge of former GDR properties) took control. In 1992, the studio was sold to a French property investment company, and Volker Schlöndorff became one of its managing directors. In 2004, the Babelsberg studios were again up for sale. Although they had attracted attention in 2003 with the promising project *In 80 Tagen um die Welt* (Around the World in 80 Days), in which parts of Berlin had been transformed into London of the Victorian era, Babelsberg had not been able to make a profit. By 2005, a rejuvenation seemed possible, however. The studio presents itself today as a "full-service provider for film and television productions."

In 1995, the centennial anniversary both of cinematography and of German film history, German film was barely alive. A hundred years earlier, in 1895, the Lumière brothers presented their cinematograph in

Stamp set from 1995 commemorating 100 years of German cinema.

Paris, and Max Skladanowsky demonstrated his Bioscop (an early film projector) in Berlin. The decades that followed had brought fame and modest fortunes, leading many to regard German cinema between 1919 and 1933 as one of the world's greatest. Paul Wegener, the Danish actress Asta Nielsen, Ernst Lubitsch, Wilhelm Murnau, Fritz Lang, and Detlev Sierck (known later as Douglas Sirk) are just a few of the names with an international reputation from the early years of UFA. Classics like *Das Kabinett des Doktor Caligary* (The Cabinet of Doctor Caligary), *Metropolis*, *Nosferatu*, *Der letzte Mann* (its English title is *The Last Laugh*), *Der Blaue Engel* (The Blue Angel), the *Doktor Mabuse* series, and *M* are part of the canon of any film history course. During the Hitler era, however, the movies made by Leni Riefenstahl in the service of the Nazi state severely tarnished the German image. After 1945, Hollywood productions began to overshadow all of Germany's fledgling attempts to regain its former status.

The division of the country was mirrored in its film industry. In the east, the Soviets recognized the great potential of film for reeducation and mass manipulation just as Hitler had done; in the west, the British and U.S. military government feared another centralization of the German film industry. Therefore, in the east, according to Corinna J. Heipcke, the Soviets decided in October 1945 "to sequester the German film companies in the Soviet zone and order a group of reliable German communists to form a committee that would prepare German film production. This committee moved into the old UFA headquarters at Berlin. They called themselves "Filmaktiv." In May 1946, Filmaktiv was granted the licence for a film production company, and the company was renamed Deutsche Film AG (German Film Corporation) (Briel 2002, 28). Only days after its creation, DEFA began producing its first film, *Die Mörder sind unter uns* (The Murderers Are Among Us), with Hildegard Knef. The films became the paradigm for the so-called *Trümmerfilme* (cinema of ruins), films dealing with the effects of World War II.

In East Germany, the positive side of the creation of DEFA in the Babelsberg studios was that the working conditions were relatively good. The technical standards were always high, DEFA was a monopoly, everything was financed by the state, and everyone had a secure job. Producers, directors, and actors were fully employed and had no need to fear for their jobs if a film was not successful. The negative side of the arrangement was state censorship. An Artistic Advisory Board (Künstlerische Rat) made sure that producers followed guidelines.

In the early postwar years until 1952, DEFA produced works primarily by directors who had not surrendered to the Nazi regime, such as Wolfgang Staudte, Erich Engel, and Kurt Maetzig, who established the tradition of antifascist films. Yet, gradually a more dogmatic approach was introduced with the goal of ideological penetration of everyday life or socialistic brainwashing. Already in June 1951, "after having successfully drawn the crowds for a month," according to Heipcke, "Falk Harnack's DEFA-film *Das Beil von Wandsbeck* (The Ax from Wandsbeck) was silently taken off the market because of 'political errors'. The unaltered, full-length version could only be shown in 1981" (Briel 2002, 28). Only a few exceptions were able to depict an authentic picture of contemporary conflicts. Examples were films by Heiner

Carow, those by Gerhard Klein and his designer Wolfgang Kohlhaase, the visual descriptions of past and present by Konrad Wolf, and the tragicomedies of Frank Beyer.

After Stalin's death in 1953 and for the following four or five years, the industry moved into a more relaxed attitude, overseen by a newly created Ministry of Culture. In 1956–1957, a few coproductions were even allowed with the French, resulting in some memorable films: *Die Abenteuer des Till Eulenspiegel / Les aventures de Till l'Espiègle* by Gérard Philipe; *Les sorcières de Salem / Die Hexen von Salem* (The Witches from Salem), with a filmscript by Jean-Paul Sartre based on Arthur Miller's *The Crucible;* and *Les Miserables / Die Elenden* with Jean Gabin. But years of leniency alternated with years of strict control, and pressure increased whenever the political elite feared change. As a result, showings of many productions were banned after the fall of Nikita Krushchev in 1965. The Central Committee decided to ban all films that allegedly fostered destructive ideologies and skepticism, such as *Karla* by Hermann Zschoche, *Das Kaninchen bin ich* (I Am the Rabbit) by Kurt Maetzig, and *Jahrgang 1945* (Age Group 1945) by Jürgen Böttcher. Only after unification in 1989 were they premiered under the title *Verbotsfilme* (forbidden films).

The West German film market, in contrast, was overwhelmed by American films. Home productions in the early postwar years were characterized by an emphasis on pure entertainment. Only a small number of films tried to come to terms with the past—for instance, Helmut Käutner's 1947 film *In jenen Tagen* (In Those Days)—or to critically appraise the present. To encourage the production of German films that might not become box-office successes, a law was introduced in 1951 to guarantee producers up to 35 percent of their production expenses if ticket sales had not produced this revenue. Although this law has since been revised, it is still a source of subsidies for local film production along with funds from the individual *Länder* (ibid., 43).

The early box-office successes were *Heimatfilme* (rustic regional romances), filled with sentiment and optimism, usually set in small towns or villages and often featuring local, traditional costumes. The most popular were the *Sissi* films about the Empress Elisabeth (known as Sissi), wife of the Austrian emperor Franz Joseph, with Romy Schneider in the title role (see 7: Celebrities). The first one appeared in 1955, and there were two sequels. Sissi of the films embodied a minor personal rebellion against a conservative society that seemed to imprison her, yet she was also depicted as a sweet little princess in a frilly crinoline. The real empress was an emancipated woman who searched for her own identity and, though beautiful, was less submissive and more confrontational than the heroine of the films. Other subgenres were similar to Hollywood soap operas and included *Arztfilme* (films about doctors in the leading role), *Karl-May-Filme* (see 6: Popular and Belletristic Literature), *Tourismus-Filme*, and the various versions of pseudo-pornographic *Schulmädchen-Reporte* (soft-porn reports about schoolgirls).

Georg Tressler's *Die Halbstarken* (The Hooligans, literally the "half-strong") (1956), addressing social questions in a realist tone; Rolf Thiele's *Das Mädchen Rosemarie* (The Girl Rosemarie) (1958), spotlighting political corruption; and especially

Bernhard Wicki's *Die Brücke* (The Bridge) (1959), reminding the audiences of the traumas of war, were the exceptions. Apparently moviegoers yearned for an identification with characters who were outside of politics. Film stars were always front-page news. Romy Schneider, Curt Jürgens, O. W. Fischer, Sonja Ziemann, and Horst Buchholz were admired and their private lives eagerly followed. Of less familiarity to the general public were the directors—for example, Rudolf Jugert, Harald Braun, Helmut Kräutner, Hans Deppe, Harald Reinl, and others.

When television became popular, it caused many cinemas to close. The project *Neuer Deutscher Film* (New German Film)—known also as *Das Neue Deutsche Kino* (the new German cinema)—as documented in the *Oberhausener Manifest* of 1962 (named after the city where twenty-six young, frustrated, and visionary filmmakers met), tried to reverse the trend. These young directors announced the death of the old cinema tradition, but the implied rebirth took a few years. Not until the later years of that decade did German cinema again gain recognition for its artistic goals as it had done in the 1920s, the era of Expressionism. Some film experts differentiate between the Young German Cinema from 1962 to 1969 and the New German Cinema of 1969/1970. Regardless of the precise labeling, the youthful artists anticipated the student revolution of the late 1960s in seeking new, fresh, and unspoiled visual images that reflected their experiences.

Interestingly enough, because traditional studios had refused to work with this avant-garde group, the TV stations supported the young filmmakers and helped launch their efforts. Rainer Werner Fass-binder was the most productive and important of these young directors. Others were Wim Wenders, Werner Herzog, Alexander Kluge, Margarethe von Trotta, and Volker Schlöndorff, but each had a different approach. Fassbinder modified the tradition of the melodrama; Schlöndorff experimented with film adaptations from literature; Kluge created fictionalized reports; and Trotta combined emotional cinema with critical reflections on society. As Martin Brady and Helen Hughes remarked: "New German Cinema was decidedly heterogeneous, with a diverse, often antagonistic group of *Autorenfilmer* (auteurist writer-directors) following their own political and aesthetic programmes. Indeed, it is really only the rejection of commercial mass entertainment cinema and a conspicuous 'literariness'" which unite the various directors and their films (Sandford 1999, 444).

Some experts predicted a true revival of the spirit of Babelsberg (the German "Hollywood") that would eventually put German filmmakers in a leading position. Even *Newsweek* contained an article about this "German Film Boom" in 1976. But, in retrospect, it seems to have been only a brief flare-up of creativity. *Die verlorene Ehre der Katharina Blum* (The Lost Honor of Katharina Blum, 1975), codirected by Volker Schlöndorff and Margarethe von Trotta, was based on Heinrich Böll's story of the same title and became part of German social history as well as film history with its depiction of the clash between society, young revolutionaries, and the right-wing press, especially *Bild* (see 6: The Press; 4: Youth Culture and the World of Intellectuals). In 1979, Schlöndorff won an Oscar for his film adaptation of Günter Grass's *Die Blechtrommel* (The Tin Drum);

in 1981, Margarethe von Trotta received the Golden Lion at the Venice Film Festival for her film *Die Bleierne Zeit* (literally, "the leaden time" but distributed in English as "Marianne and Juliane"), a film about the Baader Meinhof gang (4: Youth Culture and the World of Intellectuals). But for a general audience, the directors were too avant-garde and subtle. Even Helma Sanders-Brahms's *Deutschland, bleiche Mutter* (Germany, Pale Mother, 1980), one of the most intimate films of the young postwar filmmakers, who tried to come to terms with the Nazi past, was not a box-office success. More and more in the late 1970s and early 1980s it seemed that the films of the young directors were appreciated only by an elitist group of moviegoers. With the death of Fassbinder in 1982, the emergence of a new political climate unfavorable to artistic experimentation and cuts in the lifeline of the filmmakers—state subsidies—another dry period set in. There were only a few noteworthy interruptions, such as Wolfgang Petersen's international success *Das Boot* (The Boat, 1981); *Die unendliche Geschichte* (The Unending Story, 1984); the critically acclaimed and commercially successful *Männer* (Men, 1985) by Doris Dörrie; and Wim Wender's *Der Himmel über Berlin* (Wings of Desire, literally "the sky [or heavens] over Berlin," 1987).

After unification, DEFA was liquidated, and in the mid-1990s (just 100 years after it began), German film was again searching for an identity. In spite of the early foundation of the Berlinale film festival in 1951, German film rarely reached a level of international fame. Most productions were only successful on a very local level. The few exceptions in recent years have been *Der bewegte Mann* (Maybe, Maybe Not) by

Sönke Wortmann in 1994, based on a best-selling comic by Ralf König; *Keiner liebt mich* (Nobody Loves Me) by Doris Dörrie in 1994; *Männerpension* (Jail Birds) by Detlev Buck in 1996; the animated *Werner—Das muß kesseln* (Werner—It's Got to Be Really Cool); *Lola rennt* (Lola Runs) by Tom Tykwer in 1998; *Bella Martha* (Mostly Martha) by Sandra Nettelbeck in 2000; and possibly the comedy *Der Schuh des Manitou* (Manitou's Shoe) by Michael "Bully" Herbig in 2000. This parody of TV westerns and Karl May films (6: Popular and Belletristic Literature) about the Old West relied heavily on puns and therefore never achieved the same success in translation that it did in the German-speaking world. The problem was similar for many films that relied on German humor, especially those by Otto Waalkes.

Likewise, films inspired by the wave of nostalgia for the former East, or *Ostalgie*, as it is termed (see 1: From Two to One), were welcomed in Germany but found limited resonance globally. The best known of these films, *Good Bye Lenin!* (2003) directed by Wolfgang Becker, produced a small ripple effect even outside Germany (winning awards from the German and European film academies). In it, a son tries to recreate the German Democratic Republic for his mother, who has come out of a coma that she had fallen into in the summer of 1989, just before the Berlin Wall came down. He fears she could not survive the shock of seeing that Germany has been unified and her favorite products lost forever, along with the Communist ideals. A less positive picture of the former GDR than the one depicted by *Good Bye Lenin!* was presented in *Das Leben der Anderen* (The Life of the Others, 2006) by the film director Florian Henckel von Donnersmarck

(b. 1973), who also wrote the screenplay for the movie. Its topic is the GDR security police (Stasi). It won the Bayerische and the Deutsche Filmpreis (the Bavarian and the German Film Prize).

Nevertheless, the market remained dominated by U.S. films. Over 80 percent of the movies in commercial cinemas came from the United States in the beginning of the new millennium—usually dubbed, rarely in the original with subtitles. Yet, at the same time, German motion pictures garnered more than fifty awards in the 2002/2003 season alone, among them the Oscar for the best foreign language film, won by Caroline Link for *Nirgendwo in Afrika* (Nowhere in Africa, 2001). *Gegen die Wand* (Head-On, 2003), a film by Fatih Akin, received many German and European awards, but had little impact beyond Europe. It only made headlines in the tabloids when it was revealed that the leading actress, Sibel Kekilli, had been also a porn star.

At the top of international interest are, not surprisingly, films about Germany's past—for instance, Margarethe von Trotta's *Rosenstrasse* (The Women of Rosenstrasse, 2003), and Volker Schlöndorff's Holocaust drama *Der neunte Tag* (The Ninth Day, 2004). *Der Untergang* (Downfall, 2004) by the producer-writer Bernd Eichinger and the director Oliver Hirschbiegel, a film about Hitler's last days, and *Sophie Scholl—Die letzten Tage* (Sophie Scholl—The Final Days, 2005), a film about the early German resistance, directed by Marc Rothemund, both won Oscar nominations for best foreign language film in 2004 and 2005 respectively. In *Der Untergang*, the Swiss-German actor Bruno Ganz portrays Adolf Hitler as "some golem or mythical dwarf—a would-be Siegfried

who has collapsed into Alberich" (Denby 2005, 259). The movie, based on solid research (primarily on Joachim Fest's books, Fest being one of the prime historians of Hitler biography) and an eyewitness report (by Hitler's private secretary, Traudl Junge), is characteristic of one aspect of *Vergangenheitsbewältigung* (coming to terms with the past) because it shows the banality of evil, to use the phrase coined by Hannah Arendt for her famous book.

The film recreates visually the fate of Joseph Goebbels's children, who became part of the literary consciousness through Marcel Beyer's book *Flughunde* (published as *The Karnau Tapes* in English, 1995). David Denby wrote in his review of the film in *The New Yorker:*

Hitler's will continues to operate even after he has lost his power. In imitation of that will, Goebbels' icy wife, Magda (Corinna Harfouch), poisons the six younger Goebbels children, one by one, because they are "too good" to grow up in a post-Nazi world. The children's death is unbelievably creepy: they are blond and cute, and they sing in unison for Uncle Adolf a few days before they die—it's as if the little Von Trapps had been silenced at last. That's a sick joke, perhaps, but you long to mock these solemn, murdering Nazi "idealists," female as well as male. The movie errs in treating even the most grotesquely sordid episodes as tragedy (accompanied by Purcell's most dignified music). . . .

By adding pathos to the collapse of Nazism, the filmmakers have come close to nostalgia, and at times one longs for a coldly malicious ironist like Brecht or Fassbinder to come in and take over. One even wants a revival of Hans-Jürgen Syberberg's "Our Hitler," from 1977, a seven-and-a-half-hour extravaganza that combined surrealist shenanigans, circus acts, puppet shows, and didactic passages, all in an attempt to place Hitler within German history and sensibility. The movie was infuriating, but at least it didn't force the audience to engage in such inanities as freshly appraising Hitler's relation to his secretary, his cook, and his dog. (*The New Yorker*, February 14 and 21, 2005, 260–261)

The German filmmaker Seyhan Derin, representing one slowly increasing sector of the film market, the films by multicultural directors, responding to an interviewer who asked whether German film had an international future comparable to the success achieved in the United States, said, "I don't believe so. Most German films are too *kopflastig* [top-heavy]. . . . But as long as they don't aspire for real success, they are fine. German filmmakers are at the moment quite happy with their market share. . . . In other countries most viewers don't care about German films, and I don't want to put myself into the position of a defense lawyer. From time to time, a film pops up that I like, for instance *Schultze Gets the Blues*." (personal e-mail, January 12, 2005). The latter was Michael Schorr's funny and sentimental tale of a forced retiree who finds a new life playing his accordion and discovering Cajun zydeco music (2003). It alienates him from his German neighbors but sends him on a journey to the swamps of Louisiana to find the heart of zydeco.

Though the Berlinale mentioned above is the most important festival for introducing new films in Germany, there are smaller festivals throughout the country. Some, such as the one held in the medium-sized town of Freiburg, receive little acclaim beyond the region, but a listing of films shown at the 2004 Filmfest is an indication of the international range as well as the broad tastes of filmgoers in that area. During the five-day festival (July 22–26, 2004), twenty-four films and one sneak preview were listed. Of the twenty-four, ten were from the United States, three from Sweden, two from Pakistan, one from France, one from Brazil, one from Austria, one from Korea, one from Great Britain, two listed as joint German/Swiss productions, and two just from Germany. Though most of these films had come out that year or the previous one, four of the U.S. films were older and had not been major international hits. One was from 1984, one from 1995, two from 1996, one from 2000, and one from 2001 (*Kino kurier*, 13, a section of *Stadtkurier*, July 21, 2004).

Yet another film festival even earned a mention in a U.S. airline magazine. The report of the Munich Film Festival was, however, designed as much to offer tourists a view of the Bavarian capital that avoided the usual clichés of dirndls, beer festivals, and Lederhosen as it was to promote films. The city itself is described as a giant stage set and listed along with Berlin and Cologne as one of Germany's media capitals and "the center of the country's film industry." The article suggests that those visiting Munich plan to attend "one of five annual film festivals, showcasing everything from documentaries to fantasy," though the eight-day Munich Film Festival is listed as the biggest. Readers learned that the opening night invitation-only party is held in the baroque setting of the Künstlerhaus am Lenbachplatz and that it often spreads outdoors to the banks of the Isar River. The southern ambiance, with outdoor cafes and beer gardens, was cited as one of Munich's advantages over the larger and more serious Berlin festival. Readers of the magazine were also encouraged to head to the outskirts of the city to Bavaria Film City to see a stunt show, a tour of the special effects studios, and the submarine used in the 1981 film *Das Boot* (Julia M. Klein, "Destination: Munich," *US Airways Attaché*, December 2004, 50–57).

Munich's history as second most important film city, with seventy-eight movie houses by 1937, was also the subject of an exhibition in the 2004 festival produced by the Academy for Television and Film (founded in 1967). This academy admits just over forty students a year from among 600 international applicants and takes a perverse pride in having rejected Rainer Werner Fassbinder years ago.

The Internet

As is clear from the title of Constantin Gillies's 2003 book *Wie wir waren: Die wilden Jahre der Web-Generation* (The Way We Were: The Wild Years of the Web Generation), the Internet is used in Germany, as elsewhere in the world, for communication, advertising, and sales and marketing (there is a German eBay). It is also, as elsewhere, an alternate outlet for the press—German newspapers and magazines have their own Web pages and often free newsletters via e-mail. However, German Web sites generally have stronger security than Web sites originating in other countries—and that is a particularly German feature. Already in the early 1980s, an organization of benevolent so-called "white" hackers, who called themselves the Chaos Computer Club (CCC), demonstrated the security problems with the first public computing networks. The famous

"BTX-Hack" by Wau Holland and Steffen Wernery in 1984 resulted in a "donation" to the club of 134,000 DM from a Hamburg savings bank. Since then, the protection of personal data has been taken very seriously in Germany. It is thanks to the active hacking community (also politically active and influencing the Green Party, in particular) that identity theft is a far less common crime in Germany than in the United States. Most German hackers are proud not only of their ability to make detailed analyses of technical links and build new gadgets but also to play an active role in society in general. This characteristic is reflected in Germany's leading computing magazine, *c't—magazin für computer technik*, which offers highly detailed technical instructions for the administration of servers and the use of programming languages. In addition, the publishers spend large sums of money conducting lawsuits to set precedents regarding freedom of information and data protection.

Advertising

Advertising (*Werbung*) in all its forms—from print media to the Internet—has been a spectacular area of growth in the past half century in Germany and has established itself—as David Head remarked—as one of the largest advertising markets in the world, just behind the United States and Japan (Sandford 1999, 7). At the end of the twentieth century, about half a million people in Germany were employed in the field of advertising, and its annual budget in 1995 was more than 25 billion euros (figured, of course, in the then still valid deutsche mark). The mass media depend on advertising for their programming.

Sports and cultural events would not be possible nowadays without company sponsorship through advertising. Advertising, with its slogans, images, narratives, and productions, influences the imagination, emotions, and behavior. Commercials both reflect and influence society and are therefore useful indicators of sociocultural changes.

Full-scale advertising began in Germany after the currency reform in 1948. Directly after the war, there was no real competition. Print advertisements simply announced the availability of a product: The best example is for the detergent "Fewa." The ad showed a box with a happy woman and the heading: "Fewa. Da bin ich wieder." (Fewa. Here I am again.) Outdoor advertising played a special role. In addition to large billboards, there were *Litfaßsäulen* (advertising pillars, named after their inventor, Ernst Litfaß [1816–1874]) as well as posters in public transportation. In the new millennium, the latter have developed into large, silk-screened images on the sides of buses in metropolitan areas. Yet billboard advertising was—and still is—much more restricted, both in size and location, in Germany than in the United States. No German highway is lined with a forest of billboards. Rather, one sees just the occasional small billboard, warning of the dangers of driving too fast.

In the early 1950s, advertisements praised their products as attractive, handy, practical, easy to use, indestructible, and versatile. Car ads stressed technical information and elegance. Romantic, impressionistic landscapes and facts about the car were juxtaposed. There were references to experts or science connected to the products. Technical-sounding jargon was used to suggest the solid scientific basis of the

Advertising pillar (Litfaßsäule) in Berlin. (Photo by D. Scholl)

products. The fact that Germans were a hardworking, down-to-earth people was used by Hubert Strauf (1904–1993), one of Germany's leading publicity experts, to create for "Coca Cola" the unforgettable slogan "Mach mal Pause—trink Coca Cola" (Take a break, drink Coke), which was used for a decade until the 1960s, when Germans were no longer as diligent. Another classic ad has fared better. *Haribo's* slogan for their golden jelly bears (see 4: From Traditional Fare to International Cuisine) was introduced in 1935 for children, expanded in 1962 to include adults, and survived the turn of the millennium: "Haribo macht Kinder froh und Erwachsene

Small highway billboard. The sign reads, *Rücksicht ist besser* (Being Considerate is Better). (Photo by A. Weiss)

tional lines—influence not only architecture but also print advertisements in the 1950s. A close collaboration between the design school in Ulm and Braun electrical products is certainly evident. In addition, there were quotations from high art—for example, surrealism and abstract art, as well as the use of antique forms. A dominant role was played between 1952 and 1955 by the kidney shape (see 4: Lifestyle and Fashion). In the mid-1950s, illustrations in advertisements became more colorful, and photographs were introduced and took the place of drawings. From the mid- to late 1950s, rhyming jingles were used in an attempt to create an impression of coziness and reliability linked to novelty and innovation. The 1950s also introduced many figures that would be directly linked to the product like mascots—for example: Bruno, the *HB-Männchen* (HB mannequin, with the initials standing for the cigarette manufacturer Haus Bergmann from Dresden, which was bought in 1932 by British American Tobacco [BAT]); the Sarotti chocolate company's image of a blackamoor, a black child dressed in exotic clothes with a turban and wide flowing pants, and the salamander Lurchi for the shoe company Salamander.

ebenso" (literally, Haribo makes children happy and adults too). In English, the slogan is slightly modified: "Kids and grown-ups love it so, the happy world of Haribo."

Cleaning products and cosmetics began early on to use celebrities for their products. All this heralded the beginning of a shift—from simply offering information about the product to creating an image for it. The soap Lux was the typical example. At first, American film stars were used (Marilyn Monroe and Elizabeth Taylor), then German film stars took over (Heidi Brühl, Hildegard Knef, and Marianne Koch, who represented the product for twenty years, and in the 1970s, Romy Schneider; see 7: Film).

Aesthetically, it was interesting to see elements of the *Bauhaus*—the clear, func-

In animated TV and cinema commercials, Bruno would encounter a problem that caused him *in die Luft zu gehen* (to blow one's stack; in German, literally, "to fly up into the air")—that is, he would, as the German expression implies, fly up into the air, often banging his head against the ceiling. A cigarette from HB would calm him, and he would float down, be happy, and find the problem easy to manage. Bruno was created by the artist Roland Töpfer (1929–1999) in 1958 for TV, and he entertained audiences (smokers and non-

Immer etwas Besonderes…

Sarotti

Die *gute* Schokolade

Bruno

Lurchi

Collage of popular German advertising characters.

smokers alike) for two or three decades. The first blow came when TV advertising of cigarettes was prohibited in 1972. By the early 1980s, Bruno was history.

The *Sarotti Mohr* for the Sarotti chocolate brand, with a name recognition of 94 percent (as stated by the Sarotti company), is an even older icon. The image was created in 1918 because—as official explanations claim—the childlike figure suggests exotic and sensuous delight without a sense of guilt. But perhaps the real reason is the fact that the owner of the company at the time, Hugo Hoffmann, lived on a street named Mohrenstrasse.

The fire salamander of the Lurchi brand represents one of the early attempts by German advertisers to use comics to attract children. The salamander's adventures were depicted in comic strips that

one could get at the shoe store and are today a major collector's item. From 1937 to 1939, five comics appeared. They were discontinued during the war but came back in 1951. In 2004, after almost seventy years, Lurchi is still alive, although he was given a facelift for the new millennium in 1999.

In 1954, the prewar level of advertising had already been surpassed, and in 1956 a new era began: Television commercials were introduced, and the demand for them increased rapidly. In 1956, about six minutes each day were reserved for commercials. This may not sound like much, but it should be remembered that the actual television programming was also restricted to just four hours a day. By 1961, there were fourteen minutes of daily commercials allowed, and in 1962, twenty minutes, as part of an early evening advertising time slot

(*Werberahmenprogramm*). The two German public television channels, ARD and ZDF, showed commercials mainly between the hours of 6 and 8 PM Mondays through Saturdays, but not on Sundays. Restrictions did not allow German television to realize its full potential until privatization of broadcasting began in the last decade of the millennium. Private broadcasting stations are permitted to use 20 percent of the daily broadcasting time for commercials, yet they also have to ensure that commercials do not impact the program content that they follow or precede. This has led to *Werbeblöcke* (block advertising), whereby several commercials are broadcast in a group, often linked by cartoons and special cartoon characters, some of which have gained cult status like ZDF's *Mainzelmännchen* (see 7: Radio and Television).

On the two public channels, programs are not interrupted at all by commercials. But, in addition to overt advertisement, there have always been various subtle product endorsements in which products are strategically placed in shows so that they cannot be overlooked by the viewers.

The formalization of the European Union in 1993 gave advertising an additional boost. As David Head remarked, in the decade between 1985 and 1995, daily newspapers maintained their dominant position, but the print media as a whole declined by 14 percent, from 70 percent to 56 percent, while television increased its share from 8 percent to 17 percent and the broadcast media as a whole from 11 to 20 percent.

Early on, television commercials emphasized the yearning for an intact world and constituted yet another attempt to suppress the past. Actors in the advertisements often sounded as if they were reading fairy tales. Products were anthropomorphized and sang and danced with smiling faces and waving arms and legs. Some products became part of a story, for which the *Heimatfilm* (see 7: Film) offered many plots. Rhyme, rhythm, and music created a light, happy atmosphere. Naïveté and pseudo-science also characterized many commercials.

In the late 1950s, a trend toward emotionality and lifestyle became noticeable. The positive aspects of life were depicted, and the taste for something special was synonymous with social distinction. The lower and higher classes were clearly separated by a burgeoning middle class. Income had increased tremendously during the 1950s, and luxury articles were in demand (see 4: Lifestyle and Fashion). There was no lack of consumer goods, and needs had to be created artificially. One needed to wear a certain dress, drink a certain type of wine, or use a particular perfume not because it was necessary but because it defined style and individuality. Cigarette ads stressed the "modern way of life," the "*Duft der großen weiten Welt*" (the fragrance of the big wide world)—as the commercials for the cigarette "Peter Stuyvesant" stated.

In the 1970s, self-irony, exaggeration, and absurdity began to appear in advertisements. Typical are those for the dark red bitter herbal liqueur Jägermeister, which depicted common people as well as celebrities before a green or brown background, looking straight into the camera, holding in one hand a bottle of the liqueur and in the other a filled glass, stating their reason for drinking Jägermeister. For instance, "*Ich trinke Jägermeister, weil mir eine Kollegin 33 Nelken zum 28. Geburt-stag geschenkt hat"* (I drink Jägermeister because a colleague of mine gave me 33 carnations for my 28th birthday), or *"Ich trinke Jägermeister, weil das der Witz der Anzeige ist"* (I drink Jägermeister because that is the point of the ad).

The following decades continued that trend. Surprise, shock, stylization, breaking of taboos, jokes, and originality were the catchwords. Perhaps the ad for the cigarette John Player Special summed it all up. It depicted in the bottom third of the ad on a black background a pack of cigarettes with a heading above it: *"John Player Special. / Wahrscheinlich irgendwie anders"* (John Player Special. / Probably somehow different). In the upper two-thirds of the ad, on a light gray background, a group of sperms lined up as in a race, with one dark-headed one being clearly ahead of the rest.

Times change, but throughout German advertising, literary references have been constant features, stressing the "culture" of the German people. A typical example is a fashion ad in the online version of the magazine *Brigitte*. It read in October 2005:

Mode & Schönheit

Augenblick, verweile doch ... :

Mode vergeht. Und Accessoires? Die bleiben länger, wenn man die richtigen aus-wählt. Wir zeigen die schönsten Klassiker dieser Saison.

(Fashion & Beauty / Moment, pray tarry ... : / Fashion changes. And accessories? They last longer if one chooses the right ones. We show you the most beautiful classic ones of this season.)

Though not everyone in Germany may have seen a production of Goethe's *Faust*, there is still a tacit assumption that readers of a popular magazine are familiar with the work. In the *Brigitte* online newsletter, the headline for an article was an indirect quote from Faust's pact with the devil that he would give up his soul if he were ever to wish to hold fast a moment that was beautiful (*Augenblick, verweile doch . . .* , Act II). In this case, the emphasis was on selecting accessories that would not go out of style too quickly. A drugstore chain also made use of a *Faust* quote for many years on its reusable cotton bags, modifying it for their purpose. The bags were printed with *"Hier bin ich Mensch, / hier kauf ich ein"* (Here I am a human being / treated as a human being, here I will go shopping), an allusion to Faust's *"Hier bin ich Mensch, hier darf ich's sein"* (Here I am a human being, here I am allowed to be one) (Act I).

At the beginning of the new millennium, the trend in advertising is even more self-ironic, with cross-cultural influences evident in visual as well as linguistic signs. When those studying sports at the university in Bremen wanted to raise funds for their own library and computing facilities, they copied an idea from a group of English women whose story had served as the theme for a popular film, *Calendar Girls*, which had been released in 2003. Like the middle-aged members of the Women's Institute, the students decided that tasteful nudity would be the way to attract attention. They would sell calendars. But these students had a major advantage over their role models. They were young and fit and had no need to hide behind strategically placed cupcakes or garden tools. Rather, they used sports equipment as their leitmotif—and to avoid going beyond the bounds of taste. The calendars were sold at a price

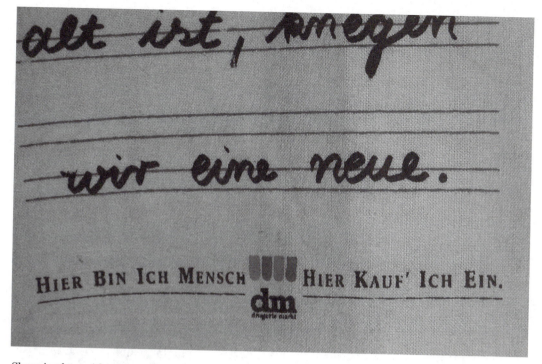

alt ist, mögen

wir eine neue.

HIER BIN ICH MENSCH ▮▮▮▮ HIER KAUF' ICH EIN.

dm
drogerie markt

Shopping bag with ad (see text).

of 19.90 euros and offered a choice of male and female models—two pages for each month. In the photos, the athletes are shown doing various sports, but lacking the usual tracksuits, leotards, etc., that most would wear. The production is black and white, elegant, and in a very large format. However, as with Denglish usage, there is a distinctly German component: The images are a nagging reminder for some of Hitler's glorification of healthy bodies and the *Kraft durch Freude* (strength through joy) movement.

In contrast to their counterparts in many other countries, German companies are not allowed to make overt comparisons between their product and similar ones made by their competitors. Also, special bonuses for buyers are limited because of a law against unfair competition. One exception was the margarine Sanella. In the 1950s,

consumers could collect pictures that came with the product and paste them into special albums and storybooks. This supposedly was a great inspiration for children to eat Sanella. In the new millennium, Lufthansa offers "Miles & More," similar to frequent flier programs offered by the other international airline carriers.

Similar restrictions apply to sales. Department stores are only allowed two major sales, the *Sommerschlussverkauf* (summer sales) in July and the *Winterschlussverkauf* (winter sales) in January. At other times, businesses may not reduce their prices by more than 3 percent. Especially strict are the *Preisbindung* (fixed prices) for books, although over the years attempts have been made to loosen the restrictions. Most of the time, these attempts have failed, because German society still realizes the value of small (often family-run) businesses that cannot compete with mega chain-stores (see 10: From "Tante Emma Laden" to Shopping Mall). But the era of the small store has passed. Large bookstores now buy slightly damaged books in large quantities and sell them at ridiculously low prices as *Schnäppchen* (special deals) to attract customers to their stores.

Celebrities

Through the media, gossip, slander, and an interest in celebrities have assumed a very special role in the postwar years. This interest is just as widespread in Germany as in the United States and other countries. There are tabloids that specialize in offering the latest news on marital spats between film stars and impending marriages or divorces—though the latter are apparently more interesting—as well as births and deaths. Many of the celebrities Germans read about are the international film stars familiar to most Western countries. Julia Roberts, for example, not only features frequently at U.S. supermarket checkout publications but also in Germany. She is also the dream woman of several fictional players of the German version of *The Dating Game* in Hera Lind's bestseller *Der gemietete Mann* (The Hired Man). However, Germany also has its home-grown celebrities, or *Promis*, an abbreviation of *Prominente*. These can be film stars, politicians and their partners, members of the aristocracy, or even bestselling writers. Hera Lind was herself often in the celebrity news until she fell from grace by abandoning her husband and four young children for a new lover. The fact that her readers knew much of her private life, because of the autobiographical na-

ture of her novels, made the split even more titillating.

One of the leading celebrities in Germany in the 1990s was Verona Feldbusch, who married the architect Franjo Pooth in 2004 and uses his name today. Born in 1968 in Bolivia, she grew up in Hamburg, where she became a seamstress and opened a boutique. Her success in beauty contests (Miss Hamburg in 1992, Miss Germany in 1993, Miss Intercontinental World in 1994, and Miss American Dream in 1995) established her fame. TV debuts followed. She became host of the series *Peep!* which created a fan club and inspired a late-night talk show, *Verona's World*, after she quit *Peep!* because it had become—as she said—too pornographic. Appearances in films and commercials were natural sequels. She made a specialty of making mistakes in German grammar and making stupid comments, cultivating her image as an erotic but dumb female. Especially popular was her slogan for a telephone company, *"Hier werden Sie geholfen!"* (Here help is waiting for you). The pun can only be appreciated by German speakers because in German, the verb "to help" is followed by a dative, but she used an accusative pronoun form, which sounded like baby talk. Another popular commercial was for spinach: *"Wann macht er denn endlich 'Blubb'?"* (When will it make the sound "blubb"?) When not enough visitors came to the Expo 2000 in Hannover, she was hired, together with Peter Ustinov, to draw the crowds.

In contrast to Austria, where the official use of aristocratic titles was abolished in 1919, Germans have had a hard time eliminating them. The appearance of a "von" or "zu" in a name is an instant mark of blue blood. In the 1980s and 1990s, a punky and spunky young woman named Mariae Gloria Ferdinanda Joachima von Thurn und Taxis was often in the headlines. She had gained notoriety not only through her marriage to Prince Johannes von Thurn und Taxis, a man thirty-four years her senior and of considerable wealth, and owner of a castle bigger than Buckingham Palace, but also for her unconventional behavior. After the marriage, she greeted the household staff in skin-tight jeans and preferred Harley-Davidson bikes to fairy-tale carriages. Her hair color changed frequently, with bright pink a frequent choice. The birthday cake she ordered for her husband's sixtieth birthday was reportedly decorated with sugar penises. The party ended, however, in 1990 when the prince died after having a second heart transplant; inheritance taxes in the amount of 65 million marks were levied. Gloria auctioned off much of the family property at Sotheby's and became a tough businesswoman. In 2000, she was featured in the portrait section of *Brigitte* in honor of her upcoming fortieth birthday, more sedate in appearance but still apparently enjoying life in her cleaned-out castle (*Brigitte* 5 [2000], 97).

One film star who was long a favorite of the gossip columns was Romy Schneider. She still has both memorabilia sold on eBay and Web sites devoted to her in spite of the fact that she died in 1982. A new book of photographs of the star was published in 2005 by Michael Petzel (*Romy Schneider: Das grosse Album—Fotografien von 1952–1959*). The daughter of another actress, Magda Schneider, Romy became famous in her role as Sissi, the Empress Elisabeth of Austria, in a series of films that came out in the mid to late 1950s. These films romanticized the empress's life, and for many, Romy Schneider was identical with the em-

Romy Schneider in 1960. (Pierre Vauthey/ Corbis Sygma)

press, and vice versa. She portrayed her as a demure, unaffected young woman who was caught up in international politics but could solve diplomatic problems through her innocence and sweet nature. At a time when cities still showed evidence of bombing and destruction, a fairy-tale princess in a frilly crinoline dress brought a welcome distraction from reality. She was shown gliding through ornate castle rooms or out riding, either in parks or with her father in the Bavarian countryside, and often wearing a dirndl (see 7: Film). The actress's real life was, however, not as idyllic. She tried to escape the typecasting as Sissi, spent much time in France, filmed with Luchino Visconti, made some English-language films, and had a rather turbulent private life. She died at the age of forty-four, less than a year after the accidental death of her fourteen-year-old son.

In February 2005, a rather different young German woman was featured in *Focus* news magazine online. The star model—or, as *Focus* described her, the "well-proportioned Top-Model"—Heidi Klum (b. 1973), frequently seen in underwear catalogs in the United States, reportedly signed on as a "brand ambassador" with McDonald's. Though one photo shows her with a single French fry in her hand, her main task is to promote the "salads plus" line. Klum reportedly claimed to appreciate the diverse offerings of McDonald's available between *Fotoshootings* (see 2: Language, Script, and Gestures). The managing director of McDonald's Deutschland told reporters that Heidi is uncomplicated and likable and has a sense of humor and that she is careful about eating a balanced diet and suits the "*Lifestyle-Marke*" of the company. Klum was no doubt selected because of her transatlantic connections to make the fast-food chain seem more German and, presumably, more attractive to the German consumer.

The other top German model dominating the headlines in the 1990s was Claudia Schiffer (b. 1971), who was for a time the best-known model in the world. She appeared on the covers of more than 500 magazines, including *Elle, Harper's Bazaar, Vogue, Cosmopolitan,* and even *Vanity Fair*—whose editorial policy refuses to depict models, so they displayed "Princess Claudia." She was also chosen in 1990 and 1991 by *People* magazine as one of the top fifty most beautiful people in the world. For years she was the fiancée of the renowned magician David Copperfield, who was able to have airplanes and the Statue of Liberty disappear. They broke up in 1999.

In recent years, the former foreign minister Joschka Fischer has been the politician to feature most often in gossip columns. *Focus* reported on a scandal over the allegedly irregular handling of visa applications in the Ukraine, which caused the opposition to call for his resignation. But the gravity of the content was accompanied by a dash of gossip, in which Fischer was called the most popular politician in Germany, in spite of not having an academic background. *Focus* also offered readers a picture of Fischer with his latest female companion, described as an exotic eastern beauty (*morgenländische Schönheit*) (*Focus*, February 16, 2005, focus.msn.de). Since the 2005 elections, the first female German chancellor, Angela Merkel, has constantly been in the headlines—for her politics, her appearance, and her private life.

Many sports figures have also gained celebrity status and had their private lives displayed on tabloids. Boris Becker, the tennis player, is regularly in headlines, though he has retired from the game, and Oliver Khan, the soccer player, was a favorite in 2005 (see also 5: Sports).

From A to Z

Actors: Actors who were not only popular on stage but also on TV included Götz George (b. 1938), Manfred Krug (b. 1937), and Mario Adorf (b. 1930), who was not only known as an international film star but also often seen on stage and TV. Hans Albers (1891–1960) was the dream of many young girls during the Nazi era. Although he kept his distance from politics, his reputation remained tainted after the war, though he retained his image as the quintessential down-to-earth German man. Karlheinz Böhm (b. 1928) became known as an actor in his role as Kaiser Franz Joseph in the Sissi-trilogy. Confronted with poverty in Africa, he founded the aid organization "Menschen für Menschen" (people for people) in 1981. Daniel Bruehl (b. 1978), the lead actor in Wolfgang Becker's *Good Bye Lenin!* (2003), was regarded in 2005 by *Time* magazine as the "New Wave Wunderkind." Heidi Brühl (1942–1991) was not only one of the beloved teenagers in the 1950s but became a successful singer and film actress. Horst Buchholz (1933–2003, born as Henry Bookholt) was the German "James Dean" and represented the rebellious young man with whom many identified in the 1950s. His first hit was the lead in *Die Halbstarken* (The Hooligans, 1956), and he enjoyed an international career matched by few other German actors.

Veronica Ferres (actual name Veronika Jansen, b. 1965), nicknamed "Superweib" (superwoman), became one of Germany's highest-paid actresses after originally being rejected by drama schools. Bruno Ganz (b. 1941), known for his sensitive and complex character portrayals on stage and in films of the New German Cinema, is regarded as one of the most distinguished German-speaking actors of his generation. He was born in Zurich. Klaus Kinski (1926–1991), an actor famous for expressing extreme emotions, became known especially through his work with the director Werner Herzog. His daughter Nastassia Kinski (b. 1961) has made films in several languages and studied under Lee Strasberg. Her best-known German movie is probably *Paris, Texas* directed by Wim Wenders. Hildegard Knef (1925–2002), whose trademark was her husky voice, was one of the few internationally recognized German film stars.

Marianne Koch (b. 1931), who received the Bundesfilmpreis (Federal Film Prize) in 1955, returned in 1985 to her original profession as a doctor of internal medicine. Heike Makatsch (b. 1971) has become one of the most popular German film actresses. Among the many roles she has played is that of Margarete Steiff in a movie about the inventor of the stuffed animals (see 10: Consumer Culture versus Green Awareness). In 2005, Makatsch published her first book *Keine Lieder über Liebe— Ellens Tagebuch* (No Songs about Love— Ellen's Diary). Franka Potente (b. 1974) was named by European Film Promotion as one of the "Shooting Stars" of European film after her performance in Tom Twyker's *Lola rennt* (Lola runs; the official English title is "Run Lola Run," 1998). Katja Riemann (b. 1963) played the lead in several important German films (*Der bewegte Mann*, literally, The Moved Man, the official English title of the movie is "Maybe, Maybe Not"; *Rosenstraße*, the English title is "The Women of Rosenstrasse") and won several important acting awards, including the Best Actress Award at the Venice International Film Festival. Heinz Rühmann (1902–1994) was one of the most popular German film actors. His career spanned about six decades with highlights in the 1930s, 1940s, and 1950s. He was known for his subtle sense of humor and for representing the common man. He is on the list of the 100 Best Germans (Knopp et al. 2003), as is Romy Schneider (1938–1982), who was typecast early on as the independent but romantic princess, playing Sissi, the Empress Elisabeth, and had a hard time gaining independence as a character actress. Hanna Schygulla (b. 1943) became known through the various films by Rainer Werner Fassbinder. Finally, Angela Winkler (b. 1944), a well-respected stage actress, became generally known through her roles in films by Volker Schlöndorff and Margarethe von Trotta.

Children's programs: One of the most well-known and popular children's programs on TV is *Die Sendung mit der Maus* (The Show with the Mouse), which has been running for thirty years and is even mentioned in the information manual for foreigners by the German government. The Web site address is www.wdrmaus.de. Another popular show is *Löwenzahn* (Dandelion). A special noncommercial TV channel for children is KiKa (*Kinderkanal*, Children's Channel). It broadcasts many educational programs (Beck 2003, 200).

Crime thrillers: The most popular TV series in this genre were *Tatort* (Crime Scene), *Der Kommissar* (The Inspector), *Der Alte* (The Old Man), and *Derrick*. *Polizeiruf 110* (Police Call 110) was one of the few East German productions that was syndicated nationwide after unification.

Directors: The best-known German directors include the following (see text [7: Film] for more information on some). Fatih Akin (b. 1973) directed *Gegen die Wand* (Head-On, 2003). Wolfgang Becker (b. 1954) directed *Good Bye Lenin!* (2003). Achim von Borries (b. 1968) won top awards with *Was nützt die Liebe in Gedanken* (Love in Thoughts, 2003). Detlev Buck (b. 1962) attracted general attention with his road movie *Wir können auch anders* (No More Mr. Nice Guy, 1993) and commercial success in 1995 with *Männerpension* (Jailbirds). His early work already had a cult following: *Erst die Arbeit und dann . . . ?* (At First Work—And then . . . ? 1984) and his first feature film, the police satire *Karniggels* (Little Rabbits, 1991). Doris Dörrie (b. 1955) is a filmmaker as well as a writer who has done many films based on her own stories. Her comedy

Männer (Men, 1985) was probably her biggest success, but her venture to Hollywood with the black comedy *Ich und er* (Me and Him) failed. Back in Germany, she continued with socially critical comedies—for example, *Happy Birthday, Türke!* (1991) based on a thriller by Jakob Arjouni (b. 1964), *Keiner liebt mich* (Nobody Loves Me, 1993), and *Nackt* (Naked, 2002). Andreas Dresen (b. 1963) was lauded for his no-nonsense approach to filmmaking.

Rainer Werner Fassbinder (1945–1982) was the main representative of the New German Cinema. Katja von Garnier (b. 1966) is best known for her film *Abgeschminkt* (Making Up, 1993). Leander Haußmann (b. 1959) was artistic director of Bochum's *Schauspielhaus* and played the lead role in Detlev Buck's *Männerpension* before having his first directing success with *Sonnenallee* (Sun Alley, 2000), based on Thomas Brussig's novel of the same name. Michael ("Bully") Herbig (b. 1968) had been familiar to Germans as a comedian before he achieved financial success in Germany with his film *Der Schuh des Manitou* (Manitou's Shoe, 2001). Werner Herzog (b. 1942) became one of the New Wave's major directors with his *Aguirre, der Zorn Gottes* (Aguirre, Wrath of God, 1972), *Jeder für sich und Gott gegen alle* (The Enigma of Kaspar Hauser, 1974), *Fitzcarraldo* (1982), and many others, often with the actor Klaus Kinski. In 2005, he presented a much discussed documentary, *The Grizzly Man*. Oliver Hirschbiegel (b. 1957) specialized in depicting extreme psychological situations, such as in *Der Untergang* (Downfall, 2004).

Romuald Karmakar (b. 1965) experimented with documentary as well as feature films. Rainer Kaufmann (b. 1959) was one of the major directors during the

1990s. His best-known film was *Stadtgespräch* (Talk of the Town, 1995). Alexander Kluge (b. 1932) was often referred to as the father of the New German Cinema. Caroline Link (b. 1964) is one of Germany's most successful young directors. Marcus Mittermeier (b. 1969) scored a surprise hit with his black comedy *Muxmäuschenstill* (a word play using the protagonist of the film, Mux, as part of the German word *mucksmäuschenstill*, which means "as quiet as a mouse," 2003). Christian Petzold (b. 1960) is popular as an actor but not yet well known outside of Germany. One of his well-known films is steeped in the German history of the RAF era, *Die innere Sicherheit* (English title: *The State I Am In*, 2000). Rosa von Praunheim (b. 1942) made films characterized by political topics that are presented in an entertaining way. Helma Sanders-Brahms (b. 1940) directed *Deutschland, bleiche Mutter* (Germany, Pale Mother, 1980). Christoph Schlingensief (b. 1960) is the *enfant terrible* of German film (and theater). Volker Schlöndorff (b. 1939), although grouped with the *Autorenfilmer* (auteurist writer-directors), gained his primary recognition for film adaptations of literary works, such as Günter Grass's *Die Blechtrommel* (The Tin Drum, 1981) and Heinrich Böll's *Die verlorene Ehre der Katharina Blum* (The Lost Honor of Katharina Blum, 1975). Hans-Christian Schmid (b. 1965) is best known for his films *Crazy* (based on a novel by Benjamin Lebert, who was Germany's youngest writer at the time) and *Lichter* (Distant Lights, 2003). Michael Schorr (b. 1965) directed *Schultze Gets the Blues* (2003).

Georg Tressler (b. 1917) directed *Die Halbstarken* (The Hooligans, 1956). Margarete von Trotta (b. 1942) was one of the major female directors of the New German Cinema. Dito Tsintsadze (b. 1957) gained recognition with *Schussangst* (Gun-Shy, 2003), a film about a conscientious objector. Tom Tykwer (b. 1965) is regarded as one of Germany's great directors of the future. Andreas Veiel (b. 1959) is regarded as one of Germany's best documentary filmmakers. Joseph Vielsmeier (b. 1939) had an international success with *Comedian Harmonists* (1997). Hans Weingartner (b. 1970) is an Austrian director. His *Die fetten Jahre sind vorbei* (The Years of Plenty Are Over; actual English title: *The Edukators*, 2004) was the first German-language film in eleven years to be invited to the Cannes Film Festival in 2004. Wim (Wilhelm Ernst) Wenders (b. 1945) was, in many ways, the embodiment of his time, caught between his German roots and his yearning for the American utopia. Many of his films were therefore marked by this dichotomy. Among his best-known films are *Die Angst des Tormanns beim Elfmeter* (The Goalie's Fear of the Penalty, 1972), based on a novel by Peter Handke (see 6: Popular and Belletristic Literature); *Im Lauf der Zeit* (Kings of the Road, 1975); *Paris Texas* (1984); *Der Himmel über Berlin* (Wings of Desire, 1987). Henner Winckler (b. 1969) directed *Klassenfahrt* (School Trip, 2002), which addressed concerns of young people. Sönke Wortmann (b. 1959) became popular with his comedies about the insecurities of young men. His biggest hits were *Allein unter Frauen* (Alone Among Women, 1991), *Der bewegte Mann* (Maybe . . . Maybe Not, 1994), and *Das Wunder von Bern* (The Miracle of Bern, 2003) (see 5: Sports).

Fees: Users of radio and TV are obliged by law to pay licensing fees collected by the

Gebühren-Einzugs-Zentrale (GEZ, Fee Collecting Center).

Genres: Some common genres in German film are: *Heimatfilme* (rustic regional romances); *Literaturverfilmungen* (literary adaptations); and *Trümmerfilm* (cinema of ruins) (see 7: Film).

Oscars and Oscar Nominations for German films: In the postwar era, fifteen German films have been nominated for an Oscar in the category Foreign Language Film; two of them went on to actually win the Oscar. They were: *Sophie Scholl—Die letzten Tage* (Sophie Scholl—The Final Days, 2005) directed by Marc Rothemund (nominee), *Der Untergang* (Downfall, 2004) directed by Oliver Hirschbiegel (nominee), *Nirgendwo in Afrika* (Nowhere in Africa, 2001) directed by Caroline Link (winner), *Jenseits der Stille* (Beyond Silence, 1996) directed by Caroline Link (nominee), *Schtonk!* (1992) directed by Helmut Dietl (nominee), *Das schreckliche Mädchen* (The Nasty Girl, 1990) directed by Michael Verhoeven (nominee), *Bittere Ernte* (Angry Harvest, 1985) directed by Agnieszka Holland (nominee), *Die Blechtrommel* (The Tin Drum, 1979) directed by Volker Schlöndorff (winner), *Die gläserne Zelle* (The Glass Cell, 1978) directed by Hans W. Geissendörfer (nominee), *Jakob der Lügner* (Jacob the Liar, 1975, GDR) directed by Frank Beyer (nominee), *Der Fußgänger* (The Pedestrian, 1973) directed by Maximilian Schell (nominee), *Die Brücke* (The Bridge, 1959) directed by Bernhard Wicki (nominee), *Helden* (literally, Heroes, but the English title is Arms and the Man, 1958) directed by Franz Peter Wirth (nominee), *Nachts, wenn der Teufel kam* (The Devil Came at Night, 1957) directed by Robert Siodmak (nominee), *Der Hauptmann von Köpenick* (The Captain of Köpenick, 1956) directed by Helmut Käutner (nominee).

Private Broadcasters: The best known private broadcasters are *RTL*, *Pro Sieben*, and *Sat1*. The best known and most controversial entrepreneur in the field of media is Leo Kirch (b. 1926), who had shares in the Axel-Springer company and in *Sat 1*. He founded *DF1* (later renamed *Premiere*), a TV pay channel in the mid-1990s, and was regarded as one of Europe's media moguls but declared bankruptcy in 2002.

Public Broadcasters: See text for *ARD* and *ZDF*. In addition, the following stations are also state-sponsored broadcasters: *DLF* (*Deutschlandfunk*, Germany Broadcast), the TV station *Phoenix*, the *Kinderkanal* (see "Children's program"), and the Franco-German TV channel *arte*.

Reception: Radio and television signals can be received through built-in antenna (or a house antenna), by digital signals, and by cable and satellite, as in the United States.

Satire: see 2: Humor and Stereotypes and Prejudices.

Sitcoms and soap operas: While sitcoms are still rare on German TV, such soap operas as *Gute Zeiten, schlechte Zeiten* (Good Times, Bad Times) of the late 1980s had a few popular precursors in the family drama series *Unsere Nachbarn heute abend* (Our Neighbours This Evening) (1954–1960) and *Familie Hesselbach* in the 1960s. *Lindenstraße*, about a Munich neighbourhood, debuted in 1985. *Forst-*

haus Falkenau (Forestry House Falkenau) focused on rural Bavaria while *Schwarzwaldklinik* (Clinic in the Black Forest) combined the doctor drama with soap opera material and beautiful Black Forest scenery.

Studios: Located between Berlin and Potsdam, Babelsberg was Germany's most important film studio. Originally built in 1911–1912 for the Deutsche Bioscop Gesellschaft (German Bioscop Corporation), before 1945 it was the production center of Universum Film AG (UFA). From 1945 to 1992, it was the home of Deutsche Film Aktiengesellschaft (DEFA). In 1992, it was sold to a French property investment firm. In the new millennium it has become a full-service provider for film and television productions.

Theater on TV: Among the theater productions that had a regular time slot on TV were productions by the Bavarian Komödienstadl, the Ohnsorg-Theater (Hamburg), and the Millowitsch Theater (Cologne).

TV personalities: Peter Alexander (b. 1926) from Austria was a trained actor but became best known as a singer of *Schlager* (see 8: Music) and presenter of entertainment shows. Alfred Biolek (b. 1934), who earned a doctorate in law, established himself as one of Germany's top talk-show masters. Lou van Burg (1917–1986) became quite popular, as could be seen in the loving epithets used by his fans: *Onkel Lou* (Uncle Lou) and *Mr. Wunnebar* (Mr. Wonderful). Those using the latter were picking up on a favorite word of his, which he always pronounced with his foreign accent. Rudi Carrell (1934–2006) began as a *Schlager* singer in his home country, the Netherlands (winning the national award in 1960). His main TV shows on German stations included *Am laufenden Band* (Without Stopping), the *Rudi Carrell Show*, and *Rudis Tiershow* (Rudi's Animal Show). His popularity was based on his charming, noncontroversial, amiable personality. Frank Elstner (b. 1942) began his term hosting the most popular German TV show of the early 1980s, *Wetten dass . . . ?* (Let's Bet That . . . ?), in 1981.

Peter Frankenfeld (1913–1979) was Germany's most popular showmaster during the early years of TV. Thomas Gottschalk (b. 1950) made the list of 100 best Germans (Knopp et al. 2003) because of his popularity with both young and old and his easygoing yet sharp-witted charm. When he began at Bavarian Radio in 1971, someone with long blond hair, flamboyant outfits, and tennis shoes could still cause a level of excitement bordering on the scandalous. Helga Hahnemann (1937–1991) was also known as "Big Helga" and, because of her family name, which translates into "rooster-man," as "Henne" (hen). Thomas Dieter Heck (b. 1937, as Carl Dieter Heckscher), as moderator for Radio Luxembourg in 1966, had the idea of playing—in contrast to the usual pop broadcasts—only contemporary popular songs by German-speaking interpreters. The plan was successful. In 1984, he received the Bundesverdienstkreuz (Order of Merit of the FRG) for his efforts in marketing the German *Schlager*. His trademark was rapid speech, which earned him the nickname of "Marktschreier" (fairground barker). Werner Höfer (1913–1997) became known to the public as the host of the first political talk show, *Der Internationale Frühschoppen* (International Midday Pint), always broadcast on Sunday at noon since 1953. It offered an international view of the political events of the day.

Günther Jauch (b. 1956) garnered almost every possible TV prize but continued to lead a life outside the limelight. Much of his income is devoted to charitable causes—a fact not known among the general public. Harald Juhnke (1929–2005), singer and actor, was loved and pitied by the whole nation, which followed his slow deterioration caused by alcoholism. Hape (Hans-Peter) Kerkeling (b. 1964) has been the insider tip for years but was never able to gain general recognition in spite of winning several official prizes. Hans Joachim Kulenkampff (1921–1998) was the second most important show- and quizmaster of the early years of TV. Petra Kusch-Lück (b. 1948), a trained nurse, began her successful radio and TV career in 1969. Robert Lembke (1913–1989) was best known to the public as a quizmaster, though his main functions over the years at Bavarian Radio were as editor-in-chief for the news and later deputy managing director. Jürgen von der Lippe (b. 1948), ex-husband of Margarethe Schreinemakers, became known as a singer, comedian, and TV moderator. Heinz Florian Oertel (b. 1927) became primarily known as a sports reporter in the GDR. Oliver Pocher (b. 1978) is one of the young newcomers on TV. He began at channel Viva and now has his own show, *Rent a Pocher*, at ProSieben. Heinz Quermann (1921–2003) was known as the "*Kulenkampff* of the GDR" as a homage to Joachim Kulenkampff, one of the best known West German showmasters.

Carolin Reiber (b. 1940) is seen by many as one of Germany's most charming moderators. Her most popular shows are about folk music (*Lustige Musikanten* [The Joyous Musicians]; *Volkstümliche Hitparade*

[Popular Hit Parade]; *Volkstümliches Wunschkonzert* [popular musical request program]). Ilja Richter (b. 1952) was one of the few TV representatives of youth pop culture. Hans Rosenthal (1925–1987) received many prizes for his showmastership and was also active as a spokesman for Jewish interests. Heinz Schenk (b. 1924) was also a singer and composer. Harald Schmidt (b. 1957) is the second TV entertainer (besides Gottschalk) voted into the group of the best-known 100 Germans (Knopp et al. 2003). Karl-Eduard Schnitzler (1918–2001) was known as "Sudel Edel" (botching nobility, "Edel" is also a funny abbreviated diminuitive form of Eduard) because of his hard-line views, which represented the official views of the GDR government. Margarethe Schreinemakers (b. 1958) became known as an engaging and controversial TV talk-show host. Vico Torriani (1920–1998) was a multitalented star, active as singer, actor, and showmaster. Wim Thoelke (1927–1995) had several major shows: *Aktuelles Sportstudio* (Current Sports News), with Rainer Günzler and Dieter Kürten; *Drei mal Neun* (Three Times Nine); and *Der Große Preis* (The Great Prize). The Italian Caterina Valente (b. 1931) helped to give German TV an international aura. (see 8: Music; 7: Celebrities).

Additional Readings

Elsaesser, Thomas. *Filmgeschichte und frühes Kino. Archäologie eines Medienwandels.* München: edition text + kritik, 2002.

Faulstich, Werner. *Filmgeschichte.* München: Fink Verlag, 2005 (UTB basics).

Fischer, Heinz-Dietrich, and Olav Jubin. *Privatfernsehen in Deutschland. Konzepte, Konkurrenten, Kontroversen.* Frankfurt: Frankfurter Allgemeine Buch, 1996.

Gerken, Jochen. *Idioten im Fernsehen von A wie Arabella bis Z wie Zietlow.* Kerpen: Gerken, 2001.

———. *Noch mehr Idioten im Fernsehen.* Bergheim: Sonnenkinder-Verlag, 2005.

Gerwin, Hanno. *Was Deutschlands Prominente glauben.* Gütersloh: Gütersloher Versandhaus, 2005.

Gries, Rainer, Volker Ilgen, and Dirk Schindelbeck, eds. *"Ins Gehirn der Masse kriechen." Werbung und Mentalitätsgeschichte.* Darmstadt: Wissenschaftliche Buchgesellleschaft, 1995.

Gudermann, Rita, and Wulff Bernhard. *Der Sarotti-Mohr. Die bewegte Geschichte einer Werbefigur.* Berlin: Ch. Links Verlag, 2004.

Habel, F.-B., and Volker Wachter. *Das große Lexikon der DDR-Stars. Die Schauspieler aus Film und Fernsehen.* Überarbeitete und erweiterte Neuausgabe. Berlin: Schwarzkopf und Schwarzkopf, 2002.

Heinmann, Thomas. *DEFA. Künstler und SED-Kulturpolitik. Zum Verhältnis von Kulturpolitik und Filmproduktion in der SBZ/DDR 1945 bis 1959.* Berlin: VISTAS, 1994.

Hickethier, Knut. *Geschichte des Deutschen Fernsehens.* Stuttgart: J. B. Metzler, 1998.

Hraab, Stevka. *Professor Zlatko. Die ganze Wahrheit.* Berlin: Eichborn, 2001.

Humphreys, Peter. *Media and Media Policy in Germany: The Press and Broadcasting since 1945.* Oxford: Berg, 1990.

Jacobsen, Wolfgang, Anton Kaes, and Hans Helmut Prinsler, eds. *Geschichte des deutschen Films.* Stuttgart: Metzler, 1993.

Kellner, Joachim, Ulrich Kurth, and Werner Lippert, eds. *50 Jahre Werbung in Deutschland 1945 bis 1995. Eine Veranstaltung des Deutschen Werbemuseums.* Ingelheim: Westermann-Kommunikation, 1995.

Kirschner, Jürgen. *Fischer Handbuch Theater, Film, Funk und Fernsehen.* Frankfurt: Fischer, 1997.

Koch, Hans J., and Hermann Glaser. *Ganz Ohr. Eine Kulturgeschichte des Radios in Deutschland.* Köln, Weimar, and Wien: Böhlau, 2005.

Kramer, Thomas, ed. *Reclams Lexikon des deutschen Films.* Stuttgart: Reclam, 1995.

Kreuzer, Helmut, and Christian Werner Thomsen, eds. *Geschichte des Fernsehens in der Bundesrepublik Deutschland.* München: Fink, 1993–1994.

Kriegeskorte, Michael. *Werbung in Deutschland, 1945–1965. Die Nachkriegszeit im Spiegel ihrer Anzeigen.* Köln: DuMont, 1992.

———. *100 Jahre Werbung im Wandel. Eine Reise durch die deutsche Vergangenheit.* Köln: DuMont, 1995.

Pflaum, Hans Günther, and Hans Helmut Prinzler. *Cinema in the Federal Republic of Germany.* Bonn: Inter Nationes, 1993.

Rösgen, Petra, Hermann Schäfer, and Jürgen Reiche. *Prominente in der Werbung. Da weiß man, was man hat.* Mainz: Schmidt, 2001.

Sandford, John. *The Mass Media of the German-Speaking Countries.* London: Oswald Wolff, 1976.

Schenk, Ralf, and Christiane Mückenberger, eds. *Das zweite Leben der Filmstadt Babelsberg. DEFA-Spielfilme, 1946–92.* Berlin: Henschel, 1994.

Strobel, Ricarda, and Werner Faulstich. *Die deutschen Fernsehstars.* Bd. 1: *Stars der ersten Stunde.* Bd. 2: *Show- und Gesangstars.* Bd. 3: *Stars für die ganze Familie.* Bd. 4: *Zielgruppenstars.* Göttingen: Vandenhoeck und Ruprecht, 1998.

Tippach-Schneider, Simone. *Das große Lexikon der DDR-Werbung. Kampagnen und Werbesprüche, Macher und Produkte, Marken und Warenzeichen.* Berlin: Schwarzkopf und Schwarzkopf, 2. Aufl. 2004.

Tuma, Thomas. "The Last of the Titans." *The Germans. Sixty Years after the War.* Spiegel Special International Edition 4 (2005): 166–169.

Weingarten, Susanne. "Wunders Never Cease." *The Germans. Sixty Years after the War.* Ed. Stefan Aust. Spiegel Special International Edition 4 (2005): 198–201.

Winterhoff-Spurk, Peter. *Fernsehen. Fakten zur Medienwirkung.* Bern: Huber, 2001.

8

The Performing Arts

Theater and Dance

The three modes of theater in Germany—*Sprechtheater*, *Musiktheater*, and *Tanztheater* (spoken theater, musical theater, and dance theater)— which include drama in the first category; operas, operettas, and other musical productions in the second; and ballet and pantomime in the third, experienced international recognition around the turn of the twentieth century and during the Weimar years, as did German film (see 7: Film). Unlike films, however, the theater's postwar recovery in both Germanys was faster and more consistently successful. Although many theaters had been destroyed in the war and resources were scarce, the reconstruction was carried out with amazing speed. Postwar theater included not only theater for adults but also for children and young people. The theater in Leipzig opened as early as 1946. And in the 1947/1948 season, "artistic personnel in German theaters already numbered 23,523—only 4,000 fewer than in 1996" (Sandford 1999, 601). People were happy to have a form of entertainment and distraction, and the theater offered this.

The role of the German theater may be misunderstood by non-Germans. It was immediately after the war and is today, in spite of all the other media offerings, a vibrant form of entertainment. To outsiders, it may seem that the theater in Germany is only for highbrow consumption. Michael Patterson and Michael Huxley argued that over the years it has "represented culture rather than entertainment" for Germans and that "Germans expect their theatres to fulfil a library function, providing them with a range of experience from the entire European theatrical heritage" (Patterson et al. 1998, 227–228). But that does not mean that theater does not have a lowbrow function, too—that is, that genuine pleasure cannot be derived from a theater production. Patterson and Huxley noted that the architecture and location of theaters in Germany differ from that of other countries: "Apart from exceptions like the Royal National Theatre in London, British theatres are usually set in a row of banks, offices and shops, distinguishable only by their neon signs and immodest advertising hoardings. In Germany most theatres are set in their own grounds, with imposing entrances, like 'majestic temples to the Muses'" (ibid., 228). Again, one could argue that it is just this central placement and pride that reflect a genuine love of theater. Of course, a few theatergoers may go to be seen as they parade through the elegant foyers of the larger city theaters at intermission, but to balance these, there are many who flock to performances in church halls or other community centers because they want to see the play, to be entertained, to enjoy innocent gossip, to be amused, and perhaps to be shocked.

The Federal Republic of Germany

In the West, subsidies allow for both affordable subscription rates and ready access to theatrical productions even in smaller towns and villages. This system of subsidies was introduced soon after the war to get things moving. The favored plays with which many theaters began their new season were classics, such as Goethe's *Iphigenie auf Tauris* (Iphigenia on Tauris), a hymn of praise to humanity, as well as Schiller's *Kabale und Liebe* (Treachery and Love) and *Don Carlos*, dramas of rebellion against an overwhelming authority. But above all, it was Lessing's *Nathan der Weise* (Nathan the Wise), with its message of religious tolerance, which filled the theaters. The play, which had as its protagonist a Jew, had been forbidden during the Nazi era and was chosen in the fall of 1945 to reopen the Deutsches Theater (German Theater) in Berlin. Fritz Wisten, who had been director at the theater of the Jüdischer Kulturbund (Association for Jewish Culture) and had survived the concentration camps, was its artistic director. Among the new theater directors was Gustav Gründgens, whose legendary produc-

tion of Goethe's *Faust* at the Düsseldorf theater in 1958 can be considered—in all its artistic greatness—characteristic of theater in Germany during the time of reconstruction. It maintained its distance from political reality and tended toward stylization and an ideology of truthfulness to the intentions of the poet. However, Gründgens' ambivalent relationship with the Nazi regime—that is, his decision to go along with the policies of the day so that he could continue his work—was criticized by many. When Bertolt Brecht returned from exile in 1948, he noted the "impertinence that they just continued as if nothing had happened but the destruction of their houses" (Simhandl 2001, 261).

In addition to the classical plays, and soon exceeding them in production numbers, were popular comedies. Peter Simhandl wrote, "Already a few weeks after the capitulation was signed, one could watch, for instance, Franz and Paul Schönthan's indestructible *Der Raub der Sabinerinnen* [Rape of the Sabine Women]. In general, a hectic activity began. Until the end of 1945, just in Berlin alone, one hundred and twenty new productions opened; two-thirds of them were boulevard comedies, musicals, and operettas" (ibid.). The trend continued, although the headlines in the feuilletons did not pay much attention to the productions. Yet, when television became part of public culture, the broadcasting vans could be seen in front of the Millowitsch Theater in Cologne, the Ohnsorg Theater in Hamburg, and the Komödienstadl in Munich, the places to see *Volksschauspiele* (plays for the people) (see 7: Radio and Television).

Theater festivals like the Salzburger Festspiele in Austria (founded in 1890 and reopened in August 1946), with its *Jeder-*

mann (Everyman), sounded existentialist themes. The Ruhrfestspiele (founded in 1947) in Recklinghausen, North-Rhine Westphalia, emphasized that it was a European theater festival reaching out to West and East European performances. The Berliner Festwochen (Berlin Festival Weeks) followed in 1951. Operas and opera festivals—for example, the famous Bayreuther Festspiele, established by Richard Wagner in 1876 and reopened in July 1951 under the baton of Wilhelm Furtwängler—were the epitome of artistic celebrations of an apolitical nature. Hitler's association with the Wagner family was quietly ignored. The new *Gesamtleitung* (directorship) was in the hands of the grandsons Wieland and Wolfgang Wagner.

The Allies supported (and initially controlled) cultural offerings, and because there were few original new German plays written and produced in the years 1945 to 1955, they added an international perspective by making their own playwrights available in translation. Hermann Glaser wrote: "The imported canon was comprised of 60 American, 98 French and 15 English plays—among them works by Thornton Wilder, Jean Anouilh, Jean-Paul Sartre and Albert Camus" (Glaser 2004, 43). The additions were welcomed because Germans had been deprived for twelve years of an international outlook. Among the few contemporary Germans whose plays were staged alongside the foreign dramas was an experienced playwright from the Weimar years, Carl Zuckmayer. He had left Germany in 1938 and had lived in Vermont in the United States as a farmer. There, in 1942, he had written *Des Teufels General* (The Devil's General), which was first performed in Zurich, Switzerland, in December 1946. The German premiere followed

one year later in Frankfurt. The play proved to be one of the most impressive theater successes in the years between 1947 and 1950. In 1955, it became a film hit with Curt Jürgens as the protagonist, General Harras, with whom many men could identify in one way or another. This hero was an apolitical person whose passion for flying led him to be seduced into serving demonic powers. Zuckmayer had modeled him after the fighter pilot Ernst Udet, who was, next to the red baron, Manfred Freiherr von Richthofen, one of the best-known war heroes of World War I.

Voices like that of Max Frisch, the Swiss playwright, in contrast, were shunned. His play *Nun singen sie wieder* (Now They Are Singing Again) had its premiere in Zurich in 1945. In it surviving fascists wrestling with their guilt are confronted by the world of the dead: twenty-one hostages who sang while they were being executed. This play was too distressing. If troubling questions were raised, they needed to be in classical guise, as in *Agamemnons Tod* (Death of Agamemnon) and *Elektra* by Gerhart Hauptmann, which premiered in Berlin in 1947. Some critics saw in Hauptmann's treatment of the myth his reaction to the barbaric times of the Hitler era and interpreted it even as "drama of resistance" (*Harenberg* 2003, 476). In Düsseldorf, a similar topic was staged with Sartre's *Die Fliegen* (The Flies; *Les mouches* in French), in which Gustav Gründgens played the lead role of Orestes. In this play, man has to take action against lawless authority, even if action means violence. Wolfgang Borchert's play *Draußen vor der Tür* (Outside of the Door), staged in Hamburg a day after his death, was more direct. Its subtitle contained a lot of truth: *Ein Stück, das kein Theater spielen und kein*

Publikum sehen will (A Play, No Theater Wants to Perform and No Audience Wants to Watch). It is the story of the soldier Beckmann, an emasculated cripple who returns home from the war. His wife has left him, his son is dead; guilt surrounds him. He tries to commit suicide and is rejected by the river. "Is there no one, no one who can give an answer?" he cries. It was haunting in a realistic way because it brought back unpleasant memories (see 1: Coming to Terms with the Past).

The Swiss playwright Friedrich Dürrenmatt seemed kinder in his comedies. The ambiguity of irony and the grotesque, the elements of the absurd that he used, allowed the theatergoer to detach the dramatic texts from the concrete political situation, to appreciate them as playful constructs in the abstract world of intellectual discourse, and to enjoy slapstick-like stage effects for their simplistic humor. His *Besuch der alten Dame* (The Visit, 1955), a parable about the moral corruptibility of people whose greed can be aroused and who fall easy prey to financial manipulation, could be seen as a satire on human weakness and folly. On the one hand, it touched on the right nerve; on the other hand, it did not overwhelm viewers with feelings of guilt or directly evoke the past that they wanted to forget. Dürrenmatt's cynical and pessimistic worldview, expressed in his remark that only comedies are suitable for the modern era and that tragedies are not feasible anymore, could be both accepted and understood by everyone because it avoided more personal and uncomfortable questions. It was ideal for the educational curriculum, and his works have become part of the canon of literary works for the high school level—and in the United States, for German college depart-

ments. The 1964 film version by Bernhard Wicki, starring Ingrid Bergman and Anthony Quinn, and Gottfried von Einem's 1971 opera based on the text have increased opportunities to discuss the play from a variety of perspectives.

Eugene Ionesco's plays also found a receptive audience in Germany. The drama of the absurd attempted to give artistic form to a senseless world, to explain the past fascist years, the epoch of inhuman pain and suffering and of unbelievable cruelty done by humans to humans, but without finger pointing. Ionesco stressed that he did not want to expose just one ideology but only evil itself, which can hide in different manifestations. Of course, German audiences saw everywhere obvious parallels to the time of Hitler, especially the depiction of an uncritical herd instinct similar to the one that made them follow the "drummer" (see Grass' *Blechtrommel* [Tin Drum], 1959), and that then made them follow the drumbeat of consumerism. But the plays did not provoke the audience, did not poke needles into barely healed wounds. Ionesco's success caused his other, older plays to be published in Germany in the same year, 1959.

From the end of the 1950s to the 1960s, German theater also became a place for questioning politics and society. The desire to overcome the trauma of the Third Reich allowed such performances to take place as *Der aufhaltsame Aufstieg des Arturo Ui* (The Rise of Arturo Ui Which Could Have Been Stopped), Brecht's parable about fascism, written in Finland in 1941 and first performed by Peter Palitzsch in Stuttgart in 1958. Harry Buckwitz had, as manager of the Frankfurt theater, prepared the ground through many productions of Brecht plays between 1951 and 1967. Buckwitz was one of the few who had kept up the tradition of the stage as a forum for political discussions. He ended his tenure in Frankfurt in 1968 with the premiere of the controversial *Viet Nam Diskurs* by Peter Weiss. Was it a play or propaganda? Peter Stein, a rising young star director, certainly stepped over the thin dividing line when he encouraged a collection of money for the Vietcong after a performance of Weiss's play in the Münchner Kammerspiele (Munich Studio Theater). He had to accept the consequences of his action and was fired.

When the 1960s rolled around, the theater changed along with dress styles and student attitudes. Fewer and fewer dresses and suits with ties were seen in the theater corridors; jeans and polo sweaters had taken their place (see 4: Lifestyle and Fashion). The student population began to dominate both the ticket sales and the program. More critical plays and social criticism were demanded. Increasingly, the German-speaking playwrights responded. Dürrenmatt's *Die Physiker* (The Physicists) presented a bleak and frightening picture of the era under the threat of the nuclear bomb. In 1962, Martin Walser's first play, a war and postwar story, *Eiche und Angora* (Oak and Angora), first performed at the Schiller Theater in Berlin, presented a response to and satire of Brecht's *Schweyk im zweiten Weltkrieg* (Schwejk in World War II, 1957). Whereas Brecht's Schwejk conforms to society on the surface only to deceive everyone behind their backs, Walser's representative is much more the plain common man: Being from the lower social classes, he is not deceptive; rather, he is streetwise but somewhat slow intellectually. He is not quick-witted enough to change his opinions from one second to the next with the political tides of the day.

He understands only too late the situations he is confronted with and what is good for him. For instance, he becomes a Nazi after the Nazis have lost power, and now his superiors—who, of course, had changed their attitude at the right time—can reprimand and criticize him.

Sparked by the demonstrations against the Vietnam War , students in Frankfurt and Berlin rebelled against the middle-class *Kulturkonsum* (cultural consumption), its affirmative attitude toward aesthetics and culture, and its festival snobbism (see 4: Youth Culture and the World of Intellectuals), which they saw symbolized in the world-famous conductor of the Berlin Philharmonic Herbert von Karajan (see 8: Music). He was regarded by the young revolutionaries as the typical representative of the apolitical artist who used music as a means to entertain the wealthy and disregard existing social problems. According to Karen Ruoff Kramer: "In keeping with an agitated rejection of 'art for art's sake' (e.g., the 'Death of Literature' controversy launched in the Journal *Kursbuch*), innovative drama of the 1960s and 1970s was characterized by an overt, left-wing political stance" (Sandford 1999, 159). Not worship but arguments began to characterize the theater scene. Erwin Piscator, who had tried in the 1920s to develop a proletarian theater as a political instrument in Berlin and who had experimented with various technical innovations, such as film projections and loudspeakers, to make political agitation more effective, had returned to Europe in 1952. In 1962, he accepted a position as theater manager at the Freie Volksbühne (Free People's Stage) in West Berlin. This position gave him the opportunity to become the "midwife" of a new German drama, the documentary drama.

Piscator staged the premieres of Rolf Hochhuth's *Der Stellvertreter* (The Deputy, 1963), attacking the pope's role during the fascist era; Heinar Kipphardt's *In der Sache J. Robert Oppenheimer* (The Case of J. Robert Oppenheimer, 1964), a play about the development of the nuclear bomb; and Peter Weiss's *Ermittlung* (Investigation, 1965), a play about the Shoah. It is based on the Auschwitz trials conducted from 1963 to 1965 in Frankfurt (see 1: Coming to Terms with the Past). Weiss's play was premiered at the same time at different theaters in West and East Germany as well as in London. The play achieved its impact because of an unemotional, objective presentation of documents, showing inhumanity disguised as bureaucratic behavior. The end of the play highlighted the general attitude of Germans, who had tried for two decades more or less successfully to leave the past untouched, when one of the accused sums up an opinion shared by many: "*Heute / da unsere Nation sich wieder / zu einer führenden Stellung / emporgearbeitet hat / sollten wir uns mit anderen Dingen befassen / als mit Vorwürfen / die längst als verjährt / angesehen werden müßten*" (Today when our nation has achieved again a leading role we should occupy ourselves with things other than accusations, which by now should be regarded as having come under the statute of limitations).

A year later, in 1966, Martin Sperr continued to ask the nagging questions about the attitude of the parent generation in his *Jagdszenen aus Niederbayern* (Hunting Scenes from Lower Bavaria), performed for the first time in Bremen, far away from its setting in the south of Germany. He presented it in the form of a folk play that seemed simple on the surface: A social study of a small backward village, which serves as a model for Germany. The year is 1948, the currency reform was successful (see 10: Consumer Culture versus Green Awareness), and political fascism has been eradicated, but the mentality of the people has not changed. Outsiders are victimized in the same way as they were under the Nazis.

With these plays by Hochhuth, Kipphardt, and Weiss, the critical folk plays by Martin Sperr, and the dramatic parables by Martin Walser, Max Frisch, and Friedrich Dürrenmatt, the German theater became a focal point of heated discussions. Especially Hochhuth was at the center of controversy. His play *The Deputy* was condemned by the Catholic Church and greeted with glee by the young people who flocked to the theaters to see it. The young student revolutionaries were confirmed in their attitude by New York's Living Theater, which had come to Berlin in 1964 to escape repression in the United States. They toured Europe from 1964 to 1970 and helped develop an alternative theater in Europe, and especially in Germany. Action theater, antitheater, happenings, demonstrations, sit-ins, occupation of buildings—all were part of the revolutionary *Gesamtkunstwerk* (synthesis of the arts), as Hermann Glaser remarked (2004, 255). In addition, the Berliner Theatertreffen (Berlin Theater Festival) had offered an outlet for the more experimental performances since 1963.

Certainly, theater and theatricality were alive in the 1960s. Peter Weiss's *Die Verfolgung und Ermordung Jean Paul Marats, dargestellt durch die Schauspielgruppe des Hospizes zu Charenton unter Anleitung des Herrn de Sade* (The Pursuit and Murder of Jean Paul Marat, Presented by the Group of Actors and Actresses of the Hospice at Charenton under the Direction of the Marquis de Sade), which premiered at the Schiller Theater in West Berlin in 1964, was typical in many ways. It belonged to the most influential plays of the 1960s and helped to shape much of political drama. Not one ideology was at the center, but an exploration of the complexity of issues. Political engagement was called for, the willingness to get involved and take a stand. It is not a play, as Weiss himself once stated, constructed in accordance with the laws of logic. It does not strive for a well-rounded plot nor for self-contained characters. It shows emotions and sequences of thought that escape rational understanding. The play was also exceptional because it offered an all-encompassing aesthetic spectacle, a combination of traditional drama, music, songs, dance, and pantomime. It was "total" theater, rare theatrical excitement having its ancestors in Expressionistic plays. Other spectacles were productions by Peter Stein, as well as Tankred Dorst's epic account of Ernst Toller's involvement in the attempt to set up a Soviet Republic in Munich in 1919, entitled *Toller* (1968). The latter offered a parable about the contrast of intellectuality and daily politics. It was premiered at the Württembergische Staatstheater in Stuttgart by Peter Palitzsch.

Theater, in its maturing process, also became self-reflective—a tendency that would continue in the years to come. In 1966, it was again the Schiller Theater that filled the headlines with the premiere of *Die Plebejer proben den Aufstand* (The Proletariat Practices the Revolution) by Günter Grass, a critical examination of Brecht's drama. The play raised the question of whether theater really wishes to—

or can—bring about social change. In the same year, Claus Peymann staged a production of Peter Handke's *Publikumsbeschimpfung* (Insulting the Audience) at the Theater am Turm, often called TaT (Theater at the Tower), in Frankfurt. In that play, theater itself, the relationship between the stage and the audience, was questioned. The anti-play caused a scandal. The TaT had established itself as one of the avant-garde theaters outside Berlin, and its production of Handke's first play exemplified a break with the older tradition of documentary theater. This Brechtian, didactic approach was, however, revived in 1967 by Rolf Hochhuth with his second play, *Die Soldaten* (The Soldiers).

It was first performed at the Freie Volksbühne in West Berlin and caused protests in England because in the play Winston Churchill was accused as having been responsible for the senseless and inhumane destruction of German cities. Almost as a contrast, Claus Peymann was back at the TaT with his second Handke play in 1968: *Kaspar*, a play experimenting with language instead of focusing on political events, and thereby questioning reality and its representation on stage. Theater, certainly, had outgrown its initial function of the postwar years—that of comforting people and reconfirming their cultural heritage—and had become an integral part of society with all its conflicts.

In 1968, the exhibition *Gesellschaftsform—Theaterform. Theaterform—Gesellschaftsform* (Social System—Theater System. Theater System—Social System) in Dortmund topicalized the interdependence of the art and the political realms and presented mixed media and multiperspective theater. It was the year when Rainer Werner Fassbinder, Hanna Schygulla, and Peer

Raben established the "antitheater" in Munich and Johann Kresnik began to set up his *Choreographisches Theater* (choreographical theater), a mixture of drama and dance, in Bremen. A year later, in 1969, Pina Bausch became artistic director of the Folkwang Tanzstudio (Folkwang dance studio) and an instructor at the Folkwangschule (Folkwang school) in Essen. She and others picked up on the German tradition of expressive dance as well as American modern dance and developed a new dance style combining elements of dance, drama, music, costumes, and conception of space. She tried to convey a new experience of the senses with the intention of provoking and irritating traditional perceptions. Her work reinterpreted and continued the work of her teacher Kurt Jooss, whose dance drama *Der grüne Tisch* (The Green Table) had made history in the 1920s. In her dance pieces, Pina Bausch presented the public with real emotions in everyday situations. Critics such as Michael Patterson and Michael Huxley saw in her work "interesting parallels with the *Volksstück*" (1998, 226). There is little disagreement in the world of dance as regards her contributions and her status. She is generally regarded as the most influential figure in late 20th century German dance, although there were and are other prominent dancers and choreographers such as Gerhard Bohner and Johann Kresnik. While Pina Bausch explored the intimacies of life and interpersonal relationships in her work, Johann Kresnik introduced political topics into his performances and became known as the choreographic revolutionary. His productions attacked capitalism as well as the corrupted form of socialism practiced in the GDR.

After 1970, two newcomers with a different agenda were added to the theatrical mix: Franz Xaver Kroetz and the Austrian Thomas Bernhard. Bernhard had his debut as a playwright with *Ein Fest für Boris* (A Celebration for Boris). Claus Peymann emphasized the absurd aspects of the play, reminiscent of Samuel Beckett. Kroetz, however, was to become probably the most successful playwright in the genre of the folk play. His play *Wildwechsel* (Game Path) premiered in Dortmund in 1971 and was the first of a long line of plays describing society at the lower end of the social ladder, depicting social needs, lack of linguistic abilities to express oneself, and sexual frustration. Just before the premiere, Marieluise Fleißer's work, folk plays filled with social critique, had been rediscovered. The first to be staged was her play *Pioniere in Ingolstadt* (Pioneers in Ingolstadt), originally written in 1928 and recast in 1968 by Rainer Werner Fassbinder, who would bring about a German film revival (see 7: Film).

The main characteristics of the 1970s in regard to theater were its richness and variety, represented by Hochhuth and Handke, Kroetz and Bernhard, and the choreographer Bausch. The Schaubühne am Halleschen Ufer (Theater on the Banks of the Halle), West Berlin, which opened in 1970, became under the directorship of Peter Stein (until 1985) and the dramaturge Botho Strauß, who held that position for four years (1971–1975), a model theater of the decade, with performances characterized by their careful analyses of the texts, precise characterization, and unforgettable images. When Botho Strauß became a playwright in his own right, his *Die Hypochonder* (Hypochondriacs), performed in Hamburg in 1972, only bewildered the audience with its intellectual wit, with the expectations and deceptions that it contained, and with its less explicitly political stance, which became characteristic of the 1970s and signaled the New Subjectivity (see 8: From A to Z, "New Subjectivity"). The main recurrent theme of Botho Strauß's plays, which confirmed his position as the most-performed playwright of the 1970s in the Federal Republic, was the inability to communicate in a continuously talkative society. Like Handke, he thematized "the diffuse socio-psychological malaise of contemporary life, isolation as the modern condition, the improbability of connection" (Sandford 1999, 160). In 1975, his play about the society of the Federal Republic in the 1950s, *Bekannte Gesichter, gemischte Gefühle* (Familiar Faces, Mixed Feelings), was staged for the first time, and his *Trilogie des Wiedersehens* (Trilogy of Meeting Again) was first staged in Hamburg in 1977. On the other end of the scale was Peter Turrini, the new enfant terrible of the German stage, who expressed his anger in a very blunt form. In 1972, he provoked the Munich audience with his play *Sauschlachten* (Slaughter of Pigs), a parable of the destruction of an outsider. Peter Zadek upset the educated audience with his Shakespearean interpretations, for example, *Kaufmann von Venedig* (Merchant of Venice) in Bochum and *Othello* in Hamburg in 1976.

Besides the theatrical scandals, there were also the political ones. For instance, in 1977, Claus Peymann directed at the Stuttgarter Staatstheater (Stuttgart State Theater) the play *Minetti*, written by Thomas Bernhard for the actor Bernhard Minetti, which led to Peymann's resignation because he had encouraged the audience through a note posted on the theater's bulletin board to give money for dental

work for members of the Baader-Meinhof gang imprisoned in the Stammheim prison (see 4: Youth Culture and the World of Intellectuals). The governor of the state of Baden-Württemberg, Hans Filbinger, in particular, made sure that Peymann's tenure would be terminated. However, a year later, Filbinger himself was forced to retire because it became known that he had been a prosecutor in the Third Reich and involved in cases of capital punishment at the end of the war. Even more damaging to his popularity was the lack of remorse expressed in his widely circulated statement, "What was legal at that time, cannot be illegal today." The play *Vor dem Ruhestand* (Before Retirement) by Thomas Bernhard is about a former Nazi who made a career as a judge in the postwar years and reminisces about the glorious past on a private level. Peymann directed the play in Stuttgart as his final farewell to that theater in 1979. Rumor had it that Filbinger was not amused by the play and its production.

In the 1980s, Franz Xaver Kroetz, Botho Strauß, and Heiner Müller attracted both applause and protests. Tankred Dorst overwhelmed both the audience and the critics in Düsseldorf in 1981 with his *Merlin oder das wüste Land* (Merlin or the Wasteland), a spectacle of Faustian proportions that presented new challenges to directors and producers and was usually—if at all—performed only in parts. Heinar Kipphardt's *Bruder Eichmann* (1983, Munich) continued the tradition of political plays, and in 1984, Harald Mueller's play *Totenfloß* (Raft of the Dead) premiered in Oberhausen. The latter saw itself as part of a growing contemporary discussion about environmental pollution. But the most controversial play was Rainer Werner Fassbinder's

Der Müll, die Stadt und der Tod (Garbage, the City, and Death), which caused a protest by the Jewish community, which opposed its anti-Semitic passages. After a closed performance for the press, further performances were stopped. The posthumous attempt to stage the play in Frankfurt failed also (Fassbinder had died in 1982). The same reasons blocked a new attempt to stage it in 1998 in the Maxim Gorki Theater, Berlin. It finally had its premiere in 1999 in Tel Aviv.

In the decade that ended with German unification, theater changed less than its audience. A high point of the 1980s was Peter Zadek's production of Frank Wedekind's *Lulu* at the Deutsches Schauspielhaus in Hamburg in 1988. Wedekind's depiction of the *femme fatale*, the woman as victim of male sexual dominance, offered Zadek and his team the opportunity for unforgettable images, using on-stage nudity in ways not done before. The poster for the play depicts a male just tall enough to stare at the pubic region of a woman's torso. Almost two decades later, Zadek's *Lulu* is still seen as a classic.

The German Democratic Republic

In the forty years of its existence (1949–1989), East German theater was highly regarded by both the people and the state. There were more subsidized theaters in the GDR than in any other state in the world. One of the reasons was that the role of the theater was to be the "partner of politics." As Dennis Tate wrote, "The cultural policymakers of Germany's new socialist regime displayed their belief in the potential of drama as an educational force by the priority they gave to reopening theatres right across their territory" (Sandford 1999, 160). Yet, the officials were cautious that the theater would not be perceived as simply an instrument of propaganda. Besides popularizing Marxism-Leninism and spreading optimism for the socialist state, limited criticism—of the type that otherwise was only expressed in the privacy of the home—was also possible. The censors recognized the delicate balancing act they had to follow. One of the functions of theater was its function as an outlet for frustration.

Bertolt Brecht's productions were the most important highlights, and his name was often surrounded by controversy. His "epic theater" was opposed to the traditional Aristotelian theater aimed at educating the proletariat. In the 1920s, he had collaborated with Erwin Piscator. Now, in the postwar years, he worked with his Berliner Ensemble at first at the Deutsches Theater, where in January 1949 he staged his anti-war play *Mutter Courage und ihre Kinder* (Mother Courage and Her Children), with Helene Weigel in the title role. In March 1954, he moved his theater company to the Schiffbauerdamm Theater, which would become its permanent home. However, many in the West had difficulties understanding his political stance. The Swiss author Max Frisch wondered aloud in 1955, when Brecht was awarded the Stalin Prize in Moscow: "Is he a coward, is he a blind man, or is the freedom of the West insufficient without the Russian money?"(quoted in Glaser 2004, 227). After the building of the Berlin Wall in 1961, theaters in the West instituted a "Brecht boycott."

The size of the audience for theater performances in the GDR was staggering. In 1955, there were 17.4 million recorded theater visits from among a population of less than 20 million (Sandford 1999, 160). In that same year, Peter Hacks moved from the FRG to East Berlin following Brecht's

Actress Helene Weigel with Bertolt Brecht in 1936. (Morechai Gorelik/AFP/Getty Images)

invitation. At first, he worked together with Brecht, and then from 1960 to 1963 at the Deutsches Theater. In 1959, however, Heinar Kipphardt, dramaturge at the Deutsches Theater in East Berlin, had left that theater and moved to West Germany. Many complex issues beyond the scope of this book have to be considered to understand these moves—in both directions. Many of Brecht's productions were seen as decadent and dangerous by the official GDR party hard-liners. One interpretation is that he considered it was worth trying to modify an existing social system in which he believed in spite of all the imperfections.

The outgoing 1950s saw a second wave of a socialist cultural revolution, the attempt to create an independent original proletarian culture and to overcome the gap between the world of material produc-tion and cultural creations. The Bitter-felder Proposal (named after the place where the guidelines were adopted) pro-posed a double strategy: Intellectuals should visit the factories to get to know the world of production, and the workers should take up pen and paper and docu-ment their experience of production in cre-ative ways. One of the results was the es-tablishment of many lay theaters and more village festivals. In 1960, the *Rügenfest-spiele* (Rügen festivals) were opened with the biggest open-air mass play of the GDR, *Klaus Störtebecker*, a ballad based on the story of the captain of a group of pirates and revolutionaries from 1400. The Bitter-felder Proposal was, however, not a pro-ductive one. The most frequently staged plays were comedies by Rudi Strahl, in which problems were addressed with humor instead of confrontation. Only one of his many productions was banned, though those of the star playwrights and producers of the GDR, Peter Hacks, Heiner Müller, Volker Braun, and Christoph Hein, frequently ran afoul of the censors.

But in spite of the difficulties these men faced, all of them embraced socialism. They saw themselves at a time of transition that was imperfect, being on a "ferry between the ice age and the commune," as Müller remarked (quoted in Simhandl 2001, 277). The fate of Müller's *Umsiedler oder Das Leben auf dem Lande* (Resettlers or Life in the Country), which depicted the consequences of agrarian reform and collectivization for the individual, was typical in many ways. After its first performances in 1961 by a student theater, the play was called anticommunistic and counterrevolutionary. Further performances were prohibited and the players forced to take part in humiliating self-critical sessions. The director lost his position and was transferred for a probationary period to a brown coal mining region; Müller was expelled from the association of writers. In 1964, he rewrote the play, which was first shown in 1976 under the title *Die Bauern* (The Farmers).

The 1970s were a time of more leniency. Willy Brandt, the chancellor of the Federal Republic, had changed the political climate through his Ostpolitik, which had brought world recognition to the GDR (see 1: From Two to One). Both German states had become members of the United Nations. Therefore, there was less talk about the leading role of the party and more about a relationship between the party and the cultural elite based on partnership. In 1972, Ulrich Plenzdorf's modern Werther-drama *Die neuen Leiden des jungen W.* (The New Sufferings of Young W.) based on Johann

Wolfgang von Goethe's novelette (1774), which had caused an uproar at the time, had its premiere in Halle, and in 1972 and 1973 fourteen different productions followed. In the play, a young man tests the limits of his society. Plenzdorf hit the right theme and his timing was good, since Erich Honecker had just promised an end to cultural taboos. Plenzdorf's protagonist expressed the popular opinion when he remarked: "They do not have anything against communism. Not a single intelligent human being can be against communism. But besides that, they are against everything else" (Simhandl 2001, 281).

In 1973, Heiner Müller's play about Germany, *Die Schlacht* (The Battle), was produced for the first time in East Berlin. It dealt with the dilemma of death and the survival instinct in the face of fascist violence and terror. The struggle for survival brings out the worst in each character, and cowardice, betrayal, brutality, and malice rule the day.

In 1980, Volker Braun's *Simplex Deutsch* (Simple-Minded German), a dramatic collage with scenes from Bertolt Brecht's *Trommeln in der Nacht* (Drums at Night), Samuel Beckett's *Warten auf Godot* (Waiting for Godot), and Heiner Müller's *Die Schlacht* (The Battle), caught the attention of the critics. And finally, *Der Bau* (The Structure) by Heiner Müller at the Volksbühne in East Berlin completed the list of important productions in that year. Especially in the 1980s, the theater, according to Patterson and Huxley, "fulfilled the function of being the debating chamber for political ideas"—besides the churches, they were the only public forums for political debate. "It was, in part at least, thanks to [this function], that the East German theatres contributed to the removal of the

Berlin Wall and the collapse of the Communist regime" (Patterson et al. 1998, 230). It was theater workers in Berlin who organized the first officially sanctioned protest demonstration in East Berlin on November 4, 1989—just days before the collapse of the Wall. The attitude that began to prevail can also be seen in Christoph Hein's play *Die Ritter der Tafelrunde* (The Knights of the Round Table), which was premiered in Dresden in 1989. By using the thin disguise of its setting in the court of Arthur, it managed to depict a government on the point of collapse. In a final confrontation with his father, Mordreth tells the old King Arthur: "It is your kingdom, father. You and your knights made it. I don't want it. . . . All this here, I don't want it" (quoted in ibid., 230).

The Berlin Republic

In 1990, Christoph Schlingensief shocked many with his cinematic interpretation of German unification in *Das deutsche Kettensägenmassaker* (The German Chainsaw Massacre), while Hans Kresnik looked back to the past when terrorism changed Germany into a police state with his dance *Ulrike Meinhof* at the theater in Bremen. They foreshadowed Einar Schleef's interpretation of Rolf Hochhuth's *Wessis in Weimar* (Westerners in Weimar), which premiered at the Berliner Ensemble in 1993. This play became symbolic in a way of the disagreements of the times, because it caused the decade-old discussion about the sanctity of the author's intention versus a director's ingenuity to flare up. Hochhuth, as always, offered a meticulously researched sequence of scenes, the epitome of documentary theater. The director Einar Schleef, however, only used about 5 percent of the text, focusing on what he saw as the important aspects and creating a

play of *Selbstzerfleischung* (self-destruction). He created real drama, but the author protested vehemently.

The revolutionary fervor of the 1960s has waned, but it certainly has left its mark on the writing of plays as well as their production in Germany. Theater is still alive and well, if no longer in the center of political discourse. One recent exception to this trend was the 2000 performance of Terrence McNally's play *Corpus Christ*, at the city theater in Freiburg, when there were protests by representatives of the Catholic Church, debates in the regional newspapers, security checks of all audience members, and, after one performance, an on-stage discussion of the issues involved.

The closing of the Schiller Theater in 1993 was a bad omen but also led to positive change. The closed Freie Volksbühne in Berlin was sold in 1999 to a private investor and since 2001 has housed the Berlin Theater Festival, thereby becoming the main stage for the Theatertreffen Berlin. It has also become profitable—a major benefit at a time when funds have been reduced and more attention is being paid to self-sufficiency. Some theaters have become very creative in this regard—for example, Halle 7 (Shed 7) in Munich, a theater run by unemployed actors and paid for by the unemployment office as a service training course. The actors do not receive a salary, but they have the chance to be discovered by the many directors visiting their performances, who now come in addition to critics and a regular audience to see the productions.

In spite of all this, Germany is still listed as having not only the best-organized theater system of any country, it has more than 800 registered publicly run and independent theaters with a total seating ca-

A modern production (2005) of Friedrich Schiller's *Die Räuber* (The Robbers) by the Berliner Ensemble (BE). Director: Hasko Weber; Karl Moor, the protagonist: Norbert Stöß (with flag in photo). Courtesy of Presse- und Öffentlichkeitsarbeit, Berliner Ensemble, Berlin (Photo by Matthias Horn.)

pacity of 276,529. It still has the greatest subsidies as well, though they vary from one region to another.

Essentially, there are three subsidized types of theater: city or municipal, state, and provincial. The first two are not unlike those in other countries, where a large city helps support its theaters and state support is given in various forms. The provincial German theaters are a special case. They are funded by the local communities, and their role is to provide small towns that have no theater of their own with accessible theatrical performances. In this re-

spect, they function like touring companies and put on productions in places such as school gymnasiums, movie theaters, and community centers, often in a different town each day. The actors travel in buses, and the scenery is set up by the company's technicians and transported in trucks. As a result, everything must be portable and designed for relatively modest conditions. One practitioner observed that it is the most exciting but also the most difficult form of theater work.

After a low point in the first years of the millennium, when numerous budget cuts had to be made (ballet performances were often the first to suffer), the situation of German theater is beginning to improve again. The need to rethink its structure and role has led to a healthy self-appraisal. It is turning away from the isolated intellectual path it had been following and is now reaching out more to the general populace, particularly the younger generation. The plays being produced are relevant both to their concerns and to their way of looking at the world, influenced as it is by the new technologies.

Music

Although German as a language for international communication is disappearing, it is still being heard on opera stages and at *Lieder* (art song) recitals. Only a few German writers can be regarded as belonging to "world literature" and are known outside of Germany, and only a few more visual artists can probably claim world status, but the music of German and Austrian composers fills concert halls around the world even today. The list of German-speaking composers includes Ludwig van

Beethoven, Wolfgang Amadeus Mozart, Sebastian Bach, Richard Wagner, Johannes Brahms, Franz Schubert, Ludwig Mahler, Richard Strauss, Arnold Schönberg, and many others. Besides its reputation for classical music, Austria is also world-renowned for its waltzes, polkas, and marches. Each New Year, the Western world listens to Johann Strauss's *An der schönen blauen Donau* (The Blue Danube) and the *Radetzky Marsch* when the Vienna Philharmonic, under the baton of the world's greatest conductors, broadcasts its New Year greetings from the Musikverein (the hall of the music society) in Vienna.

This repertoire of classical and romantic music was also one of the elements that the older generation, those who lived through the war, needed for survival—even if they did not care much about this musical heritage. It was something that helped them to accept that they were German and gave them something to be proud of, even though Franz Liszt's *Les Préludes* had been used to broadcast special victory announcements by the army, and compositions by Beethoven and Wagner had been boomed into each home through the *Volksempfänger* (people's radios) during the last months of the war. Added to the repertoire after 1945 were the composers who had been shunned during the Hitler years, such as Arnold Schönberg. Yet, dominance was given by the educated, middle-aged middle class to traditional classical composers and such festivals as the Bayreuth Wagner festival and the Salzburger Festspiele (Salzburg Festival). As Holger Briel pointed out, "Only a small market segment would be taken up by avant-garde music from composers such as Karlheinz Stockhausen, Hans Werner Henze, Wolfgang Rihm, and Bernd Alois Zimmermann" (Briel 2002, 98).

The general population listened to oldies, local folk music, the various *Tanzorchester* (dance bands), and *Schlager* (popular songs). The general theme of these can be summarized in a popular children's rhyme: "*Heile, heile Gänsje, / Es is bald wieder gut, / Es Kätzje hat a Schwänzje / Es is bald wieder gut, / Heile, heile Mausespeck / In hundert Jahr is alles weg*" (Get better, get better, [my] little goose / Everything will be better soon / The little cat has a little tail / Everything will be better soon / Get better, get better, [my] plump little mouse / In a hundred years all is gone). The more banal, lighthearted, and unpretentious the songs were, the better. They helped to create a dream world of forgetting. References to exotic utopias also filled the early songs of the 1950s and can be traced back to a single record, the "Caprifischer" (Fishermen on Capri Island) (Durrani 2002, 200). It had already been produced in 1943, but Benito Mussolini's downfall and the ensuing war with Italy had stopped its release. In 1947, there were no other new records on the market, and this one not only became a best-seller but established the genre of "hit music" in Germany (ibid.).

A typical representative of this *Fernweh* (wanderlust, see 5: Vacations and Travel), which at the same time also contained a hefty dose of *Heimweh* (homesickness), was Freddy Quinn. His record "Heimweh" was the "all-time best-selling Schlager (8 million copies sold)" (ibid., 202). Other songs of his—for example, "Heimatlos" (Homeless)—were almost as successful. "Unter fremden Sternen" (Under Foreign Stars) achieved total sales of 4 million copies and remained a top hit for six weeks in 1959. All of his songs struck the right nerve. They, and the songs of the Schlager genre in general, reflected "the moral disorientation of post-war Germany" (ibid., 201). Disregarding their artistic qualities, the Schlager were a true mirror of German society at large and in this way a genuine artform, although they had zero impact outside the German-speaking nations. Within Germany they flourished for years and were even broadcast in the 1950s and 1960s in some villages from the still existing loudspeaker systems installed on rooftops that had been used as sirens in case of air attacks during the war. These had been retained as the primary communication system for official announcements by the local administrations, replacing the bell-ringing clerk walking through the streets and reminding people of the various official deadlines. Now the beginning of a Schlager would precede the voice of the village clerk coming from the loudspeaker with its news.

Besides Freddy Quinn's expressions of yearning, a good recipe for success was a touch of *Schnulze* (tearjerker) and a touch of parody, a good portion of *ansteckende gute Laune* (contagious cheerfulness), and the creation of pastiches, German folksong and the foreign all rolled into one. The result of this combination was Bill Ramsey, the American who celebrated Germanness with a bit of naughtiness—as expressed in his song "Die Zuckerpuppe aus der Bauchtanzgruppe kenne ich aus Wuppertal!" (That Sugar Baby from the Belly Dance Troupe Was an Acquaintance of Mine from Wuppertal!) (ibid., 206).

Finally, in the early postwar years Conny Froboess and Peter Kraus, the ideal couple, rose to fame (see also 7: Film). She sang: "*Kinder, wär das wunderschön, wenn auf dieser Welt / alle Menschen sich versteh'n, wie's die Jugend hält, / denn wir pfeifen gut und gern auf die Politik, / uns verbindet nah und fern unsere Musik*"

(Kids, how wonderful it would be/ if everyone understood each other in this world the way young people do./ For we don't give a hoot about politics,/ we from near and far are united by our music). It was well intentioned and cute, but once rock 'n' roll arrived, the appeal of home-grown hits for teenagers was gone (see 4: Youth Culture and the World of Intellectuals).

For most of the young Germans growing up in the postwar years, the "in" music was American popular music, rock 'n' roll, jazz, and swing, which they listened to on the American Forces Network (AFN) and the British Forces Network (BFN). They did not understand most of the lyrics, but the music nevertheless resonated with their emotions—and scared their parents' generation. Actually, wholesome fun was the motto, the policy also found in the youth magazine *Bravo* (see 6: The Press), the favorite paper for teenagers at the time. It seemed like a fairy tale come true that Elvis Presley was close by in the late 1950s, stationed in Germany. Yet, in the first two postwar decades, American English was still "exotic." It had not yet pervaded everyday life, and, according to Christoph Dallach, many "Anglo-American hits had to be covered in the local lingo to acquire mass-market appeal in Germany. . . . At the same time, many international greats like Elvis Presley, the Beatles, Johnny Cash, The Beach Boys and The Supremes allowed themselves to be pressured into making German tracks by their record companies" (Dallach 2005, 196). But this attitude soon changed and the predominance of American music continued for the following sixty years. It was not long before German bands began imitating their American models. Among the first singers were Peter Kraus, styled as the German Elvis Presley,

The band Die Ärzte in Freiburg, 2004. (Collage based on photos by D. Miller)

and Ted Herold. They sang in German—their lyrics often pretty pathetic. As Osman Durrani remarked: "Ted Herold's *'Ich bin ein Mann'* [I am a man] consists of little more than the endlessly repeated affirmations of the singer's manhood: (*'Warum behandelst du mich wie ein großes Kind? / Meine Küsse brennen heißer als Wüstenwind'*) (Why do you treat me like a grown-up child? / My kisses burn hotter than the desert wind)" (Durrani 2002, 205). Kraus's and Herold's successors started writing their lyrics in English because, supposedly, the German language was not suited for the syncopated rhythms that had evolved from jazz—a claim that has been argued, confirmed, and negated again and again.

Today, the American control of the German music market is still strong. There are no German tracks by U.S. singers anymore but—instead perhaps—a new self-assuredness of German groups can be discerned. The United States is not a "dream" or a utopia for the young Germans at the beginning of the twenty-first century as it was for the postwar generation. It is an empire, an economic, military, and cultural power

that needs to be respected but not loved. Christoph Dallach began his survey of German music for a *Spiegel* special edition (2005) on *The Germans—Sixty Years after the War* with the observation: "The proudest domestic triumph in many years nearly went unnoticed—despite attempts by the record industry to talk it up for years. Last September, albums by German musicians suddenly found themselves among Germany's top 10: CDs by bands and solo artists with names like *Silbermond, 2raumwohnung, Gentleman, Söhne Mannheims, Die Ärzte, Reamonn* and *Max Herre*. . . . Critics are raving about young musicians in groups like *Mia, Juli* and *Virginia Jetzt!*, and the albums are selling well. . . . Now, suddenly, German rock is cool" (Dallach 2005, 194). And not only are German lyrics "in" among both teens and forty-somethings but they even have a patriotic ring to them—something unheard of in the past decades.

How did this transformation happen? Will it last, or is it only a short-lived phenomenon? Didn't critics dismiss German popular-music bands (as well as German avant-garde composers) and lament the minimal impact they were having on the global music world—in spite of the fact that the German past was filled with music and that Germany is, sixty years after World War II, the third-largest market for music in the world after the United States and Japan?

Many observers of the music scene in Germany had blamed the minor global role of German music in the second half of the twentieth century, a general impoverishment of musical life, on a clear division in taste. As Annette Blühdorn stated, "Since the beginning of the twentieth century it has become common practice in the German-speaking countries to differentiate between *E-Musik* (*Ernste Musik*, serious music), *U-Musik* (*Unterhaltungsmusik*, light music), and *Volksmusik* (folk music)" (Sandford 1999, 427). E-Musik comprises classical and avant-garde music; U-Musik includes popular songs, pop, rock, and dance music; and Volksmusik refers to "musical traditions which originated in past centuries from the lower strata of society" (ibid., 228). This subset includes songs as well as instrumental music, often for dancing. Traditional instruments are, for instance, the accordion, the harmonica, the zither, the dulcimer, the shawm (which is used particularly at Carnival time in southwestern Germany [see 5: Holidays and Local Festivals]), and various types of horns, such as the alpine horn. The often cited examples that overcame these boundaries were Marlene Dietrich's chansons or Bert Brecht's and Kurt Weill's "Macky Messer" (Mack the Knife), made popular in the United States by Sammy Davis, Jr. They were heard all over the world by all social classes. It was music that incorporated cabaret songs, dance music, popular music,

jazz, and marches. It was right for its time, the 1920s and 1930s, and, in the case of Marlene Dietrich after her comeback, also briefly in the 1960s. But it was not a long-term recipe for success. Each generation has to find its own sound. And though it is debatable what role the division between E-Musik and U-Musik plays, it is a division that is true not only for Germany but for the West in general.

In any case, most music critics agree that orchestras from German-speaking cultures—such as the Leipziger Gewandhaus Orchestra, the Berlin Philharmonic, and the Vienna Philharmonic—and individual conductors, such as Kurt Masur, are recognized as German and have a global audience. They are seen as mediators of the classical musical heritage and as such enjoy a high status in the music world. They belong to the concept of *Bildung* (high culture and education); their music is *Bildungsmusik* (educationally valuable music); and therefore they are supported by the state. In the 1990s, the state paid for 121 concert halls and 141 professional symphony orchestras and ensured that the players were financially secure. They have the status of lifelong civil servants. Certainly, a player appointed to such an ensemble is free of any money worries for the rest of his or her life. However, the positions are extremely competitive. Exceptional talent, diligence, and hard work are essential.

Nevertheless, even E-Musik faced a challenge in the new millennium. Simon Rattle, music director of the Berlin Philharmonic since the 2002/2003 season, began a project to popularize classical music again by organizing special rehearsals that could be attended by young people between the ages of ten and twenty-two to introduce them to classical music in a playful way. Institutions

Violinist Anne-Sophie Mutter. (Soeren, Stache/epa/Corbis)

such as the Deutsche Bank (German Bank), realizing that culture should not be left completely up to the state, began to sponsor Rattle's project entitled Zukunft@BPhil (Future@BerlinPhilharmonic). Of course, young conductors such as Rattle are also aware of the rapid changes in the global music industry and in musical tastes—music is more than tradition. All types of music fuse into each other. Indeed, crossover is becoming increasingly the norm. In a 2003 issue, *Brigitte* interviewed the violinist Anne-Sophie Mutter, another artist who has been instrumental in making classical music both popular and accessible, and who has acknowledged the validity of different approaches to music. She talked about her (then) latest album, *Tango, Song and Dance*, made with her husband, André Previn, in which she added Gershwin to her repertoire. She also told the interviewer about her love of jazz as well as of the music of the Beatles and the Rolling Stones.

For many, the era of the *Liedermacher* (literally, songwriters) in the 1960s and 1970s also played a key role in the changes that took place on the German music scene. The term *Liedermacher* emphasized the craft of making a song rather than the poet's inspiration as the basis for art. It had a Brechtian feel to it and was reminiscent of Brecht's neologism *Stückeschreiber* (writer of plays) for *Dramatiker* (dramatist). Rumor has it that the term *Liedermacher* was coined by Wolf Biermann, who worked in the 1950s at the Berliner Ensemble. Certainly, like Brecht's plays and the songs in these plays, the songs of the Liedermacher tried to make the listeners aware of social problems, force them to become critical of their surroundings, and encourage them to become politically active. They were primarily influenced by the United States, but this time by American folk music and protest songs, by writer-composer-singers such as Joan Baez, Pete Seeger, Bob Dylan, Phil Ochs, and Tom Paxton. They were influenced as well by French chansons. But the influence did not extend to the language. The Liedermacher's songs were in German. Indeed, they had to be if their protests were to be understood by all of their audience. Franz Josef Degenhardt, the oldest of this group; Wolf Biermann, who emigrated from West to East Germany in 1953 and was expatriated in 1976 from the GDR; Reinhard Mey; and Hannes Wader were among the most prominent and popular.

Similarly, German rock and electronic music of the late 1960s and early 1970s gained some international recognition—as its name, *Krautrock*, derived from the English nickname for Germans as *Krauts*, indicates. Early on, the name connoted the negative traits of pathos, ponderousness, and tenseness as well as artificially forced rhythms. As Christian Graf noted, the term was also used in the title of a song by the band Amon Düül I in 1969 (Graf 2002, 195). But whatever its initial implications, the negative connotation changed in later years and stood for progressiveness and a willingness to experiment. Martin Brady, based on studies by Julian Cope, sees Krautrock

as being influenced by music "ranging from 'The Velvet Underground' to 'New Music' (most famously Karlheinz Stockhausen's *Hymnen*, 'Anthems for Electronic and Concrete Sounds')." It prefigured "Punk, New Wave, ambient and electronica, groups including *Kraftwerk*, *Can*, *Faust*, *Neu* and *Tangerine Dream*." It was "not remotely 'happy'—soaring, idealistic and hard as nails" (Briel 2002, 79). The most successful and colorful band was the Scorpions. Founded in 1965, and seen by many as the most representative Krautrock group, the band became Germany's internationally most successful hard-rock band. It gave large concerts in Great Britain, Japan, and the United States. After several high and low points during a period of over three decades, the group succeeded in staging a comeback in 2000 in a joint concert with the Berlin Philharmonic at the World Expo in Hannover—overcoming the above-cited division between E-musik and U-musik.

Udo Lindenberg—the first of the few German "*Rock Superstars*"—was the most successful individual performer in Krautrock. Like the Scorpions, he had a somewhat rocky career. After a failed start with songs in English, he apparently realized that "it is much better to express oneself in a language that one knows" (Graf 2002, 211) and became the spokesman of his generation. Mega-concerts, organized and staged with the help of such leading theater directors as Peter Zadek (see 8: Theater and Dance), and banal films alternated with one another. When he was awarded the Bundesverdienstkreuz am Band (High Order of Merit of the Federal Republic of Germany), this only added to his egomania.

The top band of the subculture in Berlin, combining rock and political rebellion, was Ton Steine Scherben (Clay Stones Shards).

One of their hits was "Macht kaputt was Euch kaputt macht" (Destroy What Destroys You, 1970), which often led to vandalism at their concerts and police interventions. Their songs and their political engagement were a result of their living environment in Berlin Kreuzberg, a workers' neighborhood, and their experience with the music industry. Life, for the average person, they realized, was hard and unjust. Therefore, they actually came to political rock against their own artistic desires, which found expression in children's records and self-reflective songs.

One of the biggest sensations that a German band ever achieved outside Germany occurred in 1975 when the Düsseldorf-based band Kraftwerk (Power Station) "garnered a slot in the U.S. top 10 with its album *Autobahn*. Popular music from Germany had not created such a stir in the U.S. since Bertolt Brecht and Kurt Weill achieved success worldwide with their *Threepenny Opera*—which had premiered back in 1928" (Dallach 2005, 196). In the meantime, Kraftwerk, the most original, most progressive, and most influential German band of the 1970s, has become a rock classic. The group's mechanical, monotonous sounds and robot-like performances captured their times in unforgettable images and sounds. The Kraftwerk members founded a new idiom for the mechanical world that had been depicted in the German Expressionist films and the futurist movement of the 1920s. Techno music—with which the group Kraftwerk is associated—was the first type of popular music that began in Germany, experienced its climax in the United States, and then returned to Germany. The term "techno" has spawned many versions and interpretations, having become a term for a world-view and not only for a musical style. The most visible manifestation of techno music was its role in the Love Parade in Berlin in the late 1990s. This event, with up to 1.5 million participants, was for a few years Europe's largest youth event. It had started as an underground weekend rave in Berlin in the late 1980s but was cancelled in 2004 and 2005 because of lack of sponsors. Even Udo Lindenberg's attempt to use his celebrity status in a plea for the relocation of the parade from Berlin to Hamburg was unsuccessful (*Focus Newsletter*, April 21, 2004).

Another musical style that came close to garnering international fame was that of the *Neue Deutsche Welle* (New German Wave, NDW). These writers insisted on using the German language for both lyrics and band names, opposing the view that German was ill-suited to rock rhythms. The New German Wave bands like Geisterfahrer (Wrong-Way Driver), Abwärts (Downwards), Deutsch-Amerikanische Freundschaft (German American Friendship), and Der Plan (The Plan) "made an inventive and often ironic use of their native tongue," according to Matthew Jefferies (Briel 2002, 103). The most famous exponent of this music was the band Ideal. As Jefferies mentioned, "Language barriers notwithstanding, the NDW quickly gained an international audience through the BBC's John Peel and US college radio" (ibid., 103). And he pointed out that critical acclaim was showered on bands such as Einstürzende Neubauten (Collapsing New Building), X-Mal Deutschland (X-Times Germany), and Die Krupps (The Krupps) by the influential British music weekly *New Musical Express*. It made no fewer than three German records "Single of the Week" during the course of 1980.

According to Jefferies, Einstürzende Neubauten, with its industrial music, shaped the taste of a whole generation and found valiant successors in bands such as And One. When the famous congress building in Berlin, which had been a gift from the United States to West Berlin (it was called the "pregnant oyster" or "Jimmy Carter's smile" by the Berlin citizens because of its oval shape), collapsed in 1980, a few musicians were inspired by that event and got together to develop a different kind of musical concept, one that could not be easily categorized, and they gave themselves a name that means "Collapsing New Buildings." They liked to use various tools and kitchen utensils as sound instruments for very special rhythmic qualities. Again, it was critics in the United Kingdom who praised their daring experiments and invented a new category for them: heady metal as a pun on "heavy metal." They toured Europe and the United States successfully, participated in art festivals such as the *documenta* (see 9: Visual Arts) as well as in the World Expo in Montreal, Canada, in 1986, and worked together on new theater productions with Peter Zadek in 1987 (see 8: Theater and Dance). Members of the audience with weak hearts were warned beforehand to take precautions. Ear plugs were handed out to all listeners because maximum loudness was part of the dramaturgy. In later productions, they incorporated metal beds and sound bites from tapes of U.S. President Ronald Reagan as well as the humming of bees. Ten years later, they were, naturally, no longer regarded as radical, but rather as popular avant-gardists. They were invited to participate in many shows and also participated in making soundtracks for films such as *Sonnenallee* (see 7: Film). In 2000,

they celebrated their twentieth anniversary with a global Internet concert, a world tour, and a new recording with the title "Silence Is Sexy."

Jefferies wrote, "By the end of 1982 the NDW meant big business, and many bands were signed by major record labels. The new-look NDW took the European sales charts by storm, giving a host of minor talents a brief taste of stardom: Trio, Peter Schilling, Markus, Hubert Kah" (ibid., 103). The movement also included Ideal, Extrabreit (Extra Wide), and Nena, with her song "99 Luftballons" (99 Balloons)—who scored the biggest international hit—and the Austrian Falco, who took his artistic name from the GDR ski jumper Falko Weispflog (Graf 2003, 84). Yet, success did not last long. By the mid-1980s, "the movement had lost most of its original vitality, and the *NDW* tag was henceforth only used pejoratively" (Briel 2002, 103). Many in the music field saw it merging with the typical German Schlager.

In East Germany, music was strictly controlled by the authorities (see 4: Youth Culture and the World of Intellectuals). As Annette Blühdorn mentioned, "In 1958 a quota system was introduced requiring 60 percent of dance and light music played in public to be produced in the GDR or other communist countries" (Sandford 1999, 429). The regime thus unintentionally helped to develop German rock in the GDR. The most popular rock bands during this time period were Puhdys and Karat. Puhdys dominated the GDR hit list in the early 1970s. In 1976, they were allowed to tour West Germany, where they "showed the Federal Republic that 'beat auf Deutsch' was alive and kicking on the other side of the Elbe" (Durrani 2002, 208). Karat followed suit and was able to place well on the West German hit charts in the early 1980s, winning two golden records.

In the 1980s and 1990s, foreign influence increased again in West (and then united) Germany, although the German language (even dialect) was used by some groups. Typical examples are the punk band Shine, the band BAP, which produced rock songs in the Cologne dialect, and the group Tote Hosen (Dead Pants). This last band was formed in 1981 and played at parties, in autonomous youth clubs, and in buildings occupied by squatters. Various types of scandals marked the group's ascent, and the band was sued because its lead singer, Campino, had impersonated Heino (see 8: From A to Z, "Performers"). But there were success stories too: The band was booked for private parties and invited to appear in theater productions and on talk shows. One of the group's German tours supported the soccer club Fortuna, which was in a financial crisis, and it began the 1990s with a top ranking in the German *Hitparade*. In 1991, a documentary film was made about the band: *Die Toten Hosen—Drei Akkorde für ein Hallelujah* (The Dead Pants—Three Chords for a Hallelujah). Campino acted in the film *Langer Samstag* (Long Saturday). The Toten Hosen hit "Sascha, ein aufrechter Deutscher" (Sascha, an Upright German) was critical of the xenophobia and growing fascism among young people in Germany. The profits from this hit were donated to the group Düsseldorfer Appell gegen Fremdenfeindlichkeit und Rassismus (The Düsseldorf Appeal against Xenophobia and Racism). Throughout the 1990s, the band fulfilled the expectations of its fans and brought international recognition to German rock and pop, continued its provocative stance, and refused to compromise beliefs to gain commercial success.

The post-unification 1990s saw the brief emergence of neo-fascist songs—for example, those by the band Böhse Onkelz (Bad Uncles), whose early music was prohibited. According to Briel, "In the meantime, their [the Böhse Onkelz] political outlook has changed somewhat and they have been allowed to publish their music once again. Also due to unification, the focus of at least some *U-Musik* shifted east, with songs such as Stefan Raab's *Maschendrahtzaun* (Wire Netting Fence) .... and Niemann's *Im Osten* (In the East) highlighting eastern experiences" (Briel 2002, 98). Although East German singer-songwriters such as Bettina Wegner and Stefan Krawczyk have lost their audiences, "the classically trained pop band *Die Prinzen* has enjoyed the biggest post-unification success" (Sandford 1999, 495). The group known in the GDR as Herzbuben (Knaves of Heart) changed its name after unification and quickly climbed to the top of the charts, either in spite of— or because of—its unusual a cappella style. As former members of the world-famous St. Thomas Boys Choir, the members had voices that were highly trained, a trait that set them apart from most singers of popular songs. Experts feared their novelty would wear off fast, but the members of the group recognized this danger and soon began to experiment with different arrangements, including collaborations with a symphony orchestra. The group's least successful record so far was its attempt at real rock 'n' roll.

In the former West Germany, a few German hip-hop bands, the German version of rap, repopularized German-language lyrics and added a critical twist to them, disproving "critics' claims that the streetwise speech-song from America's ghettos could not be transposed into sprechgesang without sounding utterly ludicrous" (Dallach 2005, 196). As the essence of rap is the personal, confessional monologue, these rap texts addressed in a very direct way the immediate concerns of the young people of the 1980s and 1990s. Examples are such bands as Die Fantastischen Vier (The Fantastic Four), Fünf Sterne Deluxe (Five Stars Deluxe), and Fettes Brot (Fat Bread), who established a reputation at least on a limited international scale. But there have been many more who have experienced a one-time meteoric rise in the German pop charts only to disappear again into oblivion, such as Tic Tac Toe, a group of three very young women who played cheeky, but also reflective, songs like "Warum?" (Why?).

On January 9, 2005, the *New York Times* Arts and Leisure section included a two-page spread on the heavy metal group Rammstein with the headline "Das Jackboot: German Heavy Metal Conquers Europe." The story referred to the uproar caused on the band's 1998 American debut tour, after which two members spent the night in jail on obscenity charges. It was noted that this was nothing compared to the reception the group received in their own country, "where people actually understand their lyrics." In addition to displaying sadomasochistic antics on stage, the band—a group of six men from the former East Germany—entertain their fans with pyrotechnics and songs about mass graves and the eroticism of power, leading many to label them neo-fascist, though they themselves emphatically deny the charge. They reportedly were puzzled that their inclusion of a clip from a Leni Riefenstahl film in one of their videos was interpreted as support of the Nazi ideals. The band's second guitarist, Paul Landers, explained that they simply wanted to be provocative at first

and were tired of the prevalent attitude of shame about being German. (See also the statements of the fashion designer Eva Gronbach in 4: Lifestyle and Fashion.) Though they may look and sound like "Fascho-rock," their publicist claims their songs have no political content whatsoever.

In any case, the group has gained a strong following in the rest of Europe, particularly in Russia, despite the fact that they only sing in German. Making the political aspect of their music even more complicated was the release in September 2004 of an album entitled *Reise Reise*, which included the song "Amerika." The title should perhaps be preceded by the prefix "Anti-." The album's title is officially translated as *Voyage Voyage*, but audiences apparently find another interpretation: arise arise. At the concert attended by the *New York Times* reporter Claire Berlinski, the lead singer, Till Lindemann, wore an imperial German military uniform, and fans began "pumping their fists into the air." The accompanying photograph of the audience immediately brought images of the official greeting gesture of the Hitler era to mind. The keyboardist wore a military helmet, and Lindemann goose-stepped about the stage. The pyrotechnics created such heat that some fans passed out and had to be taken out on stretchers. Berlinski noted that when the band sang "Amerika," their antiaggression stance was difficult to discern. She pondered: "If this is their pacifism, the mind boggles at what their aggression might look like." The tame, sentimental songs of Peter Alexander or Nena's "99 Luftballons" are a far cry from this "music of brutal ambiguity," said Berlinski.

While in the 1960s and 1970s, much of the popular music was identified with a rebellion against the older generation and symbolic of finding one's own space, in the 1990s and the beginning of the new millennium popular music has been integrated into the mainstream and commercialized to serve as the *Schrittmacher der Innovation unserer Wirtschaft* (pacemaker of the innovation of our economy), as Wolfgang Clement, at the time secretary of the economy of North-Rhine Westphalia, announced in 1997 (Kemper et al. 1999, 12). As Sabine Schmidt mentioned, the "music cable channel Viva aided the rise in popularity of German music. Started in 1993 (Viva II debuted in 1996), Viva plays 40 percent local product, with an emphasis on dance and pop." And she continued: "DJs like West Bam or Marusha, and Viva VJs like Heike Makatsch and Stefan Raab have replaced musicians as pop stars" (Sandford 1999, 495).

In contrast to earlier decades, the new music scene is extremely diverse. Heavy metal is split into black metal, death metal, thrash, doom, glam, grind core, hardcore, speed metal, and noise core. Techno has, on the one hand, a hyperfast gabber style (a distorted kick sound changing to an almost melodic tone) and, on the other, a meditative trance style. And the switchover from one type of music to another is constantly occurring. Today, Brit-popper is in, tomorrow postrocker or drum 'n' bass (Kemper et al. 1999, 17).

Next to this multitude of musical styles are folkloristic styles, and high on that list is klezmer music. As in other areas, multiculturalism is alive and well in the German music world, though not without some sensitive issues and questions (see 4: Multicultural Society). An article in the *New York Times* in August 2004 reported that throughout Germany crowds flock to hear klezmer music, a genre that has its roots in the now lost Jewish communities, or shtetlach, of Eastern Europe. One can listen to the music live in Berlin every night of the week. Record sales are strong, and one label director has named Germany the strongest klezmer market in the world, pushing even the United States into second place. The appeal of the music, combining rhythms that set feet tapping with images of old-fashioned wedding celebrations, is not hard to understand, but in Germany the situation is more complex. The historical context simply cannot be forgotten (see 1: Coming to Terms with the Past). There are some who argue that klezmer music never was part of the German Jewish tradition and that it is therefore just as new to Germany as it would be to, say, France or England, but the specter of the Nazi concentration camps adds complex overtones to the performances. The *Times* reported that at performances at a restaurant named Shakespeare's and at the Ettersburg Palace, both located in or near the city of Weimar, few in the enthusiastic audience were Jewish. Weimar might be seen as a particularly sensitive city for such music, with the Buchenwald concentration camp just a few miles away, but it has nevertheless been the site of a month-long klezmer workshop for several years. At these gatherings, musicians—mostly German and mostly in their twenties and thirties—study Yiddish songs, Yiddish language, music, and dance from a primarily American-Jewish faculty.

Klezmer music was introduced (or reintroduced, depending on one's perspective) to Germany in the 1980s by groups such as Brave Old World, an American klezmer group, the leader of which runs the Weimar workshops. The reception was overwhelming then and has remained enthusiastic. Heiko Lehmann, a German bassist, is cited by the *New York Times* as saying that klezmer was "the first Jewish thing aside from guilt that the Germans got after the war." The Israeli clarinetist Giora Feidman defined klezmer less as a genre than a "musical-spiritual approach" (*New York Times* August 29, 2004, 24) and preached a doctrine of musical inclusion and bridge building. By the 1990s, thanks to workshops led by the American-Jewish performers and Feidman, essentially German klezmer groups were springing up. The music has now been incorporated into public ceremonies, particularly those focusing on German-Jewish reconciliation.

Not all are happy with this situation, however. Iris Weiss, a German-Jewish writer and cultural activist, noted that this kind of klezmer "helps Germans to identify with Jewish victims rather than the perpetrators of the atrocities" and "to avoid confrontation with their own family history." (ibid.). She also pointed out that klezmer music was not particularly popular with German Jews before the war and that they were far more likely to listen to Beethoven. She has described the situation as a "Jewish Disneyland" (ibid.), a distortion of the true culture that has vanished. By branding the Eastern European tradition as German, she feels that a stereotype is being created that obscures the rich history of German Jews. And yet, those Germans who have immersed themselves in the music and its history and culture find they have learned to correct previously held ideas, particularly of Jewish people as victims. These musicians, born long after the war, also welcome the way the music has opened up the dialogue between Germans and Jews. A transplanted Yiddish poet, born in Vienna, but—at the time of the article—living in the Bronx, eighty-four-year-old Beyle Schaechter-Gottesman, participated in the 2004 Weimar workshop. Seeing how moved young Germans were by her songs gave her an optimistic view of the popularity of klezmer music. She expressed the hope that finally her culture would become better known and better understood outside the Jewish world.

From A to Z

Actors and actresses: A few whose careers were more dominated by the stage than the film are: Elisabeth Flickenschild (1905–1977), known for her interpretation of all the major classical roles in German theater; Therese Giese (1898–1975), remembered best through her roles in plays by Bertolt Brecht and Friedrich Dürrenmatt; Gustav Gründgens (1899–1963), politically controversial but acclaimed as both an actor and director; the Austrian Fritz Kortner (1892–1970), the grand old man of both German theater and of film, who established a reputation as an actor as well as a director, at first in the Weimar years and then, after his return from Hollywood, in the postwar era in West Germany; Bernhard Minetti (1905–1998), attacked for his participation in an antisemitic Nazi movie, but rehabilitated for his impressive performances in Thomas Bernhard's plays; Anne Tismer (b. 1963), who was honored by the magazine *Theater heute* in 2003 as the best actress; Helene Weigel (1900–1971), first director of the Berliner Ensemble, wife of Bertolt Brecht and familiar to many in her role as mother in Brecht's

Mutter Courage und ihre Kinder (Mother Courage and Her Children).

AFN: American Forces Network. The two radio stations AFN and BFN (British Forces Network) were probably the most important mediators of a new culture that would shape Germany (see 7: Radio and Television; 4: Youth Culture and the World of Intellectuals).

Alienation: see *V-Effect*.

Ballet: Among the best-known German ballet ensembles was John Cranko's (1927–1973) highly acclaimed Stuttgart Ballet, which put German dance back on the international map and William Forsythe's (b. 1949 in New York) Frankfurt Ballet. See also Dance Theater.

Bands: Some of the important German bands of the late twentieth and early twenty-first centuries are as follows. Abwärts (Downwards), founded in 1979, was the favorite band of German subculture in the early 1980s. After 1984, the group seemed for a short time to be part of the New German Wave, and in the early 1990s the metal sound seemed to attract them. Amon Düül II (the name goes back to the Egyptian sun god "Amon" and a Turkish mythological figure) was founded in 1969 by Chris Karrer (b. 1947) after he left Amon Düül I, which he had inspired in 1967. The first group became primarily political, and Karrer wanted to concentrate more on musical experiments. Die Ärzte (the Medics), founded in 1982, quickly became the cult band of the Berlin punk scene. Over the years, the group became more professional, and its members are now seen as the grandmasters of German pop bands.

Some of their songs—for example, "Geschwisterliebe" (Sibling Love)—sparked vehement discussions; other songs were put on the index by the Bundesprüfstelle für jugendgefährdende Medien (Federal Control Agency for Media Harmful to Young People; see 3: The Legal System) because of references to sodomy. The resulting headlines helped the band's ranking. After a breakup, the group reunited in 1993 and regained the top spot on the lists of German hits. And One, founded in 1990, found a niche for itself between electronic body music, electropop, and industrial rock.

BAP took its name from the Cologne dialect, in which *Bap* means "father." The rock group, founded in 1978, showed that even a dialect band can advance to more than regional fame, especially if it adds a translation into standard German on the covers of its disks. Since the early 1980s, BAP's German tours have attracted an ever-increasing audience. Social critique remained the group's identifying feature; the songs focus on the lower classes with their small dreams and big disappointments. A documentary about the band directed by Wim Wenders premiered at the Berlinale in 2002. Beginner is a German-language hip-hop band from the Hamburg area. It began in 1991 under the name "Absolute Beginners" and rapped in a mixture of English and German, but then the members decided to rename themselves and only use German lyrics. Blumfeld is a band that belongs to the brooding rock intellectuals of the so-called Hamburg School. Böhse Onkelz (Bad Uncles) is a band that, from its beginnings in 1979, was seen as neo-fascist and banned by all official agencies and music stores. Its music is a mixture of punk, rock 'n' roll, and heavy rock with speed and thrash elements. The group's first songs were put on the index of the Federal Control Agency for Media Harmful to Young People as spreading violence and sexism. The members tried to distance themselves from this image but were nevertheless stopped—by, among others, Udo Lindenberg—from participating in a festival devoted to "Rock against the Right." The result of these various actions was that their music sold even better and their reputation grew. In the meantime, they have moved further to the center politically and no longer arouse such controversy. Brave Old World is a U.S. band that is popular in Germany for its klezmer music.

Can, regarded by some as Germany's most progressive band (Graf 2002, 85), became a legend in the late 1960s and early 1970s soon after the group's formation. The band established itself internationally as the underground band for intellectuals. Although band members changed relatively frequently, there were usually a few members from other countries such as the United States and Japan. Their main fan base was in the United Kingdom, where music critics appreciated their very special rhythms and daring musical experiments. Deutsch-Amerikanische Freundschaft (German American Friendship, D.A.F.) was founded in 1978 by Robert Görl (b. 1955) and Gabi Delgado-Lopez (b. 1958). The latter was born in Spain. Their biggest hit was in 1981, "Alles ist gut" (All Is Well), for which they received the Deutscher Schallplattenpreis (German Record Prize). They were also featured prominently in music magazines in the United Kingdom. But stamina was lacking, and they dissolved the band after a German tour. The attempt by Delgado to found DAF Dos in 1996 failed.

Einstürzende Neubauten (Collapsing New Buildings) was known as an innovative band (see 8: Music). Extrabreit XXL (Especially Wide XXL), founded in 1979, was a relatively traditional rock band with a very unstable career. Its biggest hits were "Welch ein Land—Was für Männer (What a Country—What Great Men, 1981) and "Hotel Monopol" (1993). Die Fantastischen Vier (The Fantastic Four) introduced hip hop to the German market. No other German band was as much talked about in the 1990s. Faust was a progressive German band, and like others of its type, it had a positive reception in the United Kingdom. The band differed from others in that it was organized by Polydor Records in 1971. These ties did not, however, guarantee record productions, and when Virgin Records declined some new recordings, the avant-garde artists dissolved the band. In the 1990s, the band was reactivated. It had a very hard sound in its first phase that mellowed in the following years. Fehlfarben (Wrong Colors) was founded in 1979 in London, where the German members of the group had experienced the English band called The Teardrop Explodes. Fettes Brot (Fat Bread) was founded in 1992 in Hamburg. It is one of the leading German hip-hop bands and known for its amusing and sometimes mystical German lyrics. Fünf Sterne Deluxe, founded in 1997, is a hip-hop group from Hamburg that gained popularity quickly and made the Hamburg dialect popular nationwide.

The New German Wave band Geisterfahrer (Wrong-Way Driver) came from Hamburg in the late 1970s. Ideal, founded in 1980, became for about three years the top band of the New German Wave, after which they discontinued performances. Juli was founded in the late 1990s under the name Sunnyglade. The members sang in English at first but then switched to German. In 2001, Sunnyglade became Juli. Karat, founded in 1975, belonged to the list of approved GDR groups in spite of its hidden criticism of the regime. The group's positive-sounding "Über sieben Brücken mußt du geh'n" (Seven Bridges You Have to Cross) was welcomed as almost an alternative anthem. In 1983, Karat became the first GDR group to receive a West German "*golden disc.*" Kraftwerk (Power Station), with its electronic music, a blend of classical avant-gardism and pop culture, emerged as the most influential band of the postwar years. Its first single, "Autobahn" (1974), a synthetic reproduction of a car trip through the Ruhr Valley, has become a classic. Die Krupps, founded in the early 1980s, played a role in the development of industrial rock. (The group's name should be familiar both to modern-day buyers of electrical appliances and World War II historians—the latter because a company of the same name was a well-known German arms manufacturer.) The band was especially popular in Japan. But the sudden popularity of the New German Wave movement forced its members to pause and take stock. They returned to the music scene in 1989 as representatives for electronic body music and included more and more elements of metal music, as, for example, in "A Tribute to Metallica." In "Final Remixes," they also used gothic, hardcore, and rap and thereby escaped any attempt at classification. After more than fifteen years of successful experimentation, the band members, who in the meantime lived in different places in the world, dissolved the group in 1998.

Mia was a group that was founded in 1998 in Berlin. Neu! (New!) was a relatively short-lived band that existed in the beginning to mid-1970s. It concentrated on recordings in a studio and not live performances. Der Plan, a band based in Wuppertal, experimented with various sounds, enriching NDW for over a decade, from the late 1970s until 1992. Popol Vuh (named after the holy book of the Quechee Indians) underwent several phases, in particular music with and without an electronic synthesizer. But in all its incarnations, the major musician was Florian Fricke (b. 1944), who had studied at the conservatory in Freiburg. The band is best known for its soundtracks for films by Werner Herzog (see 7: Film). Die Prinzen (The Princes) sang a cappella (see 8: Music). Puhdys, a GDR rock band, was founded in Berlin in 1969. It served as proof of the tolerance of the GDR regime, which allowed the group to perform abroad. Rammstein is a group whose success is to some extent rooted in the fact that its "members conform to the stereotype of the average German found in many countries around the world: battle-crazed, mindless, hulking huns who spew flames and blast out lines like 'Ein Mensch brennt' (Someone's on fire) over an infernal racket," according to Christoph Dallach. He continued, "Beyond the carping, though, Rammstein does stage a fantastic show; even today its Teutonic blend of Wagnerian pomp and rock insanity captivates Americans and Brits alike" (Dallach 2005, 196). Reamonn is a German band founded in 1998 that took its name from its lead singer, the Irishman Reamonn Garvey (abbreviated "Rea"). Rosenstolz began in 1991 in Berlin, when Peter met Anna, and is still going strong in 2005. The Scorpions became the best-known German hard-rock band internationally.

Silbermond (Silver Moon), an East German band, began in 2000 as the rock group JAST and sang in English. In 2001, it switched to using German and took the new name. Silly, founded in 1978 in East Berlin as Familie Silly (The Silly Family), developed into one of the boldest and most progressive GDR bands. Söhne Mannheims (Sons of Mannheim) was the idea of Xavier Naidoo, who founded the band in the city of Mannheim in 1995. Tangerine Dream belonged to the early electronic pioneers of the late 1960s. It has had different members over the years. Electronic meditations, cosmic music, and electronic improvisations were characteristic of their work. Praised in the United Kingdom as one of the most promising bands of the world in 1974, the group was also lauded by the *Süddeutsche Zeitung* (see 6: The Press) as the "pacemaker of futuristic music." In the United States, it was placed into the New Age category and achieved a high point by being nominated in 1993 for a Grammy award. Tic Tac Toe became the big hit in 1996 and 1997. The three-girl group had tremendous success with its first singles and won many prizes. In 1997, they separated. Two of them formed the group Tic Tac Two, but their success did not continue. Ton Steine Scherben (Clay Stones Shards) was Germany's top political rock group. Its members got together in 1970. Their first song, which became a cult song and made them famous, signaled their agenda: "Macht kaputt was Euch kaputt macht" (Destroy What Destroys You). Many concerts were marked by political discussions. Under the name Corny, Ernst & Scherben, they produced the campaign song "Das ist unser Land" (That's Our Country) for the Green Party in the early 1980s (see 10: Consumer Culture versus Green Awareness). The band dissolved when head singer and founder Rio Reiser (actual name: Ralph Möbius, 1950–1996) decided to begin a solo career in 1983. In 1996, on the occasion of his death, the ex-members formed a new band, Neues Glas aus alten Scherben (New Glass from Old Shards). Tote Hosen (Dead Pants) gained fame in the 1980s and sustained it during the 1990s (see 8: Music). Trio was founded in 1979 by Stephan Remmler (b. 1946), Gert "Kralle" Krawinkel (b. 1949), and Peter Behrends (b. 1947) and performed for the first time in a bar on Christmas in 1980. The designer Klaus Voormann (b. 1938), who had designed Beatles covers and worked for Heinz Rudolf Kunze, Marius Müller-Westernhagen, and many others, joined them as their creative artist. Soon they were regarded as the *Neue Deutsche Fröhlichkeit* (New German Joyfulness), an alternative to the New German Wave. Their biggest hit was "Da Da Da—ich lieb dich nicht, du liebst mich nicht" (I Don't Love You, You Don't Love Me, 1982). Unfortunately, they were not able to sustain their creative efforts and quietly called it quits.

Virginia Jetzt! (Virginia now!) was founded in 1999 in the Brandenburg region. Wir sind Helden (We Are Heroes), a Berlin-based group, had its successful debut in 2003 with *Die Reklamation*. They rate with lead singer Judith Holofernes as one of the big surprises of the first years of the millennium. X-Mal Deutschland (X-Times Germany), an all-woman band founded in 1980, was regarded in Germany as a band of dilettantes but welcomed in the Netherlands and the United Kingdom, where it was seen as a representative of the ending punk era and the beginning of NDW. The group broke up in 1989. Finally, 2raumwoh-nung is a pop duo that began in 2000.

Cabaret/Satire: See 2: Humor and Stereo-types and Prejudices.

Composers: Some of the most important composers of serious music (Ernste Musik, or E-Musik) in Germany since the turn of the twentieth century are as fol-lows. Boris Blacher (1903–1975), director of the Berlin Conservatory, was always ready for another musical experiment. Paul Dessau (1894–1979) was in exile in the United States, where he met Bertolt Brecht. His collaboration continued after their return to the GDR, until Brecht's death. Violeta Dinescu (b. 1953 in Bucharest, Romania) belongs to a young generation of composers active in various genres, including works for children, speaking a new musical language of ex-pression with reminiscences of the now classical tradition of modernity. Hanns Eisler (1898–1962) composed first in the twelve-tone style. He lived in the United States in exile and collaborated with Brecht. After his return to East Germany, he worked in the field of applied music and also wrote the music for the GDR's new na-tional anthem (see 2: Symbols and Memo-rials). Wolfgang Fortner (1907–1987) be-longed to the leading music theorists. Karl Amadeus Hartmann (1905–1963) was the Expressionist among the modern com-posers. Hans Werner Henze (b. 1926) is Germany's leading contemporary opera composer. Paul Hindemith (1895–1963) emigrated to the United States in 1940. Mauricio Kagel (b. 1931) is seen first and foremost as an "iconoclast, whose innova-tive musical and theatrical compositions

struck at the very heart of the cultural pre-tensions of Western German society" (Sandford 1999, 332). Giselher Klebe (b. 1925) was a major representative of operas based on literature and composed in a twelve-tone style. Carl Orff (1895–1982) is known even to a general audience. His name is often mentioned on classical radio stations, although his fame rests on one work only: *Carmina Burana*, first per-formed in 1937. In Germany, he is known through his contributions to music educa-tion, in which he encourages all children to participate in music-making by playing var-ious simple, and primarily rhythmic, instru-ments. Aribert Reimann (b. 1936), known in musical circles as an opera composer and pianist, was also an accompanist to Dietrich Fischer-Dieskau (see "Perform-ers," below). Wolfgang Rihm (b. 1952) is one of the promising new stars of contem-porary German classical music, especially in neo-tonal or neo-romantic music.

Arnold Schönberg (1874–1951) was the founder of the concept of twelve-tone mu-sic. Karlheinz Stockhausen (b. 1928) is one of the best-known composers of his gener-ation. Many of his serial and electronic compositions are seen as paradigms of the genre. His *Hymnen* for electronic sound, soloists, and (in the third part) orchestra combines forty national anthems in a plea for world peace. The third part was first performed in 1971 at Lincoln Center by the New York Philharmonic orchestra. Kurt Weill (1900–1950) helped to popularize jazz rhythms. Bernd Alois Zimmermann (1918–1970) was especially known for his brilliant musical collages. Udo Zimmermann (b. 1943) was successful—for a short time even on an international scale—with his opera *Die Weiße Rose* (The White Rose,

1986), based on the history of the Scholl siblings (see 1: Coming to Terms with the Past). (See also "*E-Musik*," "Performers," below.)

Concert halls: As Bettina Brockerhoff-MacDonald mentioned in her survey, "In Germany today there are approximately 121 government-subsidized opera houses and concert halls and 146 professional orchestras, as well as more than 700 music schools, hundreds of music festivals, music libraries, music councils and other musical organizations" (Sandford 1999, 110). Especially noteworthy of the postwar concert halls are the Neues Gewandhaus (literally, new cloth hall, named after its original function, namely as a place for the weavers' guilds to sell their products during the Middle Ages) in Leipzig and the Philharmonie in Berlin (see 9: City Planning and Architecture).

Conductors: The following short list includes primarily the names of conductors of the last six decades who are well known to a general audience. Karl Böhm (1894–1981) was a legend in his own time and always welcome as a guest conductor after he retired from his official music director posts in Dresden and Vienna. Christoph von Dohnányi (b. 1929), from a famous family of composers and politicians, led the Hamburg State Opera in the late 1970s and early 1980s and was conductor of the Cleveland Symphony until the new millennium. Wilhelm Furtwängler (1886–1954) was regarded as the leading and most controversial German conductor of his time. Herbert von Karajan (1908–1989), leader of the Berlin Philharmonic (since 1955) and the Vienna State Opera (since 1956), as well as director of the annual Salzburg Festival (since 1956), was the ultimate symbol of classical music in Germany. (see 4: Youth Culture and the World of Intellectuals; 5: Holidays and Local Festivals). Kurt Masur (b. 1927) was not only a leading figure in East German musical life but also involved in the upheavals of 1989 (see 1: From Two to One). After reunification, he became music director of the New York Philharmonic (1991–2002).

Dance Theater: In 1972, Gerhard Bohner (1936–1992) became the director of the newly founded dance ensemble at the state theater in Darmstadt, Hesse. He was the first to name his group *Tanztheater*. The concept of a "dance theater," in contrast to a traditional ballet, dates to the 1920s when Kurt Jooss (1901–1979) developed a new form of dance not based on the typical stylized repertoire of ballet steps and choreography but on gestures and movements found in everyday life. The essence of dance theater was a return to a more natural language of the body. In 1967, Pina Bausch (b. 1940) and Johann Kresnik (b. 1939) created their first dance productions, which are regarded as the beginning of postwar German dance theater. Other major dancers of the last seventy years include: Reinhild Hoffmann (b. 1943) in Bremen and Bochum, Susanne Linke (b. 1944) in Essen, and the English dancers Rosamund Gilmore and Vivienne Newport. A new generation included Wanda Golonka (b. 1958), Urs Dietrich (b. 1958), Joachim Schlömer (b. 1962), Daniel Goldin (b. 1958), Mark Sieczkarek (b. 1962), and Mitsuro Sasaki. The newest talent that has emerged in the last decade and critics regard as one of the most promising young dancers is Henrietta Horn (b. 1968), who has returned to the expressive dance style of the 1920s. In choreography, Sasha Waltz (b. 1963) has attracted much attention in the last few years. See also Ballet.

Directors: A few prominent theater directors are (for film directors see 7: Film): Ruth Berghaus (1927–1996); Harry Buckwitz (1904–1987); Frank Castorf (b. 1951); Jürgen Flimm (b. 1941); Gustav Gründgens (1899–1963); Johann Kresnik (b. 1939); Hans Neuenfels (b. 1941); Thomas Ostermeier (b. 1968); Peter Palitzsch (b. 1918); Claus Peymann (b. 1937); Erwin Piscator (1893–1966); Peer Raben (b. 1940); Einar Schleef (1944–2001); Cristoph Schlingensief (b. 1960); Peter Stein (b. 1937); George Tabori (b. 1914); Bernhard-Klaus Tragelehn (b. 1936); Robert Wilson (b. 1941); Fritz Wisten (1890–1962); and Peter Zadek (b. 1926). Tabori was also active as a playwright. One of his works, *Mein Kampf* (My Struggle), which premiered at the Wiener Akademietheater in 1987, was a tightrope act between memories and grotesque comical alienation. Wilson was a U.S. citizen but active in Germany.

Documentary drama: In addition to Rolf Hochhuth, Heinar Kipphardt, and Peter Weiss, who are generally considered the major playwrights of the genre, one should also include Hans Magnus Enzensberger, who wrote *Das Verhör von Habana* (Havana Hearing, 1970).

Dramaturge: In contrast to most theaters in English-speaking countries, in German theaters the dramaturge usually plays a pivotal role. He or she aids the artistic director in the selection of plays, helps to as-

sign directors, prepares information on the play for the actors and production staff, and contributes extensive program notes. The dramaturge is also closely involved with the actual production. Many theaters have special dramaturges for outreach programs to various community groups, especially schools. They inform the teachers about the productions of the upcoming season, distribute educational materials, and set up school partnerships for selected productions. A class can accompany the production, watch rehearsals, and talk with the production staff, actors, and directors after a performance. General discussions are also organized by the dramaturgical staff, often involving the press and theater managers.

E-Musik: Short for *Ernste Musik* (serious music). As the influential music critic and historian Kurt Pahlen stated, "Probably coming centuries will wonder why there had been these progressive people and institutions for contemporary music.... An age that does not understand and even rejects its own music has to be actually pretty sick" (Pahlen et al. 1996, 614). Annette Blühdorn summarized the situation: "Whilst leading composers were trying to find radically new, authentic forms of musical expression, public musical culture in the 1950s began to reestablish itself on the basis of traditional *E-Musik*." She saw modern music as an expression of "the fundamentally uprooting and destructive experience of modernity" (including the Holocaust) and the rejection as a suppression of this past (Sandford, 1999, 427–428). (See 1: Coming to Terms with the Past; "Composers," above, and "Performers," below.)

Epic theater: A term used by Bertolt Brecht to stress the "epic" qualities of his plays and productions in opposition to the traditional theater of his time, which he called "dramatic" or "Aristotelian." Sometimes he had the actors speak directly to the audience to avoid allowing them to enter the illusionary world of the stage and identify with the characters. His aim was to awaken the critical faculties of the audience, who would always regard the play as a play—that is, a demonstration of a point made by the playwright. (See also "V-Effekt," below.)

Festivals: Important theater and music festivals in the German-speaking countries are as follows. The Bayreuther Festspiele was founded 1876 for the exclusive production of works by Richard Wagner (1813–1883). Since its reopening in 1951 under the directorship of Wagner's heirs, it has been maintained as a cultural mecca for high society and, to some extent, for artistic innovation. The Darmstadt/Kranichstein International Holiday Courses for New Music (Darmstädter/Kranichsteiner Internationale Ferienkurse für Neue Musik), founded in 1946, were the most influential postwar events for contemporary music during the first two decades of their existence. Organized by the Internationale Musikinstitut Darmstadt (IMD, International Music Institute Darmstadt), they still attract many young composers and musicians. Mülheimer Theatertage is held in Mülheim, North-Rhine Westphalia, in May and June each year. It typically focuses on playwrights and their plays (only contemporary German plays are invited) rather than directors and their productions. The Munich Biennale, founded in 1988, is an important platform for musical experimentation. The Passionsspiele (Passion Play) in Oberammergau, Bavaria, has been staged almost every ten years since 1634. The citizens made a vow in 1633 to put on these performances each decade in order to prevent the pestilence that had almost destroyed their community. Ruhrfestspiele Recklinghausen was founded in 1948 for the workers in the Ruhr area. The intention was to introduce a wider and more general audience to classical as well as modern theater. The Salzburger Festspiele was founded by Max Reinhardt in 1920. Since 1964, German productions have competed with each other at the Theatertreffen (Meeting of Theaters) in Berlin.

Journals/yearbooks: They are the best sources for up-to-date information on theater in the German-speaking world. They contain reports of productions, theater reviews, festival schedules, photos of performances, biographies of actors and directors, and sometimes preprints of plays. The best-known journal in the FRG is *Theater heute* (Theater Today). It was continued after unification. The equivalent journal in the GDR was *Theater der Zeit* (Theater of the Times). The leading yearbook is the *Deutsche Bühnenjahrbuch* (German Theater Almanac) published in Hamburg by the Verlag der Bühnenschriften-Vertriebsgesellschaft (publisher of the distributing company for theatrical texts) since 1889.

Krautrock: The term is used today by the general public in a very generic way for German rock bands in general. Experts, in contrast, limit the term often to a more specific experimental rock music scene of the 1960s and 1970s including such bands as Amon Düül II, Can, Faust, Kraftwerk, Neu!, Popol Vuh, and Tangerine Dream. (See "Bands" above).

Liedermacher: Song writers. In addition to the Liedermacher mentioned in the text, the most popular were Georg Danzer, Konstantin Wecker, Klaus Hoffmann, Kristin Horn, Ina Deter, and the feminist group Schneewittchen (Snow White). As Richard J. Rundell wrote: "Chanson Folklore International festivals at Burg Waldeck in the Hunsrück were epochal events from 1964 to 1969 for the identity of German *Liedermacher*" (Sandford 1999, 377). Rundell also listed two additional groups: (1) the song writers with more subjective and personal texts who were popular: Rainhard Fendrich, Ludwig Hirsch, Herbert Grönemeyer, Georg Danzer, and Christof Stühlin; and (2) a small number of right-wing groups of the early 1990s: Endsieg (Final Victory), Störkraft (Jamming Power), Volkszorn (People's Rage), and Böhse Onkelz (Bad Uncles) (ibid., 377; see also "Bands," above, and "Performers," below).

Neue Deutsche Welle: New German Wave, a short-lived trend at the end of the 1970s and beginning of the 1980s based on traditional beats. It influenced German rock through its naive (sometimes funny) songs and simple Schlager-like musical structures (Graf 2002, 267).

New subjectivity: The term, reminiscent of the *Neue Sachlichkeit* (new Objectivity) in the art of the 1920s, could actually better be described as "New Sensibility" or "New Inwardness" because it is concerned primarily with personal experience and the nature of individual identity. The main rep-

resentatives of the approach for the theater were Botho Strauß, Thomas Bernhard, and Peter Handke.

Opera: The operatic tradition boomed after the war because of state subsidies, although the end of the war also marked the end of a musical era. The deaths of Richard Strauss (1864–1949) and Hans Pfitzner (1869–1949) in 1949 marked the end of a late and post-Romantic tradition, but their works and the operatic canon remained a staple in the repertoire of opera houses. In the FRG, experiments were encouraged, but much of the audience resisted. Cologne was an exception and became a major musical capital for new opera in a way that paralleled its importance for modern art (see 9: Visual Arts). In the GDR, satire was sometimes used to test the boundaries of state tolerance.

Orchestras: As Jonathan West pointed out, "The *International Who's Who in Music* lists 169 orchestras [in Germany] (as against 10 for Austria, 19 for Switzerland and 45 for France)" (Sandford 1999, 457). Most of them were founded in the nineteenth century. Even small towns in Germany are sometimes blessed with an international group of players. The leading orchestras are the Berlin Philharmonic, founded in 1863; the Dresden Philharmonic, 1871; the Hamburg Philarmonic, 1829; the Leipzig Gewandhaus Orchestra (literally, cloth-hall orchestra), which grew out of the Leipzig Collegium Musicum, originally directed by Georg Philip Telemann (1681–1767) and Johann Sebastian Bach (1685–1750); the Munich Philharmonic, 1924; the North German Radio Symphony Orchestra, 1951; the Sächsische Staatskapelle Dresden (Saxonian State Orchestra of Dresden), which goes back to the sixteenth century; and the Vienna Philharmonic, 1842.

Performers: In *Ernste Musik* (*E-Musik*), or serious music, among the many great singers, at least five need to be highlighted, especially because their names have become part of the German musical subconscious. Dietrich Fischer-Dieskau (b. 1925), who had one of the most outstanding voices of the postwar years, popularized the German *Lied* (art song) tradition with his songs by Franz Schubert (1797–1828), Robert Schumann (1810–1856), and Hugo Wolf (1860–1903). His popularity can be measured by the fact that his name was featured in a popular mystery novel, *Der Hahn ist tot* (The Rooster Is Dead, 1991) by Ingrid Noll (b. 1935; see 6: Popular and Belletristic Literature). In that work, a dog is given the name Dieskau because of his sonorous bark. Anneliese Rothenberger (b. 1924) became the spokeswoman for classical music for a general audience with her *Evergreen* shows on TV (see 7: Radio and Television). The tenor Rudolf Schock (1915–1966) was regarded by many in the first two decades after the war as the German Caruso. Elisabeth Schwarzkopf (b. 1915) was the best-known German soprano in the 1940s and 1950s. In addition to these earlier singers, at least one young classical instrumentalist should be mentioned: Anne-Sophie Mutter (b. 1963). At age seven she won the federal music contest, and again in 1974. She was exempted from school and at the age of thirteen invited by Herbert von Karajan to play with the Berlin Philharmonic. Concerts with all major orchestras and many honors have followed. (See also "Composers" and "*E-Musik*," above.)

There are also a few performers in *U-Musik* (short for *Unterhaltungsmusik* [light music]) who could be regarded as the "classical" singers of the genre. Above all is Marlene Dietrich (1901–1992), the embodiment of the *chanteuse*, an icon. There are others who could be considered the more "regular" performers (including the *Liedermacher* [see above]). The Austrian Peter Alexander (Peter Alexander Neumeyer, b. 1926) became popular in Austria as well as in Germany as an actor, singer of Schlager, and showmaster. Wolf Biermann (b. 1936) was a multitalented artist and political activist. His life has become a legend. He was a singer, a composer, a writer, and a performer. He moved at the age of seventeen to East Germany, worked at the Berliner Ensemble (see 8: Theater and Dance), and became—together with his friend Robert Havemann—a leader of GDR dissidents. He expatriated in 1976. In the FRG, he was controversial. Peter Barker mentioned in an article Biermann's support of the Gulf War in 1991. He apparently linked "the supply of chemical weapons from West Germany to Iraq with Nazi atrocities against the Jews" (Sandford 1999, 61). Roy Black (1943–1991) was one of the top popular singers in the 1960s, loved especially by middle-aged women with daughters and, therefore, was often called the favorite son-in-law of the nation. He is on the list of the 100 Best Germans (Knopp et al. 2003), as is Dieter Bohlen (b. 1954), who is regarded as one of the most successful German composers and who made the group Modern Talking the most controversial pop group in the 1980s and 1990s.

Eva Briegel (b. 1978) is the lead singer of the band Juli. Howard Carpendale (b. 1946), born in Durban, South Africa, started his German career in the late 1960s with German versions of popular songs and mellow, soft rock ballads. In 1970, he won the first prize at the German Schlager festival. Thereafter, he began to write and compose his own songs. He ended his career officially in 2003. Franz Josef Degenhardt (b. 1931) is one of the founders of the Liedermacher movement. Although he completed his doctorate in law, he only practiced for a few years and then devoted himself to composing songs, writing novels, performing, and being politically active. Jürgen Drews (b. 1945, although he used to give 1948 as his birthdate) began his musical career in 1967 and his solo career in 1976. His bucolic, idyllic Schlager gave him a certain popularity. In Majorca, he became a symbol for German tourism. Falco (Johann Hölzel, b. 1957) helped to make NDW an international success and stood in the international limelight briefly himself. Conny Froboess (Cornelia Froboess, b. 1943) became a child star in 1951 with her song "Pack' die Badehose ein" (Take the Swimsuit Along). A few years later, she and Peter Kraus were seen as Germany's dream couple in movies such as *Wenn die Conny mit dem Peter* (When Conny Is Together with Peter). In 1962, Conny won the Schlager festival, but with the arrival of the Beatles, her time as a singer was over. She devoted her later life to acting in films and on stage.

Herbert Grönemeyer (b. 1956), whose birth certificate lists him as Herbert Arthur Wigley Clamor Grönemeyer, grew up in a well-situated middle-class family with the standard piano lessons as a teenager. During his music and law studies, he was invited by Peter Zadek (see 8: Theater and Dance) to work at the Bochumer Schauspielhaus (Bochum theater) as a musical director and actor. After a successful beginning at the theater and later as film actor (especially his role as a young officer in the film *Das Boot;* see 7: Film) and as a member of the jazz-rock big band Ocean, he began his solo career in 1985 and became one of Germany's most successful rock artists. His "4630 Bochum" was on the national list of hits for seventy-nine weeks. His rare performances were sold out—in 1991, he sang for 700,000 people in Berlin at the large Open Air Festival. After a break following the deaths of his wife and his brother, who both died from cancer, he focused even more on his work and continued his career with a new version of Trio's hit song "Da Da Da." In 2000, his Hannover concert, in which he performed together with the Hannover Pops orchestra, was filmed.

Nina Hagen (b. 1955), the stepdaughter of Wolf Biermann (see "Performers," above), became in 1976, after her immigration to West Germany, the undisputed queen of German punk rock. Heino (Heinz-Georg Kramm, b. 1938), whose trademarks are his blond hair and a pair of sunglasses, was voted in 2003 into the group of the 100 best Germans (Knopp et al. 2003). This shows that he is not only a favorite with grandmothers but also the younger generation. In 1965, when he began his career, he was regarded—in the words of Matthew T. Grant—as "the healthy antidote to fashionable beat hysteria." But forty years later, he is both "a caricature and pseudomod icon of *Schlager* culture" (Sandford 1999, 541). Heintje (since 1976 Hein Simons, b. 1955) began his Schlager career when he was twelve years old and soon had several gold and platinum records. At fifty, in 2005, he was still going strong. Ted Herold (b. 1942) was one of the musicians to get rock 'n' roll rolling in Germany. Max Herre (b. 1973) is regarded by some as Germany's best rapper.

Hubert Kah (b. 1961) was able to place high on the German hit charts in 1982 during the NDW era, but unable to repeat his initial successes. He produced several more creative works, even experimenting with crossover music, producing a record together with the Vienna Philharmonic in 1996. Peter Kraus (b. 1939) began his career in 1954 as a young film actor. The music industry saw in him a German Elvis Presley. Next to Ted Herold, he helped to establish rock 'n' roll in the country. He and Conny Froboess became the most admired singers and film actors of the late 1950s. Stefan Krawczyk (b. 1955) is a Liedermacher, writer, and cabaret artist. He began his musical career in 1980. After his songs were forbidden in the GDR, he was only able to perform in churches, and in 1988 he was exiled. His songs often have a lyrical quality, and his stated goal is to reach the totality of a human—not only the political aspect. Heinz Rudolf Kunze (b. 1956) was called by the newspaper *Hamburger Morgenpost* "*Der Preuße des Pop*" (The Prussian of Pop). By others he was seen as the stiff intellectual, the *Oberlehrer* (high-school teacher), or Germany's pop poet par excellence. He showed his talents in various areas—as writer, journalist, and poet—and experimented with rock and entertaining pop. His profuse output includes not only songs but also many volumes of poetry and translations of musicals.

Although Kunze was not included in the list of the 100 best Germans (see Knopp et al. 2003), James Last (b. 1929), the great old man of big band music in Germany, and Udo Lindenberg were. Udo Lindenberg (b. 1946), the "self-proclaimed godfather of German rock" (Sandford 1999, 378), has had his share of awards and honors. His trademarks are not only his fedora but also a healthy display of ego (see 8: Music). As Matthew T. Grant remarked, "His career has spanned more than two decades and his live performances have become legendary for their spectacular excess" (ibid., 378). Peter Maffay (Peter Alexander Makkay, b. 1949) was born in Romania but came to Germany in 1963 and established himself as one of the great German rock singers. Heike Makatsch (b. 1971) at first studied politics and sociology at the university and took on an apprenticeship as a dressmaker. These attempts at a career were unsuccessful, however, and from 1995 to 1996, she was presenter of the German Chartshow Bravo TV. Her career continued as a VJ, talk-show host, and interviewer of celebrities for Vivam, the German MTV clone. In 2001, she was named as one of European film's rising stars in a European Film promotion. Markus (Markus Mörl, b. 1959) became known briefly for his NDW hit "Ich will Spaß" (I Want to Have Fun, 1982). Marusha (family name: Gleiss, b. 1966) became a top DJ. Her DJ career began in 1991. In 1994, her own techno hits won platinum and gold, and in 1995 she was awarded several prizes. Reinhard Mey (b. 1942) was one of Germany's best-known singer-songwriters following his debut in the mid-1960s, but his songs are regarded by some as bordering on Schlager and lacking in political commitment. Marius Müller-Westernhagen (b. 1948), celebrated as "*Rock-Triumphator*" and "*Marius Müller Superstar*," was Germany's most successful rock singer. He combined this talent with a career as a film actor in the 1980s. After his marriage in 1990, he withdrew for a few years from the public. His comeback was greeted with mixed reviews. Many saw in him just a well-versed professional pleasing the masses.

Xavier Naidoo (b. 1971) is a German soul singer. Nena (Gabriele Susanne Kerner, b. 1960) was the "girlie" of 1980, the star of NDW. She scored several hits in the early 1980s and the critics raved. Her unforgettable "99 Luftballons" (99 Balloons) became a hit in Germany, Great Britain, and the United States. Several ups and downs in her musical career and her private life led, however, to a successful comeback in 2002. Nicole (b. 1964, last name: Hohloch) was the first German to win the Grand Prix d'Eurovision de la Chanson (Grand Prize of the Eurovision Song Contest) in 1982 with her song "Ein bisschen Frieden" (A bit of Peace). She is on the list of the 100 Best Germans (Knopp et al. 2003). Kai Niemann (b. 1973) founded his first band in 1991. His biggest hit so far has been "Im Osten" (In the East). Tilmann Otto (b. 1968) sings under the name "Gentleman." He is from Cologne but sings reggae. Freddy Quinn (b. 1931), a son of an Irish salesman and an Austrian mother, was raised in New York, then in Vienna, where he was adopted by a Viennese aristocrat. His life was colorful: He was a school drop-out, a circus worker, a sailor, a member of the Foreign Legion, an entertainer in Hamburg's red-light district, and finally a top Schlager star. One of his big hits was "Heimatlos" (Homeless).

Stefan Raab (b. 1966) has become a cult figure for the new "fun generation." Originally trained as a butcher to take over the family business, he began his career in 1993 as a television moderator. The following years were filled with provocative ideas and hit songs. His newest idea was the "Bundesvision Song Contest" in 2005 for ambitious young musicians. Bill Ramsey (b. 1931) came to Germany as a GI and worked at the American Forces Network. Soon he was part of the Frankfurt jazz scene as a vocalist. In 1957, he settled in Germany for good. Peter Schilling (b. 1961) achieved several hits in the 1980s and 1990s—some overseas, especially in the United States and Japan. His best-known NDW song is "Major Tom." Caterina Valente (b. 1931) is known in Germany primarily as a Schlager singer, but her repertoire is much wider. She has recorded songs in twelve languages and is primarily an interpreter of South American music. Hannes Wader (b. 1942) began his Liedermacher career in 1969. His songs were based on traditional German folk songs, and his repertoire also included songs based on German Romantic poets as well as political songs. His latest CD contains only Schubert songs. Konstantin Wecker (b. 1947) has achieved recognition in various areas: as Liedermacher, as composer for film music (for example, *Die Weiße Rose*, 1983; see 7: Film), and as actor and poet. Bettina Wegner (b. 1947) returned to West Berlin in 1983 after encountering increased difficulties in the GDR because of her various protests and songs. WestBam (Maximilian Lenz, b. 1965) takes his name from an abbreviation of his home state, Westphalia, and his African role model, Afrika Bambaataa. Starting in 1983 he became Germany's most successful and popular DJ. He is also cofounder of Berlin's Indie Dance label, Low Spirit. In 1996, he received the highly esteemed cultural award from Berlin's biggest daily paper (Berliner Zeitung, BZ). Among his big successes are "Sunshine," the official Love Parade Hymn of 1997.

Playwrights: Modern playwrights of some of the favorite plays in the German repertoire (and a few additional important plays not mentioned in the text) include the following. Thomas Bernhard (1931–1989) (*Der Weltverbesserer* [Starry-Eyed Idealist], 1980, with a starring role for Bernhard's friend, the actor Bernhard Minetti; *Der Theatermacher* [The Theater Maker], Salzburg, 1985; *Heldenplatz* [Place of Heroes], Wiener Burgtheater, 1988, directed by Claus Peymann, a critical look at anti-Semitism and the authoritarian attitude in Austrian society, which provoked public protests); Wolfgang Borchert (1921–1947); Volker Braun (b. 1939); Bertolt Brecht (1898–1956); Tankred Dorst (b. 1925) (*Parzifal*, Hamburg Thalia Theater, 1983, directed by Robert Wilson); Friedrich Dürrenmatt (1921–1990, Swiss); Rainer Werner Fassbinder (1945–1982); Marieluise Fleißer (1901–1974); Max Frisch (1911–1991, Swiss); Günter Grass (b. 1927); Peter Hacks (1928–2003); Peter Handke (b. 1942, Austrian); Gerhart Hauptmann (1862–1946); Christoph Hein (b. 1944); Rolf Hochhuth (b. 1931) (*Die Juristen* [The Lawyers], Hamburg, 1980; *Unbefleckte Empfängnis* [Immaculate Conception], West Berlin, 1989); Elfriede Jelinek (b. 1946); Heinar Kipphardt (1922–1982); Karl Kraus (1874–1936); Franz Xaver Kroetz (b. 1946) (*Nicht Fisch nicht Fleisch* [Neither Fish nor Meat], Düsseldorf, 1981); Harald Waldemar Mueller (b. 1934); Heiner Müller (1929–1995) (*Germania Tod in Berlin* [Germania Death in Berlin], Munich, 1978; *Quartett*, Bochum, 1982); Franz Schönthan Edler von Pernwald (1849–1913) and Paul Schönthan Edler von Pernwald (1853–1905) (brothers who wrote the popular farce *Der Raub der Sabinerinnen* [Rape of the Sabine Women], 1884); Ulrich Plenzdorf (b. 1945); Gaston Salvatore (b. 1941, Chilean) (*Stalin*, West Berlin, 1987); Martin Sperr (b. 1922); Rudi Strahl (1931–2001); Botho Strauß (b. 1944) (*Kalldewey, Farce*, Hamburg, 1982); Erwin Strittmatter (1912–1994); Peter Turrini (b. 1944, Austrian); Martin Walser (b. 1927); Frank Wedekind (1864–1918); Peter Weiss (1916–1982) (*Trotzki im Exil*, 1970, in Düsseldorf, which caused a confrontation between the political leaders and the artistic avant-garde); Carl Zuckmayer (1896–1977).

Political theater: Although the concept is as old as theater itself, the term in Germany goes back to Erwin Piscator's book *Das politische Theater* (The Political Theater, 1929). In the modern German-speaking world of theater, the term applies primarily to works by Bertolt Brecht, Max Frisch, Peter Weiss, Rolf Hochhuth, and Heinar Kipphardt.

Productions: German productions are prepared meticulously; rehearsal time is usually about six weeks. Michael Patterson and Michael Huxley remarked: "Once the curtain opens, the stage will usually be seen to be much larger than in a British theatre, the sets more opulent, the lighting more complex. The choice of play will not have been limited by an 'economic' size of cast, and the actors will perform with intelligence and discipline but will often lack that winning presence of their Anglo-Saxon counterparts, whose future livelihood, after all, depends on their need to please" (Patterson et al. 1998, 229). No doubt some would argue with this final comment.

Protest songs: They were a product primarily of the 1960s and 1970s and part of the revolt against the parent generation (see 4: Youth Culture and the World of Intellectuals). Protests were directed against the destruction of the environment and thereby related to the Green movement (see 10: Consumer Culture versus Green Awareness), against war, against restrictive laws, and, in the 1980s, against unemployment. The way unification was achieved was the focus of later songwriters (see 1: From Two to One).

Punk: In imitation of the British punk movement, German punk culture developed in the late 1970s in urban centers. It was primarily an expression of opposition without presenting alternatives. Bands such as Die Toten Hosen and Die Ärzte are affiliated with this movement (see "Bands," above).

Record labels: Electrola, Polydor, and Telefunken were—both before World War II and in the postwar years—the leading German record companies, but they had a difficult time reaching an international audience. The most influential German punk label is Zickzack Records. IC Records (Innovative Communication), owned by Klaus Schulze, became important for the NDW.

Repertory theater: The repertory system is common to most German theaters. It requires constant set changes, much storage space for props and costumes, and sufficient rehearsal space. It is only possible with a large standing ensemble of actors, directors, musicians, and dancers. Subsidies provide a certain security for artists (in contrast to the typical hire-and-fire system prevalent in Britain and the United States)—the expectation of security being a feature characteristic of German society (see 2: Stereotypes and Prejudices). As Michael Patterson and Michael Huxley

pointed out, these subsidies amount to "about seven times the amount of public funding the United States provides for all the arts, and the Berlin Opera House alone receives almost as much as the British Arts Council has at its disposal for all the theatres it supports. The German theatergoer pays normally about a third of the actual economic cost of a theatre ticket, and in the former German Democratic Republic it was only about a tenth" (Patterson et al. 1998, 228). In the opinion of many critics, especially from an Anglo-Saxon cultural background, these subsidies are not always beneficial to artistic endeavors. Richard Lord wrote: "The *Stadttheater* (Municipal theatres) are top heavy in their distribution of government largesse, resulting in a superficially impressive glitz and much stretching room for the artists' imagination" (Lord 2004, 219). German critics and scholars as well as German theater professionals might not agree with these opinions.

Schlager: Popular song. The term is related to another: *Schnulze* (tearjerker), which is a subcategory of the genre. Actually, the name Schlager means "hit." Its origins are seen in popular melodies and operettas of the late nineteenth century as well as in the cabaret and operetta tradition of the 1920s and 1930s with singers such as Marlene Dietrich. For many music lovers, Schlager (and especially the sentimental version, the Schnulze, or schmaltzy pop tune) is synonymous with kitsch. In this vein, Schlager can be seen as a superficial popularization of other musical genres, such as folk music. (See also Neue Deutsche Welle.)

Schwank: Farce. The best-known stages for farce are the Millowitsch Theater in

Cologne, the Ohnsorg Theater in Hamburg, and the Komödienstadl in Munich.

Song writers: See "*Liedermacher*," above.

Stage designers: Among the best-known modern German stage designers are César Klein (1876–1954), Ernst Stern (1876–1954), Emil Pirchan, Ludwig Sievert (1887–1966), Josef Fenneker (1895–1956), Rochus Gliese (1891–1978), Caspar Neher (1897–1962), Theo Otto (1904–1968), Franz Mertz (1897–1966), Wilfried Minks (b. 1931), Erich Wonder (b. 1944), and Karl-Ernst Herrmann (b. 1936).

Techno music: This style is regarded as a primarily German musical development on the border of E-Musik and U-Musik. Karlheinz Stockhausen's musical experiments played a crucial role in its development, influencing, above all, the group Kraftwerk. Besides being a musical style, the term has been transferred to a general cultural phenomenon.

Theaters: With such a wealth of theaters in Germany, it is impossible to list all of them, but a few, particularly those in Berlin, deserve special mention. Some regard that city as the indisputable capital of German theater. The Freie Volksbühne (Free People's Stage), with its very special history of being founded in 1890 by Social Democrats to provide easy theater access for the working class, achieved international fame and controversy in the mid-1960s with the world premieres of documentary dramas by Rolf Hochhuth, Heinar Kipphardt, and Peter Weiss, directed by Erwin Piscator. The Schaubühne am Lehninerplatz (Theater on Lehnin Square, originally located on Halleschen Ufer—the riverbank of the Halle) was and is known for its cutting-edge performances. The Theater des Westens (The Theater of the West, a musical theater) is known instead for its popular shows. The GRIPS Theater is regarded by many as "Germany's foremost theatre company for children and young people" (Sandford 1999, 267).

The Deutsches Theater (German Theater) has been renowned since the outgoing nineteenth century and linked to many famous German artistic directors. Therefore, it was very appropriate that it was the first German theater to reopen after 1945. It was also the home of the Berliner Ensemble (BE) until the group moved into the Theater am Schiffbauerdamm in 1954. Bertolt Brecht and his wife, Helene Weigel, turned this new venue into a theater legend with their "model" performances of Brecht's plays, radical adaptations of works from the classical canon, and promotion of GDR playwrights (for example, Erwin Strittmatter). Although the theater has had its ups and downs since Brecht's death, many names connected to the BE play an important role in German theater history: Benno Besson, Peter Palitzsch, Manfred Weckwerth, Ruth Berghaus, Heiner Müller, Peter Zadek, and since 1999 Claus Peymann.

Outside Berlin, the top theaters are: the *Deutsches Schauspielhaus* (German Theater) and the *Thalia Theater* in Hamburg, the *Schauspiel Frankfurt* (Frankfurt Theater), the *Theater am Turm (TaT*, Theater by the Tower) in Frankfurt, which was closed in 2004 and reopened later under new management, the *Schauspielhaus Düsseldorf* (Düsseldorf Theater), the *Nationaltheater* (National Theater) in Mannheim, the *Kammerspiel* (Studio Theater) and the *Bayerisches Staatsschauspiel* (Bavarian State Theater) in Munich, *Schauspielhaus Bochum* (Bochum Theater, for a long time ranked as one of Germany's most innovative theaters), the *Schauspielhaus Leipzig* (Leipzig Theater), the *Deutsches Nationaltheater* (German National Theater) in Weimar.

V-Effekt: Bertolt Brecht's theory of drama and staging techniques has influenced a whole generation of postwar theater designers, performers, and directors, though he developed it even before World War II. His notion of *Verfremdung*, translated by some as "alienation," by others as "distantiation," has as its goal to make the audience look critically at the issues presented to them on stage and not let themselves be emotionally overwhelmed by the performance.

Volksstück: Literally, people's play. Going back to prewar writers such as Marieluise Fleißer (1901–1974) and Ödön von Horváth (1901–1938), this genre has become a staple on German stages through the works of Martin Sperr (b. 1944), especially his *Jagdszenen aus Niederbayern* (Hunting Scenes from Lower Bavaria, 1966); Rainer Werner Fassbinder (1945–1982), who introduced Fleißer again to a German public; and Franz Xaver Kroetz (b. 1946).

Volkstümliche Musik: Folkloristic music. In contrast to genuine *Volksmusik*, the folkloristic music that has become extremely popular since the late 1980s (on, for example, TV shows such as *Musikantenstadl* [musicians' shed] with Karl Moik) is seen by music critics and scholars as merely reproducing stereotypes. It is thereby related to the German Schlager.

Additional Readings

Bärnreuther, Andrea, and Peter-Klaus Schuster, eds. *Das XX. Jahrhundert. Kunst, Kultur, Politik und Gesellschaft in Deutschland.* Herausgegeben im Rahmen der Jahrhundertausstellung der Nationalgalerie Berlin "Das XX. Jahrhundert. Ein Jahrhundert Kunst in Deutschland." Köln: DuMont, 1999.

Beson, Manfred. *Lexikon Pop. Ein Sachwort-ABC der Unterhaltungsmusik von Operette und Schlager bis Folk, Jazz und Rock.* Wiesbaden: Breitkopf und Härtel, 1977.

Brauneck, Manfred, and Gérard Schneilin, eds. *Theaterlexikon I. Begriffe und Epochen, Bühnen und Ensembles,* 4th ed. Reinbek bei Hamburg: Rowohlt, 2001.

Calandra, Denis. *New German Dramatists.* New York: Grove Press, 1983.

Cope, Julian. *A Krautrocksampler: One Head's Guide to the Great Kosmische Musik, 1968 Onwards.* Calne: Head Heritage, 1996.

Dahlhaus, Carl, and Hermann Danuser, eds. *Neues Handbuch der Musikwissenschaft.* 13 vols. Vol. 7: *Die Musik des 20. Jahrhunderts.* Laaber: Laaber Verlag, 1984.

Dahlhaus, Carl, and Hans Heinrich Eggebrecht, eds. *Brockhaus-Riemann Musiklexikon.* Mainz: Atlantis-Schott, 2001.

Dallach, Christoph. "The Sound of Music." *The Germans. Sixty Years after the War.* Spiegel. Special International Edition 4 (2005), 194–196.

Durrani, Osman. "Popular music in the German-speaking world." *Contemporary German Cultural Studies.* Ed. Alison Phipps. Oxford: Oxford University Press, 2002, 197–218.

Farin, Klaus, Henning Flad, and Frauke Stuhl, eds. *Reaktionäre Rebellen. Rechtsextreme Musik in Deutschland.* Archiv der Jugendkulturen. Bad Tölz: Tilsner, 2001.

Fischer, Hermann. *Volkslied, Schlager, Evergreen. Studien über das lebendige Singen aufgrund von Untersuchungen im Kreis Reutlingen.* Tübingen: Tübinger Vereinigung für Volkskunde, 1965.

Fischer-Lichte, Erika. *Die Entdeckung des Zuschauers. Paradigmenwechsel auf dem Theater des 20. Jahrhunderts.* Tübingen and Basel: Francke, 1997.

―――. *Kurze Geschichte des deutschen Theaters*. Tübingen and Basel: Francke, 1999.

Fischer-Lichte, Erika, Doris Kolesch, and Christel Weiler, eds. *Transformationen: Theater der neunziger Jahre*. Berlin: Theater der Zeit, 1999.

Fischer-Lichte, Erika, Friedemann Kreuder, and Isabel Pflug, eds. *Theater seit den 60er Jahren. Grenzgänge der Neo-Avantgarde*. Tübingen and Basel: Francke, 1998.

Flood, John L., ed. *Kurz bevor der Vorhang fiel: Zum Theater der DDR*. Amsterdam: Rodopi, 1990.

Goethe-Institut, ed. *Tanztheater heute. Dreißig Jahre deutsche Tanzgeschichte*. Seelze/Hannover: Kallmeyer, 1999.

Graf, Christian. *Rocklexikon Deutschland*. Berlin: Schwarzkopf und Schwarzkopf, 2002.

―――. *Das NDW Lexikon*. Berlin: Schwarzkopf und Schwarzkopf, 2003.

Griffiths, Paul. *Modern Music: A Concise History*, rev. ed. London: Thames and Hudson, 1994.

Harenberg Schauspielführer, 3., vollständig überarbeitete und erweiterte Auflage. Geleitwort von Will Quadflieg. Dortmund: Harenberg, 2003.

Hasche, Christa, Traute Schölling, Joachim Fiebach, and Ralph Hammerthaler, eds. *Theater in der DDR: Chronik und Positionen*. Berlin: Henschel, 1994.

Innes, Christopher. *Modern German Drama*. Cambridge: Cambridge University Press, 1979.

Irmer, Thomas, and Matthias Schmidt. *Die Bühnenrepublik. Theater in der DDR*. Berlin: Alexander Verlag, 2003.

Jansen, Wolfgang, ed. *Unterhaltugstheater in Deutschland. Geschichte, Ästhetik, Ökonomie*. Berlin: Weidler Buchverlag, 1995.

Kayser, Dietrich. *Schlager, das Lied als Ware. Untersuchungen zu einer Kategorie der Illusionsindustrie unter besonderer Berücksichtigung des Musikmarktes der Bundesrepublik Deutschland*. Stuttgart: Metzler, 1975.

Klotz, Volker. *Bürgerliches Lachtheater. Komödie, Posse, Schwank, Operette*. Reinbek: Rowohlt, 1987.

Krekow, Sebastian, Jens Steiner, and Matthias Taupitz. *Das Neue HipHop Lexikon*. Berlin: Schwarzkopf und Schwarzkopf, 2003.

Kühn, Volker, ed. *Hierzulande. Kabarett in dieser Zeit. 1970–2000*. Neuausgabe. Frankfurt am Main: Rogner und Bernhard bei Zweitausendundeins, 2001.

―――, ed. *Wir sind so frei. Kabarett in Westdeutschland. 1945–1970*. Neuausgabe. Frankfurt am Main: Rogner und Bernhard bei Zweitausendundeins, 2001.

Lennartz, Knut. *Vom Aufbruch zur Wende. Theater in der DDR*. Seelze, Velber: Erhard Friedrich, 1992.

Metzger, Werner. *Schlager. Versuch einer Gesamtdarstellung unter besonderer Berücksichtigung des Musikmarktes der Bundesrepublik Deutschland*. Tübingen: Tübinger Vereinigung für Volkskunde, 1975.

Mühe, Hansgeorg. *Unterhaltungsmusik. Ein geschichtlicher Überblick*. Hamburg: Kovac, 1996.

Niketta, Reiner, and Eva Volke. *Rock und Pop in Deutschland*. Essen: Klartext, 1994.

Nyffeler, Max. *Liedermacher in der Bundesrepublik*. Bonn: Inter Nationes, 1978–1983. With six audio cassettes.

Patterson, Michael. *German Theatre Today: Post-War Theatre in West and East Germany*. London: Pitman, 1976.

Patterson, Michael, and Michael Huxley. "German drama, theatre, and dance." *The Cambridge Companion to Modern German Culture*. Ed. Eva Kolinsky and Wilfried van der Will. Cambridge: Cambridge University Press, 1998, 213–232.

Profitlich, Ulrich, ed. *Dramatik der DDR*. Frankfurt: Suhrkamp, 1987.

Schlicher, Susanne. *TanzTheater. Traditionen und Freiheiten. Pina Bausch, Gerhard Bohner, Reinhild Hoffmann, Hans Kresnik, Susanne Linke*. Reinbek bei Hamburg: Rowohlt, 1987. (Rowohlts Enzyklopädie/Kulturen und Ideen).

Schmidt, Jochen. *Tanzgeschichte des 20. Jahrhunderts in einem Band*. Mit 101 choreographischen Porträts. Berlin: Henschel, 2002.

Schmidt-Mühlisch, Lothar. *Affentheater: Bühnenkrise ohne Ende?* Ungekürzte, leicht

veränderte Ausgabe. Frankfurt/Main and
Berlin: Ullstein, 1992.

Schwab, Lothar, and Richard Weber.
Theaterlexikon, 2d ed. Frankfurt: Cornelsen
Scriptor, 1992.

Sebald, Winfried Georg. *A Radical Stage:
Theatre in Germany in the 1970s and
1980s*. Oxford: Berg, 1988.

Simhandl, Peter. *Theatergeschichte in einem
Band*, Aktualisierte Auflage. Mit Beiträgen
von Franz Wille und Grit van Dyk. Berlin:
Henschel Verlag, 2001.

Stuber, Petra. *Spielräume und Grenzen:
Studien zum DDR-Theater*. Berlin: Ch.
Links, 1998.

Sucher, C. Bernd, ed. *Theater Lexikon.
Autoren, Regisseure, Schauspieler,
Dramaturgen, Bühnenbildner, Kritiker*, 2nd
ed. München: Deutscher Taschenbuchverlag,
1999.

9

Visual Arts and Architecture

Visual Arts

Before World War II, Germany was a mecca for artists and contributed much on an international scale: *Jugendstil* (known as Art Nouveau in the French- and English-speaking world), Expressionism, Dadaism, and Bauhaus. Even after World War I, art played an important role—particularly as a means of coping with the horror of the battles in the trenches and the tremendous suffering, as depicted in the paintings of Otto Dix. Immediately after World War II, however, the situation regarding art can best be described as a void: Much of the art that had not been destroyed had disappeared; and the atrocities of World War II seemed to many artists incompatible with the sensitivity of art. Yet, at the same time, art was called upon to help with the rebuilding of a new state and with the challenge to keep the memory of these atrocities alive—to be an eternal reminder of human destructiveness. One of the most convincing works, an icon of the aftermath of the war, was, as Heinrich Klotz pointed out (2000, 358), Richard Peter's (1895–1977) photograph *Windrose III:* the view of a destroyed Dresden from the rooftop of the town hall, with the sculpture of an angel in the foreground whose gesture expresses the bewilderment, the sense of loss, he feels about the devastation below. A verbal parallel is Bertolt Brecht's diary entry about Germany's devastated capital, which captured well the feeling of the time when he wrote: "berlin, an etching by churchill after an idea by hitler. / berlin, the pile of rubble near potsdam."

More than six decades later, at the beginning of a new millennium, German art is in the international headlines again. It is termed the "Kraut Art Kraze" (Knöfel 2005, 184), picking up the Krautrock phenomenon that rocked the music world from the 1960s to the 1980s (see 8: Music). Harald Fricke wrote, "At art fairs, the German galleries put up 'sold' signs almost right away. The market and museums are scrambling for young artists from Germany. The 'old' art heroes, too, are still highly rated. Where does this new craving for paintings come from? How can it be satisfied?" (Fricke 2005, 41). How did the rejuvenation happen?

The challenge awaiting the arts in 1945 was picked up by several artists in both East and West Germany. In the Soviet-occupied territories, the Kulturbund zur demokratischen Erneuerung Deutschlands (Cultural Association for the Democratic Renewal of Germany) was founded in 1945. It was inspired by the poet Johannes R. Becher, who later became the culture minister of the GDR. In the same year—even before new political parties had been established—a group of artists who called themselves *der ruf* (The Call) opened their first exhibition in Dresden. They were followed by many others in the eastern and western parts of the occupied German territories. Often, the words *Sezession* (Secession) and *sozialistisch* (socialistic) appeared in the names of the new art groups, which signaled their way of thought. In Cologne, the gallery Der Spiegel (The Mirror) presented international art not seen in years past. German Expressionism was among the works and paintings of German artists in exile.

In general, in the late 1940s and 1950s, West Germany had to make up for lost time. It had to catch up with the international art scene. Abstract art as well as sculptures and paintings influenced by the Bauhaus movement experienced a revival. Old masters, such as Oskar Schlemmer, were compared to international artists, such as Henry Moore (1898–1986). Wassily Kandinsky, Paul Klee, and the Russian Kasimir Malevich found admirers and followers. It was a time of retrospectives and a time of imitation. New, original German art was not in the eye of the public, and it was not a topic of general conversation and debate. Two exceptions were Willi Baumeister and Ernst Wilhelm Nay. Both became models for the young postwar generation and posi-

tive links to Germany's past. Yet, the event that made the fundamental difference for German art was the first *documenta*, the internationally respected German art show that opened its doors for the first time in 1955. The initiators, the artist Arnold Bode and the art historian Werner Haftmann, had as their goal to "document" contemporary art in a free Western society. The art spectacle therefore had a political as well as an aesthetic agenda. It can be seen as an act of political rehabilitation of West Germany. For the general German population, the show offered a lesson in art history because the so-called "degenerate art" could now be placed in its international context. In the barely restored museum Fridericianum in Kassel, defamed works by Wilhelm Lehmbruck and Oskar Schlemmer dominated the staircase, and German abstract art—for instance, Fritz Winter's *Komposition vor Blau und Gelb* (Composition before Blue and Yellow)—was proudly displayed together with works by internationally renowned artists (Klotz 2000, 367). Certainly, the art show helped to reestablish West Germany as a player on the international art scene. Because of the *documenta*, spectators, art dealers, and avant-garde artists alike were attracted to West Germany again.

Whereas painters needed only canvas and paint to realize their inner images, sculptors found themselves in more of a dilemma in the immediate postwar era. They depended on the availability of various materials and suitable public space, both in short supply after the war. There were neither private patrons nor state commissions. One of the results of this situation was that it led also to an artistic stagnation. The few works created were traditional. Kerstin Mey characterized the situation as follows: "Measured and timeless images of man citing the tradition of the nude figure, inward calmness and spirituality marked the work of an older generation of artists such as Kolbe, Scheibe, Marcks, Mataré and—from the early 1960s onwards—Seitz and Grzimek" (Sandford 1999, 556). Hans Uhlmann's and Karl Hartung's abstract metal objects were the exception and not the rule.

Fortunately, when reconstruction began to boom, public sculpture also began to receive its share of attention because a fixed percentage of the construction cost of public buildings had to be spent on art. However, this law was much too rigid. The results were often rather strange artistic solutions—a small stained-glass window here, an obligatory but not well integrated ornament there. The favorite forms were "associative organic objects or reduced sculptural core forms, followed by more open and complex sculptural structures under the influence of Art Informel" (ibid.).

In the German Democratic Republic, official art was socialist realism. Art, and not only art, was regarded as a tool to reeducate its citizens (see 8: Theater and Dance). As Hermann Glaser noted, the state tried to force its ideology onto art and thereby onto its citizens. "The ideas in art have to follow the marching orders of the political struggle" was the motto given by Otto Grotewohl, the prime minister of the GDR, in 1951 (see 1: From Two to One). Walter Ulbricht, the Communist Party secretary, stated: "We don't need pictures of moonlit landscapes nor rotten fish or something similar. . . . The grey-in-grey-painting, which is an expression of the capitalistic decline, stands in stark opposition to the new life in the German Democratic Republic" (Glaser 2002, 278–279). From the be-

ginning, according to Kerstin Mey, "the instructive potential of representational sculpture was appropriated by the state" (Sandford 1999, 557). The truth of this statement can be seen in memorials for the victims of the Nazi dictatorship—for instance, in the Buchenwald memorial by Fritz Cremer and in the statues of the new heroes, stylized workers and peasants marked by social and historical attributes. In painting, it was the historical depictions of victorious workers and farmers that came closest to the taste of the ruling class. The emphasis was on "victorious" and "positive" images—and certainly not on critical works depicting the social struggle in unheroic and satirical or Expressionist ways, as had been done by artists such as Otto Dix, George Grosz, John Heartfield (who lived from 1950 until his death in 1968 in the GDR), Käthe Kollwitz, and Ernst Barlach. These old masters were quite different in their stylistic approach but were all seen as "formalistic" and disqualified as "bourgeois" (Klotz 2000, 389).

Abstract art was seen as completely irrelevant, as missing the essential human element—a criticism also used by some in the West. The result of this attitude by the political leaders of the GDR was that some artists submitted to the state's guidelines and became accomplices, whereas others went into inner exile, retreating from public life. Some resisted, some resigned, many fled to the West (among them Georg Baselitz, A. R. Penck, Sigmar Polke, and Gerhard Richter), and some became part of a semiofficial underground movement, which was to a certain extent tolerated in some political circles critical of the official party line. And then, of course, periods of strict censorship alternated with periods of greater leniency (see 7: Film). Bernhard

Heisig, for instance, at one time lost his position as president and professor at the art school in Leipzig in the 1960s because, as the accusation stated, the workers depicted in his paintings lacked the required heroism and seemed defeatist. Yet, in the 1970s, he was reinstated and honored as one who understood how to enter into a dialogue with the questions of the time (Glaser 2002, 303).

Still, artists in the GDR had—according to Heinrich Klotz (2000, 390–395)—more freedom to engage in subjective interpretation of the state regulations than they had had under the Third Reich. Good examples are the works by Werner Tübke and Wolfgang Mattheuer, who—like Heissig—were praised as well as criticized. Both remained true to realism in regard to technique, but the content of their pictures had often little to do with a true depiction of reality or with the stylized, realistic praise of workers and farmers. In surrealistic fashion, they estranged their subjects. Tübke had a tendency to use medieval and even religious iconography. Mattheuer, in contrast, was sometimes reminiscent of Salvador Dali. Some of his paintings are full of irony—for instance, his well-known *Hinter den sieben Bergen* (Behind the Seven Mountains), showing in the foreground an almost empty highway leading to the mountains in the distance, behind which a large bare-breasted woman, an obvious reference to Eugène Delacroix's *Liberty Leading the People* (1830), emerges, running toward the viewer with colorful balloons in her hands (instead of the banner Delacroix's heroine is carrying).

Much of the GDR's art can thus be regarded as *Auftragskunst* (commissioned art) (see Flacke 1995) stylizing an idealized reality. It was "understood" by the people but discarded by art critics as "banal." Art in West Germany, in contrast, became to a large extent separated from the general population. It was art for the experts, the intellectuals, the art critics, the galleries, and the art investors. Only from time to time when a scandal made headlines in the popular press did a larger segment of the general public become aware of the new art scene of the postwar years. Nevertheless, the movements that developed were avant-garde in the best German art tradition. There was, for instance, a group of West German artists who gathered in Düsseldorf in 1957 in the studio of Otto Piene who were going to make "art history." Known by the name "Zero," they followed quite a different route from the GDR's Auftragskunst. They wanted to stimulate a dialogue between artists and scientists and chose, therefore, the name for their group from the countdown of a rocket launching. Connected to the international art scene, in close collaboration with leading European artists like Yves Klein (famous for his monochrome paintings in white, red, and blue) and Lucio Fontana (known for cutting into canvases), they introduced a radically enlarged conception of art to Germany. As Daniel Koep wrote, they "aimed for increased sensibility in human perception, working with monochrome or mechanically structured surfaces, light and kineticism" (Sandford 1999, 663). According to Irit Rogoff, they saw art not as reproducing reality but "as a generator of limitless ideas" (Rogoff 1998 , 275). They wanted to obliterate reality and transform physical matter into a weightless field of energy. The concrete physicalness of the *Doni of Willendorf*, one of the oldest sculptures ever found, dating back 25,000 years, was transformed, for instance, into barely distinguishable internal

Venus (or Doni) of Willendorf. (Ali Meyer/ Corbis)

contours. As Rogoff mentioned in her survey of modern German art, this feature made it a good example "of this attempt at creating an immaterial work of art" (ibid.).

Not canvas and paints were their tools but light and the blue sky. "Zero x zero = art" was their art equation. Piene, for instance, worked with screens and painted light images onto walls; Heinz Mack used silver foil and experimented with reflections. One of his grandiose projects was the placement of huge silver steles in the desert from which the sun rays were dispersed in an almost metaphysical splendor (Klotz 2000, 386). Günther Uecker, who joined the group in 1961, specialized in "nail paintings," the nails replacing paint. Unfortunately, the traditional German Michel (see 2: Symbols and Memorials), the state officials, could not quite follow their ideas and

playfulness. An installation for children, created in 1961 by Piene, Mack, Uecker, and Joseph Beuys in the Roland Schule in Düsseldorf (a building designed by Paul Schneider-Esleben [1915–2005], a classic example of the architecture of the 1950s), was removed by the school board as dangerous for the children (ibid., 384–385).

In the early 1960s, Germany—that is, primarily West Germany, with its art centers in the Ruhr area—was again recognized by international artists. New inspiration for painting also came through photography. Many critics regard the revival of figurative oil paintings in the 1980s as a consequence of the work by photographers such as Bernd Becher (b. 1931) and Hilla Becher (b. 1934), active since the 1960s, who influenced a whole generation (Bernd Becher taught at the Düsseldorf Art Academy from 1976 to 1996). It was not only the individual photo but the placement of photos next to each other that created new aesthetic experiences. For instance, their thematically closed series of industrial architecture—such as their series devoted to gas tanks (shot as neutral records of a past)—created through their serial placement "a work of vibrating yet austere poetry" (ibid., 432). Their students Thomas Struth (b. 1954), Thomas Ruff (b. 1958), and Andreas Gursky (b. 1955) all followed their example, though in different ways, with each one specializing in a particular area: Ruff as a photographer of portraits; Struth documenting the relationship between art and viewer in art galleries; Gursky "dismembering and atomizing the depicted world into a pointillistic pattern of people and objects in order to, then, combine it again to a new unity" (ibid.).

A different kind of poetry is also found in the work of Gerhard Richter. With his combination of large abstract paintings and blurred photographic images, he encompassed the whole universe of painting in a playful manner (ibid., 411). Playfulness and irony, including self-irony, were also characteristic of Sigmar Polke, who—like the U.S. pop artist Roy Lichtenstein—created photo-paintings. But he did not make use of the dot of the print screen. Rather, his paintings resembled enlarged photoprints. Consumerism as well as art itself became the objects of his irony. He thus developed a "revived modernity," as some critics saw it.

Besides still images and photo-paintings, video art evolved in the 1960s. In Düsseldorf, the second most important Ruhr town besides Cologne, the first gallery for video art was opened by Gerry Shum. And in Wuppertal, another town in the Ruhr area, the Korean Nam June Paik, who worked together with the composer Karlheinz Stockhausen at the WDR studios for new music in Cologne, became the first in 1962—together with Wolf Vostell—to stage an exhibition of television sculpture, displaying small monitors as part of the performance. The Spichernstreet 18 in Cologne where Wolf Vostell (the *uomo universale*, as Klotz called him, because he was involved in many art forms and inspired many colleagues) and Stefan Wewerka (a multitalented designer) lived between 1959 and 1971 became an international meeting place for artists. Here, they looked at the world with completely fresh eyes. Everyday objects were rethought by Wewerka, and unorthodox results were achieved, such as chairs made from one winding pipe, or fan-shaped office desks. Again and again, Wewerka addressed the basic problem of how to cope with one's surroundings.

All this provided fertile ground for Fluxus, a German art movement that became known to the general public primarily through John Lennon's wife Yoko Ono, who made headlines in the German popular press. A first Fluxus festival was staged in Wiesbaden in 1962, and the movement spread rapidly to New York City. Similar to the Dada movement of the first decade of the twentieth century, in Fluxus "social goals often assumed primacy over aesthetic ones," as Robert Atkins remarked. He continued, "The main aim was to upset the bourgeois routines of art and life. Early Fluxus events—guerrilla theater, street spectacles, concerts of electronic music— were aggressive demonstrations of the libidinal energy and anarchy generally associated with the 1960s. Rather than an alliance with popular culture, Fluxus artists sought a new culture, to be fashioned by avant-garde artists, musicians, and poets" (Atkins 1990, 80). Klotz had an opposing view. He saw a contrast to Dada, regarding Fluxus not primarily as a provocation but as an attempt to include the audience in the act of the creation of an art work, performance, or "happening" (Klotz 2000, 380).

Fluxus gained only limited popular attention, and the attention it did get was primarily in the Ruhr area. But on October 3, 1963, the whole nation was informed about another scandal. The *Bild* headline (see 6: The Press) read: "Shock in the Art-Gallery—200 Invited Guests Stunned—Senator for Culture Refuses to Comment." The state prosecutor confiscated two paintings; a court case regarding dissemination of obscene pictures followed. The cause was a set of paintings by Georg Baselitz, especially his *Die große Nacht im Eimer* (The Large Night in the Bucket). The German idiom "*im Eimer sein*" means, literally, "to be in the bucket"—that something is broken, is not worth anything anymore and can be thrown into the trash can. The painting depicted in muted colors and in rough brush strokes a life-sized man without a shirt standing upright in front of a dark green background with his left hand holding a huge erect penis sticking out of his shorts. *Bild* regarded it as obscene and pornographic. Art critics called it bad painting, art colleagues saw it as reactionary. Abstract Expressionism was "in," as well as the pure colors of Yves Klein and Lucio Fontana who influenced the group Zero. Jürgen Klauke, another enfant terrible of the West German art scene, explained later his own aggressive actions—ridiculing the church and state authorities—by referring to Baselitz's provocative painting: It was a revolt against the do-gooders, the war-generation who knew everything better, acted as authority figures, and had nothing better to do after the war and after all the pain they had caused than to devote their lives in the postwar years to work and consumerism. They acted, he said, as if the past had not happened. They—who had caused millions to die and perverted the meaning of the word "humanity"—made a fuss about so-called "obscenity." This stance against the parent generation was part of a general revolt (see 4: Youth Culture and the World of Intellectuals).

Another event in the art world that caused a scandal typical of the times was the installation of *Sauber* (Clean, 1966) by Hans Peter Alvermann. It was based on a poem by the political *Liedermacher* (song writer) Wolf Biermann (see 8: Music) and showed an assemblage consisting of a bourgeois dressing table, a faucet, and a mirror with a light, all surrounded by two flags. One is the flag of the FRG (see 2: Symbols and Memorials), the other a red flag with a white circle and the black swastika of the Nazis. On either side of the flags are drawers hung onto the wall. In one is the bust of a woman with the letters *SAU* (a word that means female pig, swine) beneath it; in the other the buttocks of a man with the letters *BER*. Together the two syllables mean "clean" (*sauber*) (Schwerfel 2000, 162–163). The implication was that at the time, the Germans saw themselves as Mr. Clean, cleaning society from all the Communists and other "revolutionaries"— put another way, people who had their own ideas and did not follow the traditional consumer work ethic. A further implication was that Mr. Clean only proved himself to be the same intolerant fascist he ever was. From the artist's perspective, the FRG and the Nazi era were not that far apart. But such an active *Vergangenheitsbewältigung* (overcoming the past, see 1: Coming to Terms with the Past) was not asked for. Officials only looked at the surface, and the display of the swastika was not allowed (Article 86 of the criminal code). As a result, even in 1999, more than three decades since the creation of this art work, the director of an art museum still had to defend himself against the accusation of spreading fascist thought by displaying it.

Law and art always have a tense relationship. While the law wants to protect order, the task of art is to test this order. Not only formal and aesthetic aspects are questioned but also social, political, and philosophical ones. West German and Austrian art continued to prove that it took these tasks, this testing and questioning, seriously in radical ways. In his introduction to *documenta 3* in 1964, Werner Haftmann could state with confidence that the maxim for the exhibition was the simple truth that "art is that which important artists create"—and he could be sure that German artists were among them. As all *documentas* showed, German art had finally, after two decades of intermission, reestablished itself as having won back its own voice. Especially Joseph Beuys and the *Junge Wilde* movement (Young Savages) made a name for themselves in the years after the mid-1960s. In Austria, Viennese Actionism expanded the definition of art and placed Austria on the art map again. This movement was Austria's most important contribution to the international development of the avant-garde. Eva Badura-Triska and Hubert Klocker explained the goals of the movement in a brief article introducing an exhibition on Viennese Actionism, "As with the contemporaneous Nouveau Réalisme, the Fluxus Movement or various forms of American Literalist Art, Viennese Actionism exceeds the boundaries of the traditional fine art genres—painting, sculpture and drawing. Artists felt that their ultimately illusionist character was no longer adequate for their purposes. Initially, these art forms were expanded by including real bodies, objects and substances and were finally superseded by working directly with the 'materials' in the form of actions in space and time" (MUMOK 2002, 5). The Actionists explored Freudian themes of erotic violence in ritualistic performances utilizing bodily materials such as blood, semen, and flesh.

Sculpture also expanded beyond its generic boundaries in the late 1960s and 1970s. The Swiss artist Jean Tinguely from Basel was one of the pioneers and was way ahead of his time with his ideas. Already in 1960, he shocked the art world when his *Hommage to New York* self-destructed at the Museum of Modern Art. And he continued his modern pilgrimage, adding to sculpture the important element of humor. His work hums and buzzes, swirls and jingles. Appropriately enough, today his home town of Basel features his *Fasnachtsbrunnen* (Fasnet Fountain) in front of the city theater and a major kinetic and auditory art object in the main stairwell of the art museum. Since 1996, the city has also had a museum devoted to the works of Tinguely and his wife, Niki de St. Phalle, which is filled with squeaking and moving art objects. Rebecca Horn, whose "urge to trace individual experience and sensuality led to an emphasis on personal style and manifested itself in the use of new media such as performance, happenings, fluxus and video" (Rogoff 1998, 279), is to some extent Tinguely's German successor, also making use of programmable machines. In one of her works, peacock feathers are raised and lowered, hammers knock in irregular intervals against a wall, and a wheelchair turns around in circles as a reminder of her film, *Buster's Bedroom.*

Pop art dominated the *documenta 4* in 1968. In the early 1970s, happenings and political provocations continued, and in 1972, *documenta 5* offered an international survey of new art, including photo-realism, which rekindled art debates about the relationship between painting and photography. The Öffentliche Kunstsammlung (Public Art Collection) in Basel showed an exhibition of the hotly discussed *Konzept-Kunst* (conceptual art). At the same time, Joseph Beuys created the Free University, a multidisciplinary informational network, and called it a "social sculpture." Beuys even reached the top spot in the international art market and was the first German to have an extensive retrospective in New

Fasnachtsbrunnen (Fasnet Fountain) in Basel, Switzerland.

York's Guggenheim in 1979. He, as few other artists have done, brought modern provocative art to the popular consciousness. When the public museum of art in Basel bought several of his works, a public outcry erupted. The citizens did not understand why taxpayers' money was being used to buy common sticks (as they saw it) placed on the wall of an exhibition hall or why it was considered art. A group of protesters dressed as "Beuyses": They put on long coats and wore Beuys's well-known hat, carried sticks, and marched during Fasnacht (see 5: Holidays and Local Festivals) to the museum. Beuys had learned about the event in advance and marched along with them, unrecognized, until they reached the museum, where everyone threw down their sticks on a pile in protest. Beuys then stepped forward to re-arrange the sticks and thereby created a new "expensive" art work. Many of the surprised protesters asked to have their coats and hats signed—accepting the comment by Haftmann that "art is that which important artists create."

Due to Beuys's activities, art became again—as it had been before World War II—provocative and political—an attempt to arouse the citizens from a passive and lethargic form of art appreciation nurtured by a bourgeois connoisseurship and consumerism. With his art, Beuys sought to change established patterns of thought, raise the awareness of the individuals so that they would be able to realize their powerlessness in modern society—without accepting it. Thomas M. Messer, the director of the Solomon R. Guggenheim Museum in New York, wrote in the introduction to the Beuys catalog:

Beuys is best known for his insistence upon freedom in the creative process and for his belief that art takes shape not only in the hands of the draughtsman, painter and sculptor, but through creative thought in general. The results of such convictions become visible, or otherwise apprehensible, in formulations that flow from the plastic realm into socio-political, public and collective situations. The gap between art and life narrows markedly at this junction, as the artist's metaphoric content comes under pressure from the wider areas of surrounding life. Within this context, order, disorder, constraint and liberty are ever-present polarities for Beuys himself and, necessarily, for those approaching his work. Beuys' art, at least as it is perceived today, is unlikely to serve those who seek the exquisitely satisfying gratification of visual harmony. The responsive viewer, on the other hand, may derive rewards that are predicated upon Beuys' own idealistic, Schillerian faith in the ameliorative, restorative and healing powers of a broadened art range and a correspondingly invigorated art form.

What matters most about this artist, who ranks today among the most persuasive formulators of contemporary ideals and aspirations, is his capacity to identify central issues and take positions that simultaneously assume creative, plastic form. The issues so perceived tend to elude conventional rationalization. Their enunciation therefore engages intuitive and spontaneous rather than analytical and preconceived levels of comprehension. In offering us daring, often as yet unimagined freedoms, Joseph Beuys' exemplary, life-predicated art reaches its furthest point of penetration. (Tisdall 1979, 5–6)

Beuys continued his activism and in 1982, in the era of the arms race, was on the political stage with his song "Sonne statt Reagan" (Sun Instead of Reagan, a wordplay on the German homonym *Regen*, which means "rain"). In the same year, he began what is probably his most popular and most spectacular work of process art at the *documenta 7*. Using the motto "*7000 Eichen—Stadtverwaldung statt Stadtverwaltung*" (7,000 Oak Trees—City Forestation Instead of City Administration), he played again with two words that sound very similar in German, yet the meaning is totally different. He had 7,000 boulders of basalt placed in front of the museum. The idea was to change this pile of rocks over time into a forest. Each person donating 500 German marks could remove one boulder and plant instead of it an oak tree at a different location with the boulder next to it. This way, he not only beautified the landscape but tried to demonstrate that each monument is made up of a living, organic part—which changes over time and is subject to death—and a solid, inorganic part, which is crystalline and therefore keeps its form, mass, size, and weight. Beuys did not live to see his artwork completed, as he died in 1986, about a year before his son Wenzel planted the last tree at the occasion of the *documenta 8*. The landscape artist Johannes Steiner, from Stuttgart, continued to collect the seeds from the oak trees and plant them in pots, which he gave to others to continue the project and plant more trees in other places.

Some of Beuys's students from the Düsseldorf Art Academy, where he taught for years, followed his lead, especially his awareness of the connection between modern and traditional art and his attempts to create "a totally original language for the dialogue between the unchanging and the new" (Rogoff 1998, 279). Among them were Markus Lüpertz and Jörg Immendorff. In spite of his early statement, "Stop painting," in 1966, and his pleading instead for political action, Immendorff soon returned to the canvas, realizing that this was his real voice. In the tradition of Otto Dix, George Grosz and Max Beckmann, the artists of the 1920s, he tried to capture the Germany of his day not in abstract color combinations but in symbolic realism. Lüpertz "used the emblems of aggressive nationalism such as steel helmets and armour to represent a form of historical bric-à-brac, an ephemeral image of junk objects which is more strongly condemnatory than any serious treatise" (ibid., 279). Anselm Kiefer, whose beginnings are reminiscent of Expressionism, was even more drawn into history, including fascist megalomaniac architecture, turning it into allegory. Robert Atkins wrote: "Obsessed with the effects of Nazism, German artists have attempted to reclaim their cultural past in a society committed to repudiating all that transpired before 1946. The paradigmatic figure in this regard is Kiefer, whose works use biblical history, historical sites, Teutonic myth, Johann Wolfgang von Goethe's Faust (1808/32), and other cultural emblems as allegories of contemporary German life. Because Kiefer's allegorical representations are unfamiliar to most of his viewers, even in Germany, they are often difficult to interpret" (Atkins 1990, 41). And Georg Baselitz, whose trademark is the upside-down painting, "translated the monumental clarity of German medieval painting into a contemporary idiom" (Rogoff 279).

This combination of old and new, the return to oil paintings, led Heinrich Klotz to regard some of the work of these artists—although most of it was already created in the early 1960s—as "examples of a postmodern neo-realism" (Klotz 2000, 408).

By the beginning of the 1980s, neo-Expressionism was in full swing. The figurative language had won the day. At about the same time, new museums were being built: In 1984, the Neue Staatsgalerie (New State Gallery) opened in Stuttgart; one year later, the museum Ludwig in Cologne, among others. Art had established itself as a mass medium again and tried to attract a wide audience with retrospectives and exciting individual shows. The "classical" modern was combined with the newest art of the time. And more than ever, artists worked not only for the private collectors but for the art repositories, the window on art for the public. Visual art, more than any other art from, is dependent on the original, which becomes an investment that only a member of the upper class or a public museum can afford. As a result, art is now advertised in economic journals and has even spawned a new industry: lease-art firms, which allow clients to borrow works of art for their office in order to appear financially stable.

One step below this are the art lovers who go to the various art fairs and subscribe to such magazines as *art*. The advertisements in these magazines show to which social class it caters: They typically tout champagne, Minolta cameras, BMW and Alfa Romeo sports cars, gold watches, and other luxury items for those who spend their leisure time on yachts and in villas. The next group collects local art or goes to antique stores: This mass market is served by Hummel figurines, decorated

Flea market pictures. (Photo by D. Scholl)

wall hangings, religious art, and art posters from various categories. Especially popular in Germany are the classical modern artists such as Pablo Picasso, Marc Chagall, Salvador Dali, and the pop artist Andy Warhol. Popular artists from the German-speaking regions include the nineteenth-century Swiss symbolist Arnold Böcklin with his all-time favorite, *Die Toteninsel* (Island of the Dead), and the modern artists, ranging from Art Nouveau to Expressionism: Paul Klee, Gustav Klimt, Max Ernst, Lyonel Feininger, Max Beckmann, Ernst Ludwig Kirchner, and Otto Dix. There is a wide range of popular motifs. The category "Nudes" is dominated by the Austrian Egon Schiele, though the young German Jens Brüggemann (b. 1968) made inroads into the category of nude photography. Posters or mass-produced oil paintings of landscapes (beach and sea, mountains, lighthouses), gardens, flowers, bars, and various animal scenes at home and in the forest (especially the *röhrende Hirsch*—bellowing stag) are another important segment (Hermand 1988, 116–121).

Though conceptual art, happenings, and installations are good for museums and art books, only paintings or copies of paintings and posters can actually be hung in the living room. For many years, abstract art in its Constructivist as well as Expressionist variety held its own next to realistic paintings of everyday life, containing a touch of sentimentality, a slight stylization à la Modigliani, and a daring splash of color. No provocation was called for, but a sense of modernity was allowed. Such art engendered a *Wir-Gefühl* (a we-feeling), an expression of belonging to a group reminiscent of the German literary Expressionists a century earlier. Not surprisingly, the slogan was used by a New York–based art gallery for a show on the newest German art trend in 2005. The slogan also characterizes those American collectors and galleries caught up in the new German art rage in the years after unification. The new paintings appear to be quoting much of the cheap generic art produced for supermarkets. They are reminiscent of the past and often depend on photography. "The paintings deliver what the name promises," as Ulrike Knöfel wrote, "meeting all the expectations placed on today's much sought-after 'Young German Art': they are colorful, largely representational and betimes nostalgically retro" (Knöfel 2005, 184).

Already before unification, and then increasingly more afterward, oil paintings, sometimes combined with photography— representing different versions of *Stille Bilder* (Silent Pictures), as the art historian Heinrich Klotz called them—became the new vogue. A. R. Penck's work combined cave painting and graffiti; Martin Kippenberger included caricatures in his paintings; and painters such as Rainer Fetting, Salomé (Wolfgang Cilarz), Helmut Middendorf, Elvira Bach, and Georg Dokupil combined "a lurid and joyous portrayal of Rock culture at its most frenzied with the depiction of grave and important issues" (Rogoff 1998, 279–280). But the real breakthrough came, according to Harald Fricke (2005), in early 2003 with exhibitions like *deutschemalerei 2003* (German Painting 2003) and *Lieber Maler, male mir . . .* (Dear Painter, Please Paint for Me . . .) in Frankfurt on the Main and "Painting Pictures" at the art museum in Wolfsburg. Daniel Richter from Berlin and Neo Rauch from Leipzig had their debut at that time. Till Gerhard, a newcomer in 2005; Cornelia Renz, whose work incorporated advertisements and caricatures; and Martin Eder can be regarded as part of the group.

When the Art Basel Miami Beach fair opened in December 2004, *Art Newspaper* gushed (as Ulrike Knöfel reported): "The Future Is German" (Knöfel 2005, 186). These artists profit, according to some critics, "from a continuing 'Eastalgia' trend in international art, that foible for all things from former East Germany" (ibid., 187; see 1: From Two to One). This seems to be true, certainly, in regard to Rauch, who helped to start the craze in the mid-1990s. He is from East Germany, and his pictures can be seen to allude to the former socialist realism. According to Fricke: "Neo Rauch offers us paintings depicting the peaceful juxtaposition of socialist workers, nostalgic filling-stations and comic-like neologisms" (Fricke 2005, 42). Eastalgia is less obvious in Till Gerhard's paintings. On the surface, they are idyllic scenes, but they nevertheless evoke the 1960s, a time when the "the world was neatly divided by an Iron Curtain" (Knöfel 2005, 185). Martin Eder seems the most contemporary, however, in evoking a loneliness in the setting of a fashion-conscious environment. *Time* magazine praised his work's "apocalyptic undertone as aptly reflecting the mood in Germany" (ibid., 188).

Only the future will tell whether the Kraut art craze will remain more than a fad. But it seems already a given that one of the most important artistic events in Germany in the 1990s was Christo's and Jeanne-Claude's wrapping of the Berlin Reichstag in 1995, an event often compared to the American Woodstock Festival in 1969 for its cultural significance.

City Planning and Architecture

In the immediate postwar years, beautification of the environment applied only to the home and garden. It was not until the 1960s that the concept was extended to city planning. Of course, directly after the war, the main concern in both East and West Germany was to build cheap living space. Renovation of old buildings was not a priority, nor were aesthetic concerns uppermost, but rather the construction of large new suburbs. Unfortunately, the social perspective was also given low priority. What was built was essentially a set of dormitories—

the Mümmelsmannsberg development in Hamburg is a good example—and they were not designed with personal contact in mind. There were no pubs or cafes where the people who had been thrown together could meet. For young people and for women who stayed at home with their children, this was particularly difficult.

In the GDR, the *Plattenbauten* (buildings made from prefabricated slabs) characterized the new developments. The result of the commercially based construction method—which considered only how to get the greatest profit from the newly created living spaces—led to the *Unwirtlichkeit der Städte* (Inhospitability of the Cities), as the culture critic Alexander Mitscherlich called one of his books. But here not all was bad. Some of the reconstruction was based on Bauhaus ideas of functionalism (the movement returned to Germany after the war and exile in the United States), though many projects used this style as an excuse for a lack of originality. In the GDR, the concept of an independent German culture of city planning, not influenced by Anglo-American ideas, was presented (Glaser 2002, 326). In contrast to the Western solution of suburbs, there was a desire to go back to the national tradition of classicism, as found in the early nineteenth century, to give Germans back their self-respect. The town centers were to become areas for political expression, demonstrations, and public festivities.

In the wake of the revolution of the 1960s in West Germany, attention was also paid to city planning. The critics' warnings had become a reality. Just as the West German suburbs were dead both day and night, so had the inner cities become centers of commerce during the day and dead at night. A new mixture of commerce and living space, of increasing car traffic, on the one hand, and pedestrian areas, on the other, became the goal. Although the American mall idea began to establish itself in some areas, inner-city revival projects were a strong counterforce. These were to have a balanced blend of shops and cafés, regular apartments, restaurants and entertainment centers, parking garages, and pedestrian areas. The emphasis on building a reliable and easy-to-use public transportation system with streetcars, buses, and taxis led to success stories such as the one in Freiburg. In many towns and cities, old and new have learned to live together. Much has been renovated. Richard Lord observed in his traveler's guide: "And if your city has an *Altstadt* (old town) section that wasn't totally destroyed by World War II bombs, you will find that storybook Germany you have always wanted to see, perhaps with buildings and streets recalling centuries past, some looking like giant gingerbread house constructions" (Lord 2004, 12–13).

City revival also led to the creation of more concert halls and museums. These are just the most recent additions, however, to a long German tradition of museums. The Deutsches Museum in Munich, for example, is a technical museum with many hands-on exhibits, including a complete coal mine to be visited. There one can see a Faraday cage, where a technician demonstrates the protective power of such a cage against even tremendously high electrical charges, as lightning strikes against it with an ear-splitting noise that children of many generations have experienced and never forgotten. Munich is also fortunate in having the *Alte* and *Neue Pinakothek* (Old and New Art Collection) with their immense art collections. And

Downtown Freiburg, Germany. (Photo by A. Weiss)

there is the Germanisches Nationalmuseum in Nuremberg. In total, today, according to Holger Briel, "Germany is home to about 3000 museums" (Briel 2002, 96).

They play an important role not only in urban Germany but also in rural Germany. Even small towns like Tübingen, home of the world-renowned Kunsthalle (art gallery), and Baden-Baden, with its Kunsthalle and since 2004 its Sammlung Frieda Burda (Frieda Burda Collection), can offer their citizens fine art. Some exceptional buildings—museums, concert halls, and sports facilities—were added in the 1960s and 1970s—for example, Mies van der Rohe's Neue Nationalgalerie (New National Gallery, built 1963–1965) in Berlin, Hans Scharoun's Berliner Philharmonie (1963), and Günter Behnisch's Olympiastadium in Munich (1972) with its tent-like roof. Throughout the 1980s, 1990s, and continu-

ing into the new millennium, a number of large-scale architectural and cultural initiatives resulted in exciting new showcases for art in Germany. Such initiatives included the Neue Staatsgalerie (new state gallery) in Stuttgart; an extension to the Hamburger Kunsthalle (Hamburg art gallery); the Museumsufer (literally, the museum bank, as a group of museums are situated on the banks of the River Main in Frankfurt), the Schirn Kunsthalle (Schirn art gallery), and the Museum für Moderne Kunst (museum of modern art) in Frankfurt; the Wallraf-Richartz-Museum/Museum Ludwig in Cologne (both museums are named after their donors); K21 Kunstsammlung (K21 art collection) in Düsseldorf; the Museum für Deutsche Gegenwartsgeschichte (Museum for Contemporary German History) in Bonn; and the renovated Museumsinsel (museum island that combines several museums in one location) and the new Jüdisches Museum (Jewish museum) designed by Daniel Libeskind in Berlin. After unification, Berlin also acquired a new "open-air" museum of what had been the Berlin Wall; one stretch of it was kept as an exhibit. In the 1990s, a number of new galleries opened, particularly in the neighborhoods of Prenzlauer Berg and Mitte, which had formerly been in the eastern part of the city. An even more recent development, which has nothing to do with city planning, is the virtual history museum mounted by the Deutsches Historisches (German historical) Museum Berlin, which gives an interactive overview of German history (see www.dhm.de).

However, not every new building in Berlin is uncontroversial. Though in many towns and villages the goal has been to blend old and new, new buildings in cities such as Berlin, where the grandiose idea always had its home, are often an attempt to make an architectural statement. Opinions are divided about the new structures in Berlin. Buildings that have been restored or recreated in a classical style, such as the Hotel Adlon, have been criticized for a lack of innovation, whereas daring new designs are often criticized for being just that. Although Norman Foster's cupola for the Reichstag is seen by most as successful (see 2: Symbols and Memorials), buildings such as the Paul-Loebe-Haus seem to be more the result of an ambition to be remembered in art history books than the desire to create a functional and pleasant working environment. Similarly, some view the buildings at the Potsdamer Platz as typical examples of U.S. dominance. To these critics, they look like "an average American mall," indicating that "Germany has lost its soul" (Rutschky 2004, 17). However, Berlin

is not the only city with striking new buildings, although it is undoubtedly—even in 2006—still the largest construction area in Europe. Janet Schayan in her article "Building with Calibre" (2005, 12–17) picked out five outstanding architectural achievements outside Berlin and only one in Berlin: The Radisson in Frankfurt on the river Rhine, called "skyshaper" because of its blue disc-like shape. Frankfurt, or "Mainhattan" as it is also known, is the only city in Germany that has a modern skyline; the Frauenkirche in Dresden, built in 1734, destroyed in 1945, and inaugurated a second time in 2005, has become a symbol for reconciliation; the small town of Herford, Westphalia, thanks to its new MARTa museum, can now proudly show off its own Gehry building. The name MARTa combines the initial M standing for "Möbel" (furniture) and ART (for art) and the small final "a" for "ambient"; in a few years, the Grüne Zitadelle (green citadel) in Magdeburg, the last building designed by the Austrian architect Friedensreich Hundertwasser (1928–2000), a pale pink building with splashes of gold, red, and blue, will show more of the green that is part of its name when the trees on its rooftop grow; the Peek and Cloppenburg department store in Cologne, designed by the Italian architect Renzo Pianoas, is a transparent curved palace with a glass façade spanning five floors; the Elbphilharmonie (philharmonic on the river Elbe) in Hamburg, which is still in the planning stages, "will be placing a futuristic glass-wave construction on top of a former cocoa warehouse in the Hafencity [harbor city] district" (ibid., 17); and finally, the library of the Free University in Berlin (nicknamed "The Berlin brain" because of its shape), designed by Lord Norman Foster.

In the new millennium, many of the German families who once lived on the outskirts of towns have moved back into town centers or right out into the country. The empty apartments left behind were often taken over by foreigners, refugee families, and asylum seekers with lots of children. As a result, they are now inhabited mainly by people whose lives are often fraught with problems. High unemployment often leads to youth drug addiction, crime, racism, and right-wing extremism.

In the countryside, not everything remained undamaged by World War II; nor were rural areas unspoiled in the years that followed. Yet, more than in the cities, one can still see in the buildings and the layout of towns and villages the regional differences caused by the landscape, the use of locally available materials, traditional building styles and techniques, and regional legal systems. The landscape dictated the form of communities, such as clusters or *Reihendörfer* (villages built along a road); the northern *Backsteingotik* (Gothic architecture built in brick); and the southern *Barock* (baroque) style. The legal system encouraged or discouraged the size of estates: In the Black Forest, for example, the large farms were traditionally inherited by the oldest son of the family and kept as a unit. In other regions, farms and fields were divided among the heirs, resulting in much smaller properties.

Owning a small property or living in an apartment is the standard for most people today in Germany, as it is in other European countries. Space is scarce; population density is high; the average density is about 230 people per square kilometer, and most look for a private space for relaxation. A huge garden only requires work. A small garden, however, allows one to be in the fresh air and catch some sunshine without becoming a serious gardener. Walls and fences with bushes and trees protect the oasis from the outside. Neatly cut grass in front and flowers signal orderliness and a love of nature. Iron gates are good as status symbols. Sociability is not excluded—Germans love parties—but it is limited to planned events. Sudden surprises and visits that disturb the routine or one's schedule are not welcome. Germans like to be in control. The same preferences are behind the German tendency to close doors. On the one hand, it is the fear of drafts (and many Germans claim to be allergic to drafts); on the other hand, only a closed door permits completely concentrated work without distraction. To knock on a door before entering a room is, for a German, a self-evident tactful mode of behavior. (See 2: Stereotypes and Prejudices.)

From A to Z

Abbreviations for housing information: Abbreviations in Germany are always especially frustrating for foreigners. Here are a few related to housing, as listed in a manual for foreigners by the German government:.

2 ZKB means two rooms plus kitchen and bathroom; 2 ZKBB means two rooms plus kitchen, bathroom, and balcony; EG means ground floor; 2 OG means second floor; DG means roof or loft apartment; VH means the front of the house (usually, at the street); HH means the backyard of the house; qm means square meter and describes the size of the apartment; KM means cold rent, that is, rent without heating costs; NK means

ancillary costs; WM means warm rent (the cold rent plus the NK ancillary costs); WBS means *Wohnberechtigungsschein*, a certificate that allows one to live in certain cheaper apartments—that is, state-subsidized apartments (Beck 2003, 151).

Abstract art: Major postwar representatives of this style were Willi Baumeister (1889–1955); Karl Hartung (1908–1967, sculptor); Ernst Wilhelm Nay (1902–1968); Hans Uhlmann (1900–1975, sculptor); and Fritz Winter (1905–1976). The most important Russian-German prewar representative, seen by many as the father of abstract art, is Wassily Kandinsky (1866–1944).

Abstract Expressionism: See "Art Informel," below.

Actionism: The idea of the artist as actor and the related interest in the artistic process led to artistic events and performances relating to spiritual, aesthetic, social, political, and psychological concerns. For instance, in 1971, Hans Haacke's exhibition about New York real-estate ownership caused a stir and was canceled by the Guggenheim Museum in New York. In Vienna, Actionism referred primarily to ritualistic performances utilizing the body and its fluids. Artists associated with the Viennese Actionism were Günter Brus (b. 1938), Otto Muehl (b. 1925), Hermann Nitsch (b. 1938), Arnulf Rainer (b. 1929), Alfons Schilling (b. 1934), and Rudolf Schwarzkogler (1940–1969) (see 9: Visual Arts). HA (Hans-Jürgen) Schult (b. 1939) became known through such works as *Schrottarmee* (Trash Army). He regards modern times, the time of consumerism, as a time of trash. People produce trash and

become trash. Therefore he installed one thousand life sized "Trash People" as an image of modern men and women at first in the Amphitheatre of Xanten in 1996. He then sent them around the world: Paris and Moscow (1999), Peking and the Chinese Wall (2001), Kairo and Gizeh (2002), Zermatt (2003), Kilkenny Castle (2003), Görleben (2004), and Brussels (2005).

Appropriation: A practice of creating a new work by taking a preexisting image from another context and combining it with new ones. German artists who frequently use this method include Sigmar Polke (b. 1942) and Gerhard Richter (b. 1932). The latter in 2005 was seen as the leader on the international art market. His works were the most expensive by a living artist worldwide. Even more so than other artists, he is a "chameleon," according to Harald Fricke, "because he not only adopts almost every art style, but also perfects them" (Fricke 2005, 40–45).

Art and technology: A movement attempting a union of art with architecture, design, and science. German artists in this vein included Heinz Mack (b. 1931), Otto Piene (b. 1924), and Günther Uecker (b. 1930).

Art Informel: A Parisian version of Abstract Expressionism emphasizing intuition and spontaneity (in contrast to the Cubist tradition). German artists in this style include: Peter Brüning (1929–1970), Karl Otto Götz (b. 1914), Hans Hartung (1904–1989), Gerhard Hoehme (b. 1920), Bernard Schultze (1915–2005), Emil Schumacher (1912–1999), Fred Thieler (1916–1999), and Wols (Alfred Otto Wolfgang Schulze, 1913–1951).

Art Nouveau: Known as *Jugendstil* in German. Its works are characterized by the use of organic imagery, emphasis of sinuous line, and union of ornament and structure. Vienna was one of its centers during the turn of the twentieth century. The paintings of Gustav Klimt (1862–1918) are reproduced on many posters, postcards, and souvenir items and belong to popular culture more than a century after their creation.

Artists' books: The term refers to works by visual artists that assume book form. Primary prototypes for contemporary artists' books include Dieter Roth's (1930–1998) multivolume collection of meticulously filed debris from the street. Other artists who have had successful books include George Brecht (b. 1924), Hanne Darboven (b. 1941), and Anselm Kiefer (see 9: Visual Arts).

Assemblage: The three-dimensional counterpart to collage (previously just called "objects"). The practice goes back to Pablo Picasso and Georges Braque and, two years later, Marcel Duchamp's "readymades." Among the German artists associated with this technique is Joseph Beuys (1921–1986), whose name could be listed with almost all modern techniques and styles. Another representative who has received special attention is Hans Peter Alvermann (b. 1932).

Associations/groups: Organizations in Germany dedicated to advancing the arts include the Kulturbund zur demokratischen Erneuerung Deutschlands (Cultural Association for the Democratic Renewal of Germany); Quadriga, with Karl Otto Götz

und Bernard Schultze, which belongs to Art Informel; *der ruf* (the call); Der Spiegel (The Mirror); ZEN, founded 1949, which has Willi Baumeister among its members; and Zero (see 9: Visual Arts).

Bauhaus: Literally, building house, a school of art with the credo "Art and Technology, a New Unity," founded by Walter Gropius (1883–1969) in 1919 in Weimar. Its ideas, which encompassed a wide range of concepts, from attempting to reinvigorate crafts production to embracing industrial technology and mass production, found a fertile ground in the United States. After 1933, most Bauhaus faculty emigrated to the United States. Artists connected to the school included the Swiss Paul Klee (1879–1940), who was also associated with the group *Blaue Reiter* (Blue Horseman); Lyonel Feininger (see "Cubism," below); and Oskar Schlemmer (1888–1943).

In architecture, the Bauhaus movement was indisputably Germany's primary contribution to art design in the twentieth century. The architect Ludwig Mies van der Rohe (1886–1969) was the last director of the school before it was shut down in 1933 by the fascists. Its internal struggles were symptomatic of a modern society. Artists such as Johannes Itten, Wassily Kandinsky, Paul Klee, and Lyonel Feininger pleaded for the subjective expression; others, such as Walter Gropius, László Moholy-Nagy, and Oskar Schlemmer, were interested in design as such, especially in terms of functionalism and mass production. Both artistic directions were based in socialist thought. In 1925, when the conservatives gained absolute control in Thuringia and Weimar (see 1: Coming to Terms with the Past), this resulted in the end of the Bauhaus in Weimar. All instructors were fired, and the Bauhaus moved to Dessau.

Body art: A forerunner of performance art in which the body of the artist is the medium. German artists in this genre included Rebecca Horn (b. 1944) and Klaus Rinke (b. 1939).

Classical stylization: Inspired by classical Greek sculpture and the ideal proportions, the style tended often to the heroic. Some sculptors associated with the style are Fritz Cremer (1906–1993, GDR), Waldemar Grzimek (1918–1984), Georg Kolbe (1877–1947), Gerhard Marcks (1889–1981), Ewald Mataré (1887–1965), Richard Scheibe (1879–1964), and Gustav Seitz (1906–1996).

Collage: A technique of attaching paper or objects to a two-dimensional surface that has been used by many artists over the centuries. The first modern collages were produced by Pablo Picasso and Georges Braque. Dadaists like John Heartfield (Helmut Herzfeld) invented a collage technique known as "photomontage" that recombines snippets of photographs into new compositions.

Collections/museums: Although Germany does not have the tradition of donors to universities as in the United States, in the arts, donors have always played an important role in building collections. The German industrialist family Thyssen-Bornemisza has one of the finest private art collections in Germany, funded by wealth accumulated in the steel industry. The Hermann F. Reemtsma Collection, based on a fortune made through the production of cigarettes, is also outstanding.

Newer collections are funded by the German sweet tooth—that is, chocolate manufacturers: the Sprengel Museum in Hannover and the Museum Ludwig in Cologne (which has risen to global prominence for modern art). The Ludwig has also opened museums in many other cities in various states, and it established the Ludwig-Institut für Kunst der DDR (Ludwig Institute for Art of the GDR) in Obernhausen in 1984. A very special collection is the one by the painter, writer, and publisher Lothar-Günther Buchheim, which has a focus on Expressionism.

Conceptual art: As Robert Atkins noted, "In Conceptual art the idea, rather than the object, is paramount" (Atkins 1990, 63). This meant that it made any activity or thought by an artist a potential work of art. As Atkins pointed out, many critics "looked at Conceptual art and saw an emperor without clothes" (ibid., 65). German artists in this category besides Joseph Beuys and Hans Haacke (b. 1936) have included Hanne Darboven (b. 1941), Dieter Roth (1930–1998), and Rosemarie Trockel (b. 1952).

Concrete art: According to Robert Atkins, the term "concrete art" refers to abstract art "that was based not in nature but in geometry and the formal properties of art itself—color and form, in the case of painting; volume and contour, in the case of sculpture." Although the term has lost currency since the 1950s, "the underlying idea that an artwork has value as an independent object, even if it doesn't illuminate social concerns or express an artist's emotions, has been extremely influential" (Atkins 1990, 66). German and Swiss artists who made the term popular were Josef Albers (1888–1976), the Swiss Max Bill (1908–1994), and Richard Paul Lohse (1902–1988).

Cubism: A movement in art initiated by Pablo Picasso (1882–1973) and Georges Braque (1882–1963) in 1907. They followed ideas by Paul Cézanne (1839–1906), who had encouraged the "dissection" of nature into basic shapes. A German American representative was Lyonel Feininger (1871–1956), with his prismatic cubistic pictures. He also taught at the Bauhaus (1919–1933) before being forced into exile (see "Bauhaus," above).

Dadaism: Dada is not just an art style but a worldview and includes paintings, collages, and mixed-media happenings. At the core of Dada stands provocation, unconventional forms created by unorthodox means. It began during World War I in Zurich, Switzerland, and rapidly spread to New York, Berlin, Barcelona, Cologne, and Paris. Among the many artists associated with Dada were Jean (Hans) Arp (1887–1966), Max Ernst (1891–1976), George Grosz (1893–1959), John Heartfield (Herzfelde, 1891–1968), Hannah Höch (1889–1978), and Kurt Schwitters (1887–1948).

Décolage: The act of removing parts of existing surfaces to uncover older layers and creating works that may depict a diachronic in addition to a spatial effect. Besides French artists, it was Wolf Vostell (1932–1998) in Germany who used this technique frequently.

Deconstruction: Estrangement of the familiar by deconstructing existing entities and assembling new, functionless units from functionalized elements. Sculptor Olaf Metzel (b. 1952) is a well-known proponent.

Einwohnermeldeamt: Registration with government offices is very important in Germany—even if one moves from one flat to another one. The registration office is generally located at the town hall (see 3: The Legal System).

Exhibitions: Hitler's shadow was felt in a very direct way in regard to modern art, which fascists had labeled *entartete Kunst* (degenerate art). It took almost a decade until the general public accepted abstract art. The most important exhibitions, organized every four to five years in Kassel since 1955, were the *documenta*. These exhibitions helped to overcome the public perceptions of the movement left over from the Nazi era.

Expressionism: Art that emphasizes emotions by distorting realistic shapes and choosing colors and arranging space in accordance with the associated emotional value. In Germany, it had its most influential periods from 1905 to 1920. See Neo-Expressionism.

Feminist art: After de-gendering art in the 1960s, an emphasis on feminist art, inspired by the idea of the Great Goddess, returned. German artists associated with that movement include Rebecca Horn, Ulrike Rosenbach, and Rosemarie Trockel.

Fluxus: Like Dada, Fluxus is more a state of mind than a style. Mixed media was the typical Fluxus format. Artists, not all of them of German origin, who played leading roles in its development are the American George Maciunas (1931–1978), who was stationed in Wiesbaden; the Korean Nam June Paik (1932–2006); the Swiss Daniel Spoerri (b. 1930); and Wolf Vostell (1932–1998). Besides Dada, Fluxus had its roots also in John Cage's (1912–1992) performances in the early 1950s at Black Mountain College, North Carolina.

Großsiedlungen: Large-scale housing estates. These changed beginning in the 1980s from bedroom communities to autonomous living areas with shops, playgrounds, and good public transport connections. In the new millennium, Freiburg has become a model for other cities, with its newest developments featuring large ecological apartment projects (Rieselfeld), an environment-friendly and child-friendly living area (Vauban), and a new solar apartment development.

High-tech art: All art produced with sophisticated technology. One of the German artists involved in this movement is Bernd Kracke (b. 1954).

Hummel figurines: Porcelain figurines collected by enthusiasts around the world. Postcards based on drawings by Berta Hummel (1909–1946), known as Maria Innocentia after she entered a Franciscan convent, came to the attention of the porcelain manufacturer Franz Goebel, who was searching for a new line of figurines, in the early 1930s. The first figurines were introduced in 1935, and their success has not diminished. Next to *Gartenzwerge* (see 5: Activities and Clubs), they have become one of the most popular German collectibles.

Industrial complexes: Abandoned complexes in Germany are being used in some cases for experimental living conditions.

Installation: Works of art made especially for a specific place and time, usually an ensemble of objects. This form of art was popularized especially by Christo in his 1995 wrapping of the Reichstag. Joseph Beuys and Hans Haacke are also main representatives of this form in German art.

Jugendstil: See "Art Nouveau," above.

Junge Wilde: The "junge Wilde" (young savages), sometimes called "neue Wilde" (new savages), recall the Fauves painters of the first decade of the twentieth century. Just as these artists were equated with "wild animals" because of the use of striking colors and bold and daring pictorial compositions, a few German painters of the 1970s were seen in a similar light because they also dared to be provocative in their paintings in regard to color and composition. Of course, six decades had passed since the Fauves and there had been also other "revolutionary" periods in the meantime, for instance, expressionism. Some critics, therefore, called the "junge Wilde" neo-expressionists. Its main representatives in Germany are Georg Baselitz and Anselm Kiefer (see "Neo-Expressionism," below).

Kinetic sculpture: A type of art that encompasses a wide variety of approaches, from constructions responsive to the natural elements (for example, the wind) to motor-driven junk sculptures. The one thing they have in common is movement. One of the prime representatives is the Swiss Jean Tinguely (1925–1991).

Kraut art: See "Young German art," below.

Manipulated photography: Whereas the photomontage combines different photo images to form a new photo, manipulated photography changes a single photo by various means. German artists in this medium include Walter Dahn (b. 1954), Astrid Klein (b. 1957), and the Austrian Arnulf Rainer (b. 1929).

Media art: A subset of conceptual art that uses the various forms of mass media as a means of artistic communication. Joseph Beuys was one of Germany's foremost media artists. Others who are associated with this form of art include Rebecca Horn (b. 1944), Ulrike Rosenbach (b. 1943), Rosemarie Trockel (b. 1952), and Stefan Wewerka (b. 1928). Trockel was regarded in 2005 as Germany's most famous woman artist (Fricke 2005, 47).

Metamorphosis: The topicalization of art as a process. Sculptor Ulrich Rückriem (b. 1938) depicted the metamorphosis of rock into sculpture by juxtaposing rough ashlars with the drill holes showing and stones polished to various degrees (Klotz 2000, 423–424).

Narrative art: The narration of a story within a painting. This type of art has a long tradition. In modern art, it takes different forms, including installations and video art, besides traditional realistic figurative paintings. Jörg Immendorff and the Swiss Grégoire Mueller belong to the group of German-speaking artists associated with this style.

Neo-Expressionism: A reaction against conceptual art and the modernist rejection of historical imagery and iconography. Neo-Ex, as it is often abbreviated, was a return to easel painting and cast and carved sculpture. Artists in this style include Elvira Bach (b. 1951); Georg Baselitz (Georg Kern, b. 1938), a top-ranked international artist, who was awarded the "Nobel Prize of the Arts" in 2004—that is, the Praemium Imperiale of the Japan Art Association; Norbert Bisky, a disciple of Baselitz, who polarizes viewers with his ambiguous pictorial idiom (Fricke 2005, 41); Jiri Georg Dokupil (b. 1954); Rainer Fetting (b. 1949); Jörg Immendorf (b. 1945); Anselm Kiefer (b. 1945); Markus Lüpertz (b. 1941); Helmut Middendorf (b. 1953); A. R. Penck (Ralf Winkler, b. 1939), who ranked in 2005 behind Gerhard Richter as number two in the *Kunstkompass*'s listing of the 100 most famous artists, published in *Capital* magazine; and Salomé (Wolfgang Cilarz, b. 1954).

Neo-Realism: A general term for figurative art as opposed to Abstract Expressionism. Also called New Realism.

Performance art: Art that may include elements of music, dance, poetry, theater, and video. The term is also used for body art, "happenings," "actions," and Fluxus events. Among many others, Jürgen Klauke (b. 1943) is active in this form of art.

Photo realism: A hyper-realist style of painting—that is, the reproduction of a photograph on a large scale.

Photography: Among the German photographers not already mentioned in the main text are the following. Anna and Bernhard Johannes Blume (both born in 1937) became known through their Kafkaesque photographic creations of an unstable world, by which they questioned the claim of truth of photography. Thomas Demand (b. 1964) was regarded in 2005 by many critics as the most progressive German photographer, or—as some contend—as a sculptor using photography. Candida Höfer (b. 1944) produces small photos, primarily of animals in cages and empty rooms, that depict a lonely world. Katharina Sieverding (b. 1944) reduced the world to herself as the sole object of contemplation. Wolfgang Tillmans (b. 1968) is regarded as the inventor of snapshot aesthetics.

Pop art: An ironic celebration of consumerism and popular culture as well as a reaction against Abstract Expressionism and its "spiritual and psychological" search. Dada belongs, certainly, to its precedents. German artists in this vein include Sigmar Polke (b. 1942).

Process art: A form of art in which the artist is only the initiator of work that unfolds over time due to natural processes of growth or decay. Besides Joseph Beuys, one of the leading German artists (but living in New York City) was Hans Haacke (b. 1936).

Socialist realism: Usually associated with glorified and sometimes stylized realistic images of the working class meant to be accessible to every viewer. The term is often used pejoratively. But not all paintings in this style are that simplistic. They are often quite complex in regard to subject matter as well as technical detail. Among the artists who were not just realist propagandists are Bernhard Heisig (b. 1925); Wolfgang Mattheuer (b. 1927); Arno Rink (b. 1940); and Werner Tübke (b. 1929).

Stille Bilder: Literally, silent paintings. As a reaction to the various art techniques that disregarded the traditional (silent) canvas, a group of young artists has consciously returned to it and made it not only the vehicle for its art but also taken it as a major topic. There are numerous important German artists in this group. The Swiss Helmut Federle (b. 1944) combined geometric forms with figures and achieved a contemplative effect, proving that even today panel painting is possible (Klotz 2000, 430). Günther Förg (b. 1952) combined painting and photography and placed framed, oversized photos next to paintings, creating a new spatial dialogue between these works. Georg Herold (b. 1947) changed the nature of panel painting by turning it into a kind of scaffolding that extends from the frame into the picture (ibid., 427). Karl Horst Hödicke (b. 1938), cofounder of the Berlin group "Vision," experimented at the borderline between abstract and concrete art. Martin Kippenberger (1953–1997) incorporated caricatures into his paintings. Imi (Wolf) Knoebel (b. 1940) for years painted series of variations of the most basic pattern for a picture: a monochrome painted surface surrounded by a frame in four colors. Albert Oehlen (b. 1954) presented computer prints of lifestyle ads.

Straight art/straight photography: It is photography that refrains from imitating paintings and rejects manipulation of negatives and prints. It is intricately linked with the ongoing debate about whether photography is art. Besides being equated with documentary photography, it is also part of the snapshot aesthetics. German-speaking artists in this group are Albert Renger-Patzsch (1897–1966) and the Swiss Robert Frank (b. 1924).

Surrealism: A movement in art characterized, according to André Breton, by "pure psychic automatism by which it is intended to express . . . the true function of thought. Thought dictated in the absence of all control exerted by reason, and outside all aesthetic or moral preoccupations" (Atkins 1990, 156). German surrealists include Jean (Hans) Arp (1887–1966), Max Ernst (1891–1976), and the Swiss Meret Oppenheim (1913–1985).

Video art: Videos are made by visual artists in a variety of ways and can be critical as well as attuned to popular culture. German-speaking artists working with video are Klaus vom Bruch (b. 1952); the Austrian Valie Export (b. 1940); Ingo Günther (b. 1957); Rebecca Horn (b. 1939); Michael Klier (b. 1943); the Austrian Richard Kriesche (b. 1940); Marcel Odenbach (b. 1953); Klaus Rinke (b. 1939); and Ulrike Rosenbach (b. 1943).

Young German art: As is often the case in art, the word "jung" (young) is applied to the most contemporary art which at a later time will be given a new designation after critics have had time to analyze the material. Therefore, most artists in the following list belong more or less to the golf generation. In contrast to young artists mentioned in other sections their main medium is the oil painting. Kai Althoff (b. 1966); Norbert Bisky (b. 1970); Martin Eder (b. 1968); Tim Eitel (b. 1971); Till Gerhard (b. 1971); Eberhard Havekost (b. 1967); Johannes Kahrs (b. 1965); Martin Kobe (b. 1973); Antje Majewski (b. 1968); Neo Rauch (b. 1970); Cornelia Renz (b. 1966); Daniel Richter (b. 1962); and Matthias Weischer (b. 1973).

Additional Readings

Atkins, Robert. *Art Speak. A Guide to Contemporary Ideas, Movements, and Buzzwords.* New York: Abbeville Press, 1990.

Burchard, John E. *The Voice of the Phoenix: Postwar Architecture in Germany.* Cambridge, MA: MIT Press, 1968.

Damus, Martin. *Malerei der DDR. Funktionen der bildenden Kunst im Realen Sozialismus.* Reinbek: Rowohlt, 1991.

———. *Kunst in der BRD, 1945–1990. Funktionen der Kunst in einer demokratisch verfassten Gesellschaft.* Reinbek: Rowohlt, 1995.

Feist, Günter, and Eckhart Gillen, eds. *Stationen eines Weges. Daten und Zitate zur Kunst und Kulturpolitik der DDR, 1945–1988.* Berlin: Nishen, 1988.

Flacke, Monika, ed. *Auftragskunst der DDR, 1949–1990.* Berlin: Deutsches Historisches Museum, 1995.

Fricke, Harald. "A Nostalgia for Oils. The German Art Miracle." *Deutschland. Forum on Politics, Culture and Business* 2 (2005): 40–47.

Glasmeier, Michael, and Karin Stengel, eds. *archive in motion. documenta-Handbuch / documenta Manual. 50 Jahre / Years documenta 1955–2005.* Göttigen: Steidl, 2005.

Homburg, Cornelia, ed. *German Art Now.* London and New York: Merrell, 2003.

Honnef, Klaus, Rolf Sachsse, and Karin Thomas, eds. *German Photography, 1870–1970.* Köln: DuMont, 1997.

James-Chakraborty, Kathleen. *German Architecture for a Mass Audience.* London: Routledge, 2000.

Joachimides, Christos M., Norman Rosenthal, and Wieland Schmied, eds. *German Art in the 20th Century: Painting and Sculpture, 1905–1985.* München: Prestel, 1986.

Klotz, Heinrich. *Geschichte der Deutschen Kunst.* Vol. 3: *Neuzeit und Moderne 1750–2000.* München: C. H. Beck, 2000.

Knöfel, Ulrike. "Kraut Art Kraze." *The Germans. Sixty Years after the War.* Ed. Stefan Aust. Spiegel. Special International Edition 4 (2005): 184–189.

Krens, Thomas, Michael Govan, and Joseph Thompson, eds. *Refigured Painting: The German Image, 1960–88*. München: Prestel, 1989.

Mitscherlich, Alexander. *Die Unwirtlichkeit unserer Städte*. Frankfurt: Suhrkamp, 1965.

Nerdinger, Winfried, and Cornelius Tafel. *20th Century Architectural Guide: Germany*. Basel and Cambridge, MA: Birkhäuser, 1996.

Pehnt, Wolfgang. *German Architecture, 1960–1970*. London: Architectural Press, 1970.

Rasp, Markus, ed. *Contemporary German Photography*. Köln, Lisboa, London, New York, Paris, and Tokyo: Taschen, 1997.

Rogoff, Irit. "Modern German Art." *The Cambridge Companion to Modern German Culture*. Ed. Eva Kolinsky and Wilfried van der Will. Cambridge: Cambridge University Press, 1998, 256–281.

Schayan, Janet. "Building with Calibre." *Deutschland. Forum on Politics, Culture and Business* 6 (2005): 12–17.

Stärk, Beate. *Contemporary Painting in Germany*. Sydney: G and B Arts International, 1994.

Thomas, Karin. *Zweimal deutsche Kunst nach 1945. 40 Jahre Nähe und Ferne*. Köln: DuMont, 1985.

10

Production and Consumption

Innovation and Production

In the nineteenth century, the designation "Made in Germany" had to be applied to German products in Britain to protect British industries from German competition. However, the industrial mark of Cain became a stamp of quality. After World War II, West German companies tried to continue the long-standing tradition and succeeded in many areas. Innovation and reliability were the hallmarks of German products. In 2005, the Federal Republic of Germany saw itself as one of the economic giants of the world. The gross domestic product (GDP) in that year rose to 2,244 billion Euros, and the national income per capita was about 20,400 Euros. (Federal Statistical Office, April 2006).

But in spite of the good official statistics and individual success stories, the German economy is not doing as well as might be hoped at the beginning of the new millennium, and innovation is needed. Heinrich von Pierer, CEO of *Siemens*, one of Germany's largest international companies, demanded that Germany's politicians rethink their strategies and invest much more in education and research. Asked what the government can learn from a company, he remarked: "What you can learn from all successful companies is that there are times when you just have to get the costs under control. . . . But that cannot be everything. At the same time, you have to concern yourself with growth—and growth comes from innovation, meaning new products and new services. . . . The proposal to create *Eliteuniversitäten* [extremely selective top universities] is not enough. Both within and between the universities one has to allow for competition. To achieve that, universities need more autonomy. . . . Education is the alpha and omega. We are also in a global competition of educational systems" (Pierer 2004, 7).

The German government, certainly, agreed. Reforms were the agenda of the Schröder government—changes have taken place in all areas of society, some for the better, some for the worse, depending on one's perspective. And the year 2004 was declared the "Year of Innovation." The chancellor was rushing from one event to the next to get the innovation offensive rolling, opening a research center in one place, celebrating the anniversary of a company in the next, and so on. Even geniuses need the right environment to flourish, and the German government has apparently been at least somewhat successful in creating that environment, judging from Germans' achievements. Karlheinz Brandenburg (b. 1954), for example, is considered the inventor of the MP3 system, the main compression system of digital audio data used today, and Christiane Nüsslein-Volhard (b. 1942) conducted research on the fruit fly *Drosophilia* that led her to discoveries in genetics. In 1995, she became the first German woman scientist to be awarded the Nobel Prize for Medicine.

Whereas Germany's northwestern regions of the Ruhrgebiet and Saarland are the centers of heavy industry, the southwest is the cradle for high-tech developments. Many see the area between Stuttgart, Baden-Württemberg, and Zurich, Switzerland, as contemporary Europe's most creative industrial area. Approximately 23 percent of the workforce in the Stuttgart region is employed in high-tech industry, giving it European leadership status. A mere two hours from Stuttgart, across the Swiss border, Basel is the center of Europe's chemical industry and the home of the best-known pharmaceutical companies, such as Hoffmann LaRoche. In the east, Dresden has established itself as the German equivalent of Silicon Valley.

Two of the more recent examples of innovation that had a huge economic success were the Swatches and the Smart cars. The Swiss clock and watch industry was once the acknowledged leader but lost ground when inexpensive quartz clocks and watches hit the market and overshadowed the expensive, handmade chronometers. A businessman named Nicolas Hayek decided to follow the trend with cheap products, but he added a twist: colorful, unusual designs, and new models being released on a regular basis, which led fans to become collectors and seek out the latest color or shape. The watch was given the catchy name Swatch and has been an outstanding success since its introduction in 1983. Hayek has sold more than 250 million watches and has become the largest manufacturer of watches worldwide. The same company then turned its attention— and the concept of cheap and colorful—to cars. Together with Daimler-Chrysler, Hayek developed a colorful small car, the Smart car. Though its fans don't collect the car in multiples, they do appreciate its maneuverability and the way it fits into parking spaces that other cars have to pass up.

As the German economy declines and the social network weakens, it may be time to check in on the best-known representative of the Golf Generation—Florian Illies—the author of two books on his generation. What is he doing with all those royalties? From the way he described his peers, one might expect him to be relaxing in some chic location, probably the island of Sylt, in stylish clothes, sipping good wine. Perhaps he is, but he's also been keeping busy with his partner, Amélie von Heydebreck. Together they have founded an art magazine entitled *Monopol* and their own publishing house (*Deutschland* October/November 2004, 63).

From "Tante Emma Laden" to Shopping Mall

Not all problems of a new society based on commercialism are easily solved, as foreigners visiting Germany have noticed. "Germany is a beautiful country," one remarked, "but you can't get anything on Sunday and you have to rush in the evening to do your shopping. Impossible! Chauvinistic! Not made for the working woman." Correct. Though bakeries open early, usually at 7 AM (in some towns and villages even at 6 AM), to make sure that most people can get a good start on the day with fresh rolls, it was not until 1996 that some shops could finally stay open until 8 PM instead of 6:30 PM and that bakeries could sell their rolls on Sundays, too. But progress arrived and will continue to make inroads. Soon there will be stores in train stations and filling stations open twenty-four hours a day, and weekends will become the main shopping days as they are in many other Western countries. Instead of window shopping, everyone will be encouraged to do real shopping. Shopping is the new civic duty to get economies booming. The new arrangements will be more convenient for most people—but not all.

In the 1970s, the revised family legislation finally recognized in legal terms that marriage is not the equivalent for the male of getting a maid. The responsibility for housework is a shared burden, as the German civil code points out. Partners are equal, and each has the right to a professional life. In the German Democratic Republic, it was understood that women and men were equal in regard to professional work. The only drawback was that women actually were expected to play a dual role: worker and housewife (see 4: Gender Equality). In both states, in real-life situations, housework, and with it shopping, was done after work as the stores were closing. The real provisions of *gleitende Arbeitszeit* (flexible working hours) were

too cumbersome for most firms. The result: the complaint about the early closing hours of stores.

But what do you do when you own a family-run business, the famous *Tante Emma* store (mom and pop store—literally, the store of Aunt Emma)? You cannot afford to hire more employees. You have to sacrifice your leisure time to make shopping more convenient for others. The arguments of the unions and the owners of small shops were not a plea for laziness or a false claim that later closing hours would mean a shift in values. Longer opening hours meant a giant step in favor of the big supermarkets. Only on a very limited scale could some of the family stores survive as specialty stores in cities. In villages, a few more survived into the new millennium. They were even able to retain their special store hours, which include long midday breaks, often from 12 noon until 3 PM, and free Wednesday afternoons. But the process away from small to big continues. Big business is certainly going to win.

When the strict laws governing shop opening hours were modified in 2003, an article in the weekly online newsletter of the popular women's magazine *Brigitte* contained a somewhat cynical report ("Länger shoppen," June 6, 2003). Though on the face of it, the longer Saturday hours would allow families to breakfast at leisure rather than rushing out to shop for the weekend before the stores closed at noon, the author focused on the problems with the new laws. Herbert Jöhris, the Geschäftsführer des Hauptverbandes des Deutschen Einzelhandels (director of the Organization of German Retailers), is quoted as predicting that most stores would still close at 6 PM. Only shopping districts in major cities and malls would remain open until 8 PM, he said. Seasonal patterns would also affect opening hours, Jöhris predicted, as would the wares sold. In his view, no one would want to buy furniture at 8 in the morning or electric drills at 7 in the evening. But perhaps the most persuasive argument made for a modified adoption of the longer hours was the attitude of the *Betriebsrat* (employee boards). If they voted against longer hours, the boss was powerless. The large Vereinte Dienstleistungsgewerkschaft e.V. (Union for Service Workers) was also cited as being against the modified hours because they would be detrimental to employees and lead to a loss of jobs. Because the length of the workweek would remain at 37.5 hours, businesses would have to develop more shifts to cover extended hours. Although the extended hours could be seen as an opportunity for more workers to be employed, the union pointed out that since the last extension of opening hours in 1996, there had been a reduction in personnel in the retail trade. This can be explained by the shift toward large, self-service discount stores as opposed to the small shops where customer service is valued. Readers of the magazine were invited to respond to a questionnaire on whether they would take advantage of the new opening hours, though the article seemed designed to emphasize the negative aspects of the new laws and encourage a negative response.

About a year later, one could read in the local Freiburg newspapers an announcement about a repeat of the recently introduced *Mega Samstag* (Mega Saturday) on May 8, 2004. What made such days "mega" was that the stores in the city center would stay open until 8 PM. But one sensed a certain skepticism about the event. The journalist noted that "all too often" the oppor-

tunity was used rather as a chance to stroll, window shop, and stop in at a cafe rather than actually to spend money. To tempt customers, there were various additional activities: wine tastings, face painting for children, and street performances. Public transportation offerings were also expanded to handle the increased traffic. The journalist ended his report by stating that if this Mega Saturday was a success, it would be repeated in October (*Freiburger Wochenbericht*, May 5, 2004, 1). At another local newspaper, however, the staff writer was more optimistic about the event, noting that a previous longer shopping day produced crowds. This writer emphasized the "multiple attractions" (*Stadtkurier*, May 5, 2004, 1). Old habits of not shopping late on Saturdays seem to die hard.

Due to the slowness of change, large U.S.-style shopping malls have only had limited success in big urban centers. In most smaller towns, the German solution to retail selling was the revival of the inner city. Planners created pedestrian areas in the center of towns that became shopping districts with outdoor cafes and restaurants (see 9: City Planning and Architecture). These pedestrian areas are also part of the city landscapes, although in big cities they often line the main avenues on both sides, as on the famous *Kurfürstendamm* in Berlin, the *Maximilianstraße* in Munich, the *Königsallee* in Düsseldorf, and the *Zeil* in Frankfurt am Main.

Consumer Culture versus Green Awareness

The terms "economic miracle" (*das Wirtschaftswunder*) and "West Germany" (*Westdeutschland*) used to be synonymous for Europeans in the 1950s and 1960s. Over the past quarter-century (1980–2005), however, one of the primary associations with "Germany" (Deutschland) is the "Green Party" (Die Grünen [The Greens]). Germany is the only state in which a party based on environmental awareness shared the powers of government even on the federal level.

Economic Miracle

The German economic miracle began on June 20, 1948, the day of the monetary reform (*Währungsreform*). Together with the hard currency, products and produce were suddenly available. They had been manufactured before with cheap money and then stored. Now companies were able to reap the long-awaited profits. The U.S. Marshall Plan for the economic recovery of Europe was the backbone. Humanitarian sentiment and *Realpolitik* had come together in a far-sighted policy. West Germany joined the Organisation for European Economic Co-operation (OEEC), then the Europäische Wirtschaftsgemeinschaft (European Economic Union, EWG). The gross national product (GNP) tripled in ten years. In spite of millions of refugees and displaced persons who had come to the FRG after the war, the unemployment rate was 0.8 percent in 1960 (Sandford 1999, 169).

The man behind all this was Ludwig Erhard (1897–1977), a spokesman for a *soziale Marktwirtschaft* (social market economy), who was able to instill confidence in the new currency through his decisive economic actions. As Marieluise Beck has explained, "The term 'Social Market Economy' refers to an economic model that allows free trade but also accommodates the regulatory and controlling functions of the state, to prevent an unsocial

distribution of wealth" (Beck 2003, 27). In this way, the social market economy is a balancing act between the interest of business and the social welfare of society. By the 1970s, West Germany, with a population of only 60 million people, had become the world's third-largest economy. During the 1980s, it even led the entire world in exports several times, although after 1965 Germany experienced the roller-coaster rides of capitalism, the ups and downs of economic cycles. Special lows were reached in 1966 and 1967, a time of social crisis with low annual growth rates and high unemployment (Hermand 1988, 22), and in 1975, which saw the first negative growth rate since World War II. In 1983, unemployment rose to 9.1 percent (ibid., 24), and in 2005 to more than 12 percent.

Material progress in the early years of the FRG was frequently described in terms of patterns of consumption. After the "eating wave" (*Fresswelle*; see 4: From Traditional Fare to International Cuisine), when people were again able to eat their fill, there followed the "clothes wave" (*Kleiderwelle*; see 4: Lifestyle and Fashion) and the "travel wave" (*Reisewelle*; see 5: Vacations and Travel). By the 1960s, the country was seen by many social critics and commentators as an archetypal consumer society (*Konsumgesellschaft*) based on the American model. A guiding principle behind the emerging consumer culture was that people who were materially satisfied could not be politically seduced by radical parties. Consumption was a good defense against both fascism and communism. Josef Neckermann (1912–1992), who founded one of the early mail-order companies and wanted to make luxury articles available to the common man and woman, became synonymous with economic success. His slogan, "*Neckermann macht's möglich*" (Neckermann makes it possible), was the leading slogan of the time. His vision broke down social boundaries and he introduced mass tourism to Germany through the Neckermann travel agency, Neckermann Reisen. Josef Neckermann's attitude as a businessman as well as his personal achievements were characteristic of the postwar generation. As a dressage rider he had won five Olympic medals, four European championships, and one world championship, and his social consciousness led him to establish a foundation for supporting less-well-off athletes. Those who had survived the war worked hard because they appreciated the chances that were given to them. They had experienced injustice and hardships, and they saw that their efforts were rewarded in the emerging democratic society.

Environmental Awareness

The children of these war survivors, however, the baby boomers, began to question their parents' material orientation and the value of consumerism. What was the price everyone had to pay for economic progress? One was monopolism, meaning that only the large companies could survive. The number of small and medium-sized businesses that went bankrupt tripled from 1965 to 1980, increasing from about 3,000 to more than 9,000. In addition, many citizens became more aware of their environment and how it was slowly being destroyed by uncontrolled material progress. Since the mid-1970s, Germans have become increasingly active in pressure groups to bring about reforms in environmental legislation that might prevent further damage as well as alleviate existing problems. These baby boomers also questioned the competitive nature underlying human relationships. They looked for new, antiauthoritarian social structures and were skeptical of the new value system in society that put property ownership and social status at a premium (see 4: Youth Culture and the World of Intellectuals). Private and political attitudes merged, and it was from such disparate groups that the Green Party evolved. In 1980, they were ready to participate for the first time in federal elections.

One especially important driving and unifying force was the opposition to nuclear energy, which had become an issue since the first reactor was built in 1960. Back then, nuclear energy was seen as the solution for an environmentally friendly energy source, but soon this utopian dream proved to be false. It was not until 1977, however, that citizens' groups such as the Grüne Liste Umweltschutz (Green Group Environmental Protection) and Atomkraft Nein Danke (Nuclear Energy No Thank You) were both able to score political gains, each winning a seat in two local elections. Other green groups followed, and in 1979 they united for the European elections as a *Listenbündnis* (loose federation of various local citizens' groups) under the banner of Die Grünen. They were able to draw more than 3 percent of the vote. Then, after a green citizens' group in Bremen succeeded for the first time in sending delegates to a state parliament, the green movement was on its way to establishing an official party in West Germany. In January 1980, the party was formally founded. It was able to win mandates that year in the state elections of Baden-Württemberg, a state known for its liberalism, but scored only a disappointing 1.5 percent in the same year in its first federal elections.

Nevertheless, the green agenda was being discussed, and the following years were marked by large demonstrations against nuclear energy and for disarmament. Surveys in 1982 showed that the general public had become very much aware of environmental questions. The term *Technik* (technology) was still associated with progress, but at the same time it was associated by 67 percent of the population with destruction of the environment and by 56 percent with *Angst* (Glaser 2002, 335). Electoral successes on local and state levels were the result of these campaigns for the greens, culminating in their winning their first seats in the Bundestag (lower house of parliament) in 1983. For many, it was a sign of real change. There was the feeling that West Germany was a place where democracy worked, where ideas from the people had an impact. Instead of formal suits and ties, the new representatives sported jeans and sweaters. They arrived on bicycles instead of in large limousines. They brought flowers from their gardens for their desks in parliament and knitted while listening to speeches.

In the following year, the party demonstrated very clearly that it was also the voice of the slowly growing women's emancipation movement. The green faction in the Bundestag elected a party executive board consisting only of women (*Feminat*). Starting in 1985, they consistently did well in elections for the European Parliament. At the same time, defeats on the state level brought about inner-party debates between the *Realos* and the *Fundis* (realists and fundamentalists). Did they want to become just another party? Or was their goal to bring about real social change? Could their ideas be realized if they decided never to participate in the

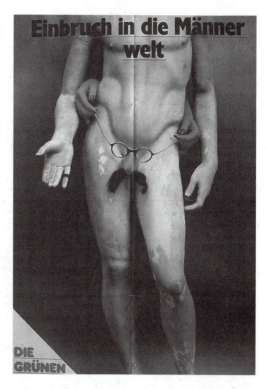

Green Party poster: *Intrusion into the Men's World.*

Regierung (executive branch of the government)? Was it possible to form a coalition with another party without giving up one's ideals? Where are the acceptable limits to compromise?

Over the years, the pragmatic politicians in the party won after many hot debates and following separate conventions held by the various factions. The idealistic wing of the party split off and founded a new group in 1991: the Ökologische Linke (Ecological Left). Joschka Fischer, the best-known Realo, went on to become the first Green Party member to accept an official position in a state government in 1985. After the elections in Hesse, the first red-green coalition, between the SPD and Die Grünen, was formed, and Fischer became minister of the environment. He took his

Solar panel on church roof in St. Georgen, Breisgau.

oath wearing blue jeans and sneakers. A few years later, his outfit changed to suits—complete with tie and vest—when, in 1998, the Green Party and the SPD formed a coalition on the federal level. Gerhard Schröder from the SPD became chancellor of the new Germany; Joschka Fischer became vice chancellor and secretary of state. In addition, two other members of the Green Party were appointed ministers.

With oil crises becoming a regular news item, alternative energy sources are becoming politically more attractive. Solar panels are becoming especially popular in Germany. More and more rooftops are now being covered with them—those of regular family homes as well as large church roofs and other buildings. They are used as architectural design elements to structure the facades of apartment buildings and appear on walls built to protect those who live near busy roads from noise pollution. Through a collaborative project sponsored by the local Green Party, a solar energy firm (Energossa) and a construction firm (Fesa GmbH) have cooperated to build new structures that dampen sound as they gather energy on the access roads to the autobahn that passes by Freiburg. The gains will be economical as well as ecological, and the project is funded through public bonds following the model established with windmills, which are sprouting up on hills and along coastlines (*Der Sonntag*, May 2, 2004, 4). In 2001, the federal government and leaders of the nuclear industry signed a contract to abandon nuclear energy over the next decades. Groups propagating alternative living styles are being encouraged. One of the centers of this type of change is Freiburg in the Black Forest. An organization called Selbstorganisierte Unabhängige Siedlungsinitiative (Self-Organized, Independent Housing Initiative, SUSI) is in many ways a typical model. Founded in 1990 as a response to free-market speculations by large real-estate companies, it realized ideas going back to the 1960s. Its goals are stated in a brochure for future members: "We wanted a better world organized in accordance with cooperative principles which would bring about a future without exploitation of human beings by human beings and without the destruction of nature."

As in other countries in the West, environmental awareness also influences food production. Organic farming has made definite inroads into the overall produce market. German agriculture has changed enormously in other ways as well over the past sixty years. A combination of new technology, intensive farming, and efficient methods of production is needed for survival, and usually it is only the larger farms that can meet these demands. But each year more local farmers' markets sprout up to compete with the supermarkets, with the result that home production accounts for more than 80 percent of Germany's food supply (some statistics list 90 percent). Even the less fertile fields are being utilized again, and not only for golf courses but for grazing sheep. Immigrants to Germany had much to do with this revival in sheep farming. A favorite food of those from the Balkans and Turkey is lamb, and in their restaurants they have reintroduced Germans to a meat that had been unpopular for years. West Germany had only about 800,000 sheep within its borders in 1970;

that figure had risen to 1.7 million by 1995. Even the romantic image of the shepherd has regained popularity (Eichheim et al. 2002, 113).

Unspoiled nature has always played a central role in the German understanding of *Heimat* (homeland). The word *Heimat* had become already in the nineteenth century the antithesis of modernity with its industrialization and urbanization. And for Germans, the trees and forests symbolize nature. The authors of the German textbook *Die blaue Blume* (The Blue Flower) summed up well the feelings Germans have for trees and forests: "They give expression to both dreams and fears." They went on to quote Elias Canetti, who said, "The Germans still like to seek out the forest where their ancestors once lived, and feel at one with the trees" (ibid., 327). And many a religious German regards *die freie Natur* (unspoiled nature) as the true church and the best place to give expression to piety, as did Joseph von Eichendorff's (1788–1857) lovable *Taugenichts* (Good-for-nothing), the epitome of Romanticism, when he joined the birds with his fiddle in praise of God.

The image of a population in love with nature is also a good counterpoint to the militaristic image Germans are confronted with all life long. Therefore, they like to hold onto the Romantic tradition with its *Blaue Blume* (Blue Flower), going back to a novel by the poet Novalis (Friedrich Leopold Freiherr von Hardenberg, 1772–1801), which stood for the yearning for the infinite, the metaphysical. It is easier to identify with theological ideas and philosophy than with the sound of sirens and bombs and the cries of victims (see 1: Coming to Terms with the Past). Not surprisingly, the Schutzgemeinschaft Deutscher Wald e.V.

(Association for the Protection of the German Forest) was founded as early as 1947, a year before the monetary reform—and two years before the establishment of a democracy—because after World War II, wood was in short supply. The German population as well as the Allies, in need of wood for fuel and for reconstruction, had felled great tracts of forest. Even the linden trees on the famous Berlin boulevard *Unter den Linden* (Beneath the Linden Trees) were cut down for fuel. The new association wanted to ensure that reforestation would be achieved, and it was—faster in fact than the rebuilding of German towns and cities. Today there is as much forest in Germany as there was 600 years ago, and in the official manual for immigrants in 2003 one could read that "nearly a third of the entire country is forested, especially in the south" (Beck 2003, 26).

The reforestation process was not without its ups and downs, however. In 1978, when the first reports appeared in the German press about the poor state of the forests, the whole nation was confounded. The term *Waldsterben* (forest dieback) was coined and immediately came into general use. The ecological movement in Germany developed more vigorously because of the threat to the forests and gained support from many groups that were usually not found on the left of the political spectrum, such as the many well-organized mountain walking and hiking clubs (see 5: Activities and Clubs). This included a large number of people. In 1994, 2 million hikers were counted on 90,000 organized hikes. Their expeditions were mainly in wooded countryside, which is crisscrossed by a multitude of well-marked trails. Many are improved with protected huts so that hikers can take a rest, as well as lookout towers

so that they can experience the calming view over a sea of treetops. Since the late 1970s, special programs have been introduced to develop sustainable forestry (ibid.).

Although Germany has become a consumer society, it is still one with a difference. On the one hand, its patterns of consumption are typical for a technologically advanced and prosperous society. The percentage of income spent on food declined, according to Stuart Parkes, "from 18.5 percent in 1991 to 16 percent in 1998," while health care outlays increased "from 3.2 to 4.5 percent over the same period" (Briel 2002, 27). On the other hand, classifying Germany as a consumer society is not totally correct. The laws that govern shopping hours (see 10: From "Tante Emma Laden" to Shopping Mall), particularly on weekends, have remained much stricter than those in Britain, the United States, and other European countries, in spite of recent liberalization. Germans also put a higher proportion of their income into savings than do citizens of other countries, particularly in the east. Parkes noted that "households with monthly incomes of more than DM 6,275 in the east saved 18.8 percent of this amount in 1997, while those in the west with more than DM 9,008 only saved 13.8 percent. Even pensioner households with incomes generally well under DM 4,000 managed to save something: 8.4 percent in the west and 9.3 percent in the east" (ibid.). Most Americans, in contrast, are in debt to their credit card companies. It is Germans' thriftiness (see 2: Stereotypes and Prejudices), some economists believe, that causes one of the economic problems in the new millennium. Sixty years after the "economic miracle," headlines reporting Germany's economic woes are multiplying: "Fears Mount That Germany Faces Recession," reported the *New York Times*, for example, on April 27, 2005.

Communication

"I will call back right away," was a common response in the United States to a caller from Germany before the 1990s. An overseas telephone call placed from Germany—and even local ones—used to be pretty expensive. The telephone was regarded as a luxury for many decades after the war, and it took older Germans many years to become comfortable chatting on the phone and using it for normal conversations. Members of the generation growing up in the 1950s learned early on to keep telephone conversations as short as possible, to have whatever documents they needed at hand before a call, and to have pencil and paper ready to take notes—to be efficient. Their children (members of the Golf Generation) have an entirely different relationship with communication technology. They are constantly available through cell phones, text messaging, and e-mail and as teenagers learned to talk for hours with their friends on the phone.

In fifty years, the world has been turned upside down. At the beginning of the new millennium, it is cheaper to call abroad from Germany than it is from anywhere else in the world. Today, a German talking to his or her friend in the United States would be the one more likely to say, "I will call back right away." The mobile telephone craze struck Germany earlier than it did the United States; the spread of Internet cafés was extremely rapid. In 2002, almost half the German population was using the Internet, according to Klaus

Lantermann, and about two-thirds of all Germans had their own mobile telephones (Lantermann et al. 2003, 248).

The change began in 1990, the 500th anniversary of the German postal service, when the Bundespost (federal postal service) was split into three separate divisions: Postdienst (mail service), Postbank (banking service), and Telekom (telecommunications). Over the next decade, the divisions were privatized, and with privatization came a new color scheme. The traditional yellow of the Bundespost was kept for the postal service, although the traditional uniforms were changed to more fashionable shirts, vests, and ties; women got more stylish skirts, blouses, and scarves. The Telekom introduced pink or lavender for the phone booths and service vehicles.

A post office sign in Frankfurt am Main. (Neil Beer/Corbis)

The black horn on a yellow background, the symbol for the post office, used to be a sign of reliability but also high costs. Though the high costs have remained, the reputation for reliability has vanished. Opinions on the privatization "success story" are divided. Certainly, it is true that post offices in small towns and villages have been closed and that letter boxes have been removed. Elderly people see these changes as a loss. Often, it is difficult to even find a post office. Post-office buildings used to be impressive—even in small villages. Now, the post office may be hidden in a mall. Businesspeople and politicians, however, see the process as a successful adaptation to new circumstances in a global environment. No one will ever know if other solutions would have been better. In Germany, as everywhere else in the world, mail service has changed drastically through computer technology—and this service, everyone seems to agree, has improved in Germany.

Today, at the beginning of the twenty-first century, phone calls are possible via landlines or mobile connections. Digital connections such as ISDN (integrated services digital network) or DSL (digital subscriber line) have become more and more popular. They give the consumer more than one phone line for parallel use. A consumer can make a phone call, access the Internet, and receive a fax at the same time. The Web site www.billiger-telefonieren.de gives an overview of rates and conditions. Another useful Web site is www.tariftip.de. A listing of phone numbers is found at www.telefonbuch.de. Although most people use a "handy" today (the German word for a cellular or mobile phone; see 2: Language, Script, and Gestures), there are still a few public phones left on streets, in train stations, and at airports. They can be operated by using coins or phone cards (prepaid cards). When first introduced with their snappy designs, these cards became collectible items and had value for some even when the calling capacity had been used up.

Public and Private Transportation

Cars

The sun was shining; it was a weekend. The little convertible puttered up the hill, and the children were happy on their *Notsitze* (emergency seats), a narrow space behind the two regular seats in front. This area was intended primarily for luggage but could also be used for additional seats, at least for small children. The seats were hard and had no cushions, but one could sit on blankets or pillows to make them a bit more comfortable. The little racing caps that the whole family wore protected their heads and ears from the wind. Suddenly, smoke and steam burst forth from under the hood. The engine was overheated. The hill was a little too steep for the engine. A rest was called for.

The convertible the family was driving was a Gutbrod, one of the many mini-sized cars that were available as well as affordable immediately after the war and that populated the streets of Germany in the 1950s. There was also the Volkswagen Käfer (VW Beetle), of course. Another was the Lloyd, often called the *Leukoplast-Bomber* (Bandaid-Bomber) because its body was made from pressed plywood covered with leather. It tried to compete with the VW, but without success. Very popular also was the DKW (which actually stands for Dampf-Kraft-Wagen, Steam Engine

BMW Isetta—vintage German Tricar. (Ulrike Hammerich/istockphoto.com)

Cars, proving its long history, but colloquially was deciphered as *Deutscher Kinderwagen*, German children's carriage). The Isetta, built by BMW (Bayerische Motorenwerke, or Bavarian Motorworks), was unusual because of its door in the front.

Similarly unique was the Messerschmitt-Kabinenroller (Karo), which looked like an airplane cockpit put on wheels. The rumor circulated that it had been built using parts of the ME 109 airplane. Driver and passenger sat behind each other; the roof was made of Plexiglas to prevent claustrophobia; the motor was in the back. Brake, accelerator, and shift petals were identical to the arrangement in other, more traditionally built cars. The gear shift was copied from a motorbike; the steering wheel was a half circle to save space. There was no reverse gear. If one wanted to drive back-

ward, one had to turn off the engine, press in the ignition button (this cannot be done with other cars and therefore this description may sound confusing), and restart the engine. It now ran in the opposite direction and one had the same number of reverse gears as one had had to go forward, that is, four. Besides the standard models, which had three wheels—two in front and one in the rear—there existed a sports model, called Tiger, that had four wheels.

There were also, of course, the Opel, the Porsche, and the Mercedes Benz for the more well-to-do, especially the *Neureiche* (nouveau riche) of the late 1950s. Mercedes, with its Silberpfeile (Silver Arrows) had reestablished its reputation as one of the world's top car makers. More important for the common man until the 1960s were the various mopeds and motor bikes.

NSU (Neckarsulmer Motorfabrik) and BMW were the best known. But with increasing prosperity, motorbikes, mopeds, motor scooters, and *Kabinenroller* (bubble cars) as the vehicles of choice lost out to the standard car. There was a clear upward trend from the mini-car to the middle-class car and then on to the status car. Cars in general had become a status symbol, and keeping up with—or being a step ahead of—the neighbors was demonstrated in part by the model one drove.

While the exotic-looking cars disappeared (the last Messerschmitt was built in 1964), the use of motorbikes was more and more limited to racing and leisure activity. The traditional motorbike manufacturers reduced their motorbike production and increased their car production. This was especially true for BMW. NSU merged in the 1960s with DKW to become Audi, which made its name by producing elegant, reliable, and progressive cars. For a few years after 1967, the company's star model was the Ro 80, the first car with a *Wankel-Motor* (rotary engine).

Car manufacturers continued to merge until finally the average person lost sight of who owned what. But a few cars gained symbolic status for particular social groups and generations: foremost, the VW Käfer; second, the Opel Manta; and third, the VW Golf. Whereas the Käfer was the protagonist of U.S. movies, especially *VW Herbie, ein toller Käfer* (Herbie, the Love Bug, 1968), and the Golf named a generation (see Illies 2001, 2003), Manta drivers became the butt of jokes because the car was seen as the typical car for the "dumb blonde," usually depicted as a hairdresser, or her male equivalent, a body-building construction worker. The jokes usually took the form of riddles such as: "Why are

Mantas now built with transparent mudguards? So that you can see the driver's cowboy boots better."

In the GDR, the main vehicle was the Trabant, affectionately known as the Trabi. This car was also the protagonist of movies, though they did not make it across the Atlantic in spite of their English titles: *Go Trabi Go* and *Go Trabi Go II*. The ingenuity of the GDR citizens to modify their national symbol knew no limits. There were stretch-Trabis, racing Trabis, and all sorts of artistic Trabis. There was also an elite car, the Wartburg, that would not have impressed many westerners but was definitely a cut above the Trabi—and out of reach for most citizens.

Beginning in the 1980s and continuing up to today, the car scene is similar to the music scene in one sense: It is completely heterogeneous. The types of cars multiplied, not only their number, and the social role of the car expanded. Once the pride and joy of the family to the point that it was given a name and meticulously washed and polished (see 2: Stereotypes and Prejudices), the family car is now a common utility vehicle. Most families in fact have more than one. Even young people own a car, and the emotional attachment is not quite the same as it used to be. The complex technologies of cars today have much to do with this development: Whereas in the past only a moderately technically minded person could tinker with spark plugs and valves, today even specialists with sophisticated diagnostic computers cannot easily locate a defect.

In the new millennium, the images of the internationally known brands—BMW, Mercedes Benz, Porsche, and Volkswagen—are perpetuated, reinforced—and now and then modified—on the firms' Web sites,

Bernd Quandt, owner of a car-rental agency, drives a lilac Trabi convertible on the island of Usedom, 2003. Since 1999 his "Fun Car Rent" offers Trabi convertibles for rent, mainly to holiday makers. (Corbis)

sometimes depending on the country in which the car is being sold. For example, in October 2005, the Mercedes home page for France opened with a chic black sporty model, whereas for the Germans, who like to travel, it was a camper; for the United States and the United Kingdom, a minivan; and for Italy, a stylish silver sports car. BMW and Mercedes Benz both stress that they are leaders in the field, makers of luxury vehicles with strong supporting service networks. Both firms offer accessories designed to convey the image of affluence and style—sunglasses, leather bags, and clothing, all with the car's logo—and proudly announce a special sales area for diplomats. BMW emphasizes its sporty image with a yachting and golf shop, along with a "Pit Shop" for car-racing acces-

sories. Predictably, the Porsche site leads one quickly to racing events, achievements, and classic models. Mercedes Benz differs from BMW in that it creates the impression that its cars serve all segments of society. The firm produces taxis, cars for driving schools, and armored cars as well as models specially equipped for the handicapped. The Volkswagen site also has a shop selling accessories—watches, pens, bags, and so on—and has recently added a larger luxury model to the line, the Phaeton. However, the Web site focuses more on the image of serviceability—like Mercedes Benz, it manufactures taxi models and cars for driving schools, but VW also offers cars equipped as emergency vehicles. In addition, the firm stresses its social conscience, the latter no doubt to balance its origins as Hitler's "car for the people." The Web site announces that VW established a fund in 1998 for making reparations to those forced to work in the factories under the Nazi regime, and it has a memorial to those workers on the property of the Wolfsburg factory. (For brief histories of the main car manufacturers, see 10: From A to Z.)

Trains

The same change in emotional attachment to cars applies to public transportation. The trains after the war with their steam engines were much more personalized in the minds of the passengers than the fast-speed trains of the new millennium. Although the ECs and ICEs of the twenty-first century have wonderful sounding names—for example, there is the EC 68 "Mozart" from Vienna to Munich—the local trains of the past were a much more distinct entity in the minds of most locals. They often had endearing names, such as the "Odenwälder Lieschen" (the little Alice from the Odenwald) which ran between the small towns of Reichelsheim and Reinheim in the Odenwald, Hesse. Because privately owned cars were not the rule, most commuters depended on trains and buses from the 1950s to the 1970s. Local train stations, even in small towns, were social centers of their communities, in addition to being impressive buildings with a top-quality bar or restaurant.

Before the creation of the two Germanys, the four occupied territories followed different policies. Whereas the Americans and the British tried to establish a working rail system early on, the French were a bit more restrictive. They prevented the continuation of a unified administration, dismantled some train facilities, and

even prohibited the use of the term *Reichsbahn* (Imperial Railway) after 1946. The Soviets, who did not object to the term, were more radical in practical matters. They ripped out almost all double tracks on the main train lines, eliminated electrification, and dismantled many local lines.

After the creation of the two Germanys in 1949, all but eight of fifty-six border crossings that had existed since the end of hostilities in 1945 were closed by the GDR. The GDR kept the name *Reichsbahn* for its railway, while the FRG adopted the name *Bundesbahn* (Federal Railway). In East Germany, the train remained the primary means of public transportation, and in the forty years of its existence, the railroad network maintained its size and the railway employees kept their jobs. In West Germany, in contrast, with the increased availability of private cars and the establishment of new airline routes, almost 3,000 kilometers of track were abolished, and freight traffic sank from 56 percent to 22 percent. By the 1970s, the train had lost its leading position, its debt increased, and the number of employees sank.

With the influx of citizens into the urban areas, the *Nahverkehr* (network of local trains) was restructured in West Germany. Because electrification, begun in the 1950s, was limited to the main lines between large cities, diesel locomotives were used. Commuter traffic was also enhanced through the use of *Schienenbusse* (rail buses) instead of trains pulled by steam engines. These rail buses had internal combustion engines that could be fueled like regular buses. They had a cab on each end so that it was easier for them to go in and out of a terminus station (*Kopfbahnhof*, literally "head station"), and they usually had only two cars instead of a row of several

Doubledecker train. (Photo by A. Weiss)

coaches. East Germany made frequent use of *Doppeldecker Züge* or *Doppelstockwagen* (double-decker trains) for regional traffic, an idea that was also adopted on a larger scale in the new Bundesbahn after unification.

As more and more steam engines were retired—the last one to go in the FRG was in 1977—the work of stokers became unnecessary. In the GDR, steam engines were used until 1988. In spite of all its innovations, however, the Bundesbahn continued to lose money, and during the 1960s and 1970s it abandoned tracks and closed stations. More flexible bus lines that could be easily rerouted according to demand were established. As with the Trans-European Express (TEE), pioneered in 1957, emphasis was laid on connecting big cities for the business traveler. In 1971, the "InterCity" trains, which ran between cities according to one-hour schedules, were introduced. Together with the "InterRegio" trains (introduced in 1988), they replaced the *Eilzüge* (faster trains that did not stop at the smaller train stations like the *Bummelzüge*, slow trains, did) and *D-Züge* (express trains). The "D" stood for *Durchgangswagen*, that is, coaches that were connected so that one could walk through the whole train. This feature, which is common today for all trains, was then limited only to these express trains. In 1991, the bullet trains of the InterCity Express (ICE), with speeds of up to 250–280 kilometers per hour, introduced a new era of travel geared to the professional. Various personal amenities as well as professional ones were incorporated, such as card-operated telephones (although they will be soon outdated because of the ubiquitous cell phones), fax machines, fully equipped offices, videos in first class beside high-tech toilets, and the standard dining cars and snack cars featuring beer on tap (although there are again and again discussions of eliminating these cars).

After unification, the railway organizations of east and west were amalgamated and fundamentally reorganized. Based on legislation passed in December 1993 (DB-Gründungsgesetz, DBGrG), the merger of the Bundesbahn and Deutsche Reichsbahn became a reality, and the new concern was privatized. The legislation, in line with a European Union directive on liberalization, separated the rail network as an independent subsidiary and divided the merged organization, the Deutsche Bahn AG, into several operating subsidiaries. Today, there are five of them: (1) DB Fernverkehr AG (long-distance passenger service), originally called DB Reise & Touristik (Travel and Tourism); (2) DB Regio (regional passenger service); (3) Railion Deutschland AG, originally called DB Cargo (freight services); (4) DB Netz und DB Station & Service (railway network and station service); and (5) the newest one, Dienstleistungen (service), for instance, rent-a-bike. The railway network of about 36,000 kilometers that is maintained by the DB is also open to other railway companies. Until 2005, there were about 300 licensed companies (Deutsche Bahn 2004, 24).

In 2003, the DB AG served about 4.6 million passengers per day (ibid.). According to Chris Flockton, "Long-distance services are expected to be profit-making while regional and local train services require heavy subsidies from the states and localities. DB plans to separate off into 38 operating companies 18,000 km of local track,

while maintaining 20,000 km as the core network. Already one quarter of the workforce, or 100,000 jobs, have been eliminated since 1994 without redundancy" (Briel 2002, 136–137). Although 2004 was not a profit-making year due to high investment for the modernization of tracks, trains, and train stations, profits are expected in 2005/2006, when DB AG (whose stocks are presently all owned by the state) will take the risk of going public with private shareholdings (Deutsche Bahn 2004, 25). The result of all of these changes is a larger number of railway lines, mergers, bankruptcies, and marketing strategies along with reductions in employees.

The smaller train stations have been closed, and the brick buildings, with their distinct architectural characteristics, are now only historical witnesses of a forgotten past in many villages. The remaining city train stations, in contrast, have been transformed into shopping malls. Perhaps the best known among them is the old Friedrichstrasse station in Berlin, through which travelers from the West had to pass to enter East Berlin during the Cold War days. Then it was a grimy, somewhat forbidding station with long underground corridors, seemingly endless stairs, and booths where stern officials took their time checking passports and visas. Now it is a glossy shopping mall with elaborately restored facades that serve as reminders of the era of the kaisers and its opening in 1882. The largest, most architecturally interesting train station in Europe just opened on May 26, 2006. Formerly known as the Lehrter Bahnhof, it is now the main Berlin railway station and has been renamed: Berlin Hauptbahnhof–Lehrter Bahnhof.

On the one hand, the DB AG has competition from other rail companies; on the other, it is involved in the business sectors of energy, telecommunications, and security and is the largest operating authority for city trains, bus services, and the military. "Rent a car" is now also a slogan of the DB (Deutsche Bahn) and Bundeswehr (army) Fuhrpark (transport fleet). The various customers, railway or military, rent their cars from car centers based on need instead of having vehicles sit around unused in barracks. The new way of thinking is based on flexibility. Rail boss Helmut Mehdorn remarked in 2004: "We would like to be in touch with the customer at the very beginning of the trip planning process and offer all the necessary services. This begins with planning the route and the choice of transportation, to internet connections and extends to car rental facilities at the train station and hotel reservations either for a vacation or business travel" (ibid., 27). "*Lückenlos mobil*" (completely mobile) is one of the slogans. This includes bicycles in a few cities from DB Call a Bike (ibid., 104), as the program is called in *Denglisch* (see 2: Language, Script, and Gestures), and it includes a global logistic system (ibid., 119–143). Certainly, a new chapter for the German rail system had begun by 1993 for which the future is hard to predict.

Boats and Planes

There were 2,200 oceangoing vessels registered with German shipping lines in 2002, and this German fleet was regarded as one of the safest and most modern in the world. Although the major European port for waterborne freight is Rotterdam, in the Netherlands, one-third of all freight shipped by water passes through Hamburg, Bremen/Bremerhaven, Wilhelmshaven, Lübeck, and Rostock, which were able to maintain an important position in the international market. The German ports are "fast ports," as Klaus Lantermann explained. This mean that "even large oceangoing vessels can be turned around within a short space of time" (Lantermann et al. 2003, 304). In addition, the canal system is constantly being improved (see 1: Overcoming Regionalism). In 1992, the opening of a canal linking the river Main with the Danube completed the waterway link between the North Sea and the Black Sea (Lewis 2001, 31). Inland waterways totaling 7,500 kilometers connect most of the large cities and industrial centers.

Since the early 1990s, major expansions in air transport have also taken place. In 1992, a new airport opened in Munich, and in 1995 Stuttgart airport was upgraded. Schönefeld south of Berlin is under construction and will become the capital's future principal airport, Berlin Brandenburg International. It is scheduled to open in 2008. As of 2005, there were thirteen airports in Germany. The largest of these by far is Frankfurt Main International, the busiest airport on the continent and well connected to the German railway system. Major trains stop at the airport—not just shuttle trains. It is also the leading air cargo center for all of Europe. Düsseldorf, Germany's second-largest airport, is usually the preferred airport for charter flights. Most of the other airports are primarily for intra-European flights. Some of these flights within Europe are extremely cheap nowadays but often connected to obscure airports. Travelers are not always aware of this and are surprised to have to pay more money for transportation from the airport to the city center than the cost of the original airfare. Deutsche Lufthansa AG was privatized in the first half of the

1990s. It now finds itself in a tough international competitive situation and is fighting for survival.

From A to Z

Agriculture: Agricultural products from Germany cover 90 percent of Germany's needs. Many products are also exported. Grains and sugar beets prevail in the north and especially in the eastern states. Vegetables, milk, and meat are produced primarily in the south. Vineyards are found along the Rhine, Main, and Mosel in Franconia, the Palatinate, the Kaiserstuhl, and Badenia (see 4: From Traditional Fare to International Cuisine). North-Rhine Westphalia has the highest rate of beer production in the country, but Bavaria (and especially Munich) are best known for their many beers and beer festivals (see 5: Holidays and Local Festivals).

Autobahn: An expressway. *Autobahn* is one of the few German words almost any foreigner knows and is synonymous to many with *freie Fahrt* (driving without speed restrictions). The feeling of freedom that Germans associate with the autobahn is found in the musical piece *Autobahn* by the techno group Kraftwerk (see 8: Music). Richard Lord wrote enthusiastically about it: "The near legendary German autobahn is the Taj Mahal, the Mecca, the Mount Everest, the El Dorado of the world's motorists. Every foreign driver has heard of it, been warned about it, been urged to dare it, and then suddenly, there you are—rolling along on the world's most famous highway. You may get your kicks on Route 66, but that autobahn offers a transcendental experience" (Lord 2004, 139). Of course, on many stretches one can drive 160–200 kilometers per hour (km/h) (96–120 mph)—or whatever speed the car is able to reach—and for many, 140–160 km/h (and not the officially recommended 130 km/h [78 mph]) are normal travel speeds—which can be very safe if everyone adheres to the basic rule of avoiding tailgating. At the same time, traffic conditions seldom allow for top speeds, and many stretches are limited to 130 km/h or even less.

The main concern for many Germans is not safety but the pollution caused by large-volume, high-speed traffic. During the summer months, when everyone is on vacation (see 5: Holidays and Local Festivals), the Autobahn is, certainly, not the fastest highway but often the largest parking lot in Europe. Until 2005, German *Autobahnen* were free of charge. Since 2005, large trucks (12 tons and up) have to pay a *Maut* (toll). In contrast to popular opinion, the Autobahn was not an "invention" of the Third Reich. One of the first streets with separate lanes for two-way traffic was the *Automobil-Verkehrs- und Übungsstraße* (AVUS) in Berlin (planned in 1907 and completed in 1921). In 1924, the planning for a network of highways began, and in 1926 the Verein zum Bau einer Straße für den Kraftwagen-Schnellverkehr von Hamburg über Frankfurt a.M. nach Basel (Hafraba e.V., Association for the Construction of a Highway for High-Speed Traffic from Hamburg via Frankfurt on the Main to Basel) was founded. It was this organization that offered the plans that the Third Reich was able to utilize once in power. (See "Highway Code," below.)

Automobile clubs: The best-known German automobile clubs are the Allgemeiner Deutscher Automobil Club (ADAC) and the Auto Club Europa (ACE).

Bagging: Primarily, customers from the United States have to get used to the fact that bagging is usually not done in German stores. Customers have to do that for themselves. Often, bags cost extra. Customers tend to bring their own shopping bags.

Bicycles: Bicycles are very popular in Germany. In many university towns, they are the main means of transportation, but they are also a favored recreational vehicle. There are many cycling lanes and routes in cities and in the countryside. For a map of these routes, see www.adfc.de, the Web site of the Allgemeiner Deutscher Fahrrad-Club (General German Bicyclist Association, ADFC).

BMW: The firm began as a manufacturer of aircraft in 1916 under the name Bayerische Flugzeugwerke (Bavarian Airplane Company) and was renamed the Bayerische Motoren Werke in 1917. One year later the firm went public. After the war, the company repaired U.S. army vehicles in exchange for permission to continue manufacturing spare parts and bicycles. In 1947, production was expanded to motorcycles, and the first ones appeared the following year. In 1994, BMW bought the British firm Rover. It acquired Rolls Royce in 1998 but sold Rover again in 2000, keeping just the Minibrand from that group (www.bmw.com).

Companies/Trademarks: Among the best-known German companies (in alphabetical order) are: **Adidas-Salomon**, the world's second largest manufacturer of sporting goods. The company dates back to 1920 when its founder and name-giver **Adi Dass**ler produced his first hand-made training shoe. The chemical company **BASF** (**B**adische **A**nilin- & **S**oda-**F**abrik) was founded in 1865. To quote their ad campaign in the United States: "At BASF, we don't make a lot of the products you buy. We make a lot of the products you buy better." The chemical company **Bayer** was founded in 1863 by Friedrich Bayer (1825–1880) and Johann Friedrich Weskott (1821–1870) and originally produced synthetic dyes. The expansion to a general pharmaceutical company began in 1881 when it was transformed into a joint stock company. Aspirin, its best known product, was launched in 1899. The tire manufacturer **Continental** was founded in 1871. **Deutsche Bank**, Germany's largest bank, was founded in 1870. **e.on** was founded in 2000 and is, five years later, the world's largest private energy provider. The "e" stands for energy, the period indicates modernity, and "on" signals an innovative start. In 2004, nine out of ten Germans were already familiar with the brand. **Henkel**, producer of *Persil* laundry detergent, was founded in the *Gründerzeit* (foundation years) by Fritz Henkel. **Merck**, one of the oldest chemical-pharmaceutical companies in the world, has its beginnings in a pharmacy established in Darmstadt, Hesse, in 1668. It became a factory in 1827. **RWE** (**R**heinisch-**W**estfälisches **E**lektrizitätswerk), one of Germany's energy giants, was founded in 1898. **SAP** (**S**ystems, **A**pplications and **P**roducts), world market leader in open, integrated software solutions for business, was founded in 1972.

The pharmaceutical group **Schering** goes back to Ernst Schering's pharmacy, which opened in 1851. **Siemens**, producer of practically everything in the field of electrotechnology and electronics, was founded by Werner von Siemens in 1847. In 1999, two German steel giants merged to form **ThyssenKrupp**, today also a high-technology enterprise. Not as powerful as the giants but nevertheless helping to represent Germany in a global market are many smaller companies (see Brand Names in chapter 5 Food): **Birkenstock** footwear celebrated its 225th anniversary in 1999. The name going back to documented shoemakers of the same name. **Faber-Castell** set the standard for all future pencils. Lothar von Faber, who took over the family business of pencil-making in the fourth generation in 1839, is credited with creating the hexagonal shape, typical for most pencils, and the scale of hardness for pencils still in use today. To protect his products from imitators, he petitioned the German Reichstag in 1874 to create a law for the protection of trademarks. The law was passed and Faber pencils belonged to the very first branded articles in the world. The name was later changed to Faber-Castell due to the marriage of his grand-daughter. For the ever popular **Hummel** figurines, see 9: Visual Arts. **Meissen**, the name of a town in Saxony, gave its name to Germany's best-known and Europe's oldest porcelain brand. It has been produced since 1710. **Melitta** coffee filters changed the way coffee was brewed. The idea of a filter was invented in 1908 by Melitta Bentz from Dresden, who was annoyed by the coffee grinds in her cups of coffee. Her solution was to drill holes into the bottom of a coffee pot and covered them with a piece of blotting paper. She and her husband,

Hugo Bentz, realized the marketing potential of this simple idea and had it patented. They started their own firm that grew into an international business. In 1925, they introduced the typical Melitta colors (red and green) and in 1932 a special font for their brand name (both are still used today). **Nivea** (from Latin meaning "snowy"), with its association of Grimm's fairy tale of "Schneewittchen" (Snow White), whose skin was "white as snow," was the first cream for adult skin care in the world when it was developed in 1912 by Oskar Troplowitz, an apothecary and owner of the pharmaceutical laboratory Beiersdorf in Hamburg. **Odol**, the mouthwash, was introduced to the market by Karl-August Lingner in 1893. The name derives from the Greek word for "tooth" (odous), and the Latin word for "oil" (oleum). **Pelikan** (pelican), synonymous with writing utensils in Germany, had August Leonardi's "magic ink" patented in 1856. It did not gel in the writing process and did not fade afterwards. Günter Wagner, a later owner of the company, chose the pelican sitting in its nest and feeding its young ones with her own blood (a symbol found in Gothic churches for Christ's sacrifice, giving his blood for mankind) as a trademark that was then registered in 1878. It was one of the very first German trademarks. **Penaten**, the baby cream, registered its patent in 1904. The wife of the pharmacist Max Riese, Elisabeth, suggested the brand name due to her interest in Roman history. "Penaten" (penates) were the household gods of the Romans, and therefore well suited for a cream for babies. **Pritt** was the first glue stick in the world in the form of a lipstick. It was patented by the Henkel company in 1969. **Teefix**, the tea bag, was patented in 1913 and played an important role in World War I for the soldiers on the front for easily prepared tea rations. The company, *Teekanne* (tea pot), is one of the oldest registered German trademarks from 1882. **Tempo**, which became the generic German term for paper handkerchiefs, was introduced in 1929 by the Vereinigte Papierwerke Nürnberg (United Paper Manufacturers of Nuremberg). Its name, Tempo, going back to a slogan of the hectic twenties: Tempo, no time, no time. **Tesa**, or **Tesafilm**, has become the generic name for adhesive tape in Germany. Introduced in 1935 as *Beiersdorf Klebefilm* (adhesive tape by Beiersdorf), it was renamed by Hugo Kirchberger, a Beiersdorf employee, in 1941 using the first two letters of the family name and the last two letters of the first name of his boss's secretary, Elsa Tesmer. **Tipp-Ex**, with its English name, still found on the shelves and desks of most offices even in the computer age, was a German invention. In 1959, Otto W. Corbs founded the firm in Frankfurt and began selling the coated paper strips that allowed for easy corrections of mistakes made on the typewriter. In the second half of the 1960s, the firm introduced the liquid Tipp-Ex that helped to cover up not only typos but also mistakes made in drawings, etc. Today, Tipp-Ex is part of the international BIC conglomerate. **Steiff** company, the popular manufacturer of toy animals (especially teddy bears) with the characteristic button in the left ear, was founded in 1880 by the dressmaker Margarete Steiff, who suffered from polio. She realized that an elephant-shaped needle pincushion was as much enjoyed by children as it was useful for adults. She therefore began producing animal toys out of felt. In 1902, her nephew introduced the bear to the ever-growing toy selection. The bear, a favorite with children, eventually became known as a Teddy bear because of cartoons showing the U.S. president Theodor Roosevelt and a small bear. In 1902, he had refused to shoot a captured bear cub during a hunting trip in Mississippi. The button in the ear of the toy animals became a trademark in 1904. **Uhu**, invented in 1932 by August Fischer, became the generic term in Germany for all-purpose glue. The name came from the powerful eagle owl, a bird of prey still existing at the time in the Black Forest, the home of the inventor. For other companies (e.g. car manufacturers), see the alphabetical entries and the index.

Consumer counseling: There are several organizations in Germany that are independent information centers for all consumers. The best known are Bundesverband der Verbraucherzentralen und Verbraucherverbände (Federal Association of the Consumer Advice Centers and Consumer Organizations) (www.vzbv.de); Stiftung Warentest (Ecology Test) (www.stiftung-warentest.de); and Öko-Test (Foundation Product Test) (www.oeko-test.de).

Currency: On January 1, 2002, the European Union adopted the euro (€) as its currency (based on the Maastricht Treaty of 1992). Twelve countries joined the Eurozone: Austria, Belgium, Finland, France, Germany, Greece, Ireland, Italy, Luxembourg, Netherlands, Portugal, and Spain. The currency has seven denominations of bills and eight different coins; the bills are 5, 10, 20, 50, 100, 200, and 500 €, and the coins are 1 € and 2 € and 1, 2, 5, 10, 20, and 50 cents. There are 100 cents in 1 €. On the front of the banknotes, the image includes windows and gateways, and on the reverse a bridge, symbolizing the European spirit of openness as well as the spirit of cooperation. The front side of each coin features one of three designs common to all twelve euro-area countries, showing different maps of Europe surrounded by the twelve stars of the EU. For the reverse side, each nation can choose motifs particular to that country.

DAX: (*Deutscher Aktienindex*) It is the German euqivalent of "Dow Jones," i.e., the leading stock index of the German Stock Exchange group. It measures changes in the value of the thirty largest German joint-stock companies.

Department stores: The main difference between U.S. and German department stores is the fact that German stores have large grocery sections and cafeterias. Even gourmet restaurants can be found in department stores. The best example is the sixth floor of the KaDeWe (Kaufhauf des Westens, Department Store of the West) in Berlin, which offers an array of gourmet foods. The best-known German chains include Hertie, Karstadt, Kaufhof, and Horten.

Deposits: Glass and other bottles or containers often have what is called a *Pfand* (deposit) (see "Recycling," below).

Deutsche Telekom: It is the largest provider of telecommunication service in Europe.

Digital service: As with most electronic ventures, digital services in Germany rely on international alliances. Derek Lewis summarized the situation this way: "By 1995 the communications market in Ger-

many had polarised into two main rivals: on the one hand the Kirch concern, which controlled access to its digital television services by its own decoder, and on the other hand the multimedia consortium MMBG (*Multimedia-Betriebsgesellschaft*) comprising mainly Bertelsmann and RTL but also including the public corporations ARD and ZDF, Deutsche Telekom and the French pay-TV company Canal plus" (Lewis 2001, 182).

Driver's licenses: Germany recognizes driver's licenses of other EU member states. All others (including the international license) are only valid for a year in Germany.

Economy: In 2003, Germany still ranked third in the world in terms of total economic output and second with regard to world trade (Lantermann et al. 2003, 234), in spite of its economic troubles caused by unification (see 1: From Two to One). The gross domestic product (GDP) per capita was 24,000 euros in 2002—that is, a total of 1,980 billion euros. While the service sector was increasing, the industrial sector, which made up one-third of the German economy, was decreasing. Germany was, behind the United States and Japan, the third-largest automobile producer. The chemical industry was also very important for exports (Beck 2003, 26). Its export ratio increased between 1991 and 2001 from 50 percent to almost 70 percent. The other leading sectors were mechanical and electrical engineering. Biotechnology was also slowly catching up. More than the economies of other nations, the German economy has an international focus; about one-fourth of all jobs depend on the export trade. According to *Facts about Germany*, the German trade surplus increased from about 11 billion euros in 1991 to around 84 billion euros in 2002. In 2001, the trade surplus had reached a record 87 billion euros (Lantermann et al. 2003, 235).

Employee qualifications: According to Klaus Lantermann (based on surveys after 2000), 84 percent of employees have vocational qualifications, and 16 percent of those have an additional degree from a technical college or institute of tertiary education (Lantermann et al. 2003, 249). (See also 3: The Educational System.)

Euratom: European Atomic Energy Community, established on March 25, 1957, at the same time as the European Economic Community (EEC). In 1967, the European Coal and Steel Community (ECSC), Euratom, and the EEC merged. The plural "Communities," as in Court of Justice of the European Communities, is an occasional reminder of the existence of more than one distinct institution. (See "European Economic Community [EEC]," below.)

Euro: The new currency of the European Union. In 2002 in Germany, the mark (Deutsche Mark, with its subdivision, pfennig [penny]) was replaced by the euro and its subdivision, the cent. (See "Currency," above.)

European Coal and Steel Community (ECSC): It was founded in 1951 under the Treaty of Paris and was based on a plan developed by the French economist Jean Monnet and endorsed by the French secretary of state, Robert Schuman. The founding members were France, West Germany, Italy, Belgium, Luxembourg, and the Netherlands. The driving force behind the

creation of ECSC was the desire to allow the German coal and steel industries to operate again to their full potentials without becoming a threat to the other European nations. This was achieved by creating a meta-national structure, the basis for the later Common Market and the European Union. (See also "Euratom," above; "European Economic Community [EEC]," below.)

European Economic Community (EEC): The ECSC of 1951, the EEC (also known as the Common Market), founded on March 25, 1957, by the signing of the Treaty of Rome, and Euratom, founded at the same time by a second Rome treaty, are the forerunners of the European Union. (See "Euratom" and "European Coal and Steel Community [ECSC]," above, and "European Union," below.)

European Union (EU): The European Union was established by the Treaty on European Union (commonly known as the Maastricht Treaty) in 1992. Its activities cover all policy areas. However, the nature of its powers depends on the powers transferred to it by its member states. The EU therefore resembles a federation (in monetary affairs and agricultural, trade, and environmental policy), a confederation (in social and economic policy, consumer protection, and internal affairs), and an international organization (in foreign affairs). A key activity of the EU is the establishment and administration of a common single market consisting of a customs union, a single currency (adopted by twelve of the twenty-five member states), a Common Agricultural Policy, and a Common Fisheries Policy. On October 29, 2004, European heads of state signed a treaty establishing a Constitution for Europe, which is currently awaiting ratification by individual member states. Unfortunately, the process ran into severe problems in 2005 after a referendum on its ratification was rejected by the citizens of two of the founding members, the Netherlands and France. The future of the constitution is therefore uncertain. Many political analysts were not surprised about the outcome of these referenda because they came at a time when the EU had doubled in size since 1992 from twelve to twenty-five member states. The enlargement brought more cultural diversity with all its positive and negative aspects. The original founders of the EU saw their role being diminished in the new EU and clearly feared a shift in policy.

Flohmarkt: Flea market. Flea markets have been popular in Germany for decades but experienced a renaissance in the new millennium. In some towns, they are open every day, but in most localities they only operate on weekends. Very often, special flea markets are organized on a monthly or irregular basis. They vary tremendously in size as well as in quality of items offered, ranging from household items to antiques, and are usually very entertaining. As in all the best flea markets, bargaining is usually an accepted part of the fun.

Gleitende Arbeitszeit: Flexible working hours. The concept was instituted in some companies to allow better coordination of household chores for working spouses and thereby to create a better working environment. All employees are expected to be physically present at work during a core time, but there are other time periods, usually at the beginning and end of the workday, that are flexible.

Godesberger Programm: Named after the town in which the program was ratified (Bad Godesberg), it proclaimed a new ideological basis for the German labor party that had its roots in both socialism and communism. After the economic successes of the conservative party (CDU), the Social Democrats (SPD) decided to move ahead and abandon some of their old socialist and communist ideals. In 1959, they embraced the concept of a social market economy and emphasized the importance of entrepreneurship, free-market competition, and freedom of choice in regard to jobs and consumption of goods.

Highway code: Germany has a reputation for fast driving (see 2: Stereotypes and Prejudices; "*Autobahn,*" above). Yet, most highways in Germany have speed limits, as in other countries. Only some parts of the Autobahn have no restrictions; on these roads, the recommended speed is 130 km/h. The speed limit within towns is 50 km/h; in many residential areas, it is 30 km/h or even lower—for example, in clearly marked *Spielstraßen* (play streets), in which cars, pedestrians, and children share the street. Outside city limits, on country roads, the speed limit is 80 km/h. The speed limits are enforced. Many towns have elaborate radar speed boxes that take a photograph of the car, the driver, and the license number and then send fines through the mail.

Inventions and discoveries: At the end of the nineteenth century and the beginning of the twentieth, German accomplishments in the fields of science and technology were impressive. Many of the inventors from the period are very much a part of the general consciousness. Some of the most noted are as follows: Carl Friedrich Benz (1844–1929) and Gottlieb Wilhelm Daimler (1834–1900), who developed the first cars (their companies merged and became Mercedes Benz); Paul Ehrlich (1854–1915), who developed chemotherapy; Albert Einstein (1879–1955), founder of the theory of relativity; Robert Koch (1843–1910), who developed modern bacteriology; Otto Lilienthal (1848–1896), who made advances in aviation technology (seen by Germans as the inventor of the airplane, which then was continued and commercialized by the Wright brothers); Emmy Noether (1882–1935), founder of modern axiomatic algebra; Max Planck (1858–1947), founder of the quantum theory; Wilhelm Conrad Röntgen (1845–1923), who invented X-ray technology; and Konrad Zuse (1910–1995), who worked on the first calculating system using binary computation, and who is seen by many Germans as the father of computers.

Konzertierte Aktion: Concerted action. This economic concept of bridging the gap between the Unternehmensverbänden (employers' associations) and the Gewerkschaften (unions) was introduced in 1968 by Karl Schiller (1911–1994), the new minister of economy and finance (who was called the *Superminister* because of the combination of two departments). He did not shy away from governmental interference in the economy, investment programs, tax changes, and regular meetings between unions and employer organizations. The result was very positive, and Schiller was able to create a new image for his socialist party as an economic innovator, the "better CDU."

Ladenschlußgesetz: Law on store closing, originally passed in 1956, modified in 2003

and 2005. It is the most berated German law by foreigners who are used to a more favorable shopping climate. Some claim that it is the most restrictive in Europe. The only exception is granted to stores in train stations and service stations. In 1993, even the highest German administrative court established the legality of after-hour sales of such items as "travel necessities" (Flippo 1999, 116). Although smaller stores close during the noon break, department stores remain open, as indicated by the sign reading "*durchgehend geöffnet*" (open without interruption).

Lufthansa: One of the world's leading airlines, Lufthansa was founded in 1926 following the merger of *Deutsche Aero Lloyd* (German Aero Lloyd) and *Junkers Luftverkehr* (Junker's Air Travel).

MAN: (**M**aschinenfabrik **A**ugsburg-**N**ürnberg) One of the leading companies in the commercial vehicles sector.

Marshall Plan: On June 5, 1947, U.S. Secretary of State George C. Marshall outlined at Harvard University his ideas of offering help to the suffering postwar nations of Europe. The Europeans—including West Germany—would be given up to $20 billion for relief if they could act as a single economic unit. Cooperation was the key. Marshall also offered aid to the Soviet Union and its allies in Eastern Europe, but Stalin denounced the program as a trick and refused to participate. Of course, the plan also benefited the U.S. economy because the money would be used to buy goods from the United States. Stressing cooperation, the Marshall Plan showed the way to a vital Europe (see "Euratom," "European Coal and Steel Community [ECSC]," and

"European Economic Community [EEC]," above, and "Schuman Plan," below).

Measurements: Germany adopted the metric system in the nineteenth century. Even the German *Pfund* (pound) fits into that system because it is exactly half a kilo, or 500 grams. The English pound is only 474 grams.

Mehrwertssteuer: Value-added tax, a type of sales tax. In Germany, the tax is already included in the price of goods and not added on as in the United States. Tourists can fill out a form that they have to hand in to custom officials at the border to be reimbursed at a later time.

Mercedes Benz: The luxury car firm founded by Gottlieb Daimler and Karl Benz in 1886. The name Mercedes was first introduced in 1899 by a businessman and racing enthusiast who had used his daughter's name as a pseudonym in a race. The first official Mercedes model was produced in 1901, and the name has been used ever since. In 1998, Mercedes Benz merged with the Chrysler Group (www.mercedes-benz.com).

Mitfahrgelegenheit: Ride-sharing. Many cities have *Mitfahrzentralen* (MFZ, carpooling centers) where drivers register who are looking for travelers to share the costs of travel.

Newspaper stands: Newspaper vendors have different names in different regions (*Kiosk, Trinkhalle, Büdchen*). They are often open late into the evening and usually sell drinks, sweets, and cigarettes in addition to the newspapers.

Online service providers: In 1984, the Deutsche Bundespost (federal postal service) offered a simple Bildschirmtext (literally, screen text; view data) service. This developed in 1991 into the more sophisticated Data Exchange für Jedermann (Datex-J), and then, since 1995, T-Online (Telekom-Online), which gives access to leading national daily newspapers and various databases. Competitors today include AOL Europa, a joint venture between America Online and Bertlesmann, and EOL (Europe Online), owned by Burda and some foreign concerns (see 6: Publishers). Online banking as well as online shopping is growing and changing rapidly (see also "Tele-shopping," below).

Patents: Besides Sweden and Finland, Germany still occupies a leading position in Europe in regard to patents. Its share of applications at the European Patent Office climbed from 8.5 percent in 1998 to about 10 percent in 2000 (Lantermann et al. 2003, 247). In mechanical engineering (especially automotive engineering), followed by chemical and electrical products, Germany is a leader in innovation.

Payments: In contrast to stores in the United States, many stores in Germany do not accept Visa, Mastercard, and Discover credit cards. The EC Card is often accepted, although cash is still usually the normal method of payment.

Porsche: The sportiest of the better-known auto brands. The firm was established in 1948, although the mastermind behind the design, Ferdinand Porsche, had been designing cars long before that for both Mercedes and Volkswagen. His son, Ferdinand

Alexander Porsche, joined the design team in the 1960s, and the company went public in 1972. The firm has continually produced both roadsters and racing cars (www. porsche.com).

Postal service: The Deutsche Bundespost handles mail, telegrams, and faxes and collects radio and television fees. Although the mail, telephone, and banking services are handled by different joint-stock companies, it is still possible to make a phone call at the post office and pay after the call has been completed—without having to have a phone card or the right number or combination of coins. The post office also handles banking and investment transactions through postal savings accounts and exchanges foreign money. *Postleitzahlen* (zip codes) were introduced in 1962, when four-digit numbers designated the various areas. In 1993, the numbers were changed to five digits. (See also 1: From A to Z, "Postal codes.")

Public transportation: Germany still prides itself on having a well-organized public transportation system. Although much has been privatized, there are so-called *Verkehrsverbünde* (collaborative ventures among several entities). Air traffic, trains, buses, trams, subways, private car rentals, and bicycle leasing may in some cities go hand in hand. In most areas, one can buy special tickets that allow the use of all public transportation for a limited region and time period. Tickets for individual rides are also usually available at ticket machines, but the cost per ride is higher with these. Unfortunately, these machines are often very confusing for foreigners with the many options offered for cer-

tain regions, conditions, and the like. Yet, many tram and bus drivers are patient and willing to help. Traveling without a ticket (*Schwarzfahren*) can result in a heavy fine.

Recycling: Germany is a leader in recycling efforts. Cities and villages have containers on the street for different sorts of glass. Each individual household is encouraged to separate recyclable items from the normal trash. There are usually several different bins (for paper and yard waste) and sacks (often yellow, for packaging of various sorts). Composting is also strongly encouraged. Packaging often has a symbol called "Green Point" (*Grüner Punkt*) indicating that it can and should be recycled. The actual garbage bins are only for *Restmüll*, that is, garbage that did not fit into one of the recycling categories. Therefore, garbage bins are small by many standards, and the special sacks for recyclables (plastics, paper, glass, and cans) are large. For some containers, particularly glass bottles, there is a deposit. These containers are often reused and are called *Mehrweg* (literally, "more way") containers. (See also "Rubbish," below.)

Regulations: Just as complex as the technological aspect of the new media is the question of its regulation. In 1996, the *Bund* (federal government) and the *Länder* (states) agreed on a first multimedia law. The states are in charge of new media services aimed at the general public, whereas the federal government regulates the services for individual subscribers. Yet, global networks require global solutions. National laws, such as Germany's law against Nazi propaganda, are difficult to enforce in the new electronic age.

Research centers: Research centers and scientific institutions are grouped together into associations. For example, the Helmholtz Association is a group of 15 research centers in six research fields, ranging from cancer research to aerospace. The Fraunhofer Society comprises 80 institutes with 12,700 experts for application-oriented research for industry and the public sector. The Leibniz Association includes 80 institutes, ranging from the humanities to economics and mathematics. Finally, the Max Planck Society has 78 research institutions with 12,300 scientists in the natural, biological, and social sciences and the humanities.

Resources: Germany's main natural resources are coal and salt, but it has almost no oil or iron. The reserves of natural gas cover only about a quarter of Germany's own needs. This lack of resources has necessarily shaped the German economy.

Rubbish: Garbage that contains poisons or chemicals (including batteries) has to be taken to special depots. Old furniture and other large appliances are called *Sperrmüll* (bulky waste) and are picked up on specific days. In some cities, special arrangements can also be made for collection. Many towns publish garbage calendars to keep everyone informed about the complex trash collection schedule. Used shoes and clothes that are still in good condition can be placed in special containers. The Red Cross, the Salvation Army, and other organizations make use of these items, sort, and resell them or use them for charity.

Sales: There used to be only two specified periods in which sales were allowed: the *Winterschlussverkauf* (winter close-out

sale) in the last week of January and first week of February, and the *Sommerschlussverkauf* (summer close-out sale) for two weeks in July and August. These arrangements, which strike foreigners as rather strange and rigid, were instituted to protect the small stores (often family-run) that could never compete with large operations. Only individual items can be marked down outside of these seasons. Globalization has changed this practice. With the exception of books, where there are still fixed prices (*Preisbindung*), reductions on individual items are possible at any time.

Schuman Plan: Since 1949, West Germany's heavy industry has been controlled by an international agency. The French secretary of state, Robert Schuman, proposed a European agency for coal and steel production in which West Germany would be a full member. It was designed to help unite Europe and prevent future wars. (See European Coal and Steel Community [ECSC].)

Shopping carts: Many stores require a deposit for using a shopping cart (the same is true with luggage trolleys in many train stations). To use a cart, the shopper must insert a euro coin into a slot at the handle of the cart, which releases a chain connecting the cart to other carts. The money is returned when one returns the cart to its original location and connects it by the chain to the other carts.

Specialty stores: Due to the dual educational system (see 3: The Educational System), there are still many specialty stores, such as butchers, bakeries, and confectioneries, in Germany. They offer excellent food (see 4: From Traditional Fare to International Cuisine), including special meat cuts and lavish cakes and pastries. The people who work in such stores are usually very knowledgeable about their field and are often products of the vocational training system.

Standort Deutschland: Investment and business location Germany. In the new millennium, German investments abroad are still higher than foreign investments in Germany, yet those investments have increased considerably since the outgoing 1990s. Since the turn of the millennium, Germany has ranked second (after the United States) in terms of investment inflows into the country. *Facts about Germany*, a publication by the Federal Foreign Office, stated: "As a result of these healthy inflows of capital, the scale of foreign investment in Germany has almost tripled since the beginning of the 1990s, from around 100 billion to 280 billion at the end of 2000. . . . The scale of German direct investments abroad almost quadrupled over the same period, namely from 150 billion to 570 billion" (Lantermann et al. 2003, 239). A survey conducted in 2004 ranked Germany third among the best business locations in the world (Hintereder 2004, 43).

Strikes: Owing to the social climate in Germany (see 3: The Social Net), which is based on a social partnership between unions and employers, the number of strike days averaged about a tenth of those in the United States (Lantermann et al. 2003, 249).

Taxis: One of the surprising first impressions of Germany for foreigners is the fact, as Richard Lord observed, "that almost all taxis are Mercedes. You knew this was a prosperous country, but this well-wheeled? Somebody will tell you before long that the government gives big tax write-offs for the purchase of these luxury cabs, which are well built to take all sorts of wear and tear. And don't forget that Mercedes is a proud German product. Still, it is impressive" (Lord 2004, 10).

Telefonkarte: Prepaid telephone cards credited with a certain amount for the small minority of people in Germany who do not have a "handy" (cell phone) and are still inclined to use a public phone. When first introduced, they were collected for their different designs.

Tele-shopping: Already in the late 1980s, the commercial television station RTL experimented with a tele-shopping service called *Teleboutique*. In 1995, a special channel for tele-shopping existed for a short time until it ran into legal problems.

Tele-working: As in many other countries around the world, in Germany more and more companies employ tele-workers— that is, employees working from a home office. This development will significantly change commerce, working patterns, and social life. It will also change education. Excellent online learning providers are already active, one of which offers opportunities to nonnative speakers to brush up their German via the Internet: www.interdeutsch.de.

Trading partners: In 2002, the list of German trading partners was headed by France, followed by the Netherlands, the United States, and Great Britain. Poland led the partners in Eastern and Central Europe, followed by the Czech Republic and Hungary. The total trade with Central and Eastern Europe accounted for almost 12 percent and surpassed the trade with North America (Lantermann et al. 2003, 236–237).

Train tickets: There is a plethora of changing options for train tickets, and it is a good idea to seek information on these at a travel agency or the station information office. There are tickets for small groups, for weekend travelers, for frequent travelers, for various age groups, and so on. Although the individual ticket may seem expensive, for smart travelers the train still is an economical way to travel. The Interrail Ticket for young people is probably the best-known option. Also very popular are the Bahn Cards that one can buy for a set fee. Depending on the type of card, one can then get a reduction of 25 percent or even 50 percent on the standard price of a ticket.

Transrapid: The magnet railway offers the fastest and most comfortable and safe means of transportation. As Klaus Lantermann stated, "Its environment-friendly technology also makes it very economical, as it is subject to almost no wear and tear and uses comparatively little energy, making it cheaper to operate than traditional railway systems" (Lantermann et al. 2003, 302).

TÜV: *Technischer Überwachungsverein*, or Technical Inspection. Cars have to pass a regular inspection in Germany to prove their roadworthiness. This is done by the TÜV, which issues a sticker indicating the length of authorization.

Verbraucherzentrale: Consumer Advice Center. This is an agency to help confused consumers find information about appliances, insurance, or almost any other topic. The center's professional staff members give advice and provide access to their copious files.

Volkswagen: Automobile manufacturer founded in 1937. Construction of the cars, designed by Ferdinand Porsche, began at the Wolfsburg plant in 1938. During World War II, the plant switched to production of armaments, and 20,000 forced laborers were employed at the firm. By the end of 2001, more than 2,050 of these workers had received reparations from the company. The firm was taken over by the British immediately after the war, returned to German management in 1949, and internationalized in 1952. Volkswagen became a public shareholding company in 1960 (www.volkswagen.com).

Additional Readings

Bank, Gerhard. *Die Deutsche Bahn aktuell. Typen, Trassen, Impressionen 1994 bis heute.* Stuttgart: Kosmos, 2003.

———. *Staatsbahnen in Deutschland.* Stuttgart: Kosmos, 2004.

Blühdorn, Ingolfur, Frank Krause, and Thomas Scharf. *The Green Agenda: Environmental Politics and Policy in Germany.* Keele, Staffordshire: Keele University Press, 1995.

Bretschneider, Rudolf. *Konsumgesellschaft.* Wien: Picus Verlag, 2000.

Deutsche Bahn AG, ed. *Die Bahn macht mobil.* Berlin: Druckhaus Kaufmann, 2004.

Dominick, Raymond H. *The Environmental Movement in Germany: Prophets and Pioneers, 1871–1971.* Bloomington and Indianapolis: Indiana University Press, 1992.

Dostal, Michael. *DB-Fahrzeuge.* Bd. 3: *Güterwagen der Deutschen Bahn.* München: Bruckmann, 2001.

———. *DB-Fahrzeuge.* München: Bruckmann, 2004.

Dostal, Michael, and Andreas Braun. *DB-Fahrzeuge*. Bd. 2: *Reisezugwagen der Deutschen Bahn*. München: GeraNova Zeitschriftenverlag, 1998.

Federal Statistical Office, Germany. Online www.destatis.de.

Gall, Lothar, and Manfred Pohl. *Die Eisenbahn in Deutschland. Von den Anfängen bis zur Gegenwart*. München: Beck, 1999.

GeraNova-Team. *Bahn Extra: 200 Jahre Eisenbahn*. München: GeraNova, 2004.

Green Party, www.gruene.de.

Hintereder, Peter, ed. "Innovation through Excellence." *Deutschland. Forum on Politics, Culture and Business* 4 (2004): 42–47.

Hooks, Mike. *Lufthansa*. Erfurt: Sutton, 2000.

Jeffries, Ian, and Manfred Melzer, eds. *The East German Economy*. London: Routledge and Kegan Paul, 1988.

König, Johann-Günther. *Global Player Telekom*. Reinbek bei Hamburg: Rowohlt, 1997.

König, Wolfgang. *Geschichte der Konsumgesellschaft*. Stuttgart: Franz Steiner Verlag, 2000.

Langenscheidt, Florian, ed. *Deutsche Standards. Marken des Jahrhunderts. Die Königsklasse deutscher Produkte und Dienstleistungen in Wort und Bild–von Aspirin bis Zeiss*. Köln: Deutsche Standards Editionen, 2003.

Lantermann, Klaus, Heiko Fiedler-Rauer, and Jens Specht, eds. *Facts about Germany*. Berlin: German Federal Foreign Office, Communications Section, 2003. See www.tatsachen-ueber-deutschland.de.

Leibniz-Institut für Länderkunde, ed. *Nationalatlas Bundesrepublik Deutschland—Unser Land in Karten, Texten und Bildern*. 6 Bände. Bd. 5: Jürgen Deiters, Peter Gräf, and Günter Löffler, eds. *Verkehr und Kommunikation*. Leiden and Heidelberg: Elsevier and Sprektrum Akademischer Verlag, 2004.

Miegel, Meinhard. *Die deformierte Gesellschaft. Wie die Deutschen ihre Wirklichkeit verdrängen*. München: Ullstein, 2002.

Owen Smith, Eric. *The German Economy*. London: Routledge, 1994.

Sarkar, Ranjana S. *Akteure, Interessen und Technologien der Telekommunikation. USA und Deutschland im Vergleich*. Frankfurt am Main and New York: Campus, 2001.

Scharf, Thomas. *The German Greens: Challenging the Consensus*. Oxford: Berg, 1994.

Siebert, Horst. *The German Economy: Beyond the Social Market*. New Haven, CT: Princeton University Press, 2005.

Steingart, Gabor. *Deutschland. Der Abstieg eines Superstars*. München and Zürich: Piper, 2004.

Wachtel, Joachim. *The Lufthansa Story: 1926–1984*, 3d ed. Lufthansa German Airlines, 1985.

Walz, Werner. *Deutschlands Eisenbahn. Lokomotiven und Wagen, Geschichte und Organisation, Kritik und Hoffnung*. Stuttgart: Motorbuch Verlag, 1991.

Wildt, Michael. *Vom kleinen Wohlstand. Eine Konsumgeschichte der fünfziger Jahre*. Frankfurt: S. Fischer, 1996.

Bibliography

Allinson, Mark. *Germany and Austria, 1814–2000*. Oxford and New York: Oxford University Press, 2002.

Ammon, Ulrich. *Die deutsche Sprache in Deutschland, Österreich und der Schweiz. Das Problem der nationalen Varietäten*. Berlin and New York: Walter de Gruyter, 1995.

Andritzky, Michael, and Thomas Rautenberg, eds. *"Wir sind nackt und nennen uns Du." Von Lichtfreunden und Sonnenkämpfern. Eine Geschichte der Freikörperkultur*. Gießen: Anabas, 1989.

Anweiler, Oskar. *Schulpolitik und Schulsystem in der DDR*. Opladen: Leske und Budrich, 1988.

Ardagh, John, and Katharina Ardagh. *Germany and the Germans*. London and New York: Penguin, 1995.

Arendt, Hannah. *Eichmann in Jerusalem. A Report on the Banality of Evil*. Revised and enlarged edition. New York: Penguin, 1977. Original edition, 1964.

Armbruster, Frank. *Politik in Deutschland. Systemvergleich Bundesrepublik Deutschland-DDR*. Kollegmaterial Politik. Wiesbaden: Gabler, 1981.

Atkins, Robert. *Art Speak. A Guide to Contemporary Ideas, Movements, and Buzzwords*. New York: Abbeville Press, 1990.

Auer, Peter, and Heiko Hausendorf, eds. *Kommunikation in gesellschaftlichen Umbruchsituationen. Mikroanalytische Aspekte des sprachlichen und gesellschaftlichen Wandels in den neuen Bundesländern*. Tübingen: Niemeyer, 2000.

Aust, Stefan, ed. *The Germans. Sixty Years after the War*. Spiegel Special International Edition 4 (2005).

Aust, Stefan, and Gerhard Spörl, eds. *Die Gegenwart der Vergangenheit. Der lange Schatten des Dritten Reichs*. München: Deutsche Verlags-Anstalt; Spiegel-Buchverlag, 2004.

Aveni, Anthony. *The Book of the Year: A Brief History of Our Seasonal Holidays*. Oxford and New York: Oxford University Press, 2003.

Baacke, Dieter. *Jugend und Subkultur*. München: Juventa, 1972.

———. *Jugend und Mode. Kleidung als Selbstinszenierung*. Opladen: Leske und Budrich, 1988.

———. *Jugend und Jugendkulturen. Darstellung und Deutung*, 4th ed. Weinheim and München: Juventa, 2004.

Bächtold-Stäubli, Hanns, and Eduard Hoffmann-Krayer. *Handwörterbuch des deutschen Aberglaubens*. 10 vols. Berlin and New York: Walter de Gruyter, 2000. (Original edition, 1927–1942)

Back, Anita, and Hermann Groeneveld. *Basler Fasnacht*, 2nd ed. Dortmund: Harenberg Kommunikation, 1989.

Bade, Klaus J., ed. *Population, Labour and Migration in the 19th and 20th Century*. Oxford: Berg, 1987.

———, ed. *Migration, Ethnizität, Konflikt*. Osnabrück: Universitätsverlag Rasch, 1996.

Bald, Detlef, and Reinhard Brühl. *Die Nationale Volksarmee—Armee für den Frieden. Beiträge zu Selbstverständnis und Geschichte des deutschen Militärs, 1945–1990*. Baden-Baden: Nomos, 1995.

Balfour, Michael Leonard Graham. *West Germany: A Contemporary History*. New York: St. Martin's Press, 1982.

Bank, Gerhard. *Die Deutsche Bahn aktuell. Typen, Trassen, Impressionen 1994 bis heute*. Stuttgart: Kosmos, 2003.

———. *Staatsbahnen in Deutschland*. Stuttgart: Kosmos, 2004.

Bark, Dennis L., and David R. Gress. *A History of West Germany*. Vol. 1: *From Shadow to Substance, 1945–1963*. Vol. 2: *Democracy and Its Discontents, 1963–1991*. Oxford and New York: Blackwell, 1989.

Bärnreuther, Andrea, and Peter-Klaus Schuster, eds. *Das XX. Jahrhundert. Kunst, Kultur, Politik und Gesellschaft in Deutschland*. Herausgegeben im Rahmen der Jahrhundertausstellung der Nationalgalerie Berlin "Das XX. Jahrhundert. Ein Jahrhundert Kunst in Deutschland." Köln: DuMont, 1999.

Baudissin, Wolf, Graf von. *Soldaten für den Frieden. Entwürfe für eine zeitgemäße Bundeswehr*. München: S. Piper, 1969.

Baumert, Jürgen, and Kai S. Cortina. *Das Bildungswesen in der Bundesrepublik Deutschland. Strukturen und Entwicklungen im Überblick*. Reinbek bei Hamburg: Rowohlt, 2003.

Bausinger, Hermann. *Typisch deutsch. Wie deutsch sind die Deutschen?* München: Beck, 2000. (Beck'sche Reihe.)

Beck, Marieluise. *A Manual for Germany. Ein Handbuch für Deutschland*. Berlin: Beauftragte der Bundesregierung für Migration, Flüchtlinge und Integration, 2003. Online: www.handbuch-deutschland.de.

Bedürftig, Friedemann. *Taschenlexikon Deutschland nach 1945*. München: Piper, 1998.

Behal-Thomsen, Heinke, Angelika Lundquist-Mog, and Paul Mog. *Typisch deutsch? Arbeitsbuch zu Aspekten deutscher Mentalität*. München: Langenscheidt, 1993.

Behrend, Hanna, ed. *German Unification: The Destruction of an Economy*. London: Pluto Press, 1995.

Beinssen-Hesse, Silke, and Catherine E. Rigby. *Out of the Shadows: Contemporary German Feminism*. Carlton, Victoria: Melbourne University Press, 1996.

Bentzien, Hans, Harri Czepuck, Gerhard Fischer, Günter Herlt, Klaus Huhn, Friedrich Wolff, and Wolfgang Wünsche. *Fragen an die DDR. Fakten und Positionen. Alles, was man über den deutschen Arbeiter-und-Bauern-Staat wissen muss*. Berlin: Das Neue Berlin, 2003. (edition ost)

Benz, Wolfgang. *Von der Besatzungsherrschaft zur Bundesrepublik. Stationen einer Staatsgründung, 1946–1949*. Frankfurt am Main: Fischer, 1989.

———, ed. *Rechtsextremismus in der Bundesrepublik. Vorrausetzungen, Zusammenhänge, Wirkungen*. Aktualisierte Neuausgabe. Frankfurt: Fischer, 1990.

———. *Gedenkstätten und Erinnerungsarbeit. Ein notwendiger Teil unserer politischen Kultur*. Wiesbaden: Hessische Landeszentrale für politische Bildung, 2001.

Benz, Wolfgang, and Edelgard Bially. *Deutschland seit 1945. Entwicklungen in der Bundesrepublik und in der DDR. Chronik, Dokumente, Bilder*. München: Moos, 1990.

Berghahn, Volker Rolf. *Modern Germany: Society, Economy, and Politics in the Twentieth Century*. Cambridge and New York: Cambridge University Press, 1982.

Berlinski, Claire. "Das Jackboot: German Heavy Metals Conquers Europe [On Rammstein]." *New York Times*, January 9, 2005, AR, 32, 36.

Besier, Gerhard. *Der SED-Staat und die Kirche. Der Weg in die Anpassung*. München: Bertelsmann, 1993.

Beson, Manfred. *Lexikon Pop. Ein Sachwort-ABC der Unterhaltungsmusik von Operette und Schlager bis Folk, Jazz und Rock*. Wiesbaden: Breitkopf und Härtel, 1977.

Bettelheim, Bruno. *The Uses of Enchantment:*

The Meaning and Importance of Fairy Tales. New York: Knopf, 1976.

Beyer, Susanne, Nikolaus von Festenberg, Volker Hage, Per Hinrichs, Ulrike Knöfel, Joachim Kronsbein, Reinhard Mohr, Johannes Saltzwedel, Mathias Schreiber, and Marianne Wellershoff. "Nobel statt Nabel." *Spiegel* 28 (2003): 124–137.

Birke, Adolf M. *Nation ohne Haus. Deutschland, 1945–1961*. Vollständige Taschenbuchausgabe. München: Goldmann, 1998.

Blühdorn, Ingolfur, Frank Krause, and Thomas Scharf. *The Green Agenda: Environmental Politics and Policy in Germany*. Keele, Staffordshire: Keele University Press, 1995.

Blum, Dieter. *Basler Fasnacht. Menschen hinter Masken*. Basel: Museum der Kulturen, 1998.

Böltken, Ferdinand. "Einstellungen zu Ausländern. Ein Vergleich zwischen den neuen und den alten Bundesländern." *Geographische Rundschau* 49 Nrs. 7–8: 432–437.

Borowsky, Peter. *Deutschland 1969 bis 1982*. Hannover: Fackelträger, 1987.

———. *Deutschland 1945 bis 1969. Darstellung und Dokumente*. Hannover: Fackelträger, 1993.

Bossler, Priska, Yannic Federer, and David Miller. "Kurzer Sitzstreik bei den 'Ärzten'. Die Punkrocker auf der Tour 'Unrockbar' in der ausverkauften Stadthalle: da hielt es keinen lange auf den Tribünenplätzen." *Jugend macht Zeitung*. Beilage der *Badischen Zeitung*, 13. May 2004, 31.

Bovenschen, Silvia, and Jörg Bong, eds. *Rituale des Alltags*. Frankfurt: S. Fischer, 2002.

Bracher, Karl Dietrich, Theodor Eschenburg, and Joachim C. Fest, eds. *Geschichte der Bundesrepublik Deutschland*. 5 Bdn. Stuttgart: Deutsche Verlangsanstalt; Mannheim: Brockhaus, 1994.

Brauneck, Manfred, and Gérard Schneilin, eds. *Theaterlexikon I. Begriffe und Epochen, Bühnen und Ensembles*, 4th ed. Reinbek bei Hamburg: Rowohlt, 2001.

Bretschneider, Rudolf. *Konsumgesellschaft*. Wien: Picus Verlag, 2000.

Briel, Holger. "The media of mass communication: the press, radio and television." *The Cambridge Companion to Modern German Culture*. Ed. Eva Kolinsky and Wilfried van der Will. Cambridge: Cambridge University Press, 1998, 322–337.

Briel, Holger, ed. *German Culture and Society: The Essential Glossary*. Oxford and New York: Oxford University Press, 2002.

Brunotte, Heinz. *Die Evangelische Kirche in Deutschland. Geschichte, Organisation und Gestalt der EKD*. Gütersloh: Gütersloher Verlagshaus G. Mohr, 1964.

Bücken, Hajo, and Dieter Rex. *Die wilden Fünfziger*. Reichelsheim: Edition XXL, 2001.

Bullivant, Keith, and C. Jane Rice. "Reconstruction and Integration: The Culture of West German Stabilization 1945 to 1968." *German Cultural Studies*. Ed. Rob Burns. Oxford and New York: Oxford University Press, 1995, 209–255.

Bundesanstalt für gesamtdeutsche Aufgaben, ed. *Facts and Figures. A Comparative Survey of the Federal Republic of Germany and the German Democratic Republic*, 3rd, revised ed. Bonn: Press and Information Office of the Government of the Federal Republic of Germany, 1985.

Bundesministerium für Gesundheit und Soziale Sicherung, ed. *Lebenslagen in Deutschland. Armuts- und Reichtumsberichterstattung der Bundesregierung*. Bonn: n.d.

Bundeszentrale für politische Bildung: www.bpb.de.

Burchard, John E. *The Voice of the Phoenix. Postwar Architecture in Germany*. Cambridge, MA: MIT Press, 1968.

Burger, Annemarie. *Religionszugehörigkeit und soziales Verhalten. Untersuchungen und Statistiken der neueren Zeit in Deutschland*. Göttingen: Vandenhoeck und Ruprecht, 1964.

Burns, Rob, ed. *German Cultural Studies*. Oxford and New York: Oxford University Press, 1995.

Burns, Rob, and Wilfried van der Will. "The Federal Republic 1968 to 1990. From the Industrial Society to the Culture Society." *German Cultural Studies*. Ed. Rob Burns. Oxford and New York: Oxford University Press, 1995, 257–323.

Büsch, Otto, and James J. Sheehan, eds. *Die Rolle der Nation in der deutschen Geschichte und Gegenwart.* Berlin: Colloquium, 1985.

Calandra, Denis. *New German Dramatists.* New York: Grove Press, 1983.

Carr, Godfrey, and Georgina Paul. "Unification and Its Aftermath: The Challenge of History." *German Cultural Studies.* Ed. Rob Burns. Oxford and New York: Oxford University Press, 1995, 325–348.

Clyne, Michael G. *The German Language in a Changing Europe.* Cambridge: Cambridge University Press, 1995.

Cohn-Bendit, Daniel, and Thomas Schmidt. *Heimat Babylon. Das Wagnis der multikulturellen Demokratie.* Hamburg: Hoffmann and Campe, 1992.

Cortina, Kai S., Jürgen Baumert, Achim Leschinsky, Karl Ulrich Mayer, Luitgard Trommer, eds. *Das Bildungswesen in der Bundesrepublik Deutschland. Strukturen und Entwicklungen im Überblick.* 2. Auflage. Reinbek bei Hamburg: Rowohlt, 2005.

Cope, Julian. *A Krautrocksampler: One Head's Guide to the Great Kosmische Musik—1968 Onwards.* Calne: Head Heritage, 1996.

Counihan, Carole, and Penny Van Esterik, eds. *Food and Culture. A Reader.* New York, Routledge, 1997.

Craig, Gordon A. *The Germans.* New York: G. P. Putman's Sons, 1982.

Cullen, Michael S. *Das Holocaust-Mahnmal. Dokumentation einer Debatte.* München: Pendo, 1999.

Czyzewski, Marek, ed. *Selbst- und Fremdbilder im Gespräch.* Opladen: Leske und Budrich, 1995.

Dahlhaus, Carl, and Hermann Danuser, eds. *Neues Handbuch der Musikwissenschaft.* 13 vols. Vol. 7: *Die Musik des 20. Jahrhunderts.* Laaber: Labber Verlag, 1984.

Dahlhaus, Carl, Hans H. Eggebrecht, and Kurt Oehl. *Brockhaus-Riemann-Musiklexikon.* Mainz: Atlantis-Schott, 2001.

Dahmen, Thomas. *Wehrdienst, Zivildienst. Das Buch zur Fernsehserie ARD-Recht.* Frankfurt am Main: Suhrkamp, 1997.

Dallach, Christoph. "The Sound of Music." *The Germans. Sixty Years after the War.* Spiegel. Special International Edition 4 (2005), 194–196.

Damus, Martin. *Malerei der DDR. Funktionen der bildenden Kunst im Realen Sozialismus.* Reinbek bei Hamburg: Rowohlt, 1991.

———. *Kunst in der BRD, 1945–1990. Funktionen der Kunst in einer demokratisch verfassten Gesellschaft.* Reinbek bei Hamburg: Rowohlt, 1995.

Dann, Otto. *Nation und Nationalismus in Deutschland. 1770–1990.* München: Beck, 1993.

de Bruyn, Günter. *Jubelschreie, Trauergesänge. Deutsche Befindlichkeiten.* Frankfurt am Main: S. Fischer, 1991.

Demm, Sabine. "Frankfurter Studentenprotest. Die Wurzeln der 'Provos'—Die 68er beeinflussten die Bewegung der 70er." *Frankfurter Rundschau,* 17. January 2001. http://www.k-faktor.com/frankfurt/studentenprotest.htm (retrieved April 15, 2005).

Denby, David. "The Current Cinema: Back in the Bunker. 'Downfall.'" *The New Yorker,* February 14 and 21, 2005, 259–261.

Denham, Scott, Irene Kacandes, and Jonathan Petropoulos, eds. *A User's Guide to German Cultural Studies.* Ann Arbor: University of Michigan Press, 1997.

Derbyshire, Ian. *Politics in Germany: From Division to Unification.* Edinburgh: Chambers, 1991.

Deutsche Bahn AG, ed. *Die Bahn macht mobil.* Berlin: Druckhaus Kaufmann, 2004.

Deutsche Gesellschaft für Freizeit (DGF). *Freizeit, Sport, Bewegung. Stand und Tendenzen in der Bundesrepublik Deutschland.* Hannover: Medienpool, Gesellschaft für Wirtschaftswerbung, 1987.

Deutscher Bundestag, ed. *Fragen an die deutsche Geschichte. Wege zur parlamentarischen Demokratie,* 19., neu bearbeitete Auflage. Katalog der historischen Ausstellung im Deutschen Dom in Berlin. Bonn: Deutscher Bundestag, Referat Öffentlichkeitsarbeit, 1996.

———, ed. *Blickpunkt Bundestag. Forum der Demokratie. Der Deutsche Bundestag in*

Berlin. Sonderheft. Köln: Media Consulta, 1999.

———, ed. *Materialien der Enquete Kommission "Aufarbeitung von Geschichte und Folgen der SED-Diktatur in Deutschland."* Vols. 3/1 and 3/2. Frankfurt: Suhrkamp, 1995.

Dieckert, Jürgen. *Freizeitsport. Aufgabe und Chance für jedermann*. Düsseldorf: Bertelsmann-Universitätsverlag, 1974.

Dieckmann, Friedrich. *Was ist deutsch? Eine Nationalerkundung*. Frankfurt: Edition Suhrkamp, 2003.

Diem, Aubrey. *The New Germany: Land, People, Economy*. Ontario: Aljon Print-Craft, 1993.

Directmedia Redaktion, ed. *Enzyklopädie der DDR. Personen, Institutionen und Strukturen in Politik, Wirtschafft, Justiz, Wissenschaft und Kultur*. Elektronische Ressource. Berlin: Directmedia Publishing, 2004.

Dominick, Raymond H. *The Environmental Movement in Germany: Prophets and Pioneers, 1871–1971*. Bloomington and Indianapolis: Indiana University Press, 1992.

Dostal, Michael. *DB-Fahrzeuge*. Bd. 3: *Güterwagen der Deutschen Bahn*. München: Bruckmann, 2001.

———. *DB-Fahrzeuge*. München: Bruckmann, 2004.

Dostal, Michael, and Andreas Braun. *DB-Fahrzeuge*. Bd. 2: *Reisezugwagen der Deutschen Bahn*. München: GeraNova Zeitschriftenverlag, 1998.

Dudenredaktion, ed. *Duden*. Vol. 5: *Das Fremdwörterbuch*. Mannheim, Leipzig, Wien, Zürich: Dudenverlag, 2001.

Durrani, Osman. "Popular music in the German-speaking world." *Contemporary German Cultural Studies*. Ed. Alison Phipps. Oxford: Oxford University Press, 2002, 197–218.

Ehlers, Frona. "Die bürgerlichen Huren." *Der Spiegel* 35 (2001): 84–90.

Eichheim, Hubert, Monika Bovermann, Lea Tesarová, and Marion Hollerung. *Blaue Blume*. München: Hueber, 2002.

Eley, Geoff, ed. *The "Goldhagen Effect": History, Memory, Nazism—Facing the German Past*. Ann Arbor: University of Michigan Press, 2000.

Elias, Norbert. *Studien über die Deutschen. Machtkämpfe und Habitusentwicklung im 19. und 20. Jahrhundert*. Frankfurt: Suhrkamp, 1989.

Elsaesser, Thomas. *Filmgeschichte und frühes Kino. Archäologie eines Medienwandels*. München: edition text + kritik, 2002.

Emmerich, Wolfgang. *Kleine Literaturgeschichte der DDR*. Leipzig: Kiepenheuer, 1996.

Eulenspiegel-Verlags-Team. *Das dicke DDR Buch*. Berlin: Eulenspiegel Verlag, 2002.

Farin, Klaus. *Jugendkulturen zwischen Kommerz und Politik*. München: Tilsner, 1998.

———, ed. *Skinhead—A Way of Life. Eine Jugendbewegung stellt sich selbst dar*. Durchgesehene, korrigierte, akualisierte Ausgabe. Bad Tölz: Tilsner, 1999.

———. *Generation-kick.de. Jugendsubkulturen heute*. München: Beck, 2001. (Beck'sche Reihe 1407.)

Farin, Klaus, Henning Flad, and Frauke Stuhl, eds. *Reaktionäre Rebellen. Rechtsextreme Musik in Deutschland*. Archiv der Jugendkulturen. Bad Tölz: Tilsner, 2001.

Faulstich, Werner. *Grundwissen MedienMedien, 5., vollständig überarbeitete und erheblich erweiterte Auflage*. München: Fink, 2004.

———. *Medienwissenschaft*. Paderborn: Wilhelm Fink, 2004.

———. *Filmgeschichte*. München: Fink Verlag, 2005 (UTB basics).

Federal Statistical Office, Germany. Online www.destatis.de.

Feist, Günter, and Eckhart Gillen, eds. *Stationen eines Weges. Daten und Zitate zur Kunst und Kulturpolitik der DDR, 1945–1988*. Berlin: Nishen, 1988.

Ferchhoff, Wilfried. *Jugend an der Wende vom 20. zum 21. Jahrhundert. Lebensformen und Lebensstile*. 2., überarbeitete und aktualisierte Auflage. Opladen: Leske und Budrich, 1999.

———, ed. *Jugendkulturen 2000*. Berlin: Sozialpädagogisches Institut, 2001.

First-Hand Information Department, ed. *Socialism: Making Culture a Way of Life. A Report from the GDR*. Berlin: Panorama, 1978.

———, ed. *Health Care in the GDR. Reports, Facts, Interviews.* Berlin: Panorama, 1983.

———, ed. *Education in the GDR. Objectives, Contents and Results.* Berlin: Panorama, 1987.

———, ed. *Young People in the GDR.* Berlin: Panorama, 1987.

———, ed. *Apprentices. The GDR in Profile.* Berlin: Panorama, 1988.

———, ed. *Culture and the Arts in the GDR.* Berlin: Panorama, 1988.

———, ed. *Farmers with a Future. Agriculture in the GDR.* Berlin: Panorama, 1988.

Fischer, Heinz-Dietrich, and Olav Jubin. *Privatfernsehen in Deutschland. Konzepte, Konkurrenten, Kontroversen.* Frankfurt: Frankfurter Allgemeine Buch, 1996.

Fischer, Hermann. *Volkslied, Schlager, Evergreen. Studien über das lebendige Singen aufgrund von Untersuchungen im Kreis Reutlingen.* Tübingen: Tübinger Vereinigung für Volkskunde, 1965.

Fischer, Johannes, ed. *Verteidigung im Bündnis. Planung, Aufbau und Bewährung der Bundeswehr, 1950–1972.* München: Bernard und Graefe, 1975.

Fischer-Lichte, Erika, *Die Entdeckung des Zuschauers. Paradigmenwechsel auf dem Theater des 20. Jahrhunderts.* Tübingen and Basel: Francke, 1997.

———. *Kurze Geschichte des deutschen Theaters,* 2. Auflage. Tübingen and Basel: Francke, 1999.

Fischer-Lichte, Erika, Doris Kolesch, and Christel Weiler, eds. *Transformationen: Theater der neunziger Jahre.* Berlin: Theater der Zeit, 1999.

Fischer-Lichte, Erika, Friedemann Kreuder, and Isabel Pflug, eds. *Theater seit den 60er Jahren. Grenzgänge der Neo-Avantgarde.* Tübingen and Basel: Francke, 1998.

Fisher, Howard D. *German Legal System and Legal Language: A General Survey together with Notes and a German Vocabulary.* London: Cavendish, 1996.

Flacke, Monika, ed. *Auftragskunst der DDR, 1949–1990.* Berlin: Deutsches Historisches Museum, 1995.

Flamini, Roland. *Passport Germany: Your Pocket Guide to German Business, Customs & Etiquette.* San Rafael, CA: World Trade Press, 1997.

Flippo, Hyde. *The German Way: Aspects of Behavior, Attitudes, and Customs in the German-Speaking World.* Reprint with revisions. Lincolnwood, IL: Passwort Books, 1999. (1st print: 1997.)

———. *When in Germany, Do as the Germans Do: The Clued-In Guide to German Life, Language, and Culture.* New York: McGraw-Hill, 2002.

Flood, John L., ed. *Kurz bevor der Vorhang fiel. Zum Theater der DDR.* Amsterdam: Rodopi, 1990.

Forrester, Ian S., and Hans-Michael Ilgen. *The German Legal System.* South Hackensack, NJ: F. B. Rothman, 1972.

Forster, Thomas Manfred. *The East German Army: The Second Power in the Warsaw Pact.* London: Allen and Unwin, 1980.

Foster, Nigel G. *German Law and Legal System.* London: Blackstone, 1993.

Foster, Nigel G., and Satish Sule. *German Legal System and Laws.* London: Blackstone, 1996; Oxford and New York: Oxford University Press, 2002.

Freckmann, Anke, and Thomas Christian Wegerich. *The German Legal System.* London: Sweet and Maxwell, 1999.

Frevert, Ute. *Women in German History.* Oxford: Berg, 1989.

Frick, Joachim. *Lebenslagen im Wandel: Determinanten kleinräumlicher Mobilität in Westdeutschland.* Projektgruppe "Das Sozio-ökonomische Panel" im Deutschen Institut für Wirtschaftsforschung, Berlin. Frankfurt and New York: Campus, 1996.

Fricke, Harald. "A Nostalgia for Oils: The German Miracle." *Deutschland: Forum on Politics, Culture and Business* 2 (2005): 40–47.

Fritsch-Bournazel, Renate. *Europe and German Unification.* Oxford: Berg, 1992.

Frogner, Eli. *Sport im Lebenslauf. Eine Verhaltensanalyse zum Breiten- und Freizeitsport.* Stuttgart: Enke, 1991.

Fuchs, Peter, M. L. Schwering, and Klaus Zöller. *Kölner Karneval. Seine Geschichte, seine Eigenart, seine Akteure.* Zweite, auf den neuesten Stand gebrachte Auflage. Köln: Greven, 1984. (Erste Auflage 1972.)

Führ, Christoph. *Schools and Institutions of Higher Education in the Federal Republic of Germany.* Bonn: Inter Nationes, 1989.

———. *On the Education System in the Five New Länder of the Federal Republic of Germany.* Bonn: Inter Nationes, 1992.

Führ, Christoph, and Iván Tapia. *The German Education System since 1945.* Bonn: Inter Nationes, 1997.

Fulbrook, Mary. *Anatomy of a Dictatorship: Inside the GDR, 1949–1989.* Oxford and New York: Oxford University Press, 1995.

Gabriel, Oscar W., and Everhard Holtmann. *Handbuch politisches System der Bundesrepublik Deutschland,* 3., völlig überarbeitete und erweiterte Auflage. München and Wien: Oldenbourg, 2005.

Gaffney, John, and Eva Kolinsky. *Political Culture in France and Germany.* London: Routledge, 1991.

Gaile, Jochen. *Wir Deutschen. Eine Reise zu den Schauplätzen der Vergangenheit.* Dortmund: Kartographischer Verlag Busche, 1991.

Gall, Lothar, and Manfred Pohl. *Die Eisenbahn in Deutschland. Von den Anfängen bis zur Gegenwart.* München: Beck, 1999.

Galle, Heinz J. *Groschenhefte. Die Geschichte der deutschen Trivialliteratur.* Frankfurt am Main and Berlin: Ullstein, 1988. (Ullstein Buch 36556 - Populäre Kultur.)

———. *Volksbücher und Heftromane. Ein Streifzug durch 100 Jahre Unterhaltungsliteratur.* Passau: Erster Deutscher Fantasy Club e.V., 1998. (Fantasia 116/117.)

Galle, Heinz J., and Markus R. Bauer. *Sun Koh. Der Erbe von Atlantis und andere deutsche Supermänner. Paul Alfred Müller alias Lok Myler alias Freder van Holk. Leben und Werk.* Zürich: ssi-media, 2003.

Gemünden, Gerd. *Framed Visions: Popular Culture, Americanization, and the Contemporary German and Austrian Imagination.* Ann Arbor: University of Michigan Press, 1998.

GeoEpoche-Team. "Deutschland nach dem Krieg, 1945–1955." *GeoEpoche. Das Magazin für Geschichte* 9. Hamburg: Gruner und Jahr, 2002.

GeraNova-Team. *Bahn Extra: 200 Jahre Eisenbahn.* München: GeraNova, 2004.

Gerken, Jochen. *Idioten im Fernsehen von A wie Arabella bis Z wie Zietlow.* Kerpen: Gerken, 2001.

———. *Noch mehr Idioten im Fernsehen.* Bergheim: Sonnenkinder-Verlag, 2005.

German Sports and Gymnastics Union of the GDR, ed. *Sport in the German Democratic Republic.* Dresden: Verlag Zeit im Bild, n.d.

Gerwin, Hanno. *Was Deutschlands Prominente glauben.* Gütersloh: Gütersloher Versandhaus, 2005.

Giersch, Herbert, Karl-Heinz Paqué, and Holger Schmiedling. *The Fading Miracle: Four Decades of Market Economy in Germany.* Cambridge and New York: Cambridge University Press, 1992.

Gieseler, Karlheinz, and Jürgen Palm. *Sport— Gesundheit—Wirtschaft. Breiten- und Freizeitsport in der Bundesrepublik Deutschland.* Köln: Deutscher Instituts-Verlag, 1985.

Gillen, Eckhart, ed. *German Art from Beckmann to Richter. Images of a Divided Country.* Cologne: DuMont, 1997.

Gillies, Constantin. *wie wir waren. Die wilden Jahre der Web-Generation.* Weinheim: Wiley-VCH and Co. KgaA, 2003.

Giordano, Ralph. *Die zweite Schuld Oder Von der Last Deutscher zu sein.* Neuausgabe. Köln: Kiepenheuer and Witsch, 2000.

Glaessner, Gert-Joachim. *The Unification Process in Germany: From Dictatorship to Democracy.* New York: St. Martin's Press, 1992.

Glaessner, Gert-Joachim, and Ian Wallace, eds. *The German Revolution of 1989: Causes and Consequences.* Oxford: Berg, 1992.

Glaser, Hermann. *Kleine Kulturgeschichte Deutschlands im 20. Jahrhundert.* München: Beck, 2002. (Beck'sche Reihe.)

———. *Deutsche Kultur. Ein historischer Überblick von 1945 bis zur Gegenwart,* 3., erweiterte Auflage. Bonn: Bundeszentrale für politische Bildung, 2003.

———. *Kleine deutsche Kulturgeschichte von 1945 bis heute.* Frankfurt: S. Fischer, 2004.

Glasmeier, Michael, and Karin Stengel, eds. *archive in motion. documenta-Handbuch / documenta Manual. 50 Jahre / Years documenta 1955–2005.* Göttigen: Steidl, 2005.

Glatzer, Wolfgang, ed. *Getrennt vereint. Lebensverhältnisse in Deutschland seit der Wiedervereinigung.* Frankfurt am Main and New York: Campus, 1995.

Glombitza, Birgit, and Christian Buß. "In Echtzeit. Der junge deutsche Film." *epd Film* 7 (2004): 8–9.

Goethe-Institut, ed. *Tanztheater heute. Dreißig Jahre deutsche Tanzgeschichte.* Seelze/Hannover: Kallmeyer, 1999.

Goldhagen, Daniel Jonah. *Hitler's Willing Executioners. Ordinary Germans and the Holocaust.* New York: Vintage Books, 1997.

Goodbody, Axel, Dennis Tate, and Ian Wallace. "The Failed Socialist Experiment: Culture in the GDR." *German Cultural Studies.* Ed. Rob Burns. Oxford and New York: Oxford University Press, 1995, 147–207.

Grabner, Wolf-Jürgen, ed. *Leipzig im Oktober. Kirchen und alternative Gruppen im Umbruch der DDR. Analysen zur Wende*, 2. Auflage. Berlin: Wichern, 1994.

Graf, Christian. *Rocklexikon Deutschland.* Berlin: Schwarzkopf und Schwarzkopf, 2002.
———. *Das NDW Lexikon. Die Neue Deutsche Welle—Bands und Solisten von A bis Z.* Berlin: Schwarzkopf und Schwarzkopf, 2003.

Grieder, Peter. *The East German Leadership, 1946–73: Conflict and Crisis.* Manchester: Manchester University Press, 1999.

Gries, Rainer, Volker Ilgen, and Dirk Schindelbeck, eds. *"Ins Gehirn der Masse kriechen." Werbung und Mentalitätsgeschichte.* Darmstadt: Wissenschaftliche Buchgeslleschaft, 1995.

Griffiths, Paul. *Modern Music: A Concise History*, rev. ed. London: Thames and Hudson, 1994.

Grimm, Jakob Ludwig Karl and Wilhelm Karl, eds. *Kinder- und Hausmärchen. Ausgabe letzter Hand mit den Originalanmerkungen der Brüder Grimm. [1857]* Band 1. Stuttgart: Reclam,1980. (Universalbibliothek 3191.)

Großegger, Beate, and Bernhard Heinzlmaier. *Jugendkultur-Guide.* 2. Auflage. Wien: Öbv und hpt, 2004. (1st ed. 2002.)

Grünberg, Horst *Soldaten des Volkes.* Berlin: Deutscher Militärverlag, 1967.

Gudermann, Rita, and Bernhard Wulff. *Der Sarotti-Mohl. Die bewegte Geschichte einer Werbefigur.* Berlin: Ch. Links Verlag, 2004.

Habel, F.-B., and Volker Wachter. *Das große Lexikon der DDR-Stars. Die Schauspieler aus Film und Fernsehen.* Überarbeitete und erweiterte Neuausgabe. Berlin: Schwarzkopf und Schwarzkopf, 2002.

Hach, Jürgen. *Gesellschaft und Religion in der Bundesrepublik Deutschland. Eine Einführung in die Religionssoziologie.* Heidelberg: Quelle und Meyer, 1980.

Hachmeister, Lutz, and Friedemann Siering, eds. *Die Herren Journalisten. Die Elite der deutschen Presse nach 1945.* München: Beck, 2002.

Hackenbroch, Veronika. "Heart with Soul." *The Germans. Sixty Years after the War.* Spiegel Special International Edition 4 (2005): 176–178.

Hafeneger, Benno, and Mechtild M. Jansen. *Rechte Cliquen. Alltag einer neuen Jugendkultur.* Weinheim: Juventa, 2001.

Haines, Brigid, and Margaret Littler. *Contemporary Women's Writing in German: Theoretical Perspectives.* Oxford and New York: Oxford University Press, 2004.

Hall, Christine. *Living and Working in Germany. Settle in Quickly and Get the Most Out of Your Stay.* 3rd ed. How to Books, 2001.

Hall, Edward T., and Mildred Reed Hall. *Understanding Cultural Differences: Germans, French and Americans.* Yarmouth, ME: Intercultural Press, 1990.

Hamann, Brigitte. *Elisabeth, Kaise wider Willen.* Wien: Amalthea, 1982.

Hancock, M. Donald, and Helga A. Welsh. *German Unification: Process and Outcomes.* Boulder: Westview Press, 1994.

Hansen, Eric T. "Typisch deutsch." *Süddeutsche Zeitung* 159 (July 13, 2004): 11.

Hardtwig, Wolfgang, and Heinrich-August Winkler, eds. *Deutsche Entfremdung. Zum Befinden in Ost und West.* München: Beck, 1993.

Harenberg, Bodo, ed. *Chronik der Deutschen.*

Dortmund: Chronik-Verlag, 1983. (Plus annual volumes 1984–2005.)

Harenberg Schauspielführer, 3. vollständig überarbeitete und erweiterte Auflage. Geleitwort von Will Quadflieg. Dortmund: Harenberg, 2003.

Harold, James, and Marla Stone, eds. *When the Wall Came Down: Reactions to German Unification.* New York and London: Routledge, 1992.

Hasche, Christa, Traute Schölling, Joachim Fiebach, and Ralph Hammerthaler, eds. *Theater in der DDR: Chronik und Positionen.* Berlin: Henschel, 1994.

Haußmann, Leander. "Es kam dicke genug." *Spiegel* 37 (2003): 220–221.

Heine, Norbert. *Deutscher Weinführer.* Stuttgart: Ulmer, 1998.

Heinmann, Thomas. *DEFA. Künstler und SED-Kulturpolitik. Zum Verhältnis von Kulturpolitik und Filmproduktion in der SBZ/DDR 1945 bis 1959.* Berlin: VISTAS, 1994.

Heise, Ulla. *Kaffee und Kaffeehaus. Eine Kulturgeschichte.* Hildesheim, Zürich, New York: Olms Presse, 1987.

Helwig, Gisela, and Hildegard Maria Nickel, eds. *Frauen in Deutschland, 1945–92.* Bonn: Bundeszentrale für politische Bildung; Berlin: Akademie Verlag, 1993.

Helwig, Gisela, and Detlef Urban, eds. *Kirchen und Gesellschaften in beiden deutschen Staaten.* Köln: Edition Deutschland Archiv im Verlag Wissenschaft und Politik, 1987.

Heman, Peter, ed. *Unsere Fasnacht.* Basel: Verlag Peter Hemann, 1971.

Hendlmeier, Wolfgang. "Die deutsche Schreibschrift von Sütterlin bis zur Gegenwart." *Die deutsche Schrift* 69 (Herbst 1983): 20–29.

Heringer, Hans-Jürgen. *Tendenzen der deutschen Gegenwartssprache.* Tübingen: Niemeyer, 1994.

Hermand, Jost. *Kulturen im Wiederaufbau. Die Bundesrepublik Deutschland, 1945–1965.* München: Nymphenburger, 1986.

———. *Die Kultur der Bundesrepublik Deutschland, 1965–1985.* München: Nymphenburger, 1988.

Hermersdorf, Martin. "Die Entwicklung der deutschen Schreibschrift." *Die deutsche Schrift* 19 (Oktober 1960): 1–20.

Herzog, Renate. *Brigitte Weihnachten.* München: Mosaik bei Goldmann, 2003.

Hettlage, Robert, and Karl Lenz, eds. *Deutschland nach der Wende. Eine Zwischenbilanz.* München: Beck, 1995. (Beck'sche Reihe.)

Heyll, Uwe. *"Wasser, Fasten, Luft und Licht." Die Geschichte der Naturheilkunde in Deutschland.* Frankfurt am Main: Campus, 2006.

Hickethier, Knut. *Geschichte des Deutschen Fernsehens.* Stuttgart: J. B. Metzler, 1998.

Hintereder, Peter, ed. "Innovation through Excellence." *Deutschland. Forum on Politics, Culture and Business* 4 (2004): 42–47.

Hitchens, D.M.W.N., Karin Wagner, and J.E. Birnie. *East German Productivity and the Transition to the Market Economy.* Adlershot: Avebury; Brookfield: Ashgate, 1993.

Hoffmann, Christa. *Stunden Null? Vergangenheitsbewältigung in Deutschland, 1945–1989.* Bonn: Bouvier, 1992.

Hoffmann, Dierk. *Die DDR unter Ulbricht. Gewaltsame Neuordnung und gescheiterte Modernisierung.* Zürich: Pendo, 2003.

Hollerbach, Alexander. *Verträge zwischen Staat und Kirche in der Bundesrepublik Deutschland.* Frankfurt am Main: Klostermann, 1965.

Holm, Carsten. "Das bringt uns gar nichts." *Spiegel* 12 (2002): 60–63.

Holz, Erlend. *Zeitverwendung in Deutschland. Berufe, Familie, Freizeit.* Stuttgart: Metzler Poeschel, 2000.

Holzweissig, Gunter. *Massenmedien in der DDR.* Berlin: Holzapfel, 1989.

Homburg, Cornelia, ed. *German Art Now.* London and New York: Merrell, 2003.

Honnef, Klaus, Rolf Sachsse, and Karin Thomas, eds. *German Photography, 1870–1970.* Köln: DuMont, 1997.

Hooks, Mike. *Lufthansa.* Erfurt: Sutton, 2000.

Horbelt, Rainer, and Sonja Spindler. *Die deutsche Küche im 20. Jahrhundert. Von der Mehlsuppe im Kaiserreich bis zum*

Designerjoghurt der Berliner Republik. Ereignisse, Geschichten, Rezepte. Frankfurt: Eichborn, 2000.

Hraab, Stevka. *Professor Zlatko. Die ganze Wahrheit.* Berlin: Eichborn, 2001.

Huck, Gerhard. *Sozialgeschichte der Freizeit. Untersuchungen zum Wandel der Alltagskultur in Deutschland.* Wuppertal: Hammer, 1980.

Humphreys, Peter. *Media and Media Policy in Germany,* 2nd ed. Oxford: Berg, 1994.

Hurrelmann, Klaus. "Youth 2005." *Deutschland. Forum on Politics, Culture and Business* 3 (2005): 40–47.

Illies, Florian. *Generation Golf. Eine Inspektion,* 5th ed. Frankfurt: Fischer, 2001. (1st ed., Berlin: Argon, 2000.)

———. *Generation Golf zwei.* München: Blessing, 2003.

Ilsemann, Carl-Gero von. *Die Bundeswehr in der Demokratie.* Hamburg: von Decker's Verlag Schenck, 1971.

Innes, Christopher. *Modern German Drama.* Cambridge: Cambridge University Press, 1979.

Inter Nationes Team, ed. *Cultural Life in the Federal Republic of Germany.* Bonn: Inter Nationes, 1993.

Irmer, Thomas, and Matthias Schmidt. *Die Bühnenrepublik. Theater in der DDR.* Berlin: Alexander Verlag, 2003.

Jacobsen, Wolfgang, and Anton Kaes. *Geschichte des deutschen Films.* Stuttgart: Metzler, 1993.

James, Harold. *A German Identity, 1770–1990.* New York: Sterling, 2001.

James, Harold, and Marla Stone, eds. *When the Wall Came Down: Reactions to German Unification.* New York: Routledge, 1992.

James, Peter, ed. *Modern Germany: Politics, Society and Culture.* London and New York: Routledge, 1998.

James-Chakraborty, Kathleen. *German Architecture for a Mass Audience.* London: Routledge, 2000.

Jansen, Wolfgang, ed. *Unterhaltungstheater in Deutschland. Geschichte, Ästhetik, Ökonomie.* Berlin: Weidler, 1995.

Jarausch, Konrad. *The Rush to German Unity.* Oxford: Oxford University Press, 1994.

Jarausch, Konrad H., and Volker Gransow, eds.

Uniting Germany: Documents and Debates, 1943–1993. Oxford: Berghahn, 1994.

Jeffery, Charlie, ed. *Recasting German Federalism: The Legacies of Unification.* London and New York: Pinter, 1999.

Jeffery, Charlie, and Peter Savigear. *German Federalism Today.* New York: St. Martin's Press, 1991.

Jeffery, Charlie, and Ruth Whittle. *Germany Today: A Student's Dictionary.* London and New York: Arnold; New York: St. Martin's Press, 1997.

Jeffries, Ian, and Manfred Melzer, eds. *The East German Economy.* London: Routledge, Kegan, and Paul, 1988.

Jesse, Eckhardt, and Armin Mitter, eds. *Die Gestaltung der deutschen Einheit.* Bonn: Bundeszentrale für politische Bildung, 1992.

Joachimides, Christos M., Norman Rosenthal, and Wieland Schmied, eds. *German Art in the 20th Century: Painting and Sculpture, 1905–1985.* München: Prestel, 1985.

Joel, Holger, ed. *Chronik des deutschen Fußballs. Die Spiele der Nationalmannschaften von 1908 bis heute.* Gütersloh and München: Chronik Verlag im Wissen Media Verlag, 2005.

Jones, Alun. *The New Germany: A Human Geography.* Chichester and New York: John Wiley and Sons, 1994.

Kaelble, Hartmut, ed. *Sozialgeschichte der DDR.* Stuttgart: Klett-Cotta, 1994.

Kaiser, Alfons. "Die Nation zieht an." *Frankfurter Allgemeine Zeitung,* 14 November 2003.

Kaiser, Karl. *Deutschlands Vereinigung. Die internationalen Aspekte.* Bergisch Gladbach: Lübbe, 1991.

Kayser, Dietrich. *Schlager, das Lied als Ware. Untersuchungen zu einer Kategorie der Illusionsindustrie unter besonderer Berücksichtigung des Musikmarktes der Bundesrepublik Deutschland.* Stuttgart: Metzler, 1975.

Kellner, Joachim, Ulrich Kurth, and Werner Lippert, eds. *50 Jahre Werbung in Deutschland, 1945 bis 1995.* Eine Veranstaltung des Deutschen Werbemuseums. Ingelheim: Westermann-Kommunikation, 1995.

Kemper, Peter, Thomas Langhoff, and Ulrich Sonnenschein, eds. *"Alles so schön bunt hier." Die Geschichte der Popkultur von den Fünfzigern bis heute.* Stuttgart: Reclam, 1999.

Kettenacker, Lothar. *Germany since 1945.* Oxford and New York: Oxford University Press, 1997.

Kirschner, Jürgen. *Fischer Handbuch Theater, Film, Funk und Fernsehen.* Frankfurt: Fischer, 1997.

Klingemann, Hans-Dieter, and Max. Kaase, eds. *Wahlen und politisches System. Analysen aus Anlass der Bundestagswahl 1980.* Opladen: Westdeutscher Verlag, 1983.

———, eds. *Wahlen und politischer Prozess. Analysen aus Anlass der Bundestagswahl 1983.* Opladen: Westdeutscher Verlag, 1986.

Klingholz, Reiner. "Deutschland 2020. Aufbruch in ein anderes Land." *Geo* 5 (May 2004): 88–94.

Klonovsky, Michael, and Martin Scherer. "Wie hältst Du's mit der Religion?" *Focus* 16 (April 10, 2004): 128–137.

Klotz, Heinrich. *Geschichte der Deutschen Kunst.* Vol. 3: *Neuzeit und Moderne, 1750–2000.* München: C. H. Beck, 2000.

Klotz, Volker. *Bürgerliches Lachtheater. Komödie, Posse, Schwank, Operette.* Reinbek bei Hamburg: Rowohlt, 1987.

Kluge, Volker. *Das große Lexikon der DDR-Sportler.* 2nd ed. Berlin: Schwarzkopf and Schwarzkopf, 2004.

Knöfel, Ulrike. "Kraut Art Kraze." *The Germans. Sixty Years after the War.* Ed. Stefan Aust. Spiegel. Special International Edition 4 (2005): 184–189.

Knoll, Joachim H. *Bildung und Wissenschaft in der Bundesrepublik Deutschland. Bildungspolitik, Schulen, Hochschulen, Erwachsenenbildung, Bildungsforschung. Ein Handbuch.* München and Wien: Hanser, 1977.

Knopp, Guido. *Die Befreiung. Kriegsende im Westen.* Berlin: Ullstein, 2005.

Knopp, Guido, and Peter Arens. *Unsere Besten. Die 100 größten Deutschen.* München: Econ, 2003.

Koch, Hans Jürgen, ed. *Wallfahrtsstätten der Nation. Zwischen Brandenburg und Bayern.* Frankfurt: S. Fischer, 1986.

Koch, Hans J., and Hermann Glaser. *Ganz Ohr.*

Eine Kulturgeschichte des Radios in Deutschland. Köln, Weimar, and Wien: Böhlau, 2005.

Kocka, Jürgen, and Martin Sabrow, eds. *Die DDR als Geschichte. Fragen—Hypothesen—Perspektiven.* Berlin: Akademie-Verlag, 1994.

Koelbl, Herlinde, and Manfred Sack. *Das deutsche Wohnzimmer.* Mit einem Beitrag von Alexander Mitscherlich. München: C. J. Bucher, 1980.

Kohl, Helmut. *A Culinary Voyage through Germany.* Commentary by Chancellor Helmut Kohl. München: Verlag Zabert Sandmann, 1996.

Kolinsky, Eva. *Women in Contemporary Germany.* Oxford: Berg, 1993.

———. *Women in 20th Century Germany: A Reader.* Manchester: Manchester University Press, 1995.

Kolinsky, Eva, and Wilfried van der Will, eds. *The Cambridge Companion to Modern German Culture.* Cambridge: Cambridge University Press, 1998.

König, Johann-Günther. *Global Player Telekom.* Reinbek bei Hamburg: Rowohlt, 1997.

König, Wolfgang. *Geschichte der Konsumgesellschaft.* Stuttgart: Franz Steiner Verlag, 2000.

Korte, Karl-Rudolf, and Werner Weidenfeld, eds. *Deutschland-TrendBuch. Fakten und Orientierungen.* Opladen: Leske und Budrich, 2001.

Koszyk, Kurt. "Presse unter alliierter Besatzung." *Mediengeschichte der Bundesrepublik Deutschland.* Ed. Jürgen Wilke. Köln, Weimar, and Wien: Böhlau, 1999, 31–58.

Kramer, Thomas, ed. *Reclams Lexikon des deutschen Films.* Stuttgart: Reclam, 1995.

Krekow, Sebastian, Jens Steiner, and Matthias Taupitz. *Das Neue HipHop Lexikon.* Berlin: Schwarzkopf und Schwarzkopf, 2003.

Krens, Thomas, Michael Govan, and Joseph Thompson, eds. *Refigured Painting. The German Image, 1960–88.* München: Prestel, 1989.

Kreuzer, Helmut, and Christian Werner Thomsen, eds. *Geschichte des Fernsehens in der Bundesrepublik Deutschland.* München: Fink, 1993–1994.

Kriegeskorte, Michael. *Werbung in Deutschland, 1945–1965. Die Nachkriegszeit im Spiegel ihrer Anzeigen.* Köln: DuMont, 1992.

———. *100 Jahre Werbung im Wandel: Eine Reise durch die deutsche Vergangenheit.* Köln: DuMont, 1995.

Krummacher, Jo, and Hendrik Hefermehl. *Ratgeber für Kriegsdienstverweigerer. Praktische Hilfe zur Vorbereitung auf das Anerkennungsverfahren.* Stuttgart: Radius, 1996.

Kühn, Volker, ed. *Hierzulande. Kabarett in dieser Zeit, 1970–2000.* Neuausgabe. Frankfurt am Main: Rogner und Bernhard bei Zweitausendundeins, 2001.

———, ed. *Wir sind so frei. Kabarett in Westdeutschland. 1945–1970.* Neuausgabe. Frankfurt am Main: Rogner und Bernhard bei Zweitausendundeins, 2001.

Kuhnhardt, Ludger. "Multi-German Germany." *Daedalus* 123, no. 1 (1994): 193–201.

Kuntz-Brunner, Ruth. *Sexualität BRD, DDR im Vergleich.* Braunschweig: Holtzmeyer, 1991.

Küster, Jürgen. *Wörterbuch der Feste und Bräuche im Jahreslauf. Eine Einführung in den Festkalender.* Freiburg: Herder, 1985. (Herderbücherei 1177.)

———. *Bräuche im Kirchenjahr. Historische Anregungen für die Gestaltung christlicher Festtage.* Freiburg: Herder, 1986. (Herderbücherei 1293.)

LaCapra, Dominick. *History and Memory after Auschwitz.* Ithaca, NY, and London: Cornell University Press, 1998.

Langenbucher, Wolfgang R., ed. *Handbuch zur deutsch-deutschen Wirklichkeit. Bundesrepublik Deutschland—Deutsche Demokratische Republik im Kulturvergleich.* Sonderausgabe. Stuttgart: Metzler, 1988.

Langenscheidt, Florian, ed. *Deutsche Standards. Marken des Jahrhunderts. Die Königsklasse deutscher Produkte und Dienstleistungen in Wort und Bild—von Aspirin bis Zeiss.* Köln: Deutsche Standards Editionen, 2003.

Langguth, Gerd. *In Search of Security: A Socio-Psychological Portrait of Today's Germany.* Westport, CT: Praeger, 1995.

Lantermann, Klaus, Heiko Fiedler-Rauer, and Jens Specht, eds. *Facts about Germany.* Berlin: German Federal Foreign Office, Communications Section, 2003. Online version: http://www.tatsachen-ueber-deutschland.de

Larres, Klaus, and Panikos Panayi, eds. *The Federal Republic of Germany since 1949: Politics, Society, and Economy before and after Unification.* London and New York: Longman, 1996.

Larsson, Rune. *Religion zwischen Kirche und Schule. Die Lehrpläne für den evangelischen Religionsunterricht in der Bundesrepublik Deutschland seit 1945.* Lund: GWK Gleerup; Göttingen: Vandenhoek und Ruprecht, 1980.

Lehmann, Hans Georg. *Deutschland-Chronik 1945 bis 1995.* Bonn: Bundeszentrale für politische Bildung, 1996.

Lehnert, Gertrud. *Geschichte der Mode des 20. Jahrhunderts.* Köln: Könemann, 2000.

Leibniz-Institut für Länderkunde, ed. *Nationalatlas Bundesrepublik Deutschland—Unser Land in Karten, Texten und Bildern.* 6 Bände. Sonderausgabe. Bd. 1: Günter Heinritz, Sabine Tzschaschel, and Klaus Wolf, eds., *Gesellschaft und Staat.* Bd. 2: Paul Gans and Franz-Josef Kemper, eds., *Bevölkerung.* Bd. 3: Klaus Friedrich, Barbara Hahn, and Herbert Popp, eds., *Dörfer und Städte.* Bd. 4: Alois Mayr, and Manfred Nutz, eds., *Bildung und Kultur.* Bd. 5: Jürgen Deiters, Peter Gräf, and Günter Löffler, eds., *Verkehr und Kommunikation.* Bd. 6: Christoph Becker and Hubert Job, eds., *Freizeit und Tourismus.* München: Elsevier und Sprektrum Akademischer Verlag, 2004.

Lennartz, Knut. *Vom Aufbruch zur Wende. Theater in der DDR.* Seelze, Velber: Erhard Friedrich, 1992.

Lewis, Derek with Johannes Schwitalla and Ulrike Zitzlsperger. *Contemporary Germany: A Handbook.* London: Arnold, 2001.

Lewis, Derek, and John R. P. McKenzie, eds. *The New Germany: Social, Political and Cultural Challenges of Unification.* Exeter: Exeter University Press, 1995.

Link, Jürgen, and Wulf Wülfing. *Nationale*

Mythen und Symbole in der zweiten Hälfte des 19. Jahrhunderts. Strukturen und Funktionen von Konzepten nationaler Identität. Stuttgart: Klett-Cotta, 1995.

Littell, Franklin Hamlin. *The German Phoenix: Men and Movements in the Church in Germany.* Garden City, NY: Doubleday, 1960.

Lohrbächler, Albrecht, Helmut Ruppel, Ingrid Schmidt, and Jörg Thierfelder, eds. *Schoa. Schweigen ist unmöglich. Erinnern, Lernen, Gedenken.* Stuttgart, Berlin, and Köln: Kohlhammer, 1999.

Lord, Richard. *Culture Shock: Germany.* Portland: Graphic Arts Center, 2004.

Loschek, Ingrid. *Mode im 20. Jahrhundert. Eine Kulturgeschichte unserer Zeit,* 5th ed. München: Bruckmann, 1995.

———. *Modedesigner. Ein Lexikon von Armani bis Yamamoto.* München: Beck, 2002.

———. *Reclams Mode- und Kostümlexikon,* 5th ed. Ditzingen: Reclam, 2005.

Lott-Almstadt, Sylvia. *Brigitte, 1886–1986. Die ersten hundert Jahre. Geschichte einer Frauenzeitschrift.* Hamburg: Gruner und Jahr, 1986.

Lowsky, Martin. *Karl May.* Stuttgart: Metzlersche Verlagsbuchhandlung, 1987. (Sammlung Metzler 231).

Ludz, Peter Christian, and Johannes Kuppe. *DDR-Handbuch,* 2., völlig überarbeitete und erweiterte Auflage. Hrsg. vom Bundesministerium für Innerdeutsche Beziehungen. Köln: Verlag Wissenschaft und Politik, 1979.

Luscher, Renate. *Deutschland nach der Wende. Daten, Texte, Aufgaben für Deutsch als Fremdsprache,* 2. Auflage. Aktualisierte Fassung 1999/2000. München: Verlag für Deutsch, 1999.

Lyons, Albert S., and R. Joseph Petrucelli II. *Medicine: An Illustrated History.* New York: Abrams, 1987.

Maaz, Hans-Joachim. *Der Gefühlsstau. Ein Psychogramm der DDR.* Berlin: Argon, 1991.

Maier, Gerhart, ed. *Die Wende in der DDR,* 2., aktualisierte Auflage. Bonn: Bundeszentrale für politische Bildung, 1991.

Marcks, Marie. *Marie, es brennt! Autobiographische Aufzeichnungen.*

München: Frauenbuch Verlag; Weismann Verlag, 1984.

Marsh, David. *The New Germany: At the Crossroads.* London: Century, 1990.

———. *Germany and Europe: The Crisis of Unity.* London: Mandarin, 1995.

McAdams, A. James. *Germany Divided: From the Wall to Reunification.* Princeton, NJ: Princeton University Press, 1993.

McElvoy, Anne. *The Saddled Cow: East Germany's Life and Legacy.* London and Boston: Faber and Faber, 1992.

McGowan, Moray, and Malcolm Pender, eds. *The Media and Society in Contemporary Germany.* Contemporary German Studies: Occasional Papers 5. Glasgow: Department of Modern Languages, University of Strathclyde, 1988.

Menke, Frank. "Narrenzahl 11 macht Rheinländer jeck. Was es mit dem 11.11. auf sich hat." Online: www.wdr.de (published on November 11, 2002; downloaded on November 1, 2004).

Merkl, Peter H. *The Federal Republic of Germany at Forty-Five: Union without Unity.* Washington Square: New York University Press, 1995.

Merkl, Peter H., and Gert-Joachim Glaessner. *German Unification in the European Context.* University Park: Pennsylvania State University Press, 1995.

Metzger, Werner. *Schlager: Versuch einer Gesamtdarstellung unter besonderer Berücksichtigung des Musikmarktes der Bundesrepublik Deutschland.* Tübingen: Tübinger Vereinigung für Volkskunde, 1975.

Meyn, Hermann. *Massenmedien in Deutschland.* Neuauflage 2004 unter Mitarbeit von Hanni Chill. Konstanz: UVK Verlagsgesellschaft, 2004.

Miegel, Meinhard. *Die deformierte Gesellschaft. Wie die Deutschen ihre Wirklichkeit verdrängen.* München: Ullstein, 2002.

Ministry of Health, German Democratic Republic. *Health Care in the German Democratic Republic.* Berlin: Panorama, 1984.

Mintz, Sidney Wilfred. *Tasting Food, Tasting Freedom: Excursions into Eating, Culture, and the Past.* Boston: Beacon, 1996.

Mitscherlich, Alexander. *Die Unwirtlichkeit unserer Städte*. Frankfurt: Suhrkamp, 1965.

Mitscherlich, Alexander, and Margarete Mitscherlich. *Die Unfähigkeit zu trauern. Grundlagen kollektiven Verhaltens*. München: Piper, 1967.

Mitter, Armin, Stefan Wolle. *Untergang auf Raten. Unbekannte Kapitel der DDR-Geschichte*. München: Bertelsmann, 1993.

Moeller, Lukas, and Hans-Joachim Maaz. *Die Einheit beginnt zu zweit. Ein deutsch-deutsches Zwiegespräch*. Erweiterte Taschenbuchausgabe. Reinbek bei Hamburg: Rowohlt, 1995.

Mohler, Armin. *Vergangenheitsbewältigung. Oder, Wie man den Krieg nochmals verliert*. Krefeld: Sinus Verlag, 1980.

Mühe, Hansgeorg. *Unterhaltungsmusik. Ein geschichtlicher Überblick*. Hamburg: Kovac, 1996.

Müller, Bernd-Dietrich, ed. *Interkulturelle Wirtschaftskommunikation*, 2. Auflage. München: Iudicium, 1993.

Müller, Helmut M. *Schlaglichter der Deutschen Geschichte*. In Zusammenarbeit mit Karl Friedrich Krieger, Hanna Vollrath, und der Fachredaktion Geschichte des Bibliographischen Instituts. Mannheim, Wien, and Zürich: Meyers Lexikonverlag, 1986.

MUMOK. *Focus 01. Rebellion & New Beginnings. The Art of the Sixties. Viennese Actionism, Fluxus, Nouveau Réalisme, Pop Art*. Museum Moderner Kunst. Stiftung Ludwig. Wien: VBK, 2002.

Musall, Bettina. "Trash and Sensual Appeal." *The Germans. Sixty Years after the War*. Ed. Stefan Aust. Spiegel Special International Edition 4 (2005): 202–206.

Naudascher, Brigitte. *Freizeit in öffentlicher Hand. Behördliche Jugendpflege in Deutschland von 1900–1980*. Düsseldorf: Bröschler, 1990.

Nees, Greg. *Germany. Unraveling an Enigma*. Boston and London: Intercultural Press, 2000.

Nerdinger, Winfried, and Cornelius Tafel. *20th Century Architectural Guide: Germany*. Basel and Cambridge, MA: Birkhäuser, 1996.

New York Times Staff. "Klezmer Music." *New York Times*, Arts and Leisure Section, August 29, 2004, 1, 24.

Niebaum, Hermann, and Jürgen Mache. *Einführung in die Dialektologie des Deutschen*. Tübingen: Max Niemeyer, 1999.

Niketta, Reiner, and Eva Volke. *Rock und Pop in Deutschland*. Essen: Klartext, 1994.

Noelle-Neumann, Elisabeth. *Demoskopische Geschichtsstunde. Vom Wartesaal der Geschichte zur deutschen Einheit*. Zürich: Ed. Interfrom; Osnabrück: Fromm, 1991.

———, ed. *Publizistik, Massenkommunikation*. Aktualisierte, vollständig überarbeitete und ergänzte Auflage. Frankfurt am Main: Fischer, 2002.

Nolte, Ernst. "Vergangenheit, die nicht vergehen will." *Frankfurter Allgemeine Zeitung* (June 6, 1986).

Nuss, Bernard. *Das Faust-Syndrom. Ein Versuch über die Mentalität der Deutschen*. Bonn: Bouvier, 1992.

Nusser, Peter. *Romane für die Unterschicht. Groschenhefte und ihre Leser*. 5., mit einer erweiterten Bibliographie und einem Nachwort versehene Auflage. Stuttgart: J. B. Metzlersche Verlagsbuchhandlung, 1981.

Nyffeler, Max. *Liedermacher in der Bundesrepublik*. Bonn: Inter Nationes, 1978–1983. With six audiocassettes.

Olszewska Heberle, Marianne. *German Cooking*. New York: Berkeley Publishing Group, 1996.

Opaschowski, Horst W. *Freizeit und Lebensqualität. Perspektiven für Deutschland*. Hamburg: BAT Freizeit-Forschungsinstitut, 1993.

———. *Neue Trends im Freizeitsport. Analysen und Prognosen*. Hamburg: BAT Freizeit-Forschungsinstitut, 1994.

Opaschowski, Horst W., and Paul Steinebach. *Literaturverzeichnis Freizeitsport*. Essen: Kommunalverband Ruhrgebiet, 1980.

Opp, Karl-Dieter, and Peter Voss. *Die volkseigene Revolution*. Stuttgart: Klett-Cotta, 1993.

Osang, Alexander. "Zu Gast im Party-Staat." *Spiegel* 37 (2003): 212–222.

Osmond, Jonathan, ed. *German Reunification: A Reference Guide and Commentary*. Harlow: Longman, 1992.

Owen Smith, Eric. *The German Economy*. London: Routledge, 1994.

Pahlen, Kurt, and Rosmarie König. *Die große Geschichte der Musik.* Erweiterte und völlig neu überarbeitete Sonderausgabe. München and Leipzig: List, 1996.

Palm, Jürgen. *Sport for All: Approaches from Utopia to Reality.* Schorndorf: Verlag Karl Hofmann, 1991.

Patterson, Michael. *German Theatre Today: Post-War Theatre in West and East Germany.* London: Pitman, 1976.

Patterson, Michael, and Michael Huxley. "German drama, theatre, and dance." *The Cambridge Companion to Modern German Culture.* Ed. Eva Kolinsky and Wilfried van der Will. Cambridge: Cambridge University Press, 1998, 213–232.

Payer, Lynn. *Medicine & Culture: Varieties of Treatment in the United States, England, West Germany, and France.* New York: H. Holt, 1988.

Peacock, Alan T., and Hans Willgerodt, eds. *Germany's Social Market Economy: Origins and Evolution.* London: Macmillan, 1989.

Pehnt, Wolfgang. *German Architecture, 1960–1970.* London: Architectural Press, 1970.

Peisert, Hansgert, and Gerhild Framhein. *Das Hochschulsystem in Deutschland.* Bonn: Bundesministerium für Bildung und Wissenschaft, 1994.

Petermann, Gustav A. *Das Dieburger Dreiecksrennen. Ein Kabinettstück des deutschen Motorsports. Aus der Motorgeschichte von 1948 bis 1955.* Darmstadt: Verlag G. A. Petermann + Walter Grimm, 1995.

Pfahl-Traughber, Armin. *Rechtsextremismus in der Bundesrepublik*, 3. Auflage. München: Beck, 2001.

———. *Antisemitismus in der deutschen Geschichte.* Opladen: Leske und Budrich, 2002.

Pflaum, Hans Günther, and Hans Helmut Prinzler. *Cinema in the Federal Republic of Germany.* Bonn: Inter Nationes, 1993.

Philipsen, Dirk. *We Were the People: Voices from East Germany's Revolutionary Autumn of 1989.* Durham, NC: Duke University Press, 1993.

Phillips, David, ed. *Education in Germany: Tradition and Reform in Historical Context.* London and New York: Routledge, 1995.

Phillips, Jennifer. *In the Know in Germany. The Indispensable Cross-Cultural Guide to Working and Living in Germany.* New York: Living Language (Random House), 2001.

Phipps, Alison, ed. *Contemporary German Cultural Studies.* Oxford: Oxford University Press, 2002.

Picht, Georg. *Die deutsche Bildungskatastrophe. Analyse und Dokumentation.* Olten: Walter, 1964.

Pierer, Heinrich von. "Es geht um die Zukunft unserer Kinder—und zwar jetzt." *Mobil* 04 (2004): 6–9.

Plonka, Kay Alexander. *Mode in D, A, CH.* Köln: Tisch 7 Verlagsgesellschaft, 2006.

Pommerin, Reiner. *Culture in the Federal Republic of Germany, 1945–1995.* Oxford and Washington, DC: Berg, 1996.

Pond, Elizabeth. *Beyond the Wall: Germany's Road to Unification.* Washington, DC: Brookings Institution, 1993.

Pötzsch, Horst. *Die deutsche Demokratie.* Bonn: Bundeszentrale für politische Bildung, 1995. (Aktualisierter Nachdruck 1997.)

———. *Deutsche Geschichte von 1945 bis zur Gegenwart. Die Entwicklung der beiden deutschen Staaten.* München: Olzog, 1998.

Probst, Lothar, ed. *Differenz in der Einheit. Über die kulturellen Unterschiede der Deutschen Ost und West.* Berlin: Links, 1999.

Profitlich, Ulrich, ed. *Dramatik der DDR.* Frankfurt: Suhrkamp, 1987.

Pross, Helge. *Was ist heute deutsch? Wertorientierung in der Bundesrepublik.* Reinbek bei Hamburg: Rowohlt, 1982.

Protzner, Wolfgang, ed. *Vom Hungerwinter zum kulinarischen Schlaraffenland. Aspekte einer Kulturgeschichte des Essens in der Bundesrepublik Deutschland.* Stuttgart: Steiner-Verlag, 1987.

Radice, Giles. *The New Germans.* London: M. Joseph, 1995.

Raff, Diether. *Deutsche Geschichte vom Alten Reich zur Zweiten Republik*, 2. Auflage. München: Hueber, 1987.

———. *A History of Germany from the*

Medieval Empire to the Present. Oxford, Hamburg, and New York: Berg, 1988.

Rasp, Markus, ed. *Contemporary German Photography*. Köln, Lisboa, London, New York, Paris, and Tokyo: Taschen, 1997.

Raven, Wolfram von, ed. *Armee gegen den Krieg. Wert und Wirkung der Bundeswehr*. Stuttgart-Degerloch: Seewald, 1966.

Redaktion "DDR," ed. *Introducing the GDR*. Berlin: Panorama, 1978.

Redaktion "DDR im Überblick," ed. *The German Democratic Republic*. Berlin: Panorama, 1986.

Rein, Gerhard, ed. *Die Opposition in der DDR. Entwürfe für einen anderen Sozialismus. Texte, Programme, Statuten von Neues Forum, Demokratischer Aufbruch, Demokratie Jetzt, SPD, Böhlener Plattform und Grüne Partei in der DDR*. Berlin: Wichern, 1989.

Reinhard, Wolfgang. *Lebensformen Europas. Eine historische Kulturanthropologie*. München: Beck, 2004.

Richter, Gert. *Erbauliches, belehrendes, wie auch vergnügliches Kitsch-Lexikon von A bis Z*. Gütersloh, Berlin, München, and Wien: Bertelsmann, 1972.

Richter, Simon. "Food and drink: Hegelian encounters with the culinary other." *Contemporary German Cultural Studies*. Ed. Alison Phipps. Oxford: Oxford University Press, 2002, 179–195.

Roberts, Geoffrey K. *Party Politics in the New Germany*. London, and Washington, DC: Pinter, 1997.

Rösgen, Petra, Hermann Schäfer, and Jürgen Reiche. *Prominente in der Werbung. Da weiß man, was man hat*. Mainz: Schmidt, 2001.

Roth, Roland, and Dieter Rucht. *Jugendkulturen, Politik und Protest. Vom Widerstand zum Kommerz?* Leverkusen: Leske und Budrich, 2000.

Rothe, Klaus. *Politik verstehen, Demokratie bejahen. Politik und politisches System in der Bundesrepublik Deutschland*. München: Olzig, 2000.

Rüdiger, Robert. *Bundesrepublik Deutschland. Politisches System und Globalisierung. Eine Einführung*. Münster and New York: Waxmann, 2001.

Ruh, Ulrich. *Religion und Kirche in der Bundesrepublik Deutschland*. München: Iudicium, 1990.

Russ, Charles V. J. *The German Language Today: A Linguistic Introduction*. London: Routledge, 1994.

Rutschky, Michael. *Wie wir Amerikaner wurden. Eine deutsche Entwicklungsgeschichte*. Berlin and München: Ullstein, 2004.

Rutz, Werner, Konrad Scherf, and Wilfried Strenz. *Die fünf neuen Bundesländer. Historisch begründet, politisch gewollt und künftig vernünftig*. Darmstadt: Wissenschaftliche Buchgesellschaft, 1993.

Sandford, John. *The Mass Media of the German-Speaking Countries*. London: Oswald Wolff, 1976.

———, ed. *Encyclopedia of Contemporary German Culture*. London and New York: Routledge, 1999.

Sarkar, Ranjana S. *Akteure, Interessen und Technologien der Telekommunikation. USA und Deutschland im Vergleich*. Frankfurt am Main and New York: Campus, 2001.

Schäfers, Bernhard. *Politischer Atlas Deutschland. Gesellschaft, Wirtschaft, Staat*, 2., aktualisierte und verbesserte Auflage. Bonn: Dietz, 1998.

Schäfers, Bernhard, and Wolfgang Zapf, eds. *Handwörterbuch zur Gesellschaft Deutschlands*, 2. erweiterte und aktualisierte Auflage. Opladen: Leske und Budrich, 2001.

Schallück, Paul. *Germany: Cultural Developments since 1945*. München: Hueber, 1971.

Schanze, Helmut, ed. *Handbuch der Mediengeschichte*. Stuttgart: Alfred Kröner, 2001.

Scharf, Thomas. *The German Greens: Challenging the Consensus*. Oxford: Berg, 1994.

Schayan, Janet. "Building with Calibre." *Deutschland. Forum on Politics, Culture and Business* 6 (2005): 12–17.

Scheib, Asta. *Eine Zierde in ihrem Hause. Die Geschichte der Ottilie von Faber-Castell*. Reinbek bei Hamburg: Rowohlt, 1998.

Schenk, Ralf, and Christiane Mückenberger, eds. *Das zweite Leben der Filmstadt*

Babelsberg. DEFA-Spielfilme, 1946–92. Berlin: Henschel, 1994.

Schlaffer, Hannelore. "Fasten, joggen, selber nähen." *Die Zeit* 20 (May 6, 2004).

Schlant, Ernestine. *The Language of Silence— West German Literature and the Holocaust.* London: Routledge, 1999.

Schlicher, Susanne. *TanzTheater. Traditionen und Freiheiten. Pina Bausch, Gerhard Bohner, Reinhild Hoffmann, Hans Kresnik, Susanne Linke.* Reinbek bei Hamburg: Rowohlt, 1987. (Rowohlts Enzyklopädie/ Kulturen und Ideen.)

Schmidt, Jochen. *Tanzgeschichte des 20. Jahrhunderts in einem Band.* Mit 101 Choreographen Porträts. Berlin: Henschel, 2002.

Schmidt, Manfred G. *Das politische System der Bundesrepublik Deutschland.* München: Beck, 2005.

Schmidt-Mühlisch, Lothar. *Affentheater: Bühnenkrise ohne Ende?* Erlangen: Verlag Straube, 1992.

Schmitz, Michael. *Wendestress. Die psychosozialen Kosten der deutschen Einheit.* Berlin: Rowohlt, 1995.

Schönbohm, Jörg. *Two Armies and One Fatherland: The End of the Nationale Volksarmee.* Providence, RI: Berghahn, 1996.

Schönfeldt, Sybil Gräfin. *Das große Ravensburger Buch der Feste & Bräuche. Durch das Jahr und den Lebenslauf.* Ravensburg: Otto Maier Verlag, 1980.

Schröder, Richard. *Deutschland schwierig Vaterland. Für eine neue politische Kultur,* 3. Auflage. Freiburg: Herder, 1995.

———. *Vom Gebrauch der Freiheit. Gedanken über Deutschland nach der Vereinigung.* Stuttgart: Deutsche Verlags-Anstalt, 1996.

Schroeder, Klaus. *Der SED-Staat. Partei, Staat und Gesellschaft, 1949–1990.* München: Econ-Ullstein-List, 2000.

Schulze, Hagen. *Germany. A New History.* Trsl. Deborah Lucas Schneider. Cambridge, USA, and London, England: Harvard University Press, 1998.

Schütz, Walter J. "Entwicklung der Tagespresse." *Mediengeschichte der Bundesrepublik Deutschland.* Ed. Jürgen

Wilke. Köln, Weimar, and Wien: Böhlau, 1999, 109–134.

Schwab, Lothar, and Richard Weber. *Theaterlexikon,* 2nd ed. Frankfurt: Cornelsen Scriptor, 1992.

Schwarz, Hans-Peter. *Die Zentralmacht Europas. Deutschlands Rückkehr auf die Weltbühne.* Berlin: Siedler, 1994.

Schwerfel, Heinz Peter. *Kunstskandale.* Köln: Dumont, 2000.

Schwitalla, Johannes. "Language Issues: Communication Problems between East and West Germans." *Contemporary Germany: A Handbook.* Ed. Derek Lewis with Johannes Schwitalla and Ulrike Zitzlsperger. London: Arnold, 2001, 238–250.

Sebald, Winfried Georg. *A Radical Stage: Theatre in Germany in the 1970s and 1980s.* Oxford: Berg, 1988.

Seegers, Lu. "Die Erfolgsgeschichte von *Hör zu!*" *Hör zu! Eduard Rhein und die Rundfunkprogrammzeitschriften (1931–1965).* Potsdam:Verlag für Berlin-Brandenburg 2001, 151–232. Available at http://www.mediaculture-online.de (accessed December 7, 2004).

Seeßlen, Georg. *Romantik & Gewalt. Ein Lexikon der Unterhaltungsindustrie.* Bd. 2. München: Manz Verlag, 1973.

———. *Orgasmus und Alltag. Kreuz- und Querzüge durch den medialen Mainstream.* Hamburg: KVV konkret, 2000.

Sereny, Gitta. *The German Trauma. Experiences and Reflections 1938–2001.* London: Penguin, 2001.

Sichrovsky, Peter. *Wir wissen nicht, was morgen wird, wir wissen wohl, was gestern war. Junge Juden in Deutschland und Österreich.* Cologne: Kiepenheuer und Witsch, 1985.

———. *Schuldig geboren: Kinder aus Nazifamilien.* Köln: Kiepenheuer und Witsch, 1987.

Siebert, Horst. *The German Economy: Beyond the Social Market.* New Haven, CT: Princeton University Press, 2005.

Sillge, Ursula. *Un-Sichtbare Frauen. Lesben und ihre Emanzipation in der DDR.* Berlin: LinksDruck, 1991.

Simhandl, Peter. *Theatergeschichte in einem*

Band. Aktualisierte Auflage. Mit Beiträgen von Franz Wille und Grit van Dyk. Berlin: Henschel Verlag, 2001.

Smith, Gordon R., William E. Paterson, and Peter H. Merkl, eds. *Developments in West German Politics.* Durham, NC: Duke University Press, 1989.

Smyser, W. R. *The German Economy: Colossus at the Crossroads,* 2nd ed. New York: St. Martin's Press, 1993.

———. *How Germans Negotiate: Logical Goals, Practical Solutions.* Washington, DC: Institute of Peace Press, 2003.

Solberg, Richard W. *God and Caesar in East Germany: The Conflicts of Church and State in East Germany since 1945.* New York: Macmillan, 1961.

Sommer, Stefan. *Das große Lexikon des DDR-Alltags.* Berlin: Schwarzkopf und Schwarzkopf, 2003.

Sommer, Theo, ed. *Leben in Deutschland. Eine Entdeckungsreise in das eigene Land.* Reinbek bei Hamburg: Rowohlt, 2006.

Sommerhoff, Barbara. *Frauenbewegung.* Reinbek bei Hamburg: Rowohlt, 1995.

Speakman, Fleur, and Colin Speakman. *The Green Guide to Germany.* London: Green Print, 1992.

Sprenger, Heinrich, Irene Charlotte Streul, and Heribert Adelt. *Von der Spaltung zur Einheit. 1945–1990. Eine deutsche Chronik in Texten und Bildern. De La Scisson à L'Unité. 1945–1990. Une chronique allemande illustrée. From Division to Unity. 1945–1990. An Illustrated German Chronicle.* Bonn: Presse- und Informationsamt der Bundesregierung, 1992.

Staritz, Dietrich. *Geschichte der DDR.* Erweiterte Neuausgabe. Darmstadt: Wissenschaftliche Buchgesellschaft, 1997.

Stärk, Beate. *Contemporary Painting in Germany.* Sydney: G&B Arts International, 1994.

Steakley, James D. *The Homosexual Emancipation Movement in Germany.* New York: Arno Press, 1975.

Steingart, Gabor. *Deutschland. Der Abstieg eines Superstars.* München and Zürich: Piper, 2004.

Stephan, Alexander, ed. *Americanization and Anti-Americanism: The German Encounter with American Culture after 1945.* New York and Oxford: Berghahn, 2005.

Stern, Susan. *These Strange German Ways.* Bonn: Atlantic-Brücke, 1994.

Stern-Team, McKinsey, ZDF, and AOL. "Wie geht's Deutschland? Deutschlands größte Umfrage. Wie wir leben. Was wir denken. Was wir wollen." *Stern* 18 (April 22, 2004): 46–62.

Stevenson, Patrick, ed. *The German Language and the Real World: Sociolinguistic, Cultural and Pragmatic Perspectives on Contemporary German,* rev. ed. Oxford: Clarendon Press, 1997.

———. *Language and German Disunity: A Sociolinguistic History of East and West in Germany, 1945–2000.* Oxford and New York: Oxford University Press, 2003.

Stölzl, Christoph, ed. *Bilder und Zeugnisse der deutschen Geschichte. Aus den Sammlungen des Deutschen Historischen Museums.* Berlin: Deutsches Historisches Museum, 1995.

Strate, Ursula, ed. *Déjà vu. Moden 1950–1990.* Heidelberg: Edition Braus, 1994.

Strobel, Ricarda, and Werner Faulstich. *Die deutschen Fernsehstars. Bd. 1: Stars der ersten Stunde. Bd. 2: Show-und Gesangstars. Bd. 3: Stars für die ganze Familie. Bd. 4: Zielgruppenstars.* Göttingen: Vandenhoeck und Ruprecht, 1998.

Stuber, Petra. *Spielräume und Grenzen: Studien zum DDR-Theater.* Berlin: Ch. Links, 1998.

Sucher, C. Bernd, ed. *Theater Lexikon. Autoren, Regisseure, Schauspieler, Dramaturgen, Bühnenbildner, Kritiker,* 2nd ed. München: Deutscher Taschenbuchverlag, 1999.

Szarota, Tomasz. *Niemiecki Michel. Der deutsche Michel. Die Geschichte eines nationalen Symbols und Autostereotyps.* Aus dem Polnischen von Kordula Zentgraf-Zubrzycka. Vom Autor für die deutsche Ausgabe überarbeitete Fassung. Osnabrück: Fibre, 1998.

Teply, Karl. *Die Einführung des Kaffees in Wien. Georg Franz Koltschitzky, Johannes Diodato, Isaak de Luca.* Wien, 1980. (Forschungen und Beiträge zur Wiener Stadtgeschichte 6).

Teuteberg, Hans Jürgen, ed. *Essen und kulturelle Identität. Europäische Perspektiven.* Berlin: Akademie Verlag, 1997.

Teuteberg, Hans Jürgen, and Günter Wiegelmann. *Unsere tägliche Kost. Geschichte und regionale Prägung.* Münster: F. Coppenrath, 1986.

Thiele, Johannes, ed. *Das Buch der Deutschen: Alles, was man kennen muss.* Bergisch-Gladbach: Lübbe, 2004. Online www.buch-der-deutschen.de.

Thomas, Carmen. *Ein ganz besonderer Saft—Urin.* Köln: Verlagsgesellschaft, 1993.

Thomas, Karin. *Zweimal deutsche Kunst nach 1945. 40 Jahre Nähe und Ferne.* Köln: DuMont, 1985.

Thränhardt, Dietrich. *Die Bundesrepublik Deutschland. Verfassung und politisches System.* München: Goldmann, 1968.

Tippach-Schneider, Simone. *Das große Lexikon der DDR-Werbung. Kampagnen und Werbesprüche, Macher und Produkte, Marken und Warenzeichen,* 2. Auflage. Berlin: Schwarzkopf und Schwarzkopf, 2004.

Tisdall, Caroline. *Joseph Beuys.* New York: Solomon R. Guggenheim Museum, 1979.

Tödtmann, Friedhelm. *Freizeitsport und Verein. Zur Situation nicht-wettkampforientierter Gruppen im Sportverein.* Frankfurt am Main: Haag und Herchen, 1982.

Tucholsky, Kurt. "Über wirkungsvollen Pazifismus." *Gesammelte Werke.* Band 2: *1925–1928.* Ed. Mary Gerold-Tucholsky and Fritz J. Raddatz. Stuttgart and Hamburg: Deutscher Bücherbund, 1960, 907–912.

Tuma, Thomas. "The Last of the Titans." *The Germans. Sixty Years after the War.* Spiegel Special International Edition 4 (2005): 166–169.

Turner, Henry Ashby. *The Two Germanies since 1945.* New Haven, CT: Yale University Press, 1987.

Ueberhorst, Horst, ed. *Geschichte der Leibesübungen.* Teilband 2: *Leibesübungen und Sport in Deutschland vom ersten Weltkrieg bis zur Gegenwart.* Berlin: Bartels und Wernitz, 1989.

Uhlmann, Lore. "Speaking in Our Own Behalf." *GDR Review* 11–12 (1989): 1.

United States Holocaust Memorial Museum. *Historical Atlas of the Holocaust.* New York: Macmillan, 1996.

Untucht, Peter. *Freiburg und die Regio.* Köln: DuMont Reiseverlag, 2003.

Viehoff, Reinhold, and Rien T. Segers, eds. *Kultur Identität Europa. Über die Schwierigkeiten und Möglichkeiten einer Konstruktion.* Frankfurt: Suhrkamp, 1999. (Suhrkamp taschenbuch wissenschaft 1330.)

Voigt, Claudia, and Marianne Wellershoff (Interviewer). "'Der Refrain des Lebens.' Der 'Brigitte'-Chefredakteur Andreas Lebert über die veränderten Ansprüche seiner Leserinnen, Feminismus im Alltag und das Glück, mit Frau zusammenzuarbeiten." *Spiegel* 19 (2004): 178–180.

Wachtel, Joachim. *The Lufthansa Story: 1926–1984,* 3d ed. Cologne: Lufthansa German Airlines, 1985.

Walz, Werner. *Deutschlands Eisenbahn. Lokomotiven und Wagen, Geschichte und Organisation, Kritik und Hoffnung.* Stuttgart: Motorbuch Verlag, 1991.

Watson, Alan. *The Germans: Who Are They Now?* Chicago: Edition Q, 1995.

Weber, Christiane, and Renate Möller. *Mode und Modeschmuck 1920–1970 in Deutschland.* Stuttgart: Arnold, 1999.

Weber, Hermann. *DDR. Grundriss der Geschichte, 1945–1990.* Vollständig überarbeitete und ergänzte Neuauflage. Hannover: Fackelträger, 1991.

Weber, Jürgen. *Kleine Geschichte Deutschlands seit 1945.* München: dtv, 2002.

Weber-Kellermann, Ingeborg. *Volksfeste in Deutschland.* HB-Bildatlas Spezial. Hamburg: HB Verlags- und Vertriebs-Gesellschaft mbH, 1981.

Wehling, Hans Georg, and Ralf Rytlewski. *Politische Kultur der DDR.* Stuttgart, Berlin, and Köln: Kohlhammer, 1989.

Weidenfeld, Werner, and Karl-Rudolf Korte, eds. *Handbuch zur deutschen Einheit. 1949– 1989–1999.* Aktualisierte Neuausgabe. Frankfurt am Main and New York: Campus, 1999.

Weidenfeld, Werner, and Hartmut Zimmermann, eds. *Deutschland-Handbuch. Eine doppelte Bilanz, 1949–1989.* München and Wien: Hanser, 1989.

Weingarten, Susanne. "Wunders Never Cease." *The Germans. Sixty Years after the War.* Ed. Stefan Aust. Spiegel Special International Edition 4 (2005): 198–201.

Weißhuhn, Gernot. *Bildung und Lebenslagen. Auswertung und Analysen für den zweiten Armuts- und Reichtumsbericht der Bundesregierung.* Berlin: Bundesminsterium für Bildung und Forschung, Referat Publ., Internetred., 2004, Stand Oktober 2004.

Weitz, Burkhard. "Ihr Vater stammt aus Ghana, seiner ist Franzose. Zwei typische Deutsche erkunden: Was ist eigentlich deutsch an uns?" Ein Interview mit Pia Ampaw und Achim Mentzel. *Chrismon* 05(2004): 22–25.

Wendt, Bernd Jürgen, ed. *Vom schwierigen Zusammenwachsen der Deutschen. Nationale Identität und Nationalismus im 19. und 20. Jahrhundert.* Frankfurt and New York: Peter Lang, 1992.

Wendt, Ingeborg. *Notopfer Berlin.* Berlin: Fannai und Walz, 1990. (Originalausgabe 1956.)

Werle, Gerhard, and Thomas Wandres. *Auschwitz vor Gericht. Völkermord und bundesdeutsche Strafjustiz. Mit einer Dokumentation des Auschwitz-Urteils.* München: C. H. Beck, 1995. (Beck'sche Reihe 1099.)

Wicke, Peter. "Populäre Musik in der Bundesrepublik Deutschland." *MIZ. Deutsches Musikinformationszentrum,* January 14, 2004.

Wickel, Horst Peter. *Ratgeber Wehrdienst.* Reinbek bei Hamburg: Rowohlt, 2000.

Wiedemann, Erich. *Die deutschen Ängste. Ein Volk in Moll,* 7 Auflage. Frankfurt: Ullstein, 1989.

Wierlacher, Alois, ed. *Kulturthema Essen.*

Ansichten und Problemfeld. Berlin: Akademie Verlag, 1993.

Wildt, Michael. *Vom kleinen Wohlstand. Eine Konsumgeschichte der fünfziger Jahre.* Frankfurt: S. Fischer, 1996.

Wilke, Jürgen, ed. *Mediengeschichte der Bundesrepublik Deutschland.* Köln, Weimar, and Wien: Böhlau, 1999.

Winterhoff-Spurk, Peter. *Fernsehen. Fakten zur Medienwirkung.* Bern: Huber, 2001.

Wise, Michael Z. *Capital Dilemma: Germany's Search for a New Architecture of Democracy.* New York: Princeton Architectural Press, 1998.

Wittmann, Reinhard. *Geschichte des deutschen Buchhandels.* München: Beck, 1991. (Beck'sche Reihe.)

Wojak, Irmtrud, ed. *Auschwitz-Prozeß 4 Ks 2/63.* Frankfurt am Main. Köln: Snoeck, 2004.

Wolfrum, Edgar. *Geschichtspolitik in der Bundesrepublik Deutschland. Der Weg zur bundesrepublikanischen Erinnerung 1948–1990.* Darmstadt: Wissenschaftliche Buchgesellschaft, 1999.

Woll, Johanna. *Feste und Bräuche im Jahreslauf,* 2. Auflage. Stuttgart: Ulmer, 1995.

Zapf, Wolfgang, ed. *Lebenslagen im Wandel. Sozialberichterstattung im Längsschnitt.* Projektgruppe "Das Sozioökonomische Panel" im Deutschen Institut für Wirtschaftsforschung, Berlin. Frankfurt and New York: Campus, 1995.

Zelikow, Philip, and Condoleezza Rice. *Germany Unified and Europe Transformed: A Study in Statecraft.* Cambridge: Harvard University Press, 1995.

Zerrahn, Signe. *Entmannt. Wider den Trivialfeminismus.* Hamburg: Rotbuch, 1995.

Ziermann, Klaus. *Romane vom Fließband. Die imperialistische Massenliteratur in Westdeutschland.* Berlin: Dietz, 1969.

———. *Der deutsche Buch- und Taschenbuchmarkt, 1945–1995.* Berlin: Wissenschaftsverlag Volker Spiess, 2000.

Zimmermann, Hartmut, Horst Ulrich, and Michael Fehlauer, eds. *DDR Handbuch,* 3., überarbeitete und erweiterte Auflage. Hrsg.

vom Bundesministerium für Innerdeutsche
Beziehungen. 2 Bde. Köln: Verlag
Wissenschaft und Politik, 1985.

Zobel, Klaus, and Rudolf Griffel. *Kleine
deutsche Typologie.* New York: Holt,
Rinehart and Winston, 1970.

Zötsch, Claudia. *Powergirls und
Drachenmädchen. Symbolwelten in
Mythologie und Jugendkultur.* Münster:
Unrast, 1999.

Zwahr, Hartmut. *Ende einer Selbstzerstörung.
Leipzig und die Revolution in der DDR,* 2.
Auflage. Göttingen: Vandenhoeck and
Ruprecht, 1993.

Index

Page numbers in **bold** indicated photographs.

About the Authors

Catherine C. Fraser is professor emerita of German and was language coordinator at Indiana University, Bloomington, IN. She has published on various aspects of teaching language with a cultural content and frequently taught courses on German popular culture.

Dierk O. Hoffmann is professor of German studies at Colgate University, Hamilton, NY. His publications include editions on Viennese and Prague literature of the turn of the 20th century, monographs, and textbooks.

DATE DUE

DEC 0 8 2015		

WITHDRAWN

OCT '07